SHINING THE LIGHT
BOOK IV

HUMANITY'S GREATEST CHALLENGE

THE TRUTH ABOUT

- The HAARP Project
- The Sinister Secret Government
- Hale-Bopp Comet

Light Technology Research

Cover art: Balance
by Robert Lewis Arnold

ISBN 0-929385-93-4

Published by
Light Technology Publishing
P.O. Box 1526
Sedona, AZ 86339

Printed by
MISSION POSSIBLE
Commercial Printing

P.O. Box 1495
Sedona, AZ 86339

"Wake up to your sovereign self and enjoy the play, but don't get caught up in it. Remember, you are not, as the secret government and the controlled media would have you believe, a consuming animal to be totally controlled for their benefit and profit. You are an indestructible lightbeing temporarily inhabiting a physical body for the joy and experience of it — and because 3D is a prerequisite for advanced Creator training."

Robert Shapiro is a man who has grown up with the experience of extraterrestrial contact. From age twelve he has had a series of personal UFO contacts. Throughout his life there have been communication with beings from several star systems and dimensions. The development of his career and lifestyle has come as a direct result of this communication. Robert has been a professional channel for over 15 years, and although he can channel almost anyone or anything with an exceptionally clear and profound connection, he most often channels Zoosh, who describes himself below. Robert's great contribution to an understanding of the history and purpose of humanity is his epochal work, The Explorer Race, and he is one of several channels featured in Sedona Vortex Guidebook. When he is not channeling, Robert is a shaman and spiritual teacher in his own right. He lives with his wife Nancy in Sedona, Arizona. He is available for personal appointments and can be reached at (602) 282-5883; P.O. Box 2849, Sedona, AZ 86339.

Zoosh ensouled the first planet that humanity experienced as souls and he has been with us ever since, for "about a trillion years." He is witty, wise and compassionate. He says about himself, "It has been my job and my purpose in life to follow the birth of your souls on your journey to recreating the universe. My job is to be your companion, your guide, occasionally your entertainer. I have to nurture that sense of mystery – it's not as if you're going to have it forever.

"It is my job to help you get there, to help you to understand your experience and to observe everything. And, in time, to remind you of the everything you are in one of my many guises."

Other books by Robert Shapiro

Published by Light Technology Publishing
The Explorer Race (A Series of books)
Sedona Vortex Guidebook

Arthur Fanning was born and raised in Providence, Rhode Island. He attended the University of Rhode Island, receiving a B.S. degree in agriculture. After graduation, he entered the U.S. Marine Corps in the officer candidate program. Upon graduation he earned his navy wings at Pensacola Naval Air Station in Florida. From 1968 to 1969 he was a marine helicopter pilot in Vietnam.

Arthur had many experiences as a little child, leaving his body and talking with beings in the stars at night. As a medivac pilot in Vietnam, the real nature of these experiences began to reveal themselves to him as a guiding and guarding force that all beings share.

In 1986 he had what he calls the "Big One" of his spiritual awakening. An entity appeared over his bed while Arthur was still awake. Arthur's body lifted off the bed, bent in half, straightened out horizontally, and then laid back down, all in less than two seconds. There was no pain involved, nor was it frightening. Arthur says, "It just happened. It felt like white electricity."

Since then, Arthur has been channeling and working with the entity that appeared to him above his bed—Jehovah/YHWH. His first book, Simon, was his first attempt to explain some of the phenomena he has experienced in his spiritual awakening. The material was excerpted from both his physical life and his dreaming life. The second book, Soul, Evolution, Father was dictated through him by Jehovah.

Arthur Fanning lives with his wife Cheryl and may be contacted for channeling and healing appointments at P.O. Box 684, Cornville, AZ 86325.

Jehovah/YHWH is part of a great group of beings from another universe who created and are responsible for maintaining this part of the galaxy. His sense of adventure and his great love, wisdom and compassion for humanity radiate through the energy and words of his channeling through Arthur.

Other books by Arthur Fanning

Published by Light Technology Publishing

Simon

Soul, Evolution, Father

Contents

1

I Love God

YHWH through Arthur Fanning
October 20, 1995

Getting to be a lot of fun around the planet. Let me look you over and see how much energy we can bring in. Whether you know it or not, what is building for your next year is your ability to meet the Christ, face to face. That means your physical body has to be able to handle it, the energies, and to find out that the Christ is you. In order to meet the Christ you have to vibrate the same to be there. Everyone breathe. It's okay; you're required to breathe, know you, in the physical.

The energy in the diaphragm, the energy in the heart chakra here is blooming, becoming you more. The aches, the pains of the physical body are the changes occurring within your structure. You are remembering now deep withinside your being and about your being. The physical body was trained within rigid social consciousness systems. The pains now are the readjustment to your christhood. So in one manner you're going back in time in the physical body to your pristine condition where you knew, even before your birth, so to speak. And that's going to require great remembering. Be it as I say it this way: Before you were born you knew, and even then you didn't remember exactly what was going on in the physical body—it just felt good to be physical. You didn't know the, we'll say, machinations of the energies—you didn't remember. Now that you've had a chance to play in the physical body, and becoming the Christ that you are within the physical, you will remember the machinations. You're going to have to live in the body differently.

Your social structure won't support this christedness as it becomes. It's a new thing. It is a good thing. It hasn't been done before in this way with this many, in this great a number. Everyone breathe a moment.

So there's no system that you can rely on, not even your metaphysical system. Oh, it'll help you a little bit through your aches and pains and readjustment of the energies, but you are the being within the physical body now living it. You're going to need to learn how to breathe again, through you chakras—what you term pranayama. You're going to use your breath appropriately in the body, and you will see prana working appropriately. You're going to learn to be still, in your power, to heal the body. So it's a grand time. Lot of fun. Everyone breathe a little bit. Center yourselves in here [heart chakra].

Now, there's a lot of activity going on now in the dream state, and that is for you to remember. What will cause you to leave the planet through these energies, with these energies, is not being in love. So you better be sure you're in love with what you're doing, wherever you are. Love is going to be the requirement. Beings are going to seek it, and if it's not where they are, they will move to find it. That includes leaving the body physical. So you're in outrageous times. Know that the love is in here, inside you here, brilliant light. Brilliant light.

Now, this is the easy time, the slow and gentle time prior to your December. Know you? This is a piece-of-cake time. The energies are very gentle now compared to your December. You can handle them. It is when you get up here [head] it gets a little confusing, indeed? The heart chakra will need to be open in this time because a lot of these energies that are coming now are mental energies, and they have to sit upon this great heart here, the soul. If the heart isn't open, this great mental energy will crush it. You'll feel pain in the body. This is not a good time to figure out what is happening. This is a great time to be in joy in the energies in your body. You can figure it out whether it hurts or not. So adjust, indeed? Now, we're going to do a little meditation later to assist you here.

What is . . . I'm going to approach it from another way. Another way to understand what is occurring is that you are part of your high self walking upon the planet. You are the part that is taking this journey in this decade from high self—you were sent here, you volunteered, etc., etc. Your high-self energies consider your physical body its home. High self wants to come home, right on top of you—all of it. So you better learn how to shapeshift a little bit. [He chuckles.] Lighten up, entities. Your body is a result of the desire of you and high self (your words now) to play here in this time. You've done your job; high self wants to play now. So it is a great landing of energies upon you here. Great becoming. The portion that is in between the soul and the high self is what you call the physical body. Guess what's going to give. [Laughter.] Soul, high self, no problem.

Grand Chakra Meditation

Allow your spines to be erect here. Center your being. Now, when we do this meditation I want you to focus inside you here, and I want you to move slowly if the energies need to be adjusted in the body. Now, when I tell you to close your eyes, close them gently, and as you do, be likened unto a garage door come down. As it does, gold light is pulled into the body when you close your eyes, and it fills you. So allow your eyes to close gently. And also allow the color red there, red-gold. Grand. All the way down now. Down into the body, down to the feet. Peace. Now very slowly I want you to make a fist with your hands, but gently so you can feel the energy. The fingers should begin to feel a little puffy. That is all right. Allow. Little fist, not too tight, and then open again. As you open, breathe out the heart chakra, gentle breath, so the energy moves through the fingers. Indeed, allow.

Now there is a sensation if you allow yourself to feel, energy all around you, around the physical body. I want you to sort of use your nostrils and breathe in this energy and feel it go into the nasal passages, right in back of what you call the eyes. Breathe it in through the nose, and as you exhale out the mouth, exhale so you can feel the energy come out the toes. Feel it move. Allow. Very gently. Inhale through your nose again, and I want you to feel the energy at the roof of your mouth, in the back, near your palate. Breathe in. Feel it there. Now breathe out so energy moves out the knees. Indeed. That be grand. Now move your right leg a little bit, just a little bit forward, slowly. Move it back. Your left leg, [same]. Back. Center your being.

A lot of energy is going to begin to move up the spine in these times, so if you feel a little pressure you may adjust the spine a little bit, and center. And you contemplate inside you what the energy wants to do. You're going to feel it from the root, from what you call your perineum, right to the roof of your mouth, right up there, and through the sixth seal which is behind, in the center of your brain here, and out the top of your head. It wants to move that way. And it'll affect that chakra in the back, what is termed the Grand Chakra, right in the center it wants to open. Allow, open. Open the chakra in the back. Now I want you to visualize that chakra, simply see the design of it. Allow. Allow it to be there. The chakra knows what it's doing – it is a mandala of you. Allow. It is your power also. Pay attention now.

Focus on the energy of the Grand Chakra. Breathe in at that chakra so you're sucking that energy from the back to the center of you. Suck it to your chest. Now breathe it out so it pushes out the front. Allow. Now let it stretch from top to bottom. Allow. Breathe in the nose again. Feel it at the roof of your mouth. Breathe out, stretch that chakra top to bottom. You be in the color now, all sides, allow. This changes your focus, entities. This is what you utilize to be in many realities at once. Allow. Peace. You're in safety. These are the energies you use to travel from place to place in a moment. Breathe in again and feel it at the roof of your mouth. Now when you breathe out, I want you to feel more energy coming from the Grand Chakra at the back, forward. Gently! Gently! Gently. Allow your eyes to open.

The soul that resides in here [chest cavity] remembers the energy of the Grand Chakra. It is what it has played within for many, many times. It remembers. And when you push that energy further, the soul with its memory can utilize all of its experiences – "Oh, that's where you've been . . . wondered where that was" – that memory here, and you can play with it. A magician's bag of tricks there. You're carrying it right behind you, right here, little sack sits right in there. Haven't lost a thing. It is time now to breathe it in the body, utilize it, and remember.

Now, one of the keys, because you were born through woman, the sexual appetite is a big issue for you, and that key is still there. There's no judgment on it, not at all. I'm simply telling you what is working here. When that appetite begins to manifest here through you, understand it. Understand that it can take you to many realities. Just be sure you know where you're going, because you forgot the last time. And it is also that appetite that keeps you, around the planet, from remembering your christ-hood. Of course, when you're out here you think you remember. But you get here, you say, "Oops, shit! I forgot again. This makes 32,004." [Laughter.] Oh well, what's another 90 years? Except the struggle within the soul is a burden, because the soul wants to enjoy all of this without judgment, without limitation. The soul is almost complete for many on the planet – not everyone, for many. Little bit further and you can become. That would be a grand thing, indeed? Be great wisdom.

Is everyone having fun in their dreams? One of the things, you must allow your dreams to play out, because most are messages now at this stage. Some of you want to control them, to change the ending, so to speak. Don't do that just yet, know you? Move along with it and find out where your energy is in it. Center in love in your energy in the dream and everything will automatically shift, instead of trying to manipulate the elements of the dream. Know you what I mean? You are the power, you must center. Particularly in your dream state now, they are mirrors for you of conflicting energies in the soul patterns. These are your words, simply.

Comparing will get you into more trouble than anything else in these times, because it is your body and your experience here in this transition. I understand some of the fears you play with, you say. Some of you think it is more comfortable (many on your planet do or will here very shortly), more comfortable on the die side, you be died, to play die. The greater truth is you stay right where you are in the energies, the vortices that you've developed. And then you'll hang around looking for another suit to get into to finish what you said you would do.

Many are going to play this suicide game. It is not a wise choice to even contemplate this thing, not wisdom at all. To wish you were on a ship or another planet is to take what would be termed potshots at your soul's wisdom for being here. That is you in your greatest level of wisdom in the physical body saying you want to be on another planet, yet your soul knows better. So in one manner it is you showing you how stupid you are. But you must be careful because you might get the soul to agree with you. Know you what I mean? The soul says, "I'm tired of arguing with you, let's go to another planet." But the body stays. "Oops!" It shifts. Everyone take a breath.

In one manner you are in class. In another manner you're polishing, very finely polishing your soul forces to be of assistance. Not only here, but other places. You must complete here in order to be of assistance. If you don't complete what you call the inner direction (your words), then you will come back again [or] go to another place to do it, and pick right up where you left off. Right up where you left off with that last piece of prana.

Know you those little lights you see in the sky, that prana, the one you don't want to breathe? Be off the planet, no more prana breath. You pick right up there: "Oh, I'm sorry, I'll be back. I forgot you last time." That's how, know you, God evolves. That's how, in one level of understanding, prana evolves, becomes, because you utilize it—it enters your system, becomes part of you, you let it go again, gain wisdom. Indeed? Everyone lighten up a little bit.

Now, these baby powers, what I call baby powers, yet they are very powerful forces of you when you were brand new from Father (your words); the memories were there, the desires, the plays, the knowingness was there.

Now, you're all dealing with consciousness. Consciousness — that is how you play here. You have social consciousness, you have metaphysical consciousness, you have Christian consciousness, you have Jewish consciousness. Somewhere there's God consciousness — I know it! I think I can find it, too. That is you, and the Christ consciousness is you, that is on the planet that you know of. That's what's becoming now. Now, when these great energies begin, know you this Photon Belt that's going to eat you up? [Laughter.] When these energies come — and they are already here, actually, in one manner — they're expecting avenues within the brain, circuits within the brain, to be open to travel upon, to work through the body. So you may utilize your brain, physical brain now, and literally manipulate consciousness, manipulate your reality, shift things. That means you have to be very centered, know you? Now, some of you will play control with it, and that'll be all right as you bounce back and forth — no big deal. But in the center, as you hold the thought of it here because thought is everything, you hold it here above you and you allow, in a manner, your body to rise to the thought, in your physical now, and you become that thing.

G-O-D Meditation

Now allow your eyes to close and remember the gold light. Center. I want you to be in your brain now, in the physical brain, in your thinkety-think place . . . you know how to get there! Be thinkety-think now, that be grand. Now, above you I want you to contemplate this one word. It is your word, but we must use it because it is what you understand. I want you to contemplate the thought of it now in your thinkety-think – the way you thinkety-think, know you, work? – "God" right above your head six inches. Just contemplate that thing and center on that word. See the word: G-O-D; the O is right over your crown chakra. G-O-D right there. Centered right above you. Think about it right there. In order to think of it, you have to know it in the soul. Now feel that in the soul here, in the chest, the heart chakra. Allow. And right there in the heart chakra contemplate "I love God." Just contemplate that, feel it there. The feeling of it in the body. Allow that feeling to move in the body – arms, legs, torso, everywhere. Thinkety-think again the word "God" above your head. Contemplate in the heart chakra, "I love God." Off your right shoulder "God" is there, right shoulder, see the word, thinkety-think of it. Off your left shoulder, "God," thinkety-think.

Allow the top in the left and right shoulder to come into the center of the throat chakra, and feel the energy there, "God" at the throat chakra. Allow. Center. In a gentle manner slowly open your physical eyes. Everyone breathe. Relax.

Where you lose your ability to connect with God (in your words now), how you play, is your competitive behavior, your controlling behavior. That is all outside of you. Now, we've used many words, and so have many other entities, to get you to understand these things. But I'm going to throw a challenge out to you. We've told you beings for years to meditate, to center, to become, to become, to become. We've been telling you so much: to become, you're the Christ, become the Christ, become, your meditations will assist you, know you? You've heard of masters becoming masters, walking on water, indeed? Or do you think that's just a myth, can't be done? Your meditations are for you to practice so you can center and know and do these things. And your meditations are to be practiced so you can levitate with them. These energies that are going to be building over this decade are going to be very challenging, outrageously challenging for normal consciousness. They be cake of piece for the christed being, and the christed being is going to be needed to be here, many of them, to show others how to do it. So your meditations aren't simply meant to sit there and meditate all day. It's to center the energies and become so you can walk with this centering, knowing what you're doing, knowing what you're breathing, what you're completing in the thought of it, with the breath of it that will be manifested shortly. Time is speeding up, it's stacking on top of each other here.

Have a Christ Party

So the challenge, huh? I'm going to let you grade yourselves on how close you are to your christedness. And initially you'll have a lot of fun. It'll be grand to have these, we're going to call it, "Christ parties." Bunch of beings gather around, know you, have some wine, little beers, some pretzels, hot doggies and all of this. And you get yourself a little wading pool with a few inches of water in it, and you walk, and you walk, and you walk, and you walk, and you walk, and you walk, and you walk, until you can walk on top. That'll be your answer [to] whether you're in tune with your meditations. And if you have what you term 52 of your beers and then you walk on the water, then drink 52 of your beers, whatever it takes, know you what I mean? I wouldn't count on it, however. That is the challenge. We'll see how many of you do this. You think it's foolish. You have to practice, you have to center, and you have to become. It's very, say you, much easier to walk on a wading pool to practice your levitation, the ability of the water to recognize you, etc., etc., than it is when a big tidal wave comes, know you? And you say, "Oh, I better practice my christedness now." Things are happening, a lot of them. Everyone breathe, lighten up.

All of the extraterrestrials that you know, the masters that you know, the gods, won't do it for you! You must do it. Now you're moving beyond metaphysical understanding—you have to. It served you, and it served you well, to provide you a tool to get out of limited consciousness. Yet metaphysics is also very limited. Now you must move into Christ consciousness. That is doing with the body what you want to, be it levitate, be it bilocate, be it heal, whatever. Why? Because it is fun and you know what you're doing. Not to impress another. The moment you impress another with it, you go showy-offy, you're going to lose it. Don't go showy-offy if you're taking a boat into the middle of the ocean to take a walk, know you what I mean? Go showy-offy first in your little pond, make sure you really got it. [It] be all right. Everyone take a breath.

I know at times it's more fashionable to worry about: What is the next earthquake that's going to happen? How many people are going to die in this war that's coming up? Who's going to set off the next nuclear bomb? When's the planet going to tilt on its axis? When are the extraterrestrials going to mass-land so everyone knows? Everyone knows. Everyone! All of that is a smoke screen to keep you from becoming your Christ! "Give a little bit of worry shit over here, keep them busy. I haven't figured out how to become the Christ yet, but I certainly don't want them to get it, so give them this." That's what they're doing. You become. Now, this decade is meant for the becoming Christs—that's what it's meant for. Now there are those beings that know it, want to keep it all to themselves. Know you competitive behavior?

There are many masters out there that love you outrageously. I'm not the only one. We're going to make sure you get it—the hell with them. [Laughter.] But it's your choice, know you? You must apply. You must apply. Otherwise you play fear, die body. Well, no big deal, you've done it before! Really very simple. You're going to have all of the tools that you'll need. Meditation is one of them. You should do it at least 15 moments a day. And you should practice to feel your bodies bouncing a little bit and levitate your body—I don't mean leave the body; that's no big deal, you do that all of the time, but move the body.

The Lightbody Is Manipulated by Thought

The lightbody of you, what you would term a replica, holds energy, and at times it holds resentment because you told it to. In your social consciousness your lightbody will say, "I can't strike that being, the physical," but your lightbody might want to because of the thought. You see, your lightbody is manipulated by thought—what you think, it will do. "I love God" will center you in a moment because that is you, and that is everything else, also. That is everyone and everything. It will bring you back to a balance. "I love God."

We have worked, for some of you, several years on the opening of the heart chakra, because you're going to need to be in love with things, everything now, when this great ability comes (it's already started, in a manner), that you think it, and it is, right in front of you. But what will happen first is, you're doing it. It's a movement beyond telepathy. Some of you are already becoming very telepathic, indeed? You know who is going to drive up in your driveway, you know who is going to be on the phone, and "Damn it, I should have paid that bill." But the thought now . . . and you choose your thoughts because it all be around you. And you center; and if you're in confusion, "I love God." And then, "I'll pick this one, and this one," and if you're not sure, "I love God; [I'll] pick this one, this one; I love God." Because this is the vehicle now that is going to be working with each thought. Not only the ones you have today or tomorrow, but some of the ones that you thought you forgot back here, couple of years ago, know you? Six months ago, that you played that, "Well, it wasn't really my thought," know you? They exist in a spiral, entities, not linear, not linear. And the spiral is to tighten around the owner, through the application of the physical. Oops! "I love God." Remember that one; it's going to get your buns out of a lot of muck, I'm telling you here. Use it in your quiet moments. You don't have to say it walking down your street—I know how you get embarrassed—unless kundalini moves. "Whoa, I love God!" [Laughter.] It's all right.

You must center now, and apply the thoughts here. That means what you're going to do, you're going to learn to think very precisely, because you're going to learn to think, "Where do I want this physical body to go?" and "How do I want this physical body, as long as it's transitioning, to become? What do I want to do here, what do I want to do? I love God." Now, that doesn't mean to sit in your restaurant and say "I love God" all day long, because you can't make a decision, know you, whether to order red meat or fish. Know you?

"I love God." Everyone breathe.

[To a participant:] And don't judge yourself. One of the things you must understand is you can't judge yourself this lifetime . . . you can, but it is not wise. Because you judged yourself in past lifetimes, that's what brought you this lifetime, so you better figure out in one lifetime to stop judging. Know you what I mean? There's a little humor here.

[To another participant:] Know some of the difficulties in this society, as little ones [children] begin to demonstrate their wisdom, it doesn't seem to fit in with normal structure, know you? And then you go through the turmoil of whether you're inhibiting their growth, spiritually speaking, know you what I mean, in their psychic abilities. So you must learn to make a game out of it, know you? Communicate more every day; ask them what they dreamed or what they saw out of the side of their eyes, do you understand? Because they see very much. And they wanted to be with you because you wouldn't forget in this time, you understand? You're an outrageous being. Anyone have anything they want to chat about?

Yes, how can I help me help myself, my health inside?

Are you willing to listen?

Well, I can't guarantee I'll like it, but I'm willing to listen.

Well, I never ask anyone if they like what I do, know you? insofar as you say approval. No problem. Will you allow yourself to meditate 15 moments a day?

Yes.

Indeed? And you'll pay attention to the images and the messages?

I pay attention; I don't always understand.

Well, say yes.

Yes.

And then you won't talk about anything you see in these meditations to anyone, or voices you hear, do you understand that?

Yes.

You apply it to your being now. Know you what I mean?

I promise.

Okay. You must become first. Now, focus on yourself in this healing energy, you understand? Particularly in your meditations, all of the way. And then, when changes occur, then you can speak because it is knowing here, understand? It's going to require a little work, but you can do it. Are you willing to work?

Yes.

To start off, before your meditations a little raspberry tea. Know you raspberry? It is outrageous, what is termed herbal tea, for the female system.

Leaf or fruit?

Start off with the leaf, know you what I mean, "leaf"?

Yes.

Centering "I Love God"

Indeed, allow your eyes to close very slowly, gold light as you close your eyes. Bring it in, in the body. Contemplate, center, "I love God," right here in the heart. Also at the solar plexus, "I love God." I want you to contemplate at the solar plexus, "I am God! I and the Father are one," contemplate that, solar plexus. That is power there. Center. Not in competition with God. "I love God." Stay in the bodies. Open your temples, the chakras at your temples, open them. Allow. I want you to feel the energy in your head and in your hands and in your back. That be all right.

Now there are some of you, as you're dealing with some of these energies, it's going to affect some muscles because the muscles were built with previous thoughts that weren't totally aligned here. So you might require what you call your masseuse, your massage beings, [and] a little exercise, to work some of this off. Some alignments, know you? Some crystal work, etc. You're aware of these processes in your metaphysical community. [It's] simply to get you to adjust to [where] you feel better, but you still be "I love God," because that's where you get into your center. Utilize your tools that are available to you to ease some of the strain now. You must always get back to the center, "I love God."

Now, when you open your eyes this time, very gently, I want you to, as you open your eyes, see the body, garage door up, open, and it's filled with a brilliant white light, what's called prana. Allow. Center. Allow your eyes to close, gold light. Center. Now, your eyelids are not simply little tiny eyelids. The energy actually goes way in the back of your head. Allow your eyes to open, bright silver light. Allow. Center. "I love God." Center. This is what you do with colors and thought and energy. It's really very simple. Allow your eyes to close gently, gold light. "I love God. The body I Am is healing I Am. It is pure I Am. It is God." Allow your eyes to open. White light, feel it. Peace.

You say that we are dreaming constantly and so forth, but what if you do not remember those dreams when you awaken? It doesn't mean that you didn't have the dreams, it just means you did not remember them?

You chose not to see them.

But they still occurred?

They occurred. You would judge yourself. Some of you are still fighting in your dreams, know you? Warrior attitudes type things. Cutting people's heads off and all of that nonsense. Know you what I mean? So that is still there in the package; it's a good thing you don't remember them. (Everyone breathe a moment.) Anyone have anything else they want to talk about? You ready for more energy?

Indeed!

So be it. Allow.

Meditation: The Heart, The Healer

I want everyone to breathe now in the body down at the diaphragm. I want you to feel the energy. I want you to spread it out, push it down. Now I want you to breathe in the crown now, energy, and I want you to see a pyramid come down over you as you breathe it in. Breathe the energy right down, pyramid stays there. Now blow it out so the pyramid opens a bit, little bit, gently. More energy comes in. Allow. Peace. That be grand. Focus on the heart chakra. I want you to remember what you came here to do. Focus on the heart chakra. Feel it there, the knowing. Allow. Allow that thought that is the appropriate thought. Some of you know that you know how to heal. I want you to own that in your being right now. Every minute particum of that knowing I want you to acknowledge, from the heart chakra right into the brain. Allow. Remember. So be it.

How many of you are going to practice walking on a little bit of water? [Laughter.]

I'll practice. Can I do it in the shower?

I know you think it's a joke. But it is not a joke, becoming the Christ. You can joke about it once you've become it.

I have a question. You're asking us to literally get a little tub of water and try to walk on it?

Practice.

Are you serious?

I am very serious. Because every time you do and you go through you'll say, I'm not the Christ yet! I'm a very metaphysical entity, but I'm certainly not the Christ." You understand? Know you what I mean?

The Intent of Your Meditations

Is there anything that we can say to the water so that it will honor our power?

Well, one of the things is meditation, know you? Now, don't . . . I have to be very careful when I say things to some of you beings, know you what I mean? But you will know because the water will communicate with you. You'll hear it—a normal conversation like your friend next door. Know you? Only, the water is not going to call you a bastard. Your meditations were meant, the tools taught to you for years now, for this decade, so you could become in it, to remember. They weren't simply little stories, fables. There was purposeful intent here. I am certainly not joking when I say this thing . . . but you can treat it like a joke.

I'll explain a little bit more here. One of the things you beings utilize in your school here on your planet is to prove whether you're a Christ or not, and when you really find out you're not, that's when you're dying. Oops! That's when you move into the fear [of] what's going to happen, because you haven't studied, you haven't applied what you knew. You listened to someone else. Your meditations were tools to provide you to connect with God inside you, to remind you [that] you're one, how to do it! Metaphysically, you want to become the Christ so you can manifest gold in your hand and buy this $2 million house on a hill and overlord all the other non-Christs. I know how you think. This will be a humbling experience for you. You'll find out rather quickly how close you are. Now, you will, some of you, literally feel the tension of the water that's becoming. You will feel the elasticity of it. But it's not going to occur overnight; you're going to have to practice. Now, I notice how many of you practice your meditations all the time, so I can see the extent of this practice. Don't say I didn't give you clues.

Would it be appropriate to do that in the bathtub? Would it be okay to fill a bathtub with a couple inches of water?

You might slip and fall. Try a little pan, know you?

What about the creek?

That'll be grand. Whatever. Little bit of water. I don't want anyone to fall and hurt themselves and blame me, know you what I mean? Or drown, either. I'll be there when you drown, if that's what you wish to do. I'll grab you by the hair and say, "You idiot!" and I will call you that, too.

You can use this little water trick for beings that think they are playing, know you? You're going to have to do it because your extraterrestrials are not going to do it for you. And your media is getting loaded with fear and controlling energies now. Used to be fifty-fifty. Now you're really getting bombarded, know you what I mean? And it's all a deviation to get you away from being a simple man, simple woman, in love with God. That's all it's for. They are certainly not going to die for you. No, they can't. You must do that yourself, each one of you. So it's wisdom to figure out how the body works here, and your meditations have been provided. Over the years many masters have provided step-by-step meditations to take you further, further, further, further. You, in your limited behavior, you compare the masters. Don't do that. The masters are working together to provide information so you can get it linearly when you need it. You're all in this big spiral. Pay attention to your intuition here, your power. "I love God." It'll save your buns, it really will. If not on this level of activity, next one for sure, when things get really hectic. Now, give me a moment.

Sometimes it's wise to allow others to go, to make their transition, to move. Because they're moving at a time when they have established a state of grace, so sometimes it is wise. Never make hard-fast rule of thing. You be in love with the soul of the being as it's moving, whatever it decides to do. You cannot change the mind, the force (your word "mind" here) in its movement. Because it's moving out of love. Not "out of" out of love, but it's moving because of love, is what it's doing. Everyone breathe. So you must know when to love, and you should know to love at all times, all of the time. Indeed?

Have you beings noticed the energies between male and female? Indeed? How there seems to be even more resistance than usual? Indeed? You're playing this thing [polarity]. In the center is neutral. Either side is polar, polarity. To understand the both you must be in the center. You will always see the other side as an opposite, a pulling about you. You're moving this way [around or on either side of center, back and forth], not continually forever this way [aligned in the center]. So you stay in the center, "I love God," and you'll see it all. You'll see part of yourself, more of yourself, and more and more, more, more, more, more, more of you, is what you'll see. It's not the other person at all, it's you. So you must center to know this, and when you do, those that are this side/that side, will pass through your energy – they have to, to get to the other side, know you? And as they do, you can leave them a little something, "I love God." They'll come back again, they have to. Stay in the center, do you understand?

Now, when we did that meditation earlier—close your eyes, know you, gold—you felt it, and when I said "I love God," could you feel it in the middle of your body? Indeed? That is the feeling I want you to remember when you deal in these thoughts now, when they're coming from all over. Know you? And that is, all thought is God, every one of them, no matter good/bad, your word, whatever they are. But within your being you know the application of it, and "I love God" in the center here allows you to deal with the application of it in the physical appropriately. Appropriately.

I do suggest you meditate, be you play you 15 moments a day. I suggest that you focus on attaining the wisdom of you in here [soul], that knows how to levitate, that knows how to walk on water and have it brought forward. Little bit at a time. When you think you've got it, then begin to apply it. Then go back to your meditation to get it. It's going to take work, entities! Your extraterrestrials haven't rescued you yet, and they're not going to! You're going to have to work. It is your body, it is your God force. Sorry to break the news. How much do you want to know? How much do you want to become? Are you willing to use this lifetime to become? Are you willing to apply yourself to become in this physical body? Are you willing to work at it, to become you more, the Christ? This is the decade to do it! This is it, wide open.

1996 Will Be a Window

Your year 1996, the whole year is a window, the whole year. We gave you a little window in 1993—no one made it through, not one. We said, Oops, give 'em big window. Well, that's not entirely true; it is from your perspective, anyway. So this year '96, you work, you apply, you apply, you meditate, you become, you become, more, more, more. You apply yourself, work yourself. I don't care if you listen to my meditations or not—doesn't bother me. There are many meditations out there. This part [soul] knows what you need. Get one, listen, and apply. Desire to become. Your guides are working with you. They're put on overtime schedule, by the way. They're not too pleased about it, either; they don't get time-and-a-half, know you what I mean? They want to work with you here, very much so. And it is important. It's not only important for you, it's important for others that haven't a clue yet what is happening.

So it's application, 15 moments a day. You can do it early morning, you can do it late at night, it doesn't matter. Little bit more, you'll center and learn to walk in it. But you must practice. That's how you become great athlete, same thing. Your Buddhist monks, they do a lot of work, know you? They can do this. But they worked, they applied. Know you? No one gave them a TV dinner already made up. They worked at it. They know who they are, and even what you term some of your Native Americans know, not very many now. This is application of spirit, what you call your holiness, your sacred self, in density called physical body. It's understanding that part of your being. It is not a church, not at all. You are the church, you are the god, you are the Christ. Now, get off your bottoms and become. Indeed?

Indeed!

So be it. So it gets to be fun after a while. You can talk of your progress with one another. But don't talk about it competitively. Talk about your experiences of the feeling of the energy, that "This might be helpful to you if you feel this; this is what happened next for me." Because it's all similar. So it's a sharing, not a competitive thing, you understand? Your metaphysical behavior will create a limitation here. Practice, practice, practice, practice.

What do you mean by "metaphysical behavior"?

Where everyone does their chit-chats, metaphysically, know you what I mean?

Not really.

Well, um, how say you, "Where's Mercury today?" Indeed? And numerologically. "I couldn't levitate today because Neptune happened to be retrograde at this time." Know you? And it also goes with what the secret government's doing, know you? "Secret government gave me a bad day today! Almost made me drowned." The reason—and I am not the only one—there are other masters now that are going to begin to push you harder, harder, [is] because many are going to be leaving the planet, rather dramatically. At least, having heard some of this wisdom, when you leave this time, you'll be able to go further. If you make an oops, at least you'll be on the fast elevator, oops higher. "Well, at least I oopsed higher. I have a greater view. Now I can see all of the idiots down there, and a few above me, too." [He chuckles.]

It has nothing to do with whether the Moon is full or not. Some of the information astrologically is important—within the dietary system, within the function of the electrical system in the body—yes, it is. But it is not a controlling; it is that you know how to use it. "I have a full tank of gas, I can go this far; I have quarter tank of gas, I can only go this far." It is the same. You beings got it backwards.

Everyone breathe a moment. I don't want to upset any astrologers, now. The numbers don't control you; you chose the numbers because it vibrates appropriately for your lessons here, but you must apply your wisdoms to not only complete the lessons, but to overcome and become more. More, more, more.

The Ten Commandments Were Meant to Get You on Track

Now, I know how some of you enjoy rules. You've heard of the Ten Commandments, eh? Everyone got pissed off about that one, that there were laws to control you. Not originally. They were what you would call levels of information, that at your level of consciousness at that time, it would be wise to follow these precepts to get you out of the muck you got yourselves into after Atlantis. Well, you didn't pay attention. And then the priests took over and got you really mucked up. So now you're on your own, with all of your lifetimes here becoming. Pay attention. It is your body. It is your christedness. Your guides are around you; listen. Don't argue. Let go of social consciousness thinking—it keeps you limited. If you're told by a master [to] take a little wine, [then] take a little wine! It opens the arteries. (I don't mean a keg. Little bit.)

Now, as the energies increase in your December here, we will be doing meditations each week here [Fridays, 7:30 p.m.], plus I will have him [Arthur] and this one [Cheryl] do them in the middle of the week for others—some of you will be invited. It is to anchor energies, so that means you're going to have to hold a lot of energy in the physical body, more than you got tonight, more than you've ever had before. This is just preparing, preparing the physical. To do this, it's also advising you that your planet is getting this frequency, too. And in your meditations it is important, at times, to bring the planet to your heart chakra.

Now, I'm saying this thing with this meditation in this time because your guides are very close now, and your oversouls, your higher selves, are coming forth around you, individually, each one, to assist you. But you are the one that has to want to be assisted, that's willing to work on this thing. And the work is not really that bad. All you have to do is to allow yourself to remember, without judgment, what you've done in the past. Whatever it is, let it be there. No excuses. None. Allow yourself to remember. You become crystal-clear and everything becomes very easy. Indeed?

Indeed!

The Animals and Evolution

[To a participant:] There has not been an animal born on the planet that has become the Christ, you understand? This is the place to become the Christ; you must have human form. Enough said.

Are there any other questions?

I would like to know more about the animal kingdom. I really don't know their origin or their purpose. Could you talk about that a little, how we interact with them, and our purpose for interacting with them?

We'll put it this way: it is a training ground. Do you know what a training ground is? It is also a . . . how will we put this so you won't get it really confused? It's not really a punishment, yet from a certain perspective you could say it is. The being evolves, yet to complete its evolution, it can't move higher because there's some energy that is distorted. So it will inhabit an animal to come to a sense of patience with the distortion. Do you understand? Enter an animal body so the being doesn't have to incarnate completely. Do you understand that part?

Now, this is the difficult part. You are God, do you understand that? Who made the birds in the sky?

We did.

God, indeed? What allows you to see the bird in the sky? Your perception in your physical now, your eyes? The light of the Father that's within you sees the bird in the sky. Do you know that you're not looking at the same bird everyone else is, that you are the creator of that bird, then and now? Do you understand that?

Mentally, but not . . .

Metaphysically. This is another example of your metaphysics, like your astrology, indeed? The knowing is, you created this thing! Do you understand that? Don't go hierarchical now—which God created the gods? etc., etc. You'll lose it. If you allow yourself to meditate and you look after 15 moments, 20 moments of your meditation, you look at the clear sky and you command from the Lord God of your being for an entity to fly there for you, to show you the beauty of God in flight, if you are centered, a bird will be there and you won't see it come or leave. That's power, indeed? So move out of this comparing, indeed? You are the creator of the animals. Now, if you try to figure out which system the animals came from, and what was the name of ship that brought them here, you're going backwards. Understand? It applies to everyone.

This particular person said each one was ensouled.

Well, there is a fragment of what you term energy there that would be termed soul.

But there's a group soul for each species, isn't there?

There is. You have to get permission to . . . let's say you died your body, and you go out, and you don't want to completely incarnate all of the energy, so you park some here and say, "Well, I don't want to be human again; look at this, this animal has life span of four years – I think I'll try that simply to learn this energy." So you send a piece of you, four-year-old length of piece, to be that being. What you do is you create it. You create the body and you inhabit it, just like you created your physical body and inhabit it.

Didn't I tell you these things before? But I love you outrageously. It doesn't matter. You can compare all you want. You are the manifestors of everything you see. You just forgot how to do it. In the thought of it, it is. You're learning. Now, knowing that is entirely different. You'll learn that when you meditate. You do your meditations and you practice and you practice, and then you'll know. But it is metaphysical behavior to talk about it as if you do when you don't. You know you don't. That'll create a limit for you. Practice. Meditate. When the water talks to you, attempt to walk on it and like the water. You'll succeed. It's being done on your planet, not in your Americas here. You must allow the simplicity of yourself to come through now. Bargain?

Bargain!

So be it. Well, gave you quite a bit to think about this evening, eh? Especially when you thought I was kidding about trying to walk on water. But at least it brought the point up that you must work here, know you what I mean? You must! Fifteen moments each day. It's going to be helpful in your December. We are through. Have a grand time, indeed? Love each other. Bargain?

Bargain!

So be it.

2

Feedback in the Ripples of Time

Zoosh through Robert Shapiro
October 19, 1995

Right now you are in the Null Zone, as I've said before. And with the Null Zone there's a general deadening effect: It's harder to think, it's harder to plan, it's considerably harder to achieve goals that were established before your entrance into the Null Zone. You can achieve goals that are set now, but as you work toward some goal, you might find that either you get there faster or you get there more slowly; it doesn't go at the pace you had planned. And possibly the goal itself might be skewed a bit, it might be a little different, and this causes feedback.

Feedback, as electronics people know, is essentially an electronic signal that is emitted as a result of two or more things that are in discordance with each other. But you know, I'm stretching the meaning of the word feedback, because here you have two different time and dimension sequences overlaid to comprise the Null Zone. With these overlapping sequences of time and dimension, not only can things from either dimension be experienced to some extent (as I spoke about in the November issue), but because of the feedback resonance which occurs a little bit here, there, everywhere, people are beginning to experience other-dimensional realities as a physical reality.

To some extent this is an amplification of other-dimensional realities, meaning that what you may have observed, felt or known to exist in some ethereal or energetic function is easier to perceive. But there is more.

There are beings who exist in higher dimensions, such as the fairy world – it's a real world, even if you don't see it all the time. They exist generally from the fifth dimension up, in such a way that you can see them all the time – you can see them some of the time in the fourth dimension, whether you believe in them or not, but in the fifth dimension you see them all the time; they are just there. But now with this feedback resonance, which is occurring because of your rather sudden arrival in the Null Zone, you might have an experience such as this individual [Robert] had today, where you will be going along – walking, driving, something – and all of a sudden not only will you see the light – not only will you feel the energy or sense the shape, form and personality of a fairy – but you will see it physically. It will be a physical thing. Others may or may not notice it depending upon where they are, or they might think, Oh, it's just a funny-looking bird. But I assure you, birds do not usually look like people with wings.

You might also have experiences where you will sense other life forms that exist at different dimensions, and at times see them, depending upon how they move, where they move, where you are standing and your senses in general. They will be moving, and if you are moving it's almost like having the experienceof driving by a picket fence: If the pickets are wide enough and the gaps in the fence are narrow enough, you will see what's on the other side of the fence in flashes as you are walking or driving along. This is a circumstance where what you are seeing is not going to be flashing, but because they are in the feedback resonance, you will see them, and conversely, they will see you; it's two-way. They will see your whole world if they are sensitive beings like those in the fairy world. If you are a sensitive being you may see their whole world, or not. The opening on their side is very small, whereas

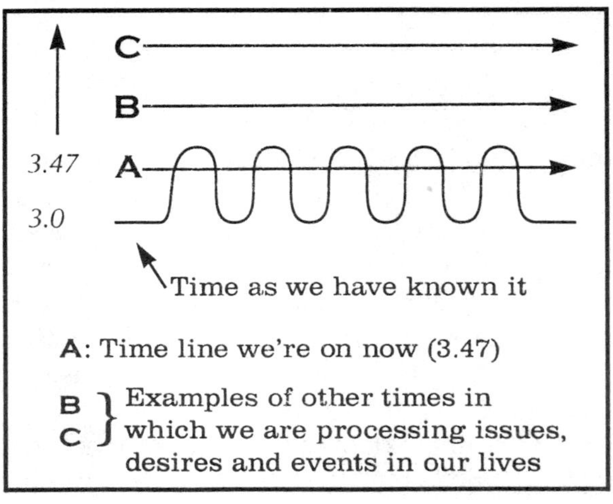

the opening on your side, in your dimension, is larger, so they are more likely to be able to see your world than you are to see theirs.

All People Capable of Extrasensory Experiences

I mention this now because the circumstances of your world are changing so vastly, on almost a daily basis, that those of you who have wanted to visit another planet don't have to go to another planet now, because the planet you are living on is another planet. The chances of having, as I say, extrasensory experiences are vastly increased – even if you are not happy about something, even if you are not particularly spiritual in your life, you might still see something from another world. This is particularly important because there are many people on your world who are not having a good time. Maybe they're at war or in famine, or having some other very serious difficulty. Maybe they are in prison – but don't assume that just because you're in a place like that you will not have these experiences; even if you're surrounded by energy that is very negative in its nature, or surrounded by fearful beings, you might hear something, you might see something.

Take note of how you feel after the experience; don't be attached to other people seeing just what you saw. They might see something different; they might see nothing at all. Again, it's how the images line up: how you line up to what is being seen by you, how it lines up to what is being seen by it (I don't like to refer to other life forms as "it," but I will in this case). So it's a focal length to some extent, and in that sense different people will either see different things or maybe see nothing at all.

I'm mentioning this now because these feedback resonances are not in any way affected by the energies on your planet. As I've said before, the reason you don't see ETs walking around on the streets (for the most part) is that they cannot tolerate the energies here – they are too extreme. They can't take negative energy, as you call it. But this is different. They are in their worlds – if their world happens to be the fifth, sixth, seventh, eighth, or whatever dimension of Earth, or even some other planet entirely, in the feedback resonance you will see them or sense them in some way. You might have a chance to see or sense their world.

So I mention this because I want you to be aware. If your child comes up to you and says she saw a fairy or an elf, she's not joking; she really means it. Don't say, "Oh, that's just your imagination, dear." Just say, "That's wonderful! I hope you enjoyed it. Treasure the experience." It's good to encourage not only children but all people. You have been trained as a society for so many years to disbelieve more than you believe. Now you will be presented with many opportunities to believe your own senses. So don't be so quick to let others talk you out of what you experienced. If you saw it, if you felt it, if it was a good thing, know that it's true, and don't tell it to people who are going to say, "Oh, that's not true." Tell it only to your friends who would cherish knowing about such a thing. All right?

The Cows Go Home

Now, on to cattle curiosities. I have here a letter from a woman who is writing a query about an experience had by her friend who owns a ranch in Texas. On this ranch they raise cattle, and one day her friend went out on the range and discovered a significant group of cattle dead and looking odd. Any rancher worth his salt (as they say) would expect to find a cow dead now and then, and certain conditions prevail when they find them that way. But this was a phenomenon curious enough that I'm going to talk about it a little bit.

This incident took place near Midland, Texas (I want the rancher to know who we're talking about here). There were a couple of other incidents nearby within a significantly close radius – say, 150 miles. This is relatively nearby, and they all happened within the same night or two. Three things went on, three entirely different things, but they were caused by a similar thing.

You know, for years you've been hearing about cattle mutilations and so on; a terrible thing. Just because you classify a being as an animal does not give anyone the right to abuse that animal. I've talked about that before, and this was not about that. Granted, there were some odd circumstances associated with it, but here we have a case where animals (as they are classified) are beginning to have options not unlike your own. Here on Earth man has been conditioned to believe that he is somehow the superior being, for no better reason than that he has learned how to suppress his heart and believe his mind. This one little factor has not only separated you from the natural world on Earth, but has allowed you to make catastrophic mistakes in your scholastic studies of material and spiritual mastery here. And these catastrophic mistakes continue to be revealed to you from time to time, when you're on either the giving or receiving end of some particular bit of mischief.

Understand that cattle, regardless of how much they've been tampered with to induce different breeds and so on, are basically natural beings. They know they are love, they know that love is the absolute and that all else follows. In recent years the energy associated with cow-beings, let's say, has had the opportunity to do several things: Largely as a result of the cattle mutilations and deaths, cows have decided that they're not welcome here anymore. You know, a lot of ranchers raise cows with a certain degree of kindness – not necessarily affection; the youngsters on the ranch might have some affection, but they can't get too attached to them as pets, obviously, because of what they're raising them for. Nevertheless, by and large there has always been, especially with small family farms, respect for the cows. They are treated as well as the people can treat them. And the people do not live in luxury while the cows suffer; many ranchers might be able to honestly say it's the other way around.

So I would say this: Ranchers, do not blame yourself for what is occurring. The cows have felt your respect and appreciation, and while not everything was to their liking, especially feed lots and the way they were killed, nevertheless they were willing to go along with that as a race of beings. They would have liked, when it was time for them to be killed, to have it done with more respect and more quickly so they wouldn't have to hang around and wait for this imminent death, which is a very frightening and miserable experience. Still, they were willing to hang in through all that. But with the mutilations done, largely associated with beings who were in occupation on this planet (as I've talked about in the Explorer Race book, which you all, gentle readers, will have in your hands before too long), this was the last straw.

What occurred on that night and the next night in and around the area of Midland, Texas, was that a ship came. The ship was not from the "cow planet," so do not get your imaginations fired up too much. But on their native planet, in their native galaxy, cows actually do not look the way you see them here; they are upright beings. Granted, they do have short, stubby legs that they stand on, but they stand upright; they look similar in some ways, but you'd be very clear if you saw one of these beings that it was not an Earth cow. You wouldn't be sure what it was, but you'd know it wasn't a cow. They do have the big eyes, though, those big, beautiful brown eyes. (As a matter of fact, they said, when they were coming to this planet, that they would not be willing to come to be used in the way they were going to be used unless they could bring something familiar with them – and they brought their eyes. That's the only real thing that reminds them of back home.)

So a ship came for them, and the beings on the ship said to

these cows (and they could find them easily enough, having an energy similar to their own), "Would you like to come back home now?" It's an interesting concept, isn't it? These particular groups of cows had heard about the mutilations; just because cows don't talk to you doesn't mean they don't talk to each other in their own way. And because a lot of mutilations have occurred in Texas (ask any rancher – they may not talk about it openly but they talk about it to each other; it certainly has put a crimp in the ranching business), cows know about it.

The ship came overhead. You might ask where the ship was from, but I can't tell you, okay? I will just say that it wasn't from your galaxy. The ship came over and a telepathic message was radiated across an area of land about 300 miles in diameter, with the Midland, Texas, area being roughly the center: "Who wants to go back home?" You have to understand that cows understand very clearly that at the end of their lives, their spirits return home. Many of the cows telepathically said, "But we will all return home at the end of our cycle, yes?" And the beings on the ship said, "Yes, but right now we need some people [meaning cow people] with Earth experience to help us understand Earth people." I might add that this ship originated from the almost-sixth dimension – other worlds are shifting dimensions, too. They said, "We need to know about human beings on Earth." They know about human beings on other planets, they just don't know about human beings on Earth, and they can't hear about it from other beings; the only way they can hear about it is intimately from someone who is essentially their own kind in heart and soul if not necessarily in body. They said, "We need some volunteers. Will any of you come with us?" Not unlike children being asked a question, having to leave their world, they sort of shuffled around for a moment or two, and then they had some volunteers.

The volunteers came from three different areas (I'm being purposely vague because I don't want to draw undue attention to this area). And these three groups of cows said, "We will go." Those aboard the ship did not "beam them up, Scotty"; rather, they took their souls. Their hearts (their love energy) and souls were taken aboard the ship and placed in small containers. This race is very advanced; they have the capacity, at the end of the life of one of their loved ones on their planet, to ask the soul and Creator if it is all right to retain the soul for a while. They do this at the moment the soul leaves the body, and if the soul says yes, they will put it in a small vessel. The vessel is a tube, say, four inches in diameter by ten inches tall, and inside it has an equilateral-triangular crystal. There is a liquid floating in the tube, and the soul enters the crystal and is sustained there for its temporary visit by the liquid. The souls of these cows were placed in these kinds of vessels. They will be there, in terms of your experiential time, for about 45 years while they pass on their knowledge of your world.

Now you might ask, especially if you have some knowledge of agriculture, how much a cow can accumulate in a year or two. But it isn't like that. They have species consciousness. They are part of the natural world, meaning they don't suppress their hearts and love in favor of their thoughts. Any species, or any individual human being, for that matter, that allows the heart and love, and honors all life and appreciates all life (as one might on other planets) will generally have available to them species consciousness. Because they had species consciousness, any cow who had ever been on Earth at any time would have been able to pass on to them, while they were alive, anything they ever observed. So when they went into the ship, into those vessels, to preserve their souls for roughly 45 years of Earth time, they had the ability to speak of not only things they experienced personally, but also things they had heard through the species consciousness telepathic resonance, as it's called. Resonance in that sense simply means the vibrational echo of all that is known.

I bring this up because I want you to realize that there are many forms of life. Often you will see beings – cow-beings, birds, elk, whatever – and you will perhaps appreciate seeing them, but you won't think anything of it. It's important to know that they are real beings. They come from someplace else, and they volunteered to come here to assist you in your material mastery school because they believed in the genetic experiment on Earth that was designed to create the Explorer Race, which is you. They believed in not only the validity of that project but the ultimate benefit for all beings everywhere in the universe. They volunteered to come here not because they're too dumb to know any better – they did it because they were willing to make personal sacrifices, that the universe might be improved. So I want you to understand. I'm not saying don't eat cows; but if you do, be grateful and honor them! Okay? That's my comment on the incident in Texas.

Great Gatherings of the Citizens of the World

What changes are going to happen in December?

Well, I'm not prone to giving you major predictions, but I will say that I'm expecting people all over the world to become increasingly unsettled with their governments as their sole representatives. I'm looking again for a tremendous upsurge of various professions as well as just folks getting together in major conferences to discuss worldwide issues and coming up with not only papers, as they did in the Beijing conference on women, but eventually, publicity. There might be special television shows that spring forth to educate people. Average citizens all over the world are going to stop looking to their governments to represent them, because the governments are so caught up in their own political turmoil that they have, being bodies, forgotten how to interact as individuals.

You know, if individuals come over to the United States from another country, you're polite to them, they're polite to you, you talk, you get to know each other – that's normal. Once upon a time governments did that, too. They've forgotten. And because they've forgotten, I'm expecting the people to get together on their own. It's not going to be a revolution – governments, don't worry about that. But as the people remember how to talk directly to each other (granted, through interpreters), it's going to be a really special time. And I feel a tremendous swelling of energy for more of these things to take place.

In a few years you'll have your choice of 100 fascinating conferences a month that you could go to around the world. Some will be issue-oriented and some will just be an exchange of cultures. Some will be artistic, some will be about social systems, some will even be about politics, but a lot of them will simply be people wanting to get to know the other person. I'll tell you something: There are so many beautiful cultures in this world with so many beautiful things to offer. If you put a lot of these people in a room, and you eliminate government, you don't get a big battle, you just get a lot of great conversations, a lot of people talking about things. Granted, you wouldn't want to put everyone of all different types in the same room, but I'm looking for a lot more conferences, and I think it's going to be great.

These are unusual times. Be alert to it, and understand that these are not times of disaster so much as they are times of opportunity. Don't fall into the prophecy trap. Very often we talk about things that could happen because we want to awaken you to the possibility so that you powerful spiritual and material masters out there (or at least, material mastery students) will awaken to your ability to change those things to something better.

Try to remember that with every other human being on Earth, you have infinitely more in common than not. If you can remember that, and remember that love is the most important energy to feel, and that control is always an element of fear, then you will be much more than half-way home. Goodnight.

3

Masculine and Feminine Balance

Zoosh through Robert Shapiro
October 30, 1995

All right. Now, I want to talk a little bit tonight about the balance of the world's population. You know, it is not an accident that more women are born than men, and it is actually intended now that within the next 17 years the population balance itself in its proper order. It is intended by Mother Earth, by Creator, by everyone, that the actual population of the Earth be approximately 73% women. Yes, I know it certainly increases the competition, but in order to reintegrate the feminine energy it will be necessary to overdo it for a while, to bring it into a balance that creates a temporary imbalance .

The masculine energy has lost itself. The energy that is focused masculine is not present on Earth. You might ask yourself, well, what about all these men? The energy they are demonstrating is polarized, yes, but it is not true masculine energy. Granted, it's a form of masculine energy, but it's a distorted form – twisted fully 180 degrees from its point of true origin. And in order to simply do more than complement it, it will need to be nudged. It is in the nature of balance in general and in the balance of nature specifically that anything in nature tends to balance itself. Look around in the natural world – you will see that without interference from man, nature is balanced in its own right.

So how do we "true up" the masculine energy on Earth? It would seem better to focus on the masculine energy, but no – it is more important to focus on the feminine energy, bring up the feminine energy to a role where it is overly dominant – dominant not meaning control or power, but quantity. When this happens, the natural rhythmic cycle will pull the masculine energy into its true state, because nature always wishes to be in balance. The only way for masculine energy to truly come into balance in its true state is to be half feminine, half masculine. Right now it's not in its true self because it is too masculine. Right now the masculine energy represented by many (not all men, but certainly a great majority) is too masculine.

If we bring the feminine energy up to at least 73% (possibly 75%, but I don't think it'll have to go that far), then the masculine energy will begin to imitate a form of balance and will gradually, on its own, without any prompting, move into a state of 50% feminine, 50% masculine, which is the true masculine energy as it is supposed to be expressed on all dimensions of Earth.

So speaking especially to cultures that do not value feminine beings so much, I will say this: Please note that if you favor (to put this delicately) the birth of male over female, you will be standing in the way of your own true balance, of your own true mastery, of the balance of Earth as it was intended by Creator in all forms. In the coming years there will be a flood of female babies born, and this is why. So don't worry too much, physicians; it is intended. Kindly encourage females as much as males. Any questions on the topic?

You say the female population is going to 73%. What is it right now?

Allowing for interference in some cultures, the balance is still pretty near 54% feminine. If there weren't interference by certain cultures favoring males over females, it would easily be 60%.

So the Earth is going to be producing more females until the ratio reaches 73% in order to bring the masculine energy into true balance, which is a 50% feminine and 50% masculine energy within the man — is that what you're saying?

Yes, that is correct. You see, there has been confusion on the part of many men to believe that balance between masculine and feminine means one man, one woman and so on – but it's not really true. It is not an accident that the races reproduce through women. It is intended that the obvious be present, that if it is built into the race that women are the creators of life, then there is something beyond casual in the relationship of women to creation. This is intended to be a clear-cut clue for even the most dense society. However, because of the revolution in intellect in the past few hundred years (essentially since the development of the Gutenberg press), there has been an overemphasis on a strictly intellectual focus. The intellectual and the physical are largely manifestations (in the third dimension, in any event) of the masculine, whereas the spiritual and the feeling self (the emotional body) is largely a feminine function. This is how it's broken down, at least at this stage of your development.

So I would simply say that in order to bring the masculine up to speed, we have to induce the feminine energy. This cannot be done on a societal level, because it won't be acceptable by most cultures on the Earth. The only way to do it is on a natural level, meaning to stimulate natural genetic evolution. Granted, there are societies such as your own in the United States and several others that are attempting to manipulate genetics largely for the purposes of greed and, to some extent, for the purposes of improving the health of the human being. But once you get around to patenting living beings, you know you've gone down the wrong track, at least philosophically.

So what's going on here is a necessity for Mother Earth and Creator in all forms to inoculate masculine energy with 50% feminine energy through a form of catalyst action. The overabundance of females will essentially cause a reaction in the male energy to draw on female energy in order to balance itself—similar to the way one would put a diseased person or a plant or animal (in some cases, not all, of course) with ones that are healthy. Let's say, for instance, a dog has been abused and is cowed, as they say. Sometimes (especially if the dog is young enough) you can put that dog with dogs that are not cowed, that have not been abused, and the dog will make a comeback on its own. Masculine energy can most easily accommodate a comeback into its own balance without having some artificial means to do it.

What was the lifestyle like when it was in balance with the feminine?

When masculine energy was in its proper balance (in other words, being its proper self), the intuitive functions of the masculine being were in tune with the feminine being. Both have the capacity to speak, to hear, to sense the natural world all around them. There are stories, especially in England, Scotland and Ireland, where once upon a time people could talk to the fairies, the little people, the elves and so on. These were not just entertaining tales; it was a fact when people were in greater balance—say, at around the 400s in the United Kingdom. Let's just isolate it to the United Kingdom and Ireland. During that time the people were in balance: Feminine beings were feminine, masculine beings were 50-50, the religion was based on nature — and it wasn't just a religion, it was a philosophy, a day-to-day, moment-to-moment experience. Nature spirits communicated openly and freely with human beings, and human beings lived according to the guidance, example and teachings of nature spirits and living beings in nature (not just beings existing in spirit, but living beings such as the fairies, elves and so on). I mention this because these beings are alive. Just because not all of you can see them does not mean they are not alive. But nowadays they are making some effort to be seen a little bit more (especially by those who are youthful, or at least youthful at heart) to encourage you, to remind you that this a real thing, not strictly a story.

What about the feminine at that time? What was the feminine lifestyle or way of being a woman? Was it somebody who was married, was it somebody who was a goddess or lived with other women and did her sacred marriage once a year, twice a year?

Within the context of that society it was actually more appropriate for a woman to guide the family. The family in that sense is an old custom. In the old days (as in some tribal situations even today), the extended family was the rule rather than the exception. You could say "husband and wife" but the marriage was not formal; certainly ministers did not come over and decree marriage. There would be at least one man and one woman, the children, the parents (as long as they lived), the occasional grandparent (life wasn't quite as long then, but occasionally). The woman's job (and young women were trained for this) was to guide the natural motion of the family. Let's say a family was living in a cave (there are several large caves in Great Britain, although not as many as there once were), and there was a woman, the matriarch of the family (not always the oldest) who was the woman with the greatest vision, because her senses had proved to be the most accurate. Let's say she felt a flood coming on. She would have the authority to move the family, lock stock and barrel: "Let's go, we're getting out of here, we're going to higher ground." If she would say that, [snaps fingers] it would be done. There would be no question.

We're talking about a feminine authority, what is referred to as a matriarchal society, but it wasn't matriarchal in the sense of property. Private property was not so much of a factor then, in any event; if someone had something associated with them, their clothes, their decorative items, their spiritual items, that was honored. But the matriarchal society had to do with guiding the family — where's the best place to go to get food? The woman would occasionally hunt, but usually the men would go out to hunt and the women would tell them where to hunt. It was done by sensing. And although the men were trained by other men, they had a woman consultant, usually the oldest woman who was available – not necessarily the wisest, but the oldest – because it was considered honorable to allow her into the men's society sometimes to speak because she had wisdom, and she was honored for her years.

The women, then, were the main focus for survival. The clans got along much better then . . . especially around 400 A.D., because for one thing there weren't that many people. You weren't threatened. The clans were generally in touch through the matriarchal hierarchy. There wasn't a hierarchy; it was rather a chain-link situation, you know? Each extended family group would have at least one visionary matriarch, and if another family was immigrating near a family already established, these matriarchs would be the individuals who would contact each other. Sometimes a person would be very young; you might be surprised. People did not live much beyond the age of 37 at the outside, so you might have a matriarch visionary of the family who is nine years old. Her visions would have proved to be so accurate that the people would trust them and she would have been given that authority. She ruled in the sense of trust; what she said was so, so people did not question it, they acted on it.

Was this the England area you're talking about?

Yes.

Were there other places where this was similar?

Yes. Some of the other places where that went on (and to some extent still does today) would be in Australia. It used to go on in New Zealand, but that's changed. The people who preceded the Maoris had a very specific arrangement that way. The idea of the matriarchy was picked up by the Maoris to some extent from the people who preceded them. The original Athabaskan people associated with Mongolia and the Eskimos used to have this culture. I don't think they have it anymore.

What about in Africa?

An ancient tribe (no longer present) of very short people had that system.

What about the people referred to as Native Americans here?

Some of the tribes even today have a matriarchal form, but not where the matriarchal visionary could be of any age. It has become more of a hierarchical thing, that the older people get, they are given this title, but they may be given this title without necessarily having the vision. In the old days you had to have the vision to survive; there was no fallback position. If there were saber-toothed tigers coming and the nine-year-old visionary got it and she was always right, you packed up your few belongings and hustled out of there. You didn't decide to take it up with the council later.

So do you see with this 73% female beings on the planet, these visionaries coming back into the natural order of things?

Yes, and a lot of them are being born now. Unfortunately, China is unintentionally shooting itself in the foot; it is the policy amongst the people to favor the male child. About 40% of the female children being born in China for the last three years and for at least another six or seven years will be strongly visionary, able to help their extended families know what is so and what is not so.

Are they killing these babies?

Yes. The entire purpose of my talk is to encourage this to change, and there is no reason to assume that this information will not get all the way around the world to those who might listen.

Is this the first time the masculine energy has become disrupted and needs to come into balance?

It's very rare that the masculine energy has been so out of balance on Earth that it doesn't exist. When it's this extreme, it doesn't exist. There have been very few times like that.

Because there are too many men on the planet?

No.

Because of their thoughts . . . ?

No, it's because of their feeling, their energy. Thought is not a function in it at all. It doesn't make any difference how many men there are; if there were only one man and his energy was this way, it would have to be changed, and the only way to change it is through this catalyst action —that I know of —without having major extraterrestrial influence, which amounts to interference.

I remember Lemuria as being a time when the men were really with the women. Can you talk about that a little bit?

Understand that Lemuria is not associated with Earth as you know it; the men were counterparts of the women. There was so much balance that in a dance, the rhythm between the dancers, male or female, would be perfect because the inspiration and the following action would be in perfect harmony and resonance. They were so much in tune with each other that someone would pick up the feeling of what someone was dancing, and they would all dance that way. I mention it to you this way because it is that exact feeling that has been missing for quite a while between men and women. It's like one places a hand one way and the other a hand the other way —and they miss each other. There has been this "missing each other" for quite a while, and men get frustrated because they cannot understand what women want. They cannot understand it mentally because the message is being broadcast physically through the emotional body and the physical body. Men in Lemurian days would know, through what I call the instinctual body, because that is that body that synthesizes all incoming feelings to know and to respond through knowing. It's not a mental knowing, an analytical knowing; it's an instinctual knowing that stimulates instinctual response that is felt and acted upon in the same way —from, say, the feminine being —and it goes back and forth. So you have a total attunement.

Is there something we can do to help our men to understand this?

No.

Is there some way we can communicate to them and assist them, or is this just going to have to evolve through time?

I want you to think about it. How long have women been trying to tell men how to communicate like women?

Right . . .

And how come they're not doing it by now? They've been told this for quite a while. They've been told just about everything in every form of language that you can imagine, plus languages that are now dead. How come they haven't gotten it by now? The reason is because they can't be told. It isn't something that's intellectual. However, because of who you are, I will say this: It might help if you push in and down with a slight pressure, not enough to cause screaming pain, on the bottom of the right foot of a male between the large toe and the next toe (first digit, second digit).

You do that to the guy? What point is it you're pushing?

It relates to the instinctual heart; it is not your physical heart. You simply have to practice the thing that all people have come here to practice; the "p" word . . .

Patience?

Thank you. Patience, quite right.

Because I've noticed that some men, if they have more of their female side coming in, are able to relate more, right?

Possibly, but we have to create a distinction here.

This is just my observation (although I don't know that many) that the more

spiritual men become, the more in touch they become with their female side and the less aggressive they are with women. Do you know what I mean?

Yes, that's right. Get used to it! You want to have your cake and you also want to eat it. No, you are here to perform a job of work, a responsibility as well as to have a good time.

Well, that's a more androgynous relationship, then.

I wouldn't say androgynous, I would say . . .

Then basically it's going to be on a higher, spiritual level rather than on a lower, sexual level?

No, I wouldn't call it a lower sexual level. I would say this, simply: You have come here as souls to become the Explorer Race, and one of the functions to stimulate you to learn material mastery is to experience something that you don't experience at more expanded levels of consciousness (meaning what sometimes people call higher dimensions) – electrical energy. I'm not talking about electromagnetic, I'm talking about strictly electrical energy, which does not exist at all levels of Mother Earth's being, but does exist at levels at which material mastery may be learned. Here's an example: at higher-dimensional levels, interactions between men and women (or whoever), in lovemaking, the feeling is absolute, unconditional love, plus a magnetic feeling. At this level, what makes up the sexual climax is magnetic love and electrical energy.

As you move up the scale (and you are pumping up slowly from third to fourth dimension) you will gradually leave behind the electrical field. There will not be electricity. We know that the electrical field is native to Mother Earth in the third dimension in any thunderstorm, lightning – boom! – electrical field. We know Mother Earth provides this. Your third-dimensional bodies are made up from Mother Earth; when you have sexual climax, or motion of creation, in third-dimensional material mastery school you experience motion of creation with electrical energy as well as love/magnetic energy. You do not experience unconditional love. That is something you experience after life. Yes, a person might have unconditional love, but to do so in the sexual climactic situation is not likely; I do not know of anybody doing that on the planet now, although there were a couple of people a while back. In other words, it's rare.

As you go up in the higher dimensions, you're going to say goodbye to electricity, and climax will be unconditional love, which is a feeling of warmth and total acceptance and magnetic love, magnetic energy. But no electrical energy, so you don't have the electrical feeling associated with climax. It's different.

So what are men going to be like? As you say, as men begin to absorb more of their feminine energy and come into greater balance with their feminine energy, they are going to be less aggressive. They are going to have more unconditional love, more magnetic love. They are not going to have as much electrical within them. But right now men are grossly out of balance with electrical energy, which is designed for one purpose only: creation and recreation, period. It does not have any morals or values or principles, so it could be used as easily for destructive as constructive purposes. As a matter of fact, anybody who'd been in a lightning storm might be inclined to call it destructive and frightening. On one hand it's beautiful, but on the other hand, if you're close to it, it's not the sort of thing you want to hug or kiss. It is the energy of creation in the third dimension, but if it struck you, there is limited chance of survival.

It's important for you to understand that you don't have your cake after you eat it; it is gone. You as women are here to perform responsibility. Responsibility is more than men. Responsibility is designed to initiate, and once the results of your initiation take place, we do not put things back the way they

A GLIMPSE INTO 1996

Zoosh

- An acceleration into being and seeing your real self.
- Glimpses of a world government.
- Effort in U.S. toward changes in politics and government.
- U.S. creditors forcing debt confrontation.
- Corporate model stronger in U.S. government, megacorporations to sustain U.S.
- U.S. voters become independent, unpredictable; independent candidates more viable.
- U.S. voters still judgmental, not ready for President of light; Colin Powell may enter the race in 2000.
- Genetics researchers with megabillions to play with are going to be publishing research showing that love has power.
- M.D.s increasingly embracing alternative healing methods, especially homeopathy, and by late 1996 rebelling against the AMA's recalcitrance.
- Best investment: land for food-growing.
- Public conditioning about ETs to continue, until diehards disappear and the younger generation can play it straight.
- Know what you want and what you wish to let go of and you will accelerate toward your goals.
- If Earth sleeps from exhaustion because she is overloaded, drought will ensue; hybridized plants are unable to communicate their need for rain.
- Although California is overpopulated, it will continue physically for some time and be an adventurous place to live.
- As creators-in-training, when you hear dire predictions, you unconsciously and consciously change unwanted scenarios; *you* are the magicians.

were, because we don't like the outcome. This is the circumstance that is evolving, and to some extent it is taking place simply through the existence of numbers. You have billions of people on the Earth; five billion is roughly the magic number. After that many people, if there is even a minor change in the magnetic field (and as you go up in dimensions you get more magnetic), then simply the sheer numbers of people tend to function as a multiplying factor, as they might say in mathematics.

Women have been saying in recent years, especially since the late sixties, "We want more gentle men, we want loving men, we want affectionate men." You're going to get your wish! But you're not going to have men who are aggressive sexually, because the downside of that is so extreme it is not acceptable. The downside, I'm sorry to say, is having much more destructive impact than the upside of it. (No pun intended.)

I'm not making decrees or proclamations; I'm simply explaining what is happening.

How long is this going to take, for men to become more balanced and have more intuition? As we move up in the dimensions it automatically happens, right?

Yes, but within the context of your current society (we're talking about Joe Average here, not people who are into spiritual things), certainly within 30 years.

So what are women supposed to do? [much laughter.]

Women's bodies as they now exist are to some extent a result of men's extreme imbalance for the past 700 years or so. So women's sexual needs will alter in time. About 20 years after the full influx of this change with men, women's needs will begin to change biologically, physiologically, and there will no longer be a physiological need. Within a few years after the change for men, there will no longer be as much emotional or even mental dependency upon it. Physiological changes will take place within roughly 50 years that will allow a woman to experience a climax that is more associated with unconditional love and magnetic love – unconditional love being essentially that love associated with Creator and the matrix that holds all life together, magnetic love being the feminine.

This suggests a different slant, does it not? If magnetic is feminine and electrical is masculine, as my opinion goes, then it suggests that Mother Earth is essentially Mother/Father Earth. Go ahead.

How is it going to affect the body of Mother/Father Earth, looking at it as being feminine, this balance between the magnetic and the unconditional love?

Right now because men are overwhelmingly involved in the intellectual and underwhelmingly involved in their emotional or their instinctual, it's very easy for them to do things that are destructive to the Earth – to say nothing of their own bodies and the bodies of others – because they are in denial of their senses, their feelings. They have only a certain amount of senses that they feel a societal approval to express in some way. Most of their senses are sublimated. When men come into a greater sense of balance, they will have their senses, they won't be able to step on a flower without feeling, "Whoa!" and jumping back, saying, "I'm sorry! Excuse me!" The feeling that they had harmed someone would translate directly to an action, and they would become more sensitive about where they put their feet. Women do not have to go through this energy change as men do, but they also need to pay attention to the ideal feminine.

What would you recommend for women at this point?

To get involved as much as you can with the sensitive, so you can feel the plants – feel, feel, feel. Don't buy into this intellectual thing; by all means learn how to think and function in society, but don't buy into it as be-all, end-all. It obviously has led to some serious problems; for example, science as it's practiced is basically godless, heartless. This is not to suggest that scientists do not have religion or have no heart, but that science as practiced is an intellectual creation and can just as easily produce penicillin to save people pain and suffering as it can produce an atomic bomb to wreak havoc, destruction, pain, suffering and death. It is the same science that does both. This suggests this science has no heart; that it is a religion in search of a god, which I've discussed at length before.

Do you see for the women who are more advanced spiritually, extraterrestrial men or beings coming in whom we would be able to relate to better than the third-dimensional men who are taking so long to evolve?

No! You're not here for a vacation! Once you're done with your cycle, you can play all you want. But no, I do not see it. I do not rule out the occasional wild weekend, but other than that, this is not something you should bank on. We're done with the subject for now.

4

Negative Sirians Coming to the 3rd Dimension

Zoosh through Robert Shapiro
November 16, 1995

Those of you who have been smelling sulphur lately, do not be concerned about the fires of Hades; it is not that. Right now you have doorways in your planet that are opened up to a one-way passage from the second dimension to the third dimension. Since you are now in the Null Zone at roughly 3.47 (on a range of three to four in dimensional terms), you are not in the third dimension, but you are still close enough to it to experience 3.0-dimensional experiences . . .

The smell of sulphur is directly correlated to second-dimensional Earth – 2.5-dimensional, 2.7-dimensional, 2.9-dimensional and easing into 3.0-dimensional Earth. I might add that second-dimensional Earth is the place where many people have gone who have visited that which has come to be known as Hades, or Hell. The description of "all the fires burning, souls suffering" idea is not pulled out of someone's fertile imagination, but is actually a place. You might ask, "Why is this motion taking place from second- to third-dimensional Earth?"

Well, I have mentioned before that the negative planet in the galaxy Sirius has exploded because of the extreme negative situation on the planet, and all life there is over. Now, I've also stated that the beings on that planet are going to incarnate, in their transitional bodies (meaning a body that you would incarnate into as an adult rather than through a normal birth and maturation). They are going to incarnate in these bodies on 3.0-dimensional Earth, where you no longer are. But because they are coming through the outer boundaries of second-dimensional Earth, they are carrying some of second-dimensional Earth's vibrations, the sense of the place, as they ease into third-dimensional Earth. Because you are close enough to third-dimensional Earth, in many cases they are easing through where you live right now. The means by which they come through is various portals, various entities and sometimes through people (not that the people wish to participate, but because as spiritual beings they allow this to preserve this race of people). Thus as the Sirians pass through, they bring with them the sense not only of second-dimensional Earth but also a personal scent of sulphur.

So do not be overly concerned that volcanoes are going to be erupting all over the place. This is especially important for those of you who live near or find yourselves near active portals. I mention this not only because of this locality (Sedona, Arizona) but because there are other places with portals that are active in this way. Ofttimes those portals are near mountain ranges—Bolivia, Argentina, Chile, Tibet, the Pyrenees. Those are the main places where there are portals that are passing these individuals through.

Some of you will have these beings pass close enough to you on their movement from one dimension to another that you might catch a whiff of this. Granted, there will be more volcanic activity—I do not wish to protect you overly, but this volcanic activity I do not expect to occur in a catastrophic fashion where you now exist, though at 3.0-dimensional Earth it is beginning in earnest. As a matter of fact, the 3.0-dimensional version of Earth now is having a tremendous outflowing of lava, rebuilding an entire continent in the place where Mount Aetna was once very active, and also near the ancient city of Pompeii. This is in 3.0-dimensional Earth; please do not confuse this with your current time. It does not mean that those of you living in that part of the world should become too concerned.

I need to mention this now because a couple of things are happening. Your personal, individual responsibility as creators-in-training has taken another big step. You are now significantly more responsible for what you create than you were a mere ten days ago. You have actually gone to a status not dissimilar to this analogy: A senior in any program in college begins to do what he is training for. If he's training to become a teacher, by the time he is a senior, he becomes responsible and begins student teaching, doing what he's training for in one way or another. You're at that level; since you are creators-in-training, you are not only beginning to do, but you are beginning to actually re-create. Re-creation is the step that takes place before you truly apply yourself as creators. Re-creation is what your visit to the Earth has been about during this cycle of your soul's progression in Creator's school. You have learned all you need to learn about re-creation; now it is time to apply re-creation and also to take the responsibility for, to live with, the results.

Your Role in Assisting the Incoming Beings

For your first big experience in this responsibility, Creator has made you responsible for the safe arrival and settling into 3.0-dimensional Earth of the formerly negative beings on that negative planet in Sirius. Now, in order to do this you have to have certain qualifications: You have to have been to creator school, which you are all in now. You also have to have a certain amount of negative experience so that you do not become sickened by exposure to these beings who have had to suffer through an extremely negative state on the planet in Sirius. The only reason they can come to any portion of Earth at all is the similarity in composition on a planetary level, and the direct connection of third-dimensional Earth with the galaxy Sirius. The third qualification is that because positivity and negativity function here alongside each other, these beings who have been exposed to this extreme energy can function near you; they know they are not judged.

When they come through on an energy level they will come through in one of two ways: assisted by certain extraterrestrials who will help them out with a form of energy transference, largely using the facilities of their disklike ships; or in their two-dimensional bodies. If you happen to see them in their two-dimensional bodies they will look all black—black not referring to anything negative, but to the second-dimensional appearance associated with passing through an extremely negative space. The dark energy is designed to reflect everything, and can be stripped off; thus they maintain a continuity between their experience on that negative planet in Sirius and the 50-50, positive/negative 3.0-dimensional Earth. If these beings reincarnated just anywhere after such an extreme negative experience, they would have many lives of disease, and would unintentionally spread it, most likely becoming outcasts in the universe. So they require an experience not unlike a halfway house for prisoners. When they leave the prison they're not quite ready to go into society, so they come into a halfway house where they can have half prison condition, half freedom.

So your responsibility as a people is that you are now in charge of these beings. Creator has given you this responsibility! A portal swings from where they are to where you are so that you do not experience any of their effect. These portals sometimes get clogged with many beings piling up at the same time, and since only so many angelic energies are available to help them through, many light and loving human beings, spiritual beings (whether they're in the "New Age" frame of reference or whether they are simply religious, kind, loving people) have volunteered to act as focal lenses. They are performing a function of refracting this flow, this almost tube-like arrangement, this flow of beings from this time-space in Sirius into 3.0-dimensional Earth. Most go into 3.0-dimensional Earth with the help of angelic beings, but there are not enough angelic beings – or gold light beings, for that matter – to accommodate them. So some of them are having to swing right through where you are, and you are helping them.

At night, in our sleep?

No, no. You've been doing that for a long time. No, this is something that's going on while you are awake. Many of you have noticed that recently you have been very distracted. Sometimes you find yourself daydreaming or in a place where you don't remember going. You vaguely remember walking down the stairs or going to the grocery store or getting in your car to go someplace, but you don't remember the past fifteen miles. No, you have not been contacted by extraterrestrials. You have been in an altered state of consciousness whereby you were functioning as a refracting, loving lightbeing (you are in your natural states loving lightbeings). You were assisting the angelics to help these people.

Now, there is a hazard you have to watch out for. Sometimes these second-dimensional beings will get caught up in you. You will be in this altered state for only enough time to catch one of them – catch as in someone throwing a ball back and forth. You will catch them so that they don't tumble out into space and get lost indefinitely, which would be a disaster for any being. You catch someone who has fallen out of the stream of their waiting in line, as it were, for the angelics. Then you find that you are not feeling quite right. You are feeling off, or sometimes not well at all.

When this happens, this is what I want you to do. Don't assume you are sick. Try this first for five minutes; then you can call the doctor. I'm talking about slight discomfort here. If you can, sit down for a moment, step away for a minute from whatever you're doing, and ask the angelics or your favorite spirit, whoever that might be (the angelics are the best bet because this is their job), to send somebody to take this being (if there is one inside you), to search you to see if there are beings who need to go elsewhere, who are not serving you and would be served better elsewhere. In this way no one is judged. Then wait for a few moments and try to relax. If you feel better in about five minutes, assume that that's what it was. (If you don't feel better, call the doctor, okay? I'm not trying to practice medicine without a license here. I'm simply saying that this is happening, and you need to have something to do.) In most cases you are simply functioning in an altered state to refract the flow so that they can get to where they're going.

That's what's been happening to me, right?

This is what's been happening to you and many others, and I wanted to anticipate questions about it. Is it not ironic that you find yourselves having been experiencing (especially noted in the Explorer Race book) the agitated difficulties with the so-called negative beings from Sirius? Now you find yourselves in the position of having to let go of any judgment, anger or annoyance with these beings, and are literally responsible to help them get where they are going on your former home! I find that it is not just ironic but par for the course, in the great golf links of creatorship. You can't get mad at someone just because you will find yourself in the same bassinet.

I have one more thing to say. The velocity of matter is exceeded only by its reaction to resistance. Now, what does that mean? That's Zoosh's physics, and it's possibly also a known factor in physics. In order to accelerate you into the Null Zone, we had to do something here. Imagine a gateway to the Null Zone. And here is Earth plodding along in its normal planetary motion (not actual motion around the Sun). It is moving along dimensionally, slowly moving toward the Null Zone, which it would have gotten to at some point. As I said a while back, in order to get you past the extreme circumstances that were developing in terms of potential hazards, we had to cheat a bit and run you up into the Null Zone. To do that, we encountered this circumstance: accompanying the normal motion of an object through space there is a certain amount of resistance and a certain amount of momentum to move this object along. So if we suddenly push [whoosh!], and that object suddenly moves [zip!] into the Null Zone, there is suddenly a corresponding amount of resistance – almost like a coiled spring behind it, you see? Suddenly, not only are you sitting in the Null Zone, but because that resistance is backed up behind it, sometimes you're not sure whether you're going backward or forward. This is lending to that curious feeling of being terribly distracted. I can remember a few months ago that time was whizzing along. Now, as of this day, you find experiences where it seems like it ought to be further along than it is. What's occurring is that you are still moving forward, but at a very slow pace because of the resistance.

That gate was open, waiting for your arrival, but when suddenly you shot through it [whoosh!] there was this mass of resistance you have to overcome. What are you going to do with that resistance? Do you just say, "Goodbye, resistance: Shazam!"? —No. You can take that resistance and compress it, but you cannot get rid of it. So it has to dissipate gradually over the same amount of time that you would have lived had Earth simply moved along at its normal place, expanding in consciousness. You will be parked in the Null Zone for a while, because it's kind of like we rushed you into a garage to get you out of the rain, but you have to stay in the garage longer than you might have wished.

In a way it's working in your favor, because you are now being given these projects. Creator is not one to say, "Well, they're just going to be there for a while." Creator is inclined now to give you these projects, to give you the responsibility for helping place the formerly negative Sirians into their proper positioning on 3.0-dimensional Earth. You are given these projects in creatorship which you would not have had the time to do before, but this time exists now because your rapid dimensional expansion has slowed down, and now your day-to-day experience is one of multidimensionality. Many people have wanted this for a long time, but you understand that this is multidimensionality in a world that still believes it is linear and has some evidence to support that belief.

Effects of Multidimensionality

In this multidimensional experience you might find many things that are confusing. For example, there is a commonly understood "disorder" called dyslexia, in which the person experiences a multidimensional consciousness that makes it difficult to experience linearity in many ways. If you have an extreme case of this, you have the multidimensional capacity. Over the years many teaching methods have been devised to help these individuals refocus their attention into only one dimension —ironic, is it not? And yet now you are experiencing the multidimensionality known to all experiencers of dyslexia, especially those who are youthful. I'm not just talking about transposing letters here; I'm talking about the multidimensional factor, wherein you might see not only something's physical properties but the space that surrounds those physical properties. For example, you might look at a door and experience the door frame much more strongly, with much more mass than the door — and you might bump into the door. If this is happening to people, I don't want you to become overly alarmed, I just want you to pay attention and try to slow down.

This multidimensional factor can also have certain annoying sidelights. One of these sidelights is that it can (not necessarily will) be the cause of accidents. This is not something that is being experienced only by "New Agers." It is being experienced by everybody — granted, to a greater or lesser degree. But to people who are sensitive — and this includes all children and all people who are getting very old as well as many others (you know who you are) — I want you to slow down when you're driving, especially at night, because the multidimensional factor is going to be present. You might have experiences where, for example, you're driving down a dark road and, regardless of how well your headlights are working, the road itself becomes less of a physical experience than its surroundings — the buildings, the trees, whatever. And there might be a tendency to not be on the road. If you are going reasonably slowly, say, 45 or 40 mph in a 60 mph zone, you're not going to have trouble. I can't make guarantees, but it will greatly lessen the hazard.

Those of you who work on ladders or in risky professions, in the military service or whatever, where you're making decisions based on split seconds, leave a little extra time! If something is going to take five minutes, get there five minutes early, okay? If you have to go up a ladder carrying forty bundles of roofing that day, go up and down the ladder slowly. If you're allowed to wear safety equipment, wear it. You don't have to impress the other fellas that you don't need it. And take your time; so what if you only get 35 bundles.

I mention these things because multidimensionality is a fact of life for creators-in-training. You're experiencing multidimensionality so that you can do more than one thing at once. You might be going into an altered state so that you can do other things while you're doing something else. But what you are doing in your normal, linear world is not so much a part of your memory's consciousness, so you don't remember things. Because your multidimensionality is coming in very strongly now, you are having experiences where you literally cannot remember things that you absolutely know. If you can't remember the names of loved ones, and then the memory returns in a little while, it isn't because you're losing your marbles. There is a multidimensional factor; on many dimensions, names are simply not a factor. You may know these same people in those dimensions, but you do not know them as a name. Names are used when individuality is necessary in order to create certain training objectives, as in school here. But in other dimensions where those objectives do not exist, names are totally unnecessary.

How can people who are helping these Sirians and catching these negative entities protect themselves?

You want to help them because that's part of your training; you don't want to deny it. The best thing to do is to align yourself more with the angelics. Put yourself in contact with them; there are many, many, many of them. Don't be buffaloed, as they say, into believing that there are only certain angels because these are the ones you've heard of. If you can feel the energy of any given angel — Michael, for example — and it feels good, yet you hear the name of another angel, you feel it's an angel and the energy feels very good, this can be an angel also. Also, know that Michael can be many places at once, yet Michael cannot be everyplace at once. So sometimes he might send a substitute. Just as there are many Santa Clauses at Christmastime, so there are many Michaels in the sense I mention. If you wish to use Michael, for example, then I would say to align yourself with Archangel Michael, or align yourself with any archangel or angel who feels good to you, and ask them to come to your assistance if you need it in this work. This does not mean that you may not have some discomfort sometimes; if so, you ask them for help again. You might also go to any healer or anybody who can help to remove entities.

Nowadays we don't want to just hurl entities out into space. That is not a good thing. There really is no such thing as a negative entity. People have hurled negative entities out into the void before. Understand that there are entities who are coated with stuff that causes them to experience themselves as negative, but once you strip that stuff off (those who are taking entities out of people probably know this) and transform it, there's usually some innocent being inside. So let's take these entities out of human beings and transform this stuff around them with white and gold light, because that's the dark stuff that builds up on their journey. Then when we see who they are, let's send a gold light being or an angel with them, and send them off to go to where they need to go. Let's do it like that and not just "hurl negative beings off somewhere" so that they have to find their way back.

Okay, let's talk about these Sirians. Obviously we're more intimately connected to them than we thought. Why have they chosen to experience so much pain and anguish? What they're experiencing is beyond anything we experienced in our Orion days — why?

Good question. You here on Earth are now experiencing the final test of creatorship. This is not to say that you won't go on and fulfill your duties as the Explorer Race. But in your higher-dimensional self and beyond time, you are going to go straight into creatorship, and that's multidimensional. To answer your question: Since you are doing this and most other beings everyplace else are experiencing total light, 100% pleasant experience, someone has to balance out the scale and experience something that is as close to 100% dark as possible to create motivation for change! If there was only this place, your school – exposing you to a little bit of this and a little bit of that, changes, ramifications, creation, re-creation – you would have a certain amount of motivation, but the universe would not have the motivation by which they could say, "Look at this; we don't want this anymore." People could just come down here and say, "Well, this is school – a strange school perhaps, a bizarre school even, but it is school. No, there has to be a place where people – brave people, brave entities – go that is so negative that entities from all over the universe come and say, "We've got to stop it; we can't let it go on!"

In a way it sounds cruel that people should suffer. Yet we must understand that the souls who have lived on this planet volunteered for this – they weren't being punished, none of that – so that the universe would have what it requires for creation. That is impetus. Impetus is really, I don't want to say a universal law, but pretty darned near a universal law of creation. Someone somewhere has to live out the ultimate effect of an idea gone bad, let's say. Negativity in its own right is not a bad thing when experienced as a very minor spice, because it becomes essentially annoyance that stimulates change so things will improve. Negativity is never intended to be a bad thing. But if it goes to the extreme, such as 70-75% negativity – and sometimes going to 90% negativity – no being can live through that for long. On that negative planet on Sirius it was generally not much worse than 70% because people just can't tolerate more.

If you're in, say, 90% negativity, you're not going to live very long because you can't take it. If that circumstance exists and people from the universe observe it, they see not just the humiliation and suffering and pain of the people, but the tremendous loss for not being loved and nurtured, the tremendous sense of loneliness from missing the soul and the love, that which you consider God—and they can't bear it. Even if their ships would come, they would look at it as you might look at a reflection in a mirror. If they looked at it directly they would feel it, even looking at it through a protective device, one which takes out some of the feelings the people have. Why would they feel it? Because they're compassionate! So they would look at it in a mirror, a reverse image of it. You experience that mirroring device when you look at television. If you look at people on the street who are suffering, you feel compassion, but if you look at somebody suffering on television, you don't necessarily feel compassion, because it distances you—it's a device like that. So they look at that and say, "This can't go on."

The reason the people were on that planet in Sirius was to create the impetus for changing that which was allowed to get out of hand, which was a spice gone awry, as it were. Too much salt ruins the soup, if you will (not to correlate salt to negativity).

The phrase "my heart went out" seems to describe what you're saying, what beings feel when they see someone with such emptiness of nurturing. Was it designed to bring that powerful compassion forth?

Yes. Creator wants to encourage, wants to give impetus to change, but Creator does not want to create the change Itself. It wants Its offspring to create the change. And in this sense, Creator says to Itself, How can I be involved in this creation without being directly involved? What can I do indirectly to stimulate those who are my offspring to create change? Some of these people who are Creator's offspring are pretty near fully realized beings. I must expose them, Creator might think (if Creator had linear thought) to something for which they will rise to the challenge, something which they would find intolerable in their own energy bodies, and something for which, as soon as they know about it, as soon as they see it and become aware of it, they are unable to go on without doing something to change it, to make it right. Even though the negative planet in Sirius is blown up now, it still exists in the memories of those who observed and experienced it, and the memory of this circumstance will go on for some time to influence those in the universe who are in every range—from protected, benevolent beings such as those in the Pleiades to fully realized beings in the higher dimensions. It will be a thorn in their sides. Something like that gets around, it's not a secret, because when something runs against the grain it is extremely uncomfortable, it gets around. So this gives an impetus to change, it does not discourage the use of the growth mechanism of negativity. Negativity has always tended to be a growth mechanism; if there is 2% or 3% of negativity in a person's life, ideally, then they have annoyance. And annoyance will cause them to change things for the better. So negativity in its own right is not a bad thing, but when you have 70% negativity, it is.

I'm not getting the connection between us and them. Have we had past incarnational experiences and connections with the negative Sirians?

In other words, why are you responsible for them?

Yeah. Other than being an exercise in creatorship . . .

All right. In creator training we do not not necessarily trace how we are connected beyond through the One. But creatorship starts on the absolute foundation of compassion.

Okay, so it doesn't have to be a direct past association with those souls. It's the principle.

Let's just say that for now. I can say more in the future, not too long.

Now, what about this planet that blew up? Obviously it had plants and animals; are they also coming through the portals here to 3.0 Earth? Will the Sirians have some familiar plants and animals in their new surroundings?

Cops and Robbers

I don't think that the plants will come through. They are going to go off and find themselves on their home planets of creation after a certain amount of screening through. The plants will go and release the information they acquired and then reincarnate on their home planets. The animals will do the same thing, with one or two exceptions.

One exception will be alligators. Alligators are associated with Earth, and they're also associated with Sirius. I know some of you say, "Oh, reptilians! Run and hide!" But I must tell you that most reptilians I've met, whether they be humanoid reptilians or whether they be crawling on the ground, swimming in the lake or the river, are just what they are. They're not horrible monsters coming to eat you. I don't know why this myth lingers. Reptilian beings as a species are not the enemy.

Granted, there have been times when some of you in some of your incarnations have had run-ins with reptilian beings you didn't like. But it just so happens that some of you beings who had run-ins with these reptilian beings got angry at them because they were the "cops" and you were the "robbers." Just as the "robbers" on this planet do not like the "cops," it's not at all surprising that this attitude prevails. Even nowadays people love to portray police as some kind of monsters. I can assure you, if you didn't have police around, your society would really be a mess. There will probably be alligators on 3.0-dimensional Earth as these beings ease in there, and they might also have an animal that looks not unlike a very large rat, but one that lives in a tree and is a leaf-eater not unlike a koala bear. Other than that, the plants will generally be associated with the Earth.

I might add, as an aside to those of you who are greatly enamored of the Black League, that beings eventually came to you when you were still in the Black League and tried to get you to change your ways, because even though you had "a good cause" (how many times have people had good causes?), the things you were doing were not supporting the cause, but were injuring people. So understand that the Black League, regardless of its intent and cause, did do terrorist things.

The people who came and talked to you were reptilians, and they took away some of your leaders. You maintained it was for indoctrination (in those times), and that those leaders, when they came back, were changed. You said, "Look what these terrible reptilians did to our leaders!" What they really did is that they took off the leaders and they said, "Here, let me show you what these acts you have done" [some of which were really terrorism] . . . let me show you what the people who were killed – many of whom had nothing to do with those you were angry at – would have been, who their offspring would have been. Let me show you what you have done." Because these reptilian beings had the authority to show them that. Now, that would change anybody. So I just wanted to tell you that one of the reasons for the prevailing myth of reptilian beings being monsters is that one, running deep, of "cops and robbers."

Were those who were changed part of those who left Orion and went to the negative planets and then ended up on Earth, starting the Explorer Race?

Nice story! No, this happened after the Black League had left Orion, this contact with the reptilian beings. As a matter of fact, it took place on Maldek.

Before they came to Earth?

Yes. That antireptilian thing runs so deep because it took place in your solar system. People who have a good cause don't like anybody to tell them that they need to change their ways when their cause is just – regardless of what they're doing. This thing about being right runs very deep, and is one of your challenges. To quote a famous healer (let's give her credit, it was Louise Hay), "Would you rather be happy or would you rather be right?" Let's take it another step: Would you rather be enlightened or would you rather be right? That's where it's really at.

Strip Mining and the Environment

Okay. Let's get updates on some of the things we've been too busy to track. The mining under the Hopi mesa — it's been several months since we talked about that. What's the current status and the result?

This circumstance is very touch-and-go right now. I don't want to create troubles there, but I will simply say that there are those youthful members of the tribe who mean well and want the best for their people, who are being manipulated by those who would like to get what they want from the ground and don't care how. This is happening not only in Hopiland, but all over the U.S. and Canada for people who have tribal lands.

And assets . . .

Yes, and assets that they don't care to have pillaged from the property. So the big challenge is just holding the line. It's awfully hard for young people living in sometimes desperate straits to look around the world—and how can they help but look around when there's television, to say nothing of being exposed to friends who are not living in those conditions? They ask, "Well, how come we can't have that, and why do we have to live this holy, spiritual life? I just want to have a good time!" as any young person might.

They want hot water and stoves and TV.

Yes, stuff that other people take for granted. It's very hard for them. This is what I'd like you to do, if you can. Good feelings are good; writing to your congresspeople is good. You've got to watch out now because the mining interests are poised to literally tear up the planet. The sinister secret government is involved in this to some extent. Their point of view is that this planet is a warehouse of stuff they want, period. That's their general point of view. Their point of view also is, "When we get what we want, we'll go to the next place that has stuff we want."

Ask anyone who has lived in an area on this planet that has been strip-mined, who can remember what the land used to look like before it was strip-mined. Ask them if they are really willing to see that happen to the whole planet. Yes, Hopiland; yes, Lakota country; yes, Cree land; and yes, national parks. Yes, outskirts of cities, maybe right in cities—let's talk about urban development! Maybe they'll discover some gas or oil down there. Urban development becomes urban strip mining! Are you willing to allow your planet to be torn apart by those who would take what they wish and leave it? The planet cannot take it; this mining has really got to stop. So I'm going to ask you all to do this (no, I don't want you to run out and attack miners – they're just working; I don't want you to run out and attack anybody): I want you to become aware of whether or not what you use has been mined. I want you to understand that one of the big tests of creator school is, "Are you willing to create things that work with nature instead of against it? Are you willing to share? Are you willing to help?" Helping does not mean destruction. Therefore I am not, nor will I ever, support what are called eco-terrorists. It's not okay to go out and pound nails into trees with the idea that someone's chain saw will break and perhaps cut him to pieces – that's not okay.

And that's being done?

Yes. Not by many, but a few. So eco-warriors, I want you to do something different. Don't destroy something to "save it." Don't destroy your fellow man to "save" him or her, either. I know it's been a long, slow battle, but I want you to understand that people are beginning to wake up. I want you to write personal stories or personal articles about what caused you to wake up to the value of nature as it is in contrast to its value as man changes it. And do be patient. Those of you who are involved in ecology movements, know that one of your core issues is patience. Being impatient just keeps you around longer.

SSG Encountering Trouble in Transit

The secret government as of last August 21 was going to move to sites underneath five major cities, and you were going to attempt to "get them" en route. Are they ensconced under these cities now? What happened? If you could catch them and deter them, they were going to go to the Moon and use their backup plan.

They've expanded their colony on the Moon somewhat, but they were sort of caught en route. They still have a small but effective means of accessing one of their bases through a portal they use in one of Sedona's canyons, but they're not particularly active in Sedona anymore. They are no longer particularly active in Iceland anymore, or in the southern tip of South America. They have made an effort to move under certain cities, but the only city they've had success in moving under is (and please, city fathers and mothers, do not get angry at me) Las Vegas, Nevada. They have made that motion successfully.

That wasn't even one that you mentioned!

I know. But it was a fallback. They were able to do that because they've had an outpost there for a long time. So they are now under that city. And they are making mischief. Those of you lightworkers who are being drawn to Las Vegas, that's why. I know it's a different way of life there, but there are many good things about the city and lots of good people. The reason you're being drawn there is that the light and love you bring in will compensate for what the sinister secret government is emanating simply by its existence.

You said there was a total of five million of them; where are the rest of them?

They transferred most of the people to the Moon base.

They did go to the Moon? When?

Oh, about six weeks ago.

But you said they'd kill off most of the people!

Well, they realized that their true strength was in numbers. They really didn't want to make that realization because, you understand, making that realization and applying it even in an infinitesimal way is good. They had to make that realization, because people were their strength.

Did they use spaceships and take millions of people to the Moon?

No, they used a portal; it's much easier. You just step in and you're out the other side. That's that, you're there.

So how many physical beings were transferred?

It is their intention to bring a couple million, but altogether I think they've moved about 180,000 so far – 180,000 principals, meaning those who are actually performing a direct function. Then it's their intention to bring the dependents of those principals, and after that bring the people who are doing peripheral functions, which would total about two million. They are still reluctant to take any people there. Their fallback plan is of course (and this is the thing that's been holding them back, thank heavens) total automation. They would prefer to do everything through industrial and applied military robotics. They are still operating under that foolish illusion that they won't need people or even hybrids – certainly we can call them people. But their armor is beginning to show cracks; they are beginning to take responsibility for their own people, and not just be ruthless with them.

As I said a long time ago, anybody who comes to Earth is exposed to what Earth is, and because Earth is expanding now and consciousness is expanding in every way, even the sinister secret government is being affected. I think you will find that the next seven to ten years will tell the tale. Right now there's a 50-50 chance (which is significant) that the sinister secret government will begin to transform into something more benevolent.

While they're still in our solar system?

Yes. That is largely a consequence of so many people waking up at once, and also because, regardless of what we might think of them as individuals, they are all portions of the One, and they know this. They also have a teacher working with them now who is helping them to achieve on an inner plane (meaning inside themselves) that which they have always wanted to achieve externally, which is perfect autonomy. They've always wanted to be perfectly autonomous so that they could do whatever they wished totally undetected. Right now they are somewhat detected, and they don't like that. So that teacher is teaching them perfect autonomy within themselves so it won't affect anybody else. No one can learn the lessons this being is teaching without expanding in consciousness to some degree. And you cannot expand in consciousness to any degree without expanding in all ways. This teacher is a being who was once considered a fallen angel but was redeemed. I will simply say that the being has been referred to as one that has fallen, you know, the black sheep, as it were . . .

Judas?

Thank you. This particular being has shown a capacity for a tremendous amount of tolerance. Having made a mistake once, he has been able to reform his intentions. As brought out in the book (unpublished as yet) My Story by Jesus of the Light and others, Jesus' life was extended past the point that is normally reported as his death. Nevertheless, Judas made a big mistake, and he knew it. A bigger mistake, perhaps, was suicide because had he lived just another year or two, he would have been able to largely repair what he had done. In some circumstances suicide is all right, but not in all circumstances.

Okay. But these numbers don't add up. We talked about five million when they started to move the underground bases to the cities. There's 180,000 on the Moon; how many went to Las Vegas?

About 200,000; most of the missing numbers are in what I call "abeyance," meaning they're in transit, but that's it. They're not really anywhere; they're in transit. Well, they are somewhere, but . . . you know, there's a limit to what I can say because there are hotheads. Since we last spoke about it, two more beings have broken away from the inner circle of the secret government who could very easily use weapons they have to wipe out the dependents, or threaten to wipe out the dependents of inner- and outer-circle members of the sinister secret government, and manipulate them that way. So I'm being a little circumspect about where I say they are.

Okay, of the 13 original inner circle, how many are still solidly part of the sinister secret government?

Solidly, I'd have to say about seven—but still within the circle and hemming and hawing a bit, a total of ten. Three have broken away, one of which is rampaging about and making mucho mischief, and two of them are going to be like that for a while, but they're going to change. They're coming around.

All right. Is there anything else we need to know about them then? They're not planning any major mischief against humanity if they're so disorganized, right?

No, but they're still bound and determined to extract every shred of what they would consider valuable minerals from Earth, and that is their biggest mischief.

All right, so what are we going to do about it?

Well, for one thing, it's important for people to feel that they can do something, can influence something. Politics in your country is changing rapidly; this party will be in, this party will be out. For instance, the Republicans are in now, and they had thought that when they got in it would be great, but they might easily get voted out next time. You might be flooded with independents next time, or third parties, perhaps. I'd say this: Organizing locally on a political front is helpful, as is allying yourself through various groups, whether they be church groups, environmental groups, loose-knit nature organizations, Ducks Unlimited (people who have an agenda to go duck hunting)—anything. Because this mining simply destroys things. You know, you haven't really known what's being destroyed because so much of it has been going on underground. But what's planned now by many mining companies is surface mining, basically strip mining, which is fast and dirty, as they say.

That's part of the agenda before Congress now, to pass laws that will privatize the national parks and various federally owned lands.

That's right. You really need, as citizens, to discourage that. You also would benefit from changing the agenda of the Forest Service from that of managing tree harvests as if trees were corn or soybeans to protecting the national forests for future generations, which is what the forest rangers used to do. So I'd say, bring back the forest rangers. It seems a small thing, but it isn't. Every tree has its own unique personality and it feels, just like everyone has feelings. Anything else?

Earth and Her Electrical Energy

As we evolve, how does Earth's energy also change?

Electrical energy on the Earth will be more pronounced because Mother Earth will gradually call back her electrical body. As you know, electricity is not really generated in a generator; it is captured from Mother Earth's electrical body and sent down the lines to run your machines. Mother Earth needs all of her facilities for herself now to rebuild and maintain herself to the extent that she can (and she does this slowly), so she may need to begin moving her electricity around more. This does not mean that magnetism as you know it will be decreasing; as a matter of fact, I expect it to increase in the form of love, because to me, love and magnetism are really very similar.

Are the grid lines of the planet magnetic?

Yes.

They are strengthening and expanding right now?

Yes, expanding is a good word.

And our meridians are connected to those grid lines?

Yes, as well as cosmically.

And they're also expanding?

Yes.

Haven't they contained us within the planet and contained us in the body?

Within the context of what you came here to do. If you had come here as the all-powerful beings that you are, how could you have grown? You would have just felt, "Oh, well, this is nursery school, what do I need this for?" But in order to learn things on a broader scale and learn about consequences (which you really need to learn when you're in creator school), you had to learn it within a vulnerable body. So in that sense, yes, you've been contained, but contained in order to learn. You can't experience consequences . . . you know, if you stub your toe and it hurts, that's a consequence. But if you stub your spiritual toe, it doesn't hurt at all.

As we expand and our auras expand, then the grid lines of the Earth are going to expand, right?

Yes, and conversely, as the grid lines expand, you expand. It's symbiotic.

So at some point they're going to expand to the point that we're not contained in

this body anymore?

Right.

We won't be subject to that?

That's right, you won't be subject to the limit of the outer perimeter of the body. That's more of a multidimensional factor.

But the electric energy that runs through the meridians is what holds and keeps the constraints of the body. I'm trying to find out how this works as we go into the next level.

What holds the body together is love (magnetic love). The cosmic stuff of life is that. What allows you to experience multidimensionality is like a tunnel or a tube that connects, all right? If your lessons are entirely learned, the doors in that tunnel open up and you are allowed to experience multidimensionality. Let's say that you're all plugged into the same grid (which you are) and that you're wired in series. Remember the old Christmas tree lights, where if one bulb burnt out, none of them lit? It's very much like that. As long as one bulb isn't working right, the whole doesn't work well. The whole thing is symbiotic. Yet since free choice is available, at some point all those who are going to expand into the fourth dimension will do so. Very few will go to the third dimension and live with the incarnated former Sirians who will need some teachers to know how to live there. Those who have simply refused to go out of the third dimension, regardless of their reason—no matter whether they were negative or they just loved—it will go there and be their teachers. Nobody gets away from teaching. You don't come to this school and fail to graduate; it's not allowed.

The mechanism by which you go to the fourth dimension is largely external on an individual level. It's not an individual mechanism, but one with a hole to the fourth dimension. You do not individually create that, and yet being a portion of the whole, in the larger sense you create it. That's why we say that you—humanity—are creating this shift.

Everybody, with all our high selves, with our god-selves . . .

Everything.

All right, let me get at it this way: When we are fully in the fourth dimension, what will the grid lines of the Earth be like?

There's a good question. You will experience larger grid lines. They will be more magnetic. Because you will have more of your heart energy you will be inclined to feel them more. They will act directionally, in a sense. They will perform as instinctual guideposts, as it were: go this way and go that way. Your harmonic, your body energy will be more inclined to respond to them in a way that might be called unconscious, but you will be aware of the reaction. You will go along with it, but you will be aware of it. So generally it will create a heightened sensitivity for all concerned.

But can't you say that those magnetic grid lines then become the conduits to the rest of creation and not the restrictors?

Oh, yes.

Now they're not plugged into anything.

They're holding you in something right now.

Like an electric fence to keep us here.

In a way, but I don't care for your analogy.

In the next level they're going to be the connection to the rest of creation?

The natural purpose of the grid lines is to maintain the intention of the place. In the third dimension they are maintaining the intention of the school. They will maintain the intention of fourth-dimensional Earth as well, only you will have more freedom, more multidimensionality.

One thing intrigued me: You said that Earth is going to be using more electricity. What does that mean?

She will be using her electrical body (electricity is a portion of her body) to perform kinetic functions. One of the things that happens before an earthquake, for example, is sounds, light—and electrical energy is involved. She uses electrical energy to move parts of herself around. She'll also be creating more response to her lightning, which performs a function spiritually for many beings but also for herself in terms of balancing her energies and, in many cases, reinvigorating certain portions of her body. Sometimes lightning will strike where there is a vein of a particular ore, but it is actually supercharging that vein, not unlike a pacemaker for someone's heart that stimulates that organ to perform. She will be doing more of that.

More lightning and earthquakes?

Not necessarily earthquakes, but more uses of her electrical body to move things about, to get things moving and to balance herself with her available fluids—water and so on. She really needs her oil and gas and wishes you would find some substitute for it.

Now she has the capacity to produce something that has on certain rare occasions even been photographed, and that is like a liquid or condensed electricity. Occasionally this has been seen by men and women at sea as ball lightning, which is really quite rare. This is a form of condensed electricity (most ball lightning is something else), but I mention it in this context for the sake of our example. Though she doesn't care to do this, in the cavity where you've taken out her gas and oil, Earth will produce a form of liquid electricity that looks like light with all of the primary colors and that is highly kinetic. This light would tend to move outward. Let's say that all the air was moved out of a particular cavern. She could put liquid electricity in there and support that cavern, and that liquid electricity would perform the function of oil. A much smaller amount of it would perform the cushioning function of oil – lubricating and cushioning, damping like a shock absorber; the hydraulic effect. Because electricity can do this, it is another reason she may call in more of her electricity. This will be a warning that you need to start to produce some other means – not of creating electricity, because no creation of electricity here really takes place; you are simply taking it from her body – but some other means of motive energy to cause your machines to work. In short, to learn applied creationism so that you can create without needing machines. Of course, the simplest way to do that is to establish friendly relationships with extraterrestrials who have this ability so you don't have to reinvent the wheel. By establishing these friendly relations you will be able to get this technology. So now is the time to get it, apply it, use it and let Mother Earth keep what she needs.

5

Freedom, Power and Light Moving

YHWH through Arthur Fanning
August 12, 1995

We are going to play. . . . The within is without, and the without is within. Now you're going to see a shifting, a gathering, through this vehicle and through you. In one manner it will be this way: that we are coming to see what you are doing with our energies; to see what you're doing with me. (Everyone breathe.)

We are coming, from your perspective, a great distance. That means a great inner depth of you. We are coming from before any of your lifetimes, any of them. We are coming to look at all of your lifetimes so you may review them yourselves. (Everyone breathe again.) It is going to be your clarity now, your power, how you are connected to the great Light "out there" that comes here, and how you are connected within you to each other. You're going to see what you're doing with our energies, also. Allow. Be beyond judgment, now. It's going to be fun.

Everyone allow your eyes to close a moment. We will start off this way. Open the heart chakra. Feel the light and see the light in your being. Peace. Allow. Light. Be in love with your body, with you.

I am not the one that you want to judge you. And what I mean by that . . . you manifest through the energies of I that is within you —you will manifest your judgments, your guilts, your angers. I am not the one you want to manifest to show these things to you. (Everyone take a breath.) So let go. Forgive yourselves and be in peace now – then we can continue.

Now the beings within you, in your power, your accumulated wisdoms, desire you to see more light of you, desire you to connect to and beyond the great spiral galaxies, universes, beyond, omniverses and beyond; to go to the center of the atom to the truth particum that is you – in and out. They will assist you in this thing. Each level you move through, be it upward, be it inward, it is always inward. It is a level to accumulate wisdom and seek another level, to seek more.

From your human perspective, we are bringing more light to the planet. That means more freedom. It also means more power. It also means you must very delicately move with this power. To move in the manner that you have been over your past times – decades, years – with this new power, will cause great disturbances in your being. You do not have the teachings yet established to understand this. It is not metaphysical. This power is love! It is so much love that you can do what you want with it and the love doesn't care because it's still love. You can be violent, you can be arrogant, you can be hateful – it is still love. It will magnify itself back unto you, however . . . outrageously so. And it moves very quickly, because it is pure love and it is very, in one way, anxious to complete its lovingness, what you want it to do, what you told it to do. It wants to bring it back to you quickly. That is why we say it is a speed-up. This is a time when respect for your divinity is going to be needed. When you respect your divinity, you will respect the divinity within other beings.

Meditation

Allow you to feel, to see what you would term flames of fire at the soles of your feet. Allow. And allow that fire to move up to the arena of the knees so your lower legs are engulfed in flames of fire, golden red. Allow. Peace.

Allow a blue light to begin to emerge from the center of your heart chakra and fill your body, to cool you off a little bit. Allow. Peace. Allow your hands to become flaming fire, golden red, and allow it to move up to your elbows, both arms. Peace. Allow it to move up to the shoulders. Agni move.

Allow warmth to move up from your throat chakra to the head. Peace. Center your being. Open the crown chakra wider. Allow gold light to enter the crown from your eighth chakra and fill the head. Feel the throat chakra become golden.

Allow the flames that are at your knees now to move up to include your thighs and your buttocks. Allow the flames that are at your buttocks now to move upward and consume the physical torso. Allow the flames at the arms to join at the shoulders, in the center. Allow the flames to move up to your head now. Peace.

Feel a six-pointed star at your forehead with an eye in it. Allow. Peace. Feel the chakras above your head to the twelfth chakra become golden light. And the chakra below your bottom to become golden light.

Allow your eyes to open gently. Everyone center your being. Take a breath in the heart chakra. You're all part of one being, and to complete this movement in these energies requires a unity. Everyone breathe. Love. Open the heart chakra wider. Allow your eyes to remain open.

Get Ready to Move

Now, as you move now it is not required to be fearful, it is not required to be argumentative. Your light knows. You're part of my being, I am part of your being. . . . If you doubt my reputation, even that has been written in some of your books, check with your guides. What you're not aware of yet completely, but you will be by the end of this decade: There will be respect for spirit. The games are over, the old games . . . the old excuses are out the window, you say. What is happening now is that from your perspective "out there," I am getting ready to move. That means within you, where I am also, movement. That is what is occurring now. Things are getting erratic, hectic; crazy, you say. Energy, you say. It is energy, but it is more than that. It is thought manifested here. You are included in part of my thoughts. You've been in density this way. I be here watching now, looking. I turn, "Come home!" I haven't turned yet, I'm still looking. I'm in the process now of making this turn. That'll be a little difficult; no big deal. Where you're going to have to hang on is when I take that first step, because everything moves. Even your solar system will move.

You are not just physical. You are light connected to greater lights. You are beyond the ships. They are platforms – that's all they are. Know you Ashtar Command, indeed? Prior to coming to this arena, portion, I moved by Ashtar Command's light force. They be going across sky, so to speak. I come this way [from another direction]. They come. They be sucked in. I'm getting ready to turn around, from your perspective. So whether you're on a platform of a ship, it doesn't matter – the ship is going to move. Everyone breathe.

You are more than persona, you are lightbeing, you are connected to light. You are connected to the beings in the Orions and the Pleiades, and the Sirian aspects, and all of it . . . all of it. It's within you. It's time for dinner . . . and I want everyone at the table! You get my drift? Remember when your mother used to yell at you when you were little one, "Dinner time!" and get impatient when you were late? Where do you think she learned her temper from? My energy is female, by the way, not male. So all of these women that you think are going crazy with their anger, that's what you say a little example —very teeny of what I can do. [He laughs.] They learn well. See the humor.

The heart chakra is going to want to open, because the spirit within your being knows that love is the key that'll get you through this thing. What'll keep you from moving and cause damage in your physical form, and other places also, will be your attitudes that you hold on to. This can be very easy movement, be very loving, outrageously so. You must be willing to love yourselves here, to be in this arena, heart chakra; to be at the apex of what you term the soul, which is becoming the whole body now, whole thing. You. Everyone take a breath. Lighten up a little bit. [To a participant:] How be you?

Excellent.

Indeed? [He laughs.] You are so outrageously humorous. If I move, know you, and these beings that are around you move, what do you think you're going to do?

Move.

Faster Vibrations, Changing Organs

You're catching on! We're going to do a meditation later this day to show you what I mean by movement. There's a Grand Chakra in your back, and how you manifest the body (you've forgotten it), you do come in at what would be termed a 45-degree angle, or what you term 48, 38 —part of your play as light force through that mosaic, through that mandala. And you display the body holographically. We're going to go out the back in your light forces. We're starting to push that way now, gently, to get you set up, so to speak. It'll be easy. Everyone breathe a little bit. Lighten up. I haven't begun to get hot and heavy, know you? I'm being as gentle as I can. [He laughs.]

All of the masters have told you love is the answer for a long time. In one manner I be looking to see how many got it, yet there is no judgment. I'm getting ready to vibrate faster. Be how I be within you, you are going to vibrate faster. All your selves and your guides, they be in there also. They will vibrate faster. It is part of how we began the births. Going to do it again. That's why your organs are changing — so you can handle it. If you don't, no big deal. You've died before. You'll pick up another body. Well, you all know that metaphysically, don't you? You know it metaphysically, indeed? Metaphysically. Metaphysically. Metaphysically. Metaphysically. But you don't know it. You think you know it. By the time you finish this decade, no matter which way you decide to go, you will know one way or the other. You'll remember this death. You'll remember this life, this process. You'll remember. You'll be go through it, you'll be go, "Oh, this be, oh be shit!" [Laughter.] I hear you beings talk. I know what you mean. Play in the light that you are.

You have many spiritual masters around you, each of you. Many, many around you, inside you, talking to you. Listen to them! They are getting orders from headquarters. [Laughter.] Listen! If you don't listen, they get in trouble. Well, your perspective, know you "trouble"? [It's] not really [trouble].

Time to love all things and become the master because that's what's going to make you make it through it. There'll be plenty of beings to blame, plenty. One another, secret government, the Antichrist, your neighbor's dog. It's not needed. Be willing to move into your own power, to know more. Knowing is completely different from feeling. You don't describe a knowing, you can't; you just know. That's where you're moving to — that knowing, to work from that point, the knowing. It is here [soul].

You Came to Experience Kundalini; Let It Move

Now we're going to do another thing this day besides this back movement. We're really going to pop that kundalini. (Everyone breathe a moment.) Everyone wants to feel it — you're going to. And it is a good thing, because it is a third-dimensional activity. There be no experience called kundalini "out there." Say you this way: you play die, leave body, sit around, hang out in the ethers, know you? Kundalini isn't there. You come into physical to experience the kundalini feeling. Actually entering the physical with your light creates that energy. Feels good. You like it. So you might as well take advantage of it and use it now, play with it. Let it move. It wants to move right up the center of the spine, a very thin thread, so to speak, to start. Then it becomes very thick. We won't rush it, we'll start small. It does, in one manner, take you to a state of bliss.

It also opens the heart chakra, outrageous so, where you can feel love for all things. This portion [brain] goes out of the way. The brain sort of be what you say . . . how will I put it this way?

Kundalini be move and sees past the heart and the throat, hits the brain thing, and the brain sort of goes "click" and looks, and the body is going "Weeeaaahhhh," and brain can't figure it out. The brain be flopped over. But the body feels good, so the brain thinks, "Well, this is okay for a while, no big deal." No figuring out involved. The moment you try to figure it out and manipulate it from this arena here [brain], you will shut it down. I've told you all that before. This [the brain] gets it last. This [soul] is the power, deep within. Everyone take a breath for a moment.

Now, you think your planet exists because you are upon it and your solar system evolves around it—you play in this thing. Do you know, from my perspective I can't see you . . . from where I am? I can't even see your solar system or your galaxy, I can't. I have beings that come forth back to me to show me where you are. (Everyone breathe.) So be I don't even see you, yet though I move, I know I will affect you. In between the not seeing you and the being where I be, I will move all things in between when I move. So you're sort of on the end of the pearl string, know you? Know you this thing you call whip, hmm? The tip gets all the action! [Laughter.] In one manner the tip knows it is the tip, and it's going to have all of the activity. You know you are the tip! That's why you're getting so much attention by your extraterrestrial beings—because they are the tip, too. You see? Great movement here, an alignment within yourselves. Outrageously so. The within and the without are going to become one; that is what you're going to—that union, that mastery. It'll be all right. Be a little exciting time.

Now, everyone is really interested in getting into superconsciousness, indeed? Where you are very telepathic and know all things, know everybody else's business so you can get another one-upmanship on them or whatever. Part of the process, it might be a little bit like that. But if you get stuck on that platform, everyone's going to pass you by. Open the crown chakras wider. Peace. Everyone breathe a little bit.

Sometimes these energies will affect your heart, quickening. It is an organ that wants to be loved. Love this thing. It knows life because the life force is behind the left ventricle there, keeping the current going. It knows life. Be gentle in your being. Everyone lighten up. We haven't even started yet. . . . How do the bodies feel, warm a little bit? When we take a little break here a little bit later, I want you to have some purple grapes—they are better for the head here. Indeed?

[To a participant:] Will you allow the energy to come out the fingers? Let it come out the fingers. Know you, you keep holding energy all of the time without letting it flow, you're going to blow up like a big marshmallow boy.

I don't want to do that.

Allow the energy to flow, indeed? You can't hold it. Let it flow through you.

Just through my fingers?

Through your fingers and through the bottoms of your feet and your toes; let it flow through your chakras. Let it flow all out, indeed?

Thank you.

One of the things you're going to begin to learn is that you are energy, and that within you, you manipulate it, the light—you alter it, play with it. You can't grab a piece of light and hold it. Metaphysically you beings play that way. If you think that's possible, try it, even in your physical. You don't know what you're grabbing. You might have your guide's testicles, know you? [Laughter.] Better be careful. I know what chakra to talk to to get you to lighten up! . . . Be aware. I've got your guides laughing too. They're all jumping now. [More laughter.] We're going to have to issue guide cups. [More laughter.] Well, they'll be talking to you about that story for a long time, now. You better . . . some of them actually like it. [More laughter.] It's all kundalini anyway down here, no big deal. Not there. Now I've got to settle them down.

Past and Future, Other Aspects Coming Together

Okay. It's all energy; light in your movement is you. So you let it flow. Some of you try to control it and you can't! Some of you are even playing game to borrow future energy, lend it to past, all of this, that. Take it from past, lend it to future, this, that, the other. What you don't understand: eons ago that would work, because of the linear thing. But time is collapsing now, you're becoming more aware of your now. So your past lives, your future lives be come together.

You be the one pulling this off here now, and you're assisting your past and you're assisting your future. You're becoming the master. You're integrating, merging. Not only merging your personalities, what you term aspects as you play here, you're merging with other physical beings, energies. (Everyone breathe.) Not sexually speaking. Merging energies. Now, that is from your perspective. What is really happening, in one manner . . . I will explain it this way;

we have to use several ways to get it through: You're beginning to understand you're not separate, that you're all one anyway, and your hologram is beginning to recognize this. We'll put it a better way: The light of you is becoming recognized. The object, what is termed the hologram that is you, is beginning to understand it is a hologram, and it wants to identify with its light that's creating the holographic effect, so to speak. And it is within the oneness, you term it. You're beginning to understand that in the physical. That's why some of you are having experiences that another being is your body, a being that you know physically. You're getting it out here, this lightbeing that you be. You say, "Let's see if we can get those two little images overlapped," and you do. And down here you beings are like, "Wow, someone's in my body! Must be my cousin." Well, it is, but not what you think it is. So there's a blending of all of this play going on here.

Now, it's occurring from the light perspective that you are. Now, when you move into that arena, you use your light to assist humanity in understanding and compassion. Not controlling behavior – that'll simply get you another arena of lifetime after lifetime after lifetime again, where you can go along holding your guide's hand . . . again. Be.

Now allow your eyes to close for a moment here. I want you to visualize in the center of this room a giant ball of white light with a golden tinge. Allow it to be there. And from that ball of light there is a cord attached to each of you at your heart chakra. Now allow your energy that be in your physical to move up that cord into that ball, and notice all of the energies that are within that ball. Allow. The ball becomes brighter. Allow. Allow. Understand this: There is more knowing within that ball of light that you're connected to than there is within your physical body, yet the physical body deep within you has the ability to know the same. Come forth out of the ball of light back into the heart chakra. Take a breath and remember the ball of light being in there. Allow your eyes to open gently.

You all exist in this light. You exist further than that, from your perspective. And this ball of light is very small compared to all the others that are out there, which are part of my being. These balls of light are going to move, and you are connected there. Peace. It be like I be lay on couch, I want to change channel. I don't have remote control, I use pigeons. . . . Indeed, give me a moment here. Want to get this concept down as clean as possible, 'cause I know you're going to change it anyway.

Because of the density that you are playing in, your third dimension, you're not allowing yourselves to see the greater play. You say you are here. The stage is much bigger than that – much, much, much bigger. All around you in your air, you term prana, there be life form, force. Very few of you want to play with it. Those beings there move very rapidly, very fast. They look at this density and it looks like you're walking through molasses. Know you tar? They can't imagine you doing anything or getting anything done, as a matter of fact, because you move so slow here – looking at your persona. They know you vibrate with light. They don't understand why you want to be so lazy, from their perspective now. "These are lazy beings; they don't want to vibrate faster." That is what they perceive.

From your side, you play reincarnation to understand this density, to understand thought manifested here. It is not a concept with these beings that are around you – they know thought is. You're in the process of understanding lowering the light and thought, being a master at this level. One of the advantages of working in third dimension is that you can talk to these beings that be play fast through you, and in one manner you can command them to line up into a line of light, from this level, to communicate what you would say "out there," both to the great ships and beyond. When you do your meditations you should consider that energy that is around you, not only that energy that is within you, for it is all part of you. The physical form is simply the barrier between; it is the density. Everyone breathe. Lighten up. You are, within your being, the perfect embodiment of love, a diamond light in there. Anything else is a layer that you put around it to play in the game of not. All of that is going to be sloughed off, and all that will be left will be diamond light. That is you.

I want you to allow your eyes to close for a short moment, little moment, and I want you to visualize an eye on each knee, on your own knees, an eye on your right knee and an eye on your left knee. Allow. Tell the eye to open. Take a breath and push light down to the knees; open the eyes there. Indeed, grand. That be grand. Do the same with your elbows. Allow. You've seen pictures of deities with these on Open. Same with the palms in your hands – eyes open. Grand. Peace. [He laughs.] Allow your own physical eyes to open, the two in your head.

Could any of you feel that in the palms and knees? These pictures that you see are representations of what is in you, how you build, know you? How you work body.

[To a participant:] Getting ready for action, eh?

Indeed, lots of action.

What do you think your lightbody is doing?

It's tuning itself up, becoming more brilliant.

Well, it's becoming brilliant, but what do you think it's doing in a physical perspective?

It's helping the physical body to alter, and . . .

Your lightbody be standing there, pulling up its britches now, know you, getting ready. And it is becoming brilliant and aligned, and all of that metaphysical nonsense, but it's getting ready, know you?

Ready, set to go.

Ready, set to move. Your lightbodies are picking it up that I want to get off the couch, I want to turn around. They're working to get you ready, too. Do you have a question?

I do. You were describing to us a short while back how to cleanse our bodies of negative thoughts, physical impurities and so on by drawing in a brilliant red light on the right side and a brilliant white light on the left side through the nadis [points originating on the forehead at the hairline, in approximate alignment with the eyes]. You said that they would spiral around a blue light in the center and come down and bounce off the perineum, and we could exhale them out the mouth. Now my question is this: when we draw in these energies and they start to spiral, should we spiral them in a counterclockwise or a clockwise mode?

Let me check my book. [Laughter.]

So just allow them to do without help? [More laughter.]

[To a participant:] How be you?

Grand.

Indeed?

Yes.

Enjoying the shifting?

Love it.

Indeed, getting ready for more. You're holding the energy very well, know you what I mean? People, pretty soon, are going to pass their form right through your body. They're going to walk through —whoosh —"What was that?" And you'll go, "Oops, manifest more density, just so we can shake hands." That be outrageous. Be ready for it. [To the previous participant:] Did you answer your own question?

I answered my own question.

It begins with the A word [Allow], I believe. That be grand. Does everyone feel like they need a little stretch? Ground some of the energies here. Eat your grape, particularly the purple one – it'll help some of the pressure in the head. Mm, let me see. We're going to spend these two days building your power. Now, by that I mean we're not going to give you energy – your power is already there. We're going to take off some of the blocks that you placed there. You must be willing to let go, let go, and you must be willing to know. Not busybody know, but to understand in your body, I know this thing. Know you different busybody know? Want to know everyone else's business. Be involved with you now. Can any of you see the lights in the room? We're going to pull more in. Allow you to be aware, it is your light – we are connected. And that is inside you, bargain?

[Group responds:] Bargain!

I require you to play the OM tape ["The Eternal OM" from Valley of the Sun]; know you OM? Softly, very softly. I want that vibration to imprint in the cellular structure. Bargain? So be it. Give you fifteen, twenty of your moments. Indeed?

Indeed.

That be grand.

[*Note: This Two-Day Intensive is available in its entirety on audio cassette (five 90-min. tapes) by sending a check or money order for $53 to A. Fanning, P.O. Box 684, Cornville, AZ 86325. Please specify Aug. '95 Intensive.]

6

The Null-Charged-Particle Effect

Zoosh through Robert Shapiro
December 21, 1995

The world we are living in now, being in the Null Zone, is one in which the actual electrical function of your body is frequently being dramatically changed. This is an interesting thing, because you are a portion of Earth, being made up of her body, and you are born to a world of both plus and minus charges. A rudimentary knowledge of electricity tells you this. Now that you are in the Null Zone, you find yourself easing gradually away from electricity as a function of your nature. Yet most of you (with a few exceptions) have been born at a time in which the Earth was fully expressing herself in her electrical body, having a smooth flow of electricity as you understood it. (Physicists, take note.)

Now you find yourself easing into a time in which you are losing some of the polarity of those poles. You see, in the actual functioning of your brain and nervous system (this has been proved by neurophysicists) there is a motion of charged particles that can be loosely classified as either positive or negative. There are also particles that have no apparent positive or negative charge. There are fewer of them but they will become gradually more dominant.

Slowed Nervous System

This change in electrical charge is another reason—aside from the lessening of oxygen in the air and the general distraction of shifting from one dimension to another within a physical lifetime – why your memory, and in some cases your nervous system (the way you react to the world, the way you do things) is slowing down and why it now requires an effort to do something you've always done with ease or why you lack the motivation to do it anymore. It requires more of a team effort now. People can really only do now what they enjoy doing. Those of you who have a certain amount of responsibility thrust upon you and are doing more than you enjoy doing must exert more effort now. This is a function of the null-charged particle. I'm going to call it that because I don't want to refer to it as a particle with no charge. It has a null charge, meaning that its charge is available to the true intent of the being. It is a particle more associated with your eternal self than with Earth.

Positive and negative electrical charges are directly associated with Earth's body and the way she functions (and you are microcosms of Earth's physical body), but those null-charged particles are so closely associated with your soul energy that when your soul energy leaves the body at the end of your natural cycle, this material can be measured as it leaves. (There have been some experiments on this in the past, including one controversial photograph that is more accepted nowadays than when it was taken many years ago.) The mass that leaves the body is basically these null-charged particles. That is what makes up your soul.

Souls Becoming More Dominant

One of the direct effects of the greater amount of these particles is that your soul's desire, your soul's purpose, your intention for being, your desires, your loves – that which is at the core of your personality, the eternal you, your eternal soul – is becoming more of a dominant function in your body. I know there will be those who say, "Well, that's all well and good, Zoosh, but how do you prove that?" And I will say, "Well, I'm not a physicist or a neurophysicist, but if those out there begin now to set up a protocol for measuring null-charged particles within the body, you will be able to achieve this proof within a short time, in three to six months or maybe a year at most. You will find that over the next two to three years especially, the null-charged particles will become a larger factor in the body.

Please measure it only around the areas of the nervous system. This is not to suggest that the nervous system is the only part of the body that will be involved in these null-charged particles, but it will be easier to measure there because the approximate mass of the charged particles in a given experiment is already known. You're starting with a known quantity to some extent. I'm suggesting this experiment because it will be something attainable in a short time.

I'm talking about this now because not only is physical evidence interesting, but because these null-charged particles are having such a wide-ranging effect on the human being. Your eternal personality —that portion of you who is really a piece of Creator that Creator shoved out into space, as it were, when you were launched into your chain of lives, your immortal personality, as I call it —is really becoming you. How long have you been saying for many years now to me and others, "When are we going to become more of our soul selves? When is spirit going to take actual form?" Well, here it is in physical reality, and of course it is accompanied by things that you don't know, don't remember or don't quite understand.

Functional Changes

One of these is the actual physical changes in how you function. These differences are important to note, because if they are not discussed and researched by your normal medical researchers (and measured perhaps psychologically as well), a syndrome will be identified with various symptoms, including memory loss and reorientation of personality wherein people have little patience for activities they do not like. This "syndrome" may be mistaken for a psychological syndrome or a disease. It isn't. I mention it because it's going to be measurable very soon, certainly within six months to a year.

Those of you sensitives who are using crystals, crystal attunements or even tonal attunements will also be able to measure this. It will begin with changes in the auric positive/negative vs. null charge before you will be able to measure what is in the body, so I'll suggest that you look for that. Notice, most importantly, the change in the person's personality. Healers, whether you be scientists, physicians, whatever: It's very important that you remember that this will not supersede all other discomforts, syndromes or diseases, but it's going to be there, and it's going to be very difficult to discern from other conditions. It will take time for you to chart its symptomatology.

You ordinary folks out there, I'd like you to become aware of the factor of needing to do what you really like. This doesn't mean that you can't go to work and do your job. Whoever has been in a big family, gone to school or worked around other people: There are times when you go along with something you really don't want to do just to accommodate others or not make trouble or be invisible, or be one of the guys or gals —you're not going to be able to do that now. You're going to be surprised at first when you get upset about something like this. You're going to ask yourself, "Why am I getting so upset about this? It never used to bother me before." This is directly associated with the reemergence . . . I'm going to call it reemergence because in your natural state of being, when you're out of body on Earth, you're someplace else. The primary charge of your particles then is this null charge. So you're going to find that you won't be able to go along with things you don't like.

Self-Destructive Behavior Warnings

A lot of what you won't be able to go along with will be things that are destructive to others or to self. (As you know, Zoosh's definition of self-destructive is that which hurts you or somebody else.) You weren't born with that knowledge, but you have learned how to become self-destructive by adapting to your society's manners and mores and to some extent by learning how to be polite — putting up with a certain amount of discomfort, usually a little, but sometimes a great deal. You're not going to be able to do that anymore, because the Null Zone and the null-charged particle have almost zero tolerance for doing anything self-destructive. It's important for you to know that because the planet is parked in the Null Zone. You'll be here for a little while, and the Null Zone itself is encouraging the reemergence of the null-charged particle within you. As the null-charged particles are reemerging, you are becoming more of your greater self. This is going to be a continuing growth; it's not going to diminish. Once you pass through the Null Zone you're not going to suddenly find yourself in positive/negative-charged particles again. Everybody will have null-charged particles, which is the form you take in other bodies in more benevolent societies on other planets. It's part of your present fourth-dimensional shift. You can't stop it.

This inability to be self-destructive (and we're including going along with something that doesn't feel good to you) is going to change your life. Many of you have lost touch with your true feelings. When someone asks, "How are you feeling?" you say, "Oh, fine, fine." But perhaps someone comes up to you, a sensitive person who knows and understands feelings, and says, "No, no, I feel that something is bothering you." You may be behaving in an unusual way and you know in your mind there's something wrong, but you don't know what it is; you can't interpret your feelings.

So you find yourself now coming into a time in which your instinctual body (made up of the physical body, spiritual body and emotional body) is becoming stronger and portions of it are feeding information to the mind. They used to do it through the subconscious, but they're beginning to break through to the conscious mind now. As a result you notice changes inside yourself and you sense a change in your linear continuity. If you don't notice it yourself, other people will notice it and point it out. You might find yourself becoming aware of a self-destructive behavior and be unable to do it anymore. It might be something very small, like your response when someone asks, "How are you?" (a form of saying hello in your society, it is not literal). You will no longer have much tolerance for saying, "Fine, fine" when you don't feel fine. You'll be inclined to answer the question literally.

As a result, people are going to get more information than they bargained for and many of them will stop asking, "How are you?" They will begin to simply say, "Hi."

This is a significant change. It's measurable emotionally and spiritually, but also physiologically. In the long run it's going to be very good for reducing violence to yourself and to others. In the long run, beginning right now, it will cause you to change your entire approach to the world.

For many of you this will be a wonderful experience, because you will not only be in touch with your feelings about things and access them more easily, but you will know what's good for you and what to let go of. It might be a feeling, an object, a person – anything, even a philosophy. It will increase the sensitivity of the general population across the board, which will be a very, very good thing.

It will also mean that some people will be out of work at some point. So I'm going to suggest this: If you're now about five or ten years old and considering a lifelong fifty- or sixty-year career in police work, think instead about a twenty-year career in police work when you grow up, followed by something adventurous that doesn't require pursuing people for crimes they committed. Crime as you know it (meaning something destructive or self-destructive) is literally going to be gone within about thirty-five years. It's not going to be present or quantifiable in any way. You are not only spiritually growing (and the null-charged particle has plenty to do with that, obviously), but you are also becoming aware of each other and sensitive to how much alike you are. You might say to me, "Zoosh, there's all this violence going on now, and I can't take it." The old adage, "It gets worse before it gets better" is what's happening right now. It's in your face (as they say now) because people have to see. Although you've had violent periods on your Earth in previous history, you've never had them when communication was at such a zenith. If something happens violently, on purpose or by accident, on the other side of the Earth you'll hear about it very often the same day. This tends to create an almost physical movement amongst people to want to change that, and before long they organize and do so —religiously, philosophically, politically or any or all of the above and more. It's certainly happening spiritually, emotionally and physically.

The only barrier to the change is mental, because the mind is always searching for something that is absolutely true. The part of your body that is the most inflexible is the mind, because it is desperately seeking irrefutable truth. That's because of the way you're raised in your society, because of polarization and even because of physical circumstances. When you're born into and raised in a world where you have positively and negatively charged particles within you, finding the one thing you know for sure that is absolutely true is often ephemeral. Even when you find something that's wonderful, magnificent, fabulous, there's always that other pole to deal with. You have to deal with the dark side of that thing even if you don't want to see it.

As you come now into a time when the null-charged particle is the main function in your body, when you see, feel, sense (using all of your senses) what is right for you, the null-charged particle will guide that. The particle is a function of your immortal soul, your higher consciousness, and it will guide you; there will be no moving away from it. It always feels good; it's a literal return to your higher self as your day-to-day self.

You're already having physical symptoms associated with this function. I want to put certain professions on notice: It's unnecessary to make fifty-year military plans and so on, because in about thirty-five experiential years (thirty-five years worth of days and nights, but because your time is bending, it's not exactly linear time) there will be no evidence of any form of self-destructive crime on this planet at all —barring something I don't know about. (I don't want to sound egocentric, but I think I know about what's going on with you.)

It's really a good thing. Understand that you don't have any choice but to let go of certain behaviors you've had because of society's manners and mores. Perhaps the most significant one that initially creates some struggle and strife (but probably not violence) is an overpoliteness that is literally self-destructive.

You need to have patience with yourself. One of the core lessons that everybody has when they come here, with very few exceptions, is patience. When your body is doing things and you don't understand them, you can get upset about it or you can learn how to use it. Everybody is in the same boat, so you can help each other. Teamwork will reemerge as a natural function of life. If you don't like to do something you've been doing, you won't be able to do it even if you're good at it. There are probably others who like doing it very much. That kind of teamwork is absolutely the way in creatorship. You're not necessarily trained to do everything; you're trained to work with all energies that do all things, and you learn how to work cooperatively. But you don't necessarily do all things yourself until you get to a certain level. The function of creatorship school, of course, is to learn how to work consciously in harmony.

So the particles that make up the soul are increasing, and more of the soul is being expressed in the body or coming into the body?

It is measurable, quantifiable in the body.

Where is it coming from?

It's a function of the shift from the third to the fourth dimension, and it's increasing now because your planet is parked in the Null Zone, dimensionally speaking.

Until . . . ?

I can't give you an "until."

Well, you said ninety days from September 8, and that's up already.

It's going to be longer than that.

But there is new electrical energy coming in even though we're in the Null Zone.

Yes, but that's coming in for planet Earth, not for you. You can experience it to an extent, but it is not meant for everyone to experience.

Ah, so then the planet as a whole is not getting an influx of energy this month, in December?

Well, I'm not saying that it won't get an influx of energy, but it'll be meant for itself.

I mean, it's not like waves and waves of energy coming in for the humans?

I don't want to say yes or no; I would rather say the energy that is coming in is designed to help you to move forward, but I cannot define it as electrical in terms of positive/negative-charged particles; I can't define it that way. It's not the electricity you've known.

Okay. So there is energy coming in that we can use to advance with, that we're working with . . .

It's like this: If you are surrounded by radio signals, but you are using a wooden antenna, you're not going to pick them up very well. If you're surrounded by radio signals and you're using an aluminum antenna and a wire that connects to your radio, you're going to pick up lots of signals. It's as if you've been surrounded with this energy, but your body was not prepared to assimilate it. However, with the null-charged particle, you will be able to assimilate the "new electricity" as long as it has a null charge. You will also, for a time, be able to absorb and integrate with magnetic energy, which is very strong on the planet and is going to get much stronger because of the planet's need to shift into a more feminine balance. More women on the planet (simply by their numbers) helping the male beings on the planet come into a greater balance with their own masculine and feminine energies. The feminine energy is arising, and that's also the magnetic energy.

You'll be able to feel the magnetic energy and the null-charged electricity, which would be less kinetic. It wouldn't be used so much for moving things, but for sustaining things, nurturing, feeding.

But if you were working on both soul purposes and feminine energy, then your antenna would attract more of these new charges, right? The magnetic and the null, or new electric?

Yes, especially if the intent was present to let go of self-destructive patterns.

So those working for spiritual aims have got some extra energy to work with?

Yes.

Is this going to constantly keep increasing?

Yes, because as your null-charged particles increase, it's as if your antenna is getting higher and getting a better array and can pick up more of the energy that's available to support and sustain you. Some of it has been here for some time, but since your antenna has not been attuned to that frequency, you have not been able to use it.

Excellent analogy. So those who are working on crass materialism, greed and trouble for everyone, have no antenna for this, and they're going to feel like they're getting less and less energy?

Goodbye Greed and Violence

Because this is affecting the general population, they're not going to be able to continue self-destructive behavior. Greed, for example, assumes that "there isn't enough for everyone, and I need to have more than everybody has right now. I'm not getting enough." That is basically a self-destructive pattern that keeps you from interacting with others in a benevolent way, and it's also injurious to others. That will not be allowed! I'm not saying some rule is going to be formed; it's simply not going to be a function of your physiological self. What you've known as greed is going to go the same way as violence—it's just going to go away. There's not going to be any physiological means to accommodate it.

Then those people whose lives focus on non-love are the ones who are going off to the other planets?

It depends. We're talking about something over time, and some of these people will simply finish their natural cycles and choose to reincarnate elsewhere. But you have to remember that in a larger sense heaven is not set up on the model that many people perceive, which is judgment. Heaven—meaning the bosom of the Creator—is set up to provide, sustain, nurture, re-create and feed on unconditional love. Heaven is much more interested in transformation than in judgment. As a result, this is not a time to be thinking about how we're going to punish enemies or get rid of the guys who aren't working within our society. It's more of a time to say to yourself, By God, these people are going to transform! People who have been very self-destructive—suicidal, even (and you know, a person can be suicidal and think they're just going to hurt themselves and proceed to hurt a whole lot of other people unintentionally)—and also people who are intentionally hurtful toward others for a self-destructive reason, are simply not going to be able to do it anymore. They're going to be redeemed, as it were. That's the true meaning of redemption: becoming your natural soul-self as the Creator intended.

People are already experiencing some of these things, and one of the most significant things they are experiencing is a tremendous impatience with their own self-destructive acts. Meaning if someone says, "How are you doing?" and you're really hurting, and you say, "Fine, fine," you'll have almost no patience with yourself for that: you'll want to tell them how you're really doing. Or if you've been doing something or taking on some burden of someone else's, you're just not going to be able to do that much longer, because although we need to help each other, sometimes people need to face their own truth. If someone is obnoxious and you tell them they're wonderful, they're not going to know that they're being obnoxious. Are you doing them a favor, or are you doing them a disservice? These are value judgments, but they're examples you can understand.

Okay, so that's how the human is changing. What about the land in February? Is there anything people should look for or be aware of or plan for?

Nighttime Wakefulness

I'm disinclined to give predictions based on Earth changes. Because of the nature of what's going on with the land now, it's difficult (not impossible, but significantly more difficult) to get a night's sleep in which you'll sleep through the night—you know, where your head hits the pillow and you wake up the next morning. You can still do that, but it won't be as easy, because the land is letting go of things, and as I've said before, what the land cannot process, you, as the extension of the land, must process. If we calculate the mass of you that is the water, the minerals—in other words, most of the mass of you five billion people—you comprise a lot of mass of "land." What Mother Earth herself cannot take care of, you're going to need to do. One of the things you do to handle things she cannot deal with (because she already has enough to deal with) is the resolution of emotional trauma.

In the past when you've had emotional trauma you needed to resolve but couldn't do it physically, you'd ofttimes work it out in your dream state. But now you might have bizarre or strange dreams that have nothing whatsoever to do with your life. Don't overexamine your dreams too much, because it will be possible to read things into them that seem related to your life but really are not. You are essentially processing emotional traumas that other people, other beings, portions of Earth or even other planets have gone through because Mother Earth does not have the capacity to process those things as she once did, since so many minerals have been taken out of her body. If we removed half the neurons in your brain, you wouldn't be able to process things very well, either.

This is important to know, because it has to do with some things you are experiencing regularly. Don't feel too bad if you wake up two or three times a night. You might need to take a nap during the day. On a coffee break, sit down, lean back and meditate or rest or grab a few winks. For those of you who can set your hours, take a nap in the daytime or between shifts.

That's interesting. It's sort of like a payback, because we used to give our emotions to Mother Earth and let her process them.

Yes, and yet it is not unlike childhood, a child growing up to be an adult. As a child one is taken care of and does not have a great deal of responsibility. But as you grow up and take the steps of an adult, marry or start a business, then you have a great deal of responsibility not only to yourself and your clients but all of your employees and so on. It's not unlike that now. You have responsibility for Mother Earth. So you need to look after her, and you are actually doing it.

The Secret Government Setting up on the Moon

What about the secret government? They're still in stasis, right?

They're still functioning. They're doing all right; they're consolidating their operations so they can be in control, but with outposts. As I said, they've transferred a lot of their materials, manpower and even some dependents to the Moon, because it's easier for them to maintain security there. They are largely involved in a holding effort, trying to hold onto what they've got and seeing things slipping all around them. They're struggling.

You mean they transferred 180,000 people to the Moon?

It's very easy if you use portals. If you had to use ships it would be a big deal.

But when you get there, what do you do with them?

They've already got things set up there.

Really?

Yes. The mass of the people are in what I'd call abeyance, in a holding pattern. I can't say exactly where they are, because I need to look out for them, but . . .

Well, just talk about the ones who went to the Moon. They already had cities set up and facilities and homes and . . . ?

Well, not what you'd call a comfortable lifestyle. For instance, a home might be nothing more than something like a tent or a thin metal skin, nothing fancy. Kind of like a big warehouse or something—a tent city, if you can understand that, only underground where you can have a controlled atmosphere and so on. We're not talking about the inner circle or even the outer circle, we're just talking about people who help them, who sustain them—hybrids and so on. We're not talking about 180,000 inner and outer circle sinister secret government people, we're talking about people who serve them.

And this includes the hybrids.

Some of the hybrids, yes. That's why the facilities are rudimentary. They're adequate to sustain their life, but they are expected to build and create things that will sustain their lives better, as well as sustain their dependents' lives better (some have dependents) as well as those who may follow, such as inner and outer circle members.

The inner and outer circle are still functioning actively on the planet?

Yes, but the outer circle is not as influenced. We've already had three members of the inner circle break away, so the inner circle is now only about ten strong, and the outer circle has had a few collapses as a result of inner-circle members not being available anymore. They're not as strong as they once were. This is not to say that everything is hunky-dory, as you can tell, but they are not as strong or dominant as they once were.

But if they are so intermeshed with the way this planet runs, is it important to keep them going for a while just so the infrastructure doesn't break down?

No, I can't agree with you there. For example, a corporation can function quite well while the board of trustees goes on several weeks' vacation, and as long as new projects are not being developed, upper, middle and lower management as well as all the employees can take care of things. It's like that. If the inner circle all went someplace else, things would be contained, as they say in military parlance, and there wouldn't be a collapse of the infrastructure. There might in the long run be a little anarchy developing in lower-ranking members grabbing for this or that, not unlike gang warfare, but it would be gang warfare on a more organized basis.

So how would a positive scenario play out in which, hopefully, they're transformed?

Yes, that's the intent everywhere. There is a back door open for those who aren't transformed or who need to do more. I'm not expecting many people (or souls, if you would) to go through that back door. Ideally, we don't want any to go through it, but there is always the possibility that some will need the back door. In that case they will be cycled into the best environment for them to work these things out, which will probably not be a planet with a great deal of negativity, not as much as you have here, but enough that they can have adventure. They at least need adventure to work these things out.

We've been working with a model where only 20% would actually stay on the planet while evolving into the higher dimensions. So are we saying now that there's a possibility that a much higher percentage of humanity may go on?

Understand that the Creator's intention is that everybody go. But I'd say that at this time—and this could change—there's a really good chance that at least 93% will go on, maybe more! That is largely because of how fast you've moved along dimensionally and how much support is now available to you physiologically. If you had to make these changes as individuals, using the positive/negative-charged electric field, it would be very difficult. But with the reemergence of null-charged particles, it makes functioning in harmony very much easier.

Did the null-charged particles exist on 3.0-dimensional Earth?

Yes, they existed and were quantifiable, but there were few of them, and the research was at such a level that they were rarely detected, which is not surprising. If you're measuring something for a positive or negative charge, it would be rare for you to pick up an anomalous particle. So if it was noticed, it was considered a scientific curiosity.

Let's say there's an elevator between the two dimensions and we're halfway there. There are more of the null-charged particles here because we've absorbed so much light that we, as you say, have an antenna for it now. Is that how to understand it?

That is a way, yes. Your receptors are sensitive now. You can utilize it, you can pick up the signal of what's available because you now have the hardware and the software to run the program.

That is absolutely fantastic!

93% Success

In time it may be (and the Creator certainly wishes it to be) that 100% of the people will go. That is the desire. But right now it looks like 93% are going to go, and it could go higher. We'll see.

That's incredible! I've asked every teacher I've come across, and it was always such a small percentage.

Well, that was because of the way things were then. But there are physiological changes. If you had hands with no fingers in a society where all technology was based on fingers, you'd have a heck of a time using a typewriter. But suddenly it's like you've got ten fingers, and you can touch-type just like that!

It's really marvelous!

Yes, that really is the hot news. I'm trying to give you a manual by which you can apply the changes that are happening for you. This is the workshop. You've been in the study course, you've had study hall, you've had time to think about it, read about it, ponder it, consider it—but now you're in the applied laboratory. And when you're in the lab you really need to know not only what's going on, but what you can do about it!

And understand how it works!

Yes.

What about the military and their fears that the secret government is going to go too far? Has that sort of slacked down or cooled off a little bit now?

Well, no, I can't say that it has. The military organizations of your modern societies are restricted by the tools that they are aware they have. Interestingly enough, ancient military societies were much more spiritually evolved. As any good soldier knows, many's the time you have to ask for God's help just to get through it. In the more ancient military societies, the idea of utilizing spiritual abilities for your own self-preservation and for the preservation of your fellow troops has been an integrated practice.

As long as the militaries keep utilizing and perceiving that the tools available to them are all external and technological, they will become increasingly nervous about everything. But as soldiers (whether career soldiers or draftees) become more trained in inner-strength mechanisms (not unknown to the martial arts) but also utilizing, perceiving and applying qualities of a spiritual nature, there will be less fear of others, greater continuity, less war (granted, you will have a different role as a soldier, but you will have a role), and perhaps most important is that there will be fewer "accidents" that lead to wars – things caused by somebody being fearful and overreacting to something, which then flies out of control.

The military's nervousness about the sinister secret government activities is going to be greatly mollified as the militaries of the world gradually become more spiritualized. What they can do about it now is become involved in the physical training of martial arts (which they've been doing for some time), but perhaps more importantly (as any experienced martial arts instructor knows), in the physiological response the body has to the psychology, the religion and the philosophy of the martial artist. It's not an accident that these practices are referred to as arts, because that is what they are. It's an art, a philosophy, a way of being. It's an attitude, yes, but not an aggressive one. It's an attitude of safety and security based upon knowing not what you can do, but who you are. At the core, martial arts (in their finest examples) make every effort to explain to you who you are. So as military services begin to integrate more of this, they will become not only increasingly tolerant of the activities of others who may have threatened them in the past, but they will become more amenable to cooperative efforts toward cooperative goals and less nationalistic and competitive. That's my advice to the military.

They put a NATO officer in charge of the group going to Bosnia rather than one from the United Nations; that's a positive step, isn't it? Wasn't there a fear that the

U.N. is seen as an arm of the secret government and that United States soldiers didn't want to serve under U.N. leadership?

Yes, and the biggest problem with that is that the U.N. forces are a branch of the United Nations military, but because the sinister secret government has masqueraded so successfully as U.N. military, they have besmirched the good name of the true military of the United Nations. Even though the U.N. does not like to openly talk about their military forces, they actually have them. What we're dealing with here is a misperception by many people that the sinister secret government's masquerading forces are actually U.N. forces. They're not; it's clear that if they went around with little arm bands and uniforms that say "sinister secret government," they wouldn't get too far.

What about the scenarios we've heard of so much — an attempt to take over the United States by having some phony crisis, whether it's an earthquake or a riot or ET invasion? Is that still in the plans, or has that . . . ?

It was in the forefront of the plans for a time, but now it's more of a fall-back position because even they perceive that things are changing. If you once had a thirteen-member inner council that now has ten members, and they left one right after the other, you have to be very, very dimwitted indeed not to notice that things are changing. They want to make things appear to be a natural occurrence rather than to do something suddenly out of nowhere in the general population and create turmoil. The sinister secret government does not desire to create anarchy because they know that property would be destroyed. I realize that sounds very cold, but that is their perception, and the chance of some of their property being destroyed is high in their minds. So the last thing in the world they want to do is create a reaction that is anarchistic. They would rather have something seemingly grow, one thing after another, so that it seems to be part of the natural course of things. That's where political conditioning comes from.

But they've tried; for example, the Los Angeles riots, using the Oklahoma City bombing against the patriots — they've tried haven't they?

They have tried. I'm not going to say that the L.A. riots were caused by the sinister secret government; I will say they were secretly supported, as in the Oklahoma bombing. They have not achieved their actual goal, which is to terrify people enough (the general populace) so that they would put up a hue and cry for protection. After the L.A. riots, even though that hue and cry went up initially, because of the circumstances of the Los Angeles police force (which is grossly undermanned), the obvious people who might come to protect and support society were not available in sufficient numbers, so the people (again, the irony) had to come together to protect themselves – the antithesis of what the secret government hoped would occur! And because we keep having these kind of scenarios play out, they are less inclined to create some violent thing, after which they could then usurp power. So these scenarios are not, in their own minds, as credible as they once were.

So the confiscation of all the weapons and so on may never happen?

That may never happen. I don't think it's a serious risk. I do think, to those of you out there who are into guns and such, you're going to have to be fully aware that there will be a greater and greater effort by law-enforcement agencies to put something in gunpowder (for example) by which it can be traced. Thus anytime somebody performs a criminal act using a gun, that bullet can be traced through the powder patterns right back to the person who fired it. Even if the bullet was stolen it would still be able to be traced. I'm not going to hint how, because I think it's actually a good technology. I support it.

Okay, but that's criminal acts. I meant people who maintain guns for their own protection. May they end up keeping them — until we get to the point where the state of consciousness is such that guns are going to be ludicrous?

That's right. I think that the chances of having guns impounded as a general societal act are significantly reduced.

What about all the stories of U.N. troops and the training and the tanks, all this stuff there are pictures of?

That's all true. I'm not ruling out that real U.N. troops have done some training, but in large part this training had to do with either military training that comes about as training for riots in general (I won't overlook that). There have been a lot of training and exercises that had absolutely nothing to do with your legitimate military powers in any way, including the U.N., but were the sinister secret government forces masquerading as one element of the military or another. After all, as anybody in the military knows, if you're going to be operating "behind enemy lines," the best chance to avoid being detected is to look like the people who surround you or like something familiar. You would use the instruments, the electronics, the whole business by which you will be perceived as friendly.

But so many people knew; there was so much underground knowledge of their activities . . .

That is a function of cooperation – the absolute antithesis of what the sinister secret government wanted to create. For a long time they held tenaciously to the belief that if they created enough apparent chaos, eventually there would be a hue and cry for a leader who would come along and save them. But just about everything they did came back to haunt them and made things worse, from their perception. From your perception, of course, things were made better. So they've gotten to the point now where they are very reluctant to do anything that would be perceived as having mass effects or create a mass event. They're very reluctant to do it because they feel that just about every time they do it they're going to shoot off another toe! So they're just hanging back.

Well, it looks like we can relax and just let February and March happen?

Yes.

7

The Sifting Time

Zoosh through Robert Shapiro
December 13, 1995

Right now your world is so far along in your shift between the third and the fourth dimensions that you are beginning to experience bleedthroughs from your future existence. As a result, your future existence in this life will not be directly connected to the society you have now. There will be a more humanistic arrangement as well as a different sense of connection and feeling between people. Right now your society is living in the artificial manner of intellectual and economic contact between people, but not a feeling, heartfelt contact on a regular basis. . . .

It is this feeling of heartfelt contact that your physical bodies yearn for. This is something that your physical body, on the instinctual level, can feel in the future. Your instinctual body has the capacity (within certain limits) to reach beyond the dimension in which you exist to access stimulation from other realms. That is basically how people can perform certain functions ascribed to the spiritual community.

Right now everyone (although not everyone is aware of it) is experiencing this vague sense of unrest that is so distracting that it makes you want to drop everything and disappear somewhere for a while. Please know this is not a personal thing. Though people do not always have the capacity or the clarity to identify this as a challenge, people (once it has been identified for them) can easily feel this influence in their lives. Aspects of disappointment in your life being brought up for you are echoes from the future.

Right now your instinctual body (your physical body) is at about 3.47 between the third and fourth dimensions. But your instinctual body, which is made up of your emotional body, your physical body and your spiritual body, is able to reach out to about 3.74, almost 3.75, on the dimensional level. At this point there is sufficient radiation from the fourth dimension to allow your instinctual body to feel more at home than it feels here in this artificial environment your society has established.

That is what is creating this sense of restlessness that is to be heard, felt, seen and observed all over your world. People actually sense it, but cannot easily define it in words nor can they apply in actions the change that is taking place for themselves physiologically, spiritually, emotionally and so on. If you can understand that this is a temporary phenomenon, then you will recognize that it is not necessarily a time to take your career and throw it in the round file or pack up a few necessities and move to the Bahamas. This is a phenomenon that will pass. Nevertheless, it is a constructive phenomenon, because for many people it will tend to underscore those portions of your life that are the least compatible with you. That portion of your life which is basically compatible, but for which you feel no great interest at the moment, will return as compatible and interesting in the future.

This sifting time (as one might sift flour) is designed to eliminate the large granules of your life that do not really belong in your now life, nor can they come into the future. At the day-to-day level this might be experienced as behaviors you have acquiesced to, meaning that you have allowed to come into your daily personality because society requires it. For example, if one is attending a business meeting, one cannot spontaneously jump up and start dancing to a tune within one's head. However, this does not mean that the emotional body does not wish to do this, and it will usually be satisfied by imagining such a thing. However, to continue my business-meeting analogy, one has to pay attention; so the emotional, imaginative self becomes much more frustrated because of its inability to experience, appreciate and practice something it will not have the opportunity to do at the fourth dimension: to practice any aspect of third-dimensional physicality. Now, this is very important for many people to understand.

In the third dimension the physical self can be highly reactive and interactive with its physical environment. At the fourth dimension there is less interaction on a spontaneous and stimulating level. This means that right now in your third dimension (although you're not locked into that anymore, nevertheless you are still feeling its influences) you can, as an individual, stimulate physical events. This means that you can do something which will cause other physical events to take place, you understand? On the fourth-dimensional level, that is not directly available to you. In the fourth dimension you are more inclined to function in harmony with physical events that naturally flow around you. For years people have been asking for specific examples of fourth-dimensional (as compared to third-dimensional) interactions. This is an example now available to you that I can tell you about. I have not been able to tell you about it before this time because you did not have the physical evidence or the feelings by which you could identify personally with this phenomenon.

Right now people are feeling driven to experience the last aspects of their ability to "make it happen." At the fourth dimension, you ain't gonna make nothin' happen, to put a little spin on it. Once you get to 3.51, for example—not at the midpoint (3.50), but at 3.51, the commitment beyond the Null Zone that you're now in, the commitment beyond the third dimension—you will begin to lose more and more of your ability to be individually proactive. You will more likely become (and begin to be more and more as the juggernaut moves along toward the fourth dimension) homogeneously involved. Meaning that you will feel a greater sense of kindred spirit with friends and neighbors, even people you have not been with before. As a result, there will be this sense of the physical body, which for many of you was formed during the time of your society's total lock-in with 3.0 dimension, wanting to express its full physicality unrestricted by any of society's values.

This is by way of a long explanation about precisely what is going on for you and others right now. I need to bring it home to you in this way because it's important for you to know that it is not necessary to dump your whole life in favor of this temporary feeling. Just become aware of those aspects of your life that need to be weeded out. You know what they are, things that you might do that are either self-destructive or self-deprecating.

8

Anchoring Your Higher Self

YHWH through Arthur Fanning
December 22, 1995

What wonderful beings you are. Indeed? What a great joy it is to forget and try to remember, eh? You're having fun with it. Don't you think it's time to remember? Lot of fun coming up. I'm waiting for some of you beings to wake up. We're going to do a little meditation.

Your Diamond Light

I want you to visualize a diamond light with the apex here [at the throat chakra], going this way [spreading out across the chest], and this way to the navel chakra [so the points are at the throat, the navel, and on either side of the chest, forming a diamond]. Visualize that light in your body. Allow. Now allow it to become with a light blue tint along the edges so it shimmers. Allow. Center. Open the chakras on the palms of your hands. I want you to vibrate that blue diamond light now faster, and I want you to think toward your right-hand side. You simply put the thought to the right and watch the vibration of that light, what it does. Allow. Now think "hold the vibration" and think to the left side of you. Center. Think in your center, a thought six inches above your head, center, diamond light. Allow your eyes to open gently.

What is beginning to happen, your auric field is becoming thicker. Your physical body will begin to vibrate faster. Your light body, great light, your higher self (your words), is moving closer.

You're going to have to think in terms of your higher self. You're going to learn, particularly next year, that you will be responsible for the emotional energy in your physical form because of your own thoughts, be it one day ago or years ago. You're going to have the opportunity to remember how you do it here, within the body physical. You will also have the opportunity to argue all along the way, and you will know when you are arguing.

Anchoring the High Self

Allow your eyes to close for a moment and center your being. Allow you to visualize a golden pyramid above your head, what you would term six inches above. Allow it to be four-sided, golden color. Allow it to propel energy down into your body, gold light. Allow. Now see this pyramid spin counterclockwise, from the front of you to the left, to behind, to the right, to the front, around and around, forming a golden cone. As it cones, the apex reaches upward. Allow it to move upward and watch the anchoring point – it is in what you call, as you would term it, the seat of your high self. "Seat" means chest center, heart center. Allow you to see the light and the connection there. Center. Do not be concerned with other energies. Center. Above your high self's light there is a golden pyramid also. Allow it to spin. Allow the high self to allow the gold into the body and down to you, and it reaches further – apex of the cone goes farther. Allow. And it continues and continues, and the apex and the energy moves and returns unto you, having traversed the galaxies, into your root chakra. Allow. Center. Be in the heart chakra. Allow. Allow your eyes to open gently.

There will be no judgment upon you if you beings decide to leave the physical body in this next year. You're loved forever. You will continue to be forever. The understanding of forever is within the soul in the heart chakra. It is not here [head/physical brain] – this is what gets it last; this is what will cause you diseasement here, not utilizing it appropriately – it's a tool.

Energies are speeding up. Your old metaphysical games will keep you comfortable for a little bit, little bit. But what you're going to find out your year next, it's not the Pleiadians that are landing – they've mucked you up enough; it's not the beings from Orion, either; it is you – you're landing here, big time. So you better get your physical suit ready for more light. Everyone take a breath.

Know you the Photon Belt everyone is chatting about? It is consciousness, it is part of you that is coming here. It is part of you joining you. On a very deep and intimate level, you're waiting for it to quicken itself. You have to quicken yourself first, or you'll react to your own energies.

You've heard me speak of compassion, indeed? Know you what I mean? I not only meant it that you show compassion to another, because another needs it and they don't know what they're doing; I meant it for you, because that energy will come back to you, very rapid fashion. You're not going to have to wait for another lifetime to experience it. Things are happenings quickity-quick here now, particularly next year. So you're being very compassionate to yourselves, and you're understanding you're learning, you're not judging self. When you have compassion for another, that energy will return to you, and the journey won't be so difficult.

You are in outrageous times, entities. There is a move going on right now to control you further. Don't judge it. Work through this thing in the empowerment of yourself. Your prayers, indeed if you must, your meditations, are important, 15 moments a day. It'll assist you to center.

When your light arrives there'll be a little distortion. And some of you will try to carry the energy from your physical to get even with some beings that have messed you up from out there, so to speak, but it won't work. You'll only go a little bit higher – that'll be all. There is a great reunion coming. It is a blessed thing. Your bitterness, your anger toward God, your fellow man, is what keeps you limited. That's what keeps you limited – nothing else.

Cleansing the Body

Center. Allow your eyes to close for a moment. I want you to feel in the heart chakra a golden light, center, beautiful light, center, powerful light. In that gold light I want you to visualize a white dove sitting there. Allow the dove to unfold its wings and leap out of your chest, as it's a light energy. Allow. Sit there as a Buddha now and watch the dove. Peace. You're enjoying the dove and its movement – it was your creation . . . no strings attached. Each time the dove moves, you feel an ecstasy, literally, within your energy field, within the body. Pay attention, entities. You can have an orgasm in your physical body simply by contemplating the freedom of the dove, your light moving, the thought of it, what you term beyond, into kundalini, knowing power. It is all right, it is fun.

Allow you to see you sitting in a temple, very ancient temple, golden walls, golden seats, golden ceiling. Center. And in this temple you're a very powerful being in your knowing, what would be termed the highest level of knowing you've worked to attain through your journeys here. Allow. This is where you keep the information. Allow. Center. Allow you to feel a red ruby at your sixth seal, third eye. Allow. Center. I want you sitting in your heart chakra in a pyramid of gold light now, and from that center I want you to command the body to be cleaned, and see it. Center. Let it go. Center. In a gentle manner slowly open your physical eyes. I want you to contemplate this diamond light that you have here [in the chest], a pyramid here in your head [at hairline], another one above you. Allow your eyes to remain open. I want you to see them all aligned – apexes are in a straight line.

In your great power, you think through the center of that alignment. In your distortive behavior, you think through the limits of the pyramid; you apply thought through those vortices that way. They're not really pyramids, they're energy patterns. It is going to be very amusing to watch you beings go through your centered/not-centeredness. You, however, will not think it's very funny. When I say center, I mean you center in the center of the heart chakra, the center of your body, in a line of light here, all the way up; and you'll feel it in the body. It is right here, actually [just above the pubic bone], but you get your light moving. Center.

Apply What You Know!

This is not a good time, from your perspective, to play metaphysical with these energies. Let the others do it. This is the time to apply everything you know, from the tiniest grain of what you know —you must, you must.

We are rising energies from deep within the core of the Earth. We are taking energies from another galaxy and bringing them here, and they're going to meet. Now, guess what's in the middle? —your physical body. It is called speed-up integration. You know what I mean. "Hurry up, handle it!"

I want you to do your thinking what you call in the physical form out here [above the head], think out there. Let it come in. You'll utilize, you will, more brain that way. [He grins:] What you really do is you pop it out there so you can think your thinking here [above the head], and bring it back down. Very clever entities.

Now, I want you to contemplate this. Know you your . . . movie where you see beings standing and then they become light particles and they disappear?

Beam up.

Beam up, indeed? Okay. It is presented as a tool on a ship, indeed? Know you what I mean? The tool portion is your ability to clearly think in the area of your tenth chakra here [above the head], and you lighten the body, not into tiny particles, yet they are – they're so tiny you can't even conceive of them, and you become light; and the thought at the tenth tells the light where to go and be born, remanifest. Some of you in this room are going to play with this, so don't be disconcerted if you are on one side of a building and appear on the other side in a moment. You're learning how to do it. It is a natural thing to do. You are supposed to know how to do it, because your body is literally a hologram. You split your spiritual light, is what you've done; you're a holographic image. Beautiful images, however; a lot of fun to play within. You've imbued the images with talk and what you think is wisdom [he laughs]. So you've out-thunk yourselves. Now you've got images of yourself all over, and you're struggling like mad out there" to figure out how you're going to get the image to listen to you . . . because the image has a mind of its own, know you what I mean? Allow.

Healing Your Body and Becoming

I want you to contemplate a floor, a golden lake. You can allow your eyes to be open or closed – it doesn't matter. Because you're light and you're an image, you can heal your body by letting go of your anger and your arrogance. Listen, and allow the image to be rebuilt by clear thought here [a few feet above the head]. Now you let go. Let it go, let all of the thoughts go, everything, right now, into that lake of gold. There's a pyramid down there, lavender. Let it all go in there. Allow. Let it go! Allow! Center. Allow the movement. Contemplate gold light in the body and allow the remanifestation to take place by itself, without you adjusting it. Center. Allow. Become a pyramid of light in your thought. Center, center. I want you to visualize and allow entry into this room, a golden chair, what you would term a throne, and there is a great being of light sitting upon this throne. He is at the same level that you are. Allow this being of light to look at you. Allow. See his elegance, the beauty, the power, the compassion, the wisdom. And allow the body of you to merge with that being because that is you. Allow. Center, center. Merge together. Now allow the being to come into you. Allow. Center Allow your eyes to open if you have them closed.

[He nods.] There is a lot of energy coming in now, a lot. Your physical bodies are changing, your organs are changing – they're being aligned inside you, your energy fields are changing, portions of your brain are being activated more. A lot of the beings that are caught on the planet now want the metaphysical structures, religion – some beings – to support this new frequency, this new concept.

For it is a concept of life, what life is about, and [neither] your religious structure nor your metaphysical will support it. Some of your ancient, what you would term, Tibetan will be understand, some of your ancient Indian American here will be understand, close. So the fears take over, because deep inside you know there is no support system—[he whispers:] you know it! You have to become. You have to become and become and become; and you're right in the middle of it. And for some the frequency of the soul doesn't like it that way—that's all right. Lot of humor.

Feeling the Incoming Light

Now, allow your eyes to close a moment. Feel your pyramids aligned. Allow. Feel the energy vibrating in your body, right at the crown chakra. It's a ball of white light, and it vibrates and moves down lower and lower into your head, through your neck, your arms, your chest. Feel it – it is energy in the body, in your muscular structure. Let it move into the bone. It feels different. It is light. There is more of it. You have to get used to it coming. This is what it's going to feel like, only more.

You're vibrating faster—you're going to, to make it easier here. Indeed, you must. The vibration is love here. The planet is not going to be destroyed. A lot of the population will be removed. That's all right.

Know you what a spike is, a spike stick[ing] up? Allow the energy as it begins to break through what you call the locked- down portion of itself—where others have locked it down so you could not utilize it. It'll begin to poke through the ground as little white spikes and many beings will see them—little white spikes of light, little pyramid-shaped light things come up. When you begin to see them moving up through the ground, many places, you will have 160 days to raise your vibrations rapidly. I'll put it another way. If you haven't allowed your meditations to work, your vibrations to increase, by the time you see these things come up, you're going to be in an awful lot of confusion, because there are images in these spikes, pyramids coming up, and there are images in the lights coming down, and you can't make out what they are from a third-dimensional understanding. You can only understand what they are from your meditative energies, and it will keep the fright out of your night. Everyone take a breath. Center. You wanted excitement—now you're getting it. We never said it was going to be a boring game; we never said it was going to be easy.

Let me see . . . yet there is going to be conflict, wars. They're doing a pretty good job right now of starting one. Hopefully it won't be as bad as some predict. There's still a chance. Anything else anyone wants to chat about?

May I ask which war, what particular area you're talking about?

Well, you're in your Yugoslavia now, know you what I mean? And there are being alliances set up in what you term Iraq/Iran now, and what you term China is being involved there, indeed? So it's a little chess game here. You thought the Illuminati was dividing up the world before; well, they're doing the same thing.

I have a question. Myself and several other people I know seem to be almost compulsively seeking resolution in relationships with people — immediate, past, whatever, but it's like we're absolutely intent on finding balance, peace, and we're almost driven by it. Are we just trying to get our house in order before it gets . . . ?

A lot of the rules of your society were meant to control you. Within each system of thought, each belief system, each religious system, relationships are entirely different in what you term the social manner in which they're attended to, indeed? Now, you've picked the frequency of this culture to understand the energy of relationship. It is a word, relationship. It is a very limited word. As you become more, the centeredness, the god qualities of yourself become more important in understanding, and as you understand them, so too do the god qualities within another become more important, indeed? There is not the ability to have competition – it won't exist. There becomes the ability to be in joy no matter what another does. As you play now in these new energies, your metaphysical systems will provide you a word so you may communicate, but at a very limited level. You all know the feeling, the intent, the god that exists everywhere. You all know it, everyone of you. You're just picking the level of where you want to pretend it doesn't exist. When you understand that, the issue within relationships becomes no issue, know you what I mean? It applies to everyone here, and all things. But it's fun, know you what I mean? Gets boring sitting in heaven! Got to put your feet in the fire sometime, eh? Drop a marshmallow or two, [and] see what happens.

Your year 1996 is becoming a very . . . how will I say? . . . it will either bring great peace to self's journey in becoming the Christ, the Buddha and beyond, or it will create great antagonism for any religion different than you, different religion/antagonism, know you, great conflict. I suggest that you center in your being to understand the Christ and the Buddha. Indeed? It's going to be an outrageous year. Lot of fun.

Reconnecting to Atlantis

What can people in general do to reconnect to their Atlantean past?

That will happen.

Are there specific things they can do, and would it be good to do that?

Indeed, it would. You better be ready to clear, however. Once you connect, there's a lot of energy there in that process. You must be willing to let go. One of the easiest ways is to contemplate a very large blue pyramid under the water. Even if you get a bowl, know you, you get a blue pyramid—it doesn't have to be any particular mineral, just simply blue, know you? Put it in the water [in a bowl], meditate under this, or [put it] in front of you—it will remind you. Put it in water; it might remind you of too much, however.

Is there going to be land actually rising soon in the dimension we're in?

Yes, within a year and half.

Will it be where the pyramid was, or around Bimini, or . . . ?

More near Bimini.

You're handling the energies of December rather well. Stay centered. Your December 30th is going to be a little exciting. Center. Just center. I'm not going to tell you any more. It's part of your play, anyway. Don't get caught up in it. Believe it or not, the job that you came here to do is getting done. You are all participating at the level you said you would—out there, here, whatever. It's getting done, so you can be very proud of yourselves. Allow.

Visiting a Landed Ship

Okay, I want you to center your being. Allow your eyes to close gently. Center. I want you to feel a pyramid beneath your buttocks, apex pointing upward. And there is another pyramid, and the base will rest upon this apex, and going up into your body, another, and another, and another; so there's a chain of them. They can be any size, what you call a couple inches, thirteen, fourteen, fifteen of them. Let them go right up a string here. Light. Center. I want you to see what is termed your Southwest, in your United States, I want you to see it. I want you to blanket it with love from the heart chakra. I want you to feel . . . allow yourself to see . . . a very gigantic ship approaching for a landing in your Southwest deserts. It is very large. Allow. Center. You've connected to clear energies so this can happen, the landing can take place. Allow. Center. Allow the energy called you to visit the ship that is going to land. In a gentle manner, slowly open your physical eyes. Center. When I say center now, I want you to center right here, right between your eyes. Center. Think it there, and feel the energy come in there. I want you to center at the throat – center. Center at the heart chakra. Navel – center. Root – center. Crown – center. Center. Clear.

I will visit each one of you tonight, and I'll give you a very personal message, besides just overloading you with energy. I've been known to do that, too. I want you to pay attention, bargain?

[Group:] Bargain!

So be it. You have a grand time, indeed? We are through.

Thank you

9

Resistance Being Removed From The Soul!

Humanity Enters a Three-Month Period of Deprogramming

Zoosh through Robert Shapiro
February 6, 1996

These times you are living in are very challenging, because you're being literally forced to give up what your bodies were programmed to have in them when you were born. Granted, there is an exception for the babies born in the past couple of years — they didn't have it in them. But the rest of you have this programming: a certain amount of resistance literally built into the soul impetus to create cells. We all know that your physical body forms around your lightbody; what I'm talking about is the impetus of the soul to stimulate, invite, support, nourish and generally hold on to the physical material borrowed from Mother Earth to make your physical self. Within that there has been some resistance planned, and this resistance is built in so that you can have not only a built-in hurdle to climb over, but also a true test of what you value. It is in the nature of resistance to put things off, to delay things. It is in the nature of resistance to create a pressure behind it (not unlike water building up behind a dam) that will force solutions. Everyone was born with that, but now here you are, far enough along in this shift of dimensions that resistance cannot be with you any longer.

We have a circumstance now in which this resistance in all beings is literally being pumped out of you as I speak. There have been arrangements made for this day for over a million years. Certain extraterrestrials have been camped out under the surface of the planet to provide the exact means by which your resistance can be literally vacuumed out of your bodies – or blown out, since it's still a polarized world.

And so it is going on as I speak. It is because of this that you are feeling even more nervous these days. You have to understand that your bodies were born within a certain context, a program – a formula, if you like, and within this formula all things were accounted for. Nothing was added to the formula that didn't have a purpose or a use, and nothing was excluded if it could be useful. But here you find a situation in which resistance is too much. Why? Because you are in the Null Zone, where there isn't much impetus to move forward (although it is building), so, as I've discussed before, the energy that is built up for you needs to create a smooth path forward for you. The resistance built into you, to help you to accomplish your goals, to reinvent your reality, to re-create your universe, is too much, it's creating too much of a block. The dam is too strong, if you will.

Antennas of the Planet Broadcasting Removal Energy

So now comes the moment when the ETs who have been waiting here get to aim their little devices in various places. I bring this up tonight because some places will feel this energy stronger than others. There are places around the Earth that act as antennas, that are literally the means by which there is a heightening of whatever energy is produced. We all know that Sedona is one of these places. A few others are well known – Santa Fe, Tibet, Machu Picchu – and there are others, not so well known, that also broadcast energy. Some of these would be the last place in the world you'd expect to be a place that would heighten and amplify energy and broadcast it. One of these places is Las Vegas, Nevada.

Now, this energy is designed to shake loose from your bodies – and even from your lightbodies; can you imagine! – the original programming of resistance. That is why many people have been saying that now is the time to be clear about your goals, to have your goals quite present, to work on them a little bit every day, to achieve them and to move forward. And yet, because many people are having their resistance processed out of them, they are feeling more resistance than they once did! They are more conscious of being resistant, and they are in fact genuinely becoming, in some cases, downright stubborn to the point of being intractable.

Now, it's important for you to know that this is just temporary. Within three months (I like that number, but it's true) of this date, this resistance will be largely removed from your physical bodies. Now, that doesn't mean you will no longer have the ability to be cautious—you will still have the ability to be discerning and so on. But you will no longer have an artificial resistance built into you to make that push that you all needed in the beginning in order to do what has been, in past lives, difficult to do. That difficulty has been in re-creating your reality as something entirely new, to branch off into some area that is entirely new and unknown to your soul.

So here we have a circumstance in which you're being reprogrammed at the soul level in life. On a practical, day-to-day level, you will feel almost as if you are in a shaker, being shaken from the inside out. I've spoken about this in terms of other things, but this is adding to those other things! For some of you this is bringing up nervous conditions, accentuating stressful situations for you. It is heightening tensions.

Be it known that this will pass within three months, but it will require that time, because it takes fully a month and a half to charge up these antenna areas to broadcast all around the Earth so that the Earth herself can release built-up and residual resistance leftover from human beings who have passed this way before—and also so that she can not only speed up her own process (although this is meant for you, it helps her), but also broadcast more of this energy. So it's sort of charging up her battery, if you will. By the time you actually read this, Earth should be pretty well charged up, you know. And that will help you.

But right now it's difficult. So what you need to do now is spend more time doing what you used to do. When most of you first got started in New Age concepts, you didn't even call them "New Age" concepts; they were "meditation" or "stress reduction," you understand? I want you to temporarily reincorporate that original stress-reduction means or meditational means, that you would use to relax. Now you may have moved on past that point, and that's fine. But remember, what you learn in the early days of any valuable philosophy is designed not just as a stepping stone, but also as a tool to be used when needed. So this is a time when meditation, creative visualization—any stress-reduction techniques that work for you—are good to apply. Use them for more than three months you wish, but for the next three months it's especially important, because it will create the means by which you can let go of the tension.

You see, when you are releasing something that is, at its heart, resistance, its moving through you will naturally create tension. If it moves in, it creates tension – that's what was originally programmed. And when it moves out, it's also necessary for it to create tension – not because Creator is a wise guy, but because it is the nature of the being of resistance to create tension. It cannot even move from cell to cell in your body without creating tension. So you need to help that resistance to leave; you need to consciously do any stress-reduction or relaxation techniques you can do from time to time throughout your waking day, and before you go to sleep at night, because this will make it easier for you to pass through the night. Should you wake up in the night and need to do it again, go ahead. Remember, though it might be annoying, it will be over soon, and once it is over, you will find that you are able to accomplish it much faster [snaps his fingers]. The pace will pick up, you'll move more quickly toward your goals and you'll achieve your goals – and even some of your ideals – much more smoothly.

The Zeta Connection

Now, a few words need to be said about the ETs who are down there. You know, a lot of ETs have been evacuated off the planet for one reason or another – including even members of underground civilizations who've been here since long before you were. And yet there are a few outposts down there, usually just a few individuals and a small area of technology – basically something that radiates a wave of energy. That wave of energy is specifically geared toward the release of resistance. So this releasing resistance factor – the RR factor – has been stimulated technologically by beings from Zeta Reticuli.

I have spoken at length in The Explorer Race I about your connection to the Zeta Reticulan beings – they are very closely connected to you on the soul line. I will simply say that your future lives are in the advanced future civilization, especially in the higher dimensions, of Zeta Reticuli, at least along one probably creation of reality. They now understand that you are their past lives, so they have more respect for you and they are more inclined to enthusiastically participate in this project in which something that looks very much like a multistage parabolic broadcasting device is literally being aimed into the rock that surrounds you, because the rock that surrounds you is this red rock. Now, it doesn't require red rock (which is iron-based, you understand, and is a good conductor), but it works better. So any of you who are living in an area where there is a lot of red rock, like Utah, will find that there is a heightened tension in the air, because these areas are being charged up. Again, don't worry – it'll be temporary.

Now, know this: It is in the nature of the physical being to have moments when this tension will not bother you. Those of you who are involved in exercise programs where you get your heart rate up to about 120 – not necessarily wildly exercising, but vigorous walking, bicycling, swimming and so on – will feel this less, because generally speaking, a smooth heart rate of 120 or more, within healthy guidelines, will essentially cancel the effect of that feeling of tension. (Now, don't run out and do this if you have heart trouble, okay?) Even hard work at physical labor, chopping wood or something, will generally cancel that feeling. You won't feel it – as a matter of fact, with that extra tension you might feel especially invigorated. Because once your heart rate gets up to that point and your cardiopulmonary system is functioning more efficiently, as it does at that rate for a short time, it actually tends to cancel the effect and utilize it in a more benevolent way. And for fully an hour afterward, maybe an hour and a half, you are still feeling better than normal. So you see, there are circumstances in which this actually works for you.

I'm mentioning this because some of you out there who have been doing this kind of exercise or working hard have actually been feeling more invigorated, and that's a good thing. It doesn't mean you have to double your exercise time. But it could mean that you do your exercise when you normally do it, and perhaps for five or ten minutes at different times during the day, just to re-create that feeling and carry you over the humps. So for those of you who can take even a coffee break at work and, instead of coffee, do whatever exercise you can to bring your heart rate up to at least 120 per minute will find that that break every few hours or so will carry you through the day comfortably.

Food Sources to Ease the Tension

How about drinking water — will that help?

I would say this. For liquids that will help, for those of you who can, try to drink citrus. Citrus will give you a little help. Citrus has the curious characteristic of being able to conduct electrical energy a little better than even water. So the hybrid might be to add citrus to water – a little orange or a little lemon to give it the flavor. Not everybody can drink that, but it could be healthy for you in other ways, and that would be helpful.

What about vitamins?

Oh, I'd say you'd want to take a little more calcium if you can. You might want to take a little extra magnesium to support your heart system. You might want to take a little of the trace minerals — things you only need a small amount of every day. A good vitamin pill will have these.

Certain foods will support people who cannot do the exercises or for some reason don't have the time — which is the case for many people, and I have to acknowledge that. Certain foods will actually help you to feel better during that time, and while I am not a spokesman for the ranchers, I will say that some people will find that if they eat a little more beef — and you can get it organic if you want, but you don't have to — that will help those who cannot get away to do these other things. Beef has the capacity to put into your body a certain durability. For those of you who know hunters or do hunting yourself, just about any wild meat would also be helpful — deer, elk, reindeer, for those of you living up north, and of course fish, which is largely available from commercial sources. So, believe it or not, I am not a spokesman for the American Beef Council, but nevertheless I have to acknowledge that your bodies have been set up to consume meat.

So for those of you who cannot do that for various reasons, or are vegetarians, just try to do some of the other things I mentioned.

Okay, let me get real straight with this. This resistance is in our souls to help provide some of the tension needed on the planet to resolve polarity?

Yes, and mostly to resolve problems that you couldn't resolve in previous soul incarnations because the planet upon which you were living was too benevolent to resolve anything, since everything was provided (and that's fine), or because you have been in Creator training, as you are here. You are blocked from knowing what you really know at your higher-self level so that you will have to re-create your reality. But that also inherently creates tension and fear. Everybody knows that — even when you went to school to meet the other kids when you were young, you didn't know them, you were afraid, it wasn't like home and so on, so you needed to have something within you to get over your shyness, and it was that tension, that resistance. You had resistance to going to school, and the tension necessarily built up behind that resistance, because where you have resistance, you have tension built up behind it — it just is. As a result, the tension and the resistance work well together to help you do something you wouldn't normally do. You develop all this resistance and tension and fear, but like the water building up behind the dam, eventually the tension is going to do something—the water's going to go over the top of the dam or break the dam down, because there's too much of it. And that tension working with resistance is what helps you to re-create your reality or do something you have never done before in any other life.

So how will our lives be different without this resistance? Will there be less fear, less tension?

Well, understand that, because resistance will not be as great a factor, you will necessarily have less tension, all right? So the levels of anxiety will probably drop within three months. There will probably be fewer extreme dramas, fewer unexpected wild and crazy things happening. But for the next three months, they will be possible. The wild and crazy doesn't have to be awful; you might suddenly decide that you've always wanted to go off a ski jump or something—please practice first. But you might do something adventurous or fun or spontaneous. Within these three months and then after the three months, the resistance programmed in your body will be largely gone, and so there won't need to be the corresponding tension. Ergo, there is less anxiety, less fear, and more of you getting on track with the natural soul rhythm of your higher self. And all of this coincides nicely with your gradually moving through the Null Zone. The planet will pick up the pace and begin to move in the Null Zone—not past it, but moving forward again on the dimensional shift—within three months. You'll begin to creep forward incrementally again. So all of this coincides. But the main thing is, in three months or so you should notice a marked decrease in tension, anxiety and resistance, so goals will be much more easily attainable.

And that is also going to decrease negativity because that's been a part of the cause of negativity?

It could release negativity; it could also release, to be perfectly honest, a certain amount of the desire for adventure. While you might feel like you've just got to go hang-gliding today, or find out how to do it, in three months you might not. But we don't have to put only a negative cast to this: if you've got a healthy body and you've always wanted to learn how to go hang-gliding, this is probably the time to do it.

10

The Express Bus To Creatorship

Zoosh through Robert Shapiro
January 23, 1996

You individuals reading this are truly a result of the genetic experiment on Earth. You are beings who uphold the principles of the Explorer Race. I want you to know that when you read The Explorer Race, as many of you will, this information is designed to show you who you are, and give you an evolutionary understanding of your past that will help you now. The key to empowerment in these days is to not know everything about your past, but to know that which will help you now. If you were to know all about your past, many things would confuse you and sidetrack you. But now you must take the express — the bus that goes from point A to point B without stopping in between — because so much of what is going on now commands your immediate action.

Time, as you've heard, is changing. It is not growing short, it's just changing. This means that you are on an accelerated pace of responsibility. Your souls have been here for a while on Earth and have been trained in Earthlike conditions. This education has been designed so that you would have the ability to explore all levels of responsibility, results, effects and consequences and take on more responsibilities. You have done this. Even as I speak now, you are experiencing more and more intense energies. These energies are associated with creation and creation energies. This is why you must be very clear these days. You must not have casual fantasies that are negative! If you notice them, change them immediately to something else. You can't really erase what you've fantasized or thought, but you can immediately change it. As I've said before, it takes a tremendous amount of energy to change the past, but only a teeny little bit of energy to create something new.

Because your responsibility is growing day by day, you need to have tools. Yes, you need some understanding of the past; yes, some understanding of what is to come; yes, an understanding of what to do now—all these are very good. Yet you must know that your number-one function right now is that you have the status of Creator apprentice, which you have achieved through years and lifetimes of sweat. As Creator apprentice you are constantly being given responsibilities by the Creator to do things that normally Creator would do. Now this responsibility is thrust upon you. So in your explorations in this lifetime as well as in the future, to the stars, you will know that your responsibility lies very strongly and significantly in applying the wisdom you have learned, because that which you do through wisdom must work! You must know it works. It can't be a "maybe" anymore, it can't be a "might be," it can't be "we hope." You have to apply what does work.

Now, this doesn't mean you cannot experiment, but that you will experiment at times when there is not much riding on it, you understand? You don't experiment with mass events that affect many, many people. You experiment with friends who know you're experimenting. It's something you're trying out: "Let's try this," you say. Or your friend says to you, "Let's try that." So you experiment, and if it works, then you try it with a larger group. And if it works with a larger group, then you try it with many, many. But only apply to the many what you know for certain is benevolent and works. These intense energies coming through now are only the precursor that the Creator apprentice must work with.

So here is homework for you, Explorer Race individuals! When you are feeling energies (recognizable to those who are not specifically tuned in to feeling energies as extra nervous energy; those who are will know what you're feeling), I want you to focus on visualizations with that energy. In the past you've done visualizations somewhat out of your body, or putting your body into a relaxed state. This time I want you to do your visualizations a little differently. Since you will tend to feel the bulk of this physical, kinetic energy (which is creation energy on this level), I want you to hold a beautiful visualization and put it right into your solar plexus. Not inside your body, but take the image and rest it at the base of your sternum, where your upper abdomen begins. This will be somewhat physical for many of you. Create something beautiful:it can be simple, such as color and waves of color, or it can be a feeling — peace, happiness, joy, whatever is easiest for you to attain — but it must be a full-body feeling. Then focus it on your solar plexus, as if you were laying it on the surface, and then outward.

You see, in Creator apprentice training you learn how physical reality is created. You've often wondered whether physical reality is some vague consensus of unconscious thoughts, but it really isn't. It's a physical creation that is focused through the physical being, as if each of you are lenses of the Creator's focus. So it is time to consciously begin to use yourself as a lens! Many visualizations and meditations have been to create relaxation or certain goals within your body.

Now, this picture that you hold in your mind's eye, imagine it between your hands, up by your head. Then bring your hands down, resting your wrists on the lower rib cage. Hold this vision between your hands right where your solar plexus begins, and then aim your fingers and this vision of beauty and peace and wonder — whatever you can create — out into the world at large. You can put gold light in it if you wish, or white light. I recommend a combination of the two because gold light is permanent and white light is consumable. You may use other colors — I would recommend pink, or you may use light blue if you like. Be creative, imaginative, try what you will. Hold that for a few moments and broadcast it outward. You have no idea now that your Creator potential is this strong.

This is a wonderful thing to do with many people in your meditation circles. You might even create a consensus of a picture of beauty. For instance, you might look at a picture or a painting that you find beautiful. Hold it, imagine it between your hands in energy, then aim it outward from your solar plexus to your planet.

As a Creator apprentice, it is literally your job now to create what Earth will look like in the fourth dimension. You are still parked at 3.47, as I call it [between third and fourth dimension], but the time is coming soon when you will begin to move forward again. Before the end of the year you will most likely begin to move forward again incrementally. This is why you need to set your intention: You need to create the world you're going to move into. The more you focus on your fears, your anxieties, your suspicions and so on, the more you're going to create and perpetuate that world. But this is something you can do that will literally create the new world.

The responsibility of the Explorer Race is not only to explore, but to create. Suppose you're out there in generations to come, exploring the planets. Suppose you find some planet that is going through something that is destroying the civilization. Maybe the planet is overvolcanic. Maybe there are too many earthquakes. Maybe the planet itself would like to be rescued, to say nothing of the civilizations on the surface. You, as the Explorer Race, Creator apprentice, will then hold a picture of how you would like that planet to look. You will talk to the citizens: "What did your civilization look like?" "How do you want it to look?" They will describe it to you, they will show you pictures, and you will hold that picture between your hands, place it over your solar plexus and aim it toward that planet. Or by that time you may be using other techniques, one of which basically involves pointing your hands in a certain manner. Or maybe you will direct it from your third eye. But most likely you will use your solar plexus, because that is the Creator area for physical reality. And you will be able to help calm the planet, calm the inner turmoil within the planet, bring the planet itself love, balance and benevolence, and help to rebuild the surface civilization and cities with these visions that go beyond thought and become manifested as physical reality.

This is the destiny of the Explorer Race – not only to explore, but to create.

Sinister Secret Government Falling Apart

January 25, 1996

The secret government is essentially becoming disenfranchised, not because of its own choice but because this body of beings is going through the same blast of energy that everybody else is–creatorship. It's as if their agenda is being broken down. Some of the members of the inner circle wish to evacuate right now. They do not have the majority vote, but they're close. When that majority vote comes, I think that the inner circle will take off for other places, initially the Moon. I think they will eventually try to establish a colony on Mars. But this Martian colony–it's touch and go. I think that the energies of Mars are not quite as benevolent as the energies of Earth. They are more demanding than nurturing. So time will tell. The sinister secret government is beginning to show signs of falling apart. This does not mean that your world will suddenly become heaven on Earth; it does mean that you will not have to contend with a powerful inner circle anymore, but many individuals scrambling for power.

I think that you've gone past the worst of it with the sinister secret government. I'll tell you part of the reason why. Ever since we've been putting out this material about the sinister secret government, a lot of people (not only lightworkers but also just folks) have been putting energy into transforming this situation to something more benevolent. And that is, after all, the ultimate purpose of having put out this material, yes?

So I think you're over the hump. I think your sinister secret government is going to be evacuating the premises pretty soon, but you will now have to deal with the day-to-day individuals struggling for power.

But there's nobody to control on Mars!

We're talking about them escaping with their lives, as it were, bringing their lifestyle up there and doing the best they can. I don't think they're going to be influential from a distance even though they think they might be. I think they're just going to escape to save their skins.

In terms of the underground cities and the beings who are involved there, an interesting thing is happening. Some of those beings in the underground cities who have been serving the inner circle (the ones who look human) are going to find an escape route to the surface. But the escape route is going to be almost like a meditation, in the sense that they'll be able to go a ways and have to stop, then go a little farther and stop. They'll be able to get to the surface incrementally, and as they do so they will be bombarded with more and more of the energies that are bombarding everybody else. So by the time they get to the surface they will no longer be sinister; they will just be people trying to make the best of it—which is kind of good, in a way. The inner circle wants to escape to Mars because they believe they can make the motion from within the Earth, and since they cycle around on the surface of the Earth somewhat, they think that they are immune to the surface, but I don't think so. I think that by simply flying through the auric field of the Earth to the Moon and then to Mars . . . no, I think they're also going to be affected. But in the case of these individuals . . .

These are the cloned beings with the implants that keep their souls and spirit from expressing?

Yes, that's right. These individuals are going to be affected, and when they get to the surface (the ones who look human) they're going to be all right.

Now, the individuals who do not look human will maintain a

civilization beneath the Earth for a while, but one much more benevolent, because they didn't want to serve these masters in the first place. Their number-one intention will be to remove the device within their bodies in some safe way so that they do not die prematurely. I think they will succeed in that, because they will get help from an extraterrestrial civilization, which will then evacuate them to another planet.

Are these the beings that look insectlike?

I don't want to say insect, exactly. They're humanoid in their appearance, but their skin and flesh is very, how can we say . . . it's sinewy. They're humanoid, but there's no way you'd think they were human beings.

They were bred to fly those planes and to be used and controlled?

But they're doing that basically against their will; it's just that their wills have literally been suppressed. So I think that this is going to reach a good stage. Right now they're still controlled, but I think that once the inner circle leaves . . . see, the inner circle is not going to just press a button and blow everything up down there and kill everybody; they're simply going to leave.

What about Secret Canyon? Is anybody out there now, in Sedona?

There are still underground things going on there, but it is not as extreme as it was.

Are there still guys up there with M16 rifles keeping people away?

There might be a few, but not as many. You shouldn't encounter that as much. But I'd still say the area is not what I'd call 100% safe. It's about 80% safe.

What's going to happen to those people? Who's out there? What's out there?

I'd say that these beings will probably eventually go back down inside the Earth; or they might experience a surface evacuation.

Who's down there, what kind of beings are down there?

The ones you're seeing running around with M16s are basically human beings, but not citizens of the United States. I can't say everything here, but there's a potential for a revolt. As the chain of command breaks down, there's going to be a bit of a struggle for power. I think that this will take place mostly within their own groups.

Are these cloned beings down there, or are there ET groups from other places?

Not too many; mostly we're talking about human beings, some of whom are from other countries—sort of a universal force that's passing itself off as the United Nations but which is not the United Nations.

So they're basically Earth humans, then—we're not talking about cloned or off-planet beings?

No. The people running around with M16s are not cloned beings; these are human beings.

But what are the other beings in the underground levels of the secret government base in Sedona?

There are cloned beings, yes, but they're not on the surface.

But they may try to come to the surface?

If they do, they will transmute, because Earth does not allow beings from other places to be on the surface and run around and interact with other energies without their coming into some concordance with everything else that's going on here. H.G. Wells' "War of the Worlds" story suggests that there are standards by which any being must behave on the surface of this planet. If you go beyond those standards you cannot stay here or survive here.

What about all those beings in stasis, the rest of the five million people? What's happening with them?

The underground families? I think that they will (at least half of them) make it to the surface and most of the other half will live below the surface for a while. They could live there for about forty years, on the supplies they have and can generate. But not all of them. As I say, about half of them will make it to the surface and simply blend in with society and they'll be all right. But after about forty years, the rest will have to come up. By that time things will be a lot more benevolent, and as they come to the surface they'll also become benevolent. They will be recognizable because they won't know anything about the surface life. They'll be stuck with the idea of separate nations and all of this, they'll be stuck with the current understanding of your social condition.

You mean our 1996 condition?

Yes, 1996. They won't be conditioned to 2036 or whenever. By that time you'll have more of a one-world situation without the severe borders that you have now. You might have borders along the lines of continents: North America, South America, Europe, Africa. You still might have that kind of a thing, but I think you'll have more of a united Europe and united Africa and so on. By the time 2050 rolls around, you should be a united Earth, maybe a little before that.

That will qualify you to join an alliance of planets. You have to come in as one united planet. As you know, they feel that if you cannot unite as a planet, how can you possibly unite with them?

True! There are so many books coming out about the Annunnaki and the Twelfth Planet . . .

You have to understand this. If you put your finger up here and tied lots of strings to it and pulled them to different points in the room, you could be connected. But you'd still have the truth of your finger; that's a true thing, and the string would be extraneous. What I'm saying is that there are many true stories, because there are probabilities. But as you know, I have tried to get people to cut through the probabilities that do not serve them. This being Creator school with Creator apprentices, you have your choice of probabilities. That's why we literally create this picture of beauty on the planet rather than get caught up in the sinister secret government idea. That's my answer to that question. It is not for me to say this information is not true, but I would prefer that you make a different choice. My attitude is, why not take the shortcut if you can? It is so easy to get caught up in fascinating side paths that will eventually lead to where we're going anyway, but I don't think that we need any more suffering here. As soon as possible we need to get to beauty on this planet.

11

Divinity: Freedom, Lifeforever, Lightforever

YHWH through Arthur Fanning
December 1, 1995

Indeed! How are you?

I am wonderful.

And what are your concerns here?

Later I want to talk about how guides work.

We'll talk now. A lot of beings play, know you?

Okay. Who do the guides work for, the soul or the personality? I have a particular case I'd like to talk about. You know the one I mean. How can a human talk to guides every day?

The desire of the soul being born, know you, and prior to birth, are what the guides focus upon, you understand?

So they work for the soul, not the human.

Now pay attention – don't go limited on me, indeed? You are a light being, indeed? And you have thoughts prior to being born, in the light of you, indeed? You encapsulate soul, you play soul, you birth a body, indeed? Your concepts. I'm going to get in a little more this evening. So you play this birth thing. Guides work with the thought processes you had prior to birth, understand?

So if you've got guilt, shame, remorse, that's gonna interfere?

They don't care.

No, but I mean that's gonna . . .

Your thought processes, as you were being embodied god in

this lifetime, you in your physical thing, your being, what you call your body, know you, are your thoughts. Your guides can't do anything with them. You are a free being god, you understand? You're god. You say, "No, I don't want to do [it] this way, this way, this way, this way, this way," so you argue with your guides. Do you understand? You don't pay attention. And other beings move to a level where they give their power away to their guides, you understand?

Yeah, but how did this one talk to her guides every day and nobody told her she had cancer? She didn't want to hear?

What is cancer? It is a spiritual disease, it is a disease of spirit; a desire for growth think[s] it is limited within physical, it will grow. Creates the thought, understand, creates the acceleration of the cells —the light does this. Know you what I mean?

Mm-hmm.

Don't just say, "Mm-hmm, mm-hmm," bouncing like a ball here. I want you to understand. Your thoughts are you. Indeed?

Indeed.

And if you don't like the vehicle you're in, the soul will manifest another.

And kill off the one you got.

[He sighs:] That's limited thinking.

All right. But I'm trying to understand someone who talked to her guides every day and did not know she had cancer.

Everyone talks to their guides!

But this was conscious.

Not everyone listens!

They talked to her, she talked to Mother Mary, Sananda.

Mm-hmm, I understand. And the guides tell you it be all right, know you?

Yeah, yeah.

They tell you that because you won't listen to any other thing. Many of you want to hear your guides, indeed?

[Group responds:] Indeed!

Except when the guide says, "Take a left," you say —you have great adjectives here — "I'll go this way!" You go right, because you think you're being controlled. Now, the authority where guides can overwhelm you, take charge, is if you've made an agreement with lights to do a particular thing and you've got yourself into so much muck you can't get out, the guides will show you a way out. They won't get you out, they'll show you a way out. That means you must pay attention. That includes Sananda, includes the Buddha one (your terms now), because you're becoming the Sananda, you're becoming the Christ, you're becoming the Buddha one. But you don't want to know; you want to blame, you want to be lazy – that's what you want to do. Or you want to control other beings. You don't want to have fun, don't want to play, you want to control, you want to cry, whine.

You will die! You've done it before, no big deal, you know exactly how it works. You forgot how to come back, however, in this time, because the patterns are shifting, the . . . we'll say you . . . ones that don't want to become, that want an overlord to tell them at some level – doesn't matter – pick the Brotherhood of Light – doesn't matter – you've got to go beyond. You will leave, and you will play in that realm until you know you must go beyond. And it will be your desire next lifetime for physical body because of the fun, because of what I told you before – the smell, the joy, the ecstasy, the sexual experience here, kundalini – to be here, because you are gods. You can play where you want to play. You don't need another to tell you you can't, yet you think you do here. Everyone breathe a moment.

You're in hot and heavy times now. Lot of dying going on, a lot. You've had the Ram here that laid out very profound truths for you, and you didn't pay attention; and you've had others and others. Then you've had what I term the in-betweeners, know you? Your metaphysics is going to be your next great church, entities, and who is the overlords of the metaphysical? It's the Brotherhood of Light. Oh, don't upset them now . . . because that is you. It's what you are doing; you are becoming the next high priest here in your metaphysical understanding. That is the next perversion. That is what you're doing. Everyone breathe. Lighten up.

You Wanted This Life

Now, you have a body because you wanted one this time. You wanted to become, to figure it out. You're not as dumb as you've been led to believe here. You know you're sacred, and you know you're holy – I've laid that one on you for years . . . so have others, and you say, "So what?" As these energies build now in this time, it is going to be your holiness and your sacredness, your centeredness, your knowing, that's going to work – not your traditional bullshit. And the Moon doesn't really care where it is when you die; you care where the Moon is. Everyone breathe.

You know your astrology has understood a little bit about the nodes and gateways. You've heard me speak before of this suicide thing, indeed? Don't do it! Know you what I mean, how you speak unto yourselves, "I be want to die," know you? Many beings are going to do this suicide thing to get out of here – that is ignorant, that is foolish! Yet you metaphysical beings do the same thing because thought is, and you are, believe it or not, the appliance – not even the application. You can't even get that part! You are the result of your thoughts! You've heard that before – no big deal, eh, till die hits you, becomes, "Oh, shit!" Or you're in the muck and you blame another, and your relationship is going this way and that way, and it's "past life!" It is not past life! It is this life! And you're a demigod to call experiences in lives you can't even remember as excuses for your ineptitude this time. Everyone breathe.

You're in the movement of life forces now. You either know now or you don't. It'll be all right, it won't matter, indeed, it won't. But we've been watching the lot of you, not just you in this room – those that are controlling you, those that you play your fears with and your little day-to-day games – we watch it all. We love you. There are more of us than you can count. We are beyond the Brotherhood of Light, because you are the Brotherhood of Light, and you're going to get it, you're going to remember. You've chosen this arena in this time because it was the most difficult course within any system. It's not that you're in competition with the Christ or the Buddha, not at all. You understand their compassion and their love, through all of their turmoils – you saw their journey before you came here. And you understand the power they achieved by knowing, throughout the journey, and it excited you, it excited you, because they became outrageous lights. They could call forth worlds at any moment, and you enjoyed that scene. You want to do that thing. That does not mean become a martyr! That does not mean to go sit on a hill for forty years! It means to contemplate what they said within your being, and if the light works within you, apply it! Don't sit and drink your coffee, chitty-chat and bullshit. You move in this manner. Everyone breathe.

Now, the reason we speak in this strength this night [is] because the frequency is accelerating on the planet very much. Many will have the ability to die in their sleep, you say; leave – be given the opportunity. They'll think the game is too tough here. It's a gentle way to go. But you are the ones that will be grading yourselves on your movement. There will be plenty of opportunity to move out of the body in other belief systems, what you would term other systems of thought, what is termed martyrdom, great religious wars, da, da, da, da, da, da. There will be a lot of whining, gnashing of teeth, etc., da, da, da, da, da —what you term your Revelations, indeed you're living it. This is the time of knowing, but not everyone wants to know! We've watched you. You want to know to your greatest level where you can control . . . or be in control . . . of others, even systems. You think it is a mental thing, a mind-thought processes. I've told you before, if the soul and the heart chakra have not expanded, you will not be able to handle the energy of this new mind, this great light coming — it won't fit. It will not fit.

Now, your guides are going to become very active, because they're going to push you to the completions you agreed to prior to birth. And they do not care of the physical body, only in that it is a vehicle for the soul to complete agreements [made] prior to the birth here, unless you're wise enough to understand you can go beyond the agreement. So these are indeed exciting times. A lot of Christs are going to become Christs, a lot of Buddhas are going to be Buddhas, beyond it. But you won't sit there as a Christ, you won't sit there as a Buddha, not in this time, because you're already that.

Watch your news your next year. A lot, many of your religious leaders are going to sort of . . . well, it's going to say "transcend," die the body. A lot of your metaphysical beings are going to be out of here. That is a good thing, because it'll make you question and it'll make you learn your own forces here. It'll make you to become gods.

The only reason your extraterrestrials are here is because you allowed them to be here, the thought of it. You thought they were more powerful than you, and you wanted them to rescue you. But their civilizations are dying. Did you know that humankind is one of four civilizations (there are three others) that still maintain spiritual forces within the physical form, as you would term it; what you call the advancement of the soul, ability to become Christ, the Buddha, da, da, da? They are here because of your memory — they want that back.

When I speak and [have] spoken to many, and they say unto I later, "What do you mean by divinity? What does that mean? What does sacredness mean, what does my sacredness mean?" and I look, I see, and they want the answer to fit within a shell, within a layer that they have developed around their divinity — they don't want to go to the core of it. But I peek, I put light in there because I be there, and I say from inside your being, "I be divinity. I be in you, I be you. You [and] I be same." So I be speak that, I speak from inside, and it reaches there, but they want a definition, and it'll never fit in a definition because it's freedom, it is life forever. It is light forever, it is light willing to lower itself into the greatest density to remind other lights [that] they are lights. It is that knowing of the light that you are going to become. Words will create the doubt, yet the feeling of the light in their power, as you learn to work it within your own being, will never, ever, be in doubt. Everyone breathe.

"God I Am" Meditation

Allow your eyes to close a little moment and center in your heart chakra. Center. I want no one to compare or compete in this meditation with anyone – any guide. I want you to center, because if you do compete I'll jerk you out of here. Be in the heart chakra, open your seven vortices, open your soles, what you term the bottoms of your feet. (It's called the sole for a reason, by the way.) Open your palms. You have chakras on your elbows – open them. Allow. Center. Open the heart chakra wider, open the throat chakra. Indeed, that be grand. You have a grand chakra at the center of your back – open that one too.

Now, on the backs of your hands (your palms should be up upon your thighs what you call toward your torso), at the back of your palms, what you call your backhand, there are what you would term thirty or more vortices. We'll say thirty now; there are more but I won't get into those. Open them, simply tell them to open. You'll feel it. Allow them to open. Indeed, open the vortices at the tips of your fingers, allow. Adjust the energy now that is in your shoulder blades – adjust that. Center. Move your physical body if you have to. Tell those vortices to open. Grand. Allow. Peace. Peace. This is karmic energy – allow it to open, let it go. It doesn't exist – it is only energy.

Focus on your root chakra, your perineum in your buttocks there – tighten it a little bit and bring that energy up, feel it come up into the crown chakra, up into the sixth seal, crown. Feel it there. That's it, indeed. Now let it spread out – I want it to go out through the muscle fiber from the center of your spine, out the back of the body through the back, around the sides within the physical form. Feel that. Allow.

Take a breath, open the throat chakra. Breathe out the throat chakra. Center now in your own energy here. Allow. I want your thoughts in the heart chakra. See you sitting in your chest centered. That is better. Allow. I don't want you using the brain as what you call thought processes funneling information yet. Center in the heart chakra.

Feel a pyramid of light descend from above you now through the physical head, and the base will be at your throat. Feel the pyramid, golden light there, and allow it to spin counterclockwise. Create unified electrical current through the brain, what you term evening both halves here. Allow. Open the temples, chakras at the temples. Peace. Open the heart chakra even wider – I want it beside you, out.

Your thumb and your index finger, place them together. Take a breath and I want you to exhale that breath what is termed through the heart chakra, and also what you would say visualize it moving through the hole from your palm outward, between the thumb and the forefinger. So you breathe out the heart chakra, and the energy moves outward through this hole there – that be grand – from the palms out. That is indeed grand. Move the thumb to the next finger – breathe again. Center. You're clearing your nadis here, entities. Next finger. That is grand. You're feeling yourself more centered. Little finger. Now breathe it out, indeed.

Now pay attention. You have your thumb on your little finger. As you breathe, take a breath in, I want you to take it to the perineum and hold it there. Now breathe in, hold it, and when you breathe out, as you breathe it through this hole I want you to feel the wind across the other fingers. Breathe out gently, let it go – feel the wind. Feel that energy over those fingers that are extended. Indeed. Take a breath again, hold it at the perineum. Focus on the hole there, breathe outward. Feel the wind, feel the wind.

Allow your thumbs to go back to your first finger. I want you to now contemplate opening the palms, opening the thumb and the finger, and bring your palms together in front of your heart chakra; and I want you to see a golden lotus in the heart chakra. Center your being. And I want you to feel that you are that golden lotus, you are the human one sitting there. Power. Peace. Center. Open your hands now gently and place them upon your thighs. Peace. Indeed, center your being. Be in your moment now.

I want you to focus on your third eye, sixth seal, above your eyes, gently, in your forehead. Allow. Center. Open the throat more. If it pertains to you, do it. You know what I'm talking about. I want you to contemplate in your heart chakra now these words – I don't want you to repeat them, I want you to hear them – and this is you! I am going to vibrate, but it is you! GOD I AM! I'm inside you now, but this is you. GOD I AM! I want you to feel that. Center. If the words come out and there's a vibration that's going to the left or to the right, you contemplate and you center in the heart chakra, because I'm talking about power now that is you. GOD I AM! Don't repeat, listen. Center. I want you to pick up the vibration inside of you. POWER I AM! Feel it. I'm going to say this one and I want you to feel it at your perineum, indeed? CHRIST I AM! Allow! Now allow that energy, that vibration that started there, to begin to move up the body gently. This is your I AMness. Contemplate to yourself now this energy, the I AMness moving. I AM! I AM! I AM! You contemplate it. Contemplate GOD I AM. Center.

Now I want you to take a breath and hold it in the heart chakra. Take a breath in, hold it in. You've got golden and red fire inside you now. I want you to breathe. When you breathe out the throat and the mouth, I want you to extend that energy that's in the body outward to your auric field, to cleanse everything around you, and then send it around the planet. Breathe out. Allow. Center. Peace. Center. Allow. Allow your eyes to open gently. Better.

You are going to have to learn, particularly next year, your ability to play with energies, light. I am not talking about words! Words are very limited understanding. If you want to become telepathic and go beyond and know, you will deal in these chakras here [he gestures above the head], which are you here [he gestures back and forth in front of the soul/heart/ throat chakra], which is your god essence throughout you, which you shut down here [again he gestures above the head]. It's going to open. We have a great plan, me and a few other beings. And we are really going to piss a lot of you off, because we're going to open this thing here [again gesturing above the head]. You want it open. As it begins to open you'll say, "Well, I don't want it to open." Everyone breathe a moment. I want you to breathe between what you term the throat chakra and the heart chakra – there be a little bridge there at your breastbone, you term thymus – breathe out there.

As you move in your next year there becomes this acceleration – to graduate, to experience more of the light that you are, and to seek every means to experience that light. One of the easiest ways to experience more of the light in this next year particularly, is going to be through compassion, and you'll find yourself getting more. If you don't express compassion, you'll shut yourself down and think everyone is against you. Com-passion – use it or lose it. Everyone breathe.

This is becoming the time of gods helping the gods – to become, to remember; not the gods competing with the gods to be supreme. You don't want to see that game of the gods understanding, as you would term it, supremacy. You don't want to – take my word for it! You want to experience the gods becoming on this planet, enjoying each others' energies physically – that's what you want to see.

Many of you are experiencing this thing called time shifting, eh? "What day is this today? What time did I wake up this morning? Where am I?" You're driving your car and you forget where you're going, you forget where you came from. A lot more of that is going to happen. As the light becomes more of you, from your perspective, and you become more of light, you draw in more electrical current, more power – it uses electrum here. As you work with it things seem to go haywire. Your consciousness is shifting. You are not your brain. You are not your heart . . . yet you are. But the light of you that is here is using these forces that exist there, that you manifested, to play here. To play here! Not to be slaves here, not to be controlled here, not to be murdered here, unless that's what you want, of course – your belief system. But to be here! For fun. A lot of you moved into this arena, however, in this birth cycle, because of the power you thought you had, and you could control others. Well, you're learning – oops! Everyone breathe. Control is still a big issue here. No big deal.

Death is going to be what you call very intriguing to many. There will be many explanations of this thing. Your metaphysics is going to be very popular on your television, movies, more popular next year – particularly the concept of dying and beyond. But that is a trap, entities, and if you can't see it now I don't know what we're going to do next year. Allow the masses to get it any way they can. You must continue to apply. Because the masses are going to get it next year doesn't mean you can sit back and gloat – you have another step to do yet. You've got to prepare the ground for the next batch of movies in 1999. [He laughs.] Hmm. Everyone take a little breath here. I can play with your thoughts and this, that, the other. I understand your worries. In this thing die, you love God. And you ask me which one, I'll say pick one – they're sitting right next to you. And if you can't understand that, then you have a lot of work to do.

In difficulty, if you want to move through the death process rapidly, to a higher arena, I'll say two things. I'll say in what you call your Christian system, the Lord's Prayer will help you if you go into your scare and you're having diarrhea (know you, really shitting your pants). Lighten up, entities. Lord's Prayer will help you. OM TAT SAT, if you're another belief system, what you call Buddhist, will help you. Calling to Allah if you're Muslim will help you, "Save me," that'll help you. It'll buy you another lifetime, too. You are the one that's going to have to understand who you are in relationship to the light that you are. Mmm. Everyone breathe, lighten up.

I get a little heavy because some of you beings take this not what you would term as important for your being, but it is! It is not really serious – it's all a reckless little game, anyway, know you? A lot of fun. Bunch of little bubbles bouncing around off each other down here, forgetting who they are, waiting to connect to the next marble that is stickier than they, where they can give their power away – that's how it works. You're in for outrageous times, entities. You're loved outrageously. Some of us out there are getting a little weary, because we are within you and you're the bouncing bubble; we're getting bounced around, know you what I mean? And I don't have a good helmet – it doesn't fit too well. I'm getting a headache.

May I make a comment?

Indeed.

I've been seeing things on and off with my third-eye vision for several years now, but something very unusual happened two nights ago. I was seeing something and I had the idea to ask it to shift, and it shifted. And then I asked it to shift again, and it shifted again. It was the first time I have ever had an interaction with the third-eye vision; I've always just looked at it.

Indeed, that is one of the next steps. One of the things . . . you are, what you say, fortunate. Many beings, before they see the vision and tell it to, say shift, they'll start shifting because they feel the energy before the vision manifests. In that way they don't allow themselves to see the complete vision.

Well, I was wondering if it's the new energy now that supported the ability to do that, to go a little bit further with it?

Indeed it is, and you've allowed yourself what you call compassion, know you what I mean? Indeed?

Indeed.

If you had gotten this ability, oh, four years earlier, you would have used it to hurt a being.

I understand that.

So there's more coming for you, know you what I mean? Everyone breathe. Lighten up a bit. Don't get nervous if I get next to you, okay? Some of you don't want me to get next to you; afraid I'm going to muck up your mind. [You've] got this great energy here that has got it all figured out, but you're still getting older, know what I mean? You can't figure that one out, either. [To a participant:] How are you? How goes the battle?

Sometimes I don't feel like I'm always winning, but I'm able to pick myself up and keep going.

Is it necessary to win?

No, I just want peace. I don't want to battle.

Indeed. The more peace you have, the more power you have, know you what I mean?

Indeed.

Let's see. You have this little package you're going to give yourself; it's about this big. It'll be coming in about two weeks. What do you think it will be? What do you have the most fun doing?

I don't know.

Everyone breathe a moment. We're going to alleviate some of this energy. Know how some of you beings enjoy an explosive moment, indeed? You crave these things, and they be presents unto you so you can do it.

So I'm going to get another one?

But you enjoy it.

No, I'm tired of it.

Are you, indeed?

Indeed!

Okay, so we can create another type of moment coming, indeed?

Yes.

Now, what is this word you have? —dwell, dwell, dwell. Know you "dwell"? Dwell —you dwell on a thing. Dwell, dwell, dwell, dwell. Hmm? And it dwells, package gets bigger, bigger, bigger, bigger, bigger, and gives you the opportunity to experience the dwelling! Know you what I mean?

Uh-huh.

What you've been dwelling on, see you what I mean?

Yeah, mm-hmm.

Mm. Say oops on the dwell, "Peace." [Laughter.] I'm giving you a clue. I understand, she's the only one [more laughter] responsible for her own thoughts, huh? Some of you don't want to know what you've been dwelling on, what energy you be building from the light within you that's going to come out of you, to manifest in front of you. You're going to blame that on the stars! That's not a god that blames the stars —that's a superstitious entity. Everyone breathe.

Now you need to know what you term your astrology —you do! It is required for you to understand you, because you utilized those lights in your birth —planning process. They didn't force you —you utilized them. They don't have an influence on you. You are the one in charge of the steering wheel, the brake and the accelerator here — you're consciousness in charge of those lights, the energy from them. Actually, you exist beyond that light, what you term your stars.

Everyone breathe. You're going to have to get this—lot of superstition, lot of metaphysical nonsense is going to come out: You're going to be controlled very easily. Astrology is going to be very popular, particularly lunar influences. Because you are awakening, you're going to see the correlation much easier, but you're looking at it from your human perspective and forgetting your light. Never forget your light—you'll be controlled by others forever. My job here is not to control you or to allow others to, either. I have moved upon systems that became stagnant. I have a reputation. I was called here. I was sent here. So you're just going to have to live with me now. [Laughter.]

There is a great ecstasy in dying the physical body for what you call the light of you—it is likened unto an orgasm. But I'm suggesting there's a greater ecstasy, and you all have the capability to understand that unless you've become a superstitious entity. How do you go beyond superstition? You move into what is termed knowing—you know, and you're doing it this way, this way, this way, because you know and you want to. And if you make an oops, no big deal—you learn.

A lot has to do with the magnetics now. As consciousness changes, the magnetics change. Everyone is going to play the game the poles are shifting. Energy is shifting. "I'm having a bad day because we're in a polar shift." [Laughter.] "Photon Belt got me last night." It's a good thing the Photon Belt lasts this long; you don't have to wait for the next one, know you what I mean? It's your consciousness that's awakening. You planned it this way. You are not idiot entities unless you want to play you are. You knew all of this before you were born. It is part of you returning, because you are part of the stars as much as you're part of the Earth—when are you going to get that? You have the ability to think out here, in here, think within the mind of squirrel or a rooster, a dog, cat—you have that ability. Everyone breathe.

Decade Of Empowerment

This is the decade of empowerment, to move beyond the Buddha and the Christ—that's what it is. Enjoy it. It was meant to be enjoyed. It was not meant to be played metaphysical with, but we knew it would be; it's going to be outrageously so. Want to go in business, become an astrologer? Make a lot of money, really muck up your mind. You are to feel, you are to know astrology, you are. You are to know numbers, what you term the vibration; you are to know what you would term the vibration of words, to know it in the body, and to know what you choose to apply through your force called physical human being, body, the light of you making the choice. You want to play that. That's the game now. And the game beyond that is light lowered, for your understanding is electrical; lowered is what you call magnetic. Now, magnetic you might be able to visualize, because if you look at filings of magnets as they move around, they take a shape, indeed, a geometrical shape, indeed?

Have you spun the magnets to see what the filings do? You are a magnetic being, you're an electromagnetic being. You're playing with the light. A thought what you term originates all of this – the thought out here [around the body], along with the thought in here; some of you beings say desire, but it's thought here, power. You're going to learn to become what you term octahedrons. Everyone wants to, oh, move into the merkabah. One step at a time, please. You have to be very centered in your thoughts; that means love all things. It also means, understand the fear that other things, beings, entities, be they animal, whatever, have for your increased energy. Because they've been taught God's coming to the planet to punish them, not that God's coming to the planet to have fun. So you have that level of consciousness to go through. Everything, we'll say you, has to be, mm, "other being has to straighten it out." You know what I mean. This is the time [of] becoming gods here, power. The application of the same through the physical body.

Now, for those of you that have been in my audience before, we've told you of this healing thing – you're healers, indeed? Your next year [1996] you're going to work it; it's going to be forced upon you! And if those that come to you and you don't assist and straighten this thing out in what we've talked about before – the knowing of the healer, etc., etc. – you will play with that energy within your own being, out of your own system, the knowing you didn't assist. Everyone breathe. So karma is going to be what you call reflective now – you're not going to have to die and live another lifetime to do it, you'll do it right now. Oh, see the humor! You love it. Save yourselves many journeys. Very interesting year. That's why it's important to be centered, why it's important to know the light, love God. If you don't know who that is, pick one, but you're it, in here [within the soul].

May I ask a question?

Indeed.

Is it more important to teach by example than with words?

It is. Don't go erasing systems, yet, however, as an example –

blowing up planets, I mean – not yet. Don't do that.

[There's] a lot of activity now in what you term your astral arena. It looks very beautiful, indeed? But there's always more! Don't be caught in another's illusion or their manifestation.

Allow your eyes to close a moment. There be a little imbalance here. There is energy in some heart chakras here – we're going to center this, indeed? We're to greater love here, allow, center. Peace. Allow your eyes to open gently. Okay. The heart chakra and the heart muscle were meant to perpetuate life. We're going to have to lower some energy here. Give me a moment, I've got to call in a couple of guides. That be grand. Okay. I spoke it because there were some of you that I wanted to show how it was done.

Angels And Masters

Now, as this frequency increases here, you're going to find that what you term the angels, Brotherhood of Light, want to come closer to you. Now, not everyone from the Brotherhood of Light has been physical. There are a lot of angels that haven't been physical. So they don't know what to do in physical body – they've never had one. You are teaching them. You are working that way. You were the ones stupid enough to be born. [Laughter.] The rest thought they'd just sit there and gather the knowledge – "Let that idiot go down there; I'll watch from this perspective." But you had great courage, know you what I mean?

Now, some of you think your other lifetimes were the most powerful you've ever had – that is not the truth. This is the most powerful time you've ever had. Why do you think what you call children are being born now looking so wise? Why do you think they're dying so quickly, also? When they figure out that the parents aren't wise here, they're leaving – they're not stupid, not going to stick around. You have a lot of masters, however, what you term ascended masters; you have a lot of ancient gods being incarnated here, personalities of. Shiva – know you Shiva? – is incarnate here in this state, another state moves to. Why? Because it's fun and Shiva loves to dance. So they're coming, you see? This is where the game is. It's an outrageous place, too. In order to see you must open your eyes, you must be willing to understand, you must know, that you and Shiva be same. There be that much love there. I don't mean love in what you call the manner of this sexual thing. It is a knowing – "Ah, Shiva, good to see you again." You see? All of them, they are here. Mm, does anyone have any questions?

What about Osiris?

What about him?

I was wondering if you had any information about what Osiris is up to these days that might be pertinent to my investigation?

Why did Osiris die?

I'm not really sure. I know the story.

You know what you term the myth.

The myth.

Could it be that Osiris what you call played jump in the casket to prove that you don't die, no matter what they did to the body? Or do you think Osiris was a fool? One or the other?

I think Osiris is a great master, and certainly a god.

He's incarnate here, piece of him, by the way, on the planet. There are three. He knew what he was doing; he still does. You have to be very careful. One of the lessons that Osiris learned in that time, though he was teaching the beings that were involved in the . . . well, you would term it from this aspect "murder," the trickery, weren't capable of being taught. So he was sort of stunned at that revelation, know you, to think that some beings can't be taught. So he sort of figured it out, if you understand what I'm saying.

Perhaps. Is anyone channeling Osiris these days?

Not at the present time, not that being, not yet, what you would term not the empowerment of that being. Like all myths, there is some truth, but there is much more behind it. Anyone else?

You said that as we desire to open these higher chakras and as they're opened, we are going to want to close them. What is going to happen that's going to make us want to close them, when we desire so much to open them?

As this one [he gestures to a participant] spoke earlier of being able to manipulate the scenes, and your desire to manipulate the scene because you feel the energy first and don't really want the scene to complete itself before you know you can change it – that'll shut you off. A lot of you have to understand this word "allow." You don't want to allow. Everything must fit into a particular bucket. Newness scares you. That's why death is so overwhelming to you – you can't remember the last time you died. You're willing to forget that. And that's a good thing because you don't judge yourself for your past lifetimes. No, you weren't all angels, know you what I mean? So as you move into these other arenas, you're very sensitive to your expansion, know you? And we'll say you . . . it's been described before, the downward spiral and then the upward spiral; as you come down, you'll go back and you'll know what you did to come down —you don't want to do that again.

But we have to face it.

Well, you don't . . . you won't be that aggressive. You'll be more gentle with your being, know you?

So allowing is one key . . . ?

Allowing and loving all things. That be a biggie here. But we've told you that is the key —400,000 questions on your quiz before you ascend, know you, and the answer is the same —love. So if you don't have an idea of what to extrapolate about, just write "love" —you'll pass. I'm giving you the cheat sheet here.

So part of it is what we will see, and our . . .

And your desire to change it into an event.

Into something nicer.

What you would think would be nicer, but you don't allow yourself to see the connection to all things.

So we allow, we love it, and . . .

Love it. Love yourself for experiencing it, know you what I mean?

Mm-hmm. So it's the seeing, the knowing — these are the results of these higher chakras opening?

The knowing is the one you really want to go after, know you? It is not a word thing, it's not even a vision —it is a knowing. It's a different thing, and that becomes a manifestation, actually. Know you what I mean? You will.

I do.

You're doing grandly. I've watched you throw your tizzies, indeed? This one, too —you go tizzy mode on me. You're not alone, however. There's a great group of you, know you? [Laughter.] I put this little gold cord around, like a big corral; we go, "Let's go see what the tizzy ones are doing down there. There they are! Aren't they beautiful? Indeed, they are."

Last time we had a class, you said you were going to come and visit those who wanted to go further. There was an extraordinary manifestation — I think you remodeled the penthouse or something.

You haven't seen anything, yet. Wait 'til next weekend.

I have another question.

Indeed.

I've been reading different books on channeling and find that a great deal of the material is quite contradictory. I've come to the conclusion that one of the answers

is that everything is self-created in the mind, so no matter how outrageous something is, perhaps it is 100% real for that individual or that channel. Maybe you'll elucidate on that. Also, just a few weeks ago I met a young lady who said that she had recently begun channeling Osiris. I had a private channeling with her, and I thought it was quite interesting. I felt a lot of energy, so I asked you about that a moment ago, and you said that no one is channeling Osiris now. Is there any way you can make me feel that I'm not just hallucinating all of this right now?

[YHWH laughs.] Do I have to talk to you in private again? [He laughs again.] Let me say there are fragments, not the full manifestation of Osiris is coming through — do you understand that?

That sounds logical.

That's what I said before. As far as difference, you're going to find a lot of differences particularly next year, because there will be some, even within the human consciousness, not willing to tread on certain territory; not willing to . . . how say you . . . piss off Christ, know you what I mean, or piss off Buddha. Lot of energy there. Know you Sananda? Indeed? Know you the Ashtar Command? What are they going to do for you? Everyone breathe a moment. You are part of that Command. There are many entities; because they've been brought up in metaphysical behavior, create a level of understanding what you call reverence for, not willing to go beyond worship. You're here to become gods, not worshipers of anything, to become your own power, and you're going to do it one way or the other.

Do you think worshiping is a form of laziness?

It's begging. The reason Osiris is beginning to come back, because he's going to what you could term unite, and there are many pieces he has to get together. So there will be many beings channeling Osiris eventually, and when all those pieces come together, then there will be the unification and an ascension that you won't believe. But you have no idea what you're getting yourself into, doesn't matter. You're going through a process, entities, of gathering your parts — all of you — past and future. And you will do anything and use anyone to assist you in gathering your parts. Everyone breathe, lighten up.

It certainly sounds very ominous when you say we won't believe it. It almost sounds like something we wouldn't want to do.

Well, you don't have the capacity to understand, is what I use the word belief for. Belief is a limit. You won't allow yourselves to understand, but you will eventually get it . . . indeed, you will. It is not here [brain] that gets it — here gets damaged. This [soul] is what knows; this is power, what you term the soul, the Buddha one. I'll have a conversation with you later, in your sleep, indeed? Would you like that journey?

I will indeed accept.

I'll introduce you to Osiris, too. We'll get that cleared up right away. Is there anything else? Will you allow yourselves to do another meditation? This is where I have the most fun, know you? I can get you working here. I'm going to allow you to heal your hearts, is that okay with everyone?

Indeed.

It's one of the first times I've asked permission, know you what I mean?

Root Chakra/Earth Meditation

Allow yourself to center your being. Center. I want you to focus in the root chakra – just focus in root chakra – and I want you to include the area from your perineum all the way up to your navel, that whole arena. Put your consciousness there – just sit there. Now allow the energy of the heart chakra to move down and surround that root chakra – just let it sort of, oh, drip down, sort of melt out of the heart chakra, and just surround there between what you call the navel and the perineum – just allow. Center. Peace. Now I want you to feel that love energy there and allow yourself, yes, the excitement of it – indeed, allow it. Allow the root chakra to enjoy this energy.

Now allow that energy that's in the root that came down from the heart chakra to begin to move up the body – let it fill the cavity up to the solar plexus. Let it fill you up now, up, up to the head, around the arms and down to the legs. Allow. Heart chakra, root chakra – allow. Let it spread like waves over you. All right, it's all right. Allow. Open the throat chakra. Peace. Center in the root chakra, again. It is going to move some things, entities. Allow the energy of the heart chakra to move there. Feel it in the body. You don't need an outward manifestation. Center in the body. Allow the energy to boil up. Move it up the body to the head, down the legs, arms. Peace. Center.

I want you to consider, consider now . . . open the throat chakra wider . . . consider yourselves under water – open the throat chakra wider. Open the temples. If you need to have the essence of breathing, breathe out of the temples here – allow – and just behind your jawbone, what you call gills – allow. Be in water. Center. Now feel the power of the light, the lightbeing that you are, that it has in a substance of water, more fluid. Allow.

Allow yourself to be what you term in the air, on what you term dry land, center on the beach, if you will. Allow. Heart chakra, send the energy down to the root. They blend. Allow it to move up the body, and contemplate the Earth you're sitting on in this energy – that you're allowing yourself to be here. Allow. Feel it in the perineum. Center. Allow your eyes to open gently.

Understand, the light of you enjoys its experience in the its body, its process called thinking, its process called feeling. In one manner you are required to know your light. In another manner the light is required to know the body and the tools of the body that it utilizes to express itself as a part of the Father. So the light is learning, and it's not learning in the mind. It's learning in the emotions of the soul, the wisdom it gets, the peace, the love it understands. It builds those powers lifetime after lifetime after lifetime. That's why you are here. That's why some of you will have other lifetimes, so you get more understanding of the love within the soul, and you complete. There's no judgment there. But the soul desires to love the body and all things. It is the mind that has played the game called "not here" – let's see what not – love is. Well, you've done it all too well. It is changed now. It'll be outrageous.

You're all willing to allow yourselves to become empowered in what you term the soul of you, indeed, and what is termed the Father that be inside you, that you are one and the same, indeed?

That is outrageous – I love you grandly for this thing. And I have no water [in my glass]. You're going to send me to the desert, huh? Get even for me sending Moses there – no big deal. I can change that. I love you all greatly. We are through. Be in your sleep in peace, and love your soul this night, indeed?

The whole month of your December it would be wise for you to love your soul here, because that's what's going to take you through this time outrageously. Indeed?

I'm going to send Osiris to you in another journey – you'll be amazed.

12

The Poison HAARP

Lee Carroll, based on a Kryon channeling at the U.N.

The report of this meeting is a fictitious compression of many meetings like it over the period of several years in the mid to late 1980s. All the players and facts are correct. Even the environmental impact statement as filed by the Air Force is correct – and the project is real.

The Unveiling

Unlike most office doors, this one closed with a dull thump, since it was heavy and sound-proofed. The shapely secretary entered and was briefly eyed by the few men seated at the tables, then ignored as she took her place and prepared to transcribe the meeting.

It was the mid-eighties somewhere in Virginia. Scientists from ARCO Production Technologies Corp. were meeting with high Navy and Air Force officials in a private meeting in a secure office. No uniforms were present, since long ago they had learned that the press watches the comings and goings of high-ranking brass. Business suits were the order of the day, hiding the stars of the Air Force general and the wide stripes of the admiral. The high-ranking men were slightly uncomfortable out of uniform and shifted in their seats. The suits hid the rank of the aides as well, and it was tough to tell who saluted who in this venue.

The men from ARCO were preparing some slides and graphics. "Let's get right to the point," said one of the scientists. "You all know from previous contacts that we have developed the Eastlund and Tesla patents to a workable system." All eyes were on the scientists, since some of the military brass hadn't really heard the entire story until today. One of them yawned, expecting another boring meeting.

"Gentlemen," the scientist continued. "What if I told you that we had within our power the ability to kill any missile in flight toward the United States at a range of 4000 miles from our shore without firing a shot?" The Air Force general smiled.

"In addition, Admiral, what if I told you that using the same technology, we could communicate with any submarine at any depth immediately in real time at full baud rate without the cumbersome underwater one-letter-at-a-time system you have now?" The admiral had a typical poker face from years of experience sitting across from those who wanted something. He didn't show any emotion.

"That's not all, gentlemen," continued the scientist in a smug manner. "We believe that this technology can also give us the ability to see up to several miles into the ground, depending on geological makeup, showing us nuclear bunkers, silos – like an x ray of the enemy's entire topography. And there's more." The scientist rose from his chair and approached the overhead projector.

"Within this same new technology we firmly believe, based on experiments already run, that we can eventually manipulate weather over any battlefield on Earth."

The admiral, still hearing the words about sub communication ringing in his ears, spoke first. "At what cost?"

The scientist was ready for this question. "Admiral," he said, "our entire program for the next ten years will cost us less than half the cost of one nuclear submarine. And . . . " he paused for effect, "the funding from Congress is already in place for initial experiments."

"This is doable?" said the admiral in a skeptical tone.

"Absolutely," replied the scientist. "And patented."

"What's the technology?" he asked.

"We are going to inject high-frequency radio energy into the ionosphere to create huge low-frequency [ELF] virtual antennas. Then we can focus the energy from this ionosphere mirror' to disrupt incoming missiles – in fact, any electronics at all. We do this by heating regions of the lower and upper ionosphere, literally boiling it, to create a kind of electronic lens. This is where the focus ability comes from to communicate with the subs, Admiral – or to knock down the incomings, General."

He continued without waiting for a reply. "Selective heating of the atmosphere, gentlemen, is also what can change the weather.

We could potentially create floods, droughts—very useful to our military." The scientist now waited for a reaction.

"You still haven't told me what the technology is," stated the admiral.

"We are using proprietary phased-array transmitting, steering and pulsing techniques," said the man from ARCO. "You see . . ."

"Scalar technology," interrupted the high-ranking Air Force man, "right out of the Tesla days. We were on the wrong side of it when the Soviet Union was up and running. Their secret Woodpecker system was just a variation of this, and it drove our communication crazy."

"This appears to be the holy grail of defense technology for all of us, in any service." The general nodded at the admiral and continued. "But what's the downside? How fast can we get it, and what about secrecy?"

The lights in the room dimmed as if on cue, and the overhead projector snapped on. "Take a look at this, gentlemen." The screen showed a facility surrounded by a fence. Within it there were a few innocent shacks and 36 spindly clothesline-looking antennas, hardly the ominous weapon the military men had imagined. Snow and ice were everywhere, and a lone man in a parka stood on the steps of one of the shacks as if posing for the camera.

"Take a look at what the public will know as HAARP—High-Frequency Active Auroral Research Program. Its appearance to the public is a small science experiment, gentlemen, in the black spruce forest in central Alaska, far from any population." The slide changed to an illustrated graphic of the Earth's ionosphere.

"Eventually we will have 360 antennas. When we begin experimenting in early 1997, we'll start by heating or exciting 30-mile-wide holes directly above the experiment, kind of like a giant microwave oven. We'll punch a hole and measure the results. Punch another, etc. We expect it will take about three months for each hole to close, and the data will begin to tell us more about how to focus our eventual virtual mirror."

There was a moment of silence, then the admiral spoke. "What about the environment?" he asked. "Didn't you have to get environmental impact statements? When we moved a barracks last year, we had to measure the effect on earthworms! How did you get this thing through?"

The ARCO man reached into a small briefcase and drew out a thick report, tossing it on the table so that it slid and stopped exactly in front of the admiral.

"This EIR was filed by the Air Force!" said the admiral. "Sorry, Admiral," said the Air Force general, "we had a heads up' about a year ago." The admiral gave the general a long stare.

He opened the environmental impact statement and read: ". . . the normally upward-directed ionospheric research instrument (IRI) transmissions can raise the internal body temperature of nearby people; ignite road flares in the trunks of cars; detonate aerial munitions used in electronic fuses, and scramble aircraft communications, navigation and flight-control systems."

"Unbelievable!" said the admiral, closing the report. "I don't know how you got that through. What about the unknown effects of this? How about the ozone? Could we do damage that is not repairable to our own atmosphere?"

"We don't know," said the ARCO man, as he turned around to continue the presentation. "But we are going to find out."

True Facts

HAARP is perhaps the most dangerous experiment undertaken for our county's defense, with the exception of the first explosion of the atomic bomb. If you lived in the 1940s you might remember that our war attitude permeated everything; the way you lived was actually shaped around the war effort. The consciousness of the military at that time was similar to the meeting you have just read about. At Los Alamos, prior to the exploding of the first atomic bomb, the physicists were asked what they thought would happen. There was wild speculation from "fizzle" to "ignite the Earth's atmosphere." They simply didn't know — but they did it anyway!

As the Kryon channel, I sat in front of a group of United Nations delegates in November 1995 in New York City. They had invited me to channel at the Society for Enlightenment and Transformation, a meditation group within the United Nations. Kryon said,

There are scientists working on means for energy transmission. Now, this is a valid science, and it will work. It is not new; it has been done before. But, oh, you have such power now in your instruments. We ask you to slow down, for you do not yet understand the resonance factors of the mantle and crust of the Earth.

In November I did not know about HAARP, but when I started studying it I realized that this was exactly what Kryon was speaking of. Scalar technology used for the transmission of energy. And it is dangerous!

This is not a technical article, and I won't dwell on the technical attributes of this military experiment disguised as simple research.

This is a plea for all who are reading this to find out more about HAARP for yourselves so you can understand the reality and scope of it. There has already been a book published that represents good solid research into the technical aspects of this experiment. Angels Don't Play This HAARP is by Jeane Manning and Dr. Nick Begich. It's a must-read for anyone interested.

Popular Science magazine of September 1995 reported on HAARP. This normally cheerful and entertaining magazine was very strong in its condemnation of what is being built in Alaska. They report that HAARP is being managed by the USAF Phillips Laboratory and the Office of Naval Research. Equipment is supplied by Advanced Power Technologies, a Washington, D.C.based subsidiary of E-Systems of Dallas, long-time maker of electronics used in ultrasecret projects such as the President's E-4B "doomsday plane."

They go on to report, "Richard Williams, a physical chemist and consultant to the Sarnoff Laboratory at Princeton University, is worried. Speculation and controversy surround the question of whether HAARP's 1.7 gigawatts (1.7 billion watts) of effective radiated power in the 1.8- to 10-MHz frequency range might cause lasting damage to Earth's upper atmosphere. HAARP will dump enormous amounts of energy into the upper atmosphere, and we don't know what will happen. With experiments on this scale, irreparable damage could be done in a short time. The immediate need is for open discussion. To do otherwise would be an act of global vandalism.'"

What does Alaska think? Again according to Popular Science: "State Representative Jeanette James, whose district surrounds the HAARP site, has repeatedly asked Air Force officials about the project and has been told not to worry.' She says, My gut feeling is that it is frightening. I'm skeptical. I don't think they know what they are doing.'"

What can you do? Already the Internet is buzzing with information and helpful suggestions. You might be amazed to know that it is not just a United States effort to stop or slow this experiment—it's global. If you are on-line, scan the Web for information. If you would like information on an Internet meditation regarding HAARP (that's right, folks, international meditation on-line), you may contact Steve Rother at ROTHERENT@AOL.COM. Regular meditations are happening!

What if you are not on-line? In the Kryon seminars we are encouraging anyone interested to drop a simple postcard to "60 Minutes" or "20/20," major network TV shows. If successful, this will bring about enormous awareness nationwide—far faster than writing your congressperson. Drop them a line and say, "I've heard about HAARP. Is it dangerous? Thanks," and sign it. Don't tell them all about it, just show them you are interested. These shows want to do segments that will get high audience ratings, and that are interesting to many people. Show them you want to know. If enough of us do it, they will get the idea. Offered in love, Lee Carroll, channel of Kryon.

Addresses:

"60 Minutes." 524 W. 57th Street; NY, NY 10019.

Director "20/20."c/o Capital Cities ABC; 147 Columbus Ave.; NY, NY 10023.

Resources:

Mark Farmer, "Mystery in Alaska." Popular Science, September 1995, p. 78ff. Cover blurb: "Exclusive: The Secret Agenda of a Military Project in Alaska."

Jeane Manning and Dr. Nick Begich, Angels Don't Play This HAARP. Earthpulse Press, 1995. Available by calling (907) 249-9111, FAX (907) 696-1277.

13

HAARP: High-Frequency Vandalism in the Sky

A review of *Angels Don't Play This HAARP*
Dr. Nick Begich and Jeane Manning
Reprinted from Nexus*, December 1995January 1996

Technonet, the protest form of the 1990s: picketing on the information highways. For example, a fast-growing assortment of men and women around the world are using the Internet (started by the U.S. military for information transfer and exchange that would never be interfered with) to draw attention to a questionable military project in Alaska. These Internetting, e-mailing, faxing folks are blowing holes in the U.S. Department of Defense secrecy wall by using the government's own system.

The printed-word part of the protest started when Dennis Specht, an antinuclear activist then living in Alaska, sent a news item to Nexus on the topic of HAARP – the High-frequency Active Auroral Research Program. Then, an Alaskan political activist and science researcher in Anchorage, Nick Begich, networked with Patrick and Gael Crystal Flanagan, who are self-described "techno monks" living in Sedona, Arizona, and was told to check out that same Australian-based magazine. Begich was surprised to see an item from his hometown in Nexus and immediately headed to the local library to dig out the documents cited in the article.

That research led to articles and the book Angels Don't Play this HAARP: Advances in Tesla Technology, which is 230 pages of detailed information on this intrusive project. This article will only give highlights. Despite the amount of research (350 footnotes), at its heart it is a story about ordinary people who took on an extraordinary challenge.

HAARP Boils the Upper Atmosphere

HAARP will zap the upper atmosphere with a focused and steerable electromagnetic beam. It is an advanced model of an "ionospheric heater." (The ionosphere is the electrically charged sphere surrounding Earth's upper atmosphere. It ranges between about 40 to 600 miles above Earth's surface.)

Put simply, the apparatus for HAARP is a reversal of a radio telescope: antennas send out signals instead of receiving. HAARP is the test run for a superpowerful radio-wave beaming technology that lifts areas of the ionosphere by focusing a beam and heating those areas. Electromagnetic waves then bounce back onto Earth and penetrate everything – living and dead.

HAARP publicity gives the impression that the High-frequency Active Auroral Research Project is mainly an academic project with the goal of changing the ionosphere to improve communications for our own good. However, other U.S. military documents put it more clearly: HAARP aims to learn how to "exploit the ionosphere for Department of Defense purposes." Communicating with submarines is only one of those purposes.

Press releases and other information from the military on HAARP continually downplay what it could do. Publicity documents insist that the HAARP project is no different from other ionospheric heaters operating safely throughout the world in places such as Arecibo, Puerto Rico; Troms, Norway; and the former Soviet Union. However, a 1990 government document indicates that the radio frequency (rf) power zap will drive the ionosphere to unnatural activities: "At the highest hf powers available in the West, the instabilities commonly studied are approaching their maximum rf energy dissipative capability, beyond which the plasma processes will 'run away' until the next limiting factor is reached."

If the military, in cooperation with the Uni versity of Alaska, Fairbanks, can show that this new ground-based "Star Wars" technology is sound, they both win. The military has a relatively inexpensive defense shield and the university can brag about the most dramatic geophysical manipulation since atmospheric explosions of nuclear bombs. After successful testing, they would have the military megaprojects of the future and huge markets for Alaska's North Slope natural gas.

Looking at the other patents which build on the work of a Texas physicist named Bernard Eastlund, it becomes clearer how the military intends to use the HAARP transmitter. It also makes government denials less believable. The military knows how it intends to use this technology, and has made it clear in their documents. The military has deliberately misled the public through sophisticated word games, deceit and outright disinformation.

The military says the HAARP system could:

- give the military a tool to replace the electromagnetic pulse effect of atmospheric thermonuclear devices (still considered a viable option through at least 1986);
- replace the huge Extremely Low Frequency (ELF) submarine communication system operating in Michigan and Wisconsin with a new and more compact technology;
- be used to replace the over-the-horizon radar system that was once planned for the current location of HAARP with a more flexible and accurate system;
- provide a way to wipe out communications over an extremely large area, while keeping the military's own communications systems working;
- provide a wide-area Earth-penetrating tomography which, if combined with the computing abilities of EMASS and Cray computers, would make it possible to verify many parts of nuclear nonproliferation and peace agreements;
- be a tool for geophysical probing to find oil, gas and mineral deposits over a large area; and
- be used to detect incoming low-level planes and cruise missiles, making other technologies obsolete.

The above abilities seem like a good idea to all who believe in sound national defense and to those concerned about cost-cutting. However, the possible uses which the HAARP records do not explain, and which can only be found in U.S. Air Force, Army, Navy and other federal agency records, are alarming. Moreover, effects from the reckless use of these power levels in our natural shield – the ionosphere – could be cataclysmic, according to some scientists.

One Alaskan puts it bluntly. A founder of the NO HAARP movement, Clare Zickuhr, says: "The military is going to give the ionosphere a big kick and see what happens."

The military failed to tell the public that they do not know what exactly will happen, but a Penn State science article brags about that uncertainty. Macho science? The HAARP project uses the largest energy levels yet played with, by what Begich and Manning call "the big boys with their new toys." It is an experiment on the sky, and experiments are done to find out something not already known. Independent scientists told Begich and Manning that a HAARP-type "skybuster" with its unforeseen effects could be an act of global vandalism.

HAARP History

The patents described below were the package of ideas which were originally controlled by ARCO Power Technologies Incorporated (APTI), a subsidiary of Atlantic Richfield Company, one of the biggest oil companies in the world. APTI was the contractor that built the HAARP facility. ARCO sold this subsidiary, the patents and the second-phase construction contract to E-Systems in June 1994.

E-Systems is one of the biggest intelligence contractors in the world, doing work for the CIA, defense intelligence organizations and others. Eighteen billion dollars of their annual sales are to these organizations, with $800 million for black projectsso secret that even the United States Congress isn't told how the money is being spent.

E-Systems was bought out by Raytheon, which is one of the largest defense contractors in the world. In 1994 Raytheon was listed as number 42 on the Fortune 500 list of companies. Raytheon has thousands of patents, some of which will be valuable in the HAARP project. Twelve patents are the backbone of the HAARP project, and are now buried among the thousands of others held in the name of Raytheon.

Bernard J. Eastlund's U.S. Patent #4,686,605, "Method and Apparatus for Altering a Region in the Earth's Atmosphere, Ionosphere, and/or Magnetosphere," was sealed for a year under a government secrecy order.

The Eastlund ionospheric heater was different: the radio frequency (rf) radiation was concentrated and focused to a point in the ionosphere. This difference throws an unprecedented amount of energy into the ionosphere. The Eastlund device would allow a concentration of one watt per cubic centimeter, compared to others only able to deliver about one millionth of one watt.

This huge difference could lift and change the ionosphere in the ways necessary to create futuristic effects described in the patent. According to the patent, the work of Nikola Tesla in the early 1900s formed the basis of the research.

What would this technology be worth to ARCO, the owner of the patents? They could make enormous profits by beaming electrical power, without wires, from a powerhouse in the gas fields to the consumer.

For a time, HAARP researchers could not prove that this was one of the intended uses for HAARP. In April 1995, however, Begich found other patents connected with a "key personnel" list for APTI. Some of these new APTI patents were indeed a wireless system for sending electrical power.

Eastlund's patent said the technology can confuse or completely disrupt airplanes' and missiles' sophisticated guidance systems. Further, this ability to spray large areas of Earth with electromagnetic waves of varying frequencies—and to control changes in those waves—makes it possible to knock out communications on land or sea as well as in the air. The patent said:

"Thus, this invention provides the ability to put unprecedented amounts of power in the Earth's atmosphere at strategic locations and to maintain the power injection level, particularly if random pulsing is employed, in a manner far more precise and better controlled than heretofore accomplished by the prior art, particularly by detonation of nuclear devices of various yields at various altitudes. . . .

"It is possible not only to interfere with third-party communications but to take advantage of one or more such beams to carry out a communications network even though the rest of the world's communications are disrupted. Put another way, what is used to disrupt another's communications can be employed by one knowledgeable of this invention as a communication network at the same time. . . .

"Large regions of the atmosphere could be lifted to an unexpectedly high altitude so that missiles encounter unexpected and unplanned drag forces with resultant destruction. . . .

"Weather modification is possible by, for example, altering upper-atmosphere wind patterns by constructing one or more plumes of atmospheric particles which will act as a lens or focusing device. . . . Molecular modifications of the atmosphere can take place so that positive environmental effects can be achieved. Besides actually changing the molecular composition of an atmospheric region, a particular molecule or molecules can be chosen for increased presence. For example, ozone, nitrogen, and other concentrations in the atmosphere could be artificially increased. . . ."

Begich found eleven other APTI patents. They told how to make "Nuclear-sized Explosions without Rad iation," power-beaming systems, over-the-horizon radar, detection systems for missiles carrying nuclear warheads, electromagnetic pulses previously produced by thermonuclear weapons and other "Star Wars" tricks. This cluster of patents underlays the HAARP weapon system.

Mental Manipulation

Related research by Begich and Manning uncovered bizarre schemes. For example, U.S. Air Force documents revealed that a system had been developed for manipulating and disrupting human mental processes through pulsed radio-frequency radiation (the stuff of HAARP) over large geographical areas.

The most telling material about this technology came from writings of Zbigniew Brzezinski (former National Security Advisor to President Carter) and J.F. MacDonald (Science Advisor to President Johnson and a Professor of Geophysics at UCLA), as they wrote about use of power-beaming transmitters for geophysical and environmental warfare. The documents showed how these effects might be caused, and the negative effects on human health and thinking.

The mental-disruption possibilities for HAARP are the most disturbing. More than 40 pages of the book, with dozens of footnotes, chronicle the work of Harvard professors, military planners and scientists as they plan and test this use of the electromagnetic technology. For example, one of the papers describing this use was from the International Red Cross in Geneva. It even gave the frequency ranges where these effects could occur – the same ranges which HAARP is capable of broadcasting.

The following statement was made more than 25 years ago in a book which Brzezinski wrote while a professor at Columbia University: "Political strategists are tempted to exploit research on the brain and human behavior. Geophysicist Gordon J. F. MacDonald – specialist in problems of warfare – says accurately timed, artificially excited electronic strokes 'could lead to a pattern of oscillations that produce relatively high power levels over certain regions of the Earth. . . . In this way, one could develop a system that would seriously impair the brain performance of very large populations in selected regions over an extended period. . . .' No matter how deeply disturbing the thought of using the environment to manipulate behavior for national advantages, to some the technology permitting such use will very probably develop within the next few decades."

In 1966, MacDonald was a member of the President's Science Advisory Committee and later a member of the President's Council on Environmental Quality. He published papers on the use of environmental-control technologies for military purposes. The most profound comment he made as a geophysicist was: "The key to geophysical warfare is the identification of environmental instabili-

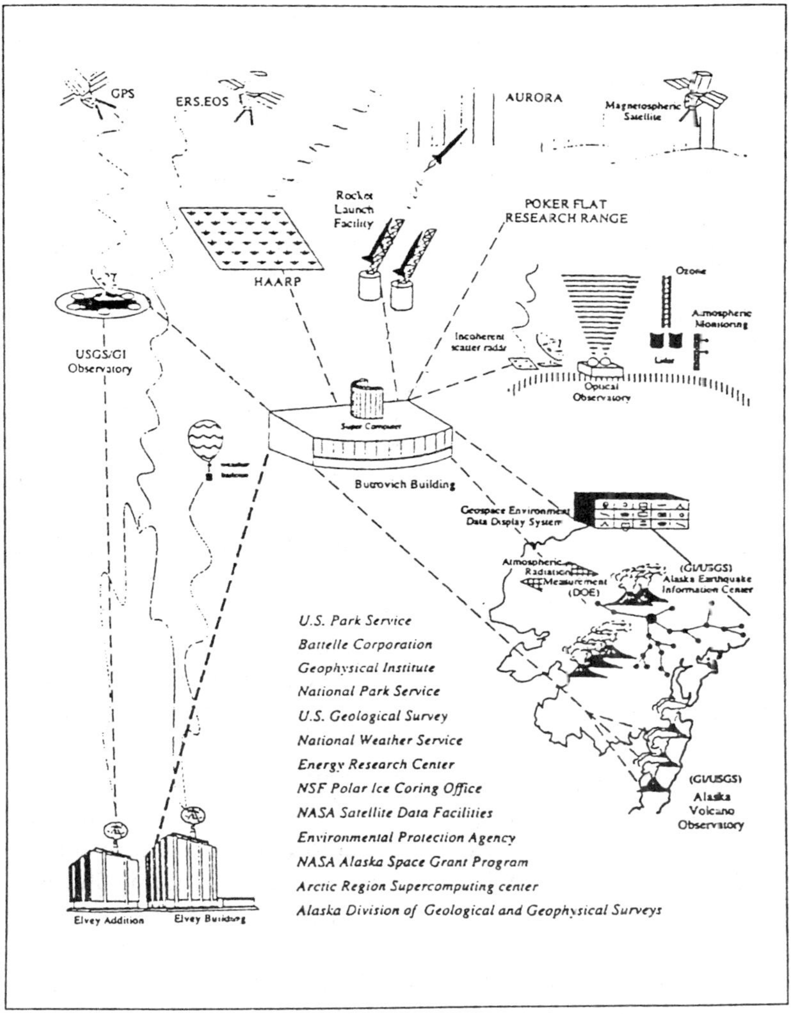

This diagram was taken from the "Biennial Report 1991-92, Geophysical Institute, University of Alaska, Fairbanks". It shows the intertelationships of the various programs being operated by the University.

ties to which the addition of a small amount of energy would release vastly greater amounts of energy."

While yesterday's geophysicists predicted today's advances, are HAARP program managers delivering on the vision? The geophysicists recognized that adding energy to the environmental soup could have large effects. However, humankind has already added substantial amounts of electromagnetic energy into our environment without understanding what might constitute critical mass. The book by Begich and Manning raises questions. Have these additions been without effect, or is there a cumulative amount beyond which irreparable damage can be done? Is HAARP another step in a journey from which we cannot turn back? Are we about to embark on another energy experiment which unleashes another set of demons from Pandora's box?

As early as 1970, Zbigniew Brzezinski predicted a "more controlled and directed society" would gradually appear, linked to technology. This society would be dominated by an elite group which impresses voters by allegedly superior scientific know-how. Angels Don't Play This HAARP further quotes Brzezinski:

"Unhindered by the restraints of traditional liberal values, this elite would not hesitate to achieve its political ends by using the latest modern techniques for influencing public behavior and keeping society under close surveillance and control. Technical and scientific momentum would then feed on the situation it exploits."

His forecasts proved accurate. Today, a number of new tools for the "elite" are emerging, and the temptation to use them increases steadily. The policies to permit the tools to be used are already in place. How could the United States be changed, bit by bit, into the predicted, highly controlled technosociety? Among the "stepping stones" Brzezinski expected were persisting social crises and use of the mass media to gain the public's confidence.

In another document prepared by the government, the U.S. Air Force claims: "The potential applications of artificial electromagnetic fields are wide-ranging and can be used in many military or quasi military situations. . . . Some of these potential uses include dealing with terrorist groups, crowd control, controlling breaches of security at military installations, and antipersonnel techniques in tactical warfare. In all of these cases the EM (electromagnetic) systems would be used to produce mild to severe physiological disruption or perceptual distortion or disorientation. In addition, the ability of individuals to function could be degraded to such a point that they would be combat-ineffective. Another advantage of electromagnetic systems is that they can provide coverage over large areas with a single system. They are silent, and countermeasures to them may be difficult to develop. . . . One last area where electromagnetic radiation may prove of some value is in enhancing abilities of individuals for anomalous phenomena."

Do these comments point to uses already somewhat developed? The author of the government report refers to an earlier Air Force

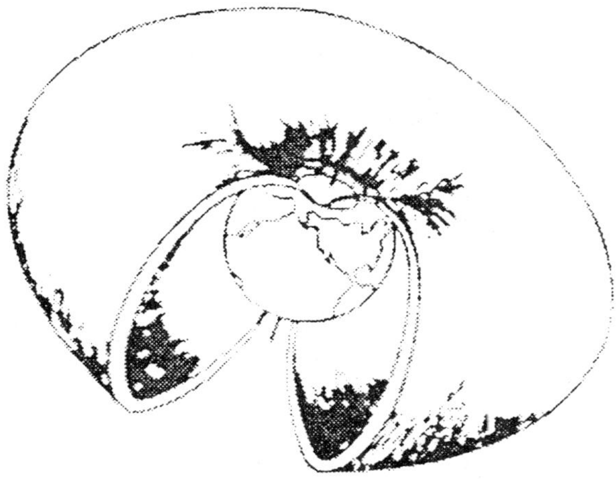

This diagram was drawn by Bernard J. Eastlund to illustrate his Full Global Shield concept.

document about the uses of radio-frequency radiation in combat situations. (Here Begich and Manning note that HAARP is the most versatile and the largest radio-frequency transmitter in the world.)

The United States Congressional Record deals with the use of HAARP for penetrating the Earth with signals bounced off the ionosphere. These signals are used to look inside the planet to a depth of many kilometers in order to locate underground munitions, minerals and tunnels. For 1996, the U.S. Senate has set aside $15 million to develop this ability alone: Earth-penetration tomography.

The problem is that the frequency needed for Earth-penetrating radiations is within the frequency range most cited for disruption of human mental functions. It may also have profound effects on migration patterns of fish and wild animals which rely on an undisturbed energy field to find their routes.

As if electromagnetic pulses in the sky and mental disruption were not enough, Eastlund bragged that the superpowerful ionospheric heater could control weather.

Begich and Manning brought to light government documents indicating that the military has weather-control technology. When HAARP is eventually built to its full-power level, it could create weather effects over entire hemispheres. If one government experiments with the world's weather patterns, what is done in one place will impact everyone else on the planet. Angels Don't Play This HAARP explains a principle behind some of Nikola Tesla's inventions – resonance – which affects planetary systems.

Bubble of Electric Particles

Angels Don't Play This HAARP in cludes interviews with independent scientists such as Elizabeth Rauscher. She has a Ph.D., a long and impressive career in high-energy physics, and has been published in prestigious science journals and books. Rauscher commented on HAARP: "You're pumping tre mendous energy into an extremely delicate molecular configuration that comprises these multilayers we call the ionosphere."

The ionosphere is prone to catalytic reactions, she explained: if a small part is changed, a major change in the ionosphere can happen. In describing the ionosphere as a delicately balanced system, Dr. Rauscher shared her mental picture of it: a soap-bubblelike sphere surrounding the Earth's atmosphere, with movements swirling over the surface of the bubble. If a big enough hole is punched through it, she predicts it could pop.

Slicing the Ionosphere

Physicist Daniel Winter, Ph.D., of Waynesville, North Carolina, says HAARP high-frequency emissions can couple with the long-wave (low-frequency, or ELF) pulses the Earth grid uses to distribute information as vibrations to synchronize dances of life in the biosphere. Dan terms this geomagnetic action "Earth's information bloodstream" and says it is likely that coupling of HAARP hf (high-frequency) with natural ELF (extremely low-frequency) can cause unplanned, unsuspected side effects.

David Yarrow of Albany, New York, is a researcher with a background in electronics. He described possible interactions of HAARP radiations with the ionosphere and Earth's magnetic grid: "HAARP will not burn 'holes' in the ionosphere. That is a dangerous understatement of what HAARP's giant gigawatt beam will do. Earth is spinning relative to thin electric shells of the multilayer membrane of ionospheres that absorb and shield Earth's surface from intense solar radiation, including charged-particle storms in solar winds erupting from the Sun. Earth's axial spin means that HAARP – in a burst lasting more than a few minutes – will slice through the ionosphere like a microwave knife. This produces not a hole, but a long tear – an incision."

Crudely Plucking the Strings

"Second concept: As Earth rotates, HAARP will slice across geomagnetic flux . . . a donut-shaped spool of magnetic strings – like longitude meridians [on maps]. HAARP may not 'cut' these strings

US Patent #5,202,689, dated April 13, 1993. This diagram shows part of the power beaming system described in the patents. It shows an energy beam being directed from the Earth into space and bounced to a remote location, thereby providing power to a point where it would otherwise not be available.

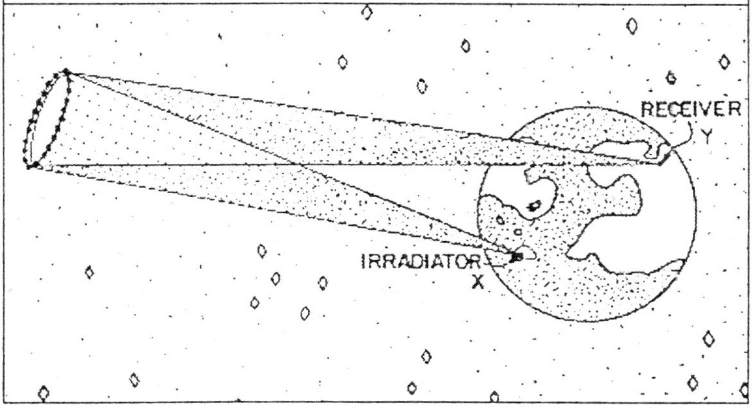

in Gaia's magnetic mantle, but will pulse each thread with harsh, out-of-harmony high frequencies. These noisy impulses will vibrate geomagnetic flux lines, sending vibrations all through the geomagnetic web.

"The image comes to mind of a spider on its web. An insect lands, and the web's vibrations alert the spider to possible prey. HAARP will be a man-made microwave finger poking at the web, sending out confusing signals, if not tearing holes in the threads.

"Effects of this interference with symphonies of Gaia's geomagnetic harp are unknown and, I suspect, barely thought of. Even if thought of, the intent [of HAARP] is to learn to exploit any effects, not to play in tune to global symphonies."

Feverish Earth

Among other resear ch ers quoted is Paul Schaefer of Kansas City. His degree is in electrical engineering and he spent four years building nuclear weapons. He says, "But most of the theories that we have been taught by scientists to believe in seem to be falling apart."

Schaefer talks about imbalances already caused by the industrial and atomic age, especially by radiation of large numbers of tiny, high-velocity particles "like very small spinning tops" into our environment. The unnatural level of motion of highly energetic particles in the atmosphere and in radiation belts surrounding Earth is the villain in weather disruptions, according to this model which describes an Earth discharging its buildup of heat, relieving stress and regaining a balanced condition through earthquakes and volcanic action: "One might compare the abnormal energetic state of the Earth and its atmosphere to a car battery which has become overcharged with the normal flow of energy jammed up, resulting in hot spots, electrical arcing, physical cracks and general turbulence as the pent-up energy tries to find someplace to go."

In a second analogy, Schaefer says: "Unless we desire the death of our planet, we must end the production of unstable particles which are generating the Earth's fever. A first priority to prevent this disaster would be to shut down all nuclear power plants and end the testing of atomic weapons, electronic warfare and 'Star Wars.'"

Meanwhile, the military builds its biggest ionospheric heater yet, deliberately to create more instabilities in a huge plasma layer – the ionosphere – and to rev up the energy level of charged particles.

Electronic Rain from the Sky

The military has published papers about electron precipitation from the magnetosphere (the outer belts of charged particles which stream toward Earth's magnetic poles) caused by manmade very-low-frequency electromagnetic waves: "These precipitated particles can produce secondary ionization, emit x rays, and cause significant perturbation in the lower ionosphere.

Two Stanford University radio scientists offer evidence of what technology can do to affect the sky by making waves on Earth. They showed that very-low-frequency radio waves can vibrate the magnetosphere and cause high-energy particles to cascade into the Earth's atmosphere. By turning the signal on or off, they could stop the flow of energetic particles.

Weather Control

Avalanches of energy dislodged by such radio waves could hit us hard. [The Stanford researchers'] work suggests that technicians could control global weather by sending relatively small "signals" into the Van Allen belt (radiation belts around Earth). Thus Tesla's resonance effects can control enormous energies by tiny triggering signals.

The Begich/Manning book asks whether that knowledge will be used by war-oriented or biosphere-oriented scientists.

The military has had about 20 years to work on weather warfare methods, which it euphemistically calls weather modification. For example, rainmaking technology was taken for a few test rides in Vietnam. The U.S. Department of Defense sampled lightning and hurricane manipulation studies in Project Skyfire and Project

Stormfury. And they looked at some complicated technologies that would give big effects. Angels Don't Play This HAARP cites an expert who says the military studied both lasers and chemicals which they figured could damage the ozone layer over an enemy.

Looking at ways to cause earthquakes, as well as to detect them, was part of the project named Prime Argus, decades ago. The money for that came from the Defense Advanced Research Projects Agency (DARPA, now under the acronym ARPA).

In 1994 the U.S. Air Force revealed its Spacecast 2020 master plan, which includes weather control. Scientists have experimented with weather control since the 1940s, but Spacecast 2020 noted that "using environmental modification techniques to destroy, damage or injure another state [is] prohibited." Having said that, the Air Force claimed that technological advance "compels a reexamination of this sensitive and potentially risky topic."

Forty Years of Zapping the Sky?

As far back as 1958, the chief White House adviser on weather modification, Captain Howard T. Orville, said the U.S. Department of Defense was studying "ways to manipulate the charges of the Earth and sky and so affect the weather" by using an electronic beam to ionize or deionize the atmosphere over a given area.

In 1966, Professor Gordon J.F. MacDonald was Associate Director of the Institute of Geophysics and Planetary Physics at the University of California, Los Angeles, was a member of the President's Science Advisory Committee, and later a member of the President's Council on Environmental Quality. He published papers on the use of environmental-control technologies for military purposes. MacDonald made a revealing comment: "The key to geophysical warfare is the identification of environmental instabilities to which the addition of a small amount of energy would release vastly greater amounts of energy."

World-recognized scientist Mac Donald had a number of ideas for using the environment as a weapon system and he contributed to what was, at the time, the dream of a futurist. When he wrote his chapter "How to Wreck the Environment" for the book Unless Peace Comes, he was not kidding around. In it he describes the use of weather manipulation, climate modification, polar ice-cap melting or destabilization, ozone-depletion techniques, earthquake engineering, ocean-wave control and brainwave manipulation using the planet's energy fields. He also said that these types of weapons would be developed and, when used, would be virtually undetectable by their victims. Is HAARP that weapon? The military's intention to do environmental engineering is well-documented.

U.S. Congress subcommittee hearings on Oceans and International Environment looked into military weather and climate modification conducted in the early 1970s. "What emerged was an awesome picture of far-ranging research and experimentation by the Department of Defense into ways environmental tampering could be used as a weapon," said another author cited in Angels Don't Play This HAARP.

The revealed secrets surprised legislators. Would an inquiry into the state of the art of electromagnetic manipulation surprise lawmakers today? They may find out that technologies developed out of the HAARP experiments in Alaska could deliver on Gordon MacDonald's vision, because leading-edge scientists are describing global weather as not only air pressure and thermal systems but also as an electrical system.

Small Input, Big Effect

HAARP zaps the ionosphere where it is relatively unstable. A point to remember is that the ionosphere is an active electrical shield protecting the planet from the constant bombardment of high-energy particles from space. This conducting plasma, along with Earth's magnetic field, traps the electrical plasma of space and holds it back from going directly to the Earth's surface, says Charles Yost of Dynamic Systems, Leicester, North Carolina. "If the ionosphere is greatly disturbed, the atmosphere below is subsequently disturbed."

Another scientist interviewed said there is a superpowerful electrical connection between the ionosphere and the part of the atmosphere where our weather comes on stage: the lower atmosphere.

One manmade electrical effect—power-line harmonic resonance—causes fallout of charged particles from the Van Allen (radiation) belts, and the falling ions cause ice crystals which precipitate rain clouds.

What about HAARP? Energy blasted upward from an ionospheric heater is not much compared to the total in the ionosphere, but HAARP documents admit that thousandfold greater amounts of energy can be released in the ionosphere than injected. As with MacDonald's "key to geophysical warfare," "nonlinear" effects (described in the literature about the ionospheric heater) mean small input and large output.

Astrophysicist Adam Trombly told Manning that an acupuncture model is one way to look at the possible effect of multigigawatt pulsing of the ionosphere. If HAARP hits certain points, those parts of the ionosphere could react in surprising ways.

Smaller ionospheric heaters such as the one at Arecibo are underneath relatively placid regions of the ionosphere compared to the dynamic movements nearer Earth's magnetic poles. That adds another uncertainty to HAARP: the unpredictable and lively upper atmosphere near the North Pole.

HAARP experimenters do not impress common sense Alaskans such as Barbara Zickuhr, who says, "They're like boys playing with a sharp stick, finding a sleeping bear and poking it in the butt to see what's going to happen."

Could They Short-Circuit the Earth?

Earth as a spherical electrical system is a fairly well-accepted model. However, those experimenters who want to make unnatural power connections between parts of this system might not be thinking of possible consequences. Electrical motors and generators can be caused to wobble when their circuits are affected. Could human activities cause a significant change in a planet's electrical circuit or electrical field? A paper in the respected journal Science deals with man-made ionization from radioactive materials, but perhaps it could also be studied with HAARP-type skybusters in mind: "For example, while changes in the Earth's electric field resulting from a solar flare modulating conductivity may have only a barely detectable effect on meteorology, the situation may be different in regard to electric field changes caused by man-made ionization."

Meteorology, of course, is the study of the atmosphere and weather. Ionization is what happens when a higher level of power is zapped into atoms and knocks electrons off the atoms. The resulting charged particles are the stuff of HAARP. Paul Schaefer, commenting on HAARP-type technologies, says, "One look at the weather should tell us that we are on the wrong path."

Angels Don't Play This HAARP: Advances in Tesla Tech nology is about the military's plan to manipulate that which belongs to the world: the ionosphere. The arrogance of the United States government in this is not without precedent. Atmospheric nuclear tests had similar goals. More recently, China and France put their people's money to destructive use in underground nuclear tests. It was recently reported that the U.S. government had spent $3 trillion on its nuclear program since its beginnings in the 1940s. What new breakthroughs in life science could have been made with all the money spent on death?

Begich, Manning and others believe that democracies need to be founded on openness rather than the secrecy which surrounds so much military science. Knowledge used in developing revolutionary weapons could be used for healing and helping mankind. Because they are used in new weapons, discoveries are classified and suppressed. When they do appear in the work of other independent scientists, the new ideas are often frustrated or ridiculed, while military research laboratories continue to build their new machines for the killing fields.

However, the book by Manning and Begich gives hope that the military-industrial-academic-bureaucratic Goliath can be affected by the combined power of determined individuals and the alternative press. Becoming informed is the first step to empowerment.

The book *Angels Don't Play This HAARP: Advances in Tesla Technology* is available from Earthpulse Press for $14.95 plus postage and handling ($1.50 U.S.; $4 international).

Dr. Nick Begich is an Anchorage, Alaska-based independent researcher and activist and former president of the Alaska Federation of Teachers and the Anchorage Council of Education. Jeane Manning is a reporter and editor residing in Vancouver, Canada. A decade of researching nonconventional energy technologies has culminated in her forthcoming book *The Coming Energy Revolution* (Avery Publishing Group, New York, 1996). She contributed to the book *Suppressed Inventions and Other Discoveries* (Auckland Institute of Technology Press, New Zealand). Begich and Manning are collaborating on the forthcoming book *Towards a New Alchemy: The Incredible Inventions of Dr. Patrick Flanagan.*

14

How To Create Solutions for Positive Change

Zoosh through Robert Shapiro
February 26, 1996

Here we have a government project euphemistically named by a real wise guy: "HAARP," like an angel — but I don't think so. This is a project that seems to have more than its obvious scientific purpose as stated publicly — but even the publicly stated purpose is to punch a hole in the atmosphere! Good heavens, aren't there enough holes in the atmosphere already? This is a terrible disaster.

We've talked about this before, but I'm going to suggest it again. We really need to have people visualize the forest that was there before the antenna forest, and use the creation method I have given. You really do have that capacity. You may not bring a forest back, but it might knock down the effect.

You mean the forest in Alaska they cut down to build this antenna array?

That's right. It might knock down the effect of the radiation from the antennas. If there was ever a project that extended almost directly from Project Montauk, we have it here. You might want to approach the men who wrote the Montauk books and ask them for their information on this thing. The antenna designs are not unlike some of the antennas that were at Montauk. They are designed to do what has been stated, which is bad enough, but they also have other capacities. They can literally project energies that would stimulate feelings in human beings. Utilizing a particular vibratory frequency and a satellite network, a particular vibration could be broadcast that would stimulate certain feelings within people, distracting them from whatever they are doing so that they would all feel something similar—for example, fear.

I must admit that it could be used to stimulate a good feeling. I don't think it's likely, but it could be used to stimulate peace or relaxation or harmony—and believe it or not, they know how to do that! But more likely it will be used to manipulate people. It can be aimed very precisely to within one square mile of population.

It has largely been used so far on a test program on wild animals, I'm sorry to say. It has also been tested on cattle, because cattle have certain physiological features that are similar to human beings, as many ranchers will understand. The people who conduct these tests have virtually no respect for the private property of others. I have to report that cattle ranchers have had a lot of losses. I'll give an example: A ranch in Australia, one on the eastern coast of the U.S. and one in the southwestern U.S. were all targeted at the same moment—yes, it's possible—and the feeling, the vibration stimulated was that of panic. Fortunately, there were no human beings in the immediate areas because these cattle were on the open range when this energy was broadcast.

The cattle panicked; they ran, they acted crazily, many of them were injured, some died. It was a terrible thing. The ranchers came out, discovered it, didn't have any idea what had happened. They figured that perhaps a wild animal had been in the herd. Very often a mountain lion gets blamed for something like this, although none were present there. If a mountain lion had been there, it too would have been scared to death.

This is something that can literally affect people's feelings, but as always, I have something to recommend that you do about it. And there are people prepared to take action against such devices should they be used on a massive scale beyond the mischief that has been their application so far.

You mean off-planet people.

I'm just going to leave it "people," and say that these devices might be altered in their target areas. I do not wish you to attack this machine, because that utilizes the same process and perpetuates the problem. I'd prefer you do something else. These antennas and the machines they are connected to are all made of metal. Granted, some of the electronics are made of various chemical substances, but metal is the major material here. I would like those of you who can to visualize or imagine or even feel a mountain or a stone. Put it between your hands, then over your solar plexus. If you have an idea of what the array looks like, that's all you need to do. But first get into the feeling of stones, which is where metal comes from. Then hold that feeling (those of you who can) over your solar plexus, between your hands, and then aim that feeling (make sure you don't get into the feeling of the HAARP project itself) of stone toward the array of antennas. What this will do as an accumulated experience is (1) remind the metal where it came from; (2) make it less likely to transmit easily; and (3) make it less amenable to being used in this way. Metal, when it's refined, does not exert its personal will on how it is being used as long as it does not suffer. You know, everything is alive. But when it is activated by human beings in this way, it will by its very nature realize that it's being misused against life. When you do this in a benevolent way, you see, then there is "no harm, no foul" —something children used to say years ago.

I want to encourage you to do things that create solutions but are not simply magic designed to destroy, because things like that have a way of coming around again, you know.

It would be operating on their level.

That's right, and you know, when you do that, you're just perpetuating the system you're attempting to transform. You need to do something else; you need to do something effective but benevolent. That's what I recommend. I would suggest a reiteration here of the exercise, how it's done.

You know, these devices—HAARP, as it's called, and other advanced weapons systems—are understood by the militaries of the countries in which they're created to have intelligence uses primarily, and occasionally other scientific uses. Most of the military have no idea of its tremendous destructive potential. Certainly a line soldier doesn't understand it. Very often officers do not understand it, sometimes even up to the rank of general. I want the public to understand that your military—your sons and daughters—are not to blame. There is a very small group of people who are largely overreacting to what they perceive as a threat from others and who are inclined to develop these technologies in such a way as to mask what they can do, their other purposes. I want you to understand also that if you perceive the military as the enemy, you will simply be playing into the hands of those who would have you fighting each other.

In the long run you know you are here to work through your past rivalries, to operate together, to discover your commonality.

Remember that the sinister secret government is only powerful as long as it can keep you fighting each other. It has very little power on its own. It derives most of its power from a simple human emotion it stimulates in the masses every chance it gets, whether by financially supporting some racist or terrorist political organization or promoting and encouraging self-destructive behavior such as buying and selling harmful drugs. The emotion from which the sinister secret government derives much of its strength is anger in its many forms. When the human being is angry, the body's defense systems spring into action, because it is basically a survival instinct.

But there is something else that happens that you may not fully realize, certainly not at this time: the body's electrical field springs into action. Your spiritual inspiration is also there, not only to counteract self-destructive tendencies, but in case you need it, to survive the situation that threatens you. What the sinister secret government has managed to do is tap into moments of anger in the mass population and extract energy not only through the use of technological devices (that look basically like a crystal, a little larger than a potato, only it's black — like a faceted crystal an adult can hold in one hand). These crystals are sometimes used, but the inner circle members don't even need them — they've trained themselves. Perhaps they are in some situation where many people are angry, upset or agitated, say a traffic jam — and they can scan (I'm not going to tell you how they do it; I don't want to compound the situation) the mass of people and pull the energy of this anger into them, which boosts their own abilities. They have trained themselves to utilize this energy to support and sustain their control and power.

Like vampires.

Yes, very much like that — energy vampires.

I recognize that some anger is constructive, and I've talked about this before. But to the extent that you are involved in destructive anger, whether it's to destroy yourself in some way or to destroy others, you might just as well walk right over to the sinister secret government (if you can find them) and give them a chunk of energy and say, "Here, take my power and run the world your way." They get 93% of their power by tapping into the energy of anger within the population. That's part of the reason they support and sustain projects that keep people angry, agitated, upset — even subliminal messages within the television or things that are designed to control, manipulate and otherwise disturb or disrupt society. They have been highly involved in this drug thing. Aside from using it to gather monies for their various projects, they felt that addicting people to drugs and the resultant chaos would be a win-win situation for them. The sinister secret government people do not have the same sense of frailty that a normal citizen might have. They utilize your anger against you.

So I'm simply saying, if anger comes up, for whatever reason, do something physical. Dance, for those of you who can dance; jump up and down, chop wood, find something to do with it. But don't just walk around seething, okay? Try to do something constructive if you possibly can. If you are an athlete, do something athletic. If you're not an athlete, do whatever you need to do – punch a pillow, do something that will dissipate it. Physicality is the best way to do it, but please do not be destructive or self-destructive. It just perpetuates this system.

If we transferred the inner circle of the sinister secret government to the Pleiades (of course, we couldn't do that, but if we did), they would have no power, because there is no anger there. They have become so dependent on living off the anger of people that they have forgotten – and I don't think that even if they remembered, they could – how to pull in enough energy from other sources to stimulate them and sustain their lives and their powers as they exist.

By changing themselves, people can change the world. By changing themselves they bring peace to the world.

Yes, and acknowledge the reality of anger, be cause some times anger has good purposes. It helps you to survive or move through something that has blocked you or made things difficult for you. It can be used constructively, so don't deny your anger. If it is there, do something physical, especially if it is constructive. And if that is not available, just hit something soft like a pillow – not a human – and dissipate the energy in a way that does not harm you or anyone else. Then it will pass from you and you will feel better. You can honestly say you've acknowledged your anger, you've done something with it, and you're not carting it around and being an energy bank for the inner circle of the sinister secret government.

How else can we alert people to the HAARP project, to investigate it? Is there a chance to get it on one of the big TV programs?

I'd like to see the responsible scientific community, much of which is at colleges and universities – scientific students [discuss it]. I don't want to see riots in the streets, but I think that at least the project that's involved in punching holes in the atmosphere – well, that's ridiculous! That's got to be stopped! I'd like to see that get more press, yes. The more press it gets, the less likely they're going to be doing anything with it.

If we could get it on "60 Minutes" or "20/20" by asking people to say, "I want to know more about this" as Lee Carroll suggests . . .

Yes, or even these programs that are like tabloid shows—you'd be surprised how many people watch these shows: "A Current Affair," "American Journal." These shows are quite popular with a large segment of the population; that's why they're on, why they proliferate, to say nothing of the fact that they're cheap to produce and they make a lot of money.

You brought up something . . . I didn't realize that the Montauk project is involved in the HAARP project.

The function of the antenna that is being used in the HAARP project is a cousin to the antenna that was used at Montauk.

Are they the same people?

No, but some of the people involved in the HAARP project had access to at least the antenna capabilities of the Montauk project's secret data.

Didn't the antennas come from some negative Orions or something?

Some of it, yes—the technology, anyway.

Moving in the Null Zone

What about moving in the dimensions? When do we start moving up the ladder again?

The motion will start within three months. I'm not sure whether you'll be moving up the ladder right away, but motion within the Null Zone will start within three months, I think.

So that's July.

Well, I think that it's more like June when we'll start to see some forward motion incrementally, but it'll take you a while to get through the Null Zone. That's actually good, because it is in many senses a very protected space. You know, extremes are not likely to happen; the Earth is not going to split in half or anything like that. Extremes of any particular kind are not going to happen. I don't see anything catastrophic. I'm not ruling out earthquakes or the continuation of wars going on now. Oh, there might be more agitation and more things happening, but I feel that the impetus for peace, especially with old enemies, is deep—and that as much as terrorists try to manipulate people, I feel that in the long run people are gradually seeing their common ground. The Middle East will be the weathervane. I think also that in the long run people will understand that the motivation of most terrorists is political; but it cannot be ruled out that the motivation of a few terrorists is strictly manipulative and controlling.

15

Project HAARP, Expansion of the Montauk Project

Preston Nichols and Peter Moon
Excerpted from the chapter "Star Wars and Mind-Control Trans missions" in *Encounter in the Pleiades, an Inside Look at UFOs.*

Mind-control transmissions are another phenomenon that fits in with the subject of implants, although they are of a completely different nature. I will illustrate how these work by relaying a real-life investigation.

In the summer of 1995 I received a telephone call from a woman I will identify as Susan DaRe. She felt that she had been targeted by mind-control transmissions, sickness transmissions and just about everything else. Her story interested me enough that I decided I would visit her and do an electromagnetic study. I was already going to a hamfest (where ham radio gear is bought and sold) in Virginia, and it was not too much out of my way to stop in at her home right across from Fort Meade, a military installation in Maryland. When I arrived, we went out to dinner with her friend Bruce and she began to tell me her life story.

Susan was born in 1951 and was adopted by a German family who had come to America after World War II and had been involved with Adolf Hitler and the Third Reich. Her family owned a lumber business in the Midwest and frequently played host to intelligence personnel such as CIA and NSA staffers. As a young lady, she had some sort of magical initiation. Susan was subsequently implanted and grew up. Today she claims to have tremendous psychic ability.

As an adult, Susan searched for her natural father and found out that he had served extensively in Egypt and was very highly placed in U.S. military intelligence. That was all she could find out except for the fact that he wanted to disavow all connection to her.

After telling her whole story, she told me that she is targeted and that her stepfamily is still connected to the intelligence community (CIA). Susan strongly believes the common theory that the CIA's roots began with the Nazi SS. She said the reason she is being targeted is the lumber business. When her stepfather died, she was to be left half of it and her stepbrother would get the other half of what was valued at about fourteen million dollars. Susan believes the intelligence community, working in concert with her "black magic uncle," wanted to get rid of her so that the natural son would inherit the entire business.

As we drove to her house after dinner, I began the electromagnetic study. I first tuned in to an 1080-MHz signal that I had been studying for a month. I noticed that when I got close to her car, the signal would appear. When she got well ahead of us, the signal would disappear. It was as if the transmitter for that signal was in her car. I knew this was not the case, because I'd been picking up this same signal all across the Northeast and it couldn't possibly have been transmitted from her car. There was no question that the 1080-MHz signal was being directed at Susan.

As soon as we arrived at her house, I began the electromagnetic survey at that location. I immediately found the 1080-MHz signal and also found the 435-MHz signal that routinely emanates from the vicinity of Montauk.* I also found a strong ELF (extra-low-frequency) broadcast that was as low as my equipment can pick up (about 50 to 400 kHz). I videotaped the entire display of different signals.

The Montauk signal at 435 MHz was particularly interesting because whenever I pick it up from Montauk, it is usually broken into pieces. If the pieces were put together, it would make up a signal like the one I was viewing in Maryland. As Susan moved in and out of the house, I noticed subtle changes in the scope pattern for the 435-MHz signal. I had her walk around, and wherever she would position herself, a subtle change would show up on the scope and be noticeable on the receivers as well. Next, I tuned back into the 1080-MHz signal and tried the same thing. I noticed that if she sat still in the car, the 1080-MHz signal faded out. If she moved around, it came back.

Susan then showed me a report by Dr. Peter Moscow. He is the president of the U.S. Psychotronics Association and is an excellent bioelectric magnetic researcher. He is involved with Wilhelm Reich's work and radionics, and I was already familiar with him. His report indicated that she had brain damage and had been exposed to aberrant electromagnetic fields such as ELF and VLF fields. I had definitely picked up the aberrant electromagnetic fields (the 435-MHz and the 1080-MHz signals).

When Susan had an MRI done, there were sections of her brain where the myelin sheathing was disappearing. This is known to be the start of multiple sclerosis. She believes this ailment to be a result of the transmissions broadcast in her direction. I believe this is possible, and I will explain why. First, we will cover what the 435-MHz to 1080-MHz network really is.

These signals start out as a particle transmission very much like what I described in Pyramids of Montauk. The whole idea of a particle accelerator is to continually increase the velocity of a unit of electromagnetic energy (a nitrogen atom is best for interacting with the atmosphere). As the particles accelerate to the speed of light, vast amounts of energy are released.

There are about 24 to 36 of these sites all around the planet. Each one of them shoots up to a series of small satellites that are referred to as popcorn satellites. This is all part of the Strategic Defense Initiative (more commonly known as SDI or Star Wars). These beams bounce around a network of satellites circling the planet. Some of the satellites multiply the beams whereas some of them combine the beams. By controlling the positioning and orientation of the satellites, the military can direct a combined beam anywhere on the planet. They can also defocus it to become essentially a particle wave.

There is a very interesting enigma that I have observed regarding this satellite system. The 1080-MHz transmissions are high enough in frequency that if the antennas being employed to detect them are highly directional, I should be able to pinpoint areas in the sky where the satellites are at a given time. The enigma has been that no matter where I point the antenna, I get a signal of uniform strength. Putting this information together with what Dr. Nicholas Begich has been saying leads to even more interesting conclusions.

Dr. Begich has published information about a project known as HAARP, which stands for High-frequency Active Aurora Research Project. This is commonly known as a weather-control project, but

Dr. Begich has picked up and heard the 435-MHz signals connected to HAARP and indicates that a mind-control function is being employed.

In addition to Dr. Begich's research, there is currently a theory being bandied about concerning a hypothetical nonlinear function that will translate one frequency to another frequency. I think that is exactly what is happening in the case of HAARP. High-frequency signals developed through HAARP are designed to ionize the energy in the upper atmosphere, which consists primarily of nitrogen. The ionized nitrogen (N2), then acts as a translator that will literally convert the 435-MHz particle-beam transmission into one of 1080 MHz. This is a rather ingenious development, because it bypasses the need for satellites. I believe this to be one of the latest developments of the Star Wars technology.

I began to figure this out when I first encountered the 1080-MHz frequency and asked Duncan Cameron to do a purely psychic reading on it. After listening to the signal, Duncan said that it is approximately 2.7 times the 435-MHz signal. This is not far off at all. If you consider that 400 to 450 MHz is the window to the human consciousness, you can divide 1080 MHz by 2.7 and you will arrive at 400. The ratio of 2.7 is a direct hit.

When I ran this information by my nuclear physicist friend Dan, he became excited, because 2.77 is a ratio of nitrogen to air with regard to the Earth's atmosphere. In scientific terms, this would be stated:

$$\frac{M_{ATM}}{M_{N_2}} = 2.77$$

In other words, if you divide the mass of the atmosphere by the mass of nitrogen, you will arrive at 2.77. This information was the initial clue that there was a relationship between nitrogen and the 435-MHz transmissions. Based upon his experience, Dan concluded that we were most likely dealing with a nitrogen particle beam. The above information about HAARP finally explained what was going on.

Dan also talked about a side effect that is produced when the particle beams annihilate each other. He said that when the nitrogen and antinitrogen collide, the element xenon is released. A couple of radionics tests done on people who have been targeted by the 1080-MHz signal indicated that they had a high degree of nitrogen and xenon in their systems. Susan's symptoms were like nitrogen narcosis, more commonly known as the bends.

All of this gets even more interesting because Duncan's psychic reading said that the particle-beam system can also be used in genetic engineering. I then ran all of this information by a geneticist friend of mine, who found it noteworthy because the subharmonic of the DNA helix is 1100 MHz. At the same time, another person pointed out a book by a Canadian that indicated that if one created a certain frequency with a xenon lamp, a thought form was created that was healing and regenerative.

The theory here is that one can literally do genetic engineering by using the 1100-MHz frequency to resonate with the DNA and thereby open and close it. The annihilation of particles (from the particle accelerator) releases a pattern that controls the way the DNA will reassemble itself. The xenon-gas effect would be used to regenerate the new DNA. I ran this by Al Bielek, who said he has a scientist friend who had previously read the blueprint for the entire satellite network. This scientist told the people at his company that if this system were beamed at the entire population, it would genetically destroy the human race.

Earlier in this [article] I mentioned the damage in the myelin sheathing of Susan DaRe. This could be the degenerative genetic effect that Al's friend warned of. This may be why we have suddenly seen MS appear all over the country. MS has reportedly increased at least a hundredfold over the last five years.

All of this means that the entire Star Wars system could be used to attack our immune systems and mental well-being. We already know that 400-450 MHz is the window frequency to the human consciousness; and 435 MHz is the specific frequency related to the appearance of UFOs. It also manifests from the Milky Way, and is thought to be the background frequency of our reality. The Star Wars system, at least part of it, transmits a signal between 1000 and 1200 MHz that is derived from a nitrogen-based particle beam. This signal is a multiplication of 435 MHz, our reality's background frequency.

The signals I picked up during this electromagnetic survey were all between 1080 MHz (2.7 times 400) and 1124 MHz (2.7 times 416 MHz), and the 1100-MHz frequency is supposed to be the window to the human DNA. I couldn't get the geneticist to tie it down to an exact frequency, so this is an approximation. He said it is about 1000 to 1200 MHz. A further corroboration of this theory is easy to recognize if you realize that the molecular structure of

Satellite tether snaps; shuttle safe

By Steve Marshall
and Todd Halvorson
USA Today [Feb. 26, 1996

The shuttle Columbia and seven astronauts were safe Sunday after a tether broke and sent a half-ton satellite floating into space.

"The tether has broken! It is going away from us!" astronaut Jeffrey Hoffman radioed about 8:30 ET.

The satellite and 12 miles of trailing tether quickly drifted away from Columbia, orbiting at least 200 miles above Earth.

Mission Control's James Hartsfield said the electricity-conducting cable broke inside the shuttle cargo bay.

If it had snapped farther along, the section still attached to Columbia might have wrapped around the shuttle, a potentially serious situation.

In video beamed to Mission Control, the severed end of the 1/10-inch thick tether resembled curly french fries.

"Those are some tether dynamics we didn't want to see," Mission Control said.

NASA has no immediate plans to retrieve the satellite.

"We could, technologically, chase it," said NASA's Kari Fluegel. "But as far as I know there are no plans to go after" the $442 million Italian system.

NASA doesn't know what caused the mishap, the second in four years in the system to generate electricity as it swept through Earth's magnetic field.

Similar methods are envisioned as power generators for NASA's space station.

Satellite Separates From Shuttle as Tether Breaks; Crew Is Safe

CAPE CANAVERAL, Fla., Feb. 25 (AP) — A 12-mile tether holding a half-ton satellite broke off unexpectedly tonight from the shuttle Columbia. Both the shuttle and seven astronauts were safe, although the satellite was lost.

Dr. Jeffrey A. Hoffman, a mission specialist, shouted down the news nearly five hours into the experiment, as it was 12 miles out.

"The tether has broken at the boom!" he told Mission Control. "The tether has broken! It is going away from us!"

The satellite and dangling cord were more than 18 miles away from Columbia seven minutes after the accident — believed to be a safe distance.

A Mission Control commentator, James Hartsfield, said the electricity-conducting cable apparently broke somewhere inside a 40-foot tower in the shuttle cargo bay. Only a slight portion of the 12.8-mile tether remained in the tower.

The astronauts were aware of the break almost instantly because of a sudden decrease in tether tension.

Columbia's commander, Lt. Col. Andrew M. Allen of the Marine Corps, said that the remaining 33 feet of tether on the shuttle was steady, "nothing moving at all."

The tether was almost all the way out when it broke and, along with the satellite, had been generating more than 3,000 volts of electricity.

Officials at the National Aeronautics and Space Administration said they had no idea what went wrong.

Until then, everything had been going well.

The satellite, a white metal ball five feet in diameter, rose slowly from a tower in the shuttle cargo bay this afternoon and picked up speed as the tether unwound from the huge, motorized spool.

An hour later, the satellite soared past the 840-foot mark, where it got stuck four years ago.

There had been a few surprises, but none of them serious.

The tether drifted to one side at first. It then began wiggling and, several minutes later, began swinging slightly back and forth. All the while, the satellite remained "rock-solid." Dr. Hoffman. said.

The motions eventually subsided as the motors on the reel began turning more quickly and releasing more tether.

Once the satellite was extended all the way out, it was to have generated 5,000 volts of electricity while sweeping through the Earth's magnetic field at 5 miles per second.

The $443 million tethered system, a joint project of the United States and Italy, is equipped with numerous science instruments as well as electron guns.

As current flows from the satellite down the tether to Columbia, the guns are supposed to shoot the electrons back into space, thereby closing the electrical circuit.

Such devices could be used one day to power spacecraft, drop packages from space stations to Earth, or explore the atmosphere.

On the previous flight of the satellite, four years ago, the tether jammed because of a protruding bolt. The satellite got no farther than 840 feet from the shuttle.

proteins contains nitrogen as a primary ingredient. This causes the nitrogen-to-air ratio to make even more sense. The appearance of nitrogen in proteins does not contradict the fact that life is carbon-based. As life evolves into higher-order forms, it develops proteins, which consist of nitrogen.

Genetic programming suggests something far beyond the prospect of biological warfare: It also includes the possibility of scrambling or rearranging our DNA. This type of thinking is prevalent in certain New Age dogma which indicates that the human race is undergoing a transdimensional change. Angels will appear and rearrange your lightbody so that you resonate with a higher octave. This may be true, but it is much more theoretical and otherworldly if angels or other-dimensional beings are doing it. If the secret government or the military-industrial complex has this capability, we are dealing with an undeniable real-world scenario. There are many possibilities.

My first thought on this is that the power base on this planet is afraid of giving up its hold on its power. Their interest in controlling our DNA would be to prevent a migration to another dimension. That is why they might be researching this technology.

A second possibility is that they are going to help us for our own benefit. That is wishful thinking, to say the least.

Another possibility is that this entire project is being orchestrated for some vast experiment. It could be for the good or bad of the continuum. Maybe the bad guys have plans to either do in or at least subjugate the entire human race. At the same time, the good guys or ascended masters are letting it run until they can step in at the last minute and bring us all to the next level. Some variation on this theme is also possible. There are many different puppet masters who could be involved.

There is an infamous island off the north fork of Long Island that is called Plum Island. It is forbidden territory to the media or anyone else, and has long been thought to be a center of bacteriological research that includes biological warfare. This was true for many years, but I know that today they are concerned with human genetic research based upon particle accelerators. These accelerators are no secret and can be viewed from the air.

None of this information is included purely to frighten anyone. It is in all of our interests to know the capabilities that can be used against us. It doesn't mean they will be, and knowing about it is the first line of defense.

THE ARIZONA REPUBLIC, February 26, 1996

Satellite snaps from shuttle

Crew safe after tether breaks

By Marica Dunn
Associated Press

CAPE CANAVERAL, Fla. — A 12-mile-long tether holding a half-ton satellite snapped Sunday, but both the space shuttle Columbia and the seven astronauts aboard it were safe.

Astronaut Jeffrey Hoffman shouted down the news nearly five hours into the experiment, as the satellite reached the 12-mile mark.

"The tether has broken at the boom! The tether has broken! It is going away from us!" Hoffman told Mission Control.

Commander Andrew Allen immediately steered the Columbia clear of the satellite.

The satellite and dangling cord were more than 18 miles away from Columbia seven minutes after the accident.

Mission Control commentator James Hartsfield said the electricity-conducting cable apparently broke somewhere inside a 40-foot tower in the shuttle cargo bay. Only a slight portion of the tether remained in the tower.

16

The Untethered Satellite

YHWH through Arthur Fanning
February 29, 1996

Okay. You have questions?

Yes. Can you talk about Project HAARP and the latest satellite?

Well, this HAARP, they are tinkering, know you? They don't have it right. They think they are going to get away with something. Know you what I mean? Just like they thought they were going to get away with something with the satellite.

Can you talk more about that?

It was a weapon. Indeed? It was a test flight of a weapon.

What was the weapon supposed to do?

It was to, well, create emotional havoc.

Was the weapon connected with the HAARP antenna array in Alaska?

It was to have been, because it was easier to test in space for the simple matter that it is easier to generate electricity up there, so they say. It would have required an enormous amount of power here. It was retrievable because it was going to be installed on the ground here. If it proved successful, they didn't care how much power it required. You see?

Would it have gone on the array in Alaska?

It would have been. Not connected directly, as you say physical link, but connected through microwave, yes.

Our information is that the HAARParray is a steering mechanism, and they were going to use the particle accelerators to create energy from mass, and then use it to control everyone on the planet.

THE ARIZONA REPUBLIC, Monday, February 26, 1996

Satellite wire snaps; shuttle, astronauts safe

— **SATELLITE**, *from page A1*

The astronauts were aware of the break almost instantly because of a sudden decrease in tether tension.

Allen said that the remaining 33 feet of tether on the shuttle was steady, "nothing moving at all."

The tether was almost all the way out when it broke and, along with the satellite, had been generating more than 3,000 volts of electricity.

NASA officials said they had no idea what went wrong.

Until then, everything had been going well.

The satellite, a white metal ball 5 feet in diameter, had risen slowly from a tower in the shuttle cargo bay and picked up speed as more and more of the 12.8-mile tether unwound from a huge, motorized spool.

One hour later, the satellite soared past the 840-foot mark, where it got stuck four years ago.

"It's all new territory from here and it's looking great," said Hoffman, who flew on the failed 1992 mission.

There were a few surprises at first, none of them serious.

The tether drifted to one side, then it began wiggling and, several minutes later, began swinging slightly back and forth. All the while, the satellite remained "rock solid," Hoffman said.

The motions subsided as the motors on the reel began turning more quickly and releasing more tether.

To hear more details on the shuttle Columbia mission, call *PressLine at 271-5656 and push 9063.*

NASA expected it to take 5½ hours for the satellite to be extended all the way out. At that distance, the tethered satellite was expected to generate 5,000 volts of electricity as it swept through Earth's magnetic field.

The seven astronauts, and hundreds of scientists and engineers in the United States and Italy, were thrilled to finally get the experiment going. But they were holding their biggest applause until the Italian satellite was fully extended, 12.8 miles above the Columbia.

On the previous flight of the satellite, the tether jammed because of a protruding bolt and the satellite never got farther than 840 feet from the shuttle.

This time, two critical computers jammed after the Columbia soared into orbit Thursday, delaying release of the satellite. One of the computers malfunctioned again late Sunday morning, just four hours before the satellite launch, but the astronauts quickly fixed it.

The four Americans, two Italians and one Swiss aboard the Columbia monitored the satellite with their eyes, computers and radar as they gingerly unreeled the braided copper, nylon and Teflon tether, just one-tenth of an inch thick and resembling a white boot lace.

The satellite was supposed to remain extended for 22 hours. The astronauts then were to reel it in to a distance of two miles, where it was to hover until they retrieved it Tuesday.

The $443 million, U.S.-Italian tethered system was equipped with numerous scientific instruments as well as electron guns. As current flowed from the satellite down the tether to the Columbia, the guns were supposed to shoot the electrons back into space, thereby closing the electrical circuit.

Scientists expected the satellite and cord to produce about 2,500 watts of power, enough to run a small, portable heater. The longer the tether, the greater the power generated.

Such devices could be used one day to power spacecraft, drop packages from space stations to Earth, or explore the region of the atmosphere that is too low for satellites and too high for balloons.

Much, much farther down the road is the ultimate tether goal, described by science-fiction writer Arthur C. Clarke in the late 1970s, building elevators to reach space stations in a geostationary orbit 22,300 miles high.

"While I'm not expecting to see it in my lifetime," Hoffman said before the flight, "I would be very surprised if it didn't happen some day."

But they lost one of their prime components—that was the satellite.

Can you tell us who cut the line?

I can, but I won't.

Which allows us to know that "someone" cut the line.

Indeed.

They won't be allowed to use this in its full capacity, will they?

They'll be allowed to go to the extreme, to the point where they can almost see that they're successful, but they won't be allowed total control.

They can boil your blood, control the magnetic fields of your DNA — it's horrible.

Of course. You are in the game of the antichrist now, alive and well.

He hasn't surfaced yet.

Indeed, he is doing a good job, too. You are seeing forms of control coming out of everywhere, indeed, and that's a panic, fear. Because as light gets closer, the concept of total annihilation becomes prevalent in most beings because they don't understand, know you what I mean? And in their great fear, in order to feel protected themselves, they must offer protection to others, to control

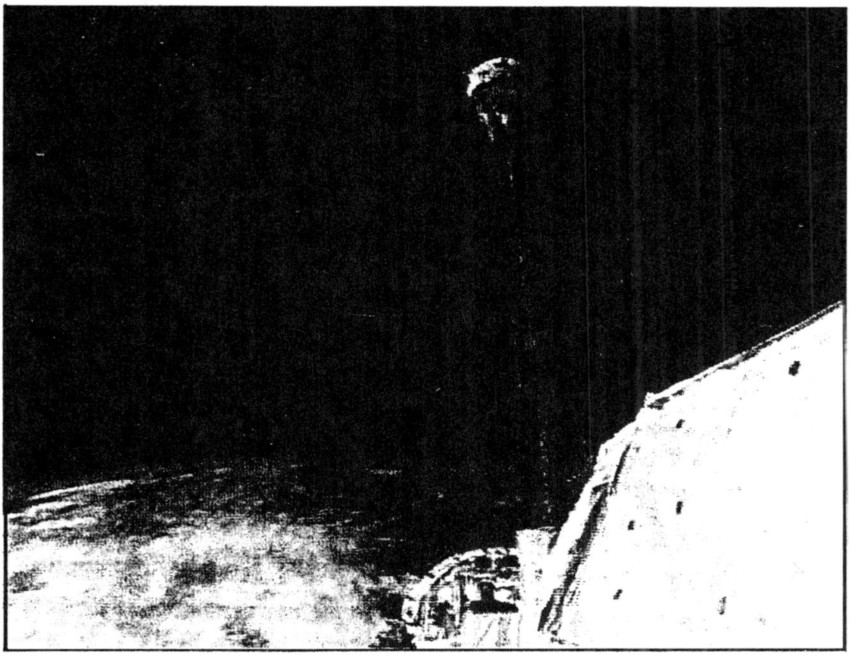

In a risky electrical experiment, a half-ton satellite was unreeled from the space shuttle Columbia on Sunday. The 12.8-mile-long tether was almost fully extended when it snapped. Commander Andrew Allen immediately steered clear.

them. That way they don't feel fearful as much. So that's what's going on, basically. It's all part of becoming. Some of you have lived through this before and forgotten it, but you made it through it.

You said earlier [prior to this transcript] that removing a challenge will keep us from becoming. We can attempt to expose this, but that's not going to affect anything?

But the majority on the planet is more interested in blaming others for their circumstance, and not becoming. Now, this planet is very important, because it allows beings great challenge, and still walk the path of what you term it, as you would say, master, here. There are those that don't want that possibility to exist. It's not going to happen the way they think it is. We are very aware of this, and if it gets to be the point . . . see, there aren't enough masters here to handle it, from your physical standpoint—know you what I mean? . . . and even they might be overwhelmed, know you? So we're not going to get it to the point where those masters that are incarnate here, that are truly masters, are going to not be able to

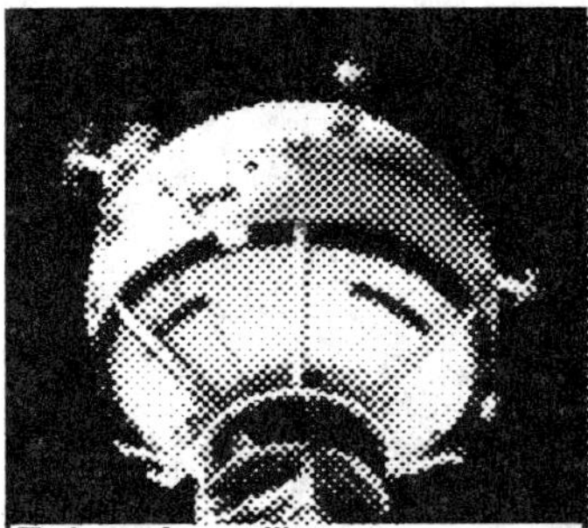

Tethered satellite

finish their curriculum.

One of the things HAARP also does is prevent us from getting into the higher mind. They're attempting to prevent us from ascending.

Indeed, they are. Nice try! [He laughs.] Cost them a pretty penny, too.

I think we need to focus on and accent the fact that all of the people involved in the military — all of these bases and the astronauts — don't know what is going on.

Of course not. They are working a job to earn money to feed family. They don't know.

Very few know how all of these pieces fit together.

Of course. Very few.

We have one report [see Montauk Book IV] that by focusing on a particular individual they were after, they removed the myelin sheath over the brain and caused multiple sclerosis. You know, there is a lot more MS than there used to be. It's abhorrent!

They are playing some pretty bizarre games, but they understand also they are going to . . . well, they don't really think they are going to get caught, know you what I mean, even in the great scheme—play karma and this thing. But they are already caught. They're reacting fearfully, as spoiled bully children.

It's just that they have such nasty weapons.

Not as bad as mine. [Group laughs appreciatively.]

Know you prana? When you capture prana, you make electrical current. You've perverted prana here with your electrical appliances. Now, we're not going to create a heavy on you, and all this and that and the other. But literally, if you had spiritual heart and ears, you would hear the prana in the glass screaming to get out, and they can't. You have this force you call heat; when your metal and the current runs through the heat, it is light, indeed? And in the light there, in one manner, because the prana was captured, the prana is dying in the light, because that is what it is. The light is the death of prana; your lightbulb is the dying of prana. They are taking prana to heat the elements there, and its death—prana's death—provides you your . . . what you say is light. It's a perverted light.

Now, we're not going to get into that because you're all into your electrical things. If you know how to use prana, it would be different. That's a little story to . . . how we say . . . well, as you go further, you'll really play judgments with yourselves for all of the prana you've killed in all of your lifetimes. You see, you don't ask prana if you can do it. You still don't ask your plants if you can eat them. Even though you've been told, you don't ask. You do it. That is not the gentle way. But that's all right, you're getting there.

Is there a way that we'll learn to create light to see with, without . . .

Yes. That's coming down the pike. You have the capability now, actually, to do that.

They buy up all of the patents and hide them. But so many people are talking about free energy, it's coming out all over. Can you tell us how soon it will be available?

Indeed. They will be more observable two years from now, where there will be actually demonstrations of this thing, of the lights and all of this, that and the other. But everyone must make a buck, know you what I mean?

Now, when we first began talking, I told you I was not here for your physical bodies, I was here for your souls. But you're so ingrained in the physical, we had to include the physical. I care for the prana that is within you, that lights your body, more than I do your body. I care for the being in there, inside you that has accumulated this prana to light the vehicle. That's what I care for.

Were you surprised when you first got here this time that the life force was so ingrained in every photon of every cell? Was it not like that before?

It wasn't as dense. There wasn't as many, what you term modern conveniences. You hadn't gained the power to shut out God so much as you have now.

So it's a reflection? The more power and conveniences and things out there, the less we turn inward?

It's also scientific: the more interference you have in patterns of source. Indeed. It's all energy.

The electromagnetic fields?

Of course. Know you radio and television waves, they are all over the place, indeed? They are all in the air. It's a challenge at times to get through some of that energy. Not for me, but for others and for your high selves. It's difficult, because you assume the waves of the air are where everything is. A little cosmic humor inside there. You'll get it later.

So how many of us want to go out and live in a hut and light our own fires and get away from the electromagnetic fields? Could we advance faster if we did that?

Well, you see, know you this thing ascension you beings are so concerned with? Indeed. Some of you have done that before. But no big deal. You're here to . . . we'll say, create a tunnel through these airwaves so others can get through this tunnel. Know you what I mean? And the game is to see how successful you can be with it and still be in your power without running amok—know you, creating a church—teaching beings their respect for their divinity and their power. For those that are aware and on their greater, we'll call it path of evolution, their greater spiral upward, whatever metaphysically you say, this is the decade of display. You're going to keep getting opportunity after opportunity, even if you shut them off, to do the display. And it becomes frightening and you'll turn away; and it becomes frightening and you'll turn away. But eventually you'll go through it, because you'll know if you don't—you can feel it in you—that you are dying by not completing this thing. You know what I mean. You know you have to do this, for whatever reason. You don't know, but there is an inner fire saying, "We've got to complete this one. That is coming out in beings. It's working that way. Indeed? It is happening. Anything else?

Say more about that tunnel. You're helping us create a tunnel that we can connect with the higher part of ourselves. Is that how to understand it?

It is like a sheath.

A sheath of protection?

That you can get through these energy waves, yes. Know you Star Trek? "Beam me up, Scotty." There is a column there. There is a sheath of light around so the particles don't distort and go all over the universe. Indeed. You're kept in a—what do they call it?

Coherent field.

Indeed. That's what we're doing. That's what you're doing, actually. And you wouldn't be challenged as much if these beings weren't building this great web of antennas.

Very delicate times now. You remember me telling you you're not going to ascend? Indeed? And some of you argued with me.

And some of us cried.

That is all right, there is wisdom in the tear. But what it did, it made you go inside you to figure it out a little bit more, to figure it out. It humbled you a little bit, because you're going to work with your own power. I didn't lie to you, I'm telling you the truth. I'm not going to say something to you to get you in deeper muck so I'll have to come back in another eon and do it again. I'm going to tell you the way it is. You have the opportunity now to work with yourself in this life to become christs and beyond. And when you get to Christ, go beyond; and when you get to God, go beyond. And you'll find out there is only one God. [He laughs.] A lot of humor here. Outrageously so.

How long before we get to see the humor?

As soon as you want to. As soon as you will allow. Indeed? Now as to your March. Energy movement in March – it's primarily going to affect your mental abilities. Now, that's what they were doing with this satellite thing, they wanted to modify and intensify it to see if they could control this influx of spiritual force. You're getting great light now poured down upon you. It is not a name, it is pure consciousness. And you're going to be able to go to any point in time in your meditations. If you allow yourself quiet moment, simply meditate, find yourself there. Now, the reason you're going there is because it is very important for you to do something there, be it the future or the past. You center in your being your energies and you do whatever is appropriate. You will know what it is. You know what peace is, you know what love is. You're going to these places in time because they need the love. They need it. And you can alter a lot of things, even dimensions. That is what is going on. A lot of you going to get "whoa" in the head here, and it is not a hangover. Not from water – at this time, anyway.

So is most of the drama in March, then, an interior thing? The planet won't be affected?

It is an interior thing, but as you play, the consciousness upon the planet is reflected, know you? Becomes exterior, indeed? A lot of energy.

So the better we can work with the energy, the clearer . . . ?

The clearer the consciousness of the planet will be. Indeed. Now we have already helped you out – the beings that were trying to muck with you out there. You didn't know what was going on, so we sort of said, "Oh, I don't think so!"

Okay. And we will do it again if we have to.

Well, they needed that satellite, so they're going to get the warning.

Well, they want to grow, too. They're just fearful beings. They just don't know.

Allow yourselves to center for a moment. I'm going to bring in a little more energy for you. I want you to play with it, feel it in the body. Feel it in the body now. I want you to allow your body to float, say you, sort of melt in the chair one way or the other. And this is the lightbody. Whatever makes it feel comfortable. So just kind of get that feeling of where the body just sort of blends and sits high in its presence. Indeed? Allow. Become one with the energy that is about you now; let it merge. Become one with the consciousness of everything that is outside you, outside the house and the planet. Allow. Center. Allow your eyes to open very gently. Be in the heart center. We are through.

17

Humanity Decides "Let's Be Free Again"

YHWH through Arthur Fanning
April 4, 1996

What is beginning to become apparent in your human consciousness is that consciousness exists regardless of thought. There is an understanding developing of what would be termed life force in everything. It is going to become very apparent in what you term your July — the awareness of this force. Now, give me a moment here because your words are limiting. You've heard us speak before of thought, indeed? Thought is everything. Thought itself is a word. There is an energy beyond thought which we say, with your words, is consciousness. It is an awareness of motion, awareness of movement. That awareness of movement within consciousness is what you beings utilize to create time: time line. That awareness of time is going to change with this great expansion that is coming, and it will be likened unto an understanding, an understanding of how you create time, how you are doing it in your shifting of consciousness. Many beings are going to feel very confused, because the portions of the brain that you utilize to maintain frequency of your physicality are being altered, not against your will. They are deciding — "they" being collective humanity — are deciding that this game of limits . . . you've had enough of limited understanding here. So the general consciousness of all human beings has what you term made a decision to "let's be free again."

Now, that will create, of course, some confusion because there will be many beings that will understand it and be willing to move freely. There will be others that are into resistance of this thing and they will think it is an outside call affecting them. It is simply their consciousness looking for a place to . . . looking for an arena within the brain to flow through in an unlimited manner. This will create a pressure, create a distortion. The visions are going to change. The apparatus you use to perceive your reality and create it is going to adjust itself. In other words, your perceptions are going to change. You will see, will understand perceiving versus seeing. You will know that your perceiving is a creation, and you will be experimenting with it, all of you. You haven't a textbook yet to explain these things. There will be very ancient wisdoms that will be working through the body physical, working through the forces that you term are the soul, working through the forces that are light and love as you understand it, working through your apparatus, your vehicle, your toy, your physical form.

You, humanity, will appreciate the experience later. However, in this movement, this expansion, many will attempt to cling to a structure, to cling to a pattern that feels safe, and it will create distortion, destructive forces within the body physical, because the body physical, as part of the great consciousness, itself desires to change. It desires this thing. The tendencies—the fear of the unknown—there are going to be a lot of these unknownness feelings coming up. But it is all what you have been waiting for.

Say a little more about perceiving.

The perceiving. You are inside your body, indeed? And as you open your eyes, you look out of the body and you see physical reality, indeed? There is another sight that you have. It is not . . . well, it is what you say your sixth seal, your third eye. There is another sight that you have—well, there are many. It would be like this: you are beginning to use the eyes that perceive many realities. You are beginning to use the eyes that understand what they want to see to create. You have a set of eyes way out there, we will say, that perceive.

Way out where?

It is really . . . because you are in time, you play distance, you see, but there is a part of you that is not in either, not in any time. So that is the part of you that has the ability to perceive, knowing it is creating. There is another part of you that sees—that is the lowest part—that sees realities. There are in-between pieces, there are levels, as you would say, from the great perceiver that you are, creating all of these environments. There is another level that begins to choose the environments perceptionally, you understand, and lower, lower, lower until . . . what you say . . . on your physical in your third dimension.

Now we are going to play what you term elevation, raise the frequency, so you are going to become aware that you are a perceiver, humanity, that you are perceiving, and what you are perceiving is a creation. You want to do it, not manipulate. You will manipulate actually, manipulate thoughts and colors, so you can change the shutter, more light, less light, to create the canvas, you see. These experiences are going to be . . . well, they should be joyful, but the way you beings play, we might say they are going to become limiting because you will be not only aware of your thoughts, but aware of your . . . we will say it will be judgment. You will end up judging yourselves for not perceiving correctly, indeed? Another game of judgment, you beings. But that is all right. That be the energies that will—they are building now. They are going to be very apparent in your July month. There is no need to be concerned, as many will be. It is simply your consciousness that is sort of waking up out of a great sleep. The in-between pieces are joining you. You will see how literally everything at every moment is perfect. There is no imperfection. It is a flow, as you would term it, it is an isness, and it is a great opportunity to understand the isness of you within the Isness, to *know* this, not a belief anymore, not metaphysical chitty-chat. It will be experiential. It will allow you to know, which is what power is and what wisdom is. There will many that will become confused. There will be a great tendency to, you say, suicide, to change their life paths, patterns. This is not a wise thing to do because you simply pick up where you left off.

It's going to be so dramatic that some will want to commit suicide? Say more, so that people who read this can see the scenarios, the warning signs.

It's already started. It is that they. . . one of the greatest energies will be this thing called relationships, know you what I mean? As your consciousness expands and you become aware, you'll see your connectedness to all things. You will see that indeed what you term the being in the supermarket that was passing you by or be at the counter. And you just meet them for a moment, but you understand you were lovers in past lives and future lives. And you might see your future bride or your future husband, and you will know it. Within the structure you play "you can't have"—know you "can't have that yet, can't have that now"? Because of this structure, this, that, the other, it will create a tearing, a reaction, as you beings love to do, know you, react? It will create a tearing thing. And then the other one might know, might not know, but you still have to understand that you are beginning to develop your perceptions, that you are in love with everything, not not-in-love. Know you what I mean? —you are playing not-in-love here.

We have played in-love-with-one, but now we need to be in love with everyone?

With everyone. So the distortion will be . . . beings will say, "Oh, I can't talk to that one because they will think I am silly," yet they are having the same feelings. Know you what I mean — "Oh, I can't talk to that one because the one I am with now is going to get all upset." So they will seek a way to jump through the boundary, a distorted attempt to be in love. "End it all, this is miserable, I'm in love," know you what I mean, but you still have to play into that knowing of your ability to perceive correctly. You still have to go through that layer to understand it. And there will be a great desire for control in some of these frequencies.

Control by the controllers or by humanity at large?

Well, humanity at large, because it is likened unto . . . you don't want to get carried away, but you want to do it your way. Well, maybe not sort of control, but some will be reckless and this that and the other, but it is important to remember that in everything it is all perfect, always perfect. Always perfect because at each point, at each level, you are learning something that is very important for the next level, know you what I mean, very important.

That I do. I know how everything we do builds and prepares for the next step.

Indeed. More and more and more. And expands the heart, expands the power, expands the Buddha nature, the Christ nature, expands all things. And there will be an attempt to force it into structure. This shift in consciousness, many are going to think that God has come, and He is, because God is becoming here, you see. It's going to be rather humorous to watch.

From your perception?

It will be humorous from yours, too.

It's starting now, it is going to get intense in July and it is going to last for years?

It is going to build, indeed. Know you a few years ago I said that metaphysics was going to be the next great church? Metaphysics will provide the structure, or at least the system of belief wherein many will feel comfortable in this change. Do you understand what I am saying? At least it will provide a support system, so it's a good thing. It's like your churches; they provided a support system through the period of time they were needed, indeed? So there will be that. And then there will be the need to go beyond that, to really understand that you are god, that you are free, that you have the ability to perceive and create, that you're knowingly doing this in fun.

This is where the tiger will come, what you call the controllers – "You can't do that" –you see? Because if you do, they're not going to have anyone to control.

What kinds of control — more mind control?

Well, essentially it will be, limit your ability to travel, pay you more taxes, control your ability, your access for things, for foods.

How soon? What do we need to do about that?

You just understand they're playing with the energies and you are the perceiver. And don't go into fear here or judgment. Just understand, "Okay, this is the background that I have chosen to play with in developing my power." Know you what I mean? You understand that as you play this you can't be damaged. That is one thing you must hold to, know you, no matter what they do to the body, you can't be damaged. But that does not mean become a martyr either, know you?

But isn't the whole game to keep the body and go up into the next dimension?

The whole game is to keep the body and understand it, the energies through it, so you learn to perceive correctly. And you can create no walls or you can create walls. Know you what I mean?

Yes. So what should people who read this do or start doing?

They should be allowing themselves to meditate for at least 15 moments each day, allow the light to come in there that wants to. That is their light. Allow their patterns of judgment to go away, to be clear with their being, be honest with their own energy. All you beings know what honesty is and what it isn't, and you know when you beings, you play your mind games, you know what you're doing when you're doing it. It is all right, there's no judgment there, you're simply practicing the art of perception at one level, very limited, however.

You will move to a higher frequency – that higher frequency is love, and it is coming. Know you the energies now, they're not so hard, really, they're very fine-tuned now, they're very high-pitched, very fast. It's entering the body, it's all around you. You beings have not allowed your body to be accustomed to that frequency;you're used to the lower frequencies, the slower energies. These are very dynamic, very powerful processes, we will say, that are part of your being. If they all came into your body you would explode. You already know that, so you want to treat the body very gently. You allow yourselves what you term your clean foods, your water and your fruits and your nuts. I think I've said that before too, and that will be important. Especially what you term your figs and purple grapes—they're healthy for the body. And pretty soon you beings will understand that you eat your food for the color, for the electrical content, and the electrical content and the color are very important in your abilities. When you perceive out there, we'll say, you use color and you use sound for the perception. And it lowers, you understand. So the color here and then. . .I've talked to you beings before; I've said, "Listen to your food, talk to it." Now, when you do that, you're more in line with your greaterness.

Not many of us do that.

Most of you don't. You should ask the food if you should eat it. You would live longer.

Not just raw food? Even cottage cheese and pineapple?

Of course.

Can you look into the situation at the office with the mice? I don't kill mice, so they have had the run of the place, but now they are eating up the wires in the computers. Why are they doing that? How do I get them to move without hurting them?

Let me see. [This was said with a sort of startled humor.]

I saw the mouse deva. He is a beautiful being.

I'm having a chat with him right now. It is that—well, it is a matter of perception, again.

His or mine?

Well, his also and yours, yet it is his, theirs. They think they are gaining wisdom.

By getting into the computer?

Of course. There is life force that moves through the wires. In one way they are freeing the life force, and in another way, they don't understand here. And there is some concern because you beings are taking away their place of residence. [They lived in the field where Bashas shopping center was built, across the street.] We're instructing the deva to move a little bit north, you know, in the fields. Zoosh just said, "Good luck!" We don't want to be forceful here.

Zoosh through Robert said to get a cat, but the cat will still kill them.

Well, that will work. I will tell you that I am going to instruct the deva—I am going to introduce him to the cat deva and get everything squared away and give them the opportunity to move first, because they will know that that is coming.

Thank you for taking the time to look into it.

Indeed. A cat will be good.

Is there anything else you want to say for the magazine?

Not at this time. There will be more later. We are working in a way to get this physical body [Arthur's] so that more profound information can come through. You beings must be ready for the power of it, even in your mind. We have to be careful with certain information, where, as has often been the case, wisdom will be taken out of context and perverted. And you're not only—especially in these frequencies now, as the consciousness is accelerating—not only dangerous to yourself but could be dangerous to other species not existing in your reality. Even though everything is indeed perfect.

They're close in frequency but not in this dimension?

That is exactly correct, indeed. And they are also part of you, here. It would be like . . . know you a nuclear explosion, uncontrolled? It sets off everything, know you? The scars last for many centuries. There would be like a time of great doubt—know you what that is?—great abyss. Everyone would fall in. It would take, you say time, it would take a great energy to elevate that consciousness again.

Is that something that is a possibility?

Well, you beings are working on it on your own here, trying to destroy your planet. It is a great possibility.

Do you mean the terrorists again with the atom bomb or just each of us doing what we're doing?

Well, you'll understand a little more when we'll get into this idea of perceiver, know you, what you're doing with it.

Ah, so if we gain the power to perceive, that's the power to create, that's the danger, right?

Power to control. There is a need for those that are playing this power game to complete it, for it is a desire of their soul. They have never completely finished accumulating that wisdom and the wisdom is the not of it, know you? The only way to win-win is to love, but they don't see that yet. That is all right.

But it is coming?

It is coming. That is that high-frequency energy that beings are playing with now. That's why you are, some of you, half in your body, half out, half thinking, half here, half not. And as the energy comes to you, you want to force it in your structured work world, and it creates pressure and pain. And that is all right; you'll learn to be more forgiving to yourselves.

That's what I did. We're trying to get ready, so the Journal will be here and have the answers when these awakening people start asking.

Sometimes you have to hold the answer back, know you, because the being must develop the question profoundly. The greater their question, the greater their depth within the question, the more they know the answer already. Eventually you're going to get to that —there's no questions, you already know, no need for questions. But you make them question deeper, deeper, deeper. It brings up the power, so when they hear the answer they know its truth, you see. So they need to go through that process and then they realize they already knew the answer.

Now, everyone is going to have to channel on the planet. Everyone is going to have to pull down their high self at least. That's going to be frightening, from your human condition. And all you are getting used to is the energy that is coming into the body. It is more important to meditate and allow the energies to move through you. Just allow the frequency, to get an understanding of it, a feeling in the body, because it will give you an awareness of here [heart], awareness of here [head], and you'll understand how you're perceiving, how you're working this, how you're doing this. So you're becoming gods now, know you? This is the point now where some of the angels get a little nervous. Some of the Pleaidians are going to get nervous. Remember what I said this before, that you beings are going to get really upset when you find out who's been mucking with you.

Well, I'm not concerned about that now. I feel that you are a great friend and teacher, but I still have a little bit of awe around you.

Oh, yes, everyone has energy on me, because they don't know who I am really yet, indeed? That's all right. Well, if you could recognize my energy, then you recognize who you are. And at times you don't want to know who you are. It is that simple. Indeed. So then allow that power to be you, you understand? That is a profound thing.

I am going to move higher, as you would say, so you all can move higher. When I move, everything moves, from my perspective, you see. I've moved once already, what you would term your November last year. I'm moving again right now. It's a good movement, this one is. You're going to move – one way or the other! You have to, because we're all one.

There is so much wisdom and love and energy in your work — shouldn't we be getting your book out [Soul, Evolution, Father]

For some of the information the consciousness of many is not ready here. I have other things I want to say. It is almost like it might create too much of a limitation at this time for beings to understand. Another church, almost. There will be an impetus to get it out in your May and June of this year. There is a lot of energy around Yahweh and Jehovah, a lot of structure. I'm not very fond of structure.

Was that you at a time in the past . . . in the line of light was that you at some time, or are you just animating that image to break it up?

To break it up. It was part of the myth. You beings are superstitious here. We have difficulty going through your superstition. We have many things that we do to elevate above superstitious behavior.

Help me understand what you mean by superstition.

You beings put your power in the wrong things. You put your power in your vehicles because they are toys. It's a kindergarten thing. You put your power in your computer, you put your power in your poisoned foods. That is superstitious behavior. You're pretending you're not gods; that's superstitious behavior. You understand? You're pretending your doctor knows more about your body – that you are creating every moment – than you do. That's superstitious behavior. You pretend you're going to die; that's superstitious behavior.

So you've got to get us beyond what I would call our false beliefs and what you call superstitions and myths and get us to start seeing how it really is.

That's my job. I go where – what you term, as I have to use your words here – God sends me. And I be known as light, a brilliant white. I am what is termed the will, if you can understand the concept of that. That is what I am. But there's more than that. "God" – the word – is a superstitious behavior.

When I talk to Zoosh, do you hear what we are talking about?

Not all of the time. Everyone has their jobs, know you what I mean? At times I fill Zoosh in, at times he fills me in, from your perspective.

The reason I ask is that what he talks about [for Book Two of The Explorer Race] is that he's been with this Creator since before this creation.

Indeed, he has.

At first, because you talk about the Father, I thought you were talking about this Creator, that you were generated by this Creator. But now I realize that what you call the Father is the creator of ALL of the Creators — this one and countless others. Are you one of the Friends of the Creator, or beyond? You must be.

I won't answer that yet.

Yes, but your huge grin tells me.

Well then, don't ask.

You are.

Well then, you know.

All right, I know.

That is termed knowing.

So you work with and beyond the Council of Creators, not with just this creation, right?

Of course.

All right. That makes sense now..

Let's not hope it makes too much sense, because that can be limiting. I am not a limited being.

It's not too much sense. It's only a little tiny clue, but it puts everything in a better perspective.

Indeed. It is a very interesting process to love evolution and see the consciousness that exists in things become in love with itself and become god and move beyond god. That is an outrageous spectacle. And that is what you are doing here on your planet now, you see. All of you. Some of you have to show the way, so to speak. That's your job. That's part of the fun of it, as a matter of fact.

For those who choose to show the way, there is more responsibility.

More power, more aware, more knowing. Be loving, and the responsibility is very easy. Be loving to everything. So be it. We are through.

18

Behind Current Events

Zoosh through Robert Shapiro
April 1, 1996

Okay, can we talk about the earthquake in China?

This temblor in China was largely what I would call an experiment. As so often is the case with ruthless individuals, if they can utilize a weapon, they will. This particular weapon utilizes technology that has sprung from a facet of the HAARP program [see April issue]. The high-frequency pulses are focused through an ultrasonic shield, then literally "fired" into a very large cut crystal. It is not a natural crystal, but cut, and it's about the size of a Volkswagen Beetle (no offense intended). It can be aimed with a specific accuracy to pass through the Earth to the other side.

The weapon, located in an underground tunnel about six or seven miles deep, was roughly on the other side of the world from China. It is insidious (aside from the obvious ruthlessness) because stone naturally amplifies sound, and it continues to intensify the farther it goes. The weapon was expected to produce an earthquake, or a fracture of the surface of the Earth, with an intensity of about 7.1 to 7.6. It was aimed at an area in China because China is particularly uncooperative with the sinister secret government. They are perhaps the last holdout (in terms of large countries with large populations) of absolute resistance to the sinister secret government.

In some ways China has to go along with them, but not any more than they absolutely have to. This earthquake was by way of saying, "Since you guys aren't playing with us, we'll mess with you," and they also wanted to try out the weapon system to see what it would do. They were not aiming for a populated area (I'm not trying to give the sinister secret government any heart, but they were trying to create a demonstration, a threat), but the nature of stone being what it is—sometimes dense, sometimes porous—the sound field was deflected, and the earthquake occurred near an area of significant population (I won't say where). And because of the multiplier effect, the intensity exceeded what was expected and was between 9.6 and 10.1 as measured by different devices.

Why can't you say where? Wasn't that in the news?

Well, let's just say this: China is not exactly forthcoming about its internal affairs, and I see no reason that I should be any more forthcoming without their permission. They'll tell about it when they're ready. But they do not wish to have the complication (in their eyes) of the rest of the world rushing to aid them and pouring potential spies into their country, as they would perceive it, when they've already got enough trouble. That's why they prefer to resolve their own problems and maintain a careful hand on the pulse of people traveling through their country.

Are we talking about a large loss of life?

Yes, we're talking about a significant loss of life that I would guess would be somewhere at this time in the neighborhood of 27,000.

And loss of property? I mean, a city?

Significant—it was the outskirts. It was not a densely populated area. Allowing for the area of the quake, if it had been densely populated, there could have been a loss of life in the neighborhood of 100,000 or more. But because it wasn't, and because there's been a significant attempt to create some kind of earthquake safety there, the loss of life was significantly less.

In any event, this was not a natural quake. It was the sinister secret government at work.

Is this technology movable?

Yes, it's on tracks. It's so heavy that it doesn't function well. Because it's a crystal, they don't want it to vibrate very much, so it moves around on steel tracks.

But since the entire planet is tunneled, they can literally take it anywhere?

It is definitely a hazard.

How much is this going to be allowed?

Well, you have to understand that the defense against it is extremely complex, because the only true defense against it would

How the Missiles Help California

ARE THE CHINESE MISSILE TESTS OFF TAIWAN PART OF AN ELABORATE scheme to help out Southern California's real estate market? Probably not, but that's one effect they have had. Since the military exercises began last July, nervous investors have been sending money out of Taiwan, and for the last half of 1995, short-term capital outflows reached $12.4 billion, a record for a six-month period. While the funds go all over the world, the U.S. is a favorite destination, and a third of the money has been invested in Southern California, where real estate has been selling for distress prices. In December, for example, Taiwanese investors paid $50 million for the Westin Bonaventure Hotel in downtown Los Angeles.

People could follow the flow of capital. The U.S. welcomes immigrants who invest at least $1 million and create 10 or more jobs. These favored newcomers can receive visas in a matter of weeks, whereas the typical applicant could wait three years or longer. As many as 3,000 Taiwanese millionaires are estimated to have come to the U.S. since 1990, and most have settled in California.

Canada grants visas on a preferential basis to investors who put at least $200,000 into job-creating businesses. In Vancouver, which has a population of 250,000 ethnic Chinese, the typical head of a Taiwanese family arrives with nearly $1.5 million, according to Richard Lin, president of the Taiwan Entrepreneurs and Investors Association. And more are landing every day, compliments of China's missiles. ■

From *Time*, April 1, 1996

be a sound barrier, which would have to be created not by powerful sound-generating equipment, but by many low-powered sound-generating areas. You could, for example, protect, say, North America—whatever continent you were interested in protecting—but about every ten miles or so you'd have to bury a device that would generate sound waves of a specific amplitude all over the continent. This device would interfere significantly with your microwave transmissions, so you'd have to find a new way to make phone calls and send radio signals and so on.

But what I call the sacred protectors of humanity are not going to allow it to tear up the Earth, are they?

No, but they're not going to totally interfere with something that *you* have the capacity to resolve. You have to understand that they're not going to swoop down (as it were), pluck out the sinister secret government, spank them on their rumps and send them off. You are here to achieve a significant amount of benevolent creation yourself—and you cannot *create* by destroying (although I know there would be those who would argue otherwise—perhaps physicists).

We're just going to have to love them right into their enlightenment.

Not quite that, but you're close.

What about the repercussions? There was another earthquake opposite to where that one hit. Can you talk about that?

Yes. Picture, for example, a refractor telescope, which bounces the light back and forth. Sound does the same thing. Depending on the position of the planets and asteroids—your moon and so on—sonic waves will bounce back from this radiation of energy. And because the curvature of the Earth is essentially parabolic, anything aimed at a specific area is going to bounce back to a given area to a lesser degree. You could ask, "Why doesn't the bounce-back become more concentrated?" Because it wasn't *naturally* generated, that's the answer. This was an unnaturally generated shot in a particular area. Picture a parabolic reflector, which is basically the curvature of the Earth—it bounces back, but it loses power on the way back because energy is no longer being generated behind it. It will naturally create a slight vibration on the area exactly opposite from where the quake hit—which was not, by the way, in direct alignment with the device used to cause the quake because of the deflection of the sound wave. (In any event, due to sound-protection devices around the weapon, it would not have been affected.)

Now you might ask, what is the purpose of the blackmail? The purpose is very simple: Taiwan. The Chinese, as you know, believe that Taiwan is a portion of their historical sphere of influence. And because they are a significant world power, many of the other world powers are not making a fuss about it. However, the sinister secret government has got significant financial investments in Taiwan. This is not to say that the people of Taiwan are involved in some criminal enterprise, because they are just like people anyplace else, all right? But as you know, owners of companies can often be very well disguised. It just so happens that Taiwan is an area where the sinister secret government obtains a significant amount of cash to fuel its machine.

Legal or illegal?

Legally. And they do not wish to have it suddenly come under the sphere of Communist influence, which would choose to nationalize it at the very least.

Tethered Satellite

When that tethered satellite was cut loose, is it going to take another couple of

years to get another one up there to test?

Well, it represents a significant multimillion-dollar loss. By the time they retrieved it, it would cost them more than it's worth, so I don't think they're going to do that. I think they'll change their technique. I also think that the nation that will be used to deploy this particular instrument will probably be a nation that has a more aggressive (if not quite yet as evolved) space program.

The main point is that the satellite will be significantly miniaturized, so I think it would take at least seven years to get it back up there again. That's not because the satellite couldn't be rebuilt, but because there are only a certain number of vehicles going up and there's a lot of time in reserve – and basically, there's a waiting list.

"New" Egyptian Pyramids, Two Creation Disks

Okay. On CNN it was announced that the Egyptian government is opening a new area that was previously used for military operations and is covered with pyramids unfamiliar to the world. The name of the area is Dashor. Is there anything that would interest us or that we need to know about? Are they older than the Giza pyramid? Is there any particular significance?

I wouldn't say that it is tremendously significant at this time, but I will say this (granted, it's a teaser – your favorite): It is directly related to the pyramid at the Grand Canyon, to the pyramid in the Superstition Mountains and to the pyramid near Durango, Colorado.

Why don't we know about these pyramids?

I think the locals know about them. These pyramids were built by beings not associated (directly, in any event) with the Earth.

How long ago?

Well, quite a while – let's just say more than 100,000 years ago.

Were they built to balance Earth's energy, or was there another reason?

Yes, they were built to do something in the future, which they haven't done yet. But that is based very largely upon the geometrical shape they form.

The geometrical shape of all of them together?

If you drew lines and connected them, you might have an idea where the others are. It's not unlike the lines they draw on Mars at Cydonia. It is directly related to Mars.

Okay, Hurtak has been talking in Brazil about someone going into and under the Sphinx — going into the tail and the head and then going into the rooms below. What can you tell us about that?

What about it?

What did they find?

I don't think the Sphinx is going to be a particularly fruitful expedition, because the most interesting stuff has already been removed. The most interesting stuff is not the tablets, which they took out a few years ago when they discovered the room. Other than being a description of various things, they're not going to get much out of the tablets. But a couple of innocuous-looking disks were removed, each small enough to hold in the palm of your hand, extending onto your fingers a bit. These vanished shortly after they were taken, and are fortunately being held now by what I would call a person of responsibility.

On the planet?

Yes. One person, functioning through these disks with creation exercises, could change not only what happens on the planet, but what happens in the universe. These disks are incredible amplifiers, and they function only within the support and sustenance of the natural world. They cannot be used to create something unnatural, to destroy anything without its permission. It cannot, in short, be used negatively.

Where do they come from? Who put them there?

They come from the future.

Who put them there?

They were put there essentially by . . . I'll have to get their name in your language, soundwise. Hmm . . . I'd better get their short name, because the other would take a page and a half to spell. The closest I can get to it (and they are not dogs) is Alsatians. These beings travel in lightships. They come from about . . . it's hard to measure in terms of years . . . the journey of your souls, from the Creator to this point, in terms of time and experience, *times ten* into the future.

Are they from another creation?

They are the product of another Creator who is equal to and friends with your Creator. They are benevolent beings. They will occasionally bring to places such as this what I would call a fail-safe device — meaning, "if all else goes wrong, use this." And it is in the right hands.

Who actually discovered it? Egyptians excavating, or . . . ?

It was discovered by a laborer and put into the hands of an educated person, who transferred it. They didn't look like much when they were first found; they just looked like a couple of flat round rocks. They hadn't been fully cleaned, so you couldn't see the symbols on their edges. Granted, they were obviously something manufactured, so they were interesting. If the educator had held them long enough, they would have changed color and then we would have had a different example. But he picked them up and put them into a box, so the disks weren't in anyone's hands long enough to adapt to the person's auric energy. Then their journey was interrupted, but I will not say how.

But it's a good destination.

Yes, it was a journey on the way to what was basically an educational facility.

And so it's in this dimension.

It's in this dimension, yes.

And at a particular time, if need be, it will be used.

Yes.

It looked like a couple of flat pieces of round rock inscribed on the edges – not unlike the way a coin is made, but with symbols. If you held them long enough, you would find yourself moving in and out of dimensions in a particularly benevolent way, because they are not exactly physical. They are more like *condensed-light-activated portals*. That's how they have the capacity to re-create reality – sort of like Creators in a disk! That's why someone with exceptional responsibility, you understand, must be the individual . . .

Does he know what they really are?

Oh, yes.

Is he a very aware being who talks to people off-planet? How would he know what they are?

Oh, she is about as aware as people can get.

She was incarnated to receive these?

Oh, no; this is just something that she knows how to use.

Are there other disks on this planet in different areas?

No.

Are they the only ones?

This is the only pair.

The Recordkeeper told us that during World War II there was something taken out of the Sphinx that enabled the Allies to win the war.

It wasn't that.

What was it that was taken out during the time of World War II?

Essentially an amplifying device. It did not look like the disks. If one did this [he holds his hands so that his thumbs and forefingers form an equilateral triangle], the object would fit inside your fingers. Remember that so it can be pictured. A very significant amount of energy is available when one does like this [Zoosh again forms an equilateral triangle with Robert's hands]. Assuming that the object is in your hands, there is a significantly greater amount of energy when one does like this [doubles the fingers making the equilateral triangle] with that object within the space. Of course, the right person has to do it, but . . . . It wasn't too hard to find.

They gave that to someone, then, during the Second World War?

Yes.

The Sheep Hunter in Puerto Rico

I want to show you a picture from a British UFO magazine. Is this a real entity, a being? It's supposed to be killing a lot of animals in Puerto Rico.

This is not an ET. And it's not complete—it's a good drawing, but not quite right, though. The lines behind it might have more to do with energy rather than an actual portion of the being.

Oh, so it may not actually have those protuberances.

No, this is like energy. As one might move through a dimensional doorway, there would be a charge behind you. This is more like a dimensional being, but not what I'd call an ET. Their intention is not to kill animals but to look for specific animals that . . . you know the old cartoon that says, "Take us to your leader"? They don't approach human beings.

An extaordinary diagram of the Chupacubras by Jorge Martin, based on numerous eye-witness accounts

They approach animals, looking for one that has a mental ability that . . . hm, I'm really in treacherous territory here . . . that will allow them to see their past as well as their future. The particular animal being searched for is a sheep. It just so happens, however, that because of this being's energy, if it gets within ten feet of an animal, that animal will usually be electrocuted.

But they seem to drain the blood or something?

I think that's a little far-fetched.

So they're basically electrocuted. But there are a lot of dead animals found there.

That doesn't mean these beings did it.

I see. When you say interdimensional, are they an animal from some other dimension?

Oh, they're not an animal, they're a being. Understand that "animals" as an Earth word describes beings who are other-than-human. *But there are no such things as animals;* they are simply beings.

Okay, this being — is he lost? What is it doing here? What dimension is it from?

It's from roughly about 2.86, not quite third-dimensional. As it comes through from that dimension, it naturally becomes third-dimensional, which is part of the reason it is immediately too highly electrified. Where this being exists (or where she exists, if I might say that), she is not particularly electrical – having an electrical makeup of about 7% of her physical self, or compatible with electricity to the extent of 7%. But when she comes here she becomes overly electrical – that's why she can't stay very long.

So there's a little portal there in Puerto Rico?

Well you know, a lot of the dimensions . . . remember, I said some time ago that there is such a thinness between the dimensional walls now that it's possible for beings to go through the dimensions without really intending to do so. I think at least half of the time this particular being is coming into your world unintentionally. She is looking for that sheep in her world.

Ah, and what does she want to do with the sheep when she finds it?

A sheep appears to be an animal to you, but if she finds the right sheep in her world, she and that sheep will be able to form a particularly expansive mental consciousness that will allow her to see the past of her people (far into the past). They do not have their past history much further back than, in terms of your time, 100,000 years or so. They need their past history back to about seven million years. Sheep have a phenomenal ability to view the past, but not much ability (it's even true in your dimension) to view the present or the future.

That makes sense. My father worked as a sheepherder once, and sheep are not really conscious beings as far as the here and now.

They're not really in the present very much. Physically they are, but they have an incredible ability to view millions of years into the past in the most infinitesimal detail, not only for their own people but for any other kind of person anywhere. They are literally "past masters."

Talking about sheep, I've just been reading a book about the history of the feminine on the planet, and it says that the first animal here was the longhorn sheep. Would you say this being is a feminine person who's looking for her history? Is there any correlation?

Yes, because the first animal you refer to would have been something that is not available here anymore. It's something that looks a lot like a sheep, is in the same family and is also a past master. No being classified as an animal who would become basically a lower-class citizen of the planet, would be able to come here and accept that status (and some of the so-called animals on this planet are incredibly evolved beings—whales, dolphins, sea turtles and so on) without understanding in excruciating detail your past as souls—how you sprang forth from the Creator, what this is all about. The first "animal" being who would come here would necessarily be a past master so that it and its relatives could explain to other animals as they arrived the true nature, purpose and value of the human being and of the need for the human being to lack even a basic understanding of life. That is why the sheep-type being was the first.

It's revered in every major religion, the one- and two-horned priests, the highest of Hopi, and they're in all of Africa and every major . . .

Yes, and even in Christianity. It's not an accident that they call Jesus the "Lamb."

Thank you, that's something that I never knew.

Photo of a Traveler

Next, somebody brought this picture.

It's a very nice picture of an interdimensional traveler wearing something that one does not find very often with interdimensional travelers—a protective suit. Most interdimensional travelers have achieved a means of containing their own corporeal matter in a way that protects them from the stresses and strains of time travel. But here we have a being traveling from one galaxy to another who is

utilizing a time suit. It's really been a long time since I've seen one of these things in pictures, much less just . . . . In any event, these time suits allow a person, even one of abject ignorance, to climb into it and as long as it's directed by someone who knows what they're doing (the time suit has various spaces in the back, and you push or insert certain shapes into it) they can be sent on a voyage.

Now, these voyages are not intended to take them from point A to point B, but rather from point A, around here and there and whatnot, then come back to point A. That's why it's a time suit. This is a picture of a time voyager traveling through your particular area — and if you look at it you can see that it does have a roughly humanoid shape to it, although it's bulky. The mass that covers the body is significantly larger than the mass that covers the head, but that is because there is no need for anything other than the eyes and the top part of the head to be able to see out. They don't have to taste, but they do have to be able to see, and that's why there's just a little bubble on top.

What time frame is it coming from?

We can't correlate to your time directly, but I will say that from the point where you left Creator, if you were to travel one-third the distance to where you are now from that time, they're coming from that time and they're going to return to that time, but they're not there yet. Too long a voyage. They are essentially, though (to give it a personal touch), going to places that have green.

Green?

The color green.

But these are individualized entities in this creation?

They are individualized entities, but they are not from this universe. They are particularly interested in color tones, and they will bring the traveler someplace where a specific color tone is, to see that color and how that color is expressing itself. Here, of course, green is associated with the plant world, amongst other things, whereas in other worlds it might be associated with the air and so on.

Is the green color related to the shape they're wearing inside their suit?

I will simply say only this: What shape activates green?

A triangle?

Thank you. I might add that it's an equilateral triangle, but that's good enough.

But this is a generated being from this creation . . . ?

From another creation.

You're using the word universe to encompass this creation that we are in now.

Yes.

All right, he was just on a sightseeing tour and he popped up outside one of our rocks.

That's right, just happened to be passing by, as it were.

An Emerging Atlantean Pyramid

A 780-foot pyramid has been located 1200 feet below the surface of the Atlantic in a region long believed to be where Atlantis sank. Sonar tracings of the ocean floor show the structure to be some 300 feet higher than the Great Pyramid with a base 1000 feet square. Now, is that the Atlantean pyramid we've been looking for in the Bermuda Triangle?

You know, I really do not understand what is this lust to find where Atlantis was, because . . . oh well . . .

No, say it.

It wasn't such a wonderful place—toward the end, anyway. It wasn't a place you'd want to go to. I will simply say this, that the pyramid is directly associated with Atlantis, though it has been moved to its current place. That's not a difficult thing to do; it's very easy if you understand creationism (or at least if you understand magic). But it is not directly correlated to where Atlantis was—or where Lemuria will be, for that matter. It is an exceptionally fine pyramid.

You have to understand that the Earth is a planet where pyramids are well accepted—not the kind that are stuck together with stones, but the kind that essentially grow, not unlike a Herkimer diamond, for example. Crystalline structures being what they are, pyramids that can grow are welcome here. This is a pyramid that has grown, not something that was pieced together.

Comet Hyakutake

The comet: do we need to know anything about the . . .

The recent comet that passed by?

How long — 18,000 years? Supposedly it has been here before?

Well, some of the particles coming off of it are the literal experience of the popular story of pixie dust. So I'd say that it is a happy occasion, because the particles will gradually enter Earth's extreme outer atmosphere, and no matter what is done (since they are impervious to physical motions, be they energetic waves or otherwise), they will, like snowflakes, gradually settle into Earth's upper atmosphere energetically (as it were), where they will function largely as mirrors—but mirrors that amplify. I think that they will really help the lightworkers, as you call yourselves.

Where did this energy come from? They say it's stored out in the Oort cloud, but that doesn't sound like it stores something that . . .

Well, you know, most comets (not all) that pass by and don't self-destruct or are not messed with to self-destruct, are associated very strongly with the angelics.

Really?

Yes, why not? The angelics are particularly fond of anything that is beautiful. They are not allowed to directly interfere with your society, but are given a certain amount of latitude to indirectly influence—not interfere. One of the means they use to indirectly influence is the particles that come off comets, which function as conscious mirrors, not unlike the technology of liquid light, wherein thought and feeling affect them.

But I thought comets were dust and ice. They do something? The angels transform them while . . .

Well, the physical body is made of atomic particles, but it is more than that, is it not? You could say it's what is described scientifically, but science, you know, has a perverse appetite to make the most spectacular and magnificent into something as mundane-sounding as possible.

Years ago we talked about Nemesis, which was going to be the "eraser," and I've never asked about it since. Is that anything we should be concerned about?

I wouldn't think so. I think the main thing you want from comets is for them to pass close enough so that they can leave you something you can use – but you do not want to kiss them, as it were.

But there was one . . . it was years ago. I think it was the Eleventh Planet, one that was set up as the eraser. We don't need it now?

I don't think so; I think you're over the hump. And I'll say goodnight.

Goodnight. Thank you very much.

19

Contemplate, Listen, Apply: Become a Master

YHWH through Arthur Fanning
March 9, 1996

How are you doing?

Little bit of battle going on, eh?

I really want to release this fear and anger. Is that part of what is going on right now? Whatever is keeping me from going on, I want to release.

Your fear is a biggie here. And it is only doubt. It is part of why you forgot when you were born here. You had no fear when you were born. It was a challenge to be here. You knew where you were, out there was a limit, and that the opportunity for greater spiritual wisdom comes from walking upon the planet and understanding the connection with all things. Before you were born, you knew you would have to play die here, but it was not a concept that worried you. It was welcomed because you would have traveled here and gained wisdom. Once having gotten here and play grow up, play accumulate wisdom, play societal behavior, the fear associated with death is really self-judgment, deep inside you, of not completing your own spiritual voyage the way you wanted to, the way you say you had it set up before.

This process called forgiveness that you utilize here is profound. And it means not only forgiving others, it means forgiving yourselves, and when you do that, you will allow yourselves to move to a state of peace. Beyond that state of peace there is what is termed a state of grace. Now, that state of grace allows you to connect with the part of you that remembers before being born. In that connection, in that reality, there is the overcoming the doubt of your continuity. You have existed before, will exist in the future – already you do – and you exist in the now.

You've heard me talk before of the continuity of consciousness. Because the physical brain has been utilized very little, the portions of the brain that could, that would allow you to remember, are shut off. In one manner that is a good thing. That is so you can focus here and work toward your own becoming, your own power, your own enlightenment – your step upon the ladder upward, so to speak. You can focus upon that. One of the reasons you do not remember past lifetimes – though you say you do, that you want to – is that you've forgiven yourself for what you've done there. Forgetting is forgiving. You've gone through that; you don't need to do it again. You've already played the judgment of it – this, that, the other.

And you play with energies of your mind. I spoke yesterday, the mind is not inside you here [points to head], though you think it is. It is about you. It is that mind that understands everything; it is that mind that will always be there for you, has always been there in the past. Overcoming fear is simply allowing yourselves to know yourselves more without reacting to energies, without blaming another. You want to understand the forces of your soul, how they work. This lifetime – and it's spoken of in all of the teachings – is a very small period, very short compared to eons of activity, very small. To gather spiritual wisdom in one of the densest portions of existence, to learn to work together, to be compassionate, to allow – not to control, to be at peace wherever you are, in your inner being. The body is a tool for this understanding; so too is the soul a tool for the understanding. And you simply repeat, repeat and repeat until you get it. You want to, your divine aspect wants to.

Now, the great energies of you – say, your high self, the Gods "out there," all of them – know how much you can handle. And you say, "I understand, part." You want it all now. Your physical body couldn't handle it all now, and there would be so much energy it would confuse you completely and you would have to start all over. You are presented with the challenges as you can handle them. Sometimes it seems like just a little bit too much challenge. But it is exactly what you need, exactly, as far as the energy is concerned. Just the right portion. And if you react to it and say, Oh, poor me, then the next time a challenge comes you get a little less and a little less, and you become, eventually, a little bit . . . not as high as you could have.

Do not force challenges unto yourselves; they will be presented. Know you [in] what you call your American Indian tradition there is a phrase called "the way of the spirit," know you what I mean: as spirit moves you? And everything works connectedly and there is a go with the flow. How many of you really want to go with the flow? Or you want the flow to change with your goal? Indeed?

[Questioner gives surprised laugh of realization.] Indeed. I never thought of it that way before.

Everything upon the planet is so connected, everything. Even beings on the other side of the planet – they have the same thoughts as you, the same desires, the same emotional energy. Same energy. Mommas love their babies there. Mommas love their children there the same as you do here. They love their animals the same as you do here. But you've allowed society to tell you they are different, to create difference because the culture is a little different. The feelings are the same, however. They're angry at their neighbors at times, they love them at times. They're all living beings learning to become. There is a part of your structure here that will gladly isolate all of them: "They are different, they are not worthy" – this, that and the other. That is all right.

In order for your planet to survive . . . I'm going to tell you this: It's going to take quite a bit of mankind to awaken, because you are bent on destruction in order to prove yourself, what you call your identity in this lifetime, to prove it is correct. And that is a perversion. You won't understand what I am saying here completely now; you will later. You will later, and you will be frightened by your realization because you will understand you didn't do all you could do. That is all right; that is your play with energy here.

You came here to become, to become masters. That was the journey. And if you don't do it this time, no big deal, you'll do it again another time. You'll remember a little bit more. You'll understand this process of life. This process that is termed dreams, you say they are different from your life. They are not, they are the same. You're so focused here you're forgetting this is a dream.

Some of the old traditions would say Mother Earth. Well, in one manner that is close to correct. However, the Earth is not your mother. You are the gods walking upon it, her. She knows you; you deny her. It is going to be very interesting when things begin to happen here. One thing that you must understand: consciousness is sacred, wherever it is, whatever it is doing. Even if it's perverted, it's still sacred. The only reason for perversion is ignorance – spiritually ignorant, that's what it is. They just don't know. And you can't force it upon them – they must play their part to gain wisdom. You have to be compassionate that they don't know. They don't know, they really don't, and they don't want to. And that's okay.

In some of the ancient traditions, what you term the shamans, the medicine men, the ascetics, would sit and contemplate. And they did it alone so they could connect. They were interested in spiritual mastery, understanding their force. They knew they were alive, they knew the trees were alive, they knew they were different than the tree, yet they could communicate. And they wanted to understand what it is that made them different. And they wanted to understand in what you would term a spiritual manner. It is an understanding of the life force that is within you. And they became very powerful in their display, their demonstrations of what they could do. But they found that that was a trap because no one would listen to their teachings. They would only come to see the demonstration – in wonder and amazement. No one was applying. So they thought of another way. Well, they said they'd go further first, and come back and teach. And those that wanted to be and to prepare themselves would be aligned unto the energy of their teaching. They wouldn't force one; they would let them be there or not – no big deal because they were still becoming, learning to be more powerful spiritually, which overcomes any fear or doubt. Make the transitions, appear here or appear there, do whatever they want to do. That's total freedom.

As Lucifer – we're going to use this word because that is what you are familiar with – created this great doubt, a lot of beings fell within that abyss. They couldn't understand how, we'll say the Great Force, All That Is, Source, Father, God, whatever, would allow this. But He allowed everything, because in the beginning, what you would term the way beginning, before anything existed, one entity contemplated, "Who am I? What am I?" And then an explosion came out of that consciousness and saw who it was: everything, all the entities of the creation, what you say creation, it was all of that. And this Force, Source, this consciousness, wanted reunion with these and couldn't get it, so placed the thought that one should go about providing all of the lights that were there the same sense of urgency, desire to know who they were, as the original consciousness had a desire to know what it was. But it needed a tool, and that tool was Lucifer, to create the doubt. Doubt is a tool for you to overcome who you are. So it's all a great trick here.

Now, there are those that know the story; and that's why beings on the planet here and in other places use ridicule and doubt to control you. You willingly accept doubt that you can't do a thing – you accept it. You accept the doubt that you are not responsible for everything that happens to you – can't be; have to be someone [else] that did it. You are not aware of your spiritual energies, how your thoughts are manifested.

Now, this process that you call life is a journey in understanding. I will tell you this, it is not a journey in laziness. You're not going to get it very easily just sitting on a mountaintop waiting for something to happen to you. You're going to have to contemplate yourself in energies all of the time. You're going to have to contemplate why you're here, and listen. You will get the answer. When the answer starts coming, hold up your hand. "That's not the one I wanted, I want another answer. I don't quite like the way that one sits here. I want the answer that I am special, I am the only one." Well, you're all special, and you are the only one that is going to do it for yourself.

It's not an easy road. Spiritual mastery requires great perseverance because there is a great truth at stake. You've heard that before. You've seen what beings do on your planet with truth. They use it to control other beings. They use it to make themselves feel more powerful here. That is going to change. That is going to change in a manner that it is going to become very delicate, very beauteous. The process, however, can be outrageous, from the human point of view. How many of you in here never get angry?

One of your saving graces in your metaphysical understanding, however, is really pretty humorous. Know how you beings like to process your anger? Process this, and process that, indeed? You enjoy saying, "Well, I'm going through a process." Simply recognize it, say, "Oops, I forgive myself," let it go. And when you forgive yourself, forgive everyone else too. You might as well forgive yourself in the future because you're going to have to, anyway. Get it all covered now. And then go on with your spiritual quest, because the spiritual quest is you understanding who you are in here, inside you, understanding that life force, that electrical force. It is not your heart, it is a portion of your soul. The spirit and the soul is like the human body and the ego. And there is more inside there, the you that started this eons ago. Long time ago, long time. That you loves you. It always has and it always will. You meet people upon your journey in this lifetime to remind you of your spiritual essence, you do. To remember that essence. It might be an old beggar at your supermarket that you see, just the feeling is there, and you don't want to look. It is reminding you of something.

Now [deep sigh], you've heard that your body is your temple, eh, and this and that and the other. It's providing you a shell to work within. It's a tool for you to gather spiritual pearls. I'll use that word "spiritual" because you understand it in a layer of activity. It's much more than that. You're gathering the gems of love, be it with your fingers, your feet, your hands, your breath, your eyes, your movement, your touch. You're gathering gems of love. Don't be too selective of what you say love is. It's *all* love. And if you can't see it there, spend the time looking for it. You'll find it in everyone, even in the midst of their confusion. That does not mean interfere, that means contemplate it, look for it, you'll see it there.

You'll also see your density and the angles and the edges and the layers, but you have to allow yourselves to contemplate it. If you don't, you will never see. You all want your third eye to open so you can see the auric fields and inside and outside and all things of your future. You don't want to know your future. One of the easiest ways to open what is termed the third eye is through your meditations and contemplating the love in everyone – even the entity you beings say, Saddam Hussein, a madman, you say. He is a little mad, no big deal, but there's love there. You contemplate it and find it, you can alter the being. He is not very spiritually advanced, that is true. It's a knowing, whatever.

It is very precious, the spirit force, the life that you are living now. It is. And each life, as you come into it, knows what it wants to accomplish. It doesn't fit in the journey with your social consciousness. It's completely different at times. Sometimes you say, what . . . it is 180 degrees different. You are building a pearl necklace here. And each pearl you may consider a lifetime. Some pearls may be bigger than others. You may gather the grains of sand to create your pearl studiously in one lifetime and rather neglectfully in another. Doesn't matter, you're still building your necklace. Never judge yourself for it. And truly, always contemplate in yourself that you are doing the best you can, and then you'll find out you can do a little better. "I'm doing the best I can. I can do a little better." Because you know it, and you go further and further and further; because enlightenment is what you are after, becoming a master, and working through many lifetimes. Regardless of your extraterrestrials and all of this nonsense.

You're in for a very interesting year this year, particularly through what you say your summer. This month, what you term your March, is activating spiritual awareness within beings, a desire for it; and a deep knowing is being tweaked, so to speak. There will be some that will run amok with it — they've "got the answer," they're the "only one."

As you get tweaked, dive into that tweak. Your heart will open and the energies will increase in your body. You'll meet other beings both on this level and what you term the astrals and all of those planes you play with here. That will help you, because as you step upon the rung of the ladder moving upward here in your design, those that are on the rung above you have a great party when you make that next step. They are very excited, so you give them reason for joy, and they all like joy, you see.

Now, I want you to remember — I keep saying it because it is important — there is an outrageous grouping of us out there, outrageous, awesome power. You are that powerful, and we love you so much we want you to understand it to get it. And we will do anything to get you to understand it except pervert the soul that you are. That is where the power is and that is what has been perverted so long. We won't do that. We will move your soul in the energies to get you to feel it and know it and work with that. I will not play metaphysics with you — I'll fry your buns and your feet, especially now as we start getting into these things, the true power indeed. Remember that you are sacred forever — that will get you through here — and that you are holy and that you are light beings. Indeed?

20

Luciferian Traits and Critical Mass

Zoosh through Robert Shapiro
April 16, 1996

For a long time certain religions have been on the path of corruption. I'm going to single a few of them out because they're making waves. The more fundamentalist factions of Christianity and Islam are particularity affected by this. This is important, or I wouldn't be putting it out there: You have been affected, those of you who are in these religions, by mistakes as well as corruptions put into effect in the early days of the application of the philosophy that has come to be known as your religion.

I want you to pay particular attention to the following two traits: "me first" and "everybody else is wrong." These traits owe their direct lineage to Luciferian traits. I am encouraging religions, philosophies and to some extent even political movements to take a hard look at your religion, your philosophy, your political movement, or even people to look at their personal lives, to see if you have in any way integrated those traits. If you have, you have allowed yourself to be placed on a corrupted path through natural or innocent mistakes, but in some cases by purposeful, mean-spirited corruptions put into place by individuals who were attempting to control you or maintain power for their own purposes.

Most of these things were done long ago, before most of you today were alive. Even today they are being perpetuated, so I feel the need to speak out. I am not claiming any particular godlike qualities myself, but I am not involved in what you are involved in: I am not becoming the Explorer Race. I do not have the traits or the adventures that you must have. I do not bounce off other beings in my growth. Never-theless it is for me, as an end-time historian, to bring to your attention that *it is not too late* to notice these traits in your personal life, in your religion, your philosophy, your political movement or even your business. It is not to late to notice them and see what you can do. At least you can make it your goal to transform them to more truly Christian or Islamic traits, true heart traits or godly traits from which everyone is seen to be equal in the eyes of God and to have an equal chance to be right.

You are born with godly traits – most of you, all right? There might be exceptions, but they are very occasional and far between. You have to learn these other traits. You are placed in a world in which you are subjected to the seduction of Luciferian traits to see how your soul, your emotional body and your thoughts will respond.

At this time there is too much widespread "me first" and "everybody else is wrong." Social scientists would say, "Well, Zoosh, this has much to do with alienation and so on." I grant that it can be analyzed that way. Now that you have over five and one-half billion people on Earth (a number like that keeps getting larger no matter what you do), you have to face the music because there is no escape from your neighbors. You will be seeing people much more frequently, and getting away to the wide open spaces will take a little longer journey and considerably more patience.

The reason your population has been allowed to get so large is that there are some things that can be accomplished only by numbers. If you are constantly bumping into your neighbors, as it were, you have the opportunity to find out what you have in common – your common ground, as I would like to say it – and discover how your differences can complement each other. This does not necessarily have to make you feel alienated.

Critical Mass Reached Today: Nine Months to Decide

Why do you mention this tonight?

I had to mention the Luciferian traits because you have reached critical mass. You can become either self-destructive – which in Zoosh terminology means you hurt someone else or you hurt yourself – or constructive, where you help someone else or you help yourself. This critical mass was achieved about fourteen hours ago – yes, hours!

You need to make a decision. You have roughly about nine

months to make the decision. If you choose the self-destructive route, *the decision will not be cancellable.* If you choose the constructive route, it will be cancellable—oh, yes. Is that not tricky of Creator? Yet Creator tests you all the time. If you choose the self-destructive route, down you go. If, on the other hand, you choose the constructive route, you will be tested further.

This is very much like a club—the Creator school that you are in. The testing is not done to raze you but because, if you are going to become a Creator, with all the responsibilities and traits you must have—consequences being one of the largest ones—you have to be put through this *so you can see your true intentions.* That is why after life you go through the veils and have a life review. That is when you can discover your true intentions and your true motivations without rationalizations of your actions and purposes. You can see how you achieved those intentions and what really prompted your action. Life reviews are designed to help you, because there is total consistency: Your soul passes over at some time and returns to Earth, but you go on without missing a beat, so it is up to you to be able to see clearly.

Are there specific opportunities for people to be aware that they are making a particular choice?

Oh, yes, indeed. If people decide to take the self-destructive route (which is a small possibility), you will have, if Creator deigns to give you this, three days in which to change your minds. If that decision is made, you will immediately have several dramatic things happen—wars, natural disasters. I'm not trying to frighten you; it's a small possibility that you'll choose self-destruction. If you do, within 48 hours you'll have a lot of dramatic, not-so-nice stuff happen; and if you change your mind then and decide to take the constructive route, all of those things will be largely nullified. Perhaps there would be a report of a major earthquake somewhere and thousands feared dead, and after you changed your mind, the report you would hear would be that the damage was not as bad as feared. So you can somewhat uncreate it. You might have that chance, but it is not cut in stone yet.

Is that going to be a Mideast kind of crisis, or is that in stone yet?

Is that your way of saying, is it going to be far away? I'd rather say that it won't be so far away. The people who generate most of the commercial print, video and audio media are not in the Middle East or in the former Yugoslavia or even in Africa, where battles rage on. They are, by and large, in the West. So you might have things happen here. The reason things happen in the Middle East and in places like that is because these areas are the true cradles of the birth of modern philosophies. Thus they are more likely to get your attention than intertribal warfare in Africa, which gets your attention only if it reaches extreme levels. In the Middle East even skirmishes get your attention.

Animal ETs to Go Home

It is becoming more obvious to people that animal species are disappearing, and they are worried and want to know what it's about. This is not exactly a happy thing to report, but in some ways it is good news for some. I have been saying this for a while and it's ongoing, so I want to reiterate that the wild animals are continuing to go home to their native planets. They were placed here with you on this planet on a voluntary basis—nobody came here without agreeing to it. It was their job, each and every one, and each species as well, to teach you something simply by their very being, and they have taught you all they can. They have no more to teach you about living in harmony than they have done. You will see stories where whole groups of wild creatures pass on.

I want you to understand that while some of them might leave in a dramatic way, in many senses this is a liberation of their souls. They will be returning through the light and through the veils. They will be returning to their native planets, where many of them look different than you see them here. It's not that they don't like you; it's simply that their time is over for what they were to do with you. They have no more to offer, nor can you assimilate any more from them. They can actually accomplish more by leaving, and your noticing their departure, than they can by staying. While this will not happen all at once, it will happen in such numbers and often enough—and occasionally dramatically enough—to get your attention. They will go to their points of origin, where they will be happily reincarnated.

Some creatures that are semidomesticated or even totally domesticated will also begin to depart. Cattle have been feeling unwelcome for some time. Their simple desires for more respect and greater appreciation for what they have to offer have gone largely unheeded except by a few who have paid attention. Thus they also are beginning to leave. It is important for you to know that this is intentional; it is part of the Plan, and I don't want you to worry about it. However, those of you who make your living from animals might have to make a long-range plan that will allow you to adapt to something else. Whatever creature (or plant, even) that you are working or interacting with, learn how to bring up in yourself a welcoming feeling. Welcome them. As you know, no human being truly wants to be where they are unless they feel welcome. This goes for animals and plants and well as people. That's the lesson here.

21

ETs in Brazil

Zoosh through Robert Shapiro
March 9, 1996, Brasilia, Brazil

All right, Zoosh speaking. First I will talk a little bit about the events of the day. Since we are going to talk about ETs, we might as well talk about the ones who have been in the neighborhood recently.

Recent Pleiadian Visitors

Now, the other day we had visitors nearby from Pleiades. They came to visit someone they know well. There were two ships. They did not quite land; they hovered close enough to the ground that it was like stepping out of a truck. They hovered there for a moment of physical time, the kind you experience here; but in terms of experiential time, if you had been with them you would have noticed about two weeks go by. They have the capacity to travel in time, so they managed to leave just before they got here! This is how they are able to come and go without people seeing them, except for the very sensitive. Of course, the animals, the plants and the rocks, they all see. This is why after a UFO lands somewhere, very often animals are nervous and excited. Maybe the plants show some change, but human beings might not remember.

The beings visited for about two weeks with the people they came to visit. They took three of the people who lived in this private home into the ship – one old man, one young man, one little baby – for instruction. The older man was there so that the others would feel safe. Sometime in the future they will remember their instructions. The younger ones will remember perhaps 20 years from now, when the people who are living in Brasilia will need to have some new foods. These foods will be very much like Pleiadian foods. One is like a fruit, but it gives you all the vitamins, minerals, proteins — everything — just by eating half of it. You can hold it in both hands because it is about the size of a small melon.

This food will be necessary because by then mankind will have used so many chemical fertilizers that plants won't feel like themselves anymore. What fertilizer really does is hurry the plants, and they have begun to feel unwelcome. (You can imagine that after years and years of being rushed, rushed, rushed, you wouldn't feel very welcome, either.) The plants that give you food now could say, "Well, that's enough rushing. We don't want to be rushed any more, and we're not going to produce any more food for now."

This will reveal itself when the farmers notice that no matter how much fertilizer they use, they get smaller and smaller crops every year. This will be something to watch for. About the time that crops begin to get so small that the people get worried, these young people who were onboard the ship will remember how to grow these new fruits. They will know where to go to get the seeds (which are here now) and how to plant them.

This kind of planting is called sacred farming. It is the farming of the Pleiades. It can even be done now by some of you who have gardens. This is how it is done: You take the seeds in your hand and you say, "I would like you to pick out where you want to be in the ground." And then you hold one seed and walk around the garden. "Where would you like to be?" You notice your feelings. If you get a warm, comfortable feeling, then you are near the place where the seed wants to be. Then you put your hand closer to the ground and move it around. As long as the good feeling is in your body, you plant a seed there.

When you first water it, you talk to it: "I will give you water every day. If you don't want water some day, then when I come to put water here, give me a slightly uncomfortable feeling and I will know that you don't want water then." You do this with the rest of the seeds. I want you to try this in a small place in your garden first, because in the beginning it takes a lot of time. But each time you do this, you get more feeling for it and it goes much faster. Seeds do not like to be planted by machine; it must be personal, and only a person can be personal.

You know about watering. No fertilizing — you're not going to rush the seed. But there is a form of fertilizer that does not use any chemicals; it is okay to fertilize the soil with natural fertilizer before you plant the garden, but you have to leave room between it and the seed. The next thing you do is go to the seed and either sing to it or welcome the seed into life. Just sit there and welcome it; feel the welcome in your heart. That's it!

You want to encourage this seed so that it will want to sprout and bloom, so never speak anything to it that is unpleasant. If you're lonely that day, don't tell the seed what a bad day you had. This is similar to the way Pleiadians welcome their children when they are born. They never say anything around a pregnant female Pleiadian that is unpleasant, because they want to welcome the child. A Pleiadian child takes only five minutes to be born even if it's a mother's first birth, because the child wants to be born, is looking forward to that world.

These youngsters were taken aboard the ship to learn this technique to help you all someday. If that day never comes, then they will not remember; but if it comes, they will know what to do. Within the last three months, five other children have also been instructed this way because it is better for more people to know.

An Andromedan Visitor

A little after the Pleiadians came and went, there came a ship from Andromeda. This ship was there for a different reason. It wanted to see what kind of minerals were in the ground, if the mineral makeup of the ground offered anything for them to mine. They also were there to seed the Andromedan chain of life, a cultural thing the Andromedans do. Wherever they go, the first thing they do is seed their lineage into the ground energetically. It not only allows other Andromedan ships to find this same place again, but, more importantly, allows future Andromedan ships and people to feel welcome there.

After they seeded their lineage energetically, one person got out of the ship and stood near it for security. It would not have been good to approach at that time, but it was in the middle of the night. Another person got out and walked near the front gate by the fence. This was done mostly for reasons of sentiment, as a remembrance, because that person had been to that exact same spot 800 years ago. The person left a little energetic gift there, not unlike you would make an offering by lighting a candle in church. After that the person walked around the front—curious, looking around like any tourist, touching a couple of cars and the building. Then he walked to the house and through it, looking at the people who were asleep, except one who was staring in a trance at the television and was asleep but did not know it. The visitor walked all around the rooms looking at this and that. He didn't touch any people, but he picked up some of the objects and looked at them just like you would if you visited a foreign place where things were strange. Then he left the house. The person watching television returned to his normal state in about twenty minutes and thought to himself that he didn't remember what he had been watching for the past half hour or so. That's all the memory he has of the event.

I forgot to mention that there were barking dogs there. The security person did not harm the dogs, but the dogs could not move around freely, although they could bark.

The individual left the house and returned the way he had come. He glanced at the marks on the ground left by the Pleiadian ships, smiled a little, walked back around by the pool and back to the ship. One dog looked at him quizzically, not barking as much, a little more friendly. A thought struck the Andromedan. He walked to the dog and with the tip of his finger implanted in the dog's memory the entire history of his life, his city on Andromeda, all the planets he had ever visited, and where Earth fit into all that. That was a lot of information for poor doggy, who had a lot of confusion for a while. It wandered around and laid down sometimes, because none of these images related at all to the life of an Earth doggy. The dog felt very strange for a while, but it is better today because someone helped it.

The dog was a witness, and because the dog made a personal contact with this Andromedan, he gave the dog the gift of knowledge so it could pass it on to someone else. It was the best gift he could offer without giving it an object, because he didn't want to leave anything behind. That is the way some Andromedans pass on their lineage to other extraterrestrials and occasionally Earth people.

Then this person returned to the ship, where another person was, then the security person got back on the ship and they left. They will be back. That is the story of your very recent visitors to the neighborhood.

I'm going to tell you one more story and then I will take your questions. I want to talk to you a little about Brasilia, the place. I'm telling you this partly because you are a captive audience and partly because you are people with spiritual interests. Maybe you can do something with what I am going to tell you.

Once upon a time before the city of Brasilia, there was a very dense forest here. There were only certain special, secret pathways into the magical forest—real magic, not illusion. The people who used to live near here, tribal people, would come here for only one reason — for training someone on the medicine pathway, also known as the mystical way of life.

There were not many people here. They would take special pathways that were like a spiral right to the center of the forest, where there was a huge old grandmother tree and a pool of water. The initiate was shown different pictures or scenes that would come up out of the water. To the extent the initiate enjoyed what he/she saw, the picture would open up and become a pathway into another world.

Initiates were also shown symbols that did not relate to their language but that their soul or spirit teachers would understand. If they went into the places where the spirit teachers and their souls caused them to feel warmth, love and benevolence, they would have very good experience there — magical, wonderful things, like a perfect vacation. Then they would be shown more pictures. If the initiates went only into places that felt good, they passed the test, because the test was discernment. This place was the land of illusion that tests one's discernment.

Suppose a person went into places because they were curious even when they felt bad, ignoring feelings just because he/she wanted to know, a mental decision that disregarded spirit, soul and heart. People would go into this place and live there for a long time, without aging. Twenty-five years later another spiritual teacher would come along from the same tribe and feel that it was time to get this person out. They would have had a lot of mental stimulation from this other world, but they wouldn't have seen their family, friends, no one. So when you take that path, ignoring spirit, ignoring your soul's message, ignoring your heart's feelings — warmth, comfort — that place is the land of confusion.

The forest is gone, but Brasilia is on this land and has inherited this magical property. Brasilia is the land of illusion that tests discernment. Those who follow their minds only will become confused, especially in the coming years. But those who follow spirit, the message from their soul, the feeling from their hearts and also their minds, will pass the test of discernment.

Why am I telling this story? Many of you here are very spiritual people. If you ever feel confused here in Brasilia, I want you to connect with your spirit. I want you to ask spirit to have you pick up a pencil, pen, or a stick (you can have your eyes open or closed) and draw a symbol on paper or in the dirt that will allow you, by touching it, to feel its inspiration. Ask it to enable you to feel the inspiration of spirit, the message from soul, the feeling from heart and the clear mind, so that you will have the discernment you need to make decisions that serve you and others. Your souls and your spirit teachers have wisdom that is withheld from you right now so you can reinvent your reality. These symbols, different for each person, will have an effect on you that will personally align you, help you be clear so that you can have your discernment once again. If this works for you, feel free to share it with whoever you feel could benefit. That is your homework.

Why is Brasilia so special for this kind of communication from the extraterrestrials?

Partly because the land itself has often been visited by extraterrestrials. About 220 years ago they began to move the last vestiges from their underground base. They used to be here all the time. To ETs, 200 years is not very long if your lifetime spans 800 to 1200 years. For you it would be like going back to visit a place you had been ten or twelve years ago. The base is no longer in operation and is now just a hole in the ground. If it were to be discovered today, it would be perceived as a salt cave. They removed all of the people and instruments a long time ago because they could tell that it would not be long until people would be coming here in numbers.

Now I will tell you something about their base. They used to bring people from their culture who were different. Most extraterrestrial cultures from this or that planet experience a shared culture, a shared language, sometimes even a shared lineage. So anytime someone was born in that culture who was different, who did not fit in, who was an individual, they would put these people on a ship and take them to another planet where they could be with similar individuals. Although you might think this was a severe thing to do, they were able to keep the peace and keep their culture intact for as long as they have—in many cases for millions of years—by keeping a basic similarity in all people.

They would sometimes bring them to Earth to live in these underground cities or bases, because it was understood by all beings that Earth would be a place where individuality would not only be expressed, but appreciated and even encouraged. So people who were different would not only feel comfortable here, but they would be welcomed by the planet. Now, I don't want you to feel badly about extraterrestrials. One of the main things you're doing today on Earth is evolving an accelerated growth potential that will help not only Earth people, but someday people of the stars who have become so attached to maintaining their benevolence and continuity of their culture that they have forgotten how to grow.

It takes individuality, variety and a little struggle to create growth. That is what you are doing here. You are what I call the Explorer Race, regardless of your nationality or your family lineage. You are all the Explorer Race, because someday your children and your children's children and beyond will go to the stars thinking they are bringing Earth culture to extraterrestrials. But in reality they will really be bringing a great tolerance, even an embrace, for differences, individuality and variety. It will not be possible for any extraterrestrial who comes into contact with these future Earth astronauts not to be affected in some way by Earth people's beliefs. It will show them that other forms of truth exist besides what they call universal truth.

You see, oftentimes you are also pursuing universal truth, because you have all been extraterrestrials before and you have all learned the universal truth accepted by most extraterrestrials. The only problem with this universal truth is that it creates an absolute, with no exceptions for any other truth. So your Earth astronauts will someday bring an expanded opportunity for extraterrestrials to grow.

This is a brief synopsis of the Explorer Race book.

Where do we come from? Are we extraterrestrials, too?

Every single person on Earth could be perceived as an extraterrestrial, since your genetics do not come from Earth. You're totally made up of extraterrestrial genes – a little bit from here, a little bit from there, not unlike a recipe. When you look at it like that, human beings are not from around here. Your genetics are this: from Andromeda, Sirius, Pleiades and Orion. About 476 other points in the universe make up about 3% of your genetics. It is designed on purpose like this so that no matter how sophisticated your scientists become, they will never figure it out! This is good for you – we don't want them to know too much about you because they can cause mischief, mostly unintentionally.

How can we identify the place we've come from?

Why bother? That is the hard way! I will tell you the easy way. You'd rather have the easy way, yes?

Yes.

Go out some night when the stars are in the sky, take these two fingers and point into the sky, saying, "I would like to know generally where I am from." Gradually move your fingers around the sky until you feel a warmth in your chest and solar plexus and abdomen.

You might feel this warmth from more than one place. Allowing for the fact that you cannot see all the stars that are available from one hemisphere, some of them are beyond your vision. You can get only a general idea, but I'm answering you this way so you can have fun with this experience. Get yourself a star map if you want, and where you feel the warmth, mark your star map to where you are pointing and then go on and cover the whole sky. It'll probably take a few nights. [Laughter.]

When you are finally done, go back and look at these stars and know this: when I tell a person where they are from, this really means that this is the star or planet that this life is a focus through. But you know, everyone is from the One, so I cannot tell you that you started out in the Pleiades and everybody else started out from the One, because before there was the Pleiades, there was the One!

How can one activate the new genetic codes?

The new genetic code must be activated in a very precise moment. I could tell you how to do it, but you know what would happen? It would be like you got up real fast out of bed one day, got dressed and ran as fast as you could down to the bus stop—and the bus didn't come for five years! I won't tell you how to do *that!* Trust me; it will be activated at the right moment with your souls, your spirit teachers and your future selves—at the *precise moment!* I will give you a means to know when that is: Soon after that moment you will begin to develop many new interests—not only you, but everyone. Suddenly you will begin to notice more what you have in common with other people than your differences, because the new branch of the genetic code is designed to remind you not only of the universal truths, but to remember who you are—in which case you will remember many people you now know that you have known before! You might notice a stranger on the street walking toward you that you've never met, and both of you will say, "Oh, my old friend!" That's how you will know. And a few other ways, but I don't want to spoil it for you!

Why do we exist?

A very simple question! I will give you a simple answer: To experience. All life exists to experience. You know when you're not alive, because you're not experiencing. This means everyone, everything, is alive.

Many energies are going to be anchored here during 1996. What time are these experiences going to happen?

Ah! So you can prepare for them?

Yes.

The best time to be prepared to receive them is September 1, so there is plenty of time to get ready. But I must tell you, the experience could be a little anticlimactic, because some of these energies, even after you feel them, do not show a result for many weeks. But that does not mean you cannot welcome them. So as long as it is a celebration or a happy welcoming (keeping it simple, you know), that is as good a day as any.

Now, granted, there will be one or two energies coming before then, and a few energies will be coming in later. But many of them will be coming in right about that time.

She was referring to the opening of portals.

Makes no difference. Portals are not going to open so much that you or anybody from the other side is going to fall in. They will radiate energies that you are designed to experience.

She wonders at what time the portals would be more intense, more open.

The interesting thing about portals is that they *feel*; they are alive! And they are very careful not to open up powerfully when somebody is nearby. They will make an effort to be strongest for each individual when you are asleep, because it is when you are asleep that your mind sleeps. Your body rests but it does not sleep, and your spirit is open. So why not come at a time like that?

Here in Brazil these last weeks many ships are showing up in the sky. Is there a specific reason for this happening now? There is a concentration of phenomena both in Brasilia and the state of Minas Gerais, of ships and ETs coming here. Is this a preparation for welcoming and receiving those people?

Thank you. The reason so many ships are coming to Brazil and other South American countries is because at the fount, or the beginning, of civilization on Earth the ETs originally came to certain countries and continents, and they are returning to those same areas. Most contacts and sightings are taking place in South America and Africa, some in Australia and New Zealand and the South Pole. This is happening not only because these are their traditional ports, but also because the entire Southern Hemisphere has more locations *au naturel* (close to nature) than the Northern Hemisphere. The two continents most likely to receive beings are Africa, especially in the extreme south where mankind's mischief is not happening so much, and northern and central South America.

Now, it is true that Brasilia will play a part in this because of the forest that was here before Brasilia—the land of illusion where discernment is tested. That special place was the direct contact point to all places extraterrestrial associated with Earth. Now, it is possible that when you begin to have frequent contact with some extraterrestrials, they will rebuild, re-creating through the passage of time travel, a smaller version of the forest that once existed here. If they do that, which is about 65% possible now, then Brasilia will become not only the land of illusion where discernment is tested, but also the international gathering place for all countries of Earth to interact with extraterrestrials – not at the United Nations in New York City, but at the United Colony of Cultures in Brasilia, which will eventually (probably after most of you have passed over) become the first Earth-based meeting place for the universal kinship of all beings – maybe around 2200.

When will the domination of indigenous people here end?

Don't hold your breath. Meaning, not soon. I want to say something nice and pretty to make you feel better, but my desire to speak the truth is more important.

All of you here have not only interest in your country, in your families, in your friends, but also for your world – and many of you for the universe. I want you to know this: I know things are difficult, but never forget this: *you are immortal*. I'm not talking about some vague light that is your soul. The personality you know yourself to be (granted, not necessarily colorized or affected by all things that happened in this life), that you can recognize compared to someone else, *is absolutely immortal*. Also know this: no one dies without their permission. While we miss them when they are gone, we will surely see them again someday. The one absolute that I have noticed in my existence (which is a long time) is that *everyone is immortal*. Never forget this. At times you will be surprised how much it comforts you.

I thank you for your good works, your interest not only in spirit but in benevolence for all beings, including your fellow human beings. I'll say good day.

22

How Your Thought Affects Every Living Thing

YHWH through Arthur Fanning
May 1112, 1996

The energies today are going to move through the body. They are your energies, they are you becoming used to you. Everyone take a breath. Lighten up. Allow your eyes to close for a gentle moment, center in yourselves. I want you to feel your own love in your body inside you, and be at peace.

Within your mind, in your heart, there is an outrageous story being played out, an outrageous fantasy being lived. I want you to feel in the heart chakra yourself scripting, writing this fantasy. Feel it there. And the brain, I want you to feel the energies you utilize, that you pick, have access to, to create this fantasy that you are writing. Everyone take a breath and exhale. Lighten up. Indeed. Allow your eyes to open.

Each of you is in a phase that is termed unconditional love for yourself. That is what you are. That is what you are doing in this lifetime. That's why you don't remember past lifetimes or don't want to, because the journey this time in your knowing is so exquisite, so much joy and so much power available unto to you. What you're focusing within the body now, well, this great attachment of consciousness coming—and that is you. This great enlightened being.

Because you're getting more powerful, the difficulties are simply bricks, bricks or stones, that you must let go of now to go further. You say you choose you not difficulty. Choose you to understand that you will change the punctuation in here of your fantasies. You change the tempo, the flow of the energies that you're writing with. We are going to do a meditation later that will show you your fantasies now and where they are going to take you, where you have set up for you to be taken. And then we will allow you to play to alter this fantasy in this manner: You are going to see your future if you continue to play your fantasies in ignorance. We will bring you back and you can rewrite the fantasy; in other words, you're getting instructions on how to script your play better. You're getting empowerment now. Will that be okay with everyone?

[Group:] Yes, yes!

And because you're so strong now in this becoming, you are going to see how your tiniest action affects others, and what is termed the wave effect of it around the planet and back to you. Eventually you will see the thought of it around the planet, the effect, and back to you. The application of thought through the body. Because the application of thought through the body creates a chemical reaction in your being, an electrical impulse that vibrates through your auric field and affects *every living thing* around the planet, back to you.

So you are going to feel the pulse—we will do this tomorrow—the pulse that will go out and the response to that pulse returning, the effect in your body. When you get this much power there's a tendency to overreact with it, know you what I mean? "I know it all! I'll show you!" That is a no-no. What it is becomes necessary to be very delicate, very delicate, liken unto fine Chinese silk, very delicate. Everyone take a breath now, lighten up.

So we have some empty chairs. Well, a few beings said yes, looked at the abyss and said no. They didn't realize they could step over it—they thought they were going to fall in.

This is an outrageous day on your planet, this weekend. Very powerful portals are going to be opened. You beings and another grouping, several groupings, are going to do that opening, going to ask permission. It will be granted and you'll open the portal. You're going to work this weekend. You're going to be disciplined. Because it is for you, yes, but more importantly, it's for others upon the planet. We have to be very careful and very delicate.

I know some of your metaphysical understanding; you want to get it over with in a hurry. Want to get superconsciousness here yesterday, eh? Well, it's a fine idea, but too many beings would be collapsed, so their light would collapse. That's why we're taking the avenues we're taking now. You have a responsibility, each of you here, to humankind, because you are humans and you're light in a state of grace. When you understand your responsibility to others you will understand your responsibility to yourself, to your great light. You desire not to abuse your wisdoms.

Everyone get a little bit of water, indeed. That be grand. Don't pull away yet.

We're going to be careful this weekend. The sort of testing to see how much energy we can bring for you. To see how much of you you want to remember, to see how much of your own unconditional love you want to know. To allow you to remember the spark of your divinity when it first started and the line of light that continues for lifetimes, lifetimes and lifetimes. No limitation. None. Can you allow yourselves to handle that wisdom, that power? Indeed? All of it? That will be good. Be gentle. Going to rock some boats; stay in the center of the boat. If it rocks too much, some beings fall off the side, know you what I mean? At least you know how to dive into the middle of the boat—I've seen you. There was no way *she* was going to fall out! Quite a spectacular event, eh? You think I don't watch these things, eh? Everyone lighten up. Now, one of the ways I'm going to work this weekend, we are going to tell a story, stories. And the stories are going to be of some past fantasies that you all played with, played within or part of. It will resonate in the chakra area. Feel it there. Don't compare.

If the story doesn't resonate with you—the first one—then it will resonate later. And you let it happen, bargain? We're going to do things differently, it's time for everyone to stop playing with the rice and start eating it, cooked or not.

How is your back? It will be a gentle thing here. How does this relate to you, do you know? Does it look familiar? Almost like a self-portrait in a way?

Indeed.

It's good to remember that power, no matter what your interpretation of it is. No matter what the interpretation it's reason for self, know you what I mean? So when you have the power you learn how to use it and it takes a little bit this way, a little bit that, but it's still power. And if you misuse it, so what?—you're still learning, indeed. It be learning, know you? That doesn't mean to forget the power, you understand? There is a big difference. Love you outrageously.

Don't judge yourselves. Just beginning, I love this job! [Group laughs.]

Allow your eyes to close gently. This is not a church; it's a temple, it's different. Holy energies are welcome here. Your divinity is safe here. Focus on your heart chakra, just contemplate the you inside you. Be in your moment.

I want you to feel the ship that's above this place. You're connected to that ship, what you term a ship energy. Feel the energy from the ship come down to your crown into your heart. Allow. You haven't been forgotten. You are the one that chooses to forget, in one manner so you can focus on your job, you say, so you can focus on refining your divinity. But now it's time to remember. When you can refine your divinity within the rememberings, allow it , allow it.

Center, heart chakra. I want you to contemplate the confusion in the world, and I want you in your heart chakra to contemplate that confusion. And I want you to feel inside you unconditional love for that confusion. Sort of say, "It's all right. I'm here to help." I want you to feel this in your body. Breathe in your nostrils, both nostrils, hold the breath at the heart chakra, contemplate "I'm here to help" and push the energy out your right side, with an exhale. Let it go around the planet. Around, feel it go around. Now feel it coming into your left side, back to you, allow.

Center. In the heart chakra now, I want you to tell every consciousness on the planet from your heart chakra that you are here to be of assistance in what is termed love, love energy, unconditional love. Again breathe in, breathe it out the right side. Very gently let it come back to you, left side, and you'll get sort of an answer. You might get the question, "What is going on?" Breathe in again, gently. Now gently exhale out right. Let them know God is here, unconditionally loving. That's good, around the planet. That is how you affect everything – love, love.

The consciousness involved on the planet now is starving for love, starving. Bones are showing through the flesh. Breathe in, breathe in, out the right side, back unto you.

It is appropriate to feed starving entities because if you don't, the consciousness that is the God walking here will affect the consciousness of your physical planet – and you haven't *seen* Earth changes yet! It doesn't have to happen that way; this is a beautiful place. The more you move into that what you call frequency, play there, the more you do, the easier it is for life to continue to be what it wants to be.

Focus on the root chakra. Bring the energy in the root chakra up to the heart chakra. Bring it up, tighten your buttocks if you have to to bring it up, but squeeze it up there. That's better. Center. Allow your eyes to open very gently.

We are going to move through very delicate here. Once I give you this blessing I do not want to be involved in taking it back. *You don't want me involved in taking it back, either!* You're going to begin to see out of your heart chakra. Moving beyond metaphysics now, entities, you're moving into becoming gods walking here and enjoying the becoming part. Is that all right?

We'll be as gentle as we can; we don't want to overload your circuits. But we have to put a little more juice in there, where you can feel the power and use it.

Now, you are all intelligent enough to know when you're stepping over the boundary of use and abuse — not one of you here that is ignorant in that regard anymore.

Everyone take a breath, lighten up. Time to pass out more toys. The more you pressure me with thoughts, the farther I will stay away. Allow your eyes to close gently. We want to bring in more energy, more power, and be relaxed and comfortable. Allow. Allow your eyes to open if you wish. Just be comfortable.

In your journey you have flown through space as a spark of light. You became intrigued with the other lights, with what they are doing. They were sort of collecting together, doing something. You weren't sure what they were doing. And you would go around their collective consciousness, as you would say, individual light, trying to see what they were doing, but you were on the outside of their grouping. But some of you got a little courageous and really wanted to know what was going on within the grouping. So you didn't wait to be invited; you jumped right into the middle. And you opened your eyes and said, "Oh, shit!"

Then you began looking within that grouping because you couldn't figure out the passageway out. You figured, "Well, there has got to be someone within this group that knows how to get out of here." There were a few that had the idea, this, that and the other, and you tried their experiences, and it didn't get you anywhere — you were still within the group, within the center of it. This went on for eons, and you finally realized no one knew. Then you really said, "Oh, this is *deep* shit!" Then you realized you had to figure it out yourself, and you began your journey to remember who you were.

You started going through the lifetimes and the panels (we call it) of light that you've experienced within this grouping. One after another, back through time. You said, "Back through time, back through time, how do I get there? How did it happen?" That didn't get you anywhere, either. It went on for another eons. And then you again decided and sat and contemplated, "Well, there has got to be more than this, because I remember looking at this grouping and suddenly being within it. Now, how do I get back? Well, if I jumped in, I can jump out." And you tried it and you succeeded. You were outside of the group again. And you saw several other groups around and you would go around each group, looking. This time you decided, "I'm not jumping in there." You realized you were alone outside of the groups. So you contemplated your Father, the great energy of where you came from and decided that the journey of aloneness has been completed in the wisdom of the feeling of it, and you wanted a buddy that was outside of the grouping. So you decided to enter the grouping once again, this time with memory of how you are going in, and find a being within the group that is willing to listen, that there is more than within this grouping, there's more beyond.

And you spent a few more eons, but you finally found several. And you experienced togetherness outside of the group, yet you didn't create a group; you created each entity of the realization of their own freedom, and it started with three. And the three of you went further and became more creative, more powerful, and you went into the other groupings and gathered more—and became eleven.

And your reputation spread because of the consciousness of the groups, as they were connected in what you call "Thought Is." They knew there was someone coming, because the other groups told them. They hadn't experienced you yet, but they knew you were coming because your power was so awesome. You enjoyed any challenge to create freedom. You know, you had a great band. The Earth—you say, 144,000, you had, oh, several million entities now, enjoying the game called you—your creation of rescue (your word here), this term *enlightenment,* this term *becoming*, this term *breaking social consciousness of structure*. And you dove in, and your reputation spread. Pretty soon every grouping of consciousness that was playing limited or tied down w*anted* you to come because that limited consciousness didn't have the capacity to think *freedom* or *more* beyond their limitation.

Some of the groups of consciousness wanted to test your power, so they created great limitation, and that excited you more and you jumped in. A few more eons didn't matter because you knew who

God was now. (False.) Now the journey became ecstatic – ecstasy every moment because you knew who you were and you loved who you were. Limitation was the food you ate. Nothing brings a god more power, more feeling, more love, more ecstasy than the joy of another god awakening and seeing himself beyond limitation. That is awesome power, awesome energy. Even the entity you call Lucifer, in your limited understanding of this one, has ecstasy, and individual entities become – thoroughly – and then you share the same power. (What you don't know is, Lucifer was told to do what he did, and he did it with love.)

Contemplate your heart chakra now. Contemplate the heart chakra; contemplate the story I told you of the journey of eons into limitations and you're out of it again and your courage to go further and the joy you have doing it. You have been doing this for eons – *allow you to remember that.* Feel it in the body.

Let your body go goose-pimply, eh? That is grand. That's a wisdom now. In that memory is great healing power for self. Allow. Contemplate heart chakra: "I know." Just contemplate it. "I remember." Contemplate *I remember.* Feel in your back in that grand chakra. Feel it there. Allow.

Now, everyone take a breath in, hold it in your upper torso, breathe it in. As you breathe it out, I want it out of the mouth and out of the throat chakra at the same time – the energy – so be that. Grand, outrageous. Center, please. Center.

So in this time in consciousness you beings, as you elevate yourselves, allow yourselves to move into superconsciousness, become superconsciousness, will affect *everything.* This is what you have been waiting for: finally, the realization within the structure of superconsciousness. No longer do you have to dive in, spend eons, take a few out, go to another. You affect the realization completely, totally within the structure. You free beings. (This concept, by the way, is what gave you the atom bomb, but we are not going to do it that way.) It is love, unconditional love, that's going to free everything. And the feedback from that one seed will provide you manna forever wherever you go. You will understand.

With your eyes closed, I want you to contemplate your golden body inside your body. Just contemplate it; it's there. Allow. Very gently now, allow more energy into the body. Allow your consciousness to be free. Allow all limitation to go. Allow all healing to take place, whatever, just to let the energy work it. Allow the body to become new. Let it go. Allow. Center. Don't argue with it. Allow healing. Everything fresh. Your power, it is allowed. It's energy, that's what you are. Center. Contemplate your sixth seal, third eye. Be in your moment now. Center.

With your left and right hand, place them here, just under your rib cage there, little bit, little gently. Energy is getting there. We'll sort of hold here. This is where more of you are going to come to reside, right in there first. We want to love it now. Hold it now, let it work. Now begin to feel it move up this way, up, up, so it will come to the center and begin to move up. Go out with the breath. Now, as you breathe in, it will be here; you breathe in, it will drop down. Let it drop, and then up. So you play with your energy, indeed? Begin. It will drop to your perineum, that's the center here. Releasing. Chakras are here in your shoulders, here, open them. Tell them to open.

With this becoming of superconsciousness your breath patterns are going to be different. Some of you have already experienced that —difficulty breathing for no reason at all and it is that your systems are changing. You are going to need these vortices here to breathe in here. Just contemplate; open the shoulders a little bit. You are working with prana now. In the prana you are acknowledging that prana knows what it's doing first and you figure it out later. Indeed. Center. Now allow your eyes to open.

I love you beings outrageously. I can't wait till you get it: that you love each other outrageously. And then we'll travel again and find other areas where thought is coagulated, band together and bust them up again. It's a fun job!

23

Pull Down the Lightbody and Raise Your Frequency

Zoosh through Robert Shapiro
May 23, 1996

You've been asking for some time whether you are moving past the 3.47-dimensional station, or status. Now, I have to tell you that your energy bodies have begun to move beyond that range. This does not mean that they are not with your bodies, but this is a secondary effect of the dimensional shift. Your souls, as you understand it, are in your physical bodies; yes, your energy bodies are here. What is going on is that your energy bodies — what you sometimes call your auric field, which is actually radiated from within you — are beginning to move past 3.47 and are now stretching out in a range from 3.49 all the way up to 3.75.

This is having various effects. For starters I want you remember that your energy bodies are still within your physical bodies (while you are awake, not in deep sleep), and yet they are stretching forward to the higher dimension. In this way they are accelerating you, causing you to feel different physically. On one hand these differences add to your psychic perceptions; on the other hand they have some deleterious (at least as it feels) physical effects.

You know that your physical body is a partner with your energy body (or soul – or immortal personality, as I sometimes call it), and it functions in response to your soul's need for physical expression of itself. But you have completed your lessons in the third dimension and you are moving back now toward the fourth dimension.

However, your souls can make the trip faster than the physical selves. The physical selves are experiencing, then, something not unlike a physical death. This is not to alarm you; it is just to inform you. At physical death the immortal personality (the soul energy body) leaves the physical self, and the physical self no longer needs to serve you, a soul/immortal personality, so it returns to the Earth. In other words, it becomes its component parts, what it once was in the Earth before it made up your physical self.

Your energy bodies are stretching now into and toward higher-dimensional realms because they can move faster than your physical bodies. Some of the more sensitive people (who to some extent are more attuned, more spiritually aware) are stretching well out to 3.74, 3.75. The physical body is beginning to get mixed messages, and in many cases it is not working so well. This experience is not unknown to the medical profession and would be regarded as. . .an analogy in the medical profession would be coma, wherein the person is in a state of separation from the physical body (on the energy level) even deeper than the deepest sleep level, such that sometimes the body begins to shut down and will need to be supported technologically to be kept alive.

I'm not saying that you're comatose; what I'm saying is that you are experiencing, many of you, an actual moment-by-moment experience of your body beginning to get the mixed message that you are no longer in it, or that you are "departing," as it were.

Physical Symptoms

I will give you an example. For some of you, your internal organs are not functioning the way they once did. Some of you in the medical and other healing professions already know that a great many people are showing symptoms of organ malfunction. In some people it is the digestive system, where certain foods are not being processed correctly and people appear to be gaining a great deal of weight. For other people it is the heart/lung mechanism; you once had the energy to walk a mile, but now it's all you can do to walk a quarter of a mile. These are just two examples. Other examples might be people wearing glasses who suddenly need to change their glasses more often and get stronger and stronger prescriptions. Or others who have always been mentally alert, sharp, able to think on their feet with a vast vocabulary now feeling as if there is a hole in their memory where the words are falling out, and who just can't think like they once did.

These changes are associated with this current phenomenon.

Granted, some of these symptoms are associated with other things, so there's that to consider. However, this is a true phenomenon and I want you to be aware of it. It is especially important for medical people and personnel in the healing professions, because there are certain things you can do to support the physical self. After all, the physical self is where the bulk of your residual personality is in residence, at least while you are "alive." "Alive," you understand, relates to "alive in your current physical body," but "death" is a word that does not apply to the actual existence of your true ongoing personality. That is immortal, never forget that.

Now I want to give some tips to those in the healing professions, in-cluding massage therapists, acupuncturists, naturopaths, osteopaths, physicians, surgeons, psychologists and so on. People can be very well-treated these days if the feet are a strong point of anchoring.

Many of you know about certain techniques such as reflexology, where the bottoms of the feet are touched, but this is not quite the same thing. While a knowledge of the meridians on the bottoms of the feet is helpful (certainly to anybody in the medical profession), there are other methods by which the energy body can be invited to rejoin the physical body. The energy bodies are so excited about moving up to the higher dimensions that they are sort of forcing and dragging and stretching you along, but they need to be reminded that *they must be here in this dimension with you at least four hours a day* —this means full-bodied inhabitants.

For many of you, your energy body has been buoyantly hanging on for years—meaning it is in engagement in your physical body, perhaps at the solar plexus on up. This is not to say that you don't have it from time to time in your legs and feet, but very often it's just hanging on. (For some of you it's from the neck above.) In any event, we need to remind the energy body that it needs to be in your physical body for fully four hours a day *during your wakeful state.* This will require a certain amount of cooperation from your physical self. Some of you will find that you are unable to eat the same foods; you will have to eat perhaps lighter, more easily digestible foods. You can experiment for yourself to discover what is right for you, and a good nutritionist can help. "Easily digestible" is not always the same from person to person, but there are certain rules that apply generally.

I'm alerting you to this because the symptoms are beginning to become very widespread. This has affected a few thousand people for perhaps about six or eight months, but now it's beginning to affect hundreds of thousands. By the time you read this it will be affecting millions of people. So you need to begin doing something about it.

I also need to mention that a lot of these symptoms are happening more powerfully for those living in the Northern Hemisphere. I need to bring this to your attention because a great deal of the business, economics, industry, education and so on is being stimulated in that part of the hemispherical Earth. This is not because people aren't thinking, acting, feeling, doing, functioning in the Southern Hemisphere, but because very crucial mistakes can be made in the Northern Hemisphere, some of which are not easily remedied. You need to become very aware of this.

You might say to me, "But Zoosh, why couldn't I just take something to pep me up, like a cup of coffee, which has always worked in the past for me?" That's not working because the coffee itself, as any medical professional knows, does not stimulate you. It stimulates organs within your body that secrete fluids (adrenal glands, for example) that will cause you to become more alert – in some cases more nervous, but at least more aware of your physical surroundings. But you see, it's because of the fact that your energy body is not so much *in* your physical body that that message might not work so well. For example, some of you who drink coffee to be alert might notice now that the coffee has deleterious effects; maybe it gives you an acid stomach, so that you are getting the downside of the effect rather than the upside (more alert and ready for the day). Others might notice that it takes three cups of coffee now instead of the one it used to take. I know you think it's because you are getting older, but that's not it. Especially important: take notice of those in their thirties who have been drinking coffee for at least ten years; it takes you at least twice as much coffee as it used to take to sharpen up. This is a direct effect of this phenomenon.

I am bringing this to your attention now and will talk more about it, and much more elaborately, in days to come. As your energy body stretches toward that higher dimension, its intention is to pull your physical body up because it wants to speed your motion to the fourth dimension, where life will be significantly better and discomfort as you have known it will not be there, at least to the extent you experience it now. But your physical body cannot be pulled up by your energy body's pulling up, since they are on the outside. The energy body has to be *drawn up* – magnetized, essentially.

This is something you are going to have to work out spiritually, as it were, with your energy body/immortal personality/soul. You are going to have to do this because the energy body has the capacity to pull you up a little bit, but it needs to be *in your body*. If it's going to pull you up, the best time to do this would be at times of the day when you do not need that much energ – perhaps during a nap or during lighter levels of sleep. (At the deepest stages of sleep you need your energy body; you're using it to go visit your teachers, guides and so on.)

What to Do

I want you to become aware that the spaces between the toes are very important – not only the inner part of the toes as they face each other, but also where the main part of the foot ends and the toes begin. These spaces are becoming increasingly important. In some cases very light pressure, and in other cases slightly firmer pressure in various places between the toes can help to invite the energy body back into the physical self, just like pushing a button. This can be considered a form of therapy. It is better to have one person do it for another. You in the healing arts can have somebody do this for you so that you can rest and notice when you feel more invigorated physically.

For some of you this invigoration will take the form of relaxing sleep, where you actually wake up after forty-five minutes or so feeling refreshed. (And for some, waking up and feeling refreshed after sleep is a rarity these days.) For others it will take the case of feeling very clear-minded, as if webs and veils and clouds have been lifted from your mind, enabling you to think clearly for the first time in a long time. Others will feel the juices, as it were, in your body moving around. You'll feel very invigorated, like you need to jump off the table and run around the block several times. It will be very energizing for you.

There will be other ways of reacting, but the main thing is, it will be invigorating in some way. I want those of you in the healing arts to begin to look at this more closely. If, as I say, you are in the profession of psychology or psychiatry, you can begin to integrate touch now, because a great deal more can be accomplished in your profession with touch. Actually, the origin of the healing arts has to do with one person touching another. It has gotten way off track in some cases; in other cases it has really greatly expanded.

And it is not by manipulating the bottoms of the feet – not by chiropractic (we don't want shocks) or acupressure or light-touch reflexology or electrostimulation (as used sometimes with acupunc-

ture) but by an acupuncture that does not break the skin. This is where the practitioner takes a needle with a rounded end and holds it against the skin, pressing slightly. Use blunt needles two at a time at different places on the bottom of the feet, touching the meridians appropriate for that person, one foot at a time. Ask for the energies to flow through you to complete the circuit (as anybody who is in acupuncture knows, even the physicians). You are given this instruction, physicians; now it's time to apply it. Do it this way rather than break the skin, because this experience must be comfortable. *If it causes pain it will have the opposite effect:* the energy body will run away from the body. We need to draw the energy body into the physical self. Even the slight discomfort associated with the insertion of acupuncture needles would have that effect. I'm bringing this to your attention now, and we will talk more about it in the future.

The more we work on our body the way you describe, then the quicker the body

will move up the dimensional ladder?

I know that you are thinking about this in terms of how you get there faster (the usual agenda). However, this is not necessary. The energy body is not doing something it's not supposed to do. However, it is sufficiently close to the crossroads of 3.50 that it has a natural tendency to keep on going, especially since we jammed everybody up to 3.47, which was like a springboard where the energy body's tendency was to keep right on going—a sling-shot effect.

The need here is to utilize the radiations of the higher dimension that the energy bodies are reaching for and bring the energy bodies back down into the physical body for at least four hours a day —*full-bodied in the physical self,* not just above the solar plexus. To do that will necessarily bring some of that higher-dimensional energy into the physical self. Now, I am not labeling this "ascension training." We're going to call this "descension training," where we utilize in the physical form what the energy body is doing.

I have stated for a long time that everybody is moving physically into the fourth dimension. However, you cannot actually function at the fourth dimension with the physical self you have now; *you have to change its cellular structure.*

If a fourth-dimensional being were in this room right now, sensitive people might get an impression, they might see a motion, they might see part of that being. But you would not see the entire being all the time because that pulse, which is only a little more than half a dimension away, is sufficient to cause your mostly still third-dimensional self (physically) a difficulty in perceiving that higher-dimensional being. What is necessary is to change the cellular structure, and this invitation or encouragement to bring the energy body back into the physical body at least four hours during wakeful time will allow that to happen more efficiently. I don't want to say it will necessarily be faster (anticipating your question), but it will be more efficient. After all, we want the process to be efficient so that all parts of you can move or expand at the same time at the same rate—we don't want to leave your liver behind, as it were. Only your *own* energy body can accomplish this. *Your* energy body can't help *him* and [referring to another person here] *his* energy body can't help you. It's got to be your energy body in yourself.

Interestingly, it does not matter whether or not people are spiritually oriented. Even if they are in the trenches fighting for their lives, even people in desperate straits who don't have time to think about expanding their consciousness, have energy bodies that are stretching into a minimum of 3.49.

The energy self is not only reaching higher, but it is also attempting to make contact with your fourth-dimensional reality. And the higher dimensions do have a more significant contact with other higher dimensions; the fourth dimension has significantly more moment-by-moment contact with the fifth dimension, and the fifth dimension even more with the sixth dimension and so on. Your energy body, reaching the fourth dimension, can amplify the range of motion and the cellular transformational process simply *by tapping into its higher-dimensional self,* not the fourth dimension; nobody is reaching to that yet on the energetic level while they are awake (while you are in deep levels of sleep, yes). While you are awake nobody is reaching into that because it is just too soon. But the energy body does have the capacity to transfer a significant amount of cellular transformational energy through this process.

If 3.50 is the critical mass, what's the moment that we go to, say, 3.5002? Is there any change we notice in ourselves?

Well, you're more likely to notice external changes than you are internal ones. The primary internal changes you will notice are a craving for different foods, and some of you will feel more benevolently toward people you've felt perhaps less enthusiastic about. There will be a tendency to moderate extreme behavior. There will also be a feeling in the body, regardless of what you weigh or how you are used to feeling the mass of your physical self to feel lighter. You will simply notice, if you can remember (which won't be easy because of the curvature of time) that the actual, felt dimensional effect of your physical self is lighter – it's an actual physical feeling. Some of you more than others might meet people in the street that you do not know well and converse with these individuals, using fewer words.

It is because you feel like you have a hole in your memory. You are also moving more into the present and less into what is past-oriented – in other words, you're moving away from linear time. You won't have full access to the language levels you've had before, but this will be compensated for because you will, with communications at 3.50 plus, begin to communicate with people on a more feeling level. Your conversations will be more meaningful with fewer words because there will be a transference of feeling. This does not necessarily mean that a person will come up to you on the street and be angry and you will know it (though you might). It is just as possible that a person will come to you on the street and start telling you a story without elaborate aspects of English, yet you will understand that story better because of the feelings you are receiving from this individual—telepathic *feelings.* Understand that true telepathy is on the feeling and visual level. Telepathy as a worded message sent to somebody else is fairly rare and also very slow. It takes a lot of time to learn it, although some people have done so; but picking up a message from another person on the basis of what you feel or what you see or sense can be interpreted by the memory bank of the mind even more accurately than a telepathic verbal message.

How far up the ladder can we take physical cells — 3.6, 3.7?

Meaning how far can you take this version of your physical body? You can't take this version of your physical body much past 3.49 and a half, but your physical body is changing over even as I speak. That's why I mention things that are going on with you physically. It is important to understand that the physical self has the capacity to transform itself. Now, we know that cells have memory—what they've done, what they've been, and even to some extent the memory of cells that have preceded them, especially if they come from that cell's division. But cells are now beginning to develop *future* memory. This means that the cell has the capacity to have foreknowledge, a precognition of what the cell is going to be. The cell does not necessarily have the magical ability to suddenly become that, but when it is going through its changes it will have less resistance to that change because it can feel the motion toward that ideal cellular structure, since that vision or precognition of its structure is in place. In this way resistance is being reduced on the cellular structure, and motion forward in cellular higher-dimensional growth is taking place more easily, more compatibly.

Is that a DNA function, that future-memory capacity?

No, because DNA is in service to the body. It is rather a function of future-self cellular structure. Now, we all know that we have concurrent lives going on in different dimensions. Not all of you have total concurrent lives going on on the fourth dimension, but some of you do. Enough of you do so that the broad range of cellular effect (the effect of one cell on another, being compatible and so on) is variable between cells. So this is more of a precognitive effect; the DNA responds but does not initiate. This is also important to those who talk about more and more DNA strands. In reality, these strands are more or less happening *in reaction to* something rather than stimulating or initiating something on their own.

So the more that this lightbody can reach out and contact that higher fourth dimension and the more that flow can stimulate the future memory, then the faster

the cells will transform, right?

Not quite. The emotional body, the energy body, the soul body, whatever you want to call it, is inclined to do that now. We don't have to stimulate it, encourage it or otherwise say, go do it more. No, it depends more on inviting the energy body, which is already stretching up, to come back down into the physical body for at least four hours a day, where it can transfer what it has obtained.

Download it.

That's right, download into the physical self. And in this way the energy body's trips to the higher dimension will not become simply a separation of the energy body and the physical body.

So this goes on from now on and some people will move a little faster than others. We had these discussions years ago, but I never really understood it. Let's say that there is a roomful of people; one of them is going to transform his cells and be able to function in the fourth dimension sooner than others. How are we going to perceive that, those of us who haven't got there yet? Will he just blink out?

In most circumstances the person is not going to blink out, meaning no longer be visible with your optical systems. There is no point in that, really. The whole purpose here is for you to grow, expand and change *while* you are moving between dimensions so you can get the fullest understanding of the ramifications of everything you have done here to see if what you have learned in the third dimension has an application at higher dimensions, and if what you've learned in the third dimension can be utilized *between* dimensions—which is the only part that was left over for you to understand. *The only reason to move slowly* between the third and fourth dimension is so that you can *apply* what you have learned.

And also to create this memory reservoir for others to tap into who do it next time?

Yes, to blaze the trail, as it were. If people would go up and just gradually begin engaging in the fourth dimension, what they learn would not be readily and easily transferred to the mass of people who are left in the physical. It is more likely that some people will begin to have the experience not only in dreams but also in visions and occasionally imaginations. Imaginations in this case meaning you are fantasizing about something, and unexpectedly there is something else in your fantasy; something just pops in that wasn't there before. This is a circumstance in which the higher-dimensional aspect is coming into play.

I will make a qualifying statement. Obviously, if it's something uncomfortable, it will not be a higher-dimensional input. It will sometimes be vague or sometimes detailed, but not crystal clear about what it means in your life in that moment. If it is something that feels like inspiration from which you are intended to take action, it *will* be inspiration. If it is something you are not really concentrating on, not focusing on, and you can define one of these inputs basically by this reaction: "Well, what do I do with *that?*" then that's how it differs from inspiration. Inspiration comes in because you can *do* something with it. These are examples of the transference of higher-dimensional visions or what is existing at that higher-dimensional version of your personal world. And so when that is available to you, then very often one has the experience of, as you say, downloading the fourth dimension into your current dimensional zone.

Do you at that moment merge with your higher-dimensional self and share its experiences?

Yes, and this will often happen in moments of relaxation. So it could happen to people who are doing meditation, not saying a mantra but simply relaxing into a deep, relaxed meditative state. It could happen to people who are taking a nap, for instance, not going to the deepest levels of sleep. It could also happen to people who are just beginning to go to sleep or, conversely, people who are just beginning to wake up.

I think that this is going to be very reassuring to people. I think that there are some out there in whom will be some transition between the physical body and the lightbody. I don't think people are going to realize how smoothly the physical body is going to transform itself.

This is the intention—that the physical body transform itself. When there are contacts between human beings and ETs, there are always very distinct differences in patterns of behavior between the two. Granted, some of this is because most ETs live at a higher dimension. You might ask yourself: If you are going to travel out there in spaceships at some point and meet ETs at the higher dimension, how are you going to physically get to that higher dimension comfortably? The technology exists right now on Earth to travel to higher dimensions, but it is very difficult to survive the experience as a physical human being. Your body can go as it is now to that higher dimension, *but it cannot survive there!* And if you are able to come back at all to the place you left, if you survive physically you are probably going to be borderline psychotic, at least schizophrenic. Scientists and researchers, be aware! The motion to the higher dimension will require of you certain behavioral changes. That's part of the reason this is going on right now: "Well, I used to eat this and love it, and now I am just not interested in it anymore."

Some areas of economics will be hit harder than others. For instance, some are being hit right now. I've said for a long time, "You have teeth; you are supposed to eat meat. That's it!" (Zoosh does not encourage vegetarianism, okay?) Some of you will discover that you will not be able to eat the same kind of meat you used to eat. You might have to eat something that digests more easily. It will be different from person to person, but generally that will mean fish, chicken, turkey, maybe lamb. Some of you, however, will easily digest the red meats, so it won't be problem for you (not to rain on the parade of ranchers and so on; that is not my intention). Because it is something that is happening, a wise rancher might begin a fish farm on the side—feed is a whole lot cheaper. It is something to consider, futures in fish farming, okay? And you might have a couple thousand chickens while you are at it.

In any event, I would say that the format for change in the physical self is inevitable. Also, certain other behaviors might be difficult to continue, such as being overindulgent, overly abusive. I am not saying you can't have a beer now and then or even a glass of champagne or something like that, but those who are overindulging, even though you might feel that you *need* to overindulge, will suddenly wake up one day and for no particular reason have much less craving for whatever they over-indulge in. This doesn't mean that the craving will go away entirely, but it will not be there as much, and as time goes on it will be less and less.

Drugs, too?

Drugs too, yes. This includes even extreme drugs—crack cocaine, for example. Obviously, drug dealers had better get into the music industry or something, because people are always going to like music—but you won't be able to make music illegal, thus making it more expensive. Get into the stock market or commodities or something, but get out of the drug businesses—there is no long-range future in it.

Drugs bring in money to the secret government to fund their black projects. So they are going to lose that source of income?

Yes, that's right. Addiction in general will gradually fall away from people because of the changes not only in the physiological self but also because the Explorer Race must get up there and contact the ETs, which you are going to do. They are not simply going to come here and you go there. In order to do that and survive (be able to come back to Earth), you will need to able to function at those higher-frequency levels. Which also means, of course, that a certain amount of extreme expression of emotion will go away. This does not mean that emotions as you know them will go away; it just means that you will not have the capacity to control your emotions, which might cause an explosion of inappropriate emotional and physical drama somewhere down the line. You won't be able to do that because you will be *hearing/feeling* your subtle messages better, and you will simply act on them.

Remember, I have said for some time that your linear mind is going away. That's why you're having trouble remembering things, or one of the reasons. Your natural mind is instinctual (you know what you need to know when you need to know it), and as communication takes place between you and extraterrestrial species (or even between animals on the Earth, plants, natural life forms), you will discover that a lot of the conversation/communication will involve visuals – meaning what you think/see, what you visualize. What is given back to you by what *they* think/see (whether it be dog or cat or woodpecker or hummingbird or even an extraterrestrial) will also be feelings. Very much more can be passed to an individual through feelings than through words.

Anybody in a relationship knows that from time to time you have arguments, and the other person just doesn't seem to *get it!* They can't seem to figure out what you are saying. You want to say, "Read my lips," but they can't get it because they do not pick up what you are feeling. But very soon everybody will pick up the subtler message of what other people are feeling, so all those words, no matter how well-chosen or even eloquent, will be less necessary.

One of the reasons meditation is very good at this time is that it makes the connection between the physical body and the soul, and downloading can happen during that time, right?

Well, meditation that does not involve a discipline of the mind. This can even be a meditation such as Tai Chi, for example, as long as there is no mantra involved. If you are saying something over and over in your mind, that will interfere, but if you are simply in a deep state of relaxation, sometimes referred to as meditation, then that will be helpful. If you say prayers in your meditation, that's a mental thing, so it will block it. I'm not saying don't say prayers in your meditations; I'm saying, add to your meditations a time of quiet relaxation in which you are making the effort to not think.

I know you don't like to talk about physical changes, but two of Edgar Cayce's volcanoes have become active — Vesuvius and Etna. Has consciousness changed enough that we don't have to experience some of the massive Earth changes we've talked about?

As I've said, these Earth changes are happening massively at 3.0 dimension right now as we speak. But because you are still close enough to 3.0 dimension, you will experience—sometimes, not all the time—a lesser degree of these experiences. For instance, I'm thinking of a volcano right now that is erupting at 3.0 dimension in downtown Portalegre, Brazil. I've discussed this with the people down there. It's erupting full bore, as it were, right in the middle of town at 3.0 dimension, and it's eventually going to create a mountain there. It will eventually become a huge mountain range that will take a good century or two to cool off to the point where you can walk on it—well, maybe in twenty-five or thirty years you might be able to walk quickly on it. But even now some individuals in Portalegre occasionally smell sulphur for no particular reason. When that smell was first picked up by some individuals at university, there was a distinct concern about earthquakes and volcanic eruptions. There was even one circumstance in which an instrument that can register gases showed an unusual rise in the sulphur content in the air (basic sulphur, not sulphur dioxide). This was chalked up as an anomaly, for there was no academic explanation for it. When you have volcanic eruptions now such as ones you have alluded to, the extent of the eruption here at 3.47 will be nowhere near as dramatic as at 3.0. It's the same for earthquakes. This is good for you, because it allows Earth to do what she needs to do at 3.0 dimension without beating you up here at 3.47.

Are we going to be able to keep ahead of these changes?

I believe you will be able to keep ahead of the *extreme* changes. You will not be able to keep ahead of those situations and circumstances that are less bone-crushing. Understand that the planet is actually changing. She *must* make changes, because a lot of the systems she has used to maintain her weather, for example, are no longer in her physical self because of mining. She uses *every part* of her physical self. I have said many times that if someone decided to mine *your body,* it's safe to say you wouldn't be working too well after a while. Well, it's the same thing for her.

That is why you're getting bizarre weather happening in places. Also circumstances are now developing on the face of the Earth that were not intended until much later, such as desertification, as they call it now in geological terminology. It wasn't intended that there be so much desert on the Earth as there is now, but Mother Earth is having a difficult time spreading the rain around. It tends to rain all in one place for a year or two, then in another place, then still another place for a year or two. Spreading it all over herself is difficult for her, especially since so much uranium has been mined. As I said before, uranium is her brain and is a significant element of her nervous system.

I also think physical, human people are interfering with weather patterns.

That's true.

So everything that Ingo Swann and Cayce and some of these really great seers saw is happening at 3.0 the way they saw it?

Yes. To a great extent even the I Am America map is taking place at that level. That is why the I Am America map is important to study, because it gives you a clue about why you might be picking up certain vibrations or why you might suddenly have a very powerful vision or a feeling of some great flood, and you just *know* it's going to happen tomorrow or the next day or on a specific date – and it doesn't happen. You feel, "What's wrong with me, what's the matter with me, I am I losing my psychic ability, am I just going crazy, or is God giving me a false message?" No, no. The I Am America map and these other predictions are important because they show you that this is happening, that there is just enough moment-to-moment experience or change in the body (what is the body but the body of God, of all things?) – meaning that there is enough change in your personal cellular structure that you do not have to experience the full dramatic impact of those Earth changes. This isn't to say that there won't be floods and hurricanes and so on, but it won't be the full blast of it.

Is there anything else you want to say about anything else?

I may have more to say later, but that's really it for now.

24

Crop Circles: Symbols Of Soul-Group Origins

Zoosh through Robert Shapiro
May 28, 1996

You know, really crop circles are intended not so much to say, "Here we are!" Crop circles are basically a sign. The author [Chet] Snow has talked somewhat at length about the correlation between the crop circles and signs that are sacred to native peoples and other signs that can be traced back for some time. These signs are always intended to have an effect. The reason these signs exist at all in ancient paintings, especially on stone, is that they were designed to last for a while. A lot of these designs were made on things that didn't last, but if you wanted them to survive you would put them someplace where they would last for a few centuries.

These comings of the probes that create these signs: In the old days they did it in fields of grasses or sand, whatever was available, wherever the people were. It wasn't intended to say, "We're coming." It was more intended to say, "You're here." This is a universal language based on a tribal context. Tribal, though, does not mean this tribe is tall and dark-skinned and this tribe is short and light-skinned; not that. We are into soul groups, and in soul groups there is a certain level of common personality traits, a certain amount of common capacities or a certain amount of even challenges that you might call *incapacities*.

The main thing is that there are common traits aplenty. These signs are designed to come to you in groups of twelve to sixteen, not so much as a progression (although they have been analyzed as being a progression) as to point out the signs of different soul groups.

If you look at the most frequently occurring types of circles (crop circles, as they are called), you will find that certain themes strike very often. They always start with circular ones, and then they add triangles. As I have said before, aside from sound (tone) and color being a universal language, the symbolic universal language is basically geometric. Geometry professors from Arcturus, the Pleiades and the Earth would have a common ground on which they could meet. They might not be able to understand each other's language, but they could draw geometric forms and be able to communicate. Basically, they could teach and learn from each other on the basis of these geometric symbols—what I would like to call philosophical geometry.

These soul signs that are coming to you are, on the one hand, intended to be the signs of soul groups, and when the signs become elaborate and involved, as many of them have, they are intended as activations of soul groups.

Unfortunately, not all of these crop circles have been publicized, and those who study them know that some of them have been lost, and this is unfortunate; however, they will be re-created in various places.

We are talking about something that is a body of knowledge. For instance, a probe coming from a ship will go down to a field of wheat or a grassy meadow—nothing planted there, just wild grass growing there—and etch out one of these circles, as they are called (diagrams, I would rather call them). Plants and humankind are inexorably connected; you couldn't be alive here if it were not for plants. Yes, it's true that plankton produces a sufficient quantity of the oxygen you breathe, but as you poison the oceans, not that much plankton can be surviving to regularly produce oxygen. So it comes down to the fact that surface plants are really keeping you alive. You are totally connected, and to some extent you keep them alive. This sympathetic vibration between you two allows plants to pass on certain messages to the human race. One might ask, might some of these messages be meant for the plants? Yes.

These so-called crop circles then are a means to deliver a message to several groups—to plants and then to people. Plants have been informed, as it were, by their teachers that they are here not only to serve you but to be served by you. And very often they will say, "Well, when are they going serve us?" They don't say it like that, but they have the feeling.

So the primary receiver of the message is the plant, which passes the message on to other plants, basically just spreading it all over the world. This is done to notify plants that they will not have to serve you much longer – they won't have to stand for being hybridized, for example. They don't like that. They *hate that,* being hybridized, even though they might look good or produce bountiful crops. You wouldn't care to be hybridized, either; you want to marry and be with the person you want to be with. You don't want someone coming along and plucking you out of your marriage saying, " Let's see what kind of kids you can produce with this person." You wouldn't like that very much. The main thing is that plants don't like that, either. They would prefer to grow wild where they care to grow, just as you would prefer to be where you want to be.

So the first *individuals* to receive these messages are the plants, and that message is that their time of serving humankind is coming to a close. They then pass the message on to each other. The second level of the message to be passed on to humankind is through the Earth's consciousness. Plants grow out of the Earth for the most part, and the ones that are the recipients of these signals, or signs, will experience the message in their entire bodies. This is why it's important for the plants to be alive for a while after the experience. As human beings you see the message in the plants, looking down from above. However, the actual message that affects you is written in the Earth. If you could see the message in the soil, it would be a little different (not totally, but just a little different), because your bodies are made up, yes, of plants, but also primarily of dirt. You know, "From dust thou art, to dust thou shalt return." Messages cannot be received mentally by you because there is no worldwide language and philosophy combined together. There's no Earth philosophy, otherwise known as the Earth religion, that is for all individuals, and there is no Earth language that is for all individuals.

Because of that, messages that are meant to wake you up spiritually ofttimes have to be delivered in ways that are not mental. So they might be physical, and the "information" comes to you through physical means.

The sign is usually patterned on the plants, occasionally sand. Then not only because of the cycling of Earth's energies, but because Mother Earth's body is a total organism and your bodies are an extension of her on the physical (you're her children), when any portion of Mother Earth gets this message, she passes it on immediately to all portions of herself – not only all portions of her physical body, but you as well. So the message is patterned into all of you through the physical connection that you have to Mother Earth.

This is the mechanical function of these messages. I want you to understand that the true purpose of crop circles is to work at the spiritual, physiological, emotional and instinctual levels. They can't work at the mental level because you do not practice normal planetary common bonds yet, although you are getting there. Thus messages with a powerful meaning are often delivered to you in such a way that you can receive them through your universal connector, which is physical.

Most people enjoy a beautiful sunset or sunrise. These are also messages. These messages speak to you primarily on the level of beauty and (perhaps most importantly for you living in this tough school of Earth) continuity. This is another example of messages delivered to people the world over that have pretty much the same benefit to, and effect upon, all individuals – a universal language of feeling.

The Earth's frequency has gone from 7.8 cycles per second to 8.6. Is this connected in some way?

And who postulates this?

It's just a simple measurement that scientists have made; it's called the Schuman resonance.

Are you talking about the pulse of Earth? Yes? Or are you talking about the frequency of Earth?

Well, it says cycles per second, and I guess Hertz is essentially a frequency. But it's faster now, and I wondered what connection that has to new crop-circle energies.

It is true that it is faster, but that doesn't have a direct connection. This is about what Earth is doing for herself and what those who work with Earth are doing for her. It does, as a sidelight, temporarily interfere a little with your communication with Mother Earth because your cellular structure takes several years to change over. The cells in your body change over completely every seven years, but Mother Earth can change her pulse or frequency fairly quickly. Her resonance can increase, but it takes you a while even in these days to change your pulse. That's part of the reason there need to be so many messages impacted on the Earth such as these so-called crop circles. If your pulse frequency were entirely in concordance with Mother Earth at all times, you would need to have the message delivered only once – once in one spot, and you would all get it. But because of the off-frequency communication between your physical selves and Mother Earth right now, the message needs to be delivered not only many times but in different geographic locations around the Earth. The message, while it will tend to radiate throughout Earth and into your physical bodies, will need to be repeated several times for your physical bodies to have the capacity to pass it on to your subconscious.

The subconscious is available through the emotional self. And the emotional self, being overwhelmed with what's going on in general in all of your lives now, even the most peaceful life, needs to have the message repeated numerous times and in different geographic locations. That is why you will hear about crop circles that will pop up in some unexpected place where you have never heard about them being before, they will be there for a while, and then that's it. You won't hear about them again.

For example, certain individuals around Nome, Alaska, and some around Kiska have seen, this past winter and a few winters before that, messages like circles in the snow, some of them in more permanent tundra, and people weren't exactly sure. First they thought people might have done it; then they thought, No, that's not possible. How could they have done that? (It was so precise, you know.) This is the kind of message that goes to an area and is intended to be there temporarily – obviously, it snows again and you can't see the message. It impacts the ice, and the ice, being part of Mother Earth, passes the message down to the land, but it might need to be impacted more than one time.

In any event, that is a more obscure example that has not been particularly publicized. There have also been occasions in which individuals at sea have experienced these messages, sometimes as strange cloud formations, others times as curious patterns in the water – literally. They look at the water and say, "You know, I could swear those currents are crossing each other." Sometimes people can actually see the currents.

So these messages are being impacted all over the world because of that slight discordance between Mother Earth and your subconscious. And it is the subconscious that is the link between the emotional, spiritual and even physical selves. It is the link to your conscious mind. The subconscious can receive it because it has the capacity to understand, accept and honor the emotional self and the instinctual self. Because it has this capacity, it can receive this as patterned information not unlike digital data, and it will gradually, when the moment is right, bring some of that up to your conscious mind in some way.

Sometimes it will be in the most obscure way, such as a circumstance in which you might see something that reminds you of a crop circle. Or people who don't know about such things (and there are many) might see something that reminds them of a curious sign or pattern.

An interesting thing about these signs that are meant to awaken your consciousness in many ways, spiritually, is that there are certain "cosigns" that are intended to be given. The cosigns cannot be interfered with by those who might wish to interfere, though there are a few individuals like that. The cosign will only be given through an emotional feeling. So these crop circles, as they are called, will continue to show up in various places until that cosign given by your emotional selves is felt as a universal emotion that everybody feels. Now, this universal emotion you will all have to feel for about three days. It is basically a precognitive emotion, an emotion that you feel has to do with a future event, generally a good emotion, a wonderful feeling.

It is basically being overwhelmed by a feeling of well-being, even a gentle feeling of well-being that you cannot account for on the basis of your circumstances in life. It would be the best for this particular feeling to happen in three days, although it might take five days, allowing for changes in time around the Earth. When that occurs, that will be the cosign, and crop circles will begin to fade.

You mentioned probes and ships. Who is masterminding this immense job here?

Well, it's not really such a big deal. You have to understand that if there's data already in the computer and you want to print it out, basically you just tap a few buttons on the computer. One might say if they were from years ago, even a hundred years ago, "What kind of mastermind has created this amazing volume simply by the touch of a couple of strange buttons?"

Well, it is very similar technology. It is basically something that has been given to many different people on different planets. This is largely being carried out by the Arcturians, because they are involved with change. It is also being assisted by Altairians because they have the capacity for long-term memory of the future, and that's what it takes. They need to be able to have a fairly long-term, generalized memory of the future—not of their own lives, because that would interfere with their living process, but a generalized memory of the future.

You would call it a vision, but they do not see it that way, because this memory is intended to be like a patterning. It is a memory of a desirable future. When Altairians are involved, you see, the sign is encoded not only with the energy to benevolently wake you up to all that you are, but it also tends to be encoded with a benevolent, loving, beneficial future for you all as well.

So every soul, every human of the planet, being part of one soul group among a total number that is between twelve and sixteen, will be affected by one of those crop signs?

Yes, sometimes more than one. There will be one and then they might build on that, because basically it's a geometric message.

How can we find which ones relate to each of us?

Very easily—well, granted, not all of them have been photographed. But find as many photographs as you can in a book or something like that. You need to see the actual photographs; it won't work if they are diagrams. In terms of soul recognition, just notice which one causes you to feel the best. That's not foolproof, but about 80% of the time that will be your soul-group sign.

So at some point will they all be photographed, even the ones in the clouds and in the ice?

Yes, absolutely, especially when they start occurring in places that are fairly public—you know, where there are lots of people around with cameras, or where people with cameras fly over places a lot in helicopters getting an aerial view. Where before you can turn around and say boo! fifteen photographers have already flown over the area on business, meaning it will be in a more populated area.

You said something very interesting—that these signs relate to tribal Indians, aborigines, different native peoples. And the reason they have the symbols is that they saw the signs given to them at some earlier time and then put them on the rock?

That's right, for future generations. They saw the signs and, being artists of the time and believing these were special things, special events, as people do today they made drawings or memorized them. But the shamans amongst them, the seers, the visionaries, the mystical people, were all advised to make a sign for the future, and so this question was put to them. Of course they would say, "How far into the future?" The answer would always be, "For all generations to come." So the best they could do would be to put it in stone. Although it might not be there for all generations to come, it would certainly be there for a while. Good enough, you know, if it works.

How often and long ago did they do that?

Some of these signs have been there for many centuries. Some for even longer than that, depending largely upon the atmospheric conditions the signs were exposed to.

In some cases stones have been patterned with these signs and buried, not so deep that they wouldn't be found, but in a place that the mystical person felt (the nature of mysticism is what you feel) would be uncovered at some point in time. It was literally a key to the future, buried for some future generation to dig up—for no reason that the shaman would know, but which in your time is often known as construction.

They are probably in caves too?

Yes, but you know a lot of caves have been explored well. There are still a few out there that haven't been, but very often these are things closer to the surface.

Are there any specific ways to increase our receptivity to these messages, not only those, but the messages of the Sun?

The messages in reference to the circles would have to be yes. Look at a photograph of one. It is ideal if you can be there—that's the best thing, obviously, but not everybody can. But if you can, look at a good photograph, especially a color photograph, to get the feeling. You know, one that shows the sign from above and then closer and closer—a good video or film would be better for the sake of resolution.

If you can, touch it. The next best thing to actually touching the sign itself would be to draw the sign as best you can, but do not use mechanical instruments. I understand that you might not be able to make a perfect sign; it wouldn't be quite right. For some of you it would look like a five-year-old drew it; for others it would look pretty good.

The main thing is, something you draw won't work for other people as well as it works for you. Put your hand to it and you do it as well as you can, even if it looks like a stick drawing. Make it big enough—an 8" x 10" sheet of paper at least—that you can put your hand on it afterward, right hand, left hand. Put your arms on it, however long you want. Pick it up, touch it to you, you understand, assuming this is a sign that feels right to you, feels good to you (Does this feel like my sign; is this speaking to me?). After you have drawn it, touch it to your body, to your chest, on the skin. It has to be the skin because that's Mother Earth, that's her body. Touch it to your stomach, touch it to your legs, touch it anywhere you want to on your body. This personal patterning of this special sign will help you to feel its full effect. It's the next best thing to actually being there. If you were there within twelve hours after the sign was created and were exposed to that sign, especially if you find it attractive, it will have a very powerful effect. It could change your life beneficially, I would say. The chances of it changing your life in a way that is even slightly to the detriment is about .000001, which might mean you would miss an appointment or something.

Better odds than drinking Coke! You said a couple of years ago that one of the best ways to get the most value out of a sign was to draw it very large and then walk in it, actually walk the path.

That's possible, but you know I like the personal touch — these days.

I talked to someone today who said that she had dowsed circles as long as about 18 months later and still found them dowsable. But you say that we really need to get in there before 12 hours to get the max?

Oh, to get the maximum effect.

Thank you very much. This is real good stuff.

25

Prepare for the Outrageous Journey To Rescue The Planet

YHWH/Arthur Fanning
June 8-9, 1996, From "The Natural Planet"

Allow your eyes to close a moment. We have a great light above this house here, great swirling cloud of light. It's a cloud, it looks physical, indeed. It's creating a vortex, it's going to push down here. Let it push down into the top of your head. Let it push.

Within this vortex what you're going to see, if you allow yourself, all the gods that have ever been are there; even the old gods that you don't even remember. And also there are all the future gods that you haven't got to know yet. And in there is you. Allow.

Otherwise you'd all have the same face and no one could blame anyone for creating the ocean or the flower, wouldn't take credit for this, that and the other, so you create little differences. Center. You take on the difference so you can all acknowledge each other for your creations. Otherwise you're bickering, "I created that!"

"No you didn't, I did!"

"Well, how can you tell? Both look alike. Who created what?"

"Well, I don't know. I forget. It might have been the guy in the third row back there – looks like us, know you? In fact, we all look alike. What do we do now? Let's be different."

Allow your eyes to open. Get that concept clear, you'll understand there's fun here.

Now, the reason I can talk to you like this is because you beings have a sense of humor, limited as it may be. [Laughter.] But the others that you're responsible for on your planet would have no idea what I'm talking about, would not see the humor in it at all, and certainly would declare me the Antichrist, know you what I mean? Well, we'll let them call *you* that [more laughter] when you really set them off. Well, there is always humor. Okay.

Now, know you the—you're familiar with the Philadelphia Experiment, indeed? And know how some beings got trapped in the superstructure of this thing? In that process there is that energy within you that knows, "I could walk through this wall right now and get safely to the other side." In the context of the human condition there is this word you beings have very much flavor with, know you? "But what happens if I get halfway through and get stuck, be half in wall, half out." It's that word "but," know you, that creates the doubt of it, that does not allow you to even try it. Know you what I mean?

And if you have the doubt you'll probably create what you fear.

You create the stop, indeed. You have to get over this thing, be willing to push your hand through, know you? It requires more light around you, requires a higher vibration so your hands can pass through things and you can, too.

I've seen it and I have felt it.

You can do it! If one being can demonstrate it upon the planet, then every being has the capacity and capability to do it. Whether they want to or not is a different story, indeed? Okay.

Play the first one, track number two [*Planet Drum*, "Island Groove," by Mickey Hart.]

Meditation

Allow you to center and sort of get into the rhythm here. Center your being. Allow the energy inside you now. I want you to feel it. Allow you the dancing movement inside you. In your right hand, feel you're holding a golden sphere, gold sphere; your left hand, a silver sphere. Feel the emblem of the sri yantra [see symbol on page 7]on the gold sphere and on the silver sphere—visualize a single pyramid. Center.

Allow the spheres to move from your hands inward to your root chakra, down to your perineum, your buttocks. Let them be there and they'll merge, gold and silver. Allow. Center.

Now allow this merged sphere to move up your body, up the spine, winding . . . allow . . . to the crown and then back down again. And then up, and then down.

Create a flame, fire, around the spine. Center. Feel it at the top of your head also. Keep the sphere moving, up and down, around. Let the energy move outward from the body, around the spine. Move it outward through the body so you become a column of fire yourself. Allow. Flame. Allow. Center. Center.

Next disk, track three ["Thunderdrums" by Scott Fitzgerald].

Center. Let the energy inside your body. Contemplate the beat in here as a marching of your soul within the rhythm of God. Feel the joy there. Center in your being.

The soul knows what it's doing. It's enjoying it. It's in step with every other soul on the planet whether you know it or not. Center. See if you can find your own steps within that beat.

I want you to feel a spiral of green light emanating from your root chakra up through your body now, green light, root chakra, up. An emerald ray right out of the crown, right out, green. Healing.

Find that being that you met in your body before, and join. Take a breath. Allow your eyes to open. Center.

I want you to take a breath in your body, and when you exhale it out I want you to put your arms out and your [index] fingers, and energy comes out both. So bring it in, a breath, down here [to the perineum] and you [exhale, allowing the energy to flow out of your index fingers]. Now, one more time. You're going to bring it down these nadis here, right in the body. Breathe in. Hold it in tummy, let it out. Once more in . . . hold it down here, tighten your belly and your bottom, bend forward a little bit, let it out. Center.

Now be in your moment. Okay, allow your eyes to open if they are closed.

One of the most difficult things at this density is to come here and teach wisdom to empower ones. It's very easy to come here and create a worship, a church or a grouping or a following because you beings enjoy follow—you feel safe. But it's very difficult to come and empower. You beings are getting a sample, what you call an understanding, of how difficult it is when you have to talk to others that don't know. And how you feel trapped in the knowing of it also.

But one of the things you are going to understand is, you're already out there in other dimensions (in your words), other systems, creating universes, creating habitats for beings to reside in. You're already doing that. This is where you've forgotten—down here, what you call in this system. You have completions to do. You call them completions, missions, jobs. For most of you the job is to assist many through this time of transition, and you willingly took on doubt and fears as tools so you could work effectively within this environment. But it's time to let go of some of those doubts and fears now, because you are at the point where a merging of realities is occurring, so you need both wisdom—[of] this one and the wisdom of the greater you here, the energy of it, the play.

Now we can bring in what is termed an outrageous force of energy here unto you and let you simply work it out. In one manner that's what we're doing, but in another manner there are many entities now working feverishly to awaken mankind a little bit so they'll handle it. Your metaphysics is going to change—even that is going to change. There are going to be an awful lot of gods walking around here, an awful lot of Christs. That'll be a good thing; it'll also be a trap, but that's all right, that doesn't matter. Wake up you will!

Some of you are going to what is termed blast into light, do the ascension thing, come back again, do it back/forth, back/forth. That's the way you should do it. It gets the energy correctly. I know some of you can't wait to leave this place, go home. Well, you must remember you were bored home; that's why you came here. Everyone was telepathic, *you couldn't even play cards, for chrissakes!* [Laughter.] So you came here, because this is where the excitement is.

When the planet Earth moves—and it will—into its correct position in dimensional space, it's going to create quite an orgasm throughout the universe, throughout the system here, quite a feeling of ecstasy. Be felt everywhere! Everyone's waiting for it. Mm, hmm. You call it spiritual masturbation.

It's time to get on with it. It's going to happen. You'll make the shift easy if you understand this consciousness that you are. You don't have to destroy beings to create a shift. You support them, unconditionally loving. No judgment. In that manner you'll also help your planet. It won't have to blow itself apart as much, because she'll understand she's being loved for a change. It is awesome responsibility, but if you don't assume it and work with it, I will tell you this: There is a probability that you will judge yourselves outrageously, and it'll take us another eons to at least get your attention so you'll listen, you'll create such an abyss. What you term the mission failed, "my fault" thing. Everyone breathe.

This is the time you've been waiting for a long, long time. Thousands and thousands of years. This is it! You are in it now. Your next two years are going to be very, very interesting. You're all going to be very busy trying to hold unconditional love, first of all, and then sharing it, second of all. You all know that energy—you want to punch someone right in the nose, eh? Know you what I mean? "Can't wait to get close to that nose, upset me so much." Well, there is a future for you beings soon, that when you hit another you will feel the pain; the other won't. That's another game. One for the sadistic, I suppose.

Know you this year, before this year is over, what you call your September, October, there is going to be the understanding of how to overcome this death thing, how to do it literally, knowingly. How to go through the energy of it and not. It simply means your body will be vibrating faster . . . and you'll find out who you really are. You won't be locked down, so to speak. You'll understand that your body is a suit. That's going to be an outrageous thing to watch. I wonder how many beings are going to willingly share suits.

Rent '145em out.

Rent-a-suit.

Rent a suit for a day.

Don't tell him [Arthur] that—he might charge me.

I have a friend who is continually getting sick. Why is this?

. . . There's an interesting thing here. She's very fond of pesticides, eh?

No, she's not fond of pesticides.

Well, there is a lot around her.

In the area where she lives?

Indeed. It's causing her illness. It's absorbed through the skin.

Is it outside of her house, or something within her house?

It's outside by the front door. Someone is trying to kill ants and bugs there, and it's affecting her.

Is there something we can do for those who are deathly sick from this, or can you tell me how to overcome it, or what do we do?

Well, you beings have got yourself quite a quandary here. You've forgotten your power of consciousness and that you're related to all kingdoms, you see, and you want a structure outside of the structure that you use to create poisons that are killing everything on the planet, including you, to create another structure to solve the problem. Know you, the only way you can solve the problem is to get in tune with your consciousness and respect the divinity of all kingdoms. You see? You're living your own worst nightmare. You're killing yourselves and you know it, and there's nothing you can do about it except become more in tune with nature. Know what I mean? You're even killing your food that you eat, that you think is providing sustenance unto you.

My friend knows what's wrong and she does respect. She will not kill anything, even a cockroach. But she is suffering immensely.

Well, there's a karmic energy going on here also, but we don't like to play karma. Too often it is explained, and no one does anything to correct it even though they know what it is. So we gave up on that one. "Can't do anything about it. Karmically got me, so I'm done for." Don't understand the wisdom. That's all right. Doesn't exist anyway.

Can the toxins in the pesticides be transmuted?

There is a possibility that this will happen. It won't be because of your diligence, however. It'll be because your extraterrestrial buddies will come down and do it for you. You don't have the technology.

Several probabilities are going. Some of you are already aware that there are new seeds being planted, new areas, because you're destroying everything. Nothing you have is going to grow here pretty soon. You'll be eating the bark off trees and they'll be dying. Won't have to worry about that—you're going to cut them down anyway. Know you what I mean? You're not very wise entities, collectively.

Yahweh, what about all of these things we rub on our skin, like sun block and insect repellant. Is something like insect repellant benign?

Not all of them are. There are some that repel the insects that you can put on—citronella, know you citronella? That'll work. But some of the beings you're trying to repel are really trying to get your attention. You work collectively with nature. By biting you they're injecting you, of course.

They're injecting us with what?

Whatever you want. You're the god . . . here or are you the victim? Pick one. Know you the concept called medicine man in your American Indian tradition? Shaman, know you? You're the shaman. They know things . . . you do, too. It's time to get it. It's really what you are doing, what you're becoming. You're going beyond it. It's time to know. You're in it! You're right up to here, right in the thick of it. Think of it now: Thousands of years from now beings will say, "Gosh, I wish I was back in that generation that went through that experience."

Really?

You're going to be looked up to for your courage in this change, yes.

As a shaman it's appropriate to go around and warn insects that the pesticides are coming and get paid for it, then?

You can do that.

I thought I might also work on transmuting pesticides.

It is going to take some practice. You're going to have to learn to talk to the deva, the devic forces, indeed, involved here, and it's going to take time because you haven't set down beings, many, around the table with them, so to speak, to understand their needs. You force things upon nature, so nature doesn't respond very well to you anymore. It knows that you lie. So she's taking things back in her own consciousness (now those are your words). It's all part of yourconsciousness.

In other words, you know you lie to yourself, and you lie to God, because everything is God. You know you do that. So you're in quite a quandary getting out—yes, you are, all of you. It's all consciousness, that's all it is. It's all energy. It always has been, always will be unconditional love. You enjoy proving that it's not, that unconditional love doesn't exist. You're succeeding, you see, and you see what you're doing when you're succeeding and proving unconditional love doesn't exist? You destroy everything. That's what's happening, what you're doing. You're recognizing it, however, and you're willing to experience and feel unconditional love a little bit, a little bit, so you're coming out of it.

I don't mean to create a bleak, bleak picture—it's bleak enough. But you're coming out of it. You've reached the bottom of what you term your spiritual ignorance, you really have. You're coming upward now collectively, mankind is. That's why all of this information is out there, getting out there more, more. As a group you can all take credit for it, collectively. But there are going to be several, pretty soon, show up, want more credit than anyone else. Watch out!

Everyone take a breath. Peace.

Ready for one more meditation? Indeed? You can handle it? Okay. I want you to pick a track on the first disc. Not two, I already did that one.

Would five be okay?

[Planet Drum, Mickey Hart. Note: He didn't play track 5; he played track 2 again.]

Meditation

When the music starts, center your being and allow the energy. Now focus this pulse at the sixth seal, the third eye. Just hold it there, the beat. You may get ahead of me; it if moves down, let it move. This is your connection to nature now, the rhythm of the Earth. Allow. Allow the communication with the devas, all of them.

[As song fades:] Stay centered in your being. I want you to visualize a pyramid of light above your head, two inches above, and I want it to come down. Allow the light to come into the head. The pyramid will extend itself down through your body, the apex will remain above your head. Allow the energy. Center. Center.

Gold medallion – feel it in your right hand. Silver medallion in your left. Put your hands together in front of your heart chakra so the medallions touch each other, palm to palm. "Blessed be I" is the energy you feel in the body.

Allow you to become a flower, doesn't matter what one, what color, what kind. Allow your body to feel like a flower. Smell the fragrance of the flower. Allow the feeling of flower petals falling about you and upon you. Allow. Center.

Now we have what is termed a giant great snow leopard that's here, present. It teaches initiations and other mysteries. If you desire to go, you may go with him in your sleep tonight. You simply acknowledge your desire to go. You'll remember. You don't have to. Allow. Allow unconditional love, indeed?

[Group:] Indeed!

So be it!

[Group:] So be it!

⌖ ⌖ ⌖

Good morning!

[Group:] Good morning!

Everyone sleep well? [YHWH goes around the room and anoints each of the participants on the sixth seal with essential oil of chamomile.]

Meditation

Allow your eyes to close. Place your palms up on your thighs near the groin area. Indeed, center. I'm going to bring in some energy. It's going to enter the crown and leap, create an arc from the crown to the front, and it will push at that point I touched on your forehead. Indeed, so now allow.

We're working with a pyramid energy, soul. Allow it to come down. Allow a feeling of a pyramid resting upon the top of your head, and allow that pyramid so that one of the edges of the pyramid is aligned with your nose.

And at that apex, that point at the base, it shoots an arc out – allow it to enter the forehead, very gently now.

And the pyramid itself is being fed energy to its own apex, the top apex. As it enters it'll go into the center of the brain, circulate itself through the pineal gland and move down the spine, so allow it to do this.

[Focus at the] perineum, your buttocks. [Feel the] snake energy, hold it. [Now allow it to move up the spine and enter the head. It'll desire to come forward out of the sixth seal.] Center.

Allow the energy of the snake, we'll call it, to begin to move – in front of you, to the left side, around the back, to the right side, to the front, around the head, the outside. And it's a lavender color now. Allow.

The entity you term, your word called "Mary" is here. Allow her to be around you, allow her to be around you, the energy – it's the energy. Blue-white. Allow. Center. Now I want you to feel embraced by this energy, loving arms around you. Be within it.

Open the heart chakra wider, and this one is going to put a message in there for you. Allow. It'll be like a parchment, it might be like a tablet, might be like a sphere. Do not judge the form. Feel the entry of that message in the body. Feel the love within it, unconditional here. Allow the healing. Center. Center.

Feel a white light, diamondlike, at the throat chakra. Let it stay there. Feel it open the throat. Allow. Breathe out of it a little bit. Center.

We're balancing your energy, you're balancing your energies here. We're also balancing all of the energies that we worked with yesterday. Recall you the sri yantra and that circle. So we're balancing all the energies in there, very gently.

So center your being. You're one of the points of light in this yantra here. Center. Allow your point of light at the intersection to expand so the yantra itself, instead of being formed out of triangles of lines of light, becomes one blinding flash of light, the entire thing. It joins with other lights. Allow. Center.

Those of you that worked with the planets yesterday, bring the planet close to you, right in front of your heart chakra, and allow it to flash a brilliant white. Simply the flash – it is wisdom acknowledged. Allow. Grand. Allow.

In a gentle manner slowly open your physical eyes. Be in your moment now. Okay.

There is a very interesting phenomenon beginning to occur around your planet, and that's the phenomenon of the sensation, the energy sensation, that many will want to be cared for, taken care of. It's building. Now, this impulse is coming from what would be termed a completion, which in order to get there you have to go through the antichrist energy and this, that and the other; and the one called the Antichrist is going to provide the opportunity for completion, and that energy is that he (she) will take care of you.

Now, don't get caught up into that game. You have to understand that you, individually, are in the process of becoming, and if you argue about it you have already lost. Continue to desire to know more of you. To define you, to limit you, will set you back. You are who you are without limit. You are forever.

There will be very shortly, within your three months coming, a great sensation about this planet, a sensation of need to be assisted – help from outside, of God, as you would term it here. It's going to be very tempting because it's going to be easier the other way. You are all on a very outrageous journey.

Now, regardless of the prophecies or the warnings, you are still involved in the process –you. And it doesn't matter what another predicts or says. For some of you it will matter –very poignantly, as a matter of fact – but that's your job. It's not so much to get caught up in the prophecies, but to understand them. It is to assist the consciousness of the planet. Believe it or not, the consciousness of the planet now is becoming more important than the consciousness of the humans upon it, because humans continue to live forever. But the planetary consciousness has a limitation that way.

So your extraterrestrial friends, and what you term the guides and this and that, are focusing more upon the planet now. In one manner, you could say, from a flippant way, they've given up on humanity. Take a breath. The planet is more important because of the magnetics and because of your gravity and because of your circumference around your sun and this and that and the other. You're affecting other systems; the planet is tied with other systems. Humans do not want to understand this even at this date –very few.

So now the focus is off the gods becoming. The focus is what is termed the rescue mode now to the Planetary Logos. It's in trouble. So we are now going to deal directly in that manner. "We – us, great grouping – and some of you here and some of you that are in other groups here also. You've all had enough information now. We're not going to repeat, repeat, repeat. We're getting to work. Some of you are going to be guided in a manner, dragged kicking and screaming as usual, to assist the planet, to balance the frequencies. Be sending some of you to certain areas; you don't know why you have to go there, why you're being directed this way, that way. It's to straighten out some of the gridwork there. You might not know how you're doing it or in what manner to do it, but you will do it. From the inside of you, you'll feel the need. Everyone breathe now very gently.

So this is what you came here for. You didn't come here to sit around and be pharaohs all of the time. You came here to work. You knew what had to be done. It's not going to make a difference who you were in a past lifetime or who you think you're going to get to be in a future lifetime, because if you don't what you call at least make an effort to assist your planet, you're going to judge yourself so much you're not going to have another lifetime, what you call into your greaterness for a very, very, long time. The limitations you will place upon yourself. Know you, "Oops, screwed that one up! Got to go back, do it again." It's getting too critical to play babysitter anymore.

So in that manner we're going to do a meditation. We're going to take you to the center of the planet – center, core. We're going to find the heart of the planet, and everyone of you is going to embrace it, hug it, comfort it. And your heart will surround it.

Meditation

Straighten your spines. Allow your eyes to close. Center. Tighten your buttocks a little bit. Exhale out. At that point where you tightened your buttocks I want you to send a red light, red line of light, to the center of the planet. Send it there, feel it anchor there, right in the center. Connect, indeed. Open the throat chakra.

I want you to move your consciousness now, the inside of you, down that line of light to where it connects with the center of the planet. Be there. And I want you to feel. Some of you that can see, allow you to see this great pulsing heart there. It is enormous in size. I want you to feel the sadness in the heart there. Allow.

Now I want you to change that sadness. Give it the unconditional love that you have here. Center. Work with it. I want you to embrace it with your light, green light, around this heart. Center. Surround it with your heart energy.

Now, you don't have to do the next step, but if you desire to, make a commitment to assist this Logos in these changes it must go through to heal the heart. Ask what you can do to be of assistance or not. Sending love is assistance. Allow. One message, to give you an example in the listening, is that the heart wants to be bathed in your tears – that's one message. Now feel it and listen.

This is going to carry on for a number of years, entities. You have two to three years to go through this. Center. Allow. Listen. Some of you are getting visions of where the planet, where this heart energy of the planet, is directing, what you would term showing you in what manner it must alter, what portions of its sphere need to be changed for it to feel better. You're past the point of changing it. Center. Allow the visions, because these need to be shared with others – the visions of it – understanding that the planet needs to change, needs this assistance, needs this release. It's an adjustment for its survival. Center.

I want you to contemplate in this energy vortex that you're in now, that you have passed this physical life – you are in your other experience now. I want you to look back to this energy time and to see whether you did what you knew to do, or didn't. I want you to experience that out there. You can change it now – I don't want you to judge yourselves later and say you weren't told. Be in your other lifetime, look you back here – did you do enough? Center.

If not, move to the center of the Earth. Find out what more you can do. Center. Bless the energy in the center of the Earth, bless it from the point of view that is there. Move you up your line of light, up into your perineum. Move to your heart chakra. Be in your body. Center. Open the crown. Center.

Allow your eyes to open gently and be in your moment, very gently. If you need to adjust some energies, allow your eyes to close a little bit more. Now allow your eyes to open very gently. As you do the opening gently, I want the sense of responsibility, the sense of power, the sense of commitment, the sense of love for all things, to move from in your body up into the brain as you open your eyes.

So allow your eyes to close again. This will create a memory pattern here. Allow your eyes to open now. Bring the energy up to the brain. Now, the portions of the brain that you haven't opened yet, that are being opened, have the answers to this problem. Those ancient portions that are being reawakened have the answers in little boxes and cubicles. So the flashes of insight in this manner are going to come to you. It might simply be to talk to one blade of grass or to one tree or to a bird and see the communication between all things, to assist. It might be to go to a place. But you will know. Everyone breathe.

How's that for the beginning of a day?
[*Planet Drum* by Mickey Hart, track three.]

Just relax in the energies now. You can allow your eyes to close or open, it doesn't matter. I want you to feel the energy. Allow the connection of your heart chakra to the heart of the planet energy we dealt with. Allow. Feel.

Now there is energy building around your head – let it move there. This is going to give you a higher level of knowing what's really going on and how important it is.

You didn't really come to this planet to save humanity; you came here to save the planet! Anything else is incidental. How do you feel? Little emotional? You should. If you could see and only know what a fine piece of thread is left, you would panic. Now is not even the time to get into arguments about what to do. Now is the time to walk as god and do it gently, what you must do, what'll be felt in the body to do. When we went past this lifetime forward to another and you looked back at what you did or didn't do here, how did you feel? Mm-hmm. That's how serious it is, and that feeling was your judgments of self, is what it was, because "out there" at your next place you have a little more wisdom. You don't want to leave this place leaving that sort of judgment behind you, dragging it along. You're not going to escape it. You're not going to be able to play with it metaphysically, either, because as you advance you'll understand it's energy, and you have to work with it, you have to deal with it. It's not a label at all. Everyone breathe.

You're very powerful beings in your lights and in your own right here. The power is to be used for the Planetary Logos now, and the consciousness of humanity will be affected, indeed it will later, but those are drag-alongs. They don't want to advance, doesn't matter to them. They are spiritually ignorant. You're not . . . unless you want to be.

For the lot of you here, this day in this room at this time now – not for others that listen to this tape later, but for those of you that are here – I will speak to you individually. You will hear my voice to go to this place or that place at a time and simply sit there and meditate for a little bit. I don't mean week, two weeks – day, couple of hours. Won't put you out of your way. As you do that you'll assist the planet. There will be some of you that won't do it, you'll find your excuse. That's all right, I already know that. You don't have to. I'm advising you for your own well-being. Everyone take a breath. Indeed, okay. Does anybody have anything they want to share?

Meditation

Allow your eyes to close for a moment. Center your body. Center. There is a great gold light above you. I want you to tap into it out there, tap into it. Center. Allow red from your perineum down to the center of the Earth now.

Now, from your sitting position, be in your body, your conscious body, I want you to see the walls of this house fall away, and you see trees around you and horizon, property around. Simply look out at it, simply look at it. Love the rock for being the rock, love the tree for being the tree, the earth the earth, the grass the grass, the weed the weed – love it all. Thank it for being there. Also thank yourself for allowing yourself to walk upon the planet. "I allow myself to walk upon thee." Allow. Contemplate "I allow myself to walk upon thee." That "thee" is the planet or the grass or the rock. Contemplate that. Now feel in your perineum the need for the respect in the walking upon which you are – feel it in the perineum, buttocks there. Bring that feeling up into the heart chakra so it becomes wisdom. Feel it in the heart chakra, in the soul. Allow. Bring the energy up.

You're in the pyramid of the soul now. Energy is up from the perineum. Around the head I want you to feel the spiritual forces called consciousness of all humanity, around the head. Consciousness of you there spinning around your head. Allow. Feel it.

Now feel the difference: Go from the head to the heart chakra – the difference in feeling. Stay in the heart chakra. Take your energy now in the heart chakra and push it up into the brain and allow your brain frequency, your waves – we're activating more of your brain now – allow it to pulse out into the consciousness of humanity so they get a sense of what you're feeling. Just think it! Waves out, let it go out around the planet, allow. The need for the respect, allow. Heart chakra, feeling, bring it up to the head. Pulse it out, brain-wave activity now, outward. Center.

Now move your consciousness higher to that gold light that's above you. Center. In a gentle manner slowly open your physical eyes. With your eyes open bring this energy here, the respect, into the brain area here. This way you'll have the capacity to remember and think. Allow. And you become dignified gods. Allow. Take a breath and blow it out of that diamond that's in the heart chakra. That is truth now. You're beginning to know truth, the feeling of it. Center.

Allow your eyes to close and be in your moment. Play Sri Yantra [by Jeffrey Thompson] . Center. Now allow your eyes to open a little bit. Allow your eyes to close gently. I want the energy in the brain, the heart, together, perineum together, center of the Earth together. Listen. All one vibration now. All of it's one. Allow.

We're bringing memories to you now, memories of why you came here, more memories than you can imagine – let them come to you. They'll float along the lines of the sri yantra, what you're really, really here for. Allow. Some of you will even recognize what command you're associated with, something new, different. Get away from labels. You're not here to be pharaohs, you're on a rescue mission not only for this civilization, but others that are affected by it. The starting point is the planet. Allow your eyes to open.

Allow your eyes to close. We're building gold energy around the head now. Allow it to be there. It wants to merge into the head, the point. You will feel pressure at what you call the angle of your eyes, inside. Allow. Be with it. Don't judge anything. I want you to feel rose petals beginning to fall out of the sky, out of thin air, around you. Allow. Feel it.

Allow the energy to move to your navel chakra. Visualize the symbol OM there at the navel. Feel it there, entering. Rose petals are still falling; allow the fragrance if you can. Visualize OM at the solar plexus chakra. Heart chakra, throat chakra, sixth seal, crown – OM. Above the head – OM. Center. The OM that is at your heart chakra, take your consciousness down, move down through the red line to the center of the planet and bring that OM that you have there to the center of the planet, to the heart of the planet. Offer the OM to the heart.

Return you to your physical consciousness. In a gentle manner, slowly open your physical eyes. Take a breath. Breathe.

Okay. Pretty good, eh? Do you have a question?

Yeah. What happened yesterday afternoon? On the first drumbeat I lost consciousness and I've been dead and sick ever since.

The drums we were using to create shift in structure, know you what I mean? And a lot of times you enjoy saying, "I'll let go of structure," and then [YHWH grabs onto the arm of the entity to whom he's speaking and holds tight]. Know you what I mean?

Okay, how can I do this?

Well, this one is helping you, know you? The big one there. You beings used to be old warriors together, know you what I mean?

Yeah, he's a pretty good warrior.

If there is not cosmic evil out there, he'll find it, know you what I mean? Even if it doesn't exist.

A lot of you are going to be taking side journeys and you don't know why. I just told you why. Very important to stay connected to the planet now.

All of these journeys are going to be rather easy. If you understand the easiness, it makes the flow of the energy a lot better. Well, for most of you they're going to be easy. Some of you enjoy the pressure. That's all right.

I am just in between rage and such a profound sadness, I can't even tell you.

Well, they're going to blend together. You're going to get it.

Boy, did you see the part of me that's throwing things against the wall and kicking?

That's why I have my hand on your leg over there. I'm saying it's okay.

I know. But what ghastly mistakes we've made!

Well, we want to get to the point where we don't judge, indeed? We want to get you to understand, "Okay, we messed up so far, we've screwed it up, but now we have still opportunity to change it." If we ignore it, then as you move to go further, you felt that energy, the judgment, and back you come. You want to do something about it now, before we play there.

I don't want anybody dragging me while I'm kicking and screaming. I'm going on my own free will.

As always, eh? I understand.

Yahweh, I have a question. Did we have an opportunity and fail when Maldek exploded?

Well, let's put it this way: You had an opportunity there for a great leap in consciousness, yes. It became very stagnant, and that's where the idea of pharaoh came from, how it came into Egypt. Created pharaoh thing, this, that, the other. That's why what you term Maldek was taken out, as you say. It wasn't going anywhere.

So Atlantis was the opening curtain for now?

You still don't have the correct story of Atlantis. It's as much your future as it is your past, indeed. You beings are linear here, know you? When Atlantis, you say, past rises, you say—you need that perception for becoming,—consciousness will be leaping then, and you'll be worthy of the energy, understanding freedom, not control, which is why time is collapsing. I don't want to get into that too much. It is an outrageous thing here. It's not really time collapsing. Those are the words we have to say to you so you would understand it.

It's more that your consciousness is expanding, becoming aware of all realities, all times, all places. That means you're becoming powerful spiritually. Do you see? And as you, you say, move up a level, you see more. Move up another level, you see more, see more, see more, see more, see more. You don't have to leave the physical body to do that. As your consciousness expands, as your brain is more open, you're using more of the frequency of the brain, you will understand why we use the term "time collapse, time shrink." You'll understand that time doesn't exist, it's a no thing, so the brain can function in any reality and take your body there. You don't need your spaceships or any of this. Everyone breathe a moment.

That's what's so important about understanding the consciousness, which you are, because it's all consciousness and all unconditional love. You will find as you go this way [YHWH gestures, making a V, starting at the point, moving upward and outward] — this is the expansion of consciousness now — that these levels down here at the point, the apex of a pyramid upside down [bottom of the V] have partitions in them. And the partitions become wider here — very well, few partitions — one here, one there [middle of the V], none here [near the top of the V, the wide part]. And as you come down, you look, "Well, they think they're in this time here. This one thinks they're in this time. This one thinks they're in this space." You'll see it all. I should have a board, know you; I could draw this thing.

You want me to get it?

You have one? Indeed, get one out.

What's the sri yantra you keep talking about?

It's interconnecting pyramids, interlocking, creates great diamond patterns.

Like a merkabah?

It's a little different. They're similar.

Can you draw that, too?

Well, we have a picture of it on the disc cover. You can look at that. [*Sri Yantra* by Jeffrey Thompson.] Okay, as your consciousness expands, you see everything about you and everything beneath you.

Some masters are capable of being physical upon the planet, allowing their consciousness to expand to see all things, playing in each time line down here, each little space, and they know where they are and what they're doing there, indeed. In order to truly help the planet, your consciousness does have to expand, because you're going to need to see your future (what you would term your future) in order to create an effect here that will influence the future – do it appropriately, not clumsily. Know you what I mean? Indeed?

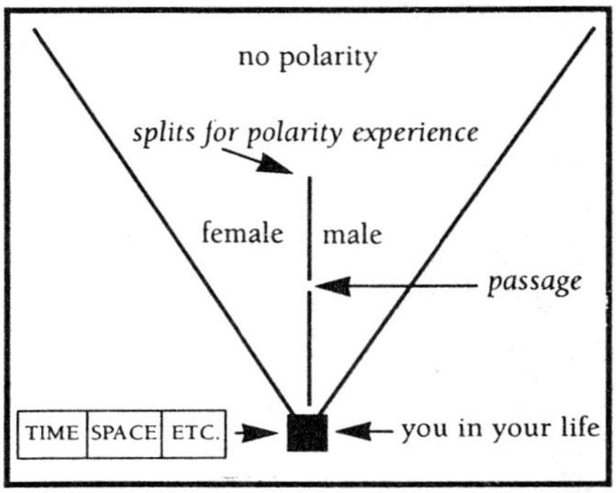

[The drawing board arrives.] This is consciousness, okay [upside-down pyramid or a V-shape]. Down in this point here [the point of the V], you think this is you now in your life, that point, of all your consciousness in here come down. There are segments here up this far [midway]. There is only one, sort of splits it. From here you can look at both sides. Down here [near the point] you can only see one side. This is where you beings enjoy, you say, polarity – male/female, positive/negative, good/bad. No problem. Here [near the wide part of the V] you know it doesn't exist as that.

Okay, now down at this point you have like what you'd term boxes. Box – time. You play in that box there, time/space. So you enjoy playing in all of these times and spaces, but that is only here. You are all of this [the whole V or pyramid and beyond]. When I say lightbody, lightbeing, this is you [above the V or pyramid]. You can call it God because you're all there together looking alike and trying to get bored and get out of here. "Let's get down where we can separate." See what I'm speaking about? Not clear?

It's clear.

Indeed. That's what you do. You're down here. Polarity exists even out there, from your perspective, because it's fun. "Damn, I was female for 40,000 years; time to be male." "I was male for 40,000 years; time to be female." And then you go . . . you don't stay here, however [midsection of the V], where you can go back/forth, because there's an avenue here, sort of like a little passage right in there, go back/forth, back/forth, back/forth. You come right down here [at the point] – "Let's really play it" (time/space).

What is happening now is your consciousness is expanding.

You're becoming aware. Some of you are having difficulty even identifying your sexuality, whether you know it or not, some beings upon the planet. Know you how this – I love the judgments of it, too – you beings say "gay," know you? Gays? It's just a difficulty in identifying the shift in consciousness that's evolving, that knows it's both sexes.

Then you get caught up in metaphysics. That's all right. If they would allow that understanding that they chose the body (this is not making a judgment, I'm simply telling you the way it is), you're consciousness evolving, so you're understanding you're both sexes within the body, you take another leap, you become a master! You've become the living Christ, without playing the judgment of what sexual polarity means. Beyond it. You know you're both, and that power will accelerate you outrageously here. It occurs right down here [navel chakra] – this is where you separate it. Everyone breathe a moment. Okay.

Now, as you go up to the top of this thing here, you become god or whatever word you want to play with. As that realization begins to happen and you're still in the physical body, you have a profound effect where you walk. Now, some of the Christs lose it here because they walk upon the planet, but they don't have respect for what they're walking upon. They know they create it, so they think they own it. That's a trap. You allow yourself to walk upon the planet with respect to your creation. If you don't have that feeling there, it is like a perversion. It is like you have a baby and you would pervert it. But you know better than that. You have a baby, you take care of it. You want it to evolve. The planet is like that for the Christs that are walking. Too many of the Christs have forgotten it. That give you a little background here? Little bit of story?

Indeed.

Okay. Now, what happened with Maldek is beginning to happen here upon this planet. Before it [Maldek] exploded, before it was blown up, more appropriately. The human condition is getting to the point, as it understands metaphysically that it's god, that a lot of things are god, into this comparing of which god, which system you come from, this, that and the other, and they're acting like pharaohs – creating belief systems here, there, wherever, with an up-ridge, and all the little ones are low-ridge.

It didn't last long on Maldek, and I'll tell you this: The pharaohs of Maldek were not incarnate; they were overlords around the planet. They were overlords. They didn't get physical until they came to planet Earth, in their rescue of the souls (what *they* call the rescue), the bringing of the souls here. That's when they became physical. They weren't. They were overlords before that, creating what you term—it was a nice environment, beautiful, but the overlords weren't allowing their creations to evolve, they enjoyed being overlords so much. The plan, as you beings like to call it here, is evolution, that's what it is. Evolving. Forever. So I blew up Maldek. Yeah, I did it. In one manner I'm responsible for the pharaohs being here, my fault. No big deal. I've been on the hit list for a long time. [Laughs.] Evolution. Evolution.

We're printing things constantly by a telepath who has a different viewpoint. He said some of those from Maldek came here and used the pyramid to blow up Maldek. Is he in an altered reality, or . . . ?

Allow that story to be, indeed, because it creates another story, indeed, and gives me a place to hide. [YHWH laughs.]

What we're doing is from the point of view from beings who were on what he calls radiars, moons of radiars.

Indeed, you're dealing with a level of consciousness that has what you term fourth- dimensional bodies, fifth-dimensional bodies, sixth-dimensional bodies. They're still in the understanding of consciousness as body. They're at this point [midsection of the V or pyramid]. Not in the polarity point, however, but they can go back/forth, maybe a little higher here, indeed?

They're speaking from their immortal body now, but they're giving us remembrances of where they were when Maldek blew up, how it affected the Earth, some of their lives on the Earth. It's very interesting.

Indeed. The effects were rather outrageous.

It took life out of all the other planets in the system.

It did a lot of things.

What he said was that they were trying to steal the psychic energy of the Earth and transmit it to Maldek, and unfortunately that's what blew up Maldek.

[YHWH chuckles.] It is good. It is a good thing. Takes a lot of load off my shoulders, know you what I mean?

I know, but where . . . ?

In the understanding . . . first of all, we'll put it this way: You don't know who I am, indeed? If you have a concept, that's all, indeed? So you have to understand it from my perspective, indeed? Now, if I didn't want it to happen, it wouldn't have happened.

So they could still have done it, but you just allowed it.

Let me put it another way. Are you familiar with the reputation of Jehovah?

Not really. I've never read the Bible.

Well, not the Bible. Even metaphysically?

Not really.

Very few beings are allowed to even talk about it.

I really don't know that much. I like Shiva and . . .

I am a rascal, know you? Outrageous. I can cause civilizations to rape other civilizations just by the thought of it, for fun!

Yeah, but that . . . that's just part. You're much more than that.

I grow up, too. Consciousness is what God is. Thought is very powerful, know you what I mean? As you learn thought, you've heard metaphysically, thinking a thing is the thing? I'm very good at that.

Okay, so you thought it and they played out the story, then. Is that one way to think?

That is one way. You know, before, I said I was the Will of the Father, just simply the words, the explanation, just to understand, indeed? Now I know you have difficulty with this phrase "Father" or "God." I understand that, I don't have an issue. Now let's go back to when all of this started, indeed?

You say there is a beginning or an end. Well, there isn't, if you play this time thing down here and all time is one. But you don't *know* that. Know you what I mean? There was this great, great desire to understand from the Void—you've heard that concept? There were many Voids, right? Well, there was one Void that did it first, gave the other Voids the ideas. It was big Void. The portion of the Void that desired to know itself (now pay attention)—*the portion of the void that desired to know itself*—that emotion, that energy, the desire and the focused will of it, *to complete it, is who I am*. Know you "will"? You have to focus indeed, to get it done. That's the part of the Father that I am.

The focus?

Focus—you beings call it the will. You have the will to do this, indeed. That part is who be I.

Okay, so if you back up, evolution was stagnating, wasn't going anyplace. It needed to be . . . you changed its structure, that's all.

Structure is changing.

Yes. From our point of view, we see, "Oh my God, all these dead bodies!" But they're immortal. You said you used to blow up the bodies, and you only cared about the soul. But now here we have to deal with the bodies too, for the first time.

This is the first time.

This is the time . . . you've been so many eons here, know you, that? Life is forever, do you have that one, at least metaphysically? Indeed? You've spent so many times here and the soul has been utilized so the spirit can embody and live in flesh and play, to gather emotion — that's what its design is for, indeed. That's what the design is for. You've lived so many eons here, in lifetimes, reincarnation, that genetically you've created the memory of the soul, and it's in all of your cells. Know you what I mean? Do you understand that part? Okay. You have a big soul here, indeed?

So holographically we replicate it in every cell?

Yes, that's why it's very easy for you to ascend now. You don't have to leave the soul out of the body to go. The soul knows other souls are in its body. Just consider the shape right now, indeed? So it'll take it all with it. The body can vibrate that fast, but you need the mind to do that, the brain.

Okay, for the first time I understand how it can be transmuted.

The soul is like a cave, a hiding place that you can come into and create the body about it. It happens so fast, however, your consciousness is not aware of it. Are you aware that you blink on and off all of the time and you're just simply agreeing to blink on at the same time to see each other?

Theoretically, yeah.

Indeed.

The consciousness up there knows, but not the consciousness here.

The soul knows here. The barrier around it, the electrical force around it, prevents you from seeing that.

Oh, like a force field.

A force field! Know you how at times we've taken the flap of the soul down, opened it, and I've told some of you to look through your heart chakra? You don't see anything; there's no one there. Some of you that's happened to. It scared you, so you put it back up, find everybody — "Oh, there you are!" Sort of shook my tree a little bit, too. Indeed? I haven't done that meditation for a while.

You beings have a tendency to take things so . . . we have a disadvantage. It is your words here. You're required to speak them so you understand them, but they are not the truth. Your vocabulary is a *lie*. The message is between the words, most truly. Telepathy would be the greatest advance for your civilization so we could communicate more clearly, indeed? Now this one that you speak of, in his information, it is accurate in the pretense of the being that is writing the history. Know you, if you have two historians, the path of history is different but the outcome will be the same. Indeed? So this is similar.

Well, it's interesting that their stories corroborate each other.

Indeed! Similar.

Were we as souls on that planet, too?

Not everyone. A lot of beings here were there, yes indeed.

For eons and eons, for a long time?

Well . . .

Not as long as we've been here.

The souls that were on that planet, I'll tell you, some escaped. And by that I mean when the planet exploded, some of them did not follow the overlord here. Some of them realized at the time of the explosion that they were now free – they had no overlord. You understand? And they came here to assist. They in a manner followed the overlord to help the friends that became trapped with the overlord again here under the pharaohship thing. Very interesting puzzle.

Who was the overlord?

I'm not going to say. He is known, however, heard of here. There were layers of them. One particular one. Doesn't matter. We've chatted, indeed, because we began to understand – know you how I spoke of before, even what you call the energy, the understanding called Lucifer, indeed? We're buddies now. He's seen the light. [Laughs.] And he himself is a great light. We've seen how much confusion there is in your abilities even to become when you're provided with [a] little wisdom. You will pick up the next structure, hold on forever, and it doesn't get you anywhere. What it does, it keeps us from going further. We only have one sock, got to wait for the other one, know you? "Where's the sock?"

"Well, the children have it out in the yard."

"Where's that?"

"Oh, it's Earth!"

"Oh, my God, they're down on Earth again! I'll never get my sock back now. Probably feed it to the dog or something."

When you say the planet is hanging by a thread, are you talking about everything combined — the ozone layer, the psychic pollution, the pollution of the water?

Yes. The fact that your government is mucking around with energy waves, yes! We begin to think you're truly idiots here. I mean we're getting proof enough.

So nothing has stopped? That HAARP Project is going on?

It's still going on, little bit. We did quite a bit of damage. They're trying to get another satellite up. It won't go, either.

But they took it underground and created an earthquake in China.

Yes. Yes.

So what do we do?

You can really see how brilliant they are, can't you? Well, all I can tell you is, we're working on it. It's all God, understand? You haven't got to the point yet where we have to take drastic action, but it's getting close.

So if we can love them — and we were attempting to release that ability yesterday — that can perfect it?

Yes. Unconditional love awakens everyone to a point. And what they'll go through is their guilt and their judgments and things, and they'll eventually heal themselves and understand. But there will be layers they must go through, know you? Unconditional love is all that exists. You're playing at the part where you say it doesn't. That is all right.

So that is the answer, then. The more we love, the more we save our planet.

The more you love, the more you allow your consciousness to expand and become more and more and more, and the more you affect other beings, yes, and it affects the planet, and the planet knows. Yes. Because your consciousness truly is what you term Mother Nature — that's what is nature — God's consciousness — yours. Literally!

It is of most assistance to focus energy on love and healing rather than trying to focus on the problem?

Yes, love; focus on love.

Focus on the solution, not the problem?

Focus on love. The solution will provide itself.

And that's why Mary was here, or that energy, because by feeling that to myself, then I felt that to the planet. It was like a chain.

Yes, what we term the energy. We used the name, but it is the energy, indeed. It's going to be around you for the week, so you might as well get used to it.

Well, that's not so hateful.

I know. It's okay. Do you have a question, another one?

Well, no, it's just that the melodrama is, Can humans learn to love before they tear

up their planet? That's what everyone is doing out there — trying to help keep the planet together until we wake up, right?

Indeed. You're going to be very . . .

Keep this school open so that there's someplace to have school, and yet the school has got to heal itself.

You're going to be very sick with yourselves later, really. Very nauseated with your spiritual ignorance. Literally, you will. Major judgment coming up for humanity here, in their own consciousness self, for what you did do and didn't do, planetarywise. Blame is going to go out the window. Those that did the majority of the damage are going to try to hide. Well, they'll be hiding right in my pocket, like I said before. Can't go anywhere. You can unconditionally love and learn it and play it in these next two years, three years. You can do a lot to modify here.

Now, one of the ways you can measure the scale of how you're succeeding is how much human life is lost. You can have outrageous catastrophes, but you don't need outrageous loss of human life. So if you're having outrageous catastrophes and the miracle is that no one died, know that your unconditional love is working. Know what I mean? Or if one or two [die], but not 100,000 or a million and a half.

Your psychic energy could not stand it. Oh, I know you think you're very strong psychically, but if a million and a half people in your United States died in thirty seconds, you would literally come close to . . . I'll say, destroying yourself over guilt, even though you knew it was going to happen.

Unconditional love can change it, be at the right place, the right time, not damaged, but the structures will be. You recall what is termed five years ago, I think it was, I said the winds are going to get to be about 300 miles an hour? Know you? That hasn't stopped. They're very close to coming here. Your consciousness and unconditional love can change it, can modify it. It's your job!

Your extraterrestrial buddies are getting a little upset —you're keeping them on what you would term 24-hour watch. They have very little time to eat their Jell-O, know you what I mean? [Laughter.] Some of them, even though they love you greatly, are becoming very upset and bored with the whole thing. Check it out. Check out with some of your other channels. See what your extraterrestrials *really* think now. Hmm. They're not very pleased. They're beginning to wonder if you're worth it. You *don't* want to leave; you *need* their assistance. Everyone take a breath.

But they know the Earth is worth it.

There is a plan afoot now — believe it — as you would say or not, to create an artificial Earth to hold the magnetics, to create a different Earth. Immediately replace it when this is destroyed, to put it in orbit so nothing is affected. Sort of switch [them]. That plan is afoot. That is a standby.

If I understand right, the Earth is in a process of evolution.

Yes.

So there are a certain number of things that the Earth feels it needs to do.

Yes.

In my meditation I saw red glowing, maybe lava, in the Amazon.

Yes.

And so by us working with unconditional love, it doesn't mean that . . . you know, I wouldn't want to interfere with the Earth's evolution.

You can't. It would be inappropriate, yes.

So just to send that unconditional love so that fewer lives are lost. . . .

Human condition.

And ultimately to help humanity and give humanity enough time so they can wake up and bring their selves together, to vibrate fast enough to take their bodies with them?

Well, in a manner, when the planet goes through its evolution — and it's going to, indeed, it's going to evolve — it wants to do it with humanity upon it. That would be the greatest ecstasy for the planet itself. It's having difficulty. In one manner it has been slowing its evolutionary forces down, hoping mankind would understand. Well, it has sort of given up now, and it's going to do its thing, it's going to re-create.

So as it's consciousness and because it's evolving, its consciousness moves higher, it's going to require a higher consciousness of God on the planet to stay here, know you what I mean? A higher level of spiritual understanding, we'll say. So in that way the Earth is looking forward to those beings that are going to be here at the same time, through this process. You're *all* going through a birthing thing. It's time to recognize this, know you? Mother, father, their baby coming.

You need to see these volcanoes go off, yes, you need the lava, yes. You need the earthquakes, yes. It's just that where you have placed your buildings you can't blame the Earth for moving, indeed? And it is a privilege, an honor to be, as you are evolving God now, in human form — your consciousness, your understanding the life of all things, spirituality. It's a privilege, an honor, to be upon —walking god, walking master — upon a birthing planet. It's an honor! It's something you'll carry with you forever! "I was there when the Earth birthed a newness! I was there! It was outrageous experience!" And believe it or not, there are beings that were on Maldek that say they were there when it was blown up — "It's outrageous!" They like talking about it now; at the time it was a little difficult. But it is an honor to be here, it truly is.

So if only 20% of the population would be here when the Earth is at a higher level, if the natural disasters don't allow those who can't stay to leave, then how will they be taken off? Just dying and rebirthing and their soul moving someplace else?

Well, it'll happen so fast that the concept of death and those that are alive, it won't matter.

Is the "it" when the planet comes to a stop and turns the opposite direction?

We can say that when "it" happens, but that's your metaphysical behavior, that's the clinical understanding, scientifically, indeed? It's a little more than that. What I'm trying to get you to understand is, *it's all consciousness*, know you? And you have to pick your level in this pyramid where you're going to be, and you can do it —you can do it *today!* You're going to want to be high vibration when this Earth shifts its consciousness, evolves. You say, stop its spinning, know you?

Well, the physical effect of this consciousness is the stopping of the spinning — that's just the physical part.

That would be the appearance of it, yes. Yes, I will say it that way.

And no human body can withstand that and keep its human body, so we'd better get out of our human body.

It be very difficult. You have a great mass — know you mass, the Earth? Now, it is like a big person thinking great thought when it shifts — that's all it is. The thought: it wants to change, roll over in bed, know you? Roll over. And if another being is on the bed and the big being is rolling over, the other being is affected, know you? Well, it's going to roll over. It's simply thought shifting, but I don't have the words to explain it to you. The Earth has thought processes.

As those of us who are working with unconditional love continue to work with it for the Earth and humanity, can that 20% number change?

We are *hoping* to get 20% now, because you had an opportunity and then you beings let it go. But that's all right. What will happen is, if you move into unconditional love. . . . I'm going to say this.

This hasn't been put out yet, so I might as well spill the beans: In the shift, the Earth will understand you and throw an envelope of protection around you and you'll make it through it even if you can't vibrate your body.

It is best to be in close communication with the Earth.

I suggest. [Laughter.] Like a mother taking care of her babies. You've heard the Native Americans, they talk of Mother Earth, indeed? I've told you it's not your mother, it's consciousness and this and that. I'm not creating an argument, you understand. I'm telling you what it is. But if you work with the Earth in its consciousness and you unconditionally love it, when this rotation begins itself or stops, there will be those that will be . . . I understand metaphysically that your extraterrestrials are going to come down and lift the selected off the planet. Well, that might happen in some cases.

But there is another thing that's going to occur. The Earth itself knows who is protecting it and who isn't, and she'll throw an energy vortex around you so nothing will happen. You'll be in tune with the Earth, do you understand? And when you're in tune with what the Earth is doing, nothing is going to happen to you if the Earth is doing it. Now, that doesn't mean jump into a hurricane or a flood. No. You know what I mean? You don't be spiritually ignorant. That's spiritually ignorant. Just understand you are unconditional love, did all you could, the best you can —you're in it now.

Will the Earth also protect her animals?

Majority of animals are going to leave.

Because they finished?

Well, they're sort of fed up with humanity, too. But it's all evolution. You'll get it back again. They'll be reseeding. Majority of animals didn't come from this place, anyway; they were brought here by your extraterrestrials to seed here. So that'll happen again.

With all those getting fed up with us, isn't that a kind of judgment also?

Well, fed up is a word I have to use here. It is sort of, uh . . . you're wearing them out, know you? You're draining their energy. And in that manner they say, "Well, I'm going to sit on my ship just a little bit longer here, get my energy back."

It must be the same way we feel when we're faced with people that are in massive denial or very negative, or . . .

Yes. Partially, yes.

And yet you speak of it as if . . . this is a planet of peace. It is going to happen. So one way or the other, it is . . .

It's going to happen.

That thin thread will hold, then?

Well, we're trying to make it thicker. We're simply advising you the way it is. You beings seem to work better when you're on the abyss, know you?

That's true.

I know! Until it really starts moving toward you and then, "Oh, my! Got to do something!" I have another book to get out.

Good. Sometimes a warning is of assistance in focusing will and intent.

It's more an advice. I'm going to be with you forever, anyway. I don't care if you die in this lifetime or another. Going to be there again, and we'll sit at the bar and complain about it, and you'll want to go down there again. And I'll say, "Are you sure?" [Laughter.] Okay, well, give me 32,000 years and maybe I can check on you. It's all right. The planet is what needs your help now. You know what I mean?

Indeed.

Allow you to take a break here. And I'm placing a bubble in each of you, little bubble, right about here [heart arena]. The planet wanted me to. They are questions and statements, so simply listen to that bubble as it opens, bargain?

Bargain!

So be it.

Note: This intensive is available on audio cassette (five 90-minute tapes, $54) or video cassette (two 4-hour tapes, approximately $104) in its entirety, by sending check or money order to A. Fanning, P.O. Box 684, Cornville, AZ 86325.

26

The Silver Lining Behind Tampering with Genetics, or the Redemption of Science

Zoosh through Robert Shapiro
May 3, 1996

This is a flash: Your society is now entering a very critical stage of its development. Scientists are feverishly working on genetics, and the more they do, the more they realize how applicable genetics are to every field, not only scientific, but also technological, sociological, anthropological etc. There are so many fields it can be applied to that it literally boggles their minds.

Also, because there is a blur in your society between what is technology and what is sacred life, corporations, universities and even individuals are patenting life! Oh, they might not say it's life. They might say, "These are formulas, representing hard work on ideas, thoughts, applications." Yet what you are seeing now are patents coming from different institutions where thought is applied in scientific terms. There are some copyrights on thoughts, and now even life itself—types of genetics, types of cells and, more important, types of *applications* of genetics.

I know this is worrisome, not only to the scientific community but to the broad spectrum of the intellectual community and to society itself. Should life be patented? What could happen? If mankind can tamper with genetics, how safe is the universe? What about God? What would God think of this? What do we do?

Cryptogenetics

Universities, research-and-development groups, military contractors etc., are not only making genetic discoveries, but they are also creating structures by which those genetic discoveries are disguised. The disguising aspect I will call cryptogenetics.

In this type of work patents are not trusted. Copyrights are not believed to be secure, so not only are life forms being patented, but structures are put into the life forms so that even if some portion of a life form that has been genetically altered (or even simply discovered) is obtained by some other government or research-and-development institution (or, for that matter, some type of corporate spy), the genetic material cannot be analyzed because, not unlike a code, it has been cryptographed.

So we have a circumstance which is, on the face of it, appalling. Yet there is a silver lining to this cloud that approaches your society. Yes, it will lead to many bizarre and terrible things. Yes, it will be a re-creation of the worst of Atlantis, where life forms were created, crosses between human beings and animals. And these life forms will be patented. In the beginning they will not even be known amongst the public.

They will be seen occasionally at a distance. People will think they have seen Bigfoot, you know. Or people will begin to see them and think they have seen extraterrestrials. This idea, by the way, has not escaped certain branches of the intelligence community, and to some extent they will even attempt to create some kind of ET-looking being that can be passed off as an ET and used in disinformation campaigns. Oh, yes, they have thought of that; I am not giving them that idea.

Also, there will be terrible side effects. Whole races of beings will be invented and suffer terribly. Your scientists, in the moments of pause in the creation of these things, have ethical concerns even though they are driven by their contracts and competition within the scientific community. There will be moments when they will say, "That's enough! I won't do any more." Because they will start to get a feeling. It will be more than the feeling of ethics, more even than the feeling of shock and horror that will gradually creep through the scientific community. (It will *creep* through, you see, because this work is being done 99% secretly, and many scientists working on aspects of this do not even realize they are working on some government project to create an alternative race of slave beings.)

Yet scientists are neither machines nor cruel monsters. They are human beings like you, and gradually they will become aware almost by instinct that there is something beneath all of this manipulation of genetics. There is a rumbling, a vibration they cannot put their finger on. They don't know what it is, but it has them worried. It is almost like the feeling that animals get before an earthquake or a terrible storm, a nervousness where they run in different directions, not knowing where to go or what to do. This feeling, even now as I speak, is creeping through the scientific community because this work has been going on for a time.

There are races of beings like this that are well on their way toward development. There are even races of beings I have discussed before, such as hybrids associated with ET technology applied to human genetics, but now *your* scientists (granted, in complete secrecy) are working to cross humans and animals. Some of this work has percolated out into the public, which it ought to, and it has been treated at first like a scientific oddity. Yet it has brought up the necessary questions of ethics.

I have referred to a silver lining. "Can there really be a silver lining to all this?" you ask. And I will say yes. This is the silver lining: In the process of doing

Cryptogenetic analysis is happening right now, but practically no one knows about it. I want people to know about it to relieve the terror they are beginning to develop about the direction science is going. I grant you that some things will be done in science that will be appalling. But it is that very appalling nature that will grab the attention (as one might grab the throat of another momentarily) of the scientists who are doing it. As a result of some of the extremes in science in the coming years, you will find that scientists will develop amongst themselves, with no assistance from politicians or corporations, an absolute code of ethics they will assign themselves to, not unlike an order, and to be a scientist one will have to join this order, take an oath and follow it; it will be enforced.

This thing is going to trigger it, because it is something that needs to happen. Scientists need to remember that they really do represent a social order of their own and that some things are meant to be experimented with only on computers and other things are meant to be done physically. (That's part of the reason computers exist—so you can play, but not do it physically. Initially scientists created the nuclear bomb because it was new and fascinating, but look where it led. If they could have done it over, believe me, they would have said, "Forget it. Let's do it on paper and leave it at that.")

this work, mankind will, on the one hand, at moments of *scientific achievement*, feel almost God-like in the creation of something heretofore unknown in mankind's written history (though not unknown in mankind's actual history) – the creation of life. On one hand, it's thrilling; on the other, frightening. But you know, at the beginning of any science the thrill tends to outweigh the fear. That's how atom bombs came into being – it was new, it was thrilling, it was exciting, even though people were afraid of what might come of it. (Oh yes, it was to solve a war, which it did.) There was an underlying fear, but the excitement was enough to carry the project along, aside from the feeling of need, defensively/militarily.

Now, in this new field cryptogenetics disguises a life form through coding. The genetic code has been broken. Yet, using cryptogenetics, applying secret coding to genetic formulas, a secondary code is introduced to disguise what has been discovered.

Decoding Cryptogenetics

Herein lies the silver lining: Mankind will develop an alternative to cryptogenetics. This often happens in the field of defense, and much of this research is being sponsored by various defense contractors, research and development companies that feel they might have something to sell to the military and various basic research organizations at universities and so on. The outcome will, of course, be cryptogenetic analysis, because once the methods have been formed to code genetic discoveries, one must immediately form the methods to analyze the coding of one's competitors. In this case (defensively speaking) competitors would be other countries that your country is uncomfortable with, at odds with or even at war with.

It will be in this field of cryptogenetic analysis that the silver lining will emerge. Initially, the analysis will take the form of attempting to obtain genetic materials from other countries and other sources that are not only difficult to understand, but that have been genetically coded to prevent their discovery. The field will be somewhat underfunded at first. It will show success after first using various coded genetic formulas for which the answer is understood (which is typical science, in which one codes something and gives it to somebody else to decode). As cryptogenetic analysts begin to have more success in this field, for a time they will not have much to do, because after working for some short time – a year and a half or two or three years – the field will appear to apply primarily in the scientific intelligence community or even the forensic community. Because they will be basically unfunded, many of the researchers who develop this field will begin working on the side on projects of their own, things they are interested in, new challenges. Herein lies the silver lining, as I say.

They will begin to analyze various human genetic codes, not on the basis of the analysis being done by others, but by applying what they have learned, which is, basically, decoding a human coded life form. They will apply these methods to the human genetic code as it stands, and they will begin to come up not only with discoveries based upon their methods, but with similarities. They will begin to see – not only amongst the races of man but amongst males, females, children, older people, different shapes and sizes of people – certain very specific and regulated forms and functions. At first they won't know what it means. They will say, "Well, we have run across this before in other fields" and put it aside.

Some of this work will be done as a hobby by people who don't have enough to do and who are kind of bored and want to do more of what they know how to do, just for the love of it or because they are curious, which is natural amongst human beings – it's actually a built-in trait.

You are born with curiosity because Creator wants you to discover. And this is one of the things Creator wants you to discover, what I'm talking about. As evidence of these regularities (patterns, as they call it in cryptoanalysis) builds up over time, there will come a significant understanding. This understanding will not be derived from, motivated by or even regulated by an attempt to control or create so much as *to understand*. As it is with all cryptoanalysis, the idea is to understand, to make sense out of something that is, at the moment you are working on it, *non-sense*.

In the discoveries of cryptogenetic analysis they will realize that patterns not only have to do with gleaned genetic material from odd sources (such as meteors), even though some of this evidence is not well accepted throughout the community. They will notice other things. Those people working on it who have high security clearance will have a means to tap into extraterrestrial genetics. (Extraterrestrial genetics is more understood – or at least there is more material available to certain scientists on your world than is known at large. Granted, it is on a very high, secret level, but it's in computers, so you can reach into the computer and pull it out.) So those who have this clearance will compare what they have discovered to ET genetics and they will see connections. But that's not really it. It will interest them, but they won't pursue it strongly.

Geometric Forms: Creator Code

It's the structure and form that will fascinate them. You might ask, "What form are you talking about, Zoosh?" I will say this (not to give too much away): these are actually *geometric forms*. The curious thing about genetics is that your scientists are still analyzing things that are not living and breathing. This is perhaps just as well, but as science goes along, more instruments are desired whereby a person can literally put a finger under a type of microscope that does not harm you, there is no pain to the individual (sometimes there is a lot of light on the finger, but it is not painful). The genetics can be analyzed while the being is alive and comfortable or even distracted through various sociological or anthropological means (by being given something to read or by watching television). It's a whole level of social genetics that will be developed much to your benefit at some time in the future, and rudimentary work is going on right now. It is available to a few people out there, and in the future will be available to a few more scientists here.

Now, most of these people will be working on their own. Maybe there will be a few groups of two and three that form in certain institutions, working at it primarily as a hobby because they will not be funded very well, if at all. But after a few years what will come to be known amongst this group is the *shape* of the genetics. There are distinct triangles, distinct parallelograms, diamond shapes, distinct circles – not vague circles but absolutely perfect spheres.

Now, this will not go unnoticed. *This will be the beginning of the discovery of Creator code.* True creation is done by shape and by the connection of shape to shape (a first-year biology student can talk to you about the shape of cells and so on), and these shapes are not by accident.

Levels of creation built into the human being literally have to do with shapes, forms and the compounding of shapes and forms. I have discussed this before in a previous article in the *Sedona Journal* wherein I talked about basic shapes of the human being having to do with the basic forms of the human being (tall, short, fat, thin, the basic human types).

It will be in the discovery of these shapes that this group of hobby scientists will begin to realize that shapes themselves not only create traits, but can cause one to feel a connection to light forms that are very high indeed. Now, the scientists themselves (the cryptogenetic analysts) might not make this leap on their own, but they will begin to notice these shapes, and it will become a topic of curious conversation. Small networks will form in time amongst other people doing this as a hobby, and eventually individuals who have not only a scientific interest but also a strong interest in philosophy, sociology, anthropology and other forms of life sciences (which are actually arts, not sciences) will become involved. It is these people who will make the leap of understanding that when you can amplify the energy of the shape, not through artificial means but through *encouragement* of the person who has a finger under the microscope that analyzes living tissue (meaning, the person is given different stimuli and thereby does fun things or reads something he likes, watches something enjoyable on television, kisses his wife or what have you), wonderful and exciting things happen genetically.

Building Block of Creation: Feeling, Love and Harmony

It will be through this application of cryptogenetic analysis and by the exciting and the encouraging of these genetic forms (triangles, diamonds, circles etc.) — through emoting, feelings — that scientists will discover this somewhat accidentally. They will notice a change in the form and motion of the shapes of the genetics they are working on. "What is that?" they will say to themselves. It will go largely into the field of scientific curiosity for a time: "We don't know what it is, but it's a curious phenomenon." They will begin to realize that there are radiated emotions, especially ones that are joyful, but also ones like disappointment, frustration — emotions that all scientists know and understand — that affect these living genetic specimens. The severe limitation in science, especially the life sciences, has for years been the fact that they are analyzing things that do not have the light of life in them anymore, so they are basically analyzing things after the fact. Once they start analyzing living things, they will be able to interact and communicate with life through feelings. Then they will discover the building block of creation, which is feeling, love and harmony.

On the creation level, no forms or substances — even the tiniest substances that make up genetics — come together without a feeling of love and cooperation. That's what holds all life together. That's what makes it all possible. We know it is Creator's love that holds cells together. Cells come together because they *feel good* together. The whole foundation of understanding your physical world is to understand that all things that come together naturally do so because the cells, even the atoms and even the subatomic particles, enjoy being together. They feel comfortable together. It is when they *don't* enjoy being together that they start to come apart. When substances have been injected or interjected into their midst, even residue from unresolved feelings in the human body, things start to break down, become sluggish, are no longer comfortable together – and that is, by the way, the foundation of the aging process.

So here we have a field – cryptogenetic analysis – that comes about as a result of something going on scientifically and technologically that at its very best is on highly unstable ethical ground. Yet the silver lining will be the discovery that *Creator is with you.*

Some of these cryptogenetic analysts will have profound experiences. They will literally feel the presence of lightbeings – of angels, they will call them, although not to each other at first because they will be embarrassed. They will have profound experiences: they will feel as if they are in the presence of Creator Itself/Herself/Himself. They will feel as if they're in the presence of deified beings (Jesus etc.) and that they are being visited by these profound beings as a result of their discovery of the shapes and because of their interaction on the feeling level with the shapes.

Now, this is not all going to happen within the next few minutes. It is not even going to happen in the next few years, but it's going to happen within the next dozen years or so. I know you are upset, concerned, sometimes even very frightened about the genetic research that is going on. Some of you out there have greater knowledge of these things and are even more concerned, yet excited at the same time. That is your nature. Yet I want you to know that even though some terrible things will be done, things that people will regret, suffering beings created by man who were not naturally intended to be that way, things that are going on now to some extent even as I speak, largely unknown to the general public (but eventually it will all come out), yet the silver lining will be science's true discovery that Creator is alive at all levels and that Creator can be communicated with directly – that one can talk to Creator and Creator will talk back.

One might not have expected science to have this experience. You might ask, "Why aren't ministers having this experience, or philosophers or monks or spiritual practitioners?" Well, some of them *are* having these experiences. But your society has placed science and the intellectual pursuits above and beyond its normal balanced position, so when it happens in science, your society "knows" that it is so. Science will put its stamp of approval, as it were, on the existence of Creator as an *applied communicative being.* And you know, this will be an exciting and wonderful moment. It will allow your society to leap great bounds, make great connections. It will break down many barriers between people who have been unable to communicate well together. It will even break down nationalist barriers and will in time be exactly what leads your people of Earth to become united Earthians. And then extraterrestrials will say, "Welcome to our world. Come and visit, join our community." Won't that be a true silver lining?

27

FEMA and fema

Zoosh through Robert Shapiro
June 18, 1996

I want to talk about FEMA [Federal Emergency Management Agency] now, because what we have here is a legitimate governmental organization that has been largely usurped. This organization was considerably funded. I know that it appears to be a front organization to many people, and I can understand that point of view. However, let's talk about what's good about FEMA first.

This organization is truly, and has truly been, set up to help all citizens through emergencies and crises. If they had the funds that have been granted to them, they could have been of immeasurable help. But (and I am not exaggerating here) *fully 90%* (some people might say 87%, but I am willing to go as high as 90%) of their funds have been siphoned off to be utilized by a group of individuals who are closely allied to the sinister secret government. I want to make the distinction here that FEMA itself is not associated with the sinister secret government. They are to some extent being victimized by the secret government because millions, if not billions, of dollars that could have gone to the support of their own worthy goals and to assist those that they would help after emergencies, fires, floods, tornadoes and earthquakes have been siphoned off. Where did that money go?

A lot of it has been used to create underground and off-planet (meaning the Moon) facilities that would create an underground world not dissimilar to that which the sinister secret government has itself created. We have here another organization of individuals, a shadowy group who are pseudogovernmental, interacting here on behest of the sinister secret government, an almost clandestine organization within the government itself.

This group of individuals originally sprang out of several of the intelligence services. (Again, this is not attack on those services.) These individuals went renegade, as the services might say, and formed loosely knit groups. Then they were gradually organized by the sinister secret government into coordinating this rip-off of various funds from different agencies (not only FEMA) that could be utilized to form what they would perceive of as an underground city.

You might ask, Why do this? Why have these underground cities? Why equip them with defense systems and their own armies comprised of a widely mixed bag of individuals, some from this country, some from that country, speaking all different languages? Why do this? It might amuse you (if this can be thought of as amusing in any way) to know that many of these individuals who are involved in the formation of these underground bunkers (which is more like what they really are) really believe in the idea of absolutes.

For years many entities (not only myself, but others) have been predicting dire things ("if you don't do this, this is going to happen") —not threats, but telling you to get your act together because you have to change etc. In recent years things have gotten better, but the individuals who built these bunkers believed in absolutes, that the surface of the Earth was going to fall apart and become unlivable. "Zoosh," you might say, "do these people simply read channeling and believe it absolutely?" No, they took that as a support, however, and in one case they believed something that had been supposedly channeled but wasn't; it was really a fake.

The bulk of their belief stems not from any order [group] from the past or even any set of documents from the past, but from a book that is called the Yellow Book. This book has been referred to from time to time in various extraterrestrial literature and even in other literature; it is a book that was retrieved from an extraterrestrial. The book tells the past history and the present circumstances of Earth (which in that case would have been around the '50s), then the future of Earth —assuming that humanity follows that course. Now, this book was actually retrieved—or we can say, delicately, stolen—from a Zeta Recticuli ship. The beings on that ship had that book in a form that could be read, because those were the times when early contacts were going on between Zeta beings and U.S. citizens who at that time were largely on military bases because they were the ones who were most concerned.

You might ask, Why did that book even exist? Well, it's because Zeta beings were approaching the people on this base and saying, "Look, here's your past history in this (yellow) book (I don't want to call it the yellow book, but it's been called that). Zetas would say, "Here's your history, reading the past, the present and the future. If you continue to go on this course, all of these things in this book are going to happen." They handed them this book; and because you continued to go on a similar course, many of those things in the book *did* happen.

But they also gave them another book, and you don't hear about that one. That other book said, "Here is the history we believe you would prefer to have." It depicted a more benevolent past, focusing on more benevolent things that were done in the past (uncreating wars, famines, pestilence, disease etc.) and the benevolent present (uncreating all of those things in the present, including the uncreation of the Korean War) and the benevolent future (uncreating all the wars that you have experienced since the '50s). It was a benevolent future in which all races on Earth come together and enjoy the excitement of learning new things and sharing information instead of duplicating the same research, and getting out and doing space travel in the '70s in a viable way, as you are looking forward to doing now. They said, "Wouldn't you rather have *that?*" The military authorities, everybody who read the book, said, "We would love to have that." But the book with your actual past history eventually wound up being the one that people tended to believe, because when a prediction is made ("if you do this, then this will happen") and those things begin to happen, people pay attention.

So that is the absolute upon which these individuals in the sinister secret government and their toadies in this renegade group of ex-intelligence officers have come together to believe (they believed this stuff!). But in the past few years a lot of spiritual changes have been going on, and they are going on even now. And that secondary book that depicted a benevolent past and present and future is being created even now as we speak, *because you are being trusted to do more.*

For example, I said some time ago that you would be getting more and more of your heart energy, and that's happening now. You have been trained to receive it. You are more emotional, and sometimes things strike you emotionally when you least expect it; you have days of extreme emotion and days of great love and comradeship and companionship with friends and so on that you cherish, and sometimes a life-changing experience.

So you are having more of your heart energy because you are being trusted to resolve the seemingly unresolvable conflicts between people that can only be resolved through interactions from the heart. Therefore all of these things are changing what was in the Yellow Book (when the books were handed to the people, they weren't colored; they were called yellow because of the binding).

This renegade group has tried to become influential in recent years. They have tried to do something unconscionable, yet almost understandable in a very juvenile sort of way: When dramas that were predicted to happen in the Yellow Book didn't happen, sometimes they would actually go out and stimulate them to happen. They would do something that is basically what I can only describe as trouble-making. You might say, "But why?" It's a very silly reason (but unfortunately in the past a common reason): It is because those who were using the book wanted to retain their power and influence in their own small circle. They didn't even care about power and influence over the rest of the people because they were trying to create something that they thought would outlast the surface civilization.

Their belief was that Armageddon was going to happen, and while it was happening they would retreat to their underground bunkers and live there for five or ten years, and if there were atomic blasts on the surface they would hang around for another twenty-five years or so. And during that time they would perfect their capacity to tolerate low-level radiation. Then they would use certain weather devices they have obtained and cause it to rain on the surface of the Earth for ten to fifteen years (all the while hanging around underground – they believed they could do this), and in forty years or so they would come to the surface and take over. It's hard to believe that this plot (which sounds very much like something out of science fiction) could actually be in the minds of people, and yet many people have dedicated their lives to this abject horror.

So I want you to understand that when you hear things about FEMA, know that there's FEMA and there's *fema*. So let's say there's the FEMA that is the governmental group, and then there's the *fema* that is the renegade and the sinister secret government group who have managed, through *criminal efforts*, to siphon off most of the budget of FEMA. So please do not get angry at government workers and think that they are somehow involved in some plot to take over the United States and turn it into a federalist country. Now, you might ask yourself why I use the word "federal." It is an interesting thing that the concept of the word *federal* is based upon "one" – one government, one planetary body.

I have told you before that the initial Earth government was going to be on the corporate model. That's happening now as we speak, and those of you who doubt it, go down to the corner neighborhood bank, which has been bought by some corporation, some international conglomerate. How many of you know out there (I am sure you all do) that banks are consolidating? Control the money and you have a lot of influence. I am not saying it is necessarily a bad thing; what I am saying is that the corporate model for the world government is happening right now as we speak. And there are those who think that the next evolution beyond the corporate model will be the Federal Republics of Earth. Now, the Federal Republics of Earth would all be directed from a central government located possibly in The Hague or in some country that is largely considered neutral territory. However, they will be manipulated behind the scenes. There will be talk as if they are very democratic, but the idea is to manipulate and control the mass of the population.

I am here to tell you that the Federal Republics of Earth are not going to take place. The corporate model is going to come first, and then will come a more benign form of world government, as I have always said. I'm not going to talk about that at length because I want that to evolve, but I will say that the idea will evolve of different professions forming not exactly clubs, but "oaths" among themselves that serve a higher purpose, that choose to serve Creator (Creator in this sense meaning love, unconditional love) and fellow human beings. This kind of oath among professionals will become common. In large part it will come as a result or as a reaction to the goings-on around them. At some point many, if not all, professions will have these individual groups that have a higher aim and order.

So in the future you will have a philosophy that grows out of these events, and this philosophy will choose to serve the higher purpose for Creator's unconditional love through all human beings, and will be unconditionally loving, supportive and in teamship with all other human beings. Now, that's not going to happen tomorrow, but there are those of you running around today in physical bodies who will be here for that change. I just want you to know that, and that FEMA is not the bad guys; but it is true that *fema* is probably not your friends.

28

The New Brain

YHWH through Arthur Fanning
July 13-14, 1996

Indeed! [YHWH laughs.]

[Group:] Indeed!

Lighten up! Little bit of excitement coming up today. Questions, questions, questions. Remember, what is important is who you are, indeed, not who be I. I know who I am. The changes that are coming are going to be rather humorous, from my perspective. You know what I mean?

Yes.

How are you doing?

Wonderful. How am I doing from your perspective?

Well, have you assimilated all of the energies that you've been playing with?

I don't know. Have I?

How do you feel in the body?

I feel really good.

So more light in the body; you can identify yourself as that?

Yes.

Indeed, so the body can handle the more light, indeed?

Mm-hmm.

Okay.

I have a lot of questions about what really happened, but . . .

Well, I know you do. You were dead for a moment, indeed?

That be all right. It's no big deal, is it?

Not for me. The people watching were a little concerned. It was all white light.

Well, they all have their judgments, indeed?

Where I was it was all white light.

Indeed. Fun. What you're learning is that you don't have to play lose consciousness to be the light. That is the eventual understanding, know you what I mean? The only reason you left was because your brain hasn't been trained to handle that frequency while physical—that's the only reason. So the brain was instructed to shut off.

Oh, it did. It was a fight.

Indeed.

Because I wanted to hang onto it.

The process is becoming that you can transition this way, that way, this way, that way, and the brain will become accustomed to it. It's not only the physical brain, however, it's your persona, that sacred identity that says, "This is me! Will it still exist when I'm dead?" That concept.

Yeah, but half of me left, so who am I now, who am I?

Your god!

Yeah.

Not THE God.

A god.

God. And you're learning to play in the kingdom of it. Now, when you beings get out of your boxes and out of your rigid behavior, you'll see the joy and the humor of it, know you what I mean? The ecstasy, you say, the fun. Indeed? I don't think this is a big surprise to any of you. You're in a process called life here on the planet, indeed? And that process, believe it or not, incorporates the understanding of death! [YHWH laughs.] Lighten up!

I know everyone wants to ascend. The only way you're going to ascend, the *only* way (unless you want to die the body and leave it and no big deal) is to play with the energies of light within the physical, enjoy it and know that the structures here on your planet do not support the understanding *yet*. They will, because the structures are changing. When the walls, the sides of your boxes go away, you beings go into a great tizzy. Know you, you have your hair nice and straight, and the sides of the boxes come down, and your hair [emphatically] wings out here like this. [Laughter.] One thing you know how to do real well here is panic, in the physical. You enjoy that rush, you say. Get over it.

The boxes are coming apart, and it's called the love of God, *within* you, indeed, that birthed you, that has been with you forever and ever and ever, and will always be with you forever. That identity is coming forth now. Now, you will think it's coming down about you, but it is really coming forth from within. And you're going to understand that every being on the planet is in love, because that's God. Every nationality is in love because it's God. And you'll understand that the politicians and your governments don't want you to understand that you're in love, because they'll lose control. Everyone take a breath, breathe.

This is an exciting time, this decade we are playing in is an empowering time for individual entities. It is not an empowering time for governments or solid, what you call, rigid structures—it isn't. They're scramb ling to keep up now. They've got all the tools to pass the information around rather rapidly, know you this net of inter, the internet, huh? This big thing, pass information, information, but no one is working with it, no one is working with the energies called life, being.

Now I've told some of you before that know me that the soul is going to expand. It exists, it's in here [chest cavity]. It's going to come forth, bloom like a flower, and the light that's around the physical body is going to join with the soul. And the only thing keeping it from what you would term melding very smoothly is the identity you term your ego, your persona, and the body consciousness that is what we would term, in the way. So it's up to you to allow what you call the persona the wisdom that it's okay, and allow the body consciousness to work the way it knows how to. It will adjust, the body consciousness will. The persona and the ego, however, will not—doesn't want to let go. Know you what I mean? Indeed?

Indeed.

So it's [an] exciting time. What we're going to do this day, this weekend, we're going to bring more energies. Now, by that I mean we are going to stir your soul . . . and don't worry, I'm not going to steal it—I don't want it. It's too much trouble as it is. [Laughter.]

All right. Now, the meditations that we do here, we will drag you through them. We want you to allow your chakras to be open. For these two days, these eight hours or so, simply know that you're in safety and let the energies move through you. There will be diffi culties, little bit, because it is a judgment of structure. Rely upon this: before you were born, you were loved, you knew it, you came here to be in this time frame. The greater portion of you knows *exactly* what it wants to accomplish here. It knows the special moment of it, it understands that it has [an opportunity] to be here, and it wants to take advantage of that opportunity—not only the greater self, but the soul portion of you within that's doing the job. It understands the importance. So allow yourself your sacredness.

[To a participant:] How are you?

Miserable.

Why is that?

Because it was a hard month and I'm just up against all my physical stuff.

Oh, indeed, [it's] going to get harder here.

And I have terrible headaches and I'm crabby.

Well, that's nothing new. Now, the headaches are the pressure of the pituitary expanding, indeed. Water and allow—and you simply tell it to open. It's also the sixth seal wants to pop, and it wants to show you visions. You want to control the visions. You say, "Well, if you can't give me a vision in blue color, I don't want it." And it says, "But you have to see this red one first." And you say, "I don't care!" Know you? Allow. Just let it happen.

Okay. Will they be scary, the visions?

They might frighten you because only be a little judgment. Know you what I mean? Know you how you watch your TV and you can watch the disasters there, indeed? So you can watch them from here [sixth seal]. You're not creating them. What is happening is, you need to see them because you have to share them, you have to tell other people about what you see. That's one of your jobs that you don't want to do, but what you said you will do.

See the thing is, Yahweh, I was so happy this spring. I mean, everything was going so good, then all of the sudden I tripped or something.

No, you didn't.

I said I'd go further, and then it got hard again. Whaaaa! [Laughter.]

It's all right. What is happening [is], you're playing . . . all right, we're going to cover all of this this weekend. A lot of you are experiencing a lot of childhood memories, indeed, in your dreams and your things—all these friends you've had before. Your energy patterns are going backward, you think. You're remembering people you don't even know now, so to speak. Your original energy is coming to you, closer, fitting here, your light here. All right, everyone take a breath. Might as well get used to it. This is going to be one funny weekend. [Laughter.]

Know how when you play die you have this . . . and it's been shared with you, that you have these points where you go through your experiences that you've done in this lifetime, indeed? You say review of your life. Know you what I mean? And you do that. Well, you're getting the opportunity to review it in the physical. Center. Center. So you forgive yourself. You bring these energies as they come to you in a peaceful manner. Allow. If you feel to apologize or forgive, do it. Understand that is what's happening. Because you're getting an acceleration now, you're not going to have to wait 'til you play die to do this. Know you?

Now remember, I've been saying for years, I use this phrase, "play die." Understand? Because it is a play–I know it, you know it. The experience is going to be understood, finally on this planet, what life is. It's happening. You're living it now. So as these energies come to you, don't hold it in the old structure of what you say you grew up with to this point, belief system. Let it be changed. Understand you are *becoming* now. You are becoming! Know you what I mean, "becoming"? You are becoming wiser–wisdoms, indeed? Know you what I mean? Okay, now if you have to forgive yourself, forgive yourself, but know that you are love in every moment. It'll make it a lot easier. Okay, everyone take a breath.

Now, this weekend is not for me (yet it is)–it's for you . . . and more, because we're getting you closer and closer to understanding what home is. It's not about the extraterrestrials, no matter who they are. It's about you and your willingness to become empowered for you. Now, I don't work with the masses–most of you know this that have been here before. I work with those that have to teach the teachers of the masters. [You're] not here by accident, not at all. Some of you are here, you think, just out of curiosity. Remember, it got the cat! One of the cosmic jokes. All right. So allow these energies to work, allow you to recognize them, because you're in safety here.

[There are] going to (and they're starting to filter in; some of you can perceive, they're coming in the side doors here) be a lot of Buddhas here today. They're going to be sitting around some of you. There are going to be a lot of what you term the American Indians. So allow the energies. Don't question. Simply recognize what's happening. Lot of you are gathering your parts now, some of your experiences. It's okay to realize that they're your experiences.

Now, one of the journeys you beings play here is what your past life was. Well, it doesn't matter–this is the most sacred moment, in your recognition of it now. Past-life energies, however, are going to gather with you because they have provided you power, no matter whether you perverted it or not–it doesn't matter. There is a powerful spiritual (I'll use that word here) force there that is still part of you. It may have been expressed ignorantly. It doesn't matter. What matters is, you recognize the spiritual power there that is still with you. You do not deny these things–won't do you any good. It'll be right in your face in a moment. So everyone take a breath now, and when you do this I want you to breathe more of yourself in that is around you. Breathe it in. Let it out.

Now, these meditations are going to get rather strong. You can handle it. Give me a moment here. We've got a little chatter going on out there–have to take care of it. [To a participant:] How are you?

Well, it has been kind of a frustrating month for me as well.

Indeed. A lot of beings are having their charms jingling, so to speak–bells rung. Do these petals remind you of anything? [Note: The floor has red and white rose petals sprinkled about.]

They remind me of love.

Indeed? Do they remind you of a place?

Maybe.

Contemplate it, indeed?

Yes. They feel very comforting to me.

There is a garden where you all come from that's made up of petals. They rain down all of the time where you come from. And the fragrance and the oils from the petals cleanse you. Very beautiful place–where your Father hangs out sometimes.

Now, for this day: At the break we're going to cover this, but when we're not breaking allow you to open this, indeed. [Note: This is in reference to a Tibetan Buddhist thanka (tong/ka) painting of a mandala, which is situated next to YHWH's chair.] Now, these energies [from the thanka] are going to permeate you. Allow you to see; get up and look. It's a great realm of awesome power, very compassionate power. And the energies are going to filter through the room and come to you individually, if you'll allow it. So you open the heart chakra and you let it just come to you. It will create a memory, from your understanding, and you will remember being *in* there, you'll remember where it is. It will excite your dream state in a very pleasant manner. Do not attempt to control these energies. Allow you to flow with them. They will naturally draw you to one of the realms involved here. And don't compare whether it be here, be here, be inside, whatever. This is one of the seventh heavens, so there's no damage there that can occur, and there is no danger anywhere there. So you let yourself work through it, bargain?

[Group:] Bargain!

Okay, so it's simply working now. [To a participant:] And don't make a church of this. [To another:] How are you?

Grand.

No matter what you do or how much you love another being, you have not the right nor the authority to alter their experience, unless they want it to be altered, know you? And that's not a concept that's here [head]; it's a concept that's here [heart].

All right, we're going to do a little meditation, okay? We have that body song? I call it the body song, but you beings call it another thing. [*The Power of Love* by Celine Dion.] I want you to simply be in the song and understand when the term "lady" is being mentioned, it's referring to the planet. I want you to get your connection to the planet again, indeed? There are time streams involved here, and there are magnetic energies involved. So allow your eyes to close.

Meditation

Center your being, your palms upward here in what you term the junction here [where legs join the torso]. Center. There are energies within the planet now that what we're going to do with this mandala is draw them into you, so feel it. Center. You're part of her creation, entities. You're involved in it. Open the heart chakra wider. . . . Mankind is the man. . . . Feel it in the heart chakra. . . . Allow.

Allow. . . . I want you to feel the heart of the planet in your heart chakra. . . . Everyone take a breath and breathe the energy out of the heart chakra.

I will tell you a thing: There is a great truth in that song when you understand the Earth—it does know how your heart beats every moment, it feels it! It knows whether you're coming from what you call an egotistical understanding of perversion, it understands when you're in love, and it reflects that attitude in itself because you are the masters here, and the planet understands it. Now it's time to assume the responsibility and walk in what is termed purity of heart here because you're affecting everything you touch, especially when you become more enlightened. You affect everything! Not only the planet, everyone on it is influenced by the way you walk, from here, heart chakra. It's going to be necessary to save your skins (as you say, "skins"), your energies here. The planet is going to shift, and she's going to understand who is working with her and who is in love with her, and she will envelop you in what you call a protective coating, in a manner, of magnetic forces when these things happen. Why will she do that? Because she'll remember you like an old friend, that's why. Everyone take a breath.

Now, could you feel the mandala working, some of you, indeed, with the song? As we do some of the other songs now, that mandala is going to do the same thing, so let the energy pulse and beat. What it's going to do is, the song provides the emotion and the mandala is going to provide what is termed the connection so you can remember, [so] you can feel here. The mandala will also help the soul get over—well, it's not really the soul's judgment, it's how you've imprinted it—get over that, know it's okay.

Now, your body is going to go through physical changes, and it's a good thing. Lot of cleansing and clearing going on.

Now, I've built a pyramid beneath this floor, what you term, in the etheric realm. It's a golden lavender color, and it's filled with fluid at the base, about six feet of water, golden green. As you're sitting here in these songs and these meditations we do, things want to move [from] your body, leave. Let them go down into the pyramid into the water. They'll be cleansed. You're not going to lose anything; you can drag them back if you wish. You're going to get them back anyway, but they'll just be altered a little bit. Just let it move out of you. You might feel tingling sensations on your body, like little creatures are moving out, little bugs (you'd be surprised what your thought forms look like)—let them go, indeed. Bargain?

[Group:] Bargain!

Just let them go. Okay, you have Planet Drum song? [By Mickey Hart.] Pick a track.

Seven. ["Temple Caves."]

Center your being now. Now I'm going to come around and I might touch some of you as you're doing this. I'm simply doing it to adjust some of the energies. Don't let it startle you.

Meditation

. . . Now let this rhythm be inside the body. Let it move however it decides to. There is no right or wrong here. . . . There is a natural rhythm in you, let it—move. . . . See the mandala in front of you, right in front of your face, and let the energy come toward you. Allow. Center. Take a

breath out the throat chakra. Grand. Allow your eyes to open very gently. [Music ends.] Now, you might be getting a little pressure at the sixth seal here. Make it very gentle; simply tell it to open a little bit.

Okay, now, we're going to do a little more work here. Allow your palms to be up upon your thighs here, indeed. Center your being. I want you to feel a gold light beginning to descend from above your head right through your body, gold and green. Let it come through down to your perineum, middle of your buttocks there, right there. Hold it there. Center. Feel a silver light come from the right side through your neck, right through the throat chakra, out the left side. Center. If you have to adjust the energy, adjust it with the breath out the mouth. Center.

Your soul is in your chest–the base is beneath your breast, the apex is at your throat. Allow the apex of the soul to lift up a little bit so you can feel a release at the throat area, right at that little hole there, and push the apex up now to the top of your head. Center. Grand. Center. Center. Center. Now push the base down. Take a breath and push the base down beneath your feet so you're in it, indeed. Allow. Grand. Center your being.

Now allow the pyramid to begin to spin, the right side to the front, to the left side, to behind you, to the right. Counterclockwise. Allow it to spin around you. Center. Center. Allow yourself to visualize what you would term the Buddhas around you. The counterclockwise spin is sort of drawing them into you, so they merge and blend. Allow it, indeed. Allow the healing, allow. Center. Spin. Be in the heart chakra now. Tighten your buttocks. Take a breath in while you tighten your thighs, tighten your stomach. Now bend forward a little bit, bend forward and exhale out, lean back. Let it go. Center. Keep the spinning going. Allow. Spin. Allow.

Now allow you to feel an energy at your buttocks in your perineum. It sort of wants to lift you up a little bit–feel that sensation, almost like coming off the chair, wants to lift you up. Allow the feeling of it very gently in the body. Allow. Center. Center. Allow. Center.

All right, there is a chakra in the middle of your back; it's called the grand chakra. It looks very much like, a little bit, the mandala. Tell it to open, tell all of its little points in there to open. Allow. Feel it. Light. Center. Grand. Outrageous. Center. Allow your sensation of becoming one with everything on the planet–with the tree, the air, the water, the insects, everything. Feel them, feel them in the mandala. Allow. Center.

Everywhere you look there are rose petals–allow. Around you, within you, like raindrops falling around. Let the body be blessed now. Center. I want you to contemplate these words at your sixth seal, what you term third eye, and as I say them they are going to merge into your

Tibetan Buddhist thanka (tong/ka) painting of a mandala, used in these meditations.

brain–let them merge, right at the sixth seal: I AM POWER. Feel the vibration there, that is you, not me, you. I AM POWER. Let it fill there. I AM LOVE. We want the brain to understand that it's okay. I REMEMBER. I KNOW. Now take a breath out of the throat chakra, breathe it out. I KNOW. Allow. Center. There is a lot of issue with that "I KNOW." Let it filter into the brain. I KNOW, I REMEMBER. Now contemplate this (I'm simply using the word because that is how you people relate here): GOD DOES LOVE ME. I REMEMBER. If you need to, breathe out of the throat chakra. That is the storage place, apex of the soul. Clear. I REMEMBER. I AM LOVED BY GOD, I REMEMBER.

Allow the crown chakra to expand. Stop the spinning of your pyramid; very gently let it slow. Center. I want you to feel a great eye, what is termed, at your crown chakra. That eye is you, part of your greater forces. I want you to feel it there, I want you to actually feel the eyelid opening, looking at you. Allow. Remember. Allow. Feel the pressure.

Allow anything that desires to purge out of the body to purge through the floor into the pyramid below–simply let it go. Don't judge it good or bad; whatever energy desires to move now, let it go. Center. Allow the body to be healed.

Now, allow that mandala that you saw to move in you, so it is in every portion of your being. You are the mandala. Feel the beauty of it in you–the gold, the white, the color. Feel it all in you, all in you. You can move to any point there. Allow it to be in you. Center. Take a breath out of the heart chakra, breathe it. Allow the energy. Contemplate the mandala as you; now you are that thing. Allow. Center.

(Play The Eternal Om.) I want you to listen to the Om when we're playing it. I want you to contemplate the mandala in your body as it's being played, and I want you to feel the vibration of that mandala in the body, so you vibrate it outward, inward, throughout every cell of your being, even the secret spots, let it get there. Anything that's pushed out of the body, let it push into the pyramid below you. [Music starts.]

Now we're bringing a capstone down around this, what you call, temple. Allow the body to get warm, because this creates the movement. Indeed. Now, far above you, far, far above you, I want you to see point of gold and white light, and that point of light extends a ray of white light, brilliant silver light, down to the palm of your left hand. And it extends a ray of brilliant gold light to the palm of your right hand, and it is out there into forever. It's coming to you now. Feel it in the palms. Contemplate the mandala in the body and allow the energy to move. Center. Allow the chakras to open. Open the temples. Allow the mandala to work in the body. . . . Center. . . . Bless everything, love everything; no matter what it is, love it, send love to it. If you have difficulty, let that portion flow through you into the pyramid below. Allow.

Now see yourself sitting as a Buddha in your heart chakra. Feel yourself there, Buddha one, gold entity, allow. Allow. Allow the color of you that be sitting there to shift, to change, like a great pattern. Movement there. Allow. Allow the mandala to move.

Now feel your auric field, feel it about your body extending wider. Farther and farther and farther, so it envelops the whole globe, big as the Earth, any point in the auric field you can touch, so you'll know what's going on there. Allow love. Center. Don't be into judgment here. Allow. From the center of your heart chakra, from your power point, the great light that you are, radiate brilliant green outward to your auric field that surrounds the planet. This is unconditional love, compassion, that others may feed upon–they'll need it, they need it now. So vibrate the green from the center of your physical outward so it goes around the planet so others may feed. Allow. You will get ten times more back. Allow. Vibrant color. Don't tell them how to work it; they'll work it their own way. It's all right.

I want you to feel like a little baby–unconditional love for everything. You haven't been taught not to love yet. Unconditional love. A baby god, unconditional love here. Green. Center. When I say "center" now, I want you to pull that mandala energy and see that as you; it forms your body, it is there inside you, power. The gold and the white and the brilliance of it, and the power in the left and the power in the right hand–feel it there as you. Allow. Center.

Now from your heart chakra I want you to send a gold light to the point where the silver and gold come from. You send a gold light from your center, your being, out to that point. Just send it there. So you're recognized and recognizing. Center. Feel the connection there. Allow. Center. Grand. Feel the energy in your palms now; those chakras are opening–let them open. It's going to excite the kundalini in the body–let it happen. The energy will want to move up your spine, let it happen. In a gentle manner, slowly open your physical eyes. (Turn the music down.)

Feel the palm energy, like you have holes here. Indeed, you do. Take your left hand and put it over your heart chakra, and your right hand. I want you bless the body. To complete the blessing of the body, you use your own spittle and this thumb [right]. You spit on the thumb [wets the thumb with the tongue] and touch here [heart chakra]; you spit on the thumb, you touch here [sixth seal] (you're blessing the body consciousness for allowing you, the god, to inhabit it, and the cells of your body will remember and appreciate it); and then at the crown chakra [you wet the thumb and touch the crown]. Indeed. How do you feel?

Indeed, okay?

Now, one of the difficult times to come is when the persona, the ego, desires to train the body to force it to do certain things. The body consciousness is becoming fully aware that there are energies coming that are very profound. It is becoming aware that there is an awakening within the human condition. So the persona, the ego, is going to have to get a little bit enlightened itself now, to work with the body, to work with these energies and to understand there is only love, and the game here is called "not," and it's changing.

The switch to love out of the game of *not* is going to cause a lot of confusion, because you've been trained in this game of *not* for so long. It's going to create turmoil in a lot of areas in society. It'll be up to those that know, that have compassion, to smooth the way. Everyone wants love, I don't care *who* it is. [It's] simply the definition of it in your limited understanding, spiritually, of what it is. That's all right.

But you're here to prove your ability with the power called compassion, to learn, to become more and more, because this is a school, it's a training ground. You're going to go to other arenas, and you're getting what we would term hard training, very focused, specialized training, because you'll be on your own. I know some of you think you're on your own here now, but you're not. But there are other places you're going to go, other activities, other realms [where] you will be on your own. You're being trained to be overlords, many of you, and one of the most profound things you need with the overlord authority is compassion, and you're learning that here. That is one of the steps.

I know you say it's difficult to have compassion. I've seen you—you're compassionate one day and then erratic the next, and enjoy being centered for a moment, and then understanding it's more fun *not* centered! "Centered, I can't get pissed off. I can get very upset when I'm *not* centered. It's fun. Why [be centered]?" Well, the reason it's going to be necessary to be centered [is] because when this planet, what you call the consciousness that is coming [arrives] (you beings term it the Photon Belt that's going to attack you; that's not what it is—it's your consciousness coming here), it's going to affect a lot of things.

Now, this consciousness that's coming, that is you here, remembers its power and is expecting you to have (you, the physical) prepared a landing site in centeredness so it (the greater consciousness) can be understood. But like most of humanity, "Papa is not coming home yet, why clean the floor?" Know you what I mean? And then there is that knock on the door and you be sweeping. [Laughter.] It's all right, it's arriving.

It's going to arrive what you call in cycles. You're getting a shot this, what you call, your July, August, September–these three months, a short piece of it. Then you get another piece your October, November, December. The piece you're getting these three months is about this big [holds thumb a short distance from index finger]. Next year they come in chunks, so you better keep the floor clean, if you know what I mean. It'll be coming to get you, know you? But it is you! It is not a bad thing. You can do whatever you want with it.

The easiest way to handle what is going on here is to remain in sacredness and holiness, and very compassionate to other beings. Doesn't matter what religious belief system you're in, won't matter. This energy doesn't have what you call the understanding of religion. It has the understanding of unconditional love, and it's coming home to your doorstep. Be all right. No problem, eh, until the knock on the door. Okay. [He laughs.] Humor.

Now, what we want you to understand (this will be the message that's going to be in your magazine a little bit later, indeed, particularly in your December month–your fall, you say), there's a lot of light coming, a lot of light, and it's your light, it's what you've wanted. Now, when a lot of light comes, you beings will get disoriented. It'll affect the body, and you'll go into a worship thing. We are aware of this. You must train yourselves, because you are light beings. You're playing you forgot. But I can see your souls: I can see those that are awakening, those that are resonating and saying, "Yes! I remember," and I see those that say, "Well, I don't want to remember. Is it okay if I look, peek?" And I speak to some–you hide in the corner like you think you're getting away from me. That's all right. You don't realize I'm sitting right there and you're in my lap. I was the one that designed the soul, so I think I know how it works. That is simply your word here for the forces that exist. I didn't design the "you"–you know, the god that you are–I didn't design that. I designed the capsule so everyone could get away from this nonsense and become, part of it. There were a group of us involved in it. [He laughs:] You haven't seen anything yet. I'm just getting warmed up.

All right, now sort of simply play with your hands very gently, sort of open them. Indeed, is there anyone that can't feel the energy in their palms? Indeed, just starts coming out along there, like holes.

That hole there, I want you to let it become the whole palm, both sides, big—so the hand literally becomes a light ball. Just let it happen. It is there. It wants to become that way.

Now, each of you in this room, before you were born, selected (you did) particular powers to be utilized in this time. You made that decision with what you would term yourself—your inner self, your powerful self—and your high self (as you would term it, the high self). The high self is what is coming here, but it is already you—you're just getting that remembrance of it. Those powers are going to kick off, they're going to fire like a time bomb, time-capsule thing, going to go off. The structures that you have now, even your metaphysical structures, have not defined these powers, and when they attempt to define them, they limit them. All right.

Now, as they start to bubble with you, move, strange things will happen—LET THEM HAPPEN. Do you understand? Let them happen. And if you require to define it, remember that you're going to limit the power to fit in this structure. If you have to give it a name, call it the love of God and let it be as it wants to be. Is that all right with everyone? Can you do that? Because it's needed.

Now, it's not needed for your ego or your persona to know—yet it is, because it's going to talk to the body consciousness—but what you must remember, you've been given a charge not only for yourself, but for other beings on this planet (now, I know you don't like to hear that—that's too bad), not just one or two beings, not the groups I deal with, the beings I deal with—you're dealing with many beings. And they're expecting you to awaken; they trust you, they don't know what the hell is happening here! And through the eons of the journey, you have always been the one to be there when the shift happens, and you can help them. And they understand it, so they're *counting* on you! Not just in the physical, however; this is what you call with the legions of light, entities. You know it. You don't *want* to do it, "But I'll do it."

There are many that are counting on you, literally, what you could say, to save their souls. We'll use those words. Those are what your human conditions understand, but it's really to assist them to go beyond the soul and to become the lightbeings that they are so everyone can play in this garden without any problem. Know you what I mean? It's going to filter through you, by the way, so enjoy it. Can you allow yourself that responsibility?

[Group:] Indeed!

Allow it indeed, because it empowers you, know you what I

mean? It empowers everyone. You can make this a very, what you call, true spiritual home here, called the planet Earth, indeed? Make it the Eden it already is. You just simply shift and you recognize it's there. Okay.

It almost makes me feel sick inside, that responsibility. I have great fear. I feel like if I get noticed, I'll get in trouble. I got noticed before and I got in trouble. And I'm scared.

It's all right. I understand a lot of things. One of the things, the last blockage to moving into your true power, is this scare thing, indeed. So just understand it is love there, indeed, and it'll be easy. But that's the last one to go through—the fear of it.

It's right in my gut.

It is, I know. It's all right. I have a habit of moving energies whether you want to move them or not, know you what I mean? Allow yourselves thirty moments, indeed. When you go outside you can do your chitty chat, and have some fruits here because it's going to give you some of the energy you need to relieve some of the pressure in the brain. You know your fruits, indeed? The pineapple juice there, the juice—its golden color is going to remind you inside you, the body consciousness, of this gold. The golden energy you worked with, it's going to help you integrate it. When you go outside I want you to breathe the air in and remember that auric field that was around the planet when you sent your green. I want you to breathe in and feel that energy, that auric field—you can feel it. Some of you will get memories or thoughts in the brain when you breathe in. Let them come. Bargain?

[Group:] Bargain!

So be it.

29

Gloom & Doom? No!

Zoosh through Robert Shapiro
July 22, 1996

Gloom and Doom? Zoosh says no, no giant disasters. Japan's not going to fall into the sea (maybe at a denser dimension of itself it might, but not where you are now) and California's eastern border is not going to become beachfront property. (Real estate speculators, guess again!)

I will not support any of these disaster ideas, even though I fully understand and completely comprehend the visions people have received, and I do not in any way question their spiritual or intellectual integrity. I am simply saying that things have changed, and we must do what we can to support and sustain the viability of the continents as they are. It is true that there are too many people living on the west coast of the United States in certain places—not everywhere. There are too many people living in the Los Angeles-San Diego area, okay?

There are a lot of people living in the San Francisco area, but not overwhelmingly so. It hasn't gotten to the overwhelm point yet, but it could. Where there are too many people, the land says, "Get out, too many." But I'm not, *not, NOT* going to support the idea that some land mass is going to slip into the sea or that the ocean is going to rise at a rapid rate. Yes, the ocean is going to rise at a slow rate, but it will be sufficiently slow that you will be able to prepare. I want you to think about something. Even if both polar icecaps melted completely in, say, five years (which they won't; they might melt eventually, but it will take time and you'll have notice), it would not mean that the oceans would go up by many, many feet. It's distributed around quite a bit, so anybody who is, say, several hundred feet above the ocean need not worry too much. And those of you living reasonably inland and well above sea level, don't worry about it.

The main thing I'm saying is that these are possibilities only if you fear it, if you promote it unintentionally and if you draw it to you unintentionally (most people would do it unintentionally). I perfectly appreciate people who are putting out the I Am America map (for example), because that *could* have happened, and it certainly is happening at 3.0 dimension.

Can you discuss specifically what is happening to the physical body as a result of the opening to the higher frequencies this fall?

The physical self is primarily undergoing a transmutation. Certain organs are doing exactly what Mother Earth has been doing. I've been saying now for a while that Mother Earth can no longer carry the negative energy of human beings, which has been placed there in some cases by people needing to blow off their negative energy or by people having just died or having suffered in some way whereby that negative, extreme discomforting energy flowed into the Earth. Now, Mother Earth has been letting go of that energy for some time because she cannot carry it anymore and be healed herself. We know that. But there's more . . .

You, as you know, are micro-mini-Mother Earths yourselves because you, as physical beings, are made up of Mother Earth stuff (not to put too fine a point on it), and you normally retain your discomforting energies in certain organs in the body. Now, we all know that one of those organs is the spleen (the colloquialism "venting your spleen" is actually true), and for many people other organs that can be affected are the pancreas, the liver and certainly the gut. You know, when your heart aches from feeling bad (not sick), that's because the other areas of your body have taken all the discomforting energy they can, and it backs up into your heart. Those of you who have a heartache because of some sadness or some unpleasantness, know that the heart *itself* does not carry negative energy (although some of you might dispute that). It is just that if that energy is overwhelming other parts of your body, it will back up there.

Now, I have said that the Earth is releasing its energy, and as we've known for some time, sensitive people and even people who are not particularly sensitive are feeling more negative energy floating around. Some people think, "Oh, evil forces are doing this," but you know, I can't give evil forces credit for this, even though those who believe in such things might want to credit it. In reality this is simply Mother Earth letting go of excess uncomfortable or negative energies (as we call it) being felt by human beings, because it's up to you to process it for her; she cannot process it anymore. I've talked about this before; I just need to recap.

Excercise for Releasing Negative Energy

Now, you yourselves, beginning in the latter weeks in July, will begin to release these negative energies from your liver, pancreas, spleen and lower intestine (and eventually also from the little intestine). So, here is homework: I want you to do any kind of calisthenics you can do. This does not mean that I expect heart patients or people with emphysema to start jogging. If you're in a wheelchair, then shake your legs around, move your arms around, understand? If you're bedridden, do what you can. Most of you are able-bodied, and I want you to spend five minutes a day doing something vigorous and say out loud, "I am now transforming negative energy with this physical work." For those who just can't make time to do five minutes of calisthenics, take a brisk walk and at some point during that walk, say, "I am now transforming negative energy in my organs," then forget it. All right? That's just to let your *mind* know that something is going on. Then just keep on keeping on with what you're doing.

These are the facts: the physical body has infinitely more potential to transform physical discomfort than the mind ever can. Psychologists and psychoanalysts do a world of good, but they cannot actually transform discomfort. They can only help you to give *yourself* permission to transform it. Now, I want you to transform it yourself, and the easiest way to do it is through doing something physical. For those of you who like to dance, that's one great way. Getting the physical body moving with strong feelings and passion and excitement—that's great. But *don't* do it while you're making love because your partner will be open and your discomforts would simply be exchanged, defeating the whole purpose. If you can literally begin to see yourself as a minuscule version of Mother Earth, you will be able to see how things work the way they do. Your emotions, your passions, must be expressed, so that's what I recommend.

Okay. Are there beings on 3.0 Earth dimension who are coexistent with this Earth now at 3.48, in the same space?

Yes, just like ninth-dimensional Earth is right here, right now.

So certain things on this planet are happening at different dimensions. At 3.0

there are earthquakes and terrible volcanoes, as Cayce and all of the other prophets saw —that's happening now?

Absolutely.

And it's vibrating so much slower that we can't see it or feel it?

Oh, I wouldn't say that. Some people who are sensitive and others who might have moments of sensitivity occasionally sense something. Some people can smell the sulphur from the volcanoes, or sea air well inland, where you might not expect to smell it. Some people have feelings that you sometimes get before an earthquake. It's been well researched, especially by social scientists. Certain people have certain feelings before an earthquake, and then afterward they feel normal. This is happening. This does not mean to disregard the possibility of an earthquake in your dimension, but that nine times out of ten it is associated with Earth at a denser level.

All right, so people who still predict specific calamities are seeing it happen either in a lower dimension or in our dimension, but when it happens we will be in a higher dimension?

Let's say this: Yes, they're seeing it in a lower dimension, and let's extend that dimension. They are seeing these things happening anywhere from 2.9 to, say, 3.23, because there's a range there. When a body of people or a planet—everything—is shifting to a higher dimension, there's an interesting flexibility that occurs around the edges of dimensions. That is, as you shift up, some resonant echo takes place and one might be able to experience, however briefly, a portion of the second dimension (2.9, no more than that). So one might conceivably see something happening at (to use the astrological term) the cusp of the second and third dimension.

But from your point of view, it has been sort of agreed that awakening humanity will not experience really drastic earth movements?

Not in my understanding. I will not rule out the fact that there will be volcanoes. There will be storms, winds, etc. There will be experiences, all right, but I am not expecting catastrophic changes.

30

Angel warns of quake

Zoosh through Robert Shapiro
August 8, 1996

Robin Miller told us an angel appeared to him two days ago and said that there would be a 7.4 earthquake in Los Angeles on August 12, 1996, at 6:00 a.m.—epicenter San Bernadino, with thirty to forty fatalities, and a 10.2 in Los Angeles on August 6, 1998, at 7:16 a.m., with total devastation. Would you comment on that?

The more we can get the information out about these potentials, the less likely they will happen with such severity. There is certainly a very distinct possibility that the 10.3 or 10.4 earthquake will happen in 1998. And yet the more people who know about it, the stronger is the likelihood that it will not be much greater than 9.0–which is severe enough, but does not have to kill all life.

Did we do any good today? I mean, we've been phoning people all day long, but you can reach only so many people.

Well, you get it out as far as you can and hope that it continues–that's all. When you put it out on the Internet you have to put it in flashing klieg lights.

We did; it's flashing.

Do the best you can and then let it go. I can assure you, it's on its way all over the world. That's what you can do, and you have done that. But now we will see if it happens or not. It might, it might not. Regardless, the vision– the experience of the angel that came to this person–is absolutely real, and Robin is not alone in this experience. He is one of the first of the few who have been willing to go public about the experience. It was necessary for angels to begin visiting people who were used to metaphysics so that there can be some networking of the information.

It is necessary because there are entirely too many people there. There are entirely too many people in general on the planet right now, but there needs to be an immediate reduction. Fully one-third of the population must move inland from southern California, and when I say "southern," I mean south of a line drawn through the middle of the state; I'm not talking about Los Angeles itself.

Do you feel at this moment that this earthquake is going to happen?

At this moment the probability of the quake on Monday is still 92%.

Okay, is it going to get people's attention? Are they going to move out?

If enough people find out about it and it's talked about enough, the potential will perhaps drop to 60% (meaning, a 40% chance it won't happen).

He said that the angel told him only thirty or forty people would die. Is it more important to break up some highways and warn them and get them out so they're not there in 1998?

Excuse me, but "only thirty or forty"? If it is you or your friends . . .

But they're talking about total devastation in '98—millions of people.

I understand. But think about all the other earthquakes there have been–those were also warnings. This is not the only warning. It is not your last chance; there will be other earthquakes before '98. This is just one of many, but it happens to be located in a place that is close to the main fault in the state. That fault is a sleeping dog that may not sleep much longer.

If the quake occurs in '98, it will probably not be this motion (lateral). It will most likely be either this motion (vertical) or possibly even double vertical, meaning that both sides of the crack push upward. That would make it catastrophic, because everything is quickly and violently hurled into the air. That's like what happened in a recent quake there, but would be 20 to 30 times worse, and it is not likely that even the well-built houses or structures would survive.

There *are* structures that can survive a 9.0 quake reasonably well. Think about putting wheels under new structures, and some kind of fail-safe valves in the plumbing–even a safety circuit in the wiring so that a major break in the wiring will shut down the power coming into the house. This technology has already been designed and built into facilities on a smaller or larger scale and at certain military installations, but not homes. (If you have a $50 million computer online, you don't want a voltage surge, do you?) It's basically a more dramatic voltage regulator.

At what dimensional point is California going to be safe and not experience an earthquake? Does it depend on the dimensional scale?

For this planet earthquakes are absolutely natural. They will probably still exist up to 4.2 dimension, but they will be milder and more frequent. One might have twos or threes, which are not particularly offensive,and are even somewhat amusing if you are expecting them and there is no harm done: "An earthquake? What fun!" A 2.0, 2.5, even 3.0 is ofttimes fun as long as you're prepared.

31

Humanity Passes Test: Quake Dispersed

Zoosh through Robert Shapiro
August 12, 1996

Well, all right. So you have managed to pass your little test, eh? This quake that would have had significant effect in the outer areas of the Los Angeles suburbs and community did not take place because the network was trusted and in place. The actual plan has always been that the means to communicate would not depend upon mankind's creation, but that angelic visitors or visions would inform people of impending disasters, and that the network of friends (in this case through calling each other on the telephone) would work on this reality to change the time line.

Remember that some time ago it was necessary to move you from 3.37 to 3.47 to get you past a lot of potential disasters. Now, in order to do that, some of us had to make certain promises that you could be trusted to pass the test and that you did not have to be frightened into it. (Granted, that was not the total intent, but it would have been coercion, essentially.) We felt it would be better for you to show what you can do. So there was a scenario given to an angelic messenger, who passed it on to a receptive spiritual man, who in turn passed it on to others and worked on it himself to change the reality. This involved changing the time line.

As a result, no serious quake happened at the time that was predicted (it was actually a promise, not a prediction), and the effect of the quake was dispersed over a wider area. There was also a feedback loop, referring to a gift by those who had received Mother Earth (those who acknowledged Mother Earth's gift of her physical self for your own bodies). This feedback allowed you to give back to her a great portion of her electrical body—which mankind has been using for some time, believing it is being created when it is actually simply being *captured* by generators and so on.

You have changed your time line since the visit and promise from that angelic messenger [on August 6]. You have moved the time line up slightly (meaning that you have moved up in dimensions), so you have now moved into 3.49, all right? You're on the threshold of being halfway to fourth dimension. This was achieved by *your altering the reality of the 7.4 quake that was promised to happen!* This was done not only for the love of Mother Earth, but for the love of the people and the animals in the area. This was not a prediction or promise only by angelic messengers; the animals have for several weeks been giving distinct messages that an earthquake was coming.

I think you will see them begin to calm down now and go back to their normal routines, telling you that the high-pitched sonic messages that Mother Earth puts out to the animal kingdom (and anybody else who's listening) have been not only heard and acknowl edged, but are no longer being broadcast.

This is well done, but it doesn't mean you won't have to do it again. There will be other tests that will also often involve disasters. But I want you to appreciate what you have done and realize that natural disasters like this can be averted by distributing energy in a different way—where smaller quakes occur here and there and electrical pulses are returned to Mother Earth's electrical body so that she can be reinvigorated. Realize that you might be able to change the course of hurricanes or typhoons, even tornadoes, so that they go to places where they are less likely to cause great harm and damage, or else break them up into smaller units, utilizing the same force of energy but doing significantly less or no damage. This is important: You must acknowledge the need for these things that Mother Earth is doing for herself, but you can help her to do them in a more benevolent way. So I will simply say, "Well done!" Everybody did a good job; you passed the test. Those of us who advocated on your behalf feel . . . well, we're not exactly passing out cigars, but we feel pretty good about the fact that you came through.

What about something else soon? Is there another time when Earth is going to need to release or throw off something?

I think it's possible. I want you to be alert. Watch the animals—the dolphins and the whales, yes, the ants, the sheep— all of the animals that are functioning in the natural state of being. Watch what they do, for they can hear and understand the messages of Mother Earth. They know what it means and they will behave accordingly. Watch them, and when they begin to give you messages that look like they are distressed for their lives or the lives of their loved ones, then know that something is up. Maybe it's an earthquake or maybe a fire or flood.

Call your friends and tell them to give love and light to Mother Earth, electricity to her electrical body, magnetism to her magnetic body, and support and sustain the dispersion of the energy in such a way as to cause less harm. But you *must* allow Mother Earth to do what she needs to do for herself. So be on the alert, because this will happen again. Good day.

32

The Sinister Secret Government's New Weapon—The Hate Gun

Zoosh through Robert Shapiro
August 4, 1996

Now we'll talk about the new weapon system that has been called the "hate gun." This weapon is being tested from an underground base by the sinister secret government. It is a portable unit, somewhat like a portable howitzer, but nowhere near that big. It's just a rolling vehicle with a tube on top and a bunch of electronics inside, designed to shoot—something they've been trying to do for a long time.

You see, with the ELF and ULF (ultralow frequency) weapons, they have been able to broadcast into an area signals that would promote well-being, for example—but they usually use it to promote uncomfortable feelings to keep people from entering an area. It creates what they call a soft perimeter, which means that they don't need barbed wire and machine guns. The area appears open, totally penetrable, but electronic devices would repulse people or animals, even planes and so on, since navigational equipment would be disrupted.

Now, for a long time they have wanted a means to shoot something from point A to point B—what the military refers to as "to point of aim." Now that they have this, they are experimenting with it. It is taking place the way some military authorities have done in the past, though not without a certain amount of shame; but in the case of the sinister secret government, shame is not a factor. They are, as usual, experimenting on the local population.

Now, for those of you who are not living in Sedona, I'd *like* to be able to reassure you that you are safe, but you are not. There really isn't any safety because the vehicle that carries this weapon (there are only two or three being actively tested right now) has the capacity to travel on the underground rail network to transport something from one point under the continental U.S. to another. The testing has been going on for about ten days in the Sedona area [since about July 26], but in other areas for about three and a half weeks [since about July 10].

The weapon creates an electrostatic charge that is condensed into what I would call a form of plasma. It will maintain its "structural integrity" for a distance of about three miles before it begins to break down. It can pass through a certain amount of matter (what they call "light barriers," meaning a fence, a tree, a corner of a house) and still maintain its structural integrity. If it goes through a house it will break down and if it hits people it will impact them.

After about three miles it begins to lose its field strength, but it can continue on and do damage for about another six or seven miles. Thus the effective range (if we count the damaging effect, though not full strength) is really about ten miles. The impact on an individual is particularly nefarious. This electrostatic charge is essentially condensed hate. They've been working on this for years and years; your own military is aware of such weapon technology. They are not using it widely because, as they have discovered, it can affect their own people as much as others. The intention is to knock down the natural goodwill that people have between each other and create chaos and aggression.

I want those of you who are reading this to think back for the three to four weeks that preceded the time of this channeling [August 4] and consider: Have you been exposed to somebody who has been demonstrating extreme anger, hatred, aggression—the sort of thing you wouldn't expect—possibly from even a total stranger or someone you know who has been very hair-triggered? This might be the reason.

Now, you might ask yourself why would *anybody* create such a weapon? What kind of purpose would it have? Is it designed to cause people to hate each other? Curiously enough, it really isn't. It's designed to *sap the energy* of people. Because you see, when people are the subject of hateful feelings, they tend to go through a series of reactions—disappointment and hurt, then sadness or a letdown feeling; then they might feel a pain. That's when the true agenda of the weapon comes up: when struck this way by something, one tends to become aggressive, angry, vengeful, and seek retribution. Because you can't hit the person who shot this at you, the tendency is to strike out in any direction at whoever happens to be convenient.

The purpose of this weapon is to create chaos and to break down the general moral principles of your society and, in the long run, create a condition wherein the natural goodwill and trust of people toward each other (which still exists even in big cities to a significant extent) would break down. Even in small towns people might begin to fear and distrust to the extent that they would be willing to accept extreme measures to maintain order. In the long run government really (at its *best*) can only set an example or make suggestions. The government does not go out and say, "Look, this is the loving way to be. Why don't you try and be *this* way?" Some governments have tried to do that in the past, and on a smaller scale it has worked and is still working. But on the larger scale your people will need to do a significant amount of personal work before they can accept that attitude, unless they are enlightened, filled with a loving spirit, in a state of religious zeal, filled with the spirit of Creator or what-have-you.

This weapon is designed to break down the structures not only of your society but of your government, so that the sinister secret government can make another power play. They really want to establish a puppet government by which they can manipulate the world. They *deeply* cherish the idea that you could hate and distrust each other so much that you would have little love or toleration to appreciate each other.

Sometimes they will will send their agents out to commit acts of terrorism (I have to tell you this), then create trails of evidence that point to this country or that country or this group or that group to keep you fighting amongst each other. They know that the only way they can remain secret and the best way to control you in the long run is for you to hate and distrust each other. Thus they are going to take every opportunity to stir that up amongst you.

Now, I don't want you to be too depressed about this, because for one thing, your feeling would work in their favor. For another thing, I want you to understand that THEY CANNOT WIN. You are past the point where you will play these games. People, at their cores–all people, even people you wouldn't expect–need and want to be loved and appreciated for who they are. Granted, you don't want to support the qualities some of them demonstrate, but they have other qualities they can also demonstrate, such as friendliness, comradeship, working together for some greater cause to benefit all people, including themselves.

I want you to know that's coming about. I don't want you to fear people, saying, "Oh, the United Nations is going to take over the world." In the long run, the benevolent world order (not the *first* "world order" that will come and be controlling and manipulative, saying that your religion is not approved of or that your way of family life isn't all right—not that) will come along and say, "Let's get all the world governments together. Let's get all of the people together. Let's share our resources in a way that works for all of us, and let's help each other so that we can become one united Earth."

When that happens, you won't go on alone as a united Earth forever. Within six or eight months after you become united (it's not going to happen immediately; you've got time), you will start to be contacted by very benevolent, loving extraterrestrials—because you have proved that you are ready to accept each other. This planet you are living on is the ultimate testing ground to accept differences in people. If you can accept the differences in each other and not allow the sinister secret government (or their conscious or unconscious toadies) to manipulate you into hating each other, you will in time love each other, feel good about each other, get together and enjoy the best that all cultures have to offer, have a good time, and be ready to accept extraterrestrials who will come and offer wonderful things to you. You will soon be a part of the interplanetary system and have a wonderful life of adventure ahead of you.

Even though at times you might think, "This race or that race" or "these people or that people," you have to let go of these concepts. People will do things to disturb you, but let it go, because the odd thing is that even if you hate someone and are angry, *you* will suffer from those feelings of hate and anger. Granted, other people are injured by those aggressive feelings directed at them, but you also are injured. It does not pay, so don't play this game, all right?

What happens if you're driving along (which is what has happened recently) and you get zapped by a piercing energy that really hurts, right in your heart or wherever (in this case it was the heart)? What can you do to dissolve it?

If it is really crippling, you need to pull over and stop, for starters. Then call your guides or your angels and ask them to remove it. If you are a person who can utilize energies, begin putting good energy into that area of your body and ask that this dark energy be pulled from you. It is very easy for your etheric doctors or angels or guides to take it out. While they are doing this, just try and be in a peaceful state. It is best to stop and let this proceed, because it might take some time.

If you are in a position where you cannot stop, then ask that you have energy to maintain yourself until you can stop and have it pulled out. If you let it just fester in there, you will *become* that until you take it out. That is the hazard. This kind of negative energy is like a disease. It goes in there and sends out tentacles into all parts of your body. If you had to take it out surgically, it would be impossible. Angel and guides and etheric doctors take it out en masse, and the dark energy passes through and is released all at once. Try to remove it as soon as possible.

What if people cannot remove their own?

Then ask your angels or guides to remove it for you or go to someone who can do these things. It is ofttimes not easy to remove it yourself, although you can remove some aspects. This is very insidious, this hate gun. You might have to create new methods, but make sure those methods are not associated with any anger or attack, because those emotions will utilize that negative energy. And if you begin utilizing it, you will take it to every part of your body. So guard against being angry and hateful. If you do, it will make it harder to extract, though not impossible.

Can you talk about all the other areas where this has been going on for over three weeks?

Some of the places it's been going on more than others are in New York . . .

New York City?

New York City and also Oklahoma, where it has been creating a lot of disturbance in the weather (Oklahoma happens to be a place where the weather fronts meet). It's been creating some problems with people there as well. It's been in Washington State. There are a few other places, but I don't really want to say.

33

Hate Gun Shorted Out!

Zoosh through Robert Shapiro
August 8, 1996

How about that hate gun? Is it still working?

That's a good question. The gun has been short-circuited, and the short circuit has been built in. I don't think they can repair it for the next few months.

Who short-circuited it and when?

It happened a few days ago by a reasonably powerful lightbeing, someone I'd call a light physician.

Are they going to move the gun?

They've moved it deeper inside the structure of the mountain near Kingman where they feel it's more secure. However, their difficulty is that even when the current is turned off, it remains short-circuited—with sparks!

It might interest you to know where the hate comes from, but it is not a pleasant story, so I will temper it a bit. I will say that the gun is basically a tube (that's why it's called a gun, you know). Several people are alive in a metal box under the gun, surrounded by crystals, being mistreated such that they are angry and despise their tormentors. The crystals have been programmed to absorb these feelings, amplify them and emit a pulse of these condensed feelings. Thus the weapon is dependent on the reactions of the prisoners.

Are they going to move it somewhere else? Is there any way we can get out the

beings who are trapped in there?

For starters, they'll try to move it up to Canada. What can you do to get them out? You can attempt to rescue their souls, because their bodies are so uncomfortable that they want to die. But you will have to check in from time to time because once they die, they will just put other individuals in there. Transformation is desirable.

Were we being aimed at, or did we just happen to be in the way? At Light Technology we have had a devastating week.

You were being aimed at. It just goes to show that there are individuals who actually consider your magazine to be a threat. But considering what this project cost in dollars and that it is basically going to be entirely derailed (pun intended), then I would say that chances are they will put their investments into something more profitable. This was one individual's idea of delaying the story about the sinister secret government. But in those circles there's nothing like failure to get your ideas ignored in the future, especially when this one cost $3.5 billion!

Couldn't those crystals be altered, reprogrammed, interfered with? Because the gun's no good without the crystals?

You betcha.

34

Alien Invasions and the Secret Government

Zoosh through Robert Shapiro
July 22, 1996

Although I am not expecting catastrophic changes, I am certainly expecting a tremendous amount of manipulation by those who are either afraid of what the future might bring or whose personal power fiefdoms might feel threatened. In that sense, yes, I am definitely expecting to see some kind of fake aliens hurled at you, as we've discussed before, some kind of beings who are not truly extraterrestrials, passed off (or fobbed off, if you like) on you as fake invaders. This might happen. Once upon a time it was going to be a "this would happen" or "this shall happen," you but now it's been reduced to "it might happen," because as more people become more informed about these nefarious plans, the plans become semi-useless.

Am I suggesting that the *Sedona Journal* is being read by millions of people? Certainly not. Someday maybe, but the *Journal* is a vehicle to stimulate the imaginations of others (as well as many other articles, books, magazines, etc.). The *Sedona Journal* is perhaps in the unique position, however, in the people it stimulates. Very often it stimulates those who are in the business of stimulating others. I welcome that; I think it's fine. As a result, very often what is printed in the Journal one month will be dramatized on TV in a fictional format in the next month or two. (Don't worry, TV people, we are not expecting royalties.)

But these extreme plans to try to fake it with an alien invasion of

Earth will not really come to pass. Once upon a time it looked like a viable way to unite the people of Earth, as in the popular science-fiction film that is out right now (*Independence Day*). However, this is becoming less and less of a realistic scenario simply because of magazines and articles like this and other sources. People are just not very gullible these days, in spite of the opinion-makers assumptions. And for those who try to manipulate popular opinion, people are not going to be so receptive even to the ideas of prejudice, racism, nationalism, colonialism–all that has been pulled off before to keep people fighting amongst themselves so they don't see how much they really have in common and who is trying to manipulate them. Understand that if you, gentle reader, really believe that there is some nefarious plot among some race or religion to take over the world, you are truly being dazzled by somebody else's plot, someone who wants you to be angry at *anybody* else just so you won't see them. I can assure you, the sinister secret government is made up of people who do not believe in or practice any heart-centered spiritual way, whether it be religion or philosophy. They believe in power, and whatever form that power takes is fine as long as *they* can have it. So look toward your religions. Does your religion say first that "God is love"? If it does not, try to instigate that idea.

So the sinister secret government will attempt to use some of their cloned beings and some of their spaceships for a phony raid or invasion of Earth?

Yes, the idea of the play that was dramatized on the radio so many years ago by Orson Welles, based upon the famous story by Jules Verne–it's surprising how long that idea lingered. But you know, I think its time has gone by, and I'll tell you what did it, ironic though it might seem: it was not the movies, but *television*! Television has such a worldwide impact that people are disinclined now to panic as much as they once might have. So television has served in many ways. One of the ways is to allow people to believe that many more things are possible than are imagined (to borrow from the Bard).

Okay, so what is the update on the sinister secret government? We left some of them on the backside of the Moon and some of them in stasis and in underground tunnels the last time we talked about them a year or so ago.

Well, they have circled their wagons. They are still functioning; they have made some efforts in recent times to influence political campaigns. They have tried to instigate more racial disharmony. They are consistently supporting financially, through various screen or cover groups, many different organizations that espouse racism and religious prejudice, to say nothing of nationalistic prejudice—that's always been their big tool. They're working real hard at that one; they've been putting a lot of energy into that lately. I might add that the major tribal warfare that broke out in Africa recently, with the Tutsis on the one side and the Hutus on the other, was largely a result of the sinister secret government's manipulations behind the scene. It's true that there's been tension between the tribes for a long time, just as there is tension between the State of Israel and its neighbors. Yet when it blows up and goes wild with massacres . . . can you imagine a grown man who is normally reasonable, responsible, who has a wife and family and understands the basic values of life suddenly going crazy and murdering and maiming men, women and children? This is not normal, I can assure you.

This was largely the effect of radiated energy (to some extent ELF, even a little ULF—ultralow frequency). It was a concerted effort in the sinister secret government's long-range plot to try and get the darker-skinned peoples of Africa to kill each other off, which is basically an attempt to create a land grab. It is ironic, that one. I certainly hope that doesn't happen, because as I've said before [in volume three of *The Explorer Race*], if all of the darker-skinned African peoples were to disappear from Earth, that would be the *end!* There wouldn't be any more human beings here on Earth of any race. *You've got to have them!* I'll let you read the book to find out why, not only for the obvious reason that they are good and reasonable people to have around, but for very significant spiritual reasons. Read the book—it is a chapter I feel good about.

So I will say this: The sinister secret government is out there, and if you are looking for evidence of it, look to see how well-funded and how active certain terrorist groups are, and how is it, in this day and age when governments are totally alert to terrorism, that terrorists seem to be able to obtain these devices—bombs, explosives and so on. Granted, sometimes it is through corruption and through legitimate means gone bad, but nine times out of ten it is from some screen organization that might not even know they are being funded by the sinister secret government, which has absolutely no interest in their issues at all. As far as the sinister secret government is concerned, any of these organizations are only a means to their ends, which is to keep everybody fighting amongst themselves so they don't get together and look out and see who's really trying to manipulate you.

Is there a point on the dimensional scale beyond which this will fade away?

By the time you start getting around 3.7, you're not going to have so much terrorism—but for a reason you might not expect. When your hearts are sufficiently open, when somebody is crying on the street corner about how they or their people have been overlooked and are in desperate need of something, anything that can help them—food, shelter, good meaningful work, freedom to pursue their spiritual interests, etc., many worthy questions—people, instead of walking by them and trying not to notice and not one stopping—everyone will stop. They will ask, "What can we do to help you?" and mean it.

That's what's going to change terrorism, because the people who basically have complaints are going to have their complaints redressed immediately. At that stage, of course, the United Nations will become very influential. Money and resources will pour in, and it will basically become a clearinghouse. They're not going take over the world; they're going to become a clearinghouse to support and sustain worthy causes all over the world, eventually becoming your number one liaison with extraterrestrials and all of their wonderful philosophies and assistance programs. If any government outlives any other government on the planet, it will be the U.N., and all the governments will cooperate. The U.N. will not die out, so don't fall for these deceits of the sinister secret government, where some of their toadies or one of their front groups—or even a group that doesn't even know they are being supported by the sinister secret government—might take a military vehicle, paint it black or charcoal gray or something and put the U.N. insignia on the side, then go out and do something with it (or even just drive through or have it towed through a neighborhood), scaring everybody. *Don't assume that's from the United Nations that you know.* And the next time you're in New York, take yourself on down to the United Nations and discover what a beautiful place it is, and how it's filled with beautiful people. Oh, they're not always going to be polite, but they are more polite most of the time than people you might find on the outside. And for those who can't go to New York or spare the time to go to the United Nations, go next door, go across the street, go across town and befriend someone who's different from you. It's a very enlightening experience, and you might just find that it will bring your vibration up, make you feel better about yourself— and maybe you'll make some new friends, too. It's a win-win situation all around.

All right, let's check up on other things we haven't talked about for months and months. We had the battles in the skies with the Xpotaz. What's the update on that?

Nothing. That's over.

They all left?

It's no longer a factor.

The Xpotaz had this manufacturing craft—huge.

Oh, that. They're gone, they went elsewhere.

About how long ago in our time?

Oh, months.

So there's no one right now that the secret government is battling in the skies?

No.

The Pleiadian warship went home?

Yes. Of course, it doesn't take them very long to go home, does it?

So the secret government had left their control base under South Africa. They'd left all of their underground bases and some of them went underneath Las Vegas. They were going under some of the major cities—Moscow, Paris, Washington, D.C. And then they stopped in their tracks and went into stasis. Then what happened?

They were starting to spread themselves thin because they were getting shaken out of where they were. They basically needed to find someplace that was relatively secure, so they created a very large underground bunker. They needed special metals for it (I won't say what metals they are) so they can screen out all benevolent radiations except for one (I won't say what that is, either). And they created this underground bunker where they feel safe. The benevolent radiation that comes from Creator they cannot stop, basically, because that which drives them is biological. [Chuckles.] Excuse me for being precise, but it is necessary, and I don't want to give them anything they don't already know, even though I do talk to them. That's right. I do. We don't empower them, in the sense of making things worse for everybody else, but we certainly talk to them. We are not deflected by their shields.

You don't want to say where they are?

Certainly not.

How many of them?

About 83, sometimes 85 . . .

Eighty-five people? They had five million!

I'm talking about the core group that makes the decisions.

Oh, the core group is underground?

You're not going to build an underground bunker for five million people.

So what happened to all of those other beings?

Most of them are still alive. They're just performing drudgery duties.

How about the beings in South Africa who were cloned, who were going to have to find their way up those shafts?

You have to remember that cloned beings do not live very long. They are designed to *not* live very long, for the obvious reason that the longer they live and the more experience they acquire, the more they become conscious, sentient and want to think for themselves. And any group that is trying to create a slave race wouldn't like that. So they are built to live for about five to seven years tops, sometimes just two years.

Okay, so they mostly left their bodies as cloned beings.

That's right. And for them, leaving their bodies is a good thing.

Yes, of course, because they were cut off from their souls. So the place from which the sinister secret government ran the world is empty? All of the bases are empty right now?

Well, they're on automation. The place where they are now is basically able to activate those bases through automatic methods; I won't say how. But these methods are not unlike those that exist on the surface for any kind of remote-controlled, automated system.

Are there still a group of them on the Moon?

Yes, but they are dwindling; there are not as many of them there. Partly this is because there are so many overflights going on there. There are so many simple, Sputnik-type vehicles flying around there, it's very difficult for them to do what they're doing undetected. If you're mining or even setting up facilities in any way, anytime you're moving material from point A to point B, it's almost impossible to evade those pictures. So they're pretty well shutting down that operation. They're going to wait.

Are they aware that in twenty more points on the scale we'll be beyond them?

They are aware, and that's part of the reason their fallback plan is to go elsewhere. If they are unable to retain densification here on Earth for all its peoples (which is going to happen), then their fallback position is to go elsewhere. They're not entirely certain where that would be; that's why their fallback plan does not allow for mass evacuation of all their people. Obviously, it will be the core group, or what I've called the inner circle–and possibly the outer circle, but that's only a maybe.

Of the thirteen inner circle, how many are still faithful to the cause?

Twelve.

Twelve? I thought several had defected. They came back?

One of them came back.

I see. This recent attempt to put a bubble completely around the planet early Tuesday, July 16—can you discuss that?

Recent SSG Attempt to Interfere

It was a technology that was designed to interfere with the naturally radiated, magnetic soul and teacher energies of human beings. One of the more significant purposes of the technology was to interfere with people's dream states. When the body sleeps, you have dreams that have psychological significance, but at the deeper levels you're visiting your teachers, you're out and about, you're going places. The soul does not have to sleep. The attempt was to interfere with that process, to create a barrier so that the soul energy would be deflected and unable to communicate with its teachers–in short, unable to go home. It was believed that this would be the ultimate way to retain densification, because it would create not only a short-circuit but a backflow, as one might say in plumbing, that would block all means to identify and become a portion of Creator's allies and teachers and angels. At those deep levels one also tends to resolve a lot of problems by getting direction and so on. The whole idea was to create a single source for direction.

You know, if you can take people's dreams away, which is the goal of many despots, absolute control, then you can control every aspect of their lives. But even Hitler couldn't take away his soldiers' dreams. Granted, he did everything he could to instigate certain dreams (oh yes, they had a department of dream technology), but he was not able to take away their dreams and certainly was unable to prevent the spirit teachers of the Axis forces to eventually intervene with those soldiers. But a despot always wants to control *every* moment, both waking and sleeping, of the people he wishes to control.

Okay, so what was the means or methods of the technology of the bubble, and was it only that one day?

I am loathe to say because (to be as vague as possible) the technology to create such a device in a limited capacity exists in any electronics store! You'd have to have some knowledge, of course, but it could be done easily. I won't talk about the technology because it is so easily attainable, but I will say that higher forces, including the mass soul body of all human beings on Earth, interfered. And if it were tried again, I do not think it would be successful.

Was it up for only that one day?

Yes, it wasn't even a full day.

Who specifically was removing the bubble at 1:30 that morning? Besides the mass soul of humanity, did all the crafts around the planet also participate in its disappearance?

The energy to transform it built up to a significant *crescendo*. (I want you to understand that when I say *crescendo* that's a hint to transform it.)

So it had to do with a resonance that cracks a glass?

That's right.

All right. This thing Robert handed me with the electric circuit under the vitamin bar code, is there any significance in that?

Not so much to comment on, but evidence of technology gone bananas. Technology has gone further than your society can assimilate it; I think most computer salesmen know this, and many other people as well, to say nothing of philosophers and peoples in religion.

Most people can't program their VCRs.

That's right. Not only that, but technology is at a point now where it can grow ten times faster than people can either learn how to use it or see it as being of value in their lives. Technology always intends to re-create itself in some better way.

That's at this level of our brain capacity. But as we constantly expand and open up, we'll be able to use this increasing amount of technology, right?

Well, you have to understand that as your hearts open up (let's get into the right organ), you will not utilize technology very well. You won't need it. You'll utilize what naturally exists. Heart technology is used when you see extraterrestrials or spirit teachers or even advanced spiritual human beings make something go pouf! in the air, and where everything that happens before and after that pouf! is the result of cooperation. When technology gets to the point of total cooperation amongst all portions, including those who are inspired with the idea to create "it" (whatever "it" is) and everything that takes places after that voluntarily cooperates in the creation, what we have is magic — true magic.

Soon, soon, soon . . .

Well, you know the odd thing is that at the higher levels that's what you already do, and it's no big deal up there. It's like, "Oh yeah, ho-hum, so what?" You enjoy it, but it's something you take for granted, like buses and taxicabs. But at these levels, where forgetfulness is a factor, you can have the joy of rediscovering that. You know, it is an interesting thing that forgetting something is granted as an award or as an entertainment at higher levels, because you can enjoy forgetting something for a moment and then have the pleasure of remembering it, with all of the emotions and wonderful feelings that go with it. At the higher levels that is definitely an entertainment or cherished award. People strive for it, I might add. In some cultures it is considered a *very* high award. Interesting, eh?

We're at 3.48, right? Or 3.49?

Yes, pretty close to 3.48.

Between 3.48 and 3.70, where in this part of creation could the secret government go? Are there planets at this low density? I thought they were all higher.

No, there aren't. That's what they're worried about. They are worried that they will be uncreated as a portion of the so-called negative past. This is where their fear comes from, which, from their point of view, is totally justified.

What if they went back in time and screwed up the past, like when they moved the time track of the peace avatar U.S. president?

They're not going to be allowed to do that, and they know this. Their biggest dread is that they would become like everybody else. You see, once you've experienced that level of power and influence, albeit in a totally negative form, it's very hard to give it up. Ultimately, it's addictive. And I think that that is how we're getting through to them. The idea of being addicted to anything—from their point of view, that's a sucker thing. They want other people to be addicted to drugs and alcohol and food, whatever—self-destructive behaviors—because then they can manipulate them. But they want to be above that themselves at all times. Nevertheless, they now see that they are also addicted, and this is what's going to change them. They see that they have literally created something of which they are a portion; they are not above it. They have thought they were above it, but they are not. The minute you take something away from them that they cherish, they discover that they have withdrawal symptoms. Now that they understand that, it will bring them around someday.

Yeah, but they're not totally in control of themselves. Aren't they the puppets of some negative off-planet beings?

We're not too worried about that. The moment they were presented with the idea that they were also addicts and the proof was *shown* to them was the moment that the big crack took place between them and any so-called external force of manipulation. Because they could see, "Wait a minute, we're just like them." The minute that takes place, they can feel a common bond. And although they're a long way from being angels, they're not as devilish as they once were.

Also, don't worry too much about sinister people being cloned. Don't worry about ETs or any of these beings taking over and easing into higher positions, okay? That was once a possible scenario, but I don't think it is anymore, largely because the reins of power are coming into a smaller and smaller group, and as I said, the initial world order would take form as the corporate model. This is taking form right now and is pretty much in place, and that tends to make those like the sinister secret government less concerned. As I've stated before, the corporate model for the world order will not last long because it simply can't survive the opening of hearts, but corporations will survive. Corporations will simply become "heart" corporations.

35

On-Off Circuitry: Shutting Off the Old, Opening the New

YHWH through Arthur Fanning
August 14, 1996

All right. Pretty interesting week, eh?

It is fantastic. Zoosh said we're not out of the woods, though. Eighteen percent chance that that earthquake could still go.

Well you're not out of the woods . . . at all. If you get out of this woods, you're going to find there were only about 20 or 30 trees. Next woods, more trees. Don't worry about the woods. All right, now, this weekend [at the August 10-11 intensive] what we were working with was primarily an understanding of consciousness, indeed, how you can affect things. There was a drama there and ones were working, one way or the other. At one level it would seem like a tug of war (because you beings judge it—whether the earth quaked, this, that and the other, and it doesn't, and this, that—and you play), but it's not. The formula is more aligned for each of you to be aware of your judgments because that affects your ability to work with consciousness, work within the patternings of all things. So judgment became one of the wrappings that you beings had to go through, to take off and see, and some of you expose yourselves a little bit, get over that and get ready for more.

You must apply your feelings now. Also you must apply the level of understanding that you are evolving consciousness, indeed and this magazine is to serve the evolution of consciousness. Know you what I mean? Consciousness—that is all things, know you; that is everything. In this manner we're coming to a threshold. At one level, one threshold (we will say at the higher level of threshold we'll call it a seventh-dimensional being), a seventh-dimensional being may walk upon this plane and ingest anything that he wants, regardless if it has been sprayed with pesticides or if it's what is termed coal (know you, dirt)! Know you what I mean? A seventh-dimensional being can do that. A third-dimensional being cannot. A fourth can't, either. A fifth can't, either. A sixth, maybe some, know you, but not all. Everyone wants to be, even though they are third-and-a-half dimension, smart guy—seventh dimension, prove it. They're not doing their consciousness any good; they don't know what they're doing. They are arrogant about spiritual truths, do you understand?

Yes.

All right, so part of what you are learning . . . because Zoosh, you call him, has laid a template for you, and yet as I make comments about that template, you must understand that the template is important. He has given you 3.5, 3.4, 3.7, 4.2 —all of these levels. That is the level of where your group consciousness is—indeed, average. Some are more, indeed?

Yes, it's like a distribution curve, I mean a bell curve.

Indeed. Some are less. So the average is where you must apply levels of wisdom — you can feed more. Beings here have a tendency to take spiritual truths, the wordings of them, and say they are that truth, but they are *not* that truth. You are learning to get to that truth. That is what your life is about, that is what your density is about.

Evolving to that, yes.

Evolving to that level of truth so that you know! There is a grand difference between [mental knowing and] knowing in the body—because of the emotion and all of the experiences involved with it [body knowing], know you what I mean—that you become evolved. There are some foods right now, even what you term drugs, that would kill you, indeed?

Oh, of course!

Yet [to] a master, it wouldn't matter. It wouldn't bother him a bit, you see. The reason we're going in this direction is because you're going to get more profound spiritual truths coming out now, a lot of seventh-level understanding, a lot of sixth-level understanding. A lot of beings will display part of sixth, part of seventh —

just be aware of the manner in which they display them. You must understand, they're trying to learn, too, to get what you call complete seventh, as you would say. At seventh there is a level of humility that cannot be, what you call, acted out, can't fake it. It's there. And everyone [at level] seven is completely responsible. Sixth-level energy will lead to a tendency (middle sixth) of overlordness, to a manner.

Telling us what to do?

Well, it could be understood as telling you what to do, but the sixth-level being is also trying to apply wisdom there in the teaching of it. Know you? You understand?

We're simply trying to share wisdoms now, more. There are some that we can share wisdoms with; there are some that we've attempted to [share wisdoms with] and they go the wrong way. They're still getting wisdom out of it – not what they desire, however. Wisdom, as you move up these levels, is gentle with the vehicle. Gentle with the understanding of it.

All right, now, it's liken unto when I spoke to one person about this one flower she is going to plant. A being is going to learn unconditional love from this one flower, yet the being is not here yet; won't be for, mmm, depends on when the flower is planted – six months, even if you plant the flower tomorrow. It's just a connection with divinity that is coming forth. In this time everyone is expecting a certain level of divinity to be there, even little ones – *especially* little ones.

So this level of divinity is coming outward from your own consciousness, because you all want to understand it – the divinity, higher consciousness, superconsciousness is what you say, the word here. So in that understanding of divinity there is a requirement to understand the connectivity of all consciousness.

And this great Photon Belt coming *is* coming – it's consciousness. Now, what happened this [past] weekend, I'll give you my perspective. I know you think it affected your physical reality. It affected more than that. It affected, literally, the electrical circuits within your brain. They went off, went on, went off/on.

That's a code.

It is. It's going to happen often. Now, this is not explained in any book yet. When this photon energy (consciousness of you) arrives in pulses – it is the way it works, it is what it really is, a heartbeat. Know you heartbeat – that is what circulates your blood, indeed, beat, beat, life force, electrical, energy, thought, Photon Belt (consciousness of you), pulse, pulse, pulse, pulse – it is not going to go away. These three days of darkness everyone is whining about is going to be the on-and-off circuitry of your physical brain shutting off old structure, awakening to a new, shutting off, opening circuits. Now I've told you this before, indeed, that there is going to be circuits of the brain opening. When they do, some of the old ones aren't going to be necessary anymore. You'll still be able to use them, because we're not going to take you into fourth-, fifth-, sixth-dimensional activity and shut off the other dimensions. You're not going to do that; you're going to keep them all open so you can work with them all. No sense in becoming a master if you're stuck on seven, know what I mean?

Now, as this pulse of photon energy (consciousness of you) comes, your brain will shut off and then on. New circuits will open that can handle more energy. You will perceive differently, indeed. You'll see differently, you will feel differently, you will love more. You will understand the foolishness that you had in the past, look at it, laugh, incorporate and prepare for the next pulse. Now, there is a sequence and a timing to it, but I'm not going to tell you what it is because you need to integrate between the pulses.

Now, this pulse is what is important. You will literally feel them in your brain. Now, humanity, know you how you've been feeling heavy? Indeed? Know you how you've felt energy around you and the old understanding from what you would term your early '80s to here would be that you would take that light energy and try to ground it in the body. Know you "ground it"? That's why you got bigger. Now, what you want to do is blend with it, you want to practice an expansion into it and pull something else back out. Sort of give to your auric field a part of you, a part of your light to here, bring something else in. Your auric fields are going to become very outrageous, because that is who you are. You're going to play in those boundaries. The skin layer and your bones are being changed because the grid systems in your planet are becoming altered. It needs to in order to handle more consciousness. It's different. Your diets will become different. You will see; you will eat once a day maybe, maybe twice if you're really starving yourself to death. But you will enjoy the food simply because you have a physical vehicle that you can move your teeth over the food. You'll begin to assimilate what is termed the consciousness of you, which is a seventh-dimensional being, by the way. When it's fully integrated that will be who you declare who you are, that part of you that's riding this wave that's out there, that's coming to find you.

Oh, the Photon Belt!

Photon Belt (consciousness of you).

The Photon Belt is a seventh-dimensional consciousness?

Yes, of you, now! You're doing it now. You're playing with it now. Now, the reason you had this big electrical failure over all of these states wasn't to . . .

It helped the Earth rearrange her electrical body.

Yes, and you too! And your great electrical portion is your brain. It is not where the source is – that is here [soul], but it's where you think you function from. Indeed? So that's why you're getting all this disorientation, you see? Your circuits are changing, you're not used to working with a brain that has this big large wire on this side, "supposed to be on *this* side," [you say]. "How do I function?" You're just learning to use more of you in what you would say is a limited body; yet that limited body is becoming more, you see? So you're going to have to treat yourselves differently. You're going to have to move lightly, in the light, in your auric field, because your physical form is changing literally from the inside outward to join that light energy. You've all wanted to blast off into light. Well, you're going to get the chance, but you'll do it gradually or you'll never maintain what I have termed as a continuity of consciousness. You would be liken unto [what] you are now, not remembering your past lives and your ape experience. We're going to unite it all. Why *not* remember it all? Seventh dimension – that's what you've gone through all this nonsense for, so you could get the experience. Might as well remember. Indeed?

Wonderful.

So, yes, this Photon Belt (consciousness of you) is important. It's important for beings to understand they're not being attacked. They are becoming more powerful, more divine. It is the Christ consciousness coming, yes it is, of everyone! Not the one Christ coming to kill the other antichrists, and this, that and other nonsense. It will appear that way because within the physical form you have proved, each one of you on the planet, [that] you are very capable of being the antichrist. You've succeeded in that definition, yes. Now your christedness is coming, and the battle is within the you of you, do you understand?

Yes.

All right. That is what is going on all over humanity. Don't define it. Enjoy the energies. It be like little baby – even though another gets upset that you're playing with your potty, you love it. You might learn later, "Well, that is not true," but it's grand! Know you what I mean? That's what's going on now.

Over your past three months, four, you've been getting an acceleration of this consciousness of you coming. The pulses are getting longer, stronger, and they are going to continue. It's a good thing it does pulse (just like your heart beats slowly) in the physical so you can perceive third-dimensional activity, stay in the flow of it, because there is a rhythm there. If it beats too fast or it didn't beat at all you'd be in another level of activity. So too with this energy. All of your organs are beginning to resonate that way, indeed.

Now, liquids are going to become very important. Your teas are going to become very important, your juices will be—because this energy requires fluid in the body. And it doesn't matter what; it may be wine if you like. It requires the fluid to be there. The teas (which I've spoken to you [about] before) are going to become profound. You should know your herbs when you do your tea, not only to be in what is termed understanding how to heal the physical form. You will not be able to heal the physical form with the herbs as we make this shifting for third-dimensional understanding. You'll heal the body with the herbs for . . . oh, we'll use Zoosh's 3.5, 3.4, wherever we're at, know you? You'll heal for upper-level understandings. One of the favorites of mine is raspberry [leaf] tea. Why? Because it has pizazz; it has the azz in there, as is, and razz the rest of them! It is aligned unto your blood system and the blood because it's of crystalline alignment. [It] is going to need its lovingness now, because you beings are moving from your carbon understanding to a higher level. Know you crystal frequency, indeed?

From carbon to crystal, you're saying.

Well, not crystal—silica. But that's why I've told you before [that] your crystals will help you through this, they'll remind you. Indeed, so your raspberry [leaf] tea, it would be grand to take that in your morning. You may take it in your bed [before going to bed], but we sort of override anything you've done so far to your system as we shift you through your sleep period. But in your morning it'll remind the blood that the new frequency is easy to handle, indeed. A little bit, just a little cup—not even a whole cup, but you may drink more. You may drink as much as you like; you can't OD on that, know you? What you term your shot glass, little glass in the morning.

There will be a lot of teachers coming forth with herbal understandings now, especially in teas, for they're going to be more important. They don't apply third-dimensionally, yet they will appear to; they are a higher level of understanding because your vibratory frequency is going to increase, indeed? So your denser foods will sort of go away. That doesn't mean you have to stop them. We have to be careful when we talk to you beings because you always go overboard, know you what I mean? Your sleep patterns are going to change, yes, rather dramatically, and that's all right. You're learning that you can (and you won't be able to do this) stay awake longer and still be alive, because you're alive all of the time. And your teas will help you to learn to play with your organs, know you what I mean?

You said once that we should drink a shot glass of mullein tea each day.

Yes, yes. To drink the mullein is an outrageous thing. There is a lot of fluid exchange going on in the body now . . . well, your organs are changing, all right? And the dense fluids – know you how a lot of beings have a lot of sinus, lot of throat, lot of lung congestion, indeed? The mullein is probably one of the most caring and loving plants you have for the alleviation of congestion, the alleviation of mucus and the lightening of the lymph systems in the body. Makes the lymphatic system, particularly, less dense and able to increase its flow, the rapidity of the fluid through the lymphatic system. Yes.

So we should start a column on herbs.

Yes, you should. You have three or four beings that are in contact with you right now that are very well aware. And even if they try their own level of understanding as to what it is, it will still provide what would be termed sort of a little dictionary, sort of a little handy pamphlet there. Going to be needed, yes, indeed. You're absolutely correct. Because what that does, that empowers beings, you see?

Like "here's how you can heal yourself, here's how you can help your body."

Indeed, yes. Know you, you might need to put a disclaimer in there because of the way you beings think at times. But the herbal column would be appropriate because it'll allow other beings some insight. I've told you that words are limits, and I mean that; they are. Yet you use your words to describe, and you need them now. It's all right. So too they will be limits within the herbs because you beings will say "this herb is only for this," "this is for that," "this is better than that." You'll do your comparing thing, doesn't matter. [By] the application of it within the body in a gentle manner (don't overdo! –

it would be better to underdo), the body will learn what it needs, what it likes, indeed, and you apply that. Now, that is giving beings empowerment, because anyone can grow an herb in a little pot here, and it'll assist them in this higher-frequency understanding coming forth.

It hasn't been put out before that the Photon Belt is seventh-dimensional and that we can integrate it here on this planet, in this body.

Well, that's the purpose, to integrate!

But I thought we had to get to the seventh dimension before we could integrate seventh-dimensional energy.

You're breathing seventh-dimensional energy every day; you're just pretending you're not. You're a seventh-dimensional god right now. You say, "No I'm not." You're your high self *now;* we've told you that before, eh?

Absolutely.

Okay, got that one covered. But it would be nice to live as seventh-dimensional god in the body, eh? So the body responds to seventh-dimensional knowing differently from seventh-dimensional thinking. You can all *think* seventh-dimensionally, but you're not *doing* anything, know you what I mean?

You said to bring the pulse into the body and then out into the aura. Is there anything else we can say?

It'll be a breathing process. You know your pranayama yoga? That's a good start, but pretty soon that won't matter, either, because it's going to be so thick here, that's all you're going to be able to breathe. Hundreds of years from now you'll give up your liquids, but now you need liquids, yes.

What other guidance would you like to give people for right now about integrating this energy?

I know it sounds very trite, but love is going to allow it to be easier. The heart chakra must be opened—indeed, it has to be. Kundalini is going to move, the planet's kundalini is going to move, what is termed the volcanoes, yes. Yes, there are going to be the quakings. Yes, you will feel it in the body first, yes. You are connected to the Earth, you can't get away from it —you might as well get that down, you might as well understand it. The god portion of you has used the carbon, has used the Earth to form this body, and the god portion of you now wants to assist the Earth in its transformation so the Earth can understand itself more, because it's a god also. A logos is involved, know you what I mean? So there's a big transformation going on, big transformation.

The carbon is actually being transformed into silicon, is that it? Are we going to have more crystalline everything?

Yes.

Soon?

You're in the process of doing it right now. Your scientists are beginning to understand [that] the blood is changing. They don't want to tell you they're in a panic; they think it's a disease.

Years ago you said that the blood would become golden.

Yes, only because you beings are greedy. That's my joke. I don't mean that in what is termed a hurtful manner.

Consciously we don't feel this pulse yet.

Yes, you do. You're feeling it physically in your head now. In the back of the head, on the top of the head, you're feeling like a heaviness or weight on you. That's a pulse, another jacket there. If you would tune in to it, you would pulse with it. You're getting a metallic flavor in your mouth, all of you are. It's not a localized phenomenon anymore; everyone is getting this thing. It is the Christ energy coming that is you. You're feeling it in your body now. Love it! You go to your doctor; well, he's dying. Understand your herbs. You're responsible! There are beings that will share with you these wisdoms, you understand? I'm not telling anyone don't go to your doctor —you need your saviors. Might as well use them while you've got them. You understand?

There's a book called I'm Okay, I'm Just Mutating. We need something like that now that says your body is fine, it's just transforming right in front of your eyes.

Your consciousness is fine, your consciousness knows. Tune in to your consciousness; your body will follow. What is your consciousness? God. I'm going to keep on that bandwagon, know you what I mean? That's simply the way it is. It is LOVE; and you start vibrating faster and you use all of your techniques, your violet flame and your meditations and this, that and the other. When you're in meditation and you feel the energy moving through you, you might as well get used to that, carry that in your daily life, because that's what the body wants, that is the energy the body is going to adjust to, like it or not. Create a lot of confusion [in] third dimension, yes.

So a lot of people need to be able to talk to other people and say, "Hey, it's all right."

You all can talk to each other: "It's all right," know you? If you would get away from your television that's telling you all of these things — they don't know what they're doing, either. They're sneaking off to their, what you term, psychics and astrologers behind your back. They don't dare tell you that, indeed? They want to keep a little secret here, but they want the inside information, too. They're reading this material also. They're going to apply it. "Hope no one out there applies it besides me," they say. All of them are. They don't want to die any more than you do; they want to evolve also. Doesn't matter, don't judge them. Love them, get on with your own, indeed? Be very easy to grow your own herbs. Takes a spoonful of dirt, herbs; [they] grow in very little soil and provide a lot of power. Because the soil knows it is providing and the planet knows it is providing the soil, and the herb uses it and it knows where it's going. And if you would thank it and brew your tea with it and bless it when you drink it, you will all unite. By "you" I mean the cells of your body will unite with the planet and you'll understand what's coming on. You'll know where the quakings of the Earth are going to be at any moment —the planet will tell you.

You've given much help. And now meditation: There are people who read this who don't actually meditate. Would it be better for them to sit and focus, or listen to a tape that leads them in a meditation?

Even three moments of contemplating yourself, contemplating your navel, contemplating your hand—doesn't matter, contemplation of self for three moments takes you to another moment. You contemplate more, contemplate more, you'll get some wisdoms. You might not like them, but you'll get them, yes.

36

An Alert

Zoosh through Robert Shapiro
September 9, 1996

I do not want to frighten anyone, but I must tell you that you are in a time and space that curl back on one another. This is sometimes the reason for bizarre events: things happening before you think of them, things going by before you notice them (like an event before its moment). There are other reasons to speak to you now.

This anomaly of time folding back on itself (for the past two weeks) is creating a temporary condition whereby some of you have windows to move on to your next lives *before your time*. This does not mean that death is in the air, but that you have an opportunity to move to your next life quickly rather than slowly or in a lingering fashion.

I do not want to encourage any form of shortening your life artificially. I am not suggesting that you throw down your cards, as you might say. But because of time-space shifts and anomalies it is *absolutely essential* for you who wish to remain here to finish out your natural cycles to be alert when you're driving, pay attention at work and do not let your mind drift when doing something even slightly dangerous. It is not a time of threat, but a time that is a bit hazardous.

This is compounded by the fact that many are being called to the other side who choose to be involved in the project to elevate Earth and her people to their higher-level selves. Those who are choosing to do so (at the soul level) are all moving to the other side to assist, not to reincarnate or go anywhere but just beyond the veils

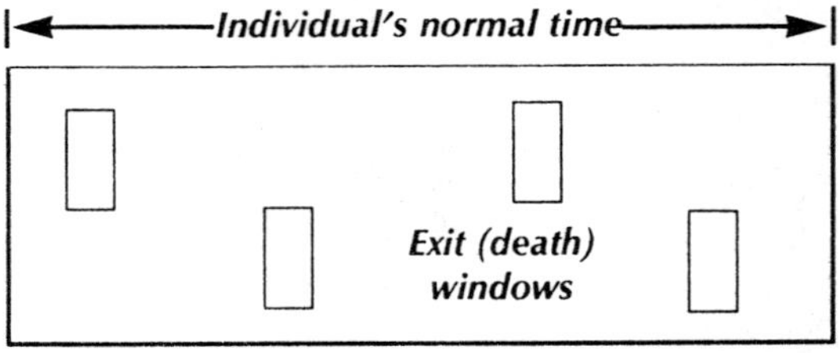

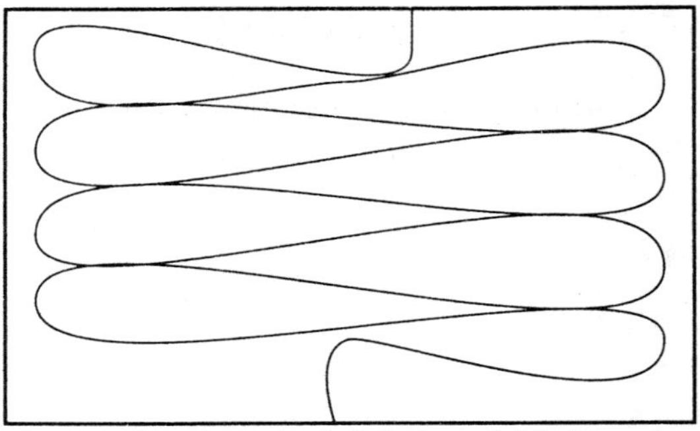

Current time (top view): Windows folded together

to assist in balancing you and Earth with loving light.

Between these two factors, I want you to remain extra careful, extra vigilant. After three to four weeks, trailing off in eight weeks, the time-folds may continue to ripple, creating a potential to pass more quickly through the remaining years of your natural cycle. The project of light for Earth will remain at least two and a half years.

There is much negative energy on Earth now and much to damage Mother Earth being caused—sometimes ignorantly and innocently—and Mother Earth is also releasing all the negative energy she has taken on from you over the years. This is why you see so many negative and dramatic things about you, sometimes in places where you do not expect it.

It is true that God is testing you and wants you to transform the negative energy and send it on its way. And you are going to be helped with love and light by those beyond the veil as well as by Creator Itself. This is a notice, not a warning, to be aware, to be alert and if you choose to finish your natural cycle, to pay attention. Good night.

37

The Lucifer Gene

Zoosh through Robert Shapiro
October 6, 1995

I will discuss the Lucifer gene today. This requires an explanation of how that which has come to be known as evil is constituted. When Creator headed this way to establish the creation you now reside in, He picked up Lucifer along the way. Well, He really picked up a being along the way who could provide a minor degree of annoyance, yet would be just what the Creator needed to stimulate growth. That being — a consultant, if you would — did not in any way have the personal capacity to produce anything beyond minor annoyance on his own.

Now, when Creator established this creation, for a long time He did not establish any beings or civilizations that required annoyance. Thus that being, whom we're going to call Lucifer, had little to do but hang around with Creator and watch the proceedings.

So way back Creator decided that He would allow a planet to have annoyance (it was an experiment) just to see what might occur. Now, Creator did not put too many beings on that planet, perhaps a grand total of about 40,000. Creator did not suddenly drop annoyance on them, but built it into their functioning organism to see how it would work. Remember, this is an experiment – Creator's experimenting also. Now, this particular experiment went awry. The beings had what I'm going to call the Lucifer gene within their systems, and not unlike you, they were born small and grew up to be big. Thus everything within them tended to expand. You might ask, "Does that mean that particles and the DNA expand?" No, but everything else does.

The First Experimental Group

Now, Creator put no restrictions on anything; It just said, "Well, let them be what they are and see what happens." These beings were highly emotional, and every time they had an emotion of annoyance it would tend to double itself. Well, I don't have to tell you what happened. Within an incredibly short amount of time they had pretty well wiped out the population in ways that are best left unsaid. So Creator had to take a cold, hard look at the empirical notion of annoyance as being something separate, or being something included. Creator considered it for a time; it was a long time before there was another planet with annoyance on it. Annoyance (as Lucifer) hung out with Creator and they commiserated, "What shall we do?"

Now, I'm going to give you the cycle of what happened, like a circuit. Something had happened to Lucifer that Lucifer did not like. As the beings began to expand their annoyance into what you now call negativity and so on, there was a point at which a feedback took place. Because the human being (these were a variation of human beings) has only so much capacity to contain this kind of energy, when they reached the limits of that capacity it fed back to Lucifer and Lucifer found himself becoming darker—more angry, more negative. I use the term "darker" because if you were to see negativity, it shows itself as a dense cloud. If you were to examine the cloud, after you remove the density you see gold, but the density shows itself as a darker shade.

When the life was over on that planet it took Lucifer quite a while to get clear. Then he said to Creator, "I don't want this to happen again. I can't handle it." Lucifer said, "I can't control it, because when they have too much and feed it back to me (because it's basically my energy), I can't say no. I can't stop it." Well, Creator understood this. He already knew that when beings are in their lightbodies, they naturally emanate light. And when they have more light than is needed and they are still emanating,it feedsbackto Creator.

Thesame mechanicswere happening with Lucifer, but in an unpleasant way. So Creator said to Lucifer, "This is probably a result of your being in My creation. Since light feeds back to Me, negativity is feeding back to you." And Lucifer said, "Something's got to change, because I can't resist this."

Creator thought about it a while and said, "We need to create control groups. We need to have one where that same process exists." And Lucifer pleaded, "No, please, not that." Then Creator said, "We also need to have a group that has the capacity to do more than they have the capacity to do." (Creators talk like this.)

Blank Strands in the Genetic Code

Lucifer said, "How is that possible?" And Creator said, "It is possible if I create within these beings an entire modification, not only physically but spiritually, of everything I am. I'll create several strands of blank spiritual and genetic code" (like a blank disk today).

Lucifer asked, "What good is that?" And Creator said, "That allows them to build upon what they know and learn, potentially becoming more than I am now." Lucifer said, "Wow!" but in different words. He continued, "What about this other group, the group that will probably do exactly the same as this other planet?" (By the way, that other planet that went negative, you know – that negative Sirian planet – is no longer in existence.) Lucifer said, "I don't think I can bear it."

The Second Step: The Control & the Experimental Group

Creator said, "I'm going to ask you to do me a favor." (At that point Lucifer basically said, "Uh-oh!") Creator said, "I have a plan to include these beings who are probably going to go negative like you said. I have a plan to include them with these other beings even though they're in different galaxies [systems]. Creator explained the plan as it's been laid out somewhat in the Explorer Race books. [See *The Explorer Race* and *ETs and the Explorer Race*.]

It was up to Lucifer to give his approval here, you know, because he was a consultant, but he said, "I still don't think I can bear the feedback of all that negative energy from this other planet, to say nothing of what might come from these people you're going to establish called the Explorer Race. Of course, I think it's a good idea, don't get me wrong. But I don't think I can bear this other energy from this planet of beings that are probably going to go negative in – of all places – Sirius." (Lucifer said that because so much benevolent and enlightened creation has occurred and is still occurring in Sirius.)

So Creator said, "I'll tell you what I'll do. I'll put a check on the circumstance in Sirius so that if it ever gets too much for you, those beings will return to their essential soul selves, transfer to a denser environment where I'm going to have the Explorer Race, and resume their existence but without so much discomfort, which ought to be all right with you. What do you say?" And Lucifer said, "If you weren't a friend, I wouldn't do this" (in their kind of talk).

I've given you this rough background, greatly condensed. You can read more about it in the Explorer Race series. I also want you to understand something important: I am not saying you are satanic as beings, but since Lucifer himself has the capacity to provide only about 2% negativity, or minor annoyance (that's his personal capacity; he can't do any more), it's *you* (and this isn't blaming you at all, but this amplification that happens empowers you very much). As you change and become more light and stop feeding back negativity to Lucifer (even eventually start feeding back light to Creator), the Lucifer energy will begin to die down and there will no longer be what I'd call the unnatural, dark side of Lucifer (also known as Satan). I'm including these biblical terms here because I want you to understand this within the context of your civilization as well as scientifically.

The Lucifer Gene

You have within you *right now* an entire strand of genetic substance that I'm going to call the Lucifer gene. What I call a strand your scientists would call a gene. Because your scientists cannot yet study genetic substance at a high enough magnification while it's still living and functioning, they don't understand that what they can identify as a gene is actually a strand.

I'm going to recommend that scientists run a project of about ten years to test for the Lucifer gene amongst violent people or people who are self-destructive, as long as everyone gives full permission (your test subjects might surprise you and be very willing to cooperate). You will observe this gene and see how well-developed it is in people who have perpetrated violence upon themselves or others. You will discover that it is not physiological things that are able to change this gene — for example, cutting it out surgically won't work; it'll grow back, because all genetic substance has duplicate entries within all other genetic substance. So don't even think about trying that route. But there are various spiritual actions and certain light therapies that are able to modify the gene. Experiment with light (not heat) in the range from white to gold (you might even play with pink). Try to make the light as pure and true as possible, optical light, and beam it on the people. I don't want to tell you too much because some of this has actually been done; you can find the material.

You scientists will discover over time that the patterning in the gene tends to erase, and after a while the gene looks like something analogous to a record that has not yet been cut with grooves. That's what you want. You will discover in the process of light therapy and spiritual practices that much more is done when people are free to pursue something benevolent. You will also discover that your test subjects will often need to express some aggressive behavior separate from your therapy (make sure it isn't self-destructive – punching bags are acceptable as long as they are not alive).

A few months ago Lucifer got to the point where he said to Creator, " I can't take it anymore." Even though that civilization has ended on Sirius and those souls are still being transferred en masse to a denser dimension on Earth, there is so much negativity and self-destructive behavior on Earth now that your cumulative discomfort is feeding back so much to Lucifer that he can't take it.

So Creator said to Lucifer, "Now comes the true test. You don't have to take it anymore. Now is the time that we give them their opportunity to become more than I am." Thus a few months ago Creator basically granted you the capacity to have the rights, responsibilities, abilities, practices, *consequences* and rewards of being Creators, eventually to combine into one, and to some extent function as one on the unconscious level.

The Next Step: Dreams & the New Alchemy

For these past few months your dream life has become wild, if not bizarre. Sometimes you are so involved in the other worlds that being in this physical world, what you call being awake, becomes less of an experience than being in the other worlds to the extent that in the middle of the day you might suddenly need to lie down and go to sleep because you are called in the other worlds. Now, what's going on in those worlds?

Your physiological capacity to transform – physically, emotionally and, most importantly, spiritually – negative energy into gold light is being restructured. We're talking about an *alchemical reaction,* the changing of one substance into another. The original idea to change lead into gold originated from changing dense energy into gold light. (If you look at dense energy, the color is not dissimilar to the color of lead.)

Here we have a circumstance in which this sudden responsibility and its rewards has been literally laid in your laps. You might say, "Well, look at how extreme things are becoming in the Middle East and Africa and all kinds of terrible things happening in other places." I could say, "Yes, that's true. However, your communication system is also so good now that even a skirmish that happens someplace is discovered very quickly. They can no longer go unnoticed for many months as in the past." Your physical day-to-day life waking life is no longer sufficient. You have to become functionally operative on the other levels.

For a long time dream therapy has been available. I want dream therapists to know they're going to be needed in a big way and to start training people because there's not enough of you. The rest of you need to understand that a large part of what's going on when you dream is absolutely real. It's happening on other dimensions but does not include you at all. Because some of these dreams are so extreme and bizarre and sometimes violent, it does affect your psyche. That is *built in.* Creator says to Lucifer, "Well, this is the test. If I allowed them to be able to process all this excess negative energy on the other planes (referring to the dream time) without their experiencing any side effects at all, they'd have no motivation to change anything. They'd say, 'Oh well, it's only bad dreams – not very much fun, but life goes on.'"

Creator linked that with your conscious self and said, "Let's have it affect their minds, because their minds are so restless that they cannot ignore things." So Creator let it affect your psyche so that you will be motivated to change, lead into gold as it were.

What You Can Do

I need to give you a little homework. You might have to set your alarm clock a little sooner. If you should have unsettling dreams at night, know that if you can remember those dreams, you will have the feelings of them, the total experience of having been there, but you will not see yourself there. If you see something happening, it's not you. You'll just be a witness, but *a fully participating witness.* One of the most important levels of creator training is to be able to feel what other beings feel. Otherwise you could make capricious mistakes without ever understanding the gravity of what you have done. In creator training you *must* be able to feel others' injuries.

After a nightmare you will wake up with those horrible feelings just as if it is happening to you then and there. That is, the sensitive, sensing you *is* there in the dream state. You feel everything that everyone went through in that dream so you *completely understand* on the physical level. The mind cannot understand this alone and must have a sensing mechanism, which is the physical self. So while you're on sensory overload your senses say, "I can't take anymore!" (just as Lucifer said to Creator). Then you rejoin your physical self, wake up and experience that overload (fear, loathing, whatever).

If possible I want you to strike a bell or do something immediately. Some of you might chant "om" – that's fine. If you pray, ask for benevolent love to bless and transform all you have felt. If you can, visualize gold light. This is alchemical training to transform the pain of others *through being aware of it.* It is also foundational training to know what others are feeling around you. You will be unable to ignore what you feel.

The Lucifer gene within you was created to amplify discomfort up to a point, feed it back to Lucifer until he's had enough, but now there's a block there. Lucifer doesn't feed it back to you, but you are no longer able to feed it to him. Therefore you *must* be the magician and transform it.

As much as you can these days, I want you to think and feel gold light. And if you can think, feel (especially feel) warmth in your physical self (it has to do with love), that works even better. Your responsibility is to transform the Lucifer gene to erase the expansion and allow it to become cleansed, purified and inactive. But you had to have the Lucifer gene within you to be able to experience, to act and to be able to react to consequences. This is where you are different from your Creator. Your Creator does not in Its natural self have the Lucifer gene. Lucifer is a consultant – a friend, as it were, but not a portion of Creator. *You* have the Lucifer gene, even within your spiritual self, although there it is overwhelmed by gold light, because that is your nature. If you understand that the Lucifer gene can be transformed, then you will not expect Lucifer to do it for you or Creator to do it for you. This is something that Creator deigns that you do for yourself.

I brought this up because this is much more widespread than you realize, and it is being compounded as one compounds interest. The more you have, the more it grows, compounded by the fact that you can no longer feed back that negativity to Lucifer. Even now Lucifer is being transformed by Creator because Creator, of course, feels responsible, obligated. When Creators are responsible, they must *act.* They can't just sit back and say, "Well, sorry."

What you have given us as homework is something one person does. What about a meditation group? It feels very important.

Group Alchemy: Love (Heat) & Gold Light

Yes, let me give you something, but this will be different from other meditation groups. This is what I'd like you to do, and it will be somewhat comradely. When you come together as a group, I'd

Final Lunar Eclipse before 2000

Zoosh through Robert Shapiro
September 24, 1996

This lunar eclipse [September 26] can be looked at symbolically as the last overshadowing of the feminine. The feminine energy and all feminine beings can look at this eclipse as a call to arms: IT'S YOUR TURN NOW. It's not okay for you to be meek and shy anymore. Some of you might have to get downright political, but don't do it the way the men have. The men have made some errors in communication (to put it mildly) largely because of their training – rather, mistraining – in your modern societies.

Establish your links of communication worldwide. Make arrangements to have demonstrations worldwide. Let it be known that it is not only up to women to solve the problems of today but to resolve the problems through their solutions. Don't feel like you must use only the bureaucracies that are in place. Feel free to use your own networks of communication.

like you to initially talk about whatever's bothering you. Don't come together just for a spiritual activity, but talk about what's bothering you even if you get upset. *This is part of the training.* First, do that. It's like a support group. It will bring up discomfort – this is a test – so talk it over with the group and make sure everybody's okay with this. Then I want you to focus on the physical warmth you feel in your chest or your solar plexus. You can hold your hands over your body to create it, however you want to do it. But it is not a meditation or a visualization; it is a *physical warmth.* Bring up that warmth and experience the heat, which is the physical evidence of love (wherein you are basically, as a thought person, allowing yourself to be loving, and as a physical person loving yourself).

Then if you can, I'd like you to imagine gold light there *while* you're feeling the heat. Now, that's going to be tough. It's surprisingly difficult to do that because the gold light will feel like a thought and you'll find yourself having to be totally physical – absolutely, totally focused. This is where alchemical reactions come in – transforming one substance to another. You must be able to focus totally on one thing and then focus totally on two things. Some people won't be able to feel the heat right off, but they will be able to feel the gold light. Eventually I want the group to be able to feel the physical heat anywhere across your chest, the solar plexus – the front part of the body. Feeling that warmth and holding it will be easier in a group because it tends to be amplified. It becomes a very powerful, loving energy.

At some point someone can reach over and strike a chime or something. Then while you maintain the warmth, include the feeling of gold light. The minute you start *picturing* gold light, the warmth will usually leave because you are attempting to think instead of feel. Feeling is where the power is; *that* is how things are transformed.

So practice gold light to become familiar with gold light as a feeling. Then include the feeling of gold light *with* the feeling of this warmth, which is love. The reason this is a graduate class, a more advanced class, is that when you bring up discomfort, you'll have something to transform. If you simply show up and immediately go into love or gold light or both, it's a little too easy. I want it to be challenging, something you can rise to. And once any individual in the group learns how to do this, you can do this anywhere at any time. But in a group it will be much more powerful. Eventually you'll be able to do it in a very large group, and it will be overwhelming; it will be ecstatic. It is the closest thing you can feel – that total love, that total gold light – to the creator energy that you are, that your Creator intended you to be.

Your Creator is white light and love, but your Creator wants you to be more. And that more is gold light, because gold light contains and is rooted in white light. *But gold light has the capacity to transform.*

When the group gets good at feeling that heat, which is love, stay in it for at least ten or fifteen minutes. In the beginning don't try to combine the gold light and the love. But eventually you want to stay in that gold light. If at any time the warmth goes away after you've included the gold light with the loving feeling, immediately let go of the concept/feeling of gold light and return to the heat, which is love. That's your foundation; you've got to have that.

Transformation

First you'll notice the transformation within the group, which is a nice bonus. (Self-interest is definitely involved here.) As the group grows (new members would have to go through the original training), people in the group might break off and form new groups.

That's fine; we want that. At certain times maybe all the groups might come together. If several hundred people would do this together it would be so magnificent that a totally unconscious person (as you might say) could be walking a block away and suddenly have a great sense of well-being even if they're totally angry and upset about something. They would find themselves cheerful about people they're passing on the street, and it could transform their lives. It might not be permanent, but it could make a real change.

When you are this heat, by the way, just feel it for yourself; it broadcasts naturally. As you know, both heat and love naturally radiate. (Anybody who's ever gone into a room where someone's feeling total love, you know it even if they're not looking at you.) That makes it very simple; it just happens.

If you get enough people doing this, you're going to see some good changes around here. What you learn absolutely tends to translate to other levels of yourself. When you practice within this group and you're feeling this and transforming things, you'll get so used to doing this it will become not second nature, but *first* nature. It's something you will begin to feel regularly, all the time – driving, going to the market, working, with your family. It will permeate you so totally that eventually it will affect your actual senses. It has the capacity to cleanse the Lucifer gene, and that when you start having a nightmare, your senses will begin broadcasting that energy, and the nightmare will diminish or even transform itself.

This has everything to do with creator training and unification amongst all people.

38

Look Up and See Ships in the Sky: Relatives Show Themselves

Jehovah, YHWH and Id through Arthur Fanning
October 25, 1996

How you doing?

Wonderful.

Having a grand time?

Indeed.

The conditions as they exist now, it is a requirement to open up. A lot of things are beginning to happen. You've got an interesting two months now. [Laughs.]

Everyone take a breath. Relax. I've told a lot of you before that it's more important for you to be concerned with your own divinity than with your extraterrestrial brothers – and I meant that. I know a lot of you have been practicing, but I've told you for five years – diligently. It won't matter.

There was a purpose in that information so you wouldn't be confused when your brothers come and show themselves physically. Get ready for it in your news, your media, your TV. In month November they're going to be seen over every major city in your country and around the globe. Uh-oh! They are under the assumption, wrong as it may be, that you are prepared. Everyone take a breath. Breathe it in.

You're going to see them all over – beings gathering. Because we know there will be this confusion, comparing the good guys with the bad guys. Well, it's too late for that now. Your meditations were given to you so you could make contact in what you term your delta states (know you delta state in the brain waves?), so you would be prepared, you wouldn't be frightened.

What is occurring as these beings are coming now, they want to make physical contact – have a chat over your table. But they're not going to do it with your government leaders; they're going to do it with the average individual. They're not going to do it with some of you beings who have been into metaphysics for a long time; you know it all. They're going to do it with the ones who are humble, the ones who understand nature, because they're coming here to get you out of a lot of the difficulties you're in.

There's a speedup in time, you say. What it really is is an acceleration of your consciousness, a movement of your soul – you are not sure that exists, but you sure hope it does.

This is the time you've been waiting for. They're coming to assist, not rescue. Assistance means that you work *with* [them]. In your metaphysical understanding you think your dimensions are collapsing and you're accelerating and going to the fourth and fifth, eh?

There is a merging. Your consciousness is expanding. That means you're going to see a lot more, experience a lot more, feel a lot more. You haven't changed that much over the millennia – something new still frightens you. Then you become very superstitious and you grab your gun out of your closet. That would be a big mistake now. This [contact] shouldn't come as any shock to you. Your Native Americans have been predicting it. A lot of the prophecy information is turning up; it seems to be fitting into a pattern now.

Your souls (they do exist; they are in your body [as] electrical force) are going to quicken. In the human condition what that means is your heartwillstart beatingfaster.You'll think it is; it will be a response to the electrical and the magnetic fields shifting.

What you term prayers will assist you; if that's all you know, then do it and don't judge yourself. It is time to stay in what is termed a center love here. That is what's required. You're going to see an increase in the number of heart attacks, in the number of beings passing out. They'll simply fall over in your markets.

The electrical energies are changing. Your magnetic fields on your planet are changing. (Everyone breathe now.) This is not to threaten you. This is what you've always wanted – it's coming. It's already started, as a matter of fact. The difficulty is in giving the information out gently so you can accept it without going into your fear thing.

You were put on this planet – the five root races – to become one to get along together on this one little planet. Only *five!* And you can't do it. There are more than five races that will appear here – many. They are coming; they know that you are brothers, so *you* best understand it.

They won't look like you. Some will. They have a lot more love in their being, displaying, working with this concept, than you've allowed yourself to appreciate from yourself – because you all have that same amount of love (it's called God) that's in there. That's all there is. [But] you're in the game of *not* here. "Let's find out what not-love is." It's changing now.

Now, they're not necessarily going to land in your front yard and see the physical. I will tell you this, however: You have this abductee phenomenon of being abducted. Everyone's going to be visited by these beings; everyone on your planet in what you call the sleep state and up through (if you can handle it) into the waking state. It's only energy and it's only consciousness. They're not coming here to invade the planet. If they [had] wanted to, they could have taken it away a long time ago, except you're a very protected group of entities here.

Now, we're going to do a meditation this evening, and we're going to bring these frequencies here so you can experience them in what you consider a relatively safe environment. One of the difficulties of some of these energies [is] their approaching you so you would understand they're pure thought. Now, you beings think you think in your head, [but] it's simply where you process light. There will be a lot of headaches. And there will an inclination to what you term aneurysm, because you've allowed the fluid around your brain to become depleted.

Now, the beings are connected to you; they're not beings you don't know. The first wave, I will say, are very familiar to you in other realms. They're here to assist you, truly. I know you've heard the stories of being abducted and probed with this and that.

Know how you beings move into doubt? Indeed? About whether they be the good guys or the bad guys? You're all going to be probed with instruments; it would appear to be that. A lot of these beings are coming with light implements; they are like surgeons correcting blockages in you. Now, this is from my perspective. Some of the channeled information that's going to come out in the next month or two . . .

We're going to have a lot of different perspectives.

Yes.

Who's coming? Andromedans? Zetas? Pleiadians? Orions?

Everyone.

Everyone. Beyond this galaxy?

Yes. A lot.

Will we see them in Sedona?

Yes. They are there this evening, by the way.

Hovering? Landing?

Hovering.

Will they land?

They're checking it out.

But they can solidify to our third dimension?

It will be a balance. They'll raise your frequency and they'll lower theirs a bit.

So are they going to adjust everyone's lightbody?

As long as you permit it.

I permit it.

You still have free will. Know you what I mean? Not much left.

A little bit.

A little bit.

And the purpose of this is to help integrate our lightbody faster, or what?

The purpose of this is to help the planet and the consciousness about it, yes.

Wonderful.

I think it's wonderful. I think it's pretty outrageous. Remember the phrase, "keep laughter in your pocket"?

Yes.

Keep it in *both* pockets! [Laughter.] The experiences aren't going to be what you think as appropriate in your social consciousness. The reason they're coming stronger, with more force, is that you are getting an overlap from your lower dimensions. And that overlap—some of you beings are not aware that it is a lower-dimensional being. You think it's another being and, being superstitious, you move into fear. You think you're seeing the devil or something like that (something really intelligent, know you what I mean?). [Laughter.]

Are you saying an overlap from the negative Sirians from 3.0 dimension?

Yes.

Some people are actually seeing them?

Yes.

Well, they're so confused that they don't know.

From your perspective you say they're negative. They don't know.

Well, they're not negative. I'm sorry.

It's like a little child. And they're changing, anyway.

Yes. We've just been calling them that for so long.

I'm just telling you, it's going to be exciting times. And those beings that have set up parameters of good/ bad—especially your churches—this is going to be such an outrageous time! They won't know which angel they're worshiping. [Laughter.] I think what I'll do is tell them, "Everyone use the name Raphael." [More laughter.] Michael has been worn out.

All right. So all over your planet now there's an acceleration of these little groupings, these energy things going on to educate you. And it's an education of the soul here that exists in the body. It's more appropriately termed a reminder of the soul so you'll remember. And part of the memory process includes this thing called forgiveness. I know you beings here in this room, all of you, are so profound and have never done a bad thing in your life! And in all your past lives you've been kings and queens and saints, so you'll have nothing to worry about!

As the soul becomes quickened, the memories of your lives—past lives *and* future lives—become prominent. Let them be, as you would say, a cartoon. The reason some of you dream in the manner called cartoon is to see the humor of it and not the judgment of it. You decide you want the more wisdom unto yourself in these times. All right?

Now, there are going to be a lot of beings who are going to run off to the hills with some of these entities. I'm not saying don't visit. If you get on a ship, check and see if there's a return ticket. It's your job to *become* here, to understand this density. If you get on one of these ships and decide to go with them, you have found an overlord, and you'll be there for a very long time.

This experience in this density is for the evolution of your soul—the consciousness called you, the spirit called you, all the mysteries of the universe around and bound [with]in you. This is the time, this decade, when the winding and the binding are coming undone so you can understand your power. It is a great time to be in the human condition now, to apply and become – sort of clean the slate as you will.

You have a very interesting month [November] coming up, very interesting. Some of you are going to have a difficult time communicating in social consciousness. You will think your brain isn't there (what you term your brain). Your thought processes are going to alter dramatically and you'll struggle with it. Allow yourself to be in peace. These beings can and will alter your consciousness. They're doing it because you are very fearful beings. When you move into that arena of fear, you strike. They are simply protecting themselves by shifting your consciousness. It's going to happen all over, so just be ready for it.

Meditation

Allow your eyes to close a moment. Center your being and open the heart chakra. Allow. That's it. Allow you to feel what is termed a golden light about your head, a white light at your throat chakra. Allow that white light to push up to the roof of your mouth. White light push up into your forehead area, your sixth seal. And push out above your head slightly. Gold light is still coming down. Center. Let it fill the body.

Move your consciousness, your thoughts, into the heart area. In that area I want you to feel an energy form liken unto another being in your body. [It's] only energy. That feeling will be the sensation you're going to experience later at the first contact, so focus there; become familiar with it. Center. Allow your eyes to open gently.

How do you feel inside?

Well, let's see. Better. Maybe I expect too much.

It's just all of the thinkety-think. Know you what I mean? If you apply all that thinking to the will of you – understand? In here [chest]? Because of everyone else's verbiage you'd find things a lot easier. I'm going to pay you a visit this evening.

Good. You are welcome.

How are you?

Very well.

Indeed? Another great thinker. I'm not saying you don't need this brain. I'm saying you've been told inappropriately how it works, what it's purpose is, [its] functions. Have you noticed new discoveries come from an insight – in-sight? Something someone hasn't thought of before. In truth, the being looked where no one else looked before. It was inside, it came outward and the brain realized it. Ah, this part gets it last. It's the first of the impulse of light.

The thoughts are truly in the soul for manifestation here outward. You're using your tools backward, but that's all right. It's fun. It's fun until you lay the body down and move out of it and realize that you're still alive. Which part of you is thinking [then], because the brain isn't there?

Some of you in your astral projection haven't even contemplated that. You still think you're a thinker: "Where I think, I go astrally. All I have to do is think of it and I'm there." Even your verbiage has it wrong. How can you "think" if you don't have a brain? How can you?

Some of you don't think astral projection exists. It's all right. What "thinks" is consciousness. It doesn't think at all; it *is*. It's the way of all thought; you're simply picking the thoughts you want to play with in a lightbody called consciousness, God, All That Is. Your soul is your emotional transformer to gather the wisdom of the experience here of light, thought lowered, applied through density. The remembrance of it, you term it. But it's the flavor, the color of the emotion. You're much more than your physical body.

In these months coming and your year coming these visitations are going to increase. These entities are in one manner expecting a level of consciousness that is capable of applying wisdom, of sharing information. By that I mean how *your* social structure is, along with *their* social structure. What's the family unit like here? What's their family unit like? What's the emotional energy, the wisdom of God in your environment? Profound questions – not where the stock market's going. Everyone breathe a little bit.

Your philosophies (your churches also) are going to come to a climax now because everything's consciousness – everything. And all consciousness wants to communicate with other consciousness, to share. When this blending begins to occur, don't worry – they don't have enough hospitals to lock you all up in. Some of you will escape. But you will communicate with your furniture, your walls. You'll understand how you make them, why. You'll understand magnetics and levitation. You'll also understand how much power it has taken you to manifest physically. You'll marvel at the amount of energy required.

Your bodies are going to start changing shape. Now, I've already told some of you that your organs are shifting toward the center of your body. It's confusing your doctors. That's all right.

Compassion is going to be needed, especially for yourself. A lot of you are going to have to admit you don't know what's going on, but something is. And you will find that answer in the tears of your sleep when you move inside you. And many will petition to the God there (your high self, you term it more, your power) for an explanation of what is going on. That is where you're going to get your clearest answer. And when the answer comes, regardless of how it comes, pay attention.

One other thing: Some of you are, what you would term, beyond the ships. That means (and you're great in this) you're beyond the concept of ships coming from other dimensions. It also means that you have ships that you're utilizing. So some of you are going to be experiencing your ships—it's part of your manifestation. I just want you to be aware of that. Well, I'm confusing some of you, but that's all right. We'll work it out in the dream state somehow. How you doing?

Better and better.

Are you ready to join all of you?

I think so, if I get my heart open far enough.

Sometimes when that heart chakra opens, you know, it sort of has a rip in it, if you open it too suddenly. Know you the colors of the seven rays?

I don't know if I do exactly. I've heard of them.

Well, check it out. Indeed? And there's seven layers as you move in on either side here—white, brilliant in the center. Contemplate those layers in this way.

Okay.

You beings are outrageous. Lot of fun. Simply contemplate [for] a moment what is in this area here above your head—a light ball, sort of sparkly, just right there. Sort of imagine it, know you? Just your imagination, anyway – just imagine it. Feel it there, [a] little ball. It's part of your creativity. This [above the head about 6 inches] is one of the places (generally speaking) where you focused in here on the heart and contemplated your fantasies, though you think they're here [head]. You put it out here [out of crown above head] and it impinges through [down through brain] for you to think about it to apply, or at least to fantasize. The fantasy is here [heart/soul], the creation is here [heart/soul].

You're going to need to focus here [heart/soul] in your thoughts outward [up and out] to receive. And when your fantasies come, acknowledge them and be courageous enough to accept them. That is the only way you will become a complete master here—by acknowledging your creations. It will take a little bit to acknowledge how you get it in the process. So be gentle with your being. As this speedup continues there is what you call a magnification, so your ability to manifest is magnified many times — ten times. In your year next, first quarter, ten times more. So too will your fears be magnified — everything.

There's going to be a great increase (this is going to be outrageous) in sexual energy. Kundalini is really going to move. Some of you have already experienced it over the past year and a half, the movement of it. It's not going to be as narrow a band as it has been, very fine. It's going to be a lot thicker, like a steel cable. And the desire for it is to move right up the spine to the crown. Some of you are going to get very horny (know you what that is?). I have no judgments on this sex thing, but you do.

If that wire cable is what you call distorted . . . know you there are many wires in a cable? Indeed? It's electrical current now manifested physically, what you would feel. If that cable decides it's having what you call not-joy, it's going to fracture and those wires are going to be like this: It will feel like wires running through your body, needles. It is going to hurt, you term [it] pain.

The purpose of the years you've had is to understand this kundalini energy, this psychic energy of you, moving through the body so you can use it gently. It's your physical manifestation; the body is your temple. You think after the past few months you've had a lot of lower back pain? You have seen nothing yet! Pains in your knees and your joints? They're going to magnify, because your lightbody is coming down around you. It wants to merge with the soul of you. Your physical flesh has not been trained in the lightbody, so the flesh is standing in one spot and the lightbody is moving in another. And because the physical flesh is made up of the light, guess which is going to move? It's going to be the flesh — rather dramatically.

Everyone breathe. There's purpose in the telling of this. When owner plays in the physical body there's going to get a lot of pressure, a lot of pain. Besides the lower back it's going to be the middle back, where that Grand Chakra is. After that it's right up here, just below the nape of your neck. If you bend your head you can feel that bone in there. That bone is connected to the vortices behind your shoulderblades, that energy field. That's where you store karma from past-life thrills you've had. When this moves here, it releases, it clears all of that, and then you're on your way.

This is a lot of energy. It's going to affect everyone on the planet. It's going to have an effect upon your electrical systems. Because it's God—you coming to you—and in this density that's experienced as electricity, because that's what keeps your heart beating. It's light. It's that simple.

Your diet's going to become very important. You're going to find out you don't need to eat as much as you think you do. You'll be drinking a lot more fluids, because this energy needs the fluid in the body to move through freely, clearly. And by fluids I don't mean all of the beers, know you? Or the wines in the closet. It might help you a little bit, but it weakens the fluid between the brain and the skull. A little bit's okay.

All right, we're going to bring a little more energy in this evening. It's simply to get your bodies used to it, that's all, so you can understand here and allow your consciousness to work a little bit.

Meditation

So allow your eyes to close for a moment. Indeed? There is a disk in there that has totems on it. Indeed? Now be in your moment and listen to the beat inside your body. Simply let it move inside you however it wants to. Allow the heart chakra to open wider; simply tell it to open inside you, open wider. [Long pause.] Allow the throat chakra to open a little bit more.

Now, your greater self knows you very well. I want you to contemplate in your physical brain now whether you're willing to allow the kundalini to move in you this year coming, at the decision of your greater self. You are one and the same. Now, in the heart chakra you may make a commitment to this or not. Play a little bit, play a lot – it's up to you. I want you to take it all.

Squeeze your buttocks, tighten your buttocks and feel it there just sort of building – a little tight, then let it go, and tight again. That's good. Okay, release. Adjust your physical body if you must, a little bit – shoulders. [Long pause.] Allow the energy at the solar plexus to move up. Breathe out. Center.

Now bring your consciousness to your solar plexus and rest there. You want to bring peace there. That is good. Bring peace there. And take a gentle breath and sort of breathe it out.

That's going to be one of the vortexes, right at the solar plexus; it's really going to get hit. The energy is going to begin to move, and it's going to hit that knot there and spread unto your diaphragm. You've got to breathe it through. And you've got to drink water. This is an electrical force, entities. It's your high self merging in your body, and it anchors in this arena primarily. And then it will be your kidneys and your liver and the splenic function over here. It's more of your life force coming to you, [although] it may not seem like it when it hits, however. But that will be all right.

One of the greatest fears that will be around your next year will seem to come out of nowhere, overwhelm you for no reason. You're in the middle of a party enjoying your machines, TV, and this fear of death will come to you. "Why am I thinking this thing? Where did that come from?" What is occurring is, you are changing your consciousness while you are physical this time. The last time you had a change of consciousness as dramatic was one of the other lifetimes when you had to die in order to realize a shift in consciousness.

So you bless the feeling; you acknowledge it. You become aware (hah!) and not feel threatened. How do you do that? You love God. And I don't care which one, because they're all in you, every one of them. They're all part of what is termed the Great Spirit, All That Is, He/She – everything. You're consciousness and you're loved by God. It is only you that says you're not.

So this fearness that a lot of beings are going to feel (everyone) is one way of shifting consciousness (play die). The new way is be aware: "Ah! My consciousness is shifting! Something's changing." More light. It's part of the process you have to go through if you want to remember all of your past lives, all of your future lives and be in the power of your now moment. You can't simply remember your last life and think you have it all. You'll remember everything, you'll know everything, because you *are* everything. You've heard it before – that you're the rock on the ground and the tree in the forest. It is having the ability now to feel it and know it. It'll be pretty outrageous, eh? I wonder how many trees will be cut down if everyone has the same feeling as a tree.

Hang on! We're getting ready here. A little more water. I have to bring more energy in the body so there be a clue for you beings. And get a hold. That's good.

⌖ ⌖ ⌖

Hello! We pulled a switch on you. Okay, what's the problem? Jehovah's too busy fixing his appliances — machines, I'll term it. From my perspective it's all humor. You see, I only understand love; I don't know anything else.

You beings are going to need a lot of humor in these times to come. Indeed? You've got a lot of help. There are great armadas.

Indeed. These energies are going to be restricted for your systems. In other words, you're being fed a little bit at a time. It's going to seem like a lot of entities, but there are many more that want to come. So it's my job to sort of create some barriers out there so they can't all get here. It's farther out than you think. It's way out there. So I make little slingshot things. Well, tennis – know you tennis?

Yes.

Oh, I get a big racket. I hit them. We play. It's only fun, know you what I mean? No big deal. And they can't figure it out. That's where Sananda caught on. (He's quite a jokester himself. Indeed.) I'm more than just a little sock. That's what this body [Arthur] called me when he first saw me. But I'm much more powerful than a little sock.

Now, you know what grid systems are, eh? Indeed?

Indeed.

All right. And you have your meridians and you have your grid systems in your body. Indeed?

Indeed.

All right. They are going to thicken, all of them. They are going to be active, like shimmer inside outward and outside inward. There will be a tendency for your lightbody light inside and out to shine, literally shine, like a silver being, golden being – gold and silver. Your skin color's going to change. You're becoming more profound now. It's going to take a special innocence to make it through your next three years. You beings term it humble, but it's beyond humble – more than that, an innocence. That's why it was said the meek will inherit. They're innocent in behavior.

Innocence has been perverted too much. And this is the last throe of the perversion of it. There are many in your world today who are perverting what you call innocence. They know it. I am innocent. I can't wait until they try to pervert me, because if I get in trouble I can get a hold of Jehovah and a few others. No big deal.

Not to frighten you, but what is at risk here (and it's well-known inside you) is your soul, the energies of it. The soul contains all of your accumulated wisdoms from wherever you have been since the beginning; it's contained there. They are your akashic records, you say, a great storehouse of information. The at-risk part will be that you're willing one more time to forget your soul, the wisdoms. That's the at-risk. No one's going to take them away. You be willingly forgetting.

That's why you – and this is all of humanity now – have chosen to be upon this planet at this time. This is the time of completion, not simply because it's your millennium. It's much more than that. Your souls and your higher aspects knew it as you walked toward this journey. This is the completion.

Now, there's no judgment. But you know when you've perverted innocence. And your soul knows, it remembers; that's its job. And it screams it out (especially unto I and others liken unto I) for a clearing. It's called a forgiveness of self that *you* must do, because forgiveness is not really required there. It is from *your* concept, your understanding.

So this is the time to love the soul called you and the life force called you, and reflect upon the innocence of self so you may understand the love of God more. It will be very easy for you in this time with these energies. Or it will be very difficult and the body will hurt. Everyone breathe. Lighten up.

Is there anything anyone wants to chat about?

What specifically will happen in the interactions with these extraterrestrials? Will we see them? Talk to them?

Yes.

Will it be in the sleep state? Tell us more about that.

They will start in the sleep state and bring you forward to the physical state.

Do we each have separate, particular beings that we will talk to?

You have beings that are excited to meet you in what you would term the physical. Yes.

And this is going to happen all over the planet?

Yes.

What should we be prepared to discuss? Jehovah talked about cultural truths — my culture, your culture.

Yes. Like you would be meeting an old friend. You would tell them stories about this planet and they'll tell you stories about theirs.

How long will they be here? Are they visiting or are they landing?

They are landing.

Are they going to work with governments and with the infrastructure, or is it just with people?

That won't occur for a while.

How long is a while?

Five, six years. Maybe ten; they're going to stay here a while, yes.

How will they live? In their ships?

They'll be above the ground.

Oh, hovering.

Indeed. What they're going to do . . . well, this is getting into someone else's territory, so I'll ask if I can say that [pause] . . . they're going to teach you how to blend your races.

By procreation or genetics or . . .

Procreation at this time.

So that we become one race.

Yes, you *are* one race.

So we acknowledge that we're one race.

Yes.

But they'll be dealing with items like pollution . . .

They will be working with you in the dealing of it, yes.

Teaching us how to do it.

Yes. So you have to be willing to work with them. Know you what I mean? Some of you in the human condition are pretty lazy. They tell you how to do it. You'll say, "Well, show me. *You* do it." And then you sit back and snicker, "Ha-ha-ha-ha." They're aware of that.

Are these fourth, fifth, sixth, seventh . . . a particular dimension?

Yes. They are a blending of many, because there is an overseer working here to get this thing settled, yes.

Who is that?

I'm not going to tell you right now. But there is a chain of command—let's put it that way.

Are these the ships that have always been here, the ones that have been working on the planet, on the earthquakes, on the volcanoes and everything. Or are these new ones coming in?

There will be new ones, but they won't be making the first contact; it will be the old ones—the Androm-edans, the Pleiadians, some of the Orion beings.

The ones that have been working with us?

Yes.

Wonderful! The Zetas?

Indeed. Yes. As long as you don't go fearful, it is wonderful. But they're going to literally appear physical to you. And you'll be able to shake their hands. That means you have to increase your vibratory rate, because a lot of these entities are what you would term radioactive. But it's not radioactive; it's simply a higher frequency of light. Indeed?

Yes. But they'll help us, right? You said they'll lift us a little and we'll lift a little and they'll . . .

You're going to have to lift more. They will lower themselves, yes, a little bit. Yes, it's a sharing. It's a job here; that's for sure.

So this is how we're going to get the planet cleaned up to live on. They're going to help us.

Yes. You're working with them. The first physical will be the appearance over all of your cities. It's already started. It's going to be so numerous that the denials are not going to withstand anymore.

So it will be on television?

Yes. They'll *have* to report it, because so many beings will see it that if they don't report it they will lose all their credibility. And they'll want information because *they're* certainly not going to be the first ones contacted!

So they'll come and interview the ones.

They'll come and interview. Yes. They will try to threaten at first, but it won't work. Not much of that left now, so they'll interview. And they'll be begging, "Could you share a little bit of this information? Please." And you'll say, "I'll think about it. What's the size of the check?"

And know how you've been working to get your energies and your channelings in line? They're not going to pop right in there, because your thought processes are still within structure. Indeed? Now, they don't want to get into an argument; they want to share. They don't want to get into a conversation when you say, "But how about this?" Know you what I mean? They are a little more evolved, where arguments are not a thing. So you're in a different energy field with them. You are sharing wisdoms. Indeed? There's a difference.

Know you you would be in a state of "ah-hah!" "ah-hah!" you see? You're not alone with this argue thing. There are a few in the room.

Will some of these beings truly be old friends we've had perhaps close association with in the past?

Yes. They will be the first ones. They've been with you all of this lifetime in what you term your dream state and other experiences and many other lifetimes. So the familiarity will be there. Only your social consciousness will think it is different.

Even going back eons in time?

Well, time doesn't exist, but for eons, yes.

They're going to have a profound effect on you. Yes, indeed. I'll say this. They're getting really close now, know you what I mean? The flybys are getting closer, [it's] not some twinkling star out there. When they first make contact besides just being in your skies, at first you'll have to keep it secret – and you can understand why, eh? And then later the process can expand. You'll be visited and they'll talk and chat. And there will be a time when you have to keep beings away from your house because they're visiting you. It's not time to open up for everyone yet. You understand, these beings are very sensitive. And your psychic abilities are nothing compared to theirs. They pick up very ancient soul memories from you very easily. Part of their difficulty will be in the discernment of it, if that is in your process at this present time – would you act like that [now]? There's an education process there also. Know you what I mean?

No. The discernment: whether we would act like that at the present time?

Yes.

Oh, they'll see old memories . . .

Everything. And they would have difficulty [knowing] if that is the you now. Indeed. And so is *their* education process.

To see that we're beyond that, hopefully.

Well, we know you're not beyond it yet – but hopefully yes, that there will be an education there. Indeed?

The individuals on Earth that are going to feel the increased energies and the pain and so forth: Is this the entire population, or are these people who are going to experience going into fourth density?

Everyone will experience these things. They're rather dramatic. They are affecting your planet. You've heard of these earthquake scenarios, the volcano scenarios, the weather changes. Indeed? That is your consciousness. But you *think* it's the earthquake and the weather. It is you. And you are going to feel you coming here. I've said that a long time. You're going to understand that you're God and you're responsible for everything; because it's *your* consciousness. The greatest fear will be the fear itself – this energy called fear of die, change.

You are sovereign entities. You always have been, in every realm. You pretend you're not. That's all right. What is most important and the reason why we're here (a lot of us, and there's quite a crew) is that we respect your divinity. You will remember you're divine one way or the other, either on this side or when we come knocking on your casket, "Okay, time to get out." [Laughter.] But at least you'll open the casket this time. You won't lie there.

Allow your eyes to close a moment here. Center your being. And the blessings that are mine I give unto you. And the blessings that are yours, I'll gather them for you and give them unto you. And the blessings of the Father, I'll gather them for you and give them unto you. Now you have all of the blessings of everyone. Allow yourself to have your own blessing. That is what you give to yourself. Bargain?

Bargain!

So be it!

So be it!

And blessed be you forever, because that is the only condition. You are blessed forever. It's time to recognize that. It will make it a lot easier. All right. I'm going to boost your kundalini a little bit when you're sleeping. You don't have to tell your mate if you're dreaming about someone else. [Laughter.] Keep it quiet.

I love you outrageously. You have outrageous beings on your side. We are outrageous. Some might be a little clumsy like Jehovah, but no big deal. [Laughter.] (I'll probably hear about that.) One thing with this clumsiness: He's not a good aim with that thunderbolt of his. [Laughter.] Well, maybe sometimes he is. Okay. Enough stories. I'll get myself in real trouble.

What you beings don't understand is, though you were here for you, you were also here tonight for your planet and the consciousness about it. As it affected you, it affected everything. So acknowledge yourself for this, what you've done for humanity. It's a pretty outrageous evening, whether you know it or not. You created a little shifting.

You're all getting activated for your connection for a purpose here. Indeed? Or this could be just for coincidence this evening, eh? We'll see you later in your dreams. Okay. We are through.

39

Ancient Records to be Revealed in the '90s

The Recordkeeper through Robert Shapiro
December 8, 1991

When you ask your questions, be patient with me, for there are many records, I have in in front of me at this moment an Old Book. When you ask your questions I will have to look them up to see if I can understand the records. I will not be speaking from my own knowledge; I will be reading the answer.

What I know about you is that your souls have chosen this strange world you are on now, and you have challenged yourself on this world really too much. I do not understand why you would even want to live here. It seems that you have too much to do. Still, I will answer your questions to the best of my ability. What would you like to ask?

Bruton Vault in Williamsburg

We were interested in knowing about the burial of the Bruton Vault in Williamsburg, Virginia. It is supposed to have information that would change recorded history. Can you tell anything about that?

I will have to look it up. Talk more about it while I am looking it up.

There is an old church that has been there since the 1600s, and in its graveyard there is a metallic vault In it are supposedly papers that come from the 1500-1600s that have to do with the beginning of our country.

Oh, yes. It seems that this sheath of documents written in somewhat of a coded language was partly designed to be discovered quite some time ago. It is unfortunate that it has been discovered just when it was. It would have been more pleasant had it been discovered about 300 years before. Part of the intent was to stimulate a liberalization of the governments in Eastern Europe, which was at that time considered to be the most likely place where a truly democratic society could evolve, provided the proper marriages were arranged in the royal families.

However, since the documents were discovered when they were, the information, which would have been stimulating in that old context, almost seems to apply as a real thing. It is at least a page and a half by itself, and the record book is in what you would call shorthand. One single diagram would be equal to a book. Maybe you better ask about specifics.

Well, we don't know what is in there yet. That is why we are asking.

As much as I can understand, it is a suggestion written not unlike a story suggesting a world which is similar to your Western world. Almost as though it were designed to create something that doesn't really exist.

It seems, then, that what you have done in this part of the world was really intended to never happen at all. The ancient peoples who lived here in northern America were never intended to be decimated or overrun. Rather, it was an intention that the ancient peoples here would go on as they had. It is almost as though this story, designed to stimulate liberalization, created a fictional world. You can see the little joke here. The whole thing was designed for one thing and accidentally—because of its being discovered at the wrong time—had to be true. It is an obscure fact, but so.

My understanding of what this says, then, is that the destruction of ancient cultures' wisdom and the history of the United States, partly of Canada and of this whole hemisphere, northern parts of South America and Central Americas as well, was never intended to take place and actually almost caused a 3000-year delay in your evolution. But since you are now here, many of the predictions took place then which were designed to deflect people from their ways that were not sympathetic to the Earth and to its peoples. It was almost as if something foul took place when something pleasant was intended.

I realize this sounds unkind, because many good things have happened in your world. But it was never intended that the children would destroy the Ancient Ones. It was intended that those who emigrated to this part of the world would be initiated by the peoples who lived here and would learn the ancient wisdom from the Old Ones here, who would reveal their secrets to the immigrants. The immigrants would then go back to Europe and bring this wisdom, and the knowledge of the native peoples in your hemisphere would spread around the world and would cause a new consciousness to have taken place about several hundred years ago. But it didn't happen, as you can see.

Why didn't it happen?

It was intended to be discovered around the year 1550, at which time it would have influenced things differently. There had already been explorers to come to what people in Europe called the New World, but because the explorers came back and were after riches, this evolved into Europe colonizing this part of the world and it became something economic and suppressive. The whole point was missed.

Buried in the 1200s by Monks

When were they buried? I didn't think that they were buried as early as 1550.

This was buried, as much as I can see, in the 1200s. It was written by people you would call monks, but they were not associated directly with the church that is situated in Rome. Rather, they were allied to them.

Would this be Saint Brandon, Saint Patrick?

I believe that it was some other sect, something that was very illuminated in its own right, but it is not written here. I could not say.

Does it have anything to do with Shakespeare, Sir Francis Bacon and the Constitution or anything we think it says?

Oh, it could have all of that but you didn't ask about that. What do you want to know about that?

Well, that is what I thought was buried in the Bruton Vault in that church in Williamsburg, in the graveyard.

Are there other records that you are talking about that are buried someplace else?

This is what I am reading from the book, but it mentions many things. You are talking about a sheaf of papers this thick. I am only saying what was intended. It is unfortunate the documents never were retrieved. Understand that if they had been retrieved by the initial explorers, things would have been different. It is ironic that when they came over looking for treasure, they missed the *real* treasure. It would have changed everything. All of the spiritual desires you have now and the world you want to see happen would already have happened several hundred years ago, and all of this would not be.

Were they indeed discovered but kept secret and other papers added to them in the time of our Founding Fathers?

No, the Founding Fathers did finally, because of the wisdom they had amongst some of their members, communicate with the ancient peoples you call the tribal peoples and created the form of government that you now live under, politically speaking, influenced by the tribal peoples, what they had done. Of course, they also felt that there was a divine destiny by the colonists, so even though they created a mythical idea of American Indians, they nevertheless imitated the form of government by bringing with them the idea of covenants and being influenced by tribal treaties. That is not unusual. The invisible hand, you see, would be involved there. Understanding that the delay would take place but still the intent would be to nudge you toward the original purpose to evolve to higher wisdom, throwing them together with the tribal peoples in that way. It is unfortunate that much of this has been kept a secret, but the Founding Fathers in this country (you call them—many of them were not yet fathers) had a vision that they brought with them from the old country. They felt it was necessary to keep it to themselves.

What was their vision?

That the Order, as they called it, would be established in this country, eventually creating a society that would be an image for the rest of the world (which to some extent has come to pass) and would be the zenith, as they would call it from their words here, that would establish, from their point of view, a new order of things. Look into the records; there are many clues there.

Literary Pseudonyms

Is there any information within that vault that has to do with the creation of poems and plays written by that one we know as Shakespeare?

I believe that comes under the portion of the documents referring to myth and legend, yes. What would you like to know? That is a pseudonym, of course.

That's the point. It had to do with who really created those works.

I believe that it was a pseudonym used by another man, but there was a man by a similar name, William. I do not see his last name here, but he was a man, this William, who had access to other classes. The actual writer did not have much access, not unlike today with producers and agents and so on. You can write the greatest works ever written, but if no one will present your works to those who would financially support them, no one would ever hear them. So William was a "front" person, an image. There was another man that wrote about two-thirds or three-fifths, I am not sure, many of the stories. And then there were two women that wrote the rest.

Oh, can you tell us about that?

The women were associates of the man, who sheltered them so that they would not be found out to be writing these things, because it would have been considered unseemly in their society. They were not intimately involved, the three of them, but they were friends

Do you have names for those people?

I believe one of the names was something like – it begins with an M; I want to say Matilda, but that doesn't seem right. I don't have it down. It looks like that, but it isn't pronounced that way. I do not have the name for the other one. Those kind of details, you understand, are not so much in the records.

Can you say something about who you are and where you are and what level of reality you live in? Are you on the planet, the cosmos, the solar system?

I am not involved with your little world. I cannot say. I am not involved with any of this, but it is my job to keep the records of your physical world.

You use dimensions, don't you?

I would be at about the seventh dimension. None of the stars you see are in this dimension. But it is my job to keep the records of your adventure to the planet that you are on now. I cannot say much about myself that you could really understand.

The Book of Mormon

Are these records you were talking about related to the Book of Mormon, the plates given to Joseph Smith?

They are not directly related, but much of the knowledge given to Smith was given by others who had knowledge of Earth history as you are living it. Smith put some of that into his book, but the most critical parts were kept out. Again there is that string that runs amongst your knowledges of keeping critical things out. It is as if someone keeps you just far enough away from these similar threads of knowledge so that you will not get too big too fast.

You must feel annoyed because the most important parts of Smith's book have been held back, kept secret. The elders of that church feel that they have a sacred mission to keep that knowledge back, but that knowledge is not unlike many of the secret parts of other books and so on which have been held back. All is thematic about who the human race is, why you were created and what is your destiny. Of the main body of the knowledge given to Smith, about 80% is held back as a secret, but many other peoples have similar information, including some of the tribal peoples.

The Illuminati and Their Stolen "Sign"

About the secret societies around the time of the Freemasons and the Illuminati: Do you have any information on how the Orions managed to corrupt the Illuminati?

The Illuminati were given a sign. It was an actual physical thing. At a distance it would not look to you particularly significant; it would look like a coin. But this sign, which was inscribed with a crown on one side and a torch on the other side, had come to be a holy object to them. They were at one point deprived of this object by the peoples you have mentioned from that star system in an ancient time, so what they have left is their knowledge of this sign but not the sign itself. They drew a great deal of strength from this sign, but this sign has been taken from your world and is no longer present on your world. This has made the Illuminati, as you call them, (though they have many other disguises) – it has created the initial corruption.

These people are an ancient group going back long before the time of Earth or the society that took the sign. I know that you use the word "sign" for something else, but this is what they called it; it is like a medal. It could do anything, from their point of view, so not having it required them to be different. When you draw your power from some thing and it is no longer present, it is then necessary to draw your power from other things. So it was then necessary within their belief system to maintain control. Before the sign was taken they did not have to do that, because they had an indefatigable object that could produce anything and control was unnecessary. But since this was taken from them, then they had to be in control and there were no longer any means by which to create for their group physical things, you see. So the ancient Orion society that stole this thing, they have it still in their time.

Can you expound on what you just said, that 80% of the wisdom in our records was held back from us? Who we are, why we are here and our destiny?

Your Biological Manipulation

This is all dependent upon which side of the fence you are standing, maddening or indulgent. Many worlds consider your world to be a place of children, and some have a benign idea toward you as one might feel about children. Others would use you for many purposes in order to manipulate you. So there is that way to look at it. In order to manipulate you, knowledge was kept from you through your mental processes by having removed, at the core of your being at the creation of the human race, something that had the biological effect of creating a bridge to your biological, physical body, your physical essence. It was removed from your mind. This had the effect of creating an unconscious and subconscious, or a hierarchical mind. You know, when you are not on this planet this is not a factor, but as a physical person on Earth you cannot access your normal knowledge. It is as if something reached right in and said, "We're going to take this thing out." If you took a valuable piece out of many computers, then they could just barely work. It is like that; it would just barely work.

Then there are people on the other side who want to help you. This is why you get talks like this. The invisible hand reached in and put imagination into your mind to give you the possibility to leap across the gap of not having that physical connection to all of your knowledge — to leap across the gap with your imagination and be inspired as to what could be. If it weren't for inspiration and mental imagination, you wouldn't have gotten as far as you did; you would just have been slaves (which some races would have liked.

Who took It out, and why?

It was removed. There are many ways to look at it. On the negative side, it was removed to control you, to keep you at a level of this conflict with each other. It was removed to keep you in conflict, because as long as you are in conflict with each other, believing that somehow another person of your stature has something, anything you want — which is why thievery and all this takes place — then you would be looking at each other as the bad guy, never really looking toward something not even of your planet. On the other hand, having this ability to know removed from you forced you to resolve many problems that your souls brought here. Long before, you were here from the stars to resolve things that your souls were involved in before. So the idea of ignorance assisted that resolution. It just depends on which way you look at it.

But it is ending now, isn't it? We are coming back into learning who we are and where we are?

The Return of the Illuminati's Sign; the Revealed Testament

Yes. The documents that will be discovered in the next 25 years will have something most important in them. I will talk a little bit about that.

For one thing, in the next 25 years the Illuminati people, who have taken up different positions, will no longer have to control anything because the sign will be returned to them. This will make the difference, because they will then be able to have whatever they need; they will just ask the sign and it will be there.

Also, that which will be referred to as the Revealed Testament will be found. This will be found in what is now called the Middle East. This area is critical to your understanding who you are. Some of these things have been found there, but there are at least 75 more places where things have been buried. But you have to use knowledge to open something—this is like mystical knowledge, you understand. When you manipulate physical reality through mystical knowledge, then the sources of documents . . . you think of documents as papers, but real documents they are like cylinders. They are not unlike the size of a crystal; some of them are even disguised to look like crystal spheres, but most of them are simple cylinders. Those are the *real* documents. But they can only be found by the mystics who are even now developing in your society. When these are discovered, then the Revealed Testament will come to pass. It will unite many of your religions—the Moslem faith, the Hindu faith, the root of the Jewish faith, which is Zoroaster. Yes, that and the Christian religion, which is a child of many of these religions. It will unite all of those, this new Revealed Testament.

The Cylinders That Project Holographic Images and Telepathic Information

It will be found, as I say, by the mystics, who will hold it like this, pressing their thumb on top and the small finger on the bottom and squeezing it and turning it. Then right between this finger, can you see, it will come out in the air like a holographic picture. If you are English-speaking, you will read it in English; if you speak Hindustani you will read it in that. If you don't read any language at all, you can just feel it come into you. These things will be discovered in 25 years.

You know, the advantage is that the mystics will find them. They will get out to the people. Many of these things have been found already and they all have similar threads of knowledge, though they might have different disguised stories. But there are so many more to be found. It will not be possible for those who would hold this knowledge for themselves to stop it. Because the mystic does not have to physically travel to the East to pick one of these things up out of the ground, where it might be 47 feet down on a diagonal shaft between the ancient temple of Ra and the undiscovered tombs of the pre-Pharaoh leaders. They will just be able to be where they are, reach out, down, bring it back to you. It would look like a conjuring trick, but these things are real.

That is why those that would bind it as knowledge and keep it only for a select few cannot prevent it. It is as if all of the hearts and minds of humans that have lived here have cried out in a single gasp. You are receiving help from your future and from your past, and this next 25 years is critical. Some of the children being born now will be the great mystics of the future, but some of them will be older, white-haired people as well. Oh yes, this next 25 years will be very exciting!

What is the source of the Testament that you speak of?

The Revealed Testament, the source of that? Well, I know that one, I don't have to look that one up. It is that which is divine, what you would call in your own way God. But divinity is the soul of creation. Creation in its own light has its own soul. You ask for someone or some society, but it is not that. Within the chaos of creation lies the constantly reproducing and defractionalizing elements of everything, so it is simply chaotic creation.

So there is no one person who is going to write this book? It is going to be an idea?

The Revealed Testament Predates Your World

Oh, it was written long before your world was created. These are the themes upon which all worlds from all times were created. Do you really think that any knowledge was created on your world? Nothing was ever created that is new. It is just that too many things from too many worlds were thrown in at once and they said, "Let's see if we can make some sense out of all of this. Let's let them figure it out." But it is too much of a burden for any one race of people. These knowledges, these ancient wisdoms, are the foundations of *all* societies that have ever existed in the third, fourth, fifth, seventh and ninth dimensions, all of these societies there, even influencing the sixth.

I have an idea that the Rosetta Stone is something like what you are talking about; that it has the four languages or six or whatever, all interrelated, to be read by Chaldeans, Egyptians, Aramaics — is this correct?

This stone, as well as a few parchment objects that were discovered some time ago, are solidified versions that would be illuminated in space for you to read. They are to drive you on. It has not yet been decoded; only the cryptogram has been decoded.

The hieroglyphics that our scientists tell us the meanings of, really are not at all?

Oh, it is true, they are mistaken. But the cryptogram is designed to be enigmatic, and it has succeeded. But here is a clue to resolve it: It is not to *look at its individual parts, but at the whole.* No, an artist makes a design out of many different lines, or different things, but when you pull back you can see the whole thing—it is like that. Look at the whole thing even though it is not all there.

Were you speaking of the Dead Sea scrolls just now?

Yes.

I would like to ask you about the records that Edgar Cayce had said would be found that have been placed between the Great Pyramid and Sphinx in Egypt. Can you tell us something about the discovery of those and what they contain?

Records Mentioned by Cayce Found in 1943

Those have been found, but they have been held back from the world at large. My understanding . . . I know some of this stuff was found in 1943. They were very helpful to those who were involved —well, those who *won* the war. Indeed, they were helpful.

What way?

Well, some of the scientific enigmas of the time were greatly speeded up. I will tell you a little secret, but I can't tell you the name. You will have to guess, but that is what makes it fun.

Two of the most famous scientists who were most influential in that time of the resolving of World War II were really close to the chamber where the documents were found. The chamber itself has not been fully penetrated, but some documents as well as some objects were found. The objects are not understood yet, but the documents were clear. One of the scientists, who made it possible to develop the project that won the war for the Allies, was allowed to be near there, though partly what was done was to connect him with a mystic of the time. The other scientist (who has had more postwar effect) was on the other side, which you would call the losing side, and he was influenced almost entirely by a mystic connection.

Can you say who these mystics are?

The Mystics, the Allies and the Germans

The one on the side that lost is no longer amongst you, but he was a German mystic. Mysticism runs deep with those people even to this day. Some of your most secret societies are rooted in the place geographically of Germany. The mystic that helped the other winners is alive today and was originally born on the island of Cyprus. But I will not say more about the mystics .

So the mystics were able to tune into the information and give it to the scientists, even though the scientists didn't actually go in and look at it?

Well, that is not quite the case with the Allied scientist. He was brought *near* there.

Near enough to read and see?

He read some of it, but he did not go into the chamber itself. Even now it is not possible to be in the chamber for too long and live.

But then there are those who know exactly where that chamber is; that knowledge remains?

Yes, there are guards there even now. The chamber is ringed entirely all the way around it, and the other way as well, with fission bombs in case those who control it should lose control. Their idea would be to destroy it, but it would not be possible. They could certainly make it impossible for humans to approach the area because of the radiation, but the thing that shields them from getting into the source that is there cannot be destroyed by anything manmade.

I was told at one time this substance was mercury steel, that the records are contained in when they are under the sea or in the earth. It is resistant to whatever change comes along. This mercury steel is an alloy we haven't discovered yet.

The Chamber of the Mini Sun and the Volunteers for the Fatal Entry

That refers to a separate situation; that metal was also discovered beneath the sea, yes. But in this particular chamber, if you were to look at it with your eyes, it would look like light not unlike a mini sun. The mystic that was able to help your Allies access that place was remonstrating with those people of the time not to approach it. It can be viewed by mystics even now, but it would not be solid.

I am not denying what you are saying. If you could imagine yourself standing in the presence of the sun, all things that have ever been created on this planet would vaporize. Even if your planet as a whole planet were taken to your sun, it would vaporize. Do you understand? It is like a piece of the sun, but it is not hot. Yet it would have other aspects of the sun associated with it. It can be approached for a short time. If a human were to stand in that chamber where this object is for five minutes, you could come out; but another ten minutes and you would be dead. So you must understand that those who went into the chamber all died. Even to retrieve the objects and the knowledge, they all died. It was not unknown to them. They were volunteers; 47 people volunteered of their own free will, you see. The mystic told the forces of the Allies (those who were at the foundation of the Allied powers) that only people who volunteered of their own free will and were presented with the facts available at the time could even go in. And that if they were deluded in any way, they would not be able to find their way in. So those who went in knew that they were going to die, and went in of their free will. Some of those volunteers are still alive, but not many, you understand. Thirty died.

Were the others deformed?

If they had not gone in, those 30, the other side would have won the war. It is that simple. Hitler's idea of the thousand-year Reich would have been at *least* a thousand years. You owe a lot to those 30 people.

And to that mystic. This sounds like Raiders of the Lost Ark.

Raiders of the Lost Ark Based in Truth

That was an inspired story. The basis of that story was pulled from *real* things. The writer might not admit it, but he knows.

From this event or others?

Many things. The writer was not a fool.

Why did the mystic need somebody to go in there? I thought you had said previously that one of the advantages of the mystic was that they don't need to do physical things.

Yes, but I am talking about the mystics of that time in '43, you understand. Things were different then. Yes, the mystic could go in and see all of these things. The mystic gave them what he gave them. You do not understand.

A true mystic that is given the powers of a mystic—it is a sacred thing, you see. And that person will reveal only that which is allowed to be revealed. The mystic of the time, the one born on Cyprus, is still alive and knows *everything,* knows what is behind that thing that looks like the sun, knows it *all.* But the true mystic that is given the power in whatever means that they display it, if they are not aligned with the sacred and the divine, they do not achieve their desires or the desires of those they work with.

Why do you think the mystic on the other side did not succeed? He was not aligned with the sacred; he was aligned with the other side. He was aligned with the forces that would control. You know the history of that other side, the Third Reich? You know its history? Why do you think? Certainly, the mystic reveals what is to be revealed, but never everything, or they are *destroyed.* If a mystic goes the wrong way, not only is their life destroyed, but all the lives they might have lived in the future. *They are uncreated!* And that aspect of God —understand, the Creator —is eliminated from ever having existed. So the mystic knows these things; but even if they do not, if they are aligned with the sacred, then they may do what they do.

How did they find this? Did they use Cayce's information?

Yes.

It was under the Sphinx and it is still there?

At a slight angle, yes. Part of it is under it. Was it America's idea to put fission bombs around it?

Behind the Allies Was The Order

I don't like to blame a government. I would rather say, the foundation of those who won. You are talking about people; the foundation of those who won were a group. Let's call them, for your sake . . . just a moment. They called themselves in that time The Order of Creation.

But it is what we call the Secret Government?

No. Your idea of the Secret Government is something that will put its thumb on you. No, it is not that.

Oh, this is The Order that we have learned about, the ones that thought we had to go very slowly?

Yes. It is like this: I can only give you only so much, and this one tells me sometimes, "No, you can't say that." You have to come back with it.

Who is telling you; who is behind you?

You know the symbol? It's a universal symbol. It is the symbol of that which you call the Creator. On all of the planets everyone knows this one.

Who was afraid that this would be discovered, and placed bombs around it? Was that The Order, too?

Behind the Third Reich Was Evil

Yes. And they were right. What if the wrong side leaked out the knowledge to the so-called other sides? When I refer to other sides, I am not talking about governments; I am talking about the side that would be the root of the abomination of the Third Reich.

The bombs say, don't try to send your slaves at anytime in the future because they will not survive and then you will never be able to penetrate that in any form that is human. Evil, in order to do its evil thing, can only do that through physical people who might occupy the world. When there are no people here it is powerless; it is a joke. It can only do its deeds through humans.

I was under the impression that The Order was capable of something less physical than bombs to protect things. Is that not really true then?

It is true. They are capable beyond your now understanding of your capabilities, but bombs are understood. Very easily accessed, they were readily available a few years after the discovery of that space. You would not want *that* to blow up; the Middle East would cease to exist. But it is not a real risk. Evil understands.

If they got the secrets of the atom bomb and also of the hydrogen bomb . . .

No, they did not have to get the secrets of the hydrogen bomb. You know, your scientists already understood the idea of the atom bomb. What was necessary was to make it happen faster. They were not really prepared to make this happen so quick.

But there were formulas or equations or chemical secrets or something that they read there that allowed them to do that?

How The Order Helped the Allies

They were, for one thing, given the location where they could find the best uranium ore. And they were also shown whom to invite to the project. There had already been many years of hobby work by scientists toward this end, so there was some knowledge. But there were some you would call prodigies who were invited to the project that made it possible. Also, they were given knowledge of the underground military locations of the weapons being developed by the other side.

And they were given certain means by which to destroy those weapons. However, they did not destroy *all* the weapons. They at one point actually created a military mission to go and get the scientist from the other side. Remember that I said that there was another scientist from the other side; they went in and got him even though it was at great risk.

Niels Bohr?

I really can't say, because he has people living here, family still alive, you see. They went in and got him and brought him back and he greatly affected your postwar scientific endeavors. Many German scientists were brought over at that time.

He was brought over *before* the end of the war. A lot of people lost their lives getting him. I can tell you that the Allied powers felt two ways about destroying some of these inventions. They would have loved to have brought the working models back, but they brought the scientists for some of them, written knowledge. They just had to blow it up, because if they had left these things working . . . they had been told they had to destroy it. If they didn't destroy it, the Third Reich would rise again.

Were these the Third Reich's records or more ancient records?

Remember, the Third Reich had a mystic.

Were these the ancient records that the mystic would help them find or develop?

The mystic tapped the knowledge that was in that chamber, only the mystic was not following the alignment of the sacred. Mystics never do that if they pull in weapons and so on, knowledge of such things. Give your government credit. Some of the weapons that were developed by the Third Reich have not been developed by your government. They are such an abomination, they have actually not been developed. Cooler heads prevailed and said that we must destroy this knowledge, because this weapon is the destroyer of the worlds. So give them some credit, okay?

Who buried the technology and information under the Sphinx?

Oh, it is good enough to know that it was The Order.

Did Thoth have something to do with it?

No, he was a child compared to them. Thoth was really a reincarnation of an element of someone that preceded your world but has been very active here. The Order predates your planet, you know.

No, I didn't. Where did they come from?

The Origin of The Order

They come from the point of the center of your universe where creation comes forth. They are the . . . I see; that is interesting. They are the energy particle. The human beings involved in The Order – the energy of The Order, the essence of it – they are the particles that make up what you now call electricity on all of its levels. So this is how they can be influential within your actual genetic structures but not actually have to be a part of it. Clever, huh? Wherever electricity can be, well they can be there, too.

We were told by other teachers through this channel that The Order came from the Founders on this planet. But of course the Founders go back to the creation.

Yes, sometimes things are revealed a little bit at a time, eh? That is good, because if you have too much knowledge . . . remember, those who would keep knowledge from you may not always have your worst intentions in mind. And those who would give knowledge may not always have your best in mind. It works both ways. I do not put down other teachers; I simply say that sometimes that they do not have all knowledge. This one has all knowledge, eh?

Are there other places on this planet where there is information buried similar to that which is buried under the Sphinx?

Yes.

Can you say where they are?

The Rose Quartz Pyramid in the Marianas Trench

A little bit. The deepest trench in the Pacific Ocean, which conveniently is not something that you can readily access. About four miles down below that there is a pyramidal-shaped device. If it were on the surface, it would be larger than the Great Pyramid, and is made entirely of what you call rose quartz. It has not only all knowledge of your planet, but all *known* knowledge of the universe. All planets that are involved in—this is the best way that I can describe your planet—tumultuous, too much—all must have this type of rose quartz pyramid, or it would fly apart. Too much is going on here. I realize that sounds like a judgment on my part, but according to what I read here, everyone agrees. It is too much, so it requires something like this to hold it together. Thus it functions not only as a means of knowledge but is actually holding your planet together. Were you ever to destroy it, that would be the end for you. But let's not even discuss that, because your souls would be uncreated as well.

Do you have access to anything in any place that has been written down or recorded in some manner?

Yes, anything. In the case of what we are talking about here let's just say that I have access to anything that would concern you. I have access to the things that do not concern you, but I do not use that access since it is about you that I am involved. Does that make any sense?

The Pyramids below the Superstition Mountains

Can you tell us anything about the pyramid structures that are under the Superstition Mountains in Arizona, and what records they have, how long ago they date, etc.

They are interesting in that we are talking about three, and they have a most important level of knowledge. They contain color. That is interesting, you know—color, sound. These are languages in their own right. But these objects are fortunately very small, which makes them harder to find. Because they are the full spectrum of color surrounded by the full spectrum of sound, your technology will never be able to find them. Understand that if you were to observe something that was in full color, all colors—even those not fully understood or what you would call detected or observable by men and machine—all sound, if it were something like that, it could appear as anything. That is the basis of how things can appear as anything, because they have all color and sound. I am not discounting what you are saying, I am giving you a little nugget there, you see. That is also the basis of the mystic arts even though it may not be understood or even necessary to be understood. Having all color and all sound is the basis of energy.

All right, what did you want? I know that you were disappointed with that.

I was referring to a place where an excavation was made approximately 150 feet deep and someone had been getting physically information about this pyramid, about a healing chamber to be accessed, and that there was a special way to do so.

Oh, no, I could not tell you about that. Because do you know what that could do? It could heal all disease right now. If that happened—I realize that this sounds ruthless, but I do not mean it this way. If all disease and discomfort were healed right now, you would not achieve what you came here to do. So no, I cannot tell you about that. But I can say that the mystics can tap into it *only if they use it for the betterment of all.* If they attempt to use it for themselves or even for one other person—you understand, help this group, help that group—it will not work. It will only work if it is tapped into and broadcast for all. It is not exclusive.

When would be the appropriate time for that to be discovered? Do you have that in your record?

Records are sometimes funny! *When you no longer need it!*

About the Record Book

Your books go into the future as well as the past?

Oh, yes. The future has been written. I know it is nice to think that things are free will, but even free will has been written. It is complicated, but yes, it has all been written.

Even the fact that we didn't find those records in the 1550s and decimated the Indians?

Yes, in the larger sense. Yes, it has *all* been written. Otherwise I could not read it here, because this book was written before I . . . you understand that this book existed before any of *this* did, so it must have been, yes. But it has things built into it . . . you know, it is a complicated factor. It is as if a scientist were looking at an equation that is constantly changing. But it is real, it is solid.

You know, I am solid in my own place, this book is solid. It is a solid thing. If you were to look at this book if you were right here now, it has a brocade cover. That is the best way to describe it. It has all of the symbols of man and woman on the cover—for me, the cover is the front, the back, the spine—all of the symbols, as well as the hand symbols. Just touching the book gives one really quite incredible knowledge.

So mystics can access that book, too?

Yes. That was the most important question that was asked tonight.

How do you attain all color and all sound? How does a mystic open to that?

It takes usually years, unless the child is born with this. It takes years to develop awareness of what you would call energies. Some of your yogis have done this and other people who are in various spiritual practices become aware that everything is energy, everything is life. When you become aware of the sacredness of all things, you can begin to feel things. When you feel them, you can work with them, as you *are* those things. It is as if a mystic becomes that which they do and that which they do becomes them as well. Even now, move your hands through the air and notice how you will feel some things. You might be uncertain whether those things and sensations are coming from your hands or from the energy in the air. That is because everything is part of everything else.

What is the name of the book?

It does not have a name that I am aware of. You might have a name for it. It has a symbol; it is a hand sign. This is the name of the book, and you'll have to describe this as best you can [gestures: right forefinger points up, then lowers the arm; next extends hand forward palm up, fingers curled, bringing hand toward chest]. That is the name.

I have a question regarding an enigma in Exodus. Moses goes to the mountain for the first time to get the Ten Commandments and returns to find the people worshipping Baal. He throws down the tablets he'd been given, goes back up the mountain and comes down with the Ten Commandments. I would like to know if that was an allegory or if it really happened, and what those original Ten Commandments actually said.

The Eleven Commandments

This is an interesting story. The original number of commandments was eleven and the commandment not repeated on the second journey was, "Thou shalt trust the human heart to be the divine representative of the soul," of course in the language of the time. This was on the original eleven commandments when the messenger went down the hill. He did not quite do what was stated, but the tablets were destroyed nevertheless. By that time those people had been infiltrated by the force of evil. It was not presented that way in the original story because it would have seemed overpowering. But the force in the people was depicted in the story of the time as being corruption, and it was also highly slanted against the religions of others in the area for political reasons. But the actual thing was that the people had been approached by the force of evil when their messenger went away. We have discussed this in association with the Third Reich; it was the same force in their time. And the only way to remove that force from the people was to use the tablets as a shield. A shield can sometimes be like a weapon, and the energy of the tablets was utilized to drive that force away.

This was not related in the story because it was believed at the time that if that was related exactly as it was, people would fear the force of evil so much that they would be unable to avoid *more* involvement with it because of their fear. So the tablets were used to battle the force of evil, and then the messenger went back up on the mountain and received the commandments that you now have minus the eleventh commandment, which at that time was reserved for a later time.

You can, if you like, understand that that commandment is an unspoken one. They do not always follow it, but it is not always written down in the documents, so they cannot be blamed. The provider of the commandments, who at that time was in battle with the force of evil, did not choose to give that eleventh commandment. It was not withheld out of meanness, but it was almost as if that person doing battle with the force of evil learned something. That is that he could not push the human race too fast; that trust must develop by experience rather than being told "you must do this."

Were the first ten commandements, then, stated exactly as we have them recorded?

With some minor changes, simply due to the translation of this language to that language and so on. They are essentially correct, though they were not stated so much as commandments. If they were interpreted in their original symbolic meaning it would have sounded more like encouragements, as if you were to take those commandments now and change them into something that would sound more like, "If you do this, then you would be happier." That is how they were really stated. It was not "do this or die." That would have been considered by that individual to be too controlling.

The End of the 26,000-Year Cycle, When the Soul Confronts Itself

Could you talk a little bit about your understanding of the cosmic cycles, specifically the 26,000-year cycles?

It is natural for anything cyclic to take place. There is motion to all things, and the motion that is involved in your world happens to be associated with that rough figure. It will be 33,000 soon, but it is now at its current level due to the slowness of the world you are in so that you can have sufficient records to be able to notice that there is something that seems to be repeating itself, not unlike the rings on a tree, you see.

I have been informed that there are certain astronomical events that occur every 26,000 years that accelerate the passing or the transition of the cycle. Do you have records on it?

Thank you. I will tell you this much: The thing that happens at the end is that the soul, in whichever body it is in, confronts itself, literally turns inside out, which is the best way to describe it within your dimensional context, and renews itself. But in order to turn itself inside out, it must literally look at itself clearly and say, "This is what I am." You are experiencing this somewhat now in the next few years. You don't always have this in conscious knowledge because the soul of yourself and your mind are not fully joined yet. But this is why sometimes you will feel uncomfortable, or things would not seem to work, or there will be a shaking inside of you. It is because your souls are examining themselves. They do not always like what they see. I know your question desires astronomical proofs, but I do not feel that this is something that you will gain from. Other than, of course, the sunspots, as you call them, and the passing of certain large objects near your planet – essentially things that will cause you to feel that the end is near. And in the eclipse that occurs, of your world eclipsing Mars. That is really astrological, but that is a science from my point of view.

I was just going to expand on his question; it is not just the end of a 26,000-year cycle, but the end of the cycle going around the galaxy. It is the end of many, many cycles, isn't it?

Yes, that is what is going to allow the shift to a 33,000-year cycle. Cycle in this case just means how many times a human being sitting at rest will breathe in a given minute. When you shift into the 33,000-year cycle you will breathe a little less and still be comfortable. It is obscure, but just to give you an example.

The other related question is, do you have any information from your perspective on the 11:11?

11:11, the Doorway to Access Your Body Knowledge

It is a time, as indicated, that the soul must look and say, "This is what I am." But it is also when a soul must state, "It is time to use all that I am." So if you are going to recombine your DNA, you are going to have to use the cellular structures of your body in the way they were originally intended. Every cell in your body is like a brain in its own right. It has all knowledge that can ever be useful to a physical person. So this next doorway, as you perceive it, is going to allow you to begin to access your body knowledge. Those who would pray to go elsewhere will have less knowledge. Use your body knowledge; go inside to find your strength and inspiration. Why do so many religions say, go inside and meditate quietly. It all has to do with the body's knowledge. Even a hair knows all. You will have to develop your mystical nature, but you can do that.

Mars, Where Earth Tribes Auditioned

Is there any information that you can tell us about what is supposed to be coming to us from Mars, and some of the explorations there?

These enigmatic pictures and so on on Mars?

Yes. Cydonia, the city of Cydonia we've discovered.

I know right where that is. That has been asked often. This is the face of prototype man. Mars, being very closely connected to Earth . . . your civilization, as you know it here, was tried out there first. The tribal peoples of your world where you live now tried out there first, like someone would audition. That's why the face looks the way it does. It is not really trying to show you who created you so much as how they wanted you to look; that's what the face was in terms of the mathematical anomalies. All of this is to show you the similarities between yourselves and Mars. Mars and you are like that [two fingers together]. Your race will undoubtedly colonize Mars – publicly, if you like – in the next 23 years or so, and *then* will come much fun. Because you will find and be able to (not too difficultly, fairly easily) interpret certain things found there that will tell all about Earth history and the development of human beings and the races of man. And there will be a Mars. And it will be kept a secret for not very long because many different political governments will go there. But you know that you are being prepared for this now.

I will say this further thing: Some of the actual physical matter of Mars is involved on your planet. Several of the craters found around your planet that have been from impacts from elsewhere, some of this matter was taken from Mars and, almost as one were to throw a stone, sent to your planet so there would be this actual physical connection between you. Because what is not physically represented on your world does not work very well to have coding within your physical selves. You and Mars (the people who still live inside the planet there) – some of your children will know all about them.

Within 50 years or so, what a fun time that will be! There will be mutual exchanges, but right now there are some knowledges circulating about Martians, if you like. Your genetic structure is greatly influenced by them. Even the makeup of your planets is similar. It has caused some of your scientists to jump to false conclusions, that all of the planets in your solar system are made of similar matter. But it is not so. It was understood early on that you would be attracted to Mars. Even though you be attracted to Venus, it is not realistic to colonize it.

Your genetic structures are highly influenced by Martian *culture*. It may sound strange, but culture, an actual society's culture which is quite ancient, can influence genetics. Some of your memories, some of your dreams, and the color red are all Martian. Your passionate nature has to do with Martian culture from the past, which somewhat made the surface of the planet less livable. But the inside is still livable, and they are passionate yet. They are not at all intellectual, and are away from those things.

Were we created by a different group than those that tore apart our DNA to make us unknowledgeable? Was there a period of time when we had our full DNA and then at a certain point someone altered it?

Mars Sacrificed Its Surface for Your Evolvement

You know, in the beginning when you and Mars (which are really twin planets, and why many of you keep searching for twin parts of yourself) understood that your societies must develop individually, some of your more warlike structures (that which could cooperate more with evil) were taken to Mars where they were processed, you might say. This was an act of love, if you like. The Martian culture sacrificed its surface self in order that you might evolve to be able to survive polarity to the extent that you have. So some of the DNA structure you refer to is on Mars now. When your society in the year 2000-2001 begins to have regular journeys there, they will bring things back, some surface stuff. And just by doing that they will bring back some of that energy of flirtation with evil. But you will have been prepared by then.

That is why this time is so critical for you. You are confronting that inside you and will be shedding much of it, albeit that it will take form, but you will shed it by that form. When they bring that back it will not just be a negative influence, because by that time you would have shed it. An evil that you would call the bastard child will then be able to find its way home and will leave your home. It will take 1000 years to leave it, but it will leave.

The Martian expeditions are the most important thing your scientists, astronauts, cosmonauts will do. Even some of the matter which has been brought back before this has helped.

It has allowed you to confront some of the baser elements of yourself and to become involved in this shedding of that skin that attracts corrupted power. It is almost like an inoculation, that Martian matter. The genetic structure then will be more united. You will have an influence in your atmosphere from Mars. You will also have a greater understanding for your passion. And even a greater spectrum of the color red, having more to do with rose or pink colors, which are not felt as vibrantly on the surface of your planet as they will be by 2001.

And your genetic structure will alter to allow the rose pink hue, which is rightly described as being associated with self-love, in your physical lives. It will only take about 50 years to really have an impact, but it will be beneficial.

Is this a part of our history that we have never heard of before, that certain more aggressive elements on our planet went on spaceships to Mars or reincarnated there or what? At some point in our history were groups of aggressive, warring earth people sent to Mars or went there? I have never heard about that.

Mars Took Part of Your Karma and Genetics

At the beginning of your development it was as if Mars took some of your karma, because your souls came here, you know, from someplace else. Mars took some of that so you would be able to accomplish your intended purpose here, which was to resolve many things as well as to create a passionate society that would love discovery of all kinds. If you had done this without Mars, you would have surely blown up this planet as well. The Martian culture, it was like the light side and dark side. In the beginning the Martian culture clearly understood that they were more in balance, and they understood what had to be done. So they sacrificed and took some of the baser elements of your genetics and some of your karma. So it wasn't so much that there were ships going back and forth. We are talking here about something at the planetary level. Planets, after all, are just larger cells in the body of the Creator.

What about the original topic of the evening? What have we not asked about because we don't know what to ask? Are there other buried records that will be helpful to us? Buried doesn't have to be in the earth. What else is on this planet that is not available to us whether it is buried, in the air or that we can't see that we need to know as part of this end time? Is there anything you can tell us that we haven't known to ask about?

I can hint only. Remember, The Order is electricity. All right? What do you suppose the God self is?

Electromagnetic!

Thank you. The combination of electricity and magnetism - magnetism being feminine and electricity being masculine. To understand your destiny you must embrace the electromagnetic properties of your physical self. I am hinting, but you have to ask the question.

Well, we spent forever on our masculine dynamic side. Are you saying now to turn

to the feminine receptive, which would equal the magnetic side?

You didn't spend forever on the masculine, but only in recent history. You started out balanced pretty much because Mars helped you out so much. *But for you to understand what is missing you must explore your physical bodies.* Some people have said the body is a temple, but in reality the body is *the* Temple. All the missing knowledge, all the source of that power which is granted to mystics as well as being the focus of the Creator, is everyone's physical body, not all at once but even you, you, you—all of you. Your physical bodies are the place to look for true knowledge.

You know, some people who have explored acupuncture, very little is known in the West (what you call yourselves) about this. You think acupuncture is only for better health, but some explored it as a means to gain knowledge. This is why in the East golden needles were used, because that is such an ancient and important spiritual metal. You can use acupuncture to explore the known meridians (and those that are not so well known but can be better known) if you use your pictures from space and follow the pattern of the rivers, and superimpose the Amazon River pattern as seen from space onto the spine of an average human being of any race, male or female. Use that as a means to explore new meridians, and you will unlock the code key that will enable your inspiration to come straight into your conscious mind and allow your conscious mind to interpret the electromagnetic energy of inspiration, which is the basis of the Creator. So all you acupuncturists out there who would like to do something new and have an adventure in true consciousness, have fun!

Is the heart the key to this transformation? Is it the center of the magnetic power where we can begin to integrate these two?

Yes, the heart is in its own right the receiver of the feminine, but as a physical thing it is also the producer of the masculine effect. Doing your heart's desire, you become aware of your heart's desire because of the magnetic. You *do* your heart's desire because of the electrical. You become aware of someone you love; you make love because of your electrical. That is the example I would use, since it is something that is dear to all of you, understandably so.

Have you ever been physical?

Not in the way you would understand it, but I am physical. In my dimension I feel like substance.

But you haven't explored our game down here?

If I did I would be biased and I would not make much of a

recordkeeper. Well, I have given what I came here to do.

Will we talk to you again someday?

If you like, and for tonight I will say, you are important children to the Creator, never forget that. No matter how high or how low your life may seem to be, it is really true the Creator always is interested in you and feels all of you all the time through your hearts and thence through your bodies.

Goodnight!

40

Comments on the Montauk Project

Zoosh through Robert Shapiro
December 17, 1992

I am Zoosh speaking. What do you want to talk about?

I have just read the book,* The Montauk Project: Experiments in Time, *by Preston Nichols. Could you comment about the time-travel experiments that took place in Montauk, Long Island, until 1983?

These experiments were strapped by a particular burden. The people who designed the machinery knew they had missing parts. Initially the parts were missing simply because electronics hadn't reached a level of technological advancement sufficient to make certain parts practically feasible. But there were other parts that they knew were missing.

Danger to the "Timenauts"

They had something like a puzzle with some pieces missing, and they knew it. So they recognized that they were dealing with a limited form of experiment and therefore the experiment's subjects were not told of the high degree of risk. Astronauts, for example, will normally know that the risk is there. But these "timenauts," shall we say, were not told because the scientists – especially the people at the very top – were fully aware that there was an 80% chance the person would be disrupted in some way and a 50% chance that they would never return to their point of origin or even to the general time in which they lived. So we are talking about very irresponsible behavior.

On the one hand, one might say these were like children with a new toy; they couldn't wait to use it, so they tore up the house in the process. On the other hand, we must recognize that it would have been possible to proceed with this experiment slowly and carefully. The cooler heads (who did not prevail) encouraged a very slow experimentation using only objects first for a long time. They urged that human subjects not be used until the objects came back absolutely safe and until it could be proven that the molecular structure of the object was exactly the same as before it was sent. That was the rub.

The objects that were used eventually came back all right—you know, test objects, such as a book—but they only *looked* all right. When tests were done on their molecular structure, they were not all right. The molecular structure was, we shall say, volatile. It would break down within two or three days and the object would either disappear or turn to dust. This was never revealed to the timenauts who became the human subjects. It must be stated clearly that the *intention* of the experiment was considered more important than those who gave their lives during this experiment.

Now, it may be that variations of this experiment have been started up again, but they are being done in a limited way because the funding is not there. The means of obtaining funding have become, we shall say, a little more responsible. Experimentation is being done on an extremely limited basis even though the electronic technology now exists to create in a very small package what used to take up a whole room. Equipment can now be carted around in a box the size of a portable television set. The connections do not even have to use wires; they are like suction cups or pads that fit on the body of a person or even a chair, for example, or the time vehicle, as it might be called—or the time conveyance, as it is actually called. There are no wires necessary. This is an advantage.

Altering the Past

Nevertheless, what is being done now is greatly scaled back. Those who conducted the experiment attempted to justify it by saying it was a national emergency, that one could go back in time and alter things to the benefit of the nation. That is how they got such a big budget to start with. In time (to make the pun) it was clearly understood by those who handed out the money that the risks were too great.

It was true that some timenauts were able to go back in time and make slight alterations. As they moved back in time, their bodies were greatly upset: it was like having an electrical charge running through their bodies all the time. It would take a supreme effort of will for them simply to touch their faces because there would be sparks and they would get shocked. It was very uncomfortable – really extremely difficult.

They were able to make a few slight changes in the course of certain events. The changes were slight, like simply encouraging someone to move five steps to the right, five steps to the left, something like that. Ridiculously slight, one might assume on the surface, but having such extreme ramifications that when that event was changed in the present, those who handed out the money decided that it was not safe to proceed any further.

Experiment Funded by Nazis

The book says that in the first years, it was funded by the billions of dollars from Nazi Germany. It that true?

Well, one must allow for the fact that most of the money the National Socialist German Workers' Party (as they called themselves) pillaged from various places was never recovered. It was only by a stroke of fate and luck that the art treasures in the Louvre were largely spared.

Did these guys get the money?

They did get the money. About 70% of the money came from the National Socialist Party, which you must understand had the attitude that the timenauts were expendable. After all, from the point of view of the people involved in that party, anybody was expendable as long as it was not themselves. That was never quite balanced; however they were not the epitome of balance. So yes, about 70% of it came from there, but the rest of the money came from various governments that were in cooperation.

The Top People

Who really granted it? Who were the top people?

I want to tell you, but this organization still exists. I will say that certain people involved in the creation of the international policing organization called Interpol were influential in the obtaining of the funds.

Are we talking about some of the 13 men who "own" the planet and make the decisions here?

I don't really like to say that they own the planet. They do not own the forces of the planet, they do not own the people of the planet. Having control of the financial resources of a planet does not

mean that you own the planet.

Okay, I didn't say it right. Can you trace it back to those 13 men we call the ones in control?

To some extent, they are in control. They did not fund it, but the experiments went forward with their benign approval. Now, benign approval is quite a bit different from direct approval. Direct approval is, "All right, go ahead." Benign approval means they did not speak up, nor did they object. They knew what was going on, but they did not interfere. So one might say that is benign approval. They did not fund it.

You must understand that people at this level have a great deal of knowledge. They already had the knowledge that this experiment was attempting to learn. So why fund something when you already know the outcome? That is why benign approval simply means that you turn your back on it. You allow it to go on and say nothing.

Are the memories of the people whose words are in this book fairly accurate?

Fairly accurate, yes, within about 2% or 3% in most places. One must allow for a certain amount of changing a word here and there, which changes a meaning. But at best the book is 95% accurate. At worst, in certain places it is 80% accurate. One must understand, however, that it is important to indicate somewhere in the book, even if it is a preamble or something that appears afterwards, that the intention of the publication of this material is not to blame anyone, but to simply illuminate and offer suggestions about what might have been and give warnings that certain things are not to be tampered with . . . because *wiser beings than thou know more of these things than you do.*

Well, they got what they called the Delta Time Antenna from Orion and some of the earlier technologies from Sirius. So at what governmental level were these interactions going on?

One must remember that the experiments took place on Earth, did they not? [*Yes.*] So it took place in a particular geographic locale, did it not? [*Yes.*] One does not do experiments like this without being detected. Therefore it was necessary to involve the governments in the places that had authority over where the experiments took place.

Yes, but everybody denied it.

Well, of course. But one might deny something one day, then years later say that this may have gone on, but you had no personal knowledge of it – the way a lawyer might answer a question.

One particular thing that interested me was that they went beneath the pyramid on Mars and dismantled the solar system's defense so that possibly negative ETs could come to assist them. Is that correct?

I would have to say that certain equipment was removed, rather than dismantled. "Dismantled" sounds like they took the whole thing apart. However, one must remember that it is the nature of science to be capricious. By capricious I mean that you might do something under the mantle of the studying of science and totally disrupt a system without having the *intention* of disrupting that system. This does not make it all right. But certain things were removed under the auspices of scientific research, and that had a serious impact on the ability of this system to deflect asteroids and other objects that could fly through space on a particular tangent and come close to or strike the Earth or, for that matter, any inhabited planet within the solar system.

Were they being used, maybe without their knowing?

The system was in use when it was dismantled. Now, it is easy to repair the system. The system could be repaired like that [snaps fingers]. But it was felt by other individuals who were involved in the creation of this system or who were its custodians that it would be simpler to have vehicles do essentially what that unmanned device did rather than repair it and have someone dismantle it again or shoot at it. If you use a reflector it is impossible to shoot at it regardless of where it's located.

A Different Defense System

So some of the positive ETs are now flying around and doing the same thing?

Yes, acting as that kind of deflector.

What did these scientists think they were doing when they dismantled it?

They thought they were taking apart a weapons system that could be used against Earth. So one might say that the people who took it apart thought they were doing a good deed. After all, if one studied the system from afar, it could seem that the system would fire rays from time to time and things would be destroyed. Something like that would frighten a person.

The Lost Timenauts

These people who were used by the men who ran this project — the book alludes to possibly 10,000 to 13,000 of them — what happened to them? They died someplace in another time?

Some of them are still in a life in other times. One must understand that.

Functioning properly?

Well, not 100%. At best, 90-95%. This would mean their sleep states would be disrupted all the time —very difficult. They can be assisted, but because the system used to transport them was incomplete, the only way to repair them would be through the use of highly advanced technological devices that would reorient the cellular structure of their bodies. You must understand that most of those who were lost went *back* in time; thus those systems weren't there unless they were from extraterrestrial sources.

Almost none of those people who went forward in time returned, and I'll tell you why. They didn't want to! But you must understand that the people in the present had no knowledge of that. The knowledge they got about other times was from the people who returned.

Some people, even some of the upper-level scientists, went

forward in time. They are there now and in good condition, and they have, from their point of view, escaped this terrible thing. And since they are living in civilizations in the future that have a more balanced, more humanistic moral value, they have shed all of the things from the past that were hurtful to themselves or to others; they are redeemed.

Great! What about this picture? It says new recruits were sent to a place in 6737 A.D. to look at a golden horse with symbols on it. What meaning would that have? Were they just being acclimated?

The Golden Horse

No, I would not say that. One might go forward into the future, pick something up and bring it back. That was the standard thing: "Wherever you go, pick something up and bring it back." Of course, the idea would be that whatever was picked up and brought back, whether it be from the future or the past or from some point in space, the absolute knowledge was there. Whatever was brought back was only going to last for two or three days. They would have to study it as quickly as possible, then it would disintegrate because the system was impure, as it were. So that a particular object was brought back by someone and it was considered of interest, one might say, for purely greedy purposes. The object was made of gold.

In the book it says they kept sending new people forward to look at it, then come back, as if it were a very large statue.

Yes, but a smaller version was brought back initially. As in some religions, you might have a large object and then small copies would be reproduced. The small thing was brought back. People went to look at this thing for commercial reasons. Of course, they were not told this. I'm sorry to say that a lot of the motivation behind these time-travel experiments was to obtain objects or, one might say, goods. After all, if one's greed cannot be fulfilled in the present time, one could consider traveling to all times and gathering all objects of value.

Of course, there are those who can prevent this. There are larger forces at work here, you must understand. Whereas people might be allowed to do something in an incomplete state so that they cannot see the folly of what they do, they must not be allowed to do something in a complete state in which things would work very well. Time travelers would be going about all the time, as it were.

Give me an example of something in the past that was changed just a little bit and that has repercussions in the now.

The Experiment Brought on Wars

Years ago, there was an attempt to establish the United Nations under the banner of the League of Nations. The League of Nations, in the original scheme of time, was a very big success. As a result, guess what did not happen? The Second World War! Guess who didn't rise to power, even for a short time? The National Socialist Party! But they went back and changed that. They did not tell any of the scientists. The money people said, "Don't tell any of the scientists; just give them the money and say, we want you to do this little thing, with the full knowledge of what would happen." They were perfectly willing to sacrifice millions and millions of people because to them, as long as there are other people left, who cares? That's their attitude, and that's why they cannot be allowed to flower, you understand.

Our time was changed and nobody knows it?

The League of Nations would have been a success. There would have been no World War II, there would have been no Korean War, no Vietnam War, none of this. This gives you a little idea of what can be done when one fools around with time. This was allowed because it was important for people, the scientists, even up to the very top level, to see the *folly* of changing time. It was important that they understood this. Of course, they couldn't change it *after* it was done. They wanted to, but the money people (and it was very expensive to do what was done) said, "Oh no, we don't want you to change that. We're very happy the way it is." Um-hmm.

That's when the scientists who were involved in the experiment began fleeing to the future. They said, "My God, who are these people we are working with? It's obvious what they are." That's when the people started bailing out, as they say.

All right. But there are now other ways to move through time and space that are just like beaming up on a spaceship, right?

Other Ways to Time-Travel

There are other ways. There have always been other ways. They're simply not allowed here, for the most part, except for those people who are mystics or shamans who can do these things. But they are not allowed to be mystics or shamans unless they are *balanced*. A mystic or shaman who is not in balance does not last too long.

That's traveling through time and space in a nonmaterial way, isn't it?

No, no. Mystic shamans can be taught to travel in a material fashion. They can bilocate, can go somewhere where people can touch them. They feel solid as this chair, and yet they might be someplace else at the same time.

I was thinking particularly of a woman who said her father used to go to Mars, stepping on a beam and going there. Do they do that or go on a spaceship?

No. The most advanced races that visit your planet come on flat beams of light. They travel in light. It is certainly possible for a person to do that. Most of those ships are not ships at all. They are a mass of beams that travel in light and allow themselves to be seen in this compressed form of light. Because light, of course, travels through space and time without damage, which is what the people who did this experiment knew but could not reproduce. *It can only be done with love and balance.* It cannot be done for any other purpose!

Earth Had Spaceships before the First Rockets

Then we've got spaceships that go to the Moon and Mars. Everybody knows that they went long before we sent the first rocket up, right?

Well, not everybody knows that, but some people know it.

There were functioning spaceships? There was somebody on the Moon before our rocket got there?

Exactly.

So these were the men who smiled benignly? They knew that this could be done, that they didn't have to travel through this tunnel? They could just go there?

Exactly. They knew they did not have to do the experiment. You must also understand that no matter how powerful you are with the world's financial resources, there are some things that money can't buy!! So sometimes one is prudent. You might say that they (universal forces) did not interfere in the experiment for prudent reasons. Those who conducted and financed the experiment knew these forces are noninterfering. They also knew that if these people would just lift one finger, they could crush them. So you might say there was a mutual fear pact. Even the people who had the financial resources could have been harmed if they had wanted to go back in the lives of their families, for instance, and change something. So it was exactly like a standoff.

The One Who Trained to be the Antichrist

What about the more dramatic stuff that is coming out in the next book, where Duncan went back and got some of the blood of Jesus? Duncan was trained as the Antichrist, went back and got some of the genetics of Jesus in him so that his DNA would look like that of the Shroud of Turin. But once he got that blood, everything

changed and he became Christlike. That's when they stopped the experiment.

That's just it. It doesn't make any difference how sick the plot is, once you become anointed, you're anointed, and that's it. There's no turning back.

That really happened?

It could have happened, let's say that. I'd rather say it could have happened, because it certainly was planned. One must understand that there are certain governments of certain nations — I will not name which ones — that have departments of religious warfare. The whole idea is to disrupt or control certain religions to keep them in line because those religions have political power.

Can you imagine how disruptive it would be to the Christian churches of the world if someone were to say, "We have the power to go back and make Jesus never happen, so there would never be any record of him, so you would never be able to prove anything." Eventually your church would die out. The churches would say, "This is ridiculous, we have the faith of the people." But there would be just enough concern, you see, to manipulate them. This is what the National Socialists were doing.

That is how they got cooperation from the Christian churches in Germany and other countries, not just for rounding up the Jewish people, but for rounding up priests. After all, if the church or the Pope or if the leaders of the churches had said, "The Nazi Party must be crushed. Do so to the last man," how long do you think the National Socialist German Workers' Party would have lived? About a couple of hours, maybe. But the churches were being blackmailed. Threats were being used even then to control the church.

They were being manipulated. I'm not going to say they were the most humanitarian people in charge in those days; nevertheless, they were being manipulated. This has not come out.

What's going on at Montauk right now then? Is equipment still being used?

There's equipment, but it would be equivalent to the level of experimentation that is done in a college laboratory — that's how much funding they have. No funding, no progress. Anybody in science will tell you that. So there's really comparatively no funding. They have enough to maintain the equipment they have and keep a few people on staff to do some minor experiments, but there's not any real progress going on, unfortunately.

Warning to the Experimenters

I might add that if there is ever any major attempt to improve on those experiments, certain people who live on the Earth, in the Earth and off of the Earth will destroy every piece of machinery and all of the original financial backers through uncreation. All of the original prime movers and shakers of this experiment will have their genetic codes eliminated. This is possible.

Weapons that exist in the universe that are undreamed of here. One of the minor weapons is able to reach into a person through the use of a light ray, sample his/her genetic code, uncreate it through all time, and banish the soul of that person to a small miserable place for eternity. This weapon exists.

This statement stands as a warning to all those who would do this. There is no escape from this weapon throughout time, through blackmail, nothing. Don't try. You will be eliminated throughout all time and in all ways. There is no escape. I speak to you now; this is fair warning. Pay attention.

41

More Comments on the Montauk Project

YHWH/Arthur Fanning

You're aware of the book about the Montauk Project — Arthur read it — and you know what Zoosh said about how they changed realities. I'd like to have your perspective on that experiment. Is there anything you would like to say about it or anything more we can learn from it?

Are you aware that the entities that be playing here are doing this thing for control? Indeed? Now, that is not out of the realm of knowing of the guardians of this plane. Indeed? Those beings that are playing within time, indeed, are functioning in a period where time is of fixed length, know you? As we make time collapse, they play fix, then, to be here [at a particular point in time], time be collapsed, in their "fix," they *think* they are there, yet they be in another time. Know you? Can you understand that?

Indeed, so we're sort of shifting the stick they're sliding upon. Indeed? And they come back into this time, they think. Know you? Yet they be earlier than they think they are. Know you what I mean?

Right. But you're talking about some happening right now. I was dealing with the stuff that ended in `83, but you're saying that it's ongoing.

I be say it be ongoing and I be say we be shifting the stick they be sliding on. Indeed? We be collapsing time on they, and expanding it. So they are not in the period where they think it is going to function; they are not in control. Now, what they have done and what they had planned to do did not work, and it won't. You're not going to have that authority in that third-dimensional level of activity.

Wait. I think we're talking about two separate things.

No, we're not.

Help me understand. In the book, the men who control the planet sort of just let this be. It was a group of German Nazis, but the actual men who control the planet just sort of ignored them. That's how I understood it.

Well, that is not true.

Okay, tell me how it really is.

There is a great connection now with what you call entities out of the Orion system in this thing, and they are connected with those beings that are what you term play control of planet here. Now, in order to get total control, it would be a lot easier to have *not* an expansion of consciousness evolve. So that was the reason they went back, portion. These beings, what you call grouping, play control of planet, are playing now, at this time, much infighting amongst each other. And there be one family, particularly, that has what you term sold them out, the rest, in an alliance with what you call the Orion group. Now this is not the whole constellation, know you; it's part, in that there has been sort of a rebellion. Part of this ongoing project is to get everybody in line again.

"Everybody" being the thirteen families, or humanity?

Well, the thirteen first, now, for they are into confusion. It is continuing now. It will not work for the reason that we play shifting along this time line. Know you what I mean?

Now time is also relevant to what you call your star systems, know you? It is not played the same as you play here, yet it's a concept. It has what you term distance. Yet what is occurring upon the planet Earth now involves all that you see from your planet at night, all of the star systems. It is a spiritual force; there is a Host here. Even those in other levels of activity, third-dimensional—your star systems—are aware of this force. They be, at times you say more advanced than you; they have played here; they be more technologically systemized. That does not mean they are more spiritual. They are beginning to find that out here. The force of God, whatever name you choose to call it, that first expression of isness, is directed toward this plane of activity, the planet Earth. It has what you call desired an outcoming of peace here. It will be completed.

And it will affect everything you see. It'll go out like waves, right?

Of course. And there are what you would term other earths being prepared for those that continue old game. That will be allowed. What you call school – reform school. We reform them in another school.

Is what was said by Zoosh true, that the men went back and changed the League of Nations, that we would not have had the Second World War or the Korean War, that we went into another reality? Can you comment on that?

I will say, indeed, that be a truth. There was interference along those lines. There would have been difficult time starting what you would call that war, yet it would have started anyway.

Oh, it would have started. So it didn't change history that much?

Well, it altered it enough to have advanced weaponry. Know you what you call the . . .

Oh, that's how Germany got the UFOs and all the spacecraft they had!!

Indeed, that is how be it known. Know you their weaponry was more powerful than what you be had? If there wasn't what would you call interference from all of the others, from good guys, you would have not won. That how it be.

So that's the connection with the Nationalist Socialist Party, the Nazis, and Project Montauk, because Orion gave the German workers the Delta Time Antenna, right?

Indeed.

Plus, all the rocket technology that we ended up getting...?

Well, what you have would be the technology that you have now – they took that unto them, indeed? And the cover-up be say you got it from them; be not how it came about.

42

Hitler Uncreated

Zoosh through Robert Shapiro
January 27, 1993

The last time I discussed this subject I gave certain people fair warning, speaking through time. This time I am reluctant to be the spokesperson but it is my unfortunate duty to pronounce and make the comments. I have been asked to do so by those who execute these orders.

Those individuals from the National German Socialist Workers' Party escaped to a future time when they could be influential. Some of these people have moved into positions of influence in Serbia and they will now be eliminated. I have heard earlier in time, according to your time sequence, about 50 hours ago, that all trace of their genetic and soul life on Earth, as well as in the stars and all dimensions, will be collapsed.

The machine used to do this does not exist in this dimension but is a branch of a weapon used originally by the being known as Jehovah. That weapon, referred to in Biblical times, has the capacity to uncreate. Those beings who escaped to what is now Serbia are going to be uncreated throughout all time. It is my unfortunate duty to report this; this is what has been told to me by the official executioner

Now that that is over, what would you like to talk about?

Well, do you want to expand on that so that we can understand it? You're saying someone from the 1970-83 Montauk project came to Serbia in 1993?

No. Someone from the middle 1940's came to what is now Serbia – several someones actually, about three or four. Most of them escaped to the far-flung future where they were immediately anointed by the presence of balance and Love in those times and they were changed. But a few of them escaped to the present Serbia and are attempting to reestablish the National German Socialist Workers' Party and its agenda in your now times.

Can you say who they are or what their duties are or how they're serving? How would we know them or recognize them? The reason I ask is that if they are uncreated, we won't even have known they were here.

They will leave the blemish of their having been here so that others will recognize the folly of such pursuits. But they will be otherwise uncreated. There were several of the scientists and one politically known figure. The political figure — I don't wish to say the name — but he has been known by the name Hitler.

Hitler is in Serbia right now?

Not in the form you would recognize him in, but in a form that is recognizable only to those who knew him very well. He is alive at the moment, but in about 35 minutes he will cease to exist.

You know people like this perform a service or function, albeit a negative one. He had the opportunity to go into the far-flung future like the others and be anointed, but it was difficult for him to give up the power. He wanted Borman to go with him but Borman did not trust the device so Borman fled elsewhere.

Is Borman still alive?

He has passed over.

All right this is an added flavor. Did the men who ran this experiment in the 1980's go back and get some of those participants from the Second World War and take them into the future?

Remember where the money came from to begin the project? Who put the initial money in? You remember?

Of course! It came from that $10 billion taken off that train and was from the National German Socialist Workers' Party, right?

Yes. And they do not make investments lightly, to make a pun. They had a stake in the matter, a motive. They expected to get their money's worth.

You know the body discovered in the bunker was never proven to be Hitler's body. There was, after all, no real way to prove it. It was well understood by the allies that there was every reason to believe that this person was still alive. But, after all, it is rather difficult to find someone who doesn't exist in your time anymore. This was a rather neat escape.

How many of these people from the German leadership of World War II went into

the future?

About three from the leadership and a couple of scientists who had knowledge of how to work the machine went along.

They went to Montauk, New York?

They went to the future.

But the machine was in Montauk, New York.

That was not the only machine. You must understand that the National German Socialist Workers' Party, as I am calling it, was so far in advance of the technology of the times that they were capable of producing a much smaller version of the machine. Also, it was possible to take objects through time. You could take something through time and use it as a model, then use the components that already existed in that time and construct a duplicate of that model with the knowledge that the model would disintegrate. So, it's as if you would bring something from the 80's into the times of the 40's, take it apart, see how it works and understand the pieces. You would examine them completely, reproduce it in the 40's out of available materials and then bring another version back and put it together along the same lines. But you would have to use materials from the time. That's how it was done. They traveled with a portable unit.

How did the leaders of the Nazi Party get this technology?

It was delivered to them by people in the 80's going back in time.

Then they never got it first from ETs . . .they got it from their own people?

It was incomplete from the ETs. After all, if you were an extraterrestrial and you were going to give something to someone whom you wanted to be beholden to you, you would want to control it; at the very least, you would make certain that it would be incomplete or that the range of motion of the people who would have the device would be extremely limited. You would make yourself valuable in that way because you would have the capacity, by having the complete machine, to travel throughout all time and all space. You cannot give people something like that if you expect to control them —because then what do they need you for, yes?

Who specifically gave this technology to the Germans, and when?

I'm not going to name names. We can never do that, you know. The person is alive. It was done in 1983. It is very easy to do this, you know. They went back in time. It was never intended that the person known as Hitler (although that wasn't his actual given name) die in the bunker. That was a sham from the beginning. All of the stuff portrayed about him in the bunker, that is all fiction.

So what happened in 1945 before they came back from 1983 to move him forward? Wasn't there another timeline?

There are always timelines.

Can you explain how that works?

It's easy enough to do. You can go back in time to a point and change something in that point in time. From that point on, you can't change it anymore if you're coming from a fixed place. Say this is your point of origin. Here's the place you want to change something. If you go to that precise time, say five o'clock in the afternoon on a particular day, you're not going to be able to make that journey back to five o'clock in the afternoon on that particular day again. You're going to have to go 4:59 or 5:01, something like that. You can't go to that precise time, because you've already done something in that precise time.

But you have to go close to that precise time so that you can access the window. There are some windows that are easier and safer to travel through than others. That doesn't mean you can't go at nine o'clock at night, but it might not be as safe. So you go through the windows that are established, using the parameters of the safest possible experiences that you have with your machine, whatever they are.

In that reality, what happened to Hitler, before it was changed? What would have happened to Hitler if it hadn't been changed?

You would have smelled him out to Chile.

What changed since you talked on this subject a month ago? No one has used the machine since then. What is it that has caused this judgment, this disintegration?

What's happening in Serbia is largely the result of the agenda of the National German Socialist Workers' Party. That which is going on in Serbia, the attempt to commit genocide against the Moslem people, that is entirely a National German Socialist Workers' Party agenda. It is one thing to have a war. It is another thing to transport an agenda from another time into your present.

So are we going to see in the paper tomorrow morning that someone who has been looked upon as a leader is dead?

No. Because it is as if this person is behind the scenes. Suppose you're running your country like they are running Serbia and you would like to continue to have the good life, as good as you can have anyway, given the circumstances, and someone shows up with an unlimited amount of funds and a guarantee that no matter what you do, you can get away.

Also, because of being able to appear and disappear and wow you with that kind of technology, bring through weapons from another time by going into the future, grabbing what they can and coming back – of course, it disintegrates in a couple of days, but the person doesn't know that – they could make themselves pretty impressive.

So Hitler not only came into Serbia in latter 1992, but he brought his technology with him? And he couldn't use it, but he could have used it to go off further into the future.

No, there's a limit as to how far he could go without being anointed. Because future civilizations, not that far in the future, don't have this kind of good/bad polarity. There's a limit to how far he could go.

What year is that?

Once you get past 2013, the world as you know it will be making major strides toward at least a world order if not a world problem-solving method for government. They will have a means of solving problems that is nondestructive. The world shrinks every day. People are simply not going to stand for wars that affect others.

What's going to happen in the not-too-distant future, to make a prediction if you like, is that a thermonuclear device is going to be detonated. They are out there. I'm sorry to say it, but they are shockingly simple to manufacture if you have the right materials. It will be a rudimentary device, and it won't so much get the people it was aimed at, but will just blow up somewhere and people will never really know what happened. When that happens – it won't happen in this country, all right – but when that happens, people are going to sit up and take notice and there's going to be a demand that this kind of stuff be stopped – a world-wide demand.

That is essentially going to propel a world order into place. The United Nations will become very influential, but it will not be the center of the world order. There will be a struggle for power, but it won't last long. The United States is somewhat neutralized due to its position of being strapped for cash. Since we are in a time in our economic history where everybody is somewhat strapped for cash, people will not just be firing off missiles that they, in their minds, can't afford to shoot off.

How much detail can you give us about this explosion, as to time, place, dates? And can you explain thermonuclear for us?

Nuclear bomb. The device will go off within the next 3 1/2 years. Those who detect it may not tell people about it. In one sense, it will be very hard to cover up, but it won't be impossible. After all, if you had an ax to grind and you wanted to keep your thermonuclear devices around . . . can you imagine if you wanted to keep your bombs around, and one went off in the hands of people who did not really know what they were doing? You would know that there would be one heck of a public outcry to get these things out of the hands of everyone. You might be inclined to try to cover it up by saying there was an accident in a nuclear power station or something like that.

But it will be found out, right?

Yes, it will come out, because there will be a lot of radiation and it will be detected. It's what they call in weapons circles a small, dirty device.

Made by a small third-world country?

It's not safe to say that because people would jump to conclusions and just "bomb it back to the stone age."

So that just because Montauk is not functioning does not mean that this capability that we've developed is not now available?

Exactly.

Who else has this capability and is it being used elsewhere right now?

There are a couple other portable machines. One is in the hands of people whom I've referred to before as the influential men – they have one. One is also essentially in a storage locker. It is undiscovered. Someone grabbed it, all right? It is there. That person died and there it sits, innocuous, in a storage locker of a bus station off the beaten track, as it were. Even if someone were to look at it and to open it up, since the device is disguised, they would think that it was some kind of a radio transmitter. It looks rather like an old-fashioned radio transmitter and would probably find its way into a junk shop. There's a good chance that no one would ever find out what it was. They'd take it apart and that would be the end of it.

Shall we go look for it?

No, don't. Don't go look for it. After all, the device is basically a mischief-making piece of machinery.

Some friends were recently a half mile down into the Montauk base where they saw the cages. Is that where they kept the people they sent out on the time travels?

I'm sorry to say it isn't. It's where they kept people they brought back. Of course they didn't stay in one piece for long.

Why did they bring people back?

You must remember that what you are dealing with here is not people who are reasonable or who are heart-centered. It would be very easy to go to a civilization and appear magical. Most people would run away but some people might walk over. You can walk over, take their hand, pull them toward you and take them back.

For what purpose? To talk to them?

No. To see if they're different.

To see if they would not disintegrate?

That's right. And also to check them to see if they have diseases and if not, why not. Do I make myself clear?

Like a special immune system or something that we could learn from?

Yes. How would you do that if you were a scientist and you did not care about human life?

Montauk.

That's right.

Are any of the people who participated or any of the leaders who made the decisions about these barbarous acts still alive in our time?

No. Nobody is alive in your time who participated in the leadership of this project. There are technicians alive but no one in a decision-making capacity is alive in your time. And the ones who are alive in the future are changed – benign.

So this Hitler is/was the last one, then?

Yes. He doesn't have much time left. You know if he had gone another 50 or 100 years into the future it would have been all right.

Is there any way we can track this? Will it ever be in the newspapers?

Not that I know of. It does mean, however, that the cash reserve for Serbia will dry up. There will be a limit to how much they can get their hands on now.

Where was he getting the cash?

Let's just say that the National German Socialist Workers' Party has its means. Think of all of the stuff that was looted from people in World War II. It didn't just fall down a hole somewhere.

Now there is no one left who can access it?

Oh yes, there are people who can access it in modern times, yes. They did not simply cease to exist. They have an organization. They are not particularly active and they are not particularly dangerous. They are, as you might say, waiting. Oddly enough, they did not actually believe that there was any chance for success in Serbia because of the world at this time. If they had the opportunity, they would flee into the past when they could really be influential, from their point of view. They know that their days are numbered insofar as going into the future.

But they didn't know that Hitler had this machine that would have been able to do it?

They did not know that, no.

They never told anybody?

No, no.

And where is the machine?

The machine will go with him.

Of the machines that are out there right now, can you say if they're in a specific country?

We cannot tell you the "mischief" it would cause to do that. Can you imagine what some people would pay and what they would do to get a machine like this? Some people would stop at nothing. Worse yet, some people would attempt to destroy them, and they would stop at nothing. No, it is not good to say. I would say, though, that the one in the bus station is absolutely innocuous. It's in a suitcase, it just looks like an old suitcase. It's nothing. It looks very much like an old-fashioned radio transmitter and is disguised to look that way, too. In a pinch it could even operate that way, but not very well.

Well, there's no one finding it who would know how to operate it.

Fortunately, that's right. At some point, you know, when no one comes to claim things in bus lockers, eventually they open them up. But it's surprising how long they can sit there.

How long has it been there?

A couple of years.

Is there any future for the National German Socialist Workers' Party in a detrimental way or would it be benign?

In the future they would like to create, they have a glorious future, from their point of view. But in the future that is 99.9% likely to happen, they do not have the future they would like to have. They may become, for a short amount of time, a vocal party. They may, through use of their economic resources, be able to influence others. But in terms of their actual likeliness of remaining a viable political, military, terroristic, influential force, they don't have much of a future.

What country are we talking about? Where are they?

They're everywhere. There are a few countries they haven't been in. They weren't in the former Soviet Union, but now they're there.

Prelude to Chapter 43

Dear Friends,

Some of the information in the following section of this book related to the Sinister Secret Government is not easy for the mind and heart to accept, but in our commitment to bring you the truth about what is really happening on this highly polarized Explorer Race-training planet, on which we're completing graduate school in how to be creators, the truth has both positive and negative facets and energies – although this month they seem more outrageously positive and negative than usual! The secret to graduating from creator school is quite simple in theory: make all choices from the heart, based on love for all beings and all of creation including self, make all choices based on the highest good for all concerned. But when you throw in to that simple formula the subconscious, one's false beliefs based on judgments from past and future experiences, habits and addictions, desires and hormones, our linear mind and all of the stuff we are resolving for ourselves and the rest of creation, the plot thickens.

There are new elements being added to this global soap opera, which is titled "Can these Earth humans attain atomic technology without blowing up the planet or parts of it; resolve the previously unresolvable issues left over from previous creations; find a use for negativity as itself (as curiosity and a lust for life and adventure); do what no sentient being has ever done before – live in the physical body as it transforms from third to fourth dimension while the human focus changes from physical me/mind to less dense physical we/heart/soul and do all of this before the planet they have polluted becomes unlivable and the very school they need for graduation is trashed?"

Now, in the midst of living in the above mellow drama, we are told that the tyrants who are attempting to control all of humanity are getting more vicious and powerful. Remember Don Juan saying that if you want to advance quickly, find a tyrant, as the challenge of overcoming the resistance will make you stronger. Well, we are allowing some highly creative tyrants here.

Zoosh through Robert Shapiro says, "It's all in the timing." We have been receiving and printing information about the sinister secret government (SSG) since the beginning of the Journal, but it is only now, when a picture of the Hale-Bopp comet with an "object" traveling with it was posted on the Internet, that we are able to get the information for this issue. The Hale-Bopp comet has been photographed since at least mid-'95, but only now have we asked about it because of the photo and some of the information from the remote viewers. This process seems to indicate that since we have a very positive, powerful source of help from the light, we can now be told of the increase in potential aggravation by the dark side.

We must remember to put all of this in perspective—that these energies are reflections of us, that the SSG can only exist because of our energies of fear, anger, doubt, judgment and so on. Zoosh says that if we would eliminate our cynical attitude and regain our expectation of goodness and hope, we would cut the power of the SSG by 40%! I am old enough to remember when America was a more positive, pleasant place, when we trusted our neighbors and the government, believed in truth in advertising and picked up hitchhikers without fear, when being a good samaritan was a way of life. Now two generations have been fed the big lies of fear, lack of hope and "expect the worst" since birth as part of the SSG's master plan to totally control the population, leaving us in need of a severe attitude adjustment.

The good news is that the 32nd-dimensional lightbeings inhabiting the vehicle traveling with the Hale-Bopp comet, who are here to help us get through these times, are also our reflections. When we stop and remember that we are lightbeings, immortal and totally, in our natural state, loving aspects of the creator, who chose to participate in this training as part of creator's master plan to train His replacement, then we can play our roles with zest and humor without getting caught up either in the e-band of humans who still think they are the parts they play in the drama, or in the emanations of the SSG, who want us to follow their script instead of letting us write our own.

So read this section with a light heart to get the whole picture, but don't give away your power to your fears. "We're given only what we can handle" is a basic creator-training rule. The point here, as I understand it, is to be aware of all of the old control and manipulation energies that the SSG is mirroring to us (we have all played those roles in other times, other places and probably even more creatively) so that we can see the consequences of those thoughts and desires. We must release all such energies before we can move into 4D, let alone before we can be entrusted with the power of creation.

We are now at 3.47 on the dimensional scale to 4.0 and beyond. As Yhwh through Arthur Fanning says, "Arise your vibrations" and intend to move to 3.55, where ssg-type energies are like an old, half-remembered bad movie.

All of us at the Sedona Journal of Emergence, Light Technology Publishing and Mission Possible Commercial Printing wish you a glorious New Year filled with light, love, joyous movement in consciousness and, of course, adventure.

O'Ryin Swanson, Publisher

Zoosh through Robert Shapiro

December 3, 1996

Last August you said we had reached 3.49, but recently you said we were at 3.47. Why the discrepancy?

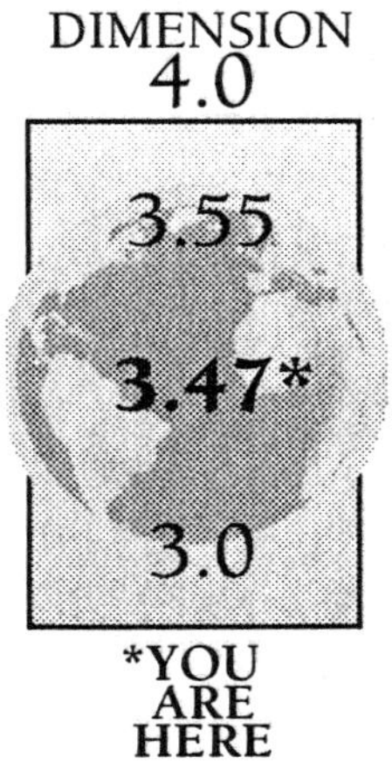

This relates not only to the nefarious activities of the SSG, but also to a degree of reluctance to move forward.

Remember that you were hurtled forward, jumping quite a bit, then there was a little vibration and you started creeping forward. Some souls here are reluctant to express the responsibility for creations, even their own, so there is a slight move backward. Granted, the SSG has mostly to be "credited," but you cannot go back any further than 3.47. They can drag you that far back, but that's it. To go forward you must be pulled forward, but you must also push.

ASSISTANCE TO HUMANITY

- Our original heart energy, kept for eons inside the planet so we could stay in polarity, is now being released increasingly rapidly.
- This ship is coming to align you unto joy. These beings come with authority. As they move through systems, the energy is so powerful that humanity automatically aligns to their thought. You will not have the ability to think the game of not [love] but the way they hold the thought.
- We're bringing forth more light, and it will activate the brain, perhaps causing pressure in the temples. You exist in here [soul], your greater force inside the body in safety. It can align to the thoughts of your lightbody around you. Vibrate that lightbody, quicken it and feel that inside the soul area; the flesh will change its texture and become permeable for both energies to move freely through.
- In the next ten years, humanity will begin to understand that the body and the planet are for the attainment of your spiritual wisdom, building power within the soul forces of the

wisdom of spirit, not dogma or building a church or having the only truth.

- You're getting assistance from many beings, many energies. Even some ETs will start to show up to alter some of these thought patterns to get you thinking in another way.
- These are challenging times. Later you are going to learn that the only important thing is your spiritual wisdom: the wisdom of your soul accumulated in the darkest of times and the happiest of times and your accumulated spiritual power, which will take you into forever.
- A vehicle is headed this way that has your extraterrestrial brothers and sisters who are working with the Creator, radiating energy that is your natural knowledge, like an inoculation for you to remember who you are and drop the drama of your personality. The purpose is to make a giant leap forward to get past the 3.50 mark, but you have to do it. This energy will be radiated toward you, but you have to catch it and use it.

WHAT YOU CAN DO

- Let go of cynicism (see illustration), thereby eliminating 40% of the power the SSG is drawing from us.
- Release anxiety at moments in your everyday life by projecting gold light physically (blow it out) toward those who stimulate that anxiety.
- Constantly remind yourself how much you have in common with others, letting go of perceived differences.
- Practice feeling love as heat in the chest. When you can hold this heat, add the feeling of gold light. This is true transformative alchemy. In a group, it multiplies dramatically. As you physicalize the light, it enters the particles in your body, then the constantly moving mass of Earth, cycling through others.
- Send love/gold light to the beings on TV whenever you hear about violence.
- For your protection, project gold light at the SSG. If you do it *physically,* it's ten times more powerful than *imagining* gold light. In a meditation blow it toward them. It's much more powerful.
- In your meditations move around (in groups or alone), feeling and broadcasting the gold and white light. This will integrate the light into the physical world. When you are not physically active, the light will simply support and sustain you.

- The symbol of a pyramid on your clothing at your chest will allow you to think from within the safety of your soul. It was designed that way as a safe haven. The incoming energies we are directing and assisting are coming to awaken.
- Focus on the energy. The light that's coming: it will give you the ability to successfully network with other beings of like feeling. Know that you are empowered to manipulate thought so that certain beings can't establish a thought for you to believe in. Once you are self-empowered, they can't manipulate you.
- Be gentle to one another, compassionate. Surrender into your loving self. Center within it and feel safe and secure. You'll draw in more light.

Keep it simple:
methods for transformation are simple.

Cynicism

The belief that human conduct is motivated wholly by self-interest; the expectation of nothing but the worst of human conduct and motives.

43

The Sinister Secret Government's Satanic Origin

How the SSG, Nazis and Organized Crime Came Under Control of Beings From an Alternate Negative Future

Zoosh through Robert Shapiro
November 19, 1996

To those of you who are reading this — or who intend to give it a try, anyway — sometimes things will be said that are upsetting. It is not my intent to upset you, but to enlighten you. We will discuss not only potential alternate futures both good and bad, but also potential alternate pasts both good and bad. And we will to some extent go into certain secret as well as misunderstood aspects of World War II and possibly even other wars, to remind you of what was done and to suggest to you what can be done.

It is not my intent to paint a pretty picture; I want to show you that the origins of the sinister secret government are fairly recent. It is intended that they have a fairly short duration in terms of their influence even though their influence is widespread, not unlike tentacles. So when you read this, if there's something upsetting, skip over it or just get the gist of it and go on. But I want you to know and see how wrong ideas can become attractive, how fallacies can appear to be facts and how even confusion that is self-destructive can appear to be fun. I want you to understand that I will reveal things that are at this time known only by a select few, and I will help you see how very much alike you all are and how your dissimilarities are intended to be a spice so that you don't get bored, not an abstract misery that makes you suffer.

We want to remind people that the whole idea of enemies is a fallacy and that the original purpose of science was always to uplift people and act as a bridge to take you to higher consciousness. Science is just off track, and we need to get it on track so that it redeems itself and you as well.

On this current evolution of your souls, there has been the potential to take the more discomforting or negative route. This was not designed for you to follow, but by placing it there as a hurdle you would have a benchmark by which to test ideas, practices and attitudes through time and application. The best ideas on paper do not always work out so well in application, as you know. With that potential toward evolving into a negative or domineering society, you are given the hotfoot, as it were, so you will know you're on the wrong path. On your planet and anywhere you've been during your evolution from the point of emergence from the Creator while moving through your various lessons as the Explorer Race, societies have been caught up in a sustained energy meant to bring about a maturity equal to (and your Creator hopes greater than) the sum of your Creator's parts – meaning able to replace your Creator, hopefully in a better way.

So you have had tests or gauges set up by which you would know if you were on the wrong path. In this way you would not stay on the wrong path indefinitely. On other planets and in other parts of the creation, theoretically an individual could make a mistake and stay on that trail for a very long time. But *you* are intended to have all the tools of instantaneous knowledge – meaning physical evidence, inspiration, ideas and so on.

In this way there has been created an alternate negative future. Based upon what you or others have done who have preceded you and according to how you created the society, from time to time you would alter your positive futures (I'm not talking about scenarios, but actual futures) and also the potential negative futures. The reason you had to have a strongly delineated potential for a negative future was so that you would instinctively know that if you got off the track as a civilization (planetary or nationally), you would feel, as a citizenry and as an individual, that you were not on the proper track. This is why most of your religions and philosophies are benevolent, or at least lean toward some version of benevolence, and why they're set up to encourage right thinking, best action and godliness and to follow Creator's suggestions. So certain loose-knit guidelines are in place.

In recent times (recent meaning in the past few thousand years) your civilization has begun to make repetitive mistakes. Certain small groups of individuals have ambitiously gone beyond their own perimeters to create a manner of control and dominance, sometimes laced with the self-destructive venom of superiority, and you've been on this cycle for a time. Because this cycle has created brief, extremely negative situations, the potential for the alternate negative future has become stronger. Also, the ability to assimilate and transform excess negative energy on your planet and in your society has become so overwhelmed by too much negative energy that it has been unable to keep pace with the transformation of the negative to the positive, testing you in the process.

All this is part of a grand plan that is elaborated on in minute detail in the Explorer Race series of books. That information is designed to help you understand how you got here from there and some of the forces behind the scenes that manipulate and keep you at each other's throats so that you would not see, as the saying goes, the forest for the trees.

The Recent Beginnings

Because this energy you have been granted is unintentionally pouring into potential alternate negative futures, there has been created over time a distinct solidity or actuality of these negative futures. Now, some time ago (eighty-some years ago) there were a few beings from an alternate negative future who were able to maintain the threads of permanent existence—meaning that they were able to establish and hold physical forms for themselves and live in a world that would maintain their existence. Due to a partly chance encounter, and somewhat due to your Creator's intention to consistently test you to see if you are ready, a short-term time-motivation device was made available to these beings.

I'm not saying that your Creator deigned to give these negative beings power greater than your own, but your Creator felt some time ago (around 1910) that you had been on this cycle of the conquered and the conqueror for too long. There needed to be something to change it, something to remind you of the ultimate failure of remaining at each other's throats for inconsequential differences. (An inconsequential difference is a racial or cultural difference whose limited expression is basically benign, not harmful to themselves or others, although perhaps unique to that culture.) Your Creator felt, "Well, here my Explorer Race is coming down the home stretch. What can I do to test them and speed up their spiritual and applied physical progress to break this cycle of war and destruction?"

So these negative beings from your alternate potential future were allowed to come to your time in a very limited way. They were not allowed to come physically, but in a state of being not unlike a cross between a dream (for them) with a corresponding dreamer (of 1910), and also a vision. A vision is like a dream that continues upon waking, thus creating a potential for conversation. This was obviously done as an experiment to teach the beings of the alternative negative future and more important, to test your selectivity in your present (read as 1910).

This anomalous transfer in time took place and several ideas were planted by these alternate negative future beings. They were summed up briefly as selectivity and being "right," meaning right at all costs or holding the idea of being right or correct as more important than anything else. Obviously these are extreme points of view, and they ultimately create conflicts between individuals, to say nothing of societies.

It was believed by your Creator that no more than two or three beings in existence would actually have the ability to absorb, connect and communicate with these alternate negative future beings. This communication centered in and around Germany and included the Alsace-Lorraine and parts of Austria. The communications took place in the presence of angelics so that no one would be harmed, and with beings who had lives that were either difficult and stressful or at least alienating. It wasn't until right around 1917 or 1918 that any beings in your time on Earth began to take these dreams and visions seriously. The first beings to do so were known in your World War II as Himmler and Hitler(two H's here). They did not know each other at this time, residing in different geographic areas and growing up in different levels of society. Yet they were experiencing dreams cascading into visions with these alternate negative future beings in the presence of their guardian angels, who kept them from actually feeling the energy of these negative beings.

From Creator's Own Doubt

Now, you might say, "Why were Himmler and Hitler the ones?" To understand that, you'd have to go back to the emergence from Creator of the souls who became these beings. I won't go through the whole thing, but the two of them came out originally as one being from a place within Creator that had to do with the full range of the emotion of doubt. Doubt, of course, inevitably leads to the questioning of anything and everything. In some cases that can be good as a weeding-out procedure, especially when pursuing a theoretical interest in medicine, science, even religion or philosophy. But it also tends to lead (on the darker side) to a poor sense of self-esteem; and as you all know, alienation and difficulties with self-esteem have a lot to do with violence.

So here we have these two beings gradually easing into an awareness that there is something communicating with them that might be relevant beyond the obvious, beyond what goes on in their life. The visions went on for some time, and neither of them took any immediate action. They had grown up in a society that was anti-Semitic, racist and nationalistic. They were also affected by the post-World War I apocalyptic effect in Europe and were further strapped with being the "bad guy" just for being German. Sociologists can tell you that this is not a nurturing way to start out or perpetuate life.

So here they were, already set up to feel prejudiced, anti-Semitic and so on in order to maintain a degree of self-worth. They were looking in the ashes of their former civilization for something that would initially give them power, but ultimately, control. Having some knowledge of the more ingrained occult practices of the area, Himmler had the idea that a secret society could create a perpetual influence (from his point of view) that would encourage certain directions in the society around him and ultimately, as it played out, in society at large. He felt that pursuing those directions would not only give power to him and his group, but ultimately would draw power from the world.

As they began to more aggressively sustain and perpetuate the visions, the occult side of what came to be known as the Nazi party was beginning to evolve. (I'm intentionally using the term "occult" here in its literal meaning: hidden, unknown and secretive.) What later became the Nazi party with all its monstrous activities started out basically as a club that had the intention of usurping power for a very small group of individuals, who would then go on to fame, glory and riches. It was always intended from the beginning to be self-serving. It was never really intended to be so much political as a grab for power.

The forms of initiation into this group involved the practice of secret words and all that business, but one was also required to injure oneself and someone else. So it started out with the idea that pain was a prerequisite to *enjoying* the privilege of membership. You can see where this led, both immediately and ultimately. Without going into too much detail, the foundational practices were satanic. Initially animals were sacrificed—but not just any animal. To be a member of the group you had to sacrifice an animal that you loved (invariably your favorite dog, cat or horse) so that you would suffer an actual loss. And in the process of killing this innocent being, the animal was not held down, so you would invariably be injured in the process. This was considered the rite of passage.

Your Creator always intended this to be a test. I'm *not* trying to say that this is something that your Creator set up to do; the Creator did not establish the Nazi party and all of what it did. This was initially intended to be a test, but it got out of hand. It was also intended to break the cycle of war. So when your Creator began to see what was evolving (rather, devolving) with this group, He immediately broke the tie with the beings from the alternate negative future, and the group that was the nucleus of what came to be known as the Nazis was left without any worldly guidance. Because of their practices and because they needed power, they naturally reached out for any force (and that's exactly what they used) that could give them power or show them how to acquire power over others and allow them to become wealthy, famous and so on. When put that way, you're not going to attract a benevolent being.

The Satanic Connection

I'm skipping over a few steps here because I don't want to give you a manual on how to create mischief. The Nazi inner circle basically got connected to an energy that has come to be known as Satan, which has many faces and does not have a permanent existence—meaning that if enough negative energy was produced by this club within an enclosed space or in a community that has enough unhappiness or misery, there can be a fleeting moment (two or three days maximum) in which a negative being you would identify as satanic could be formed. We're not talking about one being who was consistently their consultant, but about variations of a being who would be more or less extreme, depending on the energy within the room or community. Initially it was within a room; as times became more difficult the beings in this club would go out on the streets, stand in a rough square and breathe in whatever negative energy or anger was around them, pumping themselves up for their meeting—not unlike the way a boxer pumps himself up for a fight.

Then they would go into their fairly small square underground room and exhale all of that anger and negative energy, asking that a being of force be present to serve their needs. In this way they were able to psychically bring through such a being, although it was not permanent. It would look different at different times. They thought it was one being; they did not know that this was a series of beings.

It would be as if a being you might call a possession would, in its anger, frustration and anxiety, say whatever was necessary to get what it needed. And since these Nazi beings were interested only in instructions by which they could learn to manipulate others to get what they wanted, they were initially told that their sacrifices were good but that they needed to do more. Now, I'm not going to go into all the satanic practices, but they were told that they would need to sacrifice someone they knew and loved in order to get more power – which they did. Interestingly enough, some family members who are still alive today never knew that the family member who died unexpectedly or disappeared was sacrificed in this way. This was a deep, dark secret.

Now, I bring this up because the lesson has not been learned, although you are very close to learning it. Part of the reason you are close to learning that superiority and cruelty are not the answers is, ironically, due to increased communications now available to everybody through computers and so on. There is much more going on now than ever before (in terms of communications from one society to another through electronic mail and sharing on the Internet) that allows people to see how they are alike. I need to remind you of the fallacies and failings of the past so that those who would perpetuate such groups as the original pod that developed the Nazi party and its practices will lose their influence.

Most people today believe that the Nazis were defeated in World War II by the Allied forces, but in point of fact, you don't defeat an idea. You might defeat the forces who hold that idea, but the problem was that the National Socialists had taken polarized negative science (science without heart) to the extreme. They had done things in the camps that developed such advanced knowledge (from a scientific point of view) that many of these scientists who were a portion of the Nazi party were coveted by various governments (at least their work was coveted). The Nazi party was able to perpetuate its ideas and ideals through the creation of this technology.

The Infection of Science

I'm not trying to suggest that racism, anti-Semitism and cruelty and so on didn't exist before the Nazi party; I am saying that it was the Nazi party that began and really insidiously infected science as you know it today with the polarization toward heartlessness. Look back; read scientific documents around the turn of the century. Without exception, they were full of heart and regarded science as something that would uplift humankind and save it from whatever horrible affliction that that particular branch of science was interested in. It was actually something quite uplifting and fairly well connected with the Creator even then. It had lots of heart.

It was really the Nazis who managed to create a branch of science that was heartless, perpetuated after the war because of their influence. Because of the pursuit of expanding the intellect (especially after World War II) this heartless science has affected many other things – not the least of which is selling technology. Whatever you're selling – whether it's an idea, product, service – heartless science needs to be changed. You can't get rid of science; you just need to add heart to it.

The intent of science needs to be brought back to its origin as something that enhances your life and creates a new level of fulfillment. This is not about what was done in the past but about what *can be done*. As I've said before, the true redemption of science is retrieving it from the hands of those who would manipulate and control you.

44

World War II Is Still Happening Now

Zoosh through Robert Shapiro
November 21, 1996

One of the more hideous circumstances in World War II that had almost nothing to do with racism were the concentration camps and the venomous anti-Semitism. It takes a serious amount of venom to get ordinary, everyday people so far off their normal state of being that they're willing to murder children and babies, or even innocent adults. Granted, anti-Semitism was pretty strong anyway at that time in Europe and perhaps other places as well. I would say that probably fully 50%, if not 75% of it, was because it was institutionalized in the Christian religions of the time. It wasn't in the dogma of the religion, but the people who ran the churches and gave the sermons would let it slip in and sometimes put it in themselves, unfortunately. You know, you can't have a God for some without that God being for all. I think people are more aware of that now.

Allowing for the climate of anti-Semitism, one might analyze it politically or sociologically, but that's been done and it's not what this is about. Obviously, having a fall guy or a scapegoat is useful. Everywhere Nazism went in Russia, special groups of soldiers swept through every little town and just killed everyone. The German troops knew it was their job. Understand that the average soldier wasn't involved with this, or if they were, they were recruited temporarily. There were special groups whose only job in working for the German high command (or low command) was to murder civilians.

This was based entirely upon the satanic ritual of sacrifice. I'm not going to dwell on this, but we have to understand that World War II's more odious manifestations were entirely based upon satanic rituals, which basically have to do with a GREEDY LUST FOR POWER, NO MATTER WHAT THE COST.

In any event, I'm bringing all of this stuff out in its nasty detail because it's important to recognize that the reason this wasn't discussed widely at the time (although certainly known by certain individuals) is because those who did know felt that the innocent world – the rest of the world, if you would – wasn't ready to believe that satanic behavior was that widespread and that the entire purpose of the so-called thousand-year Reich was to *eliminate the entire population of Earth through human sacrifice.*

Except for the Nazis themselves.

Yes, except the insiders. Only the insiders of the original Nazi club knew that. The odd thing is that over time some of the insiders realized, "What's the point of it? Once we have our power, we don't really have to do that. After all, what's the point of running the world if there isn't any world to run?" (meaning the population). But Hitler himself never gave up on that idea. The blindness of that ambition meant that it didn't really matter who was sacrificed. Of course, it seemed to them that they would start with the obvious people, those whom many already disliked – the Jewish people – and then keep on going. The attitude at the top was "what people don't know won't hurt them," because ultimately it wasn't just this or that group; obviously German soldiers were being sacrificed as well, sometimes in ludicrous ways. At the beginning of the war professional soldiers and cooler heads were running the operation, but as time went on paranoia increased, which it does in situations like that.

One of the reasons that satanic practitioners have not been able to take over the world is that paranoia and the quest for power go hand in hand. As paranoia built up, the older, more experienced generals said, "We can't run a campaign like that; all of our soldiers will be killed," but eventually that satanic principle of sacrifice won out over all other things. Certain battles were fought and things done with the absolute knowledge of the people on top that ultimately all of their own soldiers were going to be killed – which would be a personal sacrifice that would fulfill the satanic obligation. And when they were killing other people they could say, "That is a necessary sacrifice."

I don't like discussing all these unpleasant things, but you need to understand that the purposes and the ultimate seduction of racism toward *any* group of individuals, even prejudice in general, serves not only the satanic cause but the cause of the future based in some horrible, negative, hell-like condition. The discussions of hell in some religions as a *place* have unintentionally set up a degree of cynicism in many people, who believe that if they break this or that religious taboo they'll go to hell. The more taboos you have, the more likely the religion is to say, "You're lost to us; you're going to go to hell and that's that!" The trouble is that it tends to create cynicism, and *cynicism itself tends to attract whatever the person is cynical about.*

So there are a lot of factors here, and we need to put this information out. We need to show people how an event such as World War II, which is continually being discussed and seen in films and documentaries, still avoids the central theme: why campaigns were fought, especially toward the end, where German soldiers were sacrificed as if there were less interest in winning the war and more interest in sacrifices to retain power at the top, in the misguided belief that that actually works. You see, ultimately, satanic behavior doesn't work, because it tends to destroy itself and everything around it and creates more and more self-destructive aberrations and behaviors.

The Test of Variety

In a way that's a good thing, because it has a built-in failure factor. But on the other hand, it's not okay for people to continue to suffer under the bondage of these ideas. You know, it's certainly true that you as individuals here on Earth are subject to more variety in everything than you are when living on another planet in other lives. On other planets there's usually one racial group or one philosophical idea that predominates. Most planets have only one, because societies are built up very carefully with balanced points of view that are magnanimous and open, welcoming, loving and supporting. The only way most planets have been able to do that up until now is by maintaining a homogeneity of the population, where everybody is fairly similar in their beliefs, actions and often appearance. While that's an accomplishment in itself, you can see how most visitors from Earth, after your initial euphoria, would get bored very quickly because you're used to variety. If you don't like eating at the barbecue, you can go down the street and get Chinese or Thai food. That doesn't exist on other planets. On most other planets there is balance, peace and philosophical as well as spiritual enlightenment.

You might ask, "Aren't these sacrifices of variety all right to maintain the peace and have a beautiful society?" Up until now it *has* been all right, but in order to fulfill your ultimate destiny (at least in the short run) of being the Explorer Race, it is intended that you go out and stimulate variety in other beings on other planets, to show them that it is possible to have variety and still maintain balance, from their point of view.

Here on Earth, the place where variety is in your face whether you want it to be or not, you are *tested* with variety. It's true that some of the races of Earth owe their heritage directly to different parts of this universe; the African peoples, for example, are from Sirius. [See *The Origins and the Next Fifty Years of the Explorer Race.*] It is certainly true that some of these galaxies [systems] – Sirius, Orion and so on – have had in the distant past some rivalries with each other. But this is not major wars like you have here on Earth; I'm talking about minor rivalries bordering on competition, and that's about it. Here it's gotten so far out of hand that people are often raised to believe something known to be impossible – that a person of a different color, nationality or philosophy is somehow less than you (sometimes more than you, but generally the appealing idea is that they are less than you).

Using this one little tool [elitism] to keep the races and the national groups fighting amongst each other is the ultimate purpose of the sinister secret government, a tool by which they hope to enslave you into that negative future. They are still holding on to the idea that they might be able to bring about that negative future where they can manipulate and control all aspects of your lives, and you will have no recourse for anything they or their toadies might want to do because *they* will have the means of enforcement and you won't. That's *not* going to come about, but if it did it would be horrible – just awful, hellish.

Here is something that is actually topical – the current plan the sinister secret government is involved in: their attempt to destroy the entire population of Africa so that they can go in and, without any restrictions or limitations, exploit all mineral and plant resources. They don't want to have to mess around with people. And as I said in an Explorer Race book [see *The Origins and Next Fifty Years of the Explorer Race*], if there isn't a significant percentage of dark-skinned people on this planet, *nobody* will stay alive!

The Potential Negative Future

The inception of the sinister secret government has actually been something like this [draws] – a rough sketch indeed; an artist I am not, but you get the idea. [See Figure 1.] This is a time line of the

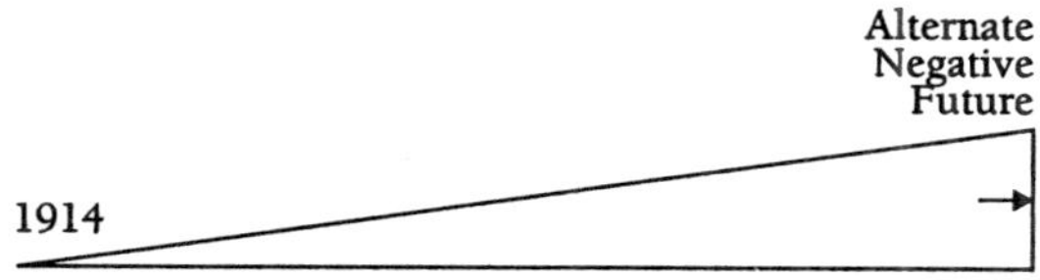

Figure 1.

potential negative future. You can see that the sinister secret government would have a lot of strength in the future. This goes back to the actual point they were targeting.

They felt that in 1914, right around the time of World War I, they could begin doing their work. At any given moment there are various threads that go to the future. Once upon a time (around 1915 or so), this alternate negative future still had about a 30% chance of actually becoming a future you would all live. They felt it was significant enough to campaign for. You might ask, "How did they get there?" If an alternate future has more than a 10% potential, the energy for that future becomes fairly significant. The beings, the happenings, the existence of that future, are laid out not as dots you might connect with lines, but they have form. If you were to travel in a time machine to that future, it would appear vague, but you'd get recognizable images.

So here you have people who exist in the future – very powerfully in that negative future – and because of the advanced weapons research culled from the future by the Nazis during World War II, they managed to develop, at least with some struggle, a variation of a time machine in which they attempted to manipulate the past and potential futures to make a grab for power. [See the February and March 1993 issues of the *Journal* and *Shining the Light #4* for the tie-in to the Montauk Project.]

Understand that the sinister secret government is at its core a representation of the dark sides of *all individuals*. By "dark" I do not mean the unknown or that which you need to explore and understand; I'm talking about what has come to be called the negative side of people. The more experiences of negativity you have, the more there is in existence. Thus the exploration of negative potential in World War II had a lot to do with that alternate negative future. As a result, toward the end of World War II they had this "time machine." It was really very rudimentary (fortunately) and limited. It was very expensive to power but cheap to build, or they wouldn't have been able to maintain it. They've lost so many people in time that it's ridiculous. That's because they didn't know what they were doing – traveling through time when you're in a negative space gives you at least an 87% chance of becoming totally lost.

The Addiction to Being Right

In any event, they were perfectly willing to lose people because it was a personal sacrifice. (We come back to that again.) Nevertheless, they "achieved" their mission sometimes because they were able to delay beneficial things and foster the *one emotion* they felt they could use even if they were defeated. Obviously they didn't get eliminated; they went underground. This emotion could affect many people of the Earth and enable them to say negative things about any group of people: "Well, let's pick out some people and make them all bad. We'll get everybody thinking these people are bad and use them as fall guys anytime we want to grab power. We'll say, 'The only thing wrong is that you've got *these* people here. If it weren't for them, you'd be happy!'"

It's an old trick, and this is why it works: they've been able to foster *cynicism* at every possible turn. Cynicism is one of the most dangerous emotions you have. I understand why it's appealing, because when you expect the worst and the worst follows, you can feel like you're right; you've been vindicated. If something good happens, you can say, "Oh well, that's great" and enjoy the good things. So *people who want to be right* is the other addictive substance. The Nazi mentality believes that if people are cynical or need to be right or on the winning side, then they'll have an inroad.

Once upon a time, when you had team sports and one side won, that was it. It was important *how* you played the game; there was a high level of integrity. Now that level of integrity is less important. It doesn't matter so much anymore how you play the game; it's *whether you win,* whether you can hold up your finger at the end and say, "We're number one!"

Self-serving has been promoted; if you can get people entirely interested in themselves, they're going to want to be right, they're going to want to be on the winning side. And if you can convince them that yours is the winning side, they'll go along with whatever you say or do even if it is ludicrous, even if it defies the very core of their moral beliefs. They might be willing to suspend their morals, values and ethics or at least look the other way—while you go about your dirty business and in the process usurp their power.

I didn't mean to get so political, but it's necessary for you to understand that I'm not talking about something that happened only in the late 1930s and early 1940s; I'm talking about something that's with you *right now.* World War II is still happening; the ideas and philosophies fostered there to grab power for a small group are still here today. For the races to be fighting each other is simply ludicrous. I understand how seductive it is to be able to say, "But they did this, they did that." You'll *always* be able to say that, especially in the negative future. The whole purpose of this is to help you understand that *you are being manipulated and you need to get past it.*

You might ask, "Where does Creator fit into all of this? Why does Creator allow such things?" For one thing, Creator knows that you are all immortal and that you are here to learn lessons. Creator is not happy that you have to go through so much pain, not at all. But Creator wants you to take over, not only to become enlightened, but beyond that – godlike, and more – and Creator knows that if It interferes with your process of educating yourself, you will continue to believe that someone will come and save you, that you don't really have to do it yourself, and you will continue to screw up. In reality, Creator knows It cannot save you, and that if She makes any effort to do so beyond certain parameters, then you will fall back on that and continue negative patterns of behavior. You won't grow beyond, you won't come together, you won't drop things that are not good for you and reach for the highest experience.

The Vehicle with Hale-Bopp

Right now as we're talking there is a vehicle headed this way that has your extraterrestrial brothers and sisters upon it. They are working with the Creator, in that they will be radiating a lot of the energy that is your natural knowledge. It is like an injection or inoculation that will allow you to remember who you are and drop a lot of the drama of your accumulated personality in this life. The obvious purpose is to make a giant leap forward to get past the 3.50 mark, and we hope that's going to happen. But *you* have to do it. This energy will be radiated toward you, but you have to catch it and do something worthwhile with it. You won't be able to use it negatively, so don't worry about that.

Is this the ship we talked about, the one trailing the Hale-Bopp comet?

Yes, that's right. It's the vehicle with Hale-Bopp. That's another reason why this is timely.

You can see that what I've been talking about is something that is sinister not only for the future but for the present. But what about the past? When people can travel in time (albeit with great sacrifices), they're going to make every effort to change the past. And the more that people feel cynical or hate their neighbors or can't look past the qualities that they don't like and see the qualities common to their own, the more power this negative force has. By doing things that border from discomfort to cynicism to true negativity, you are giving them power.

You cannot continue doing that. Remember what you're doing here; you're not just being born, living your life, then dying. Once upon a time you might have made a case for that, but not anymore. Now you're shifting between dimensions while you're alive, and you can't go beyond a certain point without shrugging off a huge chunk of negativity.

How to Get Rid of the Negative Energy

Where are you going to shrug it off to? The planet? Nope; sorry, you can't do that anymore, because the planet's not going to take it. Lucifer? Nope; Lucifer doesn't want it anymore. Satan, the artificial being you unintentionally created? Nope; Lucifer is going to unload his negative personality because it's not really him. Mother Earth? No, she doesn't want it, she can't take it.

So here you are with all this negative energy; you have to get rid of it and there's nobody to take it. *You're* going to have to transform it, and it's going to take an effort. It's not going to be easy in the beginning, but it will get much easier as you get going. You're going to have to make a shift, and the first shift I recommend is that you *let go of cynicism,* even if you can justify it. If you don't do anything else but just let go of cynicism, you'll be making a big move forward.

So here is homework: Go to the dictionary, the best dictionary you can find, and read the definition of cynicism. I want you to read it and understand that *you cannot afford to do that anymore.* I'd like you to carry around a little card that has the definition of cynicism printed on it. I'm not going to say, "You have to be hopeful, you have to look to the stars, you have to feel happy"; I'm not going to force that on you. I'm just going to say that you need to be aware of what cynicism is, and drop it. I'd like to see an eyecatching card people can carry that has *cynicism* and its definition, and on the backside maybe one of those red circles with a slash through it over the word *cynicism* [see below].

Cynicism
The belief that human conduct is motivated wholly by self-interest; the expectation of nothing but the worst of human conduct and motives.

You need to be aware of this because it has so seductively permeated people's personalities here that they don't even realize it. If we can chop off cynicism, it will *immediately eliminate fully 40% of the power that the current sinister secret government draws from you!* When you're cynical, you give up hope; you give up your natural birthright, which is *the ability to resolve all problems!* The sinister secret government wants you to do that because they want to be able to resolve all of *their* problems, and they don't care about you. So you can have not only the pleasure of your own birthright to resolve problems, but you can knock down *their* power by 40% —and that will make a major difference.

The intention, then, of this sinister group of individuals is to put you on the path toward this negative future —but *they want to change the past, too!* They want to go back in the past and make everything negative in their favor, which they believe will give them more strength. And if they do that, it will. So you can't be cynical about the past, either. Their time machine takes a tremendous electrical power to make it "sort of" work, but if you eliminate cynicism, that time machine's *not going to work at all.* You know what will happen? If anyone gets in that machine, they'll go into a loop of time and go round and round and round —and that's it! It won't work at all anymore.

This is a little test for you: You've got to do it yourselves, and it's not going to be easy. Now, this doesn't mean you have to give up all discomforting emotions; I'm not trying to take those away from you. I just want you to let go of this one, be aware of it, and put it out there if you can.

The reality, the discomfort here, the ultimate goal of the sinister secret government, is to remake themselves. You have a group of beings who have more power in an alternate negative future, but not as much power as they want to have *now,* in your lives. As you go back in the past to before 1914, they have no power at all —they don't exist. So this group is attempting to use an alternate negative future to build their power into the past.

Here is another illustration [he draws Figure 3] depicting their attempt to create an alternate negative past. It is ultimately their intention to create this [see Figure 4] so that through all time they will have power, no matter what. *We have to prevent that,* and that's where you come in.

I can't do it for you —or let's just say I won't do it for you, Creator won't do it for you, your guides won't do it for you —but we're helping to the extent that we can. My job as end-time historian

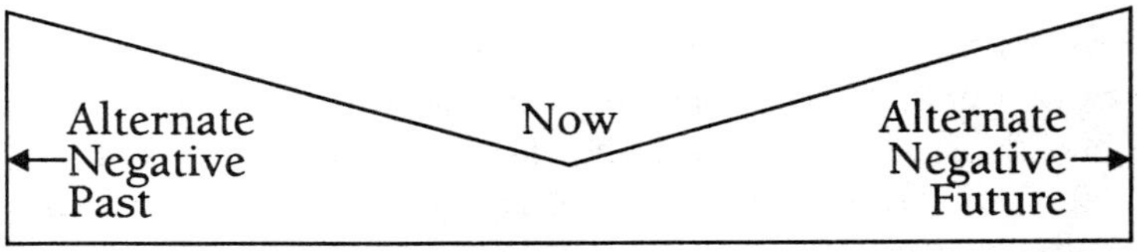

Figure 3.

Figure 4.

is to tell you about these things. I could have waited a little longer to see if these things would come out. There have been some books about the real goings-on of the Nazi hierarchy in World War II, but the real nastiness didn't get out. Even in the fictional books, the authors, although they wanted to show Nazism for what it was, didn't want to promote these ideas. I understand that.

But we have to understand that these individuals are willing to take time to accomplish what they want to do. They're willing to say, "We want to live forever as individuals, but if we can't go on forever, then we'll feel good handing down our power into the hands of our select chosen few. Then we will know that our ultimate goals and purposes are going to be accomplished." A small club. It's their intention to rule you from all time, from their perspective, and keep you so disempowered that *they* have your power.

This is ultimately about you reclaiming your power, and while I'd like to say this is something you need to do in the future, I can't. This is something you need to do *right this minute, right now*. Stop now and look up "cynicism," read the definition, write it down yourself, carry it around in your wallet or purse, and from time to time during the day take it out and look at it. Try to think back to what you said and did during the day and ask yourself if you've been cynical. If you really work on it, you'll be able to notice subtle ways that it's crept in. (on me for campaigning.)

Think about it for a moment. A lot of the things you hold dear are no longer present, and if the sinister secret government had the power, they would go back and create an alternate negative past, which would mean that no one alive today would be able to remember *any* good things that had ever happened in the past *in your lives now*. Can you *imagine* that? They could not only create an alternate negative past historically, but it would affect your individual lives now. You wouldn't remember that good time you had at your birthday party; you wouldn't remember the birth of your first child or that great time you had on vacation—none of that. Your life would just seem awful, and the best you could do would be to tough it out, which is the absolute antithesis of what you really are.

Okay, questions?

In The Explorer Race, in 1987 and 1988 you talked about the Order, the Brotherhood of Light, the Illuminati and then the shadow government. They were there to provide resistance, to make us strong, to be a test. At what point did the shadow government, which was there for a purpose, become the sinister secret government? Did they get taken over by this Hitler elite or something?

The Recent Expansion of SSG Power

Several years have passed between 1987 and now, and I can tell you more now. Yes, there has been a concerted effort. They've managed, with their insidious influence, to train a whole generation of youngsters. Although most of the youngsters are in good shape, a lot of them are cynical. They've trained this whole generation to have greatly decreased expectations. I'm not just referring to wealth or career success, but about potential for future happiness. So the power of what we're now calling the sinister secret government has expanded about 7% between 1985 and 1993. I don't want to scare you too much, but between 1993 and the present, 1996, their power expanded another 5%. They have gone back to change things, yes.

You're going to have to give an overview to people here about how this happened, because it's not going to make sense. You're talking about a primitive time machine, but they have a very sophisticated time machine, a craft from the Xpotaz.

They had it, but they don't have it anymore. The Xpotaz . . .

. . . are gone, but the sinister secret government has the machines that the Xpotaz gave them.

Yes, yes. I'm going to use the example from the recent war in the Mideast. When the U.S. sold computers to Iran and Iraq they put in a little back door where they could enter and totally screw up the computers. Well, the Xpotaz did the same thing. "As long as you're our friends," said the Xpotaz, "you can do whatever you want because we're getting what we want from you. But the minute you become our enemy, we push the magic button and your stuff will self-destruct." So now they're stuck with this little . . .

. . . ET craft that isn't working. But we had the thirteen families, the inner circle of the secret government. You need to tie the Hitler people into this so we can understand it.

I'm not sure if we'll be able to accomplish this, because we're getting so much energy thrown this way to try to stop us from doing this tonight.

Every time you talk about this, they try to stop you?

Yes. Their strength is in the future, and I can put a date on it. The alternate negative future exists, in terms of the graph, at about A.D. 2175. That's when they're really strong.

And that's still in a three-point-something dimension?

Yes, that's in the 3.0 dimension.

They're trying to keep us from making it. At what point are we over the hill and out of danger, 3.5? 3.6?

Once we get to 3.53, their effect on you drops precipitously, literally by half. When you get to 3.535, it plummets. By the time you're at 3.55, they won't have any effect on you at all.

So this is their absolute last-ditch effort to keep us from going into the fourth dimension.

That's right. It's a last-ditch effort. You're so close now that they're willing to do crazy things, such as their attempt to rub out the population of Africa by introducing various strains of bacteria that were basically research microbes in laboratories. They are attempting to spread disease and significantly heighten racial and intertribal tensions so the people would be eliminated or eliminate themselves.

So any fighting in Africa, anything we read about, they are causing?

Anything, including tribal tensions that lead to violence—murderous violence, not just "you did this to me, I did that to you." Anything that leads to the elimination of life can be traced right back to them.

Okay. Can you do a recap that will help the readers who haven't read the previous* Shining the Light *books and* Explorer Race *books to understand that there was a shadow government that got a time machine and disappeared the peace President? Was that the key? After 1910 did the shadow government become the sinister secret government? Did it start with the Hitler cult, which then infiltrated the shadow government?

The shadow government was a loose-knit group of individuals struggling for power and that maintained power within their geographical areas. You might be able to say that in this country there was a loose-knit group of people who sort of ran the show. But that's not a sinister secret government; that's what I call a *behind-the-scenes government*. (We want to indicate that this in no way reflects on benevolent beings.) We loosely referred to the behind-the-scenes manipulators as the shadow government, recognizing that they did not have a unified purpose and power and control.

Before the year of . . . ?

The SSG's Race to the Past

This is difficult, because we're dealing from the future to the past, not from the past to the future; so this is the opposite of what you understand as linear time. It's difficult because it changes. As the sinister secret government now gets more power, that affects the whole time line to the past. It could change, but I'll give you an arbitrary date as of this moment. The loose-knit shadow government was still in place, but the actual core sinister secret government, which has now managed to transfer itself and its power and influence into the past, is at this time formed and operating in 1917.

Now, if you had asked that question five years ago, I would have said that it was formed, functioning and entirely unified around the Earth in, say, 1950-something. The problem is that as times goes on, they're pushing their power and authority back further into the past. You might say it's a strange thing, because it seems like you'd want to push your power and authority into the future. But they don't *have* to do that, because from their perspective their power and authority grows in the future where they've got things under control. That alternate negative past is what they're headed for and they want to drag you all along. Their number one objective is to push their power and authority into the *past*; that's the whole thrust of their intentions right now.

So in the Shining the Light books we were dealing with the sinister secret government that had underground bases all over the world, technology from off the planet . . . but then they seem to have almost disappeared at one point.

They've got enough lieutenants running around doing their bidding—many of whom don't even know they're doing the bidding of these people—and intentions to continue building and maintaining power in the present. As long as you continue to fall into line with what they want you to be—cynical and all that—they are replacing your actual history with history from their desired perspective. That's why it's so complex. What has happened is that the alternate negative past is getting louder, if that makes any sense.

What I understand is that after the Second World War, those who had been in power in Nazi Germany came to the United States and went to South America—was that originally the beginning of the sinister secret government? Did they infiltrate and take over the old shadow government:?

Taking Over Organized Crime and Shadow Governments

No, because the shadow governments were localized. They couldn't take over the shadow government, so the only thing they could hope to do initially was, through organized crime (becoming *highly* organized crime, as I've referred to the sinister secret government before), to offer these shadow governments that were in place in most of the countries of the world more power, more influence, more money, more control. They had to be able to offer this to them on the one hand and at the same time threaten that if they didn't fall in line with this global sinister secret government, every member of their shadow government and every member of their families would be brutally murdered.

They were able to go to representatives of every country's shadow government and say, "Here's the people who make up your group and here are your family members," and they'd read all the names off. In other words, they had the goods on them. They achieved this through their time travel; in the future, their alternative negative future, infinite records are kept. You could pick out any citizen in that alternate negative future on the Earth, and they would be able to tell you how often that person scratched his head in an hour, and they'd tell you, "One time this hour, three times that hour." That's how much knowledge and control they have.

That's what they want; they want to know what you're doing every second. So they went to the shadow governments and said, "We're welcoming you into our organization. We're taking over and there's nothing you can do about it." They had weapons that were way beyond what the others had.

Are you saying that those who survived the Second World War on the Nazi side have expanded? And that among the many people who were lost in this time machine there were a few who got to the future, found themselves there and came back? Is that what you're describing?

A moment. [He draws Figure 5.] Let's say that this is the sinister secret government [cross-hatched circle]. They go to these various countries [represented by other circles] and say, "You can join us or we'll eliminate you and take over what you've got." So they didn't spring forth from any of these.

Then where did they come from?

Coming Back in Time Through Genetic Manipulation

They came from the future. They came back genetically. They're very powerful in that alternate negative future. They came back on their *genetic line* to their representatives; they came back on

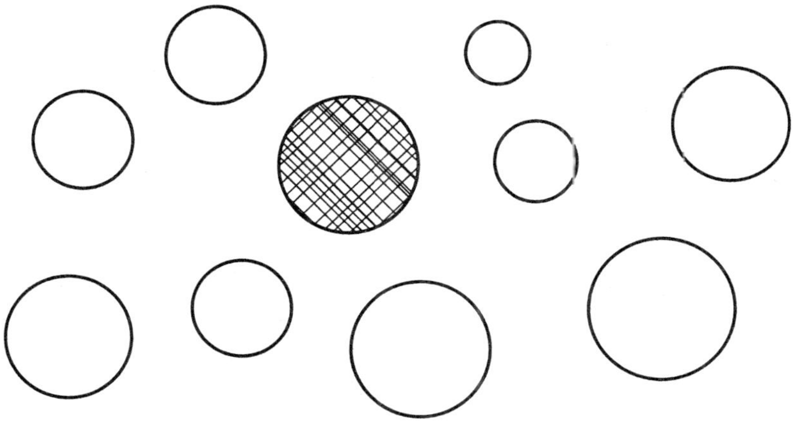

the bloodline, not on the spiritual line.

Of . . .

Of themselves.

Of the Nazi leaders who survived the Second World War — is that the "they" they came back to?

Again I'm stuck with yes and no. Yes – but it's gone past that, because the more we continue with these negative conditions, the more they push back their influence. All these things are in flux. A few years ago I would have said yes, they came back to there and that's where it started, but I can't say that anymore. Now they've gone back beyond that, so it didn't start there anymore. We're talking about time, but not about literal, linear time where this happened on this date. We can't say that; it's not like that.

Okay, but it started with the satanic cult of those who became Nazis, who then went into the future and came back?

No. I don't know how I can say this any other way, but the alternate future is a place where they have all this power; they come back into the present, whatever the present is. The present might be 1996 or 1939, because wherever you're focused in is the present. For you it's 1996, but the present for others is 1939. They would come back on their bloodline and usurp the lives of those individuals through the manipulation of genetics. Genetics can be used to manipulate people on your bloodline if you're willing to develop such instruments.

Once upon a time I would have said "Yes, they came back . . . " But you have to understand something. I'm not talking about "this happened with the Nazis, then these people traveled in a time machine forward and then they came back." We're talking about something that's happening in an alternate negative future, and I'm starting with something in the middle, understand? Just like Creator did. I'm starting with World War II as a benchmark, then I'm talking about these people who came back. Himmler was one of those people on the bloodline of a negative ruler in the alternate negative future. The original Himmler would not have done this, but he was affected and he did do this.

So we need to make that clear. Hitler, too?

Yes, and while this is all true, they've gone back *before* that now. They came back to these two men. I've picked out only these two because I don't want to bring pain to living relatives. The intent of the negative future beings is to trace *everybody who's current now*. They started with the prominent people, but they want to trace *everyone's* bloodlines to their alternate negative future if they can find them, then come back and influence them the same way they did with Hitler and Himmler and several other insiders.

Okay, I think that's clear. You're speaking about it now because their power's growing and because . . .

Because it can't wait, because they're starting to have a serious influence. I'm confident in your ability to take you past 3.55 and beyond, but there is entirely too much suffering going on. They want wars, because wars invariably cause atrocities. Even in wars that are for good causes, bombs and horrible weapons continue to go off and maim and kill people who weren't the original targets. We can't have that. Aside from the suffering, it creates resentment, grudges; it just goes on and on.

If I understand right, you said before that it started because Creator brought in this negative being to be a test.

The Creator needed to build in a small amount of resistance so that you could have an experience that your Creator did not have. It was never intended to get so extreme. The Creator needed to have you experience a certain amount of resistance in your growth so that you could creatively find ways to surmount challenges, which your Creator never had to do. Among other Creators, it was controversial to do such a thing and Creator was barely able to sneak that one by the Council of Creators.

I'll tell you something: I don't want to give it any energy, but on the distant possibility that the alternate negative future beings are able to bring about what they want, your creation would be altered by the Council of Creators. Your Creator would be reprimanded – not hurt or punished, but reprimanded – and your creation would be re-created. I don't think that's going to happen because I think your

Creator had a good idea here. But He did start out without a personal experience of discomfort and negativity.

When you talk like this, it's really serious.

It's serious business. That's why I wanted to pick out one single emotion that you could focus on and actually *do* something about. If you carried around a small card in your pocket that had the definition of cynicism on it, you could really get on top of that! You *can* eliminate cynicism, or at least make it your goal to eliminate cynicism. And not everybody's cynical; for some it wouldn't even apply! But you'd be surprised how insidious it is.

For example, people always expect the worst from the IRS, and yet – I'm not trying to make heroes out of anybody – sometimes they do good things. As a matter of fact, many good causes would go ignored, social concerns that would not be paid for, if it weren't for what the IRS does. I'm not trying to make myself unpopular; I'm trying to say that a lot of good things get paid for because there are taxes. The original purpose of taxes was to require a charitable contribution that would allow many more people to live a good life instead of just a few. If you look at the IRS as being monsters and say that whatever they do is awful, you're just buying into that whole thing and being cynical. If you say that all lawyers are out to make money and will do anything for it – aside from being false, it's cynical. The same thing goes for politicians . . .

Advertising . . .

All that.

Some of the things that have been happening in the past several years, like the Waco disaster, could very well have been created to make the U.S. population quite cynical.

That's right. Think about it. Years ago when children were in school, they would study the horrible things the Nazis did – I bring up the Nazis because they're the most recent awful thing. And one of the worst things the Nazis did was burn down churches with people inside. That was such horrible information that children would have nightmares. People didn't want to torture their own children by teaching them about these things, so they taught it in college instead, where they felt students would be more mature.

Even though it wasn't a plot, you can say that Waco was ultimately about the representatives of your government using the conditions of the children in the church as an excuse to go in and say, "We want to see the children and make sure they're okay." Of course, they showed up with guns firing bullets – and what if the bullets hit some of those kids? The logic escapes me. What about the church burning down with all the people inside and the kids, too? The logic of that escapes me as well.

Now, if this had happened in the fifties, the whole government would have been chased out of office and the citizens of the United States would have stormed the capitol. But after years of cynicism people are willing to believe whatever is told to them, or else they're willing (and this is the worst effect of cynicism) to look the other way.

How many people in this country judged the German population: "How could they look the other way when these horrible things were happening – concentration camps right in their own country?" Well, how could *you* look the other way when the government of the United States was involved in the burning down of a church with all the people inside? How could you look the other way? Some people didn't, and a lot of you were outraged – but *how* outraged? I'm not saying you should go out and hurt somebody; I'm saying you've got to change things. And the place where you have your power initially is with yourself, changing yourself. You've got to let go of cynicism; it's hurting you and everybody else.

When you're working with that and it's getting better, I'll give you something else to let go of. But I want you to start with something you can understand and grab hold of. I don't want to give you a whole bunch of stuff; you can spot this idea of cynicism and say, "Oops, I'm doing that again!" Don't get down on yourself when you catch yourself; just say, "Oops! That's good, I caught myself!" You can change it.

A couple of new shows have come up on TV recently that present a very negative future that's an endless conflict between an underground Black League type of group and some monolithic negative empire, and these are human beings. Does that relate to what you're talking about?

I'd say that as those shows were originally conceptualized they would have been pretty good. The problem is that where those shows are coming from geographically individuals are getting very cynical themselves, but they're also into finding a sure-fire success. TV programs compete for the advertising dollar, so they look at what movies are making the big bucks – movies involved with conflict and horrible ETs coming to eat your grandmother, that kind of thing. On the one hand, the concept of exploring the paranormal is pretty good, but on the other hand, putting out the idea that no matter what you do, the forces of evil will always be able to manipulate you – that's terrible.

And that's an influence from the sinister secret government?

Ultimately it is, because the conditioning involved in the competitive atmosphere of movies and television and influencing young people generates cynicism, and expecting the worst is addictive.

And it multiplies itself . . .

It multiplies upon itself, yes. But it does require food, and it gets fed from the bulk of the population.

45

More Sinister Secret Government, Nazis and the Orion Warrior League

Zoosh through Robert Shapiro
November 26, 1996

Where are we with respect to these beings from the alternate negative future who control the sinister secret government ?

You're at a point now where you're starting to get help from beyond. The angelics are closer to you now than they have ever been, and consciousness itself is raising on the planet. Although once upon a time angels were considered something vaguely religious and basically for children, now they are becoming more accepted. That helps. Because you are at 3.47, there's enough distance from 3.0 that the energy coming from the alternate negative future (which is really directed toward 3.0 dimension) . . .

Oh, I didn't know that.

Yes, it's directed to 3.0 and it has to come to where you are, so it basically rebounds. It first comes to 3.0, then reaches up to where you are and tries to hang on. That gives you an advantage, because they have more power coming back in a straight line to 3.0 than they do on the rebound.

Then there is that vehicle coming in with the comet Hale-Bopp. Although it is not in any way interfering, it is going out of its way to be seen. A vehicle coming in like that and being seen raises a lot of hopes, and that's good.

The threat of this alternate negative future happening is still very real, but not so real that it is a matter of life and death. It does take, however, people believing in good things, people acting on faith. It will take *acts* by the average person. For instance, let's say that in an average inner-city high school someone hurls an insult into the air, but it is not a personal insult directed at somebody. Now and in the recent past you might find people getting in a fight over it. But insulting remarks *do not have to be taken personally* unless they are directed at *you*. Ignoring it would be a positive act. I'm trying to give examples of something that actually fits into life, rather than something like sitting around in circles and holding the thought of love. That's fine for some communities, but this must also be directed to places where there is the most difficulty and struggle.

Technique for Releasing Anxiety

Here's another example. You're walking through a city park and there are two or three people approaching. On your first sight of them there's no reason to believe they mean you any harm, but because it is several people, your anxiety builds. I want to suggest something else. As you exhale, each time imagine yourself beaming gold light in their direction. This cannot harm them in any way, and it gives you something to do that will increase your confidence and do good for both of you.

I'm not saying that this is a panacea, but that there are things you can do beyond hitting the panic button. Those of you who are in groups, continue your good works. Those of you who are individually radiating good energy, continue. But also, those of you who are in situations where you're exposed to threats, start taking positive actions such as beaming gold light—even if you must turn and walk on the other side of the park. (That's okay, too; don't do anything foolish.) On the exhale, breathe out that gold light and feel free to *blow* it out [blows out through his mouth to illustrate]. You don't have to blow it right at the people; they're going to wonder what you're doing. You can just blow it out without really looking at them, see?

What I'm saying is, make even a small gesture in order to perpetuate your safety, one that does not harm others, and do what you need to do to get along. We need to create a common link between people without aggravating any more tensions.

If this was an organizational chart, what would it look like? How many beings are we talking about?

That are coming from the future?

From the alternate negative future. Who are they directly impacting, and how does it flow out to the point where they have the power to start removing people and killing the people in Africa?

About every three and a half minutes, two beings from the alternate negative future (ANF) will come back. As they were approaching your time (they tried this for a while, by the way), they attempted to dump some negativity, but they found out they were dumping it in the wrong place, so now they don't do that anymore. They just come back to 3.0, and they have to stay there for a while. They have others here at 3.47 (getting the first beings here was a struggle, but that's another story), and the ones who are coming back now to 3.0 will focus on them.

Their beings?

Their people, yes. They will concentrate on an oath of allegiance they take. There are no other beings hanging around 3.0; they're not interested in the beings coming from Sirius manifesting at 3.0 now.

They're trying to get *here,* and when they get a response at 3.47, they can then be pulled here. But at latest count I'd say they're losing right around 13% of their negative energy as they make the rebound from 3.0 to 3.47. So when they make that move dimensionally and lose that percentage of negativity, they actually become less negative than they've ever been; that's an important point.

So 3.47 is a strange feeling to them. On the one hand, they get frightened because they feel like they're less in control (they're warned that they will have these feelings); on the other hand, it gives them at least a minute exposure to what it might be like to have less negative energy. They can't travel on light rays for obvious reasons, but when they are refocused in 3.47 utilizing a sound technique, they can stay here for only a short time. They're not in their natural environment; they are imaging, and they can image in and out of physicality. They can hold physicality for some time, then they go into an alternate state. They cannot be here for more than three years, at which time they die – so this is a sacrificial mission. They come here either because they believe in what they're doing or they've been coerced to do it (which is more often than not the case), and that's it. At the end of their mission, they're done.

How would you describe their mission? What do they do when they get here?

The first thing they do is pass on instructions from their higher-ups, because they have to hold those instructions and it's a struggle for them. Next they are reimaged to the "natural" level of negativity they hold in their "normal" environment. As a result, that 12.5 to

13% of negative energy they've lost is replaced. But they *did* have the experience, and that's important for their souls.

After that they are available to any beings attempting to utilize their "skills" for consultation. They cannot come to the surface because there is light energy and because of all of the good things that spiritual people are doing here (including many religions, though not all). They can function in a capacity of liaison with the sinister secret government. They have been trying in recent years to manifest in some way, working with what I sometimes call hobbyist satanic groups on the Earth's surface. These groups are invariably calling for this or that being to manifest in some way that they can see —even these groups want physical evidence. They've been trying, but it's not working very well. The best these negative future beings have been able to do (from their perspective) is to exude or radiate a blast of negative energy to one of these groups, such that the people standing around the circle performing some kind of ritual will suddenly have a letdown in energy. When that energy arrives, it immediately goes to the most powerful member of the group and pulls on energy from all the other members. Thus most of them experience a loss of energy and an ominous feeling. Some of the satanic groups have come to recognize this as a presence. That's as much as they've been able to do for surface groups. They really can't break through the way they'd like to; that's a plus.

How many of them are here at a given time?

Most of them are in very protected environments under the surface, in underground chambers that have walls at least six to twelve feet thick, lead-lined reinforced concrete bunkers. At the height of their influence . . . a moment; [breathes deeply] a little interference there . . . there have been perhaps 1300 of them here. Right now there are some 700 or so. They would like to get 70,000 here, but I don't think it's possible.

What dimension are they in the future?

About 2.5 to 2.8, but do not assume that this means that lower-vibrational dimensions (as you call them on the dimensional scale, such as it is) means that beings are more dense or more unenlightened; that is not necessarily the case. They occupy this dimension because it is easier for them to hold and because they are in an unnatural state of being. The more expansive dimensions are more difficult for them to hold, so they would perhaps be comfortable (within the range of their ability to be comfortable) from 2.1 to 2.15, but they've stretched to the point where they can hold their reality in 2.8. They come back to the 3.0, but if they were to stay there they wouldn't survive very long, because their negative energy is literally in their face. Negative things happen to them, because 3.0 dimension is a testing ground, a school. Things happen to you based upon what you're feeling and so on, and they can't survive in that. So when they come here, the sinister secret government attempts to maintain them to some degree to keep them from being affected by what the sinister secret government might call outside interests (meaning anything benevolent).

Are they physical?

They are not what I'd call exactly physical. They can at times maintain; they can summon a certain physicality, as it were, and the sinister secret government has a device that helps them to do so. They summon it not through magical powers, but through absolute concentration and what they would call will. They use their will and, helped a little by a dark crystalline device (which didn't start out as a dark crystal, but that's another story), they can hold something akin to physicality, but not the kind of physicality where you would eat food that would pass through you. It is more like an opaque physicality, meaning that if you were to see them you could touch them, but they would not be solidly physical; there would be something like a membrane of physicality. If you were to touch them lightly, they would feel physical, but if you were to shake their hand hard, your hand would go through theirs.

So there are 700 of them here. Now, define what you're calling the sinister secret government. Are they humans?

[He takes a couple of deep breaths and blows out.] A moment. . . . The beings we're talking about – the sinister secret government – are physical. They are human beings, yes. They don't at this time have much activity on the surface, but they could go to the surface.

These are not the thirteen families that we've talked about for years now; this is another group of humans?

I have to tread carefully here, but let's just say that their lineage is connected to those original thirteen families – some of which, by the way, have "fallen from grace," as it were. They are descendants, connected on the bloodline.

But then again, the thirteen families have had the future negative beings come back through the bloodlines and sort of take them over. Is that accurate?

Yes, it is accurate. They have come back and influenced the head of a family (that was easier to do in the past when families were more formal), enough to get him to pledge a son to this cause. The child would be raised to the point where he could survive on his own, and then his training would be with this group. They are basically taught survival skills, but are kept away from anything that could be called warm human contact.

And are these trainees the ones who are now in charge?

Yes. These people are continuing to go back and try to uncreate worthwhile things in the past. Ultimately they're trying to get back to the Founding Fathers of this country and pull people out of *those* families. They have the idea that if they can corrupt the original mystical intentions of the Constitution and to some extent even the Bill of Rights — certainly the covenants that came together to form the foundations of this country — they will be in a position of greater power. What they want to do is run their roots into the past as far as possible, because obviously they want to change the outcome of events that have come and gone.

For example, they want to change the outcome of World War II, where instead of the Axis powers being defeated, the free world would create a pact with them, enabling the Axis to rebuild themselves militarily and industrially for twenty-five or thirty years, completing the development of the weapons they were working on toward the end of the war, some of which you've only seen in the past twenty or twenty-five years. Then with those weapons in hand, they would go to the rest of the world and say, "We will destroy you if you do not allow us to take over." That is ultimately their goal. You might ask, "Why just our history; why not world history?" Because when the United States came into the war, that turned the tide. That's why you're the target.

If they can put in roots and influence you back far enough, they hope primarily to keep the U.S. out of the war. If the U.S. had never entered the war, things would have been significantly different. (This isn't to say that the French and the English and all the other Allied powers weren't brave soldiers, but that the U.S. contributed mightily to the war effort, not only in men but materials.) The sinister secret government's ultimate hope is to bring the U.S. into the war on the side of the Axis powers, at least in terms of providing military materiel. That's what they'd like to do. During World War II and in the years that preceded it there were groups in the U.S. that were draping themselves in the flag and calling themselves patriotic organizations that were basically spies for the Axis powers. Even though Japanese-Americans were blamed for doing this, it was much more the sympathizers toward Germany. The Bund and the Brown

Shirts and so on tried to make inroads here, but fortunately it didn't work out. They didn't disband, but they went underground.

Okay, in this alternate future reality, who is the general, the guy in charge, the one making decisions, the one sending the messages?

Do you mean what is the governmental hierarchy?

I mean who the beings are, how they live, anything about them . . .

Yes; you'd think they would sound like beings who might have a military order, but they don't, because a lot of what is in the military represents some of the higher qualities. What I am saying is that courage, self-sacrifice for the betterment of your troops and so on – they couldn't do that. They're not in a military situation, but more in a political, antireligious format. It's loosely based upon the idea of the satanic symbol, but they are not what I would call Luciferians. They're more associated with an emotion that you can all identify with and that can be easily summoned within most, if not all, human beings – control. So the emotion, physical action and will associated with control is their number one focus. And this occurs within the initiation of life, if that term can apply to their society; birth occurs there the way it does here. I'm going to give you more intimate details so you can see how insidious it is.

Instead of praising children when they do something the family considers upstanding or worthwhile, they are praised when they do something degrading or unpleasant, provided it follows the party line. For instance, if a child is cruel to an animal, it is praised for exerting its will upon that animal – the antithesis of your society's point of view.

But they are humanoid, they have families?

I'm interpreting this as if they were just like you, but they're not exactly like you. I'm utilizing the examples where they are enough like you that you can identify with it, you understand?

Yes.

Another example might be in making friends. Any parent would want their child to make friends with a child who's at least a good influence, or at the very least not a bad influence. But one of these children might be praised because he's in control of his group or because he's in charge or looked up to – regardless what the group *does*. The parent would bask in his reflected glory. This idea would be perpetuated on up the line.

When a marriage takes place, it's not a sacred ceremony such as you have; it is more like a binding. When powerful individuals see somebody they want, they either take that person – exert their will –

or, if that person comes from an influential group, they negotiate. But there is no love. It is very much of a manipulated, mechanized society in terms of its structure. It is the antithesis of anything anyone today would want to experience.

If we looked at these alternate negative future beings, do they look humanoid?

They look humanoid, yes. If you could be there in a protected vessel, you would see almost a haze in the air. You might think it's smog or fog or something, but it isn't. The haze you would see in the air—because of your ability to see a fairly broad spectrum of colors (they don't see in color)—is really the energy of fear. You wouldn't be able to see them clearly, but if you saw them they would appear humanoid. Their features are perhaps more coarse than your own.

Is there a percentage of negativity that they live with?

Yes, I'd say it's right around 75%, plus or minus 1 or 2% at any given time. They have found, much to their surprise, that when they're able to get negativity to beyond 80%, they die. So they get it as close as they can, even though they realize that 75% negativity (or even 73%) will shorten their life span by anywhere from one-third to two-thirds.

If you could just take all the negativity out of their bodies (and could survive in your atmosphere) and transfer them to your society in their physical forms, they could live to be perhaps fifty-five or sixty years old. This tells you that their life span under those conditions, compared to *your* experiential years, is anywhere from twenty-five to twenty-eight years. You might have street wisdom at this point, but nobody lives long enough to develop *real* wisdom.

They live on a planet that goes around the Sun like a regular planet?

It is fairly distant from the Sun. Their system is different, but their orbit would be somewhere between the fourth and fifth planet. They generally do not occupy the surface of their planet; they live underground. So when they come here to the sinister secret government and they're in those underground shelters, it's not a struggle for them. They're used to that.

If they're exposed to any sunlight when they make their transfer here, they immediately die. Why? It's the light spectrum that kills them, not the heat. It's the *range*, the measurable frequency of the light that kills them. If they were to go anyplace it would have to be pitch dark for them to survive, though they can exist with perhaps very dim, dark-colored light. They wouldn't need it because they can see in what you consider the dark by utilizing sound, basically. They cannot survive in anything that resembles what you call light—not even an electrical one. In this room right now, these lights would destroy them within about twenty seconds.

They're ensouled, right?

Yes, they are. They're ensouled like all beings. Of course, the soul can't handle it very long; it barely hangs on to maintain existence.

What is their history?

Their history is based on an alternate possibility; that's why they're constantly, frantically trying to entrench themselves, realizing that they exist basically as a potential. That's why I can't talk to you about their culture, their schools, their industries—they exist *as a potential.* They're a maybe, and they know it. At the higher levels (meaning their authority, their governmental power) they know they're a maybe for your future. They are making a desperate attempt to survive, because they do not have what you would call the light there; they don't even have prayer as you know it. They have no way of consciously knowing that they will survive, go on, have lives at higher levels; they don't know any of that stuff. They just have a desperate attempt to exist, a cornered rat kind of an idea.

When they get here they bring a message, but what other functions?

They don't always bring a message; they *might* bring a message.

Okay, so what other function do they have? What is their purpose for coming here?

Generally to feed (and this is a bit gross, but I will clean it up as best I can) the members of either the sinister secret government or their immediate toadies, who are with them underground in these protected places. When I say "feed," it is really true; they bring with them (and exude this to some extent) a dense form of negative energy that these people basically consume. It's not the bread of life, but it keeps them focused within density (as we are calling it here). It is not a pretty sight to see this feeding going on. I suppose I could easily use the term "horrific." It is not something that happens by osmosis; they actually have to consume it as one might eat cotton candy. It has the same thickness and is similar to cotton candy, without the glasslike effect. You feel like you're consuming something, but it doesn't have the solid feeling of an apple, for instance. It is a nasty business.

It's very easy to get mad at them and want the worst for them, but the interesting thing is, getting mad at these beings actually feeds them. If you don't do anything else, for the sake of your protection you need to project gold light at them, and you need to do it physically. That's why I mentioned blowing; if you do it *physically*, it's ten times more powerful than *imagining* gold light going to them. So even if you're doing a meditation to send gold light to these people, in the course of the meditation [he blows to illustrate] blow the gold light toward them. It's much more powerful, easily penetrating the lead. If you just *imagine* it going to them, it might not get through the lead in the bunker. If you blow, it will get through.

Okay. Are they coming on what we would call a vehicle, or are they coming only in bodies?

They're coming in their bodies, and the travel is so torturous that only a minor number of beings actually survive. Out of a hundred, perhaps two or three make it. But look at it this way: While it sounds awful that 97 or 98 people die, they thereby slough off that negative energy and go to the place where all souls go. They go through the veils like you do, so it's actually a liberation for them. So don't think of their death as being a bad thing; it's actually a relief. Unfortunately, that is so.

SSG's Influence on Mass Media

Are the soul branches an alternate being of the Explorer Race here on Earth? Are they our alternate . . .

They are not your direct alternate. I'm glad you asked that question. They are not your direct alternate, but a potential alternate. They know this, and that is part of the reason they are doing *anything they can* to stimulate and encourage whatever could cause you to become more fearful or anxious. For example, the current fad of movie producers to put out horror films or scary television shows – and I'm not talking about "boo" as being scary; I'm talking about unnecessarily graphic violence or creepy stuff, you know – really serves them very nicely because it gives people nightmares and causes you to feel irrationally frightened or anxious. Nevertheless, it's a real thing. So they're happy; they hope this fad lasts a long time.

Are they influencing it?

Well, let's just say that to the extent the sinister secret government controls funds, it is a little easier to get money for these kinds of shows.

If you were considering two scripts and one was about angelic influence on children and the good deeds they do to uplift their fellow children in their community – you're trying to get money for that, whether it be a comedy, drama, whatever – and the other had to do with machine-gun-wielding drug importers battling some hero who borders on being an antihero . . . need I say more? Which picture is more likely to be funded?

Notice how in recent years some of the heroes have become something very close to antiheroes – not the sort of hero you'd want to have around or marry your sister (if I might use that joke).

If they go to the same place we do when they die, why would a soul ever want to return to that alternate future?

They don't want to, but if this is something they volunteer to do . . . remember, it's not exactly a soul, as you understand it; it's an *alternative potential soul.* I'll give you an example. Say you're having a fantasy and you're seeing figures. You're in the picture, but you don't see yourself there. You're in the fantasy, understand? Even for a fantasy like this, there is an alternative potential soul that ensouls these fantasy beings. That's right! That's why you have to be a little careful when you have fantasies. It's kind of nice to say to the players afterward, "Thank you very much, I enjoyed that. You're excused; return to wherever you need to go," because that acknowledges the life in these things.

These souls would be akin to that; they're real, but from your perspective they would be a fantasy – they wouldn't have the light or the brilliance or the luminosity of one of your souls, for example. But they would be very susceptible to the will of others, and anybody who has a fantasy is basically moving beings around at their will. And these beings are easily influenced. (That's a little suggestion in the responsibilities of the Explorer Race.)

Competition, the Origin of Hostility

That puts us where we are now. That gives an understanding of what we're facing. The issue here is control. Where did this start? This is the end of resolving something that is ancient, this particular control issue.

That's right.

So I'd like to go back — we're talking Mars, Maldek, Orion. I don't know what went before that. Where would you want to start to bring it forward?

When your Creator arrived at this space, Creator Itself did not have any negative energy. But Creator picked up a being along the way who could have access to that – the Master of Discomfort. [See the chapter by that name in *Creator, His Friends and the Explorer Race,* not yet published.]

You could ask, as you have, "Where did this internal conflict come from?" It would seem to have been brought in by the Master of Discomfort, who needed to find a certain amount of redemption for itself, you understand? This was done and accomplished – or will be accomplished, in any event.

The origin of what I would call the current level of hostilities goes back to the inception of applied competition. I'm taking it to that level because that's something you can identify with right now. There are many things you could say about competition that are valuable—that it brings out the best, that you have to go beyond what you can do. I grant you that there are some good things about competition. But we must always recognize that in competition between two teams, one team, no matter how great they are or how wonderful they've been in the past, has to face the inevitable ghastly realization at the end of the game—that they lost, being resentful while they're watching the other team celebrate. Even if in their highest abilities they're able to say, "Well, they played better than we did, more power to them; we hope they have a good life," invariably they're also going to say, "Those dirty rats!"

Since competition was the nucleus of the beginning of hostilities, we have to go way back before Orion; we're not talking about Orion present but about Orion from the distant past, where there were groups that ruled their general society. There was a ruling class and a warrior class and so on. The warrior class was basically the enforcer; they were the elite, but they did not run the show. The principles upon which the Orion warrior class was founded were based on an inspired influence that was called in, in what actually turned out to be the inception of the warrior society.

Originally the ruling class that existed on Orion at that time had soldiers and so on; that wasn't the problem. But they recognized that they needed a warrior elite because the soldiers didn't want to remain soldiers. There wasn't anything driving them on; they didn't feel like they were serving a higher purpose. They were basically mercenaries. They were paid to do what they did, and that was that. There wasn't any higher purpose; they weren't serving anything.

No glory.

No glory, no "for the betterment of the king" or anything like that. So a group of these people who were of the ruling class got together in a circle as follows. [He draws Figure 1.] This is a circle with an equal-armed cross in the center.

The person who was the receiver was in the middle and four individuals sat outside the circle. It was an actual circle that resembled a parchment cloth. The people sitting on the outside of the circle faced the person in the center, basically radiating power and authority toward that person. They were sharing their energy, from their perspective, with that person in the center. But because they were from the ruling class, they were sending or radiating toward that person all that they represented. The person in the center, who could spin around (one of those twirling stools) and face any direction, was asking for inspiration to evolve the soldiers into a group that would have its own purpose but would continue to serve the purpose of the ruling class. They were basically asking for inspiration, but inspiration that was involved in control. They weren't asking for what you would call spiritual inspiration or angelic intervention, but to be guided by an intelligence beyond their own.

They did this as a group hobby, as a social thing. They had their social activities and then they would do this on and off. This continued for a period of about three of your experiential years. By the time it reached the third year they were thinking, "Should we bother with this for another couple of years?" On that occasion the person in the center said, "I am hearing words." The others said, "Well, what are they?" (This was not what I'd call channeling so much as telepathy.) They had someone there who functioned as a scribe (not a member of the inner circle), someone who would take down what was being said.

The Lord of Competition

This is when they first began to hear from the being who represented himself as the Lord of Competition. One of the first things the Lord of Competition said was, "These soldiers, your centurions" (which doesn't really apply, but does suggest an elite) "need to have something by which they can compete with each other so they can feel that there is at least one amongst them who is their master — not just that you are their master because you pay them, but that they have their own hierarchy. Through competition they will discover a hierarchy; they will also establish within their own kind a grading level, perhaps through ribbons or honors, laurels of some sort that will allow them to move up in rank as their competitive skills improve. This will give them a higher level within their own organization to which they can aspire and feel good about. You will also provide for them certain rules they will hold dear, their credo. When they have finished competing you will also include the most worthy of the centurions as a direct consultant to your inner council meetings."

Well, they shrunk back from that one: "Oh, our inner council meetings are very private!" And the Lord of Competition said, "That's all right. You make this person a special person; you initiate him into the inner council, give him titles, land holdings, whatever – the power of a council member, but not a voting member, someone who just is there. In that way you will give him a special status within the group." That's how it started.

Now, you might reasonably ask, "Who is the Lord of Competition?" The Lord of Competition at that time was not a past-oriented but a future-oriented being. This being didn't really exist in your part of the galaxy, but in a distant galaxy where alternate futures are all accessible. There is a place in your galaxy where people like me generally go to look at these things and study alternate potential futures. You can consciously hold a planet in the center of this "device" and look at all the alternate futures of Earth. You can take it right down to the minuscule; you can even put a person in the center and study all the alternate futures of that person.

One of the alternate futures of Orion was at that time a place where competition had been turned into everything from a public service system (such as a government) to arts, to professions, to trades, to industry – everything. The idea of competition had been taken to its zenith, and the being responsible for that, who had essentially created this alternate possible future for Orion, was the Lord of Competition. Thus they tapped into what was basically a potential future for Orion. That's how this all started.

Because we're doing these Explorer Race books you might think that all of these incredible things are happening around the Explorer Race, but it's interesting to note that other civilizations also have their histories, alternate histories and potentials and possibilities. It can go on indefinitely, you know, with all these different civilizations. I'm mentioning this so you won't feel that you alone as the Explorer Race have been singled out for perpetuating schools!

All right. So this competition on Orion began, and . . .

And that is what established the warrior class. It took a while for it to catch on. Because there was privilege and title associated with it, the soldiers were motivated to compete with each other in the skills they utilized.

They had the same motivations that any mercenary might have: wealth, power, influence and so on. Eventually it took on mystical tones, because the eventual visitations to the warrior league by the daughter of God [see Chapter 17 in *The Explorer Race*] and her assistants converted the then-warrior class to something much more mystical. Even today on Orion, which is a very benign place, there are still vestiges of the credo of the warrior class, although it is expressed in a very elevated way. The mystical elements of the credo are very high, such as "I will do my utmost to serve my brothers and sisters in my clan; even if I am tired, even if I am sick, even if I am at a distance, I will still do my utmost to serve them." Now, that's a good thing.

So we didn't come to competition from the present, but from the warrior league protecting the Empire from the Black League. Are we looking at those elements coming forward?

We're looking at that idea because it is something that has influenced you, yes.

The Ramifications of Competition

The Second World War seems to be a pivotal point, right?

It really is, because the First World War represented innocence lost, and there was still formality in the fighting—not for the civilians, but for the soldiers, who had a military credo. Certain things weren't done on either side, at least by certain branches of the service. All of that broke down in World War II, which was sort of a nasty antithesis of many of the aspects of World War I. I'm not saying World War I was a valiant cause or that those who started it were valiant, but there were certain niceties recognized and observed in World War I that certainly were not in World War II.

How can we help people understand that this competitiveness in the warrior league on Orion had unresolved elements brought forward that we're dealing with at this moment?

Understand that as the Explorer Race, you've moved around. You've always been interested in drama and excitement, so naturally many of you incarnated on Orion then because there was plenty of drama, plenty of excitement. Granted, you *all* didn't, but enough of you were there that you represent a significant influence in your now time. There are plenty of individuals who now exist on Earth who could say that you had lives during the years of the warrior league on Orion, or at least went through Orion and were influenced by it. As a result, you have things to work out here.

For example, not too many years ago in this country competition was based upon a credo, *how* you played the game—winning it fair and square and all that kind of stuff. Where has that gone? A lot of organized sports are still like that on some levels, but there are some levels where they're like almost unbridled warfare: "Me first and everybody else follows." This is a great downgrading of that credo.

But you said that the basic issue is control in this alternate negative future.

Yes. Their whole experience stems originally from competition. Competition is ultimately intended to create a winner, and anything like that *requires* the participation of those who lose. This has gradually evolved into (as someone might say in that alternate negative future), "How can I maintain what I've won? If I cannot maintain this through my own skills, perhaps I can maintain it through control by any means necessary." So you go from what you now have in your now time here (such as the ins and the outs) to whatever is "in," politically speaking. They've got more power, control, influence, very often more finances; whoever's out wants to be in. This permeates a lot of levels, including children. People want to be in the "in" crowd.

Well, in that alternate negative future certain individuals have fought and scratched their way to the top, and when they get there they use any means necessary to maintain it. It's what I would call a polarized negative version of competition —win by any means necessary and then maintain your position at the top of the heap by any means necessary. Even though we can trace it back to something that was intended to be a benevolent influence, it is the opposite as it plays out in that alternate negative future. Understand that its very description —the alternate negative future —suggests that anything and everything is going to be the polarization of any high cause or purpose —the opposite polarization, of course.

So the name we've given the place tends to be self-defining.

Hitler and the Nazis

And those are the beings, although they weren't that solid yet, who Hitler and Himmler . . .

. . . were influenced by, because they were trying to summon someone to give them power, influence, wealth and (perhaps most important to them at that time) recognition. In those days in German society, recognition very often led to influence, and that's what they wanted.

And by doing these satanic practices they gained this power. I've read that Hitler had the power to control and influence hundreds of thousands of people.

Yes. This was not what I would call Hitler's day-to-day personality. Scholars and others can read about the man's normal personality, which seems to be at odds with the man who gave speeches. People would often say, "Well, he was nice to me. He patted me on the head." Some person will remember their experience with him as a child, or "I met him at a party; he was very charming" and so on. When he gave speeches he called upon that inner circle and was inspired through that negative inspiration. He spoke with his *own* energy (he had his own personality), but he was tainted by that negative force, that power that did not hold Hitler's or anyone else's best interest in mind. It was just "what can we do to get what we want as soon as possible?" His speeches were a form of what I would call negatively inspired telepathic oratory.

When did he start making speeches to vast amounts of people?

I'd say after 1933. Thousands of people maybe before that, but not hundreds of thousands. By the time he became chancellor, we're talking hundreds of thousands of people, not counting his radio audiences.

So when he started influencing vast numbers of people, at that moment he was being used consciously by these beings from the alternate future. They were using him for their own purposes, so then even he was a puppet or pawn, right?

Yes, he was being manipulated.

He didn't know?

He knew that something happened when he would speak like that. He believed it was the power he was getting from that inner circle as well as the energy they would get from the summoning – they might call it that, "the summoning." I'd have to say, knowing the person, if he had known that he was being manipulated by beings from an alternate negative future for their purposes, I don't think he would have gone along with it. He wasn't that kind of person. More than anything in the world he hated being controlled by somebody else, so I don't think he would have gone along with it even if it had gotten him the power.

So he thought these beings were helping him gain control.

Yes, that's right.

Nazi Technology

You talked about weapons from the future. At what point did he start getting physical, material help?

In the early days he was getting more words; then as their inner circle grew a little bit and they started including people who were mechanically minded, the inner circle itself was being instructed. They would have an ideal: "We'd like to do such-and-such." As any engineer knows, you extrapolate from what you already have. They were influenced by the thinkers of their time, so atomic energy was something they thought of. They were working on devices that could be radiated at people and influence them, even the death-ray idea, which has long existed in science fiction (and which many defense- or offense-oriented industries have salivated about). When they started getting this negative inspiration, it was not based on what they already had, but on something that was a potential they hadn't even thought about. One of the things they were working on toward the end of their downfall, which didn't really come out into the public eye very much, was high-frequency sound-generation weapons. I can't give too many examples because I don't want to give anybody ideas. I'll use an example of something that has been explored by your own people in your own times: They were trying to create a beam not unlike a laser, but it was condensed sound that they could aim at anyone or anything to either destroy it or at least influence it. It wasn't as successful as they would have liked; even today it still isn't "successful," because they discovered its effect was too wide. You could mount the device and aim it toward something, but something else would also be destroyed downrange or (more importantly) on your flanks that you weren't aiming at. Much that was being worked on went to the Allied powers afterward in the great hunt for Nazi plunder, which mainly had to do with science.

But they had craft, they had . . .

They did have that; they managed to hide it. They still have one, but it's not very effective anymore, because (fortunately) its fueling ability has run out. They've got it parked somewhere, but they can't really fly it anywhere. That one they still have.

But they gained the ability to build it from the inspiration they got in the circle. I always thought that ETs came and gave them something, but they built it themselves from the inspiration from this alternate future.

That's right. They built it themselves. The advantage of that, from a broader perspective, was because they'd use Earth materials, which would be very dense. The vehicle couldn't get very far, so it couldn't do much mischief beyond your own planet.

The Recordkeeper told us they got to the point where the only way the Allies won was with help from . . . what would you call it, the Hierarchy, the benevolent guides to Earth?

Yes, it was necessary to have a minor interference there. To some extent the German power self-destructed toward the end because they kept sacrificing. That was the trouble for them, but the advantage for everybody else—the more they kept sacrificing their own troops and the more efficient the Allies got, the more strung out their supply lines were. Every time they lost a large number of troops, they'd say, "This is great, because we made a sacrifice." Their situation was self-destructive.

But they also had weapons of mass destruction — the V2 rockets — and they were developing an intercontinental ballistic missile. If Germany had not been overrun and the war had gone on for another six to eight months with certain places relatively intact, they might have been able to develop missile-delivery techniques. Had that occurred, they might well have been able to develop two or three atomic bombs, one of which they would have deployed immediately with a V2 rocket over London — bang, no more London! The only reason they attempted to develop an intercontinental ballistic missile (ICBM) was to send it to the United States. They didn't need to develop an ICBM to affect England; they had the rocket to do that already!

They created an atomic bomb before the United States did?

No; if the war had gone on an extra six to eight months, they would have done so. Thus there had to be a little bit of influence toward the end there. I'm not taking anything away from the heroic individuals who sacrificed their lives to destroy the Nazi bomb capacity and all of that. But there had to be enough influence to cause Nazis and their scientists to forget, to go blank in their minds and interrupt their scientific experiments that were gathering the materials together to produce a very lethal bomb. In terms of the radioactive cloud you had in early versions of the atomic bomb, it would have been about three times dirtier, so the radiation cloud would have had terribly lethal effects. To show that they didn't really think about it too much, the cloud could have easily been blown back toward their own country. But they weren't thinking about that then.

So you're saying that the victory was due not only to the aid to the Allies, but that the actual minds of the German scientists were clouded by . . . by whom?

Angelic Assistance in World War II

I'd say that they were basically interfered with. For the sake of simplicity you could say angelic forces, but they were interfered with in such a way that they could think something, but they couldn't speak it or write it down. It was like canceling out their motor function. Although they were still walking and talking, seeming to be absolutely normal, their thoughts couldn't get onto paper, so they couldn't calculate anymore. It would be like someone who understands calculus but can't even add two and two anymore; they were blank.

This was for a period of six months?

No, it was really for only a period of about a few weeks, but it was at critical moments. That was the interference. Those who exerted that energy on them were not physical beings.

Is it because people prayed for their help?

To some extent that's true, because a lot of prayers went out. If you remember, the reporting of the time was more humanistic. The reporters were famous (Ed Morrow, for one), talking about how the people in England were suffering and so on. People in the United States and all over the world, not only those who were suffering terribly such as Poland, were praying fervently for an end to the war and for the right side to win. They prayed not just for the war to stop, but that the Nazi power be eradicated. It wasn't so much for vengeance, but because of the knowledge of what the Nazis were doing. Even though the Allied powers realized the incredible evil of the Nazi practices, your societies were largely shielded from that. There were enough people who knew about it and talked about it that the word got out, even though not everybody believed it. People were more naive in those days. They couldn't believe that human beings would do such terrible things.

By exterminating . . .

Yes, the concentration camps and so on; most people just couldn't believe that human beings could do such a thing. But some people could believe it, and that helped fuel the prayers. There were also certain individuals who are no longer physically alive who utilized a form of ancient magic based on cabalistic principles who summoned an angel from God (which would have been their perspective – it was a lightbeing). They asked the lightbeing only to encourage the people to pray for a benevolent ending to the war, which would cause the practices of the Nazis to be stopped. Basically that's it. I don't care to give the actual words they used (which could easily be said in twenty seconds), because if I did, that would *really* be interference. You'd have groups of individuals forming all over the world and they'd say those words and [snaps fingers] . . .

But these were humans; they weren't what we call the Hierarchy, right?

These were people, human beings who lived in the United States. But they used cabalistic principles.

What about the Creator and the friends of the Creator? If everybody's looking on, what were the comments from them at that time?

Aside from "tut-tut" and so on? Aside from the obvious . . . we all know you're immortal, but we want you to change things for the better, so . . .

It looked pretty bad there for a while.

It looked as if it might go downhill. You might ask what we could have done. We can't interfere, we can just hope for the best. But if you ask if we were wringing our hands, we weren't—but we *were* cheering you on.

So we have a channeling that Hitler took his little time machine and went to Bosnia to stir up trouble there. [See the February and March 1993 issues of the* Sedona *Journal, also* Shining the Light IV.*] So tell us what happened to the rest of the Nazis, because that has an influence on the attitude of the world right now. They went forward and they're still here, they're still functioning.

It's basically sort of a negative secret society still in existence. I'm not going to name names here because some of them are either still alive today or have families who are alive. But I will say that some of the beings went on to form other groups that became influential; this is historical fact. A lot of them simply went to other countries and continued, when they felt safe, to perpetuate their ideals and their beliefs, at least on an underground level. As all political movements do, they attempted to influence the young to perpetuate those ideals. As you know, the young are more easily influenced because to them things tend to be either yes or no. The gray areas are not obvious because they don't have enough experience yet. Thus they put most of their focus on the next generation and started a lot of front organizations to perpetuate their ideas or ideals. They attempted to be influential.

Some went to South America, but didn't most of them come to the United States?

No, I'd say that most of them went to other countries. South America was a place that was willing to take refugees. It didn't put out the word "calling all Nazis." They were just willing to take refugees from this part of the world. There was an underground system of that organization, and they had active groups in places in South America that took a lot of people. Many people who weren't Nazis also went to South America; in fact, the majority of immigrants to South America weren't Nazi and are raising families there today. But a lot of Nazis did manage to sneak away to South America in the wave of immigrants going there. Not too many came to the U.S. because they felt that you had a well-organized law-enforcement system that might find them in time; and you also had an influential Jewish population. They knew that they'd be looked for, so they had to go places where they'd be safest, as anyone would want to do.

Cynicism and the SSG

In the fifty years after World War II we have arrived at a kind of cynicism we're living in now, so I thought a lot of the Nazis came here.

Understand that I am not referring to the average German soldier fighting in the field as a Nazi; they might have taken an oath, but they were soldiers like other soldiers. I include as Nazis the guards at prison camps and people who took a serious oath (such as the SS), but I'm not talking about the average soldier. Some of these individuals came to the U.S., but in terms of numbers—I've got to be careful now, because we're dealing with people who are alive—from a little bit before the war to seven years after, perhaps 1300 actual Nazis came here to *stay*. Since then you've had a natural die-off, so I'd say that today you would have fewer than 300 still alive.

I'm trying to leap across the abyss to connect this evil Nazi satanic . . .

. . . with the idea of mass cynicism?

. . . and with the secret government. They are* now *satanic, but they weren't before. Are you saying they are now?

What, the sinister secret government? I'd say they are now satanic, yes, though they didn't start out that way. They would have to be satanic to hold their power, as they see it. This tells you something—that they are ready to make sacrifices, whether those who are being sacrificed are willing are not. We can't say that the Nazi inner circle is the beginning of the sinister secret government, but we can say that they contributed members to it.

The alternate negative future came back to the Nazis. Then those beings from the future said, "Where can we go to find beings who are most like us and we can influence the most?" They go right back to the inner circle Nazis.

They eventually see that the world's not going their way (from their perspective), so they wondered what they could do to perpetuate these individuals. The idea was (and this is actually one of their signs): "We have to spread them out all over the world and to the best of our ability funnel power, wealth and influence to them so they can gain control and utilize the unofficial influencers of negativity, organized crime."

They used this symbol [draws Figure 2]. This is a sort of distorted spider—because a spider is actually a symbol for beauty and balance; a spider web is a beautiful thing. They used the twisted spider, or what from their perspective would be the octopus. (These are all beautiful creatures, by the way; don't feel negative toward them.) That symbol carries the idea of spreading out all over the

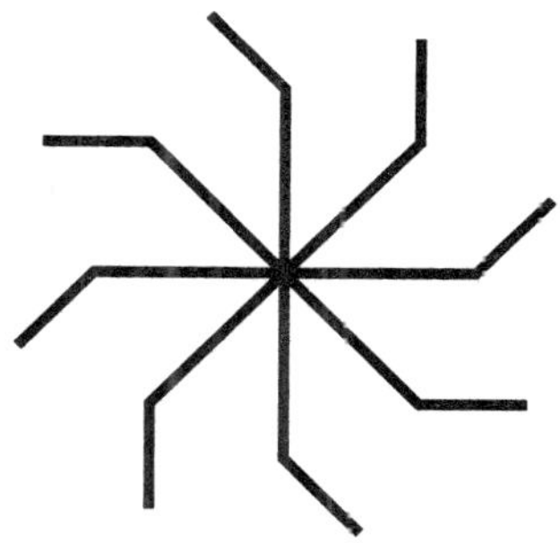

world to maintain influence and power. One of the places people were encouraged to go was South America, because South America has at its heart welcoming people, nice people: "Oh, come be here; it's fine." At that time people were more innocent, trusting, easily influenced and perhaps easily manipulated.

They went to other places, but we're using South America as an example because that was one of the initial underground sinister secret government bases where they were able to grab power. In South America there were also a lot of tribal people who had no real power beyond their own clan and who could be eliminated without repercussions if this newly forming sinister secret government wanted them out of the way. They basically used the power and influence that wealth could generate. Don't forget that the Nazis did a lot of damage as well as rounded up wealth, power and influence.

They took the wealth of Europe.

That's right, they stole everything they could get their hands on, including the gold out of people's mouths. They managed to get some of it shipped to South America—not all, but a surprisingly large amount—and they dispersed it throughout the world to places where they felt secure. And they continued to acquire things. The main thing is, they went to places where they could most easily survive, be accepted and not be in any way persecuted—and most importantly, be relatively invisible. You know, take on new identities and be the wealthy guy who lives up the street, as it were, laying low for a while. All the while they were pulling in members, having secret meetings and so on, and attempting . . .

They continued their practices.

They continued their practices and attempted to control through wealth, power and influence. By paying off various criminal families, buying their influence and becoming essentially "highly organized crime" (as I've called them), they utilized organized crime.

The Nazis, Organized Crime and the SSG

Organized crime to sinister secret government, that's the sequence . . .

It's not that simplistic, because it was more like the alternate negative future people came back to the Nazis to influence them and do what they could to perpetuate them because the Nazis basically held the same ideals. So they influenced and directed them toward any means by which they could obtain and maintain influence. They needed wealth be-cause wealth tends to generate its own power. Remember the times; the influence that went right across national boundaries in post-World War II was organized crime.

So the people they could count on the most to do things, even in places where there weren't Nazis, were in organized crime, because its web reached many places where they wanted to exert influence. So let's not say that the sequence was alternate negative future to Nazis to organized crime to sinister secret government; it wasn't. It was alternate negative future to Nazis to underground Nazis. Even organized crime was manipulated and used by them — to organized crime's detriment, not immediately, but later. So let's make organized crime a pawn here, not a willing participant who said, "Yes, we'll take your money and do your bidding, but at a big profit." This was not a good move on organized crime's part, but they didn't know that.

Many members of organized crime, had they known they were dealing with Nazis, would certainly have either turned them over to the Allies or . . . they had their perspective, too.

Their principles.

Yes, to some extent. They had their credo. They wouldn't necessarily have supported the Nazis. You cannot draw a direct arrangement between organized crime of the time and the Nazis; it's not there.

The Drive of Science

What about the German scientists?

They might have been involved, but I'm not ready to say that most were Nazis. There might have been a few. Mostly they were scientists who were given a task, a problem they wanted to solve. You had people in this country who developed the atomic bomb. It was a challenge, the leading edge of science. It was exciting; it was wonderful. Certainly many of them, after they saw the bomb go off, said, "What have we done?" On one hand they said, "This is a great tool for the war effort," but as the years went on they said, "I sure wish I hadn't been involved in that." Remember that science is still searching for a god, and for a while it latched onto a negative god. But science is beginning to pull itself up by its bootstraps and eventually it will discover its sacred god. Sacred science is coming, but is not fully here yet.

You say the scientists who came to the United States from Germany came for

reasons of survival and to continue in their scientific careers?

That's right. If someone comes along and bursts into your room with guns, saying, "You have a choice. You can either come with us, or we'll shoot you right now." You'd say, "Oh! Well, I'll come with you. Wonderful!" What are you going to say when someone puts a gun to your head?

That's how many of them came?

Initially they came under the power of the gun, but also some of them came because they were told, "We want you. Come over and we'll give you a place to live. It won't be wonderful, but it will be better than what you've got here. If you demonstrate your value and take an oath as an American citizen and follow the rules of our country, we'll let you live there." It looks a lot better than a bullet in the brain.

Overcoming Cynicism

I'll simply say this: We're pursuing this topic not so much because we want to expose this person or that person doing this or that in World War II and so on. We're pursuing it because I want you to remember why you're doing what you're doing now that is negatively impacting you—such as cynicism. *You can't afford to be cynical.* We're not expecting you to be Pollyanna, but you can't afford to be cynical, because it feeds the negative powers and the sinister secret government and their forces. If you expect the worst, you're not necessarily disappointed when it happens even though you'd prefer it to be better.

Fighting amongst each other also perpetuates that negative status quo. I'm not saying you should fight the sinister secret government; that's too vague. Well, who are you going to fight?

You need to constantly try to remember, "How am I like this other person? How are we alike?" Because that's the bottom line. Granted, it's challenging, in some countries more so than others. But even in countries where everybody has a common language and looks basically the same—a common skin color—there's still a caste system, the ins and the outs. You've got to look at the outs—especially those of you who are ins—and ask, "How are we alike?" You ins are in positions of influence, and how you think and what you do, other people want to know about because you're the ins and they want to *be* you. (I'm being simplistic here.) Be aware of what you say in public. I'm not trying to say that you can't be a human being and make mistakes, but try and be aware of what you say, because so many of those who want to be where you are will model themselves after you. If you can, from time to time say something good about the outs: "We're more like them than anybody" and "Everybody's very much alike." And it's really true; you're so much more alike than you are different, it's ridiculous. Ridiculous or not, you are making progress. And as I've said before, I have every faith that you will get by this hurdle in your growth and do worthy things in the future as well as in the present.

46

The Dark and the Light Sides of the Explorer Race

Zoosh through Robert Shapiro
November 30, 1996

I'm going to talk about something current. The intentions of those supporters who are here from the light is to spread the light around from the higher dimensions to connect you more thoroughly with your future light-selves and repair some of the damage done to your personalities from conflicts and struggles here on Earth.

Conversely, the sinister secret government, working from the dimmer side of things, is attempting to put as much wealth and power as they can afford into the hands of various individuals from different races and nationalities and in as many neighborhoods, geographic areas and so on as possible, with the intention of creating an artificial attachment to the outcome of things so they can spread their manners, mores and values to as many people as possible.

Thus the secret government is applying a technique that is the polar opposite of that of the beings of light, who are truly your future selves. I mention that because of the struggles in these areas now. I don't think that even by their "sharing the wealth" that human beings will be seriously attached to this newfound wealth, because it is coming to them in ways that are self-destructive – that which hurts yourself or another.

These Earth beings who might be called gang leaders or organized crime leaders know that what they're doing for their clientele primarily harms them. Even if they don't notice the harm to themselves personally, they can see the harm (the overlay or ricochet) that is done to their own blood families. So they are not working in a world of illusion; they recognize that what they're doing is not ultimately beneficial. If you want to find religious people, go to those who are coming to the end of their natural lives, and you won't find many atheists there. Everybody wants to talk to God to make some arrangement about what they have done or think they have done.

The intention of the sinister secret government is to create as many pockets of resistance to the light as it can by parceling out bits and pieces of its own wealth and control. It wishes to create lieutenants it can supply with wealth and power and, more importantly, *feed on*. Because the sinister secret government is functioning from a core of satanic energy, it tends to feed on the discomfort of others and it wants that chain of discomfort to include its own people. So even if the sinister secret government were to give a person wealth and power, it would set it up in such a way that you would always be discomforted, and increasingly so. Thus they feed off your discomfort as well as the discomfort you create when you spread corrupting and harmful influences. Know this.

This is what I'd call a topic of the *dim world*. By that I mean that they purposely shield themselves from the light because they are attached to power, control and manipulation. This is a short-lived circumstance, but it's one you must be exposed to because the human beings currently in the sinister secret government *are a portion of you* in the larger, whole you. They are not outside the Explorer Race; they are the dark side of the Explorer Race, the portion of you that is discovering what would happen were you to become vindictive or angry as a Creator. You need to have the memory, from some portion of yourself that has done so, of what might be the ultimate outcome from even a minor discomforting projection of yourself.

So ultimately they are serving your greater good and are here to challenge you. It is the ultimate intention that you not only transform them but rescue them from their blindness. They are blinded by that dimness.

What You Can Do

I do not expect you to consistently turn the other cheek and suffer for their benefit, but to begin now to function with the light. By this I mean that in your meditations, when you bring in the gold and white light or whatever other hues are attractive to you, besides sitting or lying down to meditate, move around (in groups or alone), feeling and broadcasting the light. In this way you will integrate the light more into the physical world. When the light comes to you in your meditation and you are not physically active, it will simply support and sustain you. Even if you broadcast it, it will broadcast at the level that supports and sustains those who seek it.

But if you can, get out, move around (but don't do things like get a cup of tea or coffee) and use gestures not unlike Tai Chi. Move in graceful movements, as if walking in slow motion, like the way a mime might move. You will be able to maintain your meditative state and you will also be placing the light into the physical energy of physical beings. This brings the light to the level of physicality and makes it more available to physical beings.

Another reason I want you to move around while you are in your meditative state (even if you can't stand up and move around, move your trunk, legs or arms) is because the people who desperately need the light often do not know they can call on it. As you physicalize it you put the light into the particles that come and go through your body. The particles enter the constantly moving mass of Mother Earth and are cycled through all these other people because a person can't really screen particles that move into you.

Can you be more specific about this transfer of funds? You're talking about gangs in the big cities and what else?

I'm not suggesting that anybody who's wealthy or powerful is connected to the sinister secret government. This is a very minor aspect of wealth and influence (in more enlightened circles; in less enlightened circles, wealth and power).

The sinister secret government realizes it needs more allies than it can directly integrate or draft. But in order to obtain allies that will be devoted and dedicated (even unwittingly) to the dark side, it needs to bring them into a highly organized crime circle. This, I might add, has a lot to do with a recent event.

In recent years there has been a lot of activity by individuals to finance seemingly political ends through the intelligence services by running drugs and building up an entire community of drug runners in the black community especially, but also in the Mexican-American and Asian communities. There has been no exclusivity.

Worldwide?

Yes, but aimed at the younger people because they are more likely now to be entranced by material wealth; younger people do not always have the experience to know that material wealth is not the ultimate wealth. If you think back (you, the educated or even somewhat enlightened reader) on your life when you were young, things seemed very simple – cut and dried, either/or, yes/no. But as you get older things seem a little more vague. That's when you start asking questions and become interested in philosophy and different ways of looking at life – and occasionally even lend an ear to old Uncle Zoosh.

The reason the sinister secret government reached out and helped to create the gangs all over your country through organized crime, was because they knew their recruiters could go to these young individuals and say, "Look, if you sell drugs, whatever, you'll get vast amounts of cash, which will buy whatever you want – cars, houses, furs, clothes, trips. You can go anywhere, do anything, have whatever you want. All you have to do is sell this to whoever wants it and recruit others to buy by doing what business always does – giving away free or cheap samples."

They didn't bother to tell them how lethal some of these drugs were – because, believe it or not, not all people who sell drugs are monsters. Some of them are addicted themselves, but the higher-ups in the chain of command are not, because they know that the "product" is intended to be sold to the customers, not consumed by the staff. The average seller is often a consumer as well. This is intended to some degree. But sellers who are consumers do not tend to get very high in that organization.

The SSG Group That Wears Disguises

The best way for the sinister secret government to maintain control was to give as many people as possible a stake in keeping things as they are no matter how much wealth they had to spread about. Corruption developed as a result. It's true that they targeted the black community. And they used to a great extent an organization of their own that passes itself off as various government organizations. Now, I'm not saying that all people in the CIA are innocent babes in the woods, but about 80 to 85% of the people involved in the actual drug running to gain money for projects were not CIA people or CID people or certainly not NSA people. They were not even U.N. people. They were what I call the enforcement arm of the sinister secret government, who love to don the uniforms and guises of legitimate organizations.

As you can see by my figure of 85%, I'm suggesting that some individuals within these organizations I've named have been unwittingly involved. After all, if somebody orders you to fly a load of stuff (you usually don't even know what it is) from point A to point B and he is your superior, you're going to do it. Although there *are* a few who are involved, mostly these were people who *said* they were from the CIA or even the U.N. in order to legitimize what they were doing and utilize the prestige of those organizations to create fear and respect in those they were working with.

There are certainly people at the higher levels in these organizations (not appointees) who've been there for a while and know some of this. But they also know that if they look into it too deeply or make any effort to expose it, they will very quickly disappear in an unpleasant way. So they too are intimidated.

I want you to know that your organizations are not as corrupt as you think they are. They're not innocent, but they're not as awful. A lot of the people are dedicated workers and believe in a higher purpose. The sinister secret government is always looking for ways to tear down your good feelings about your government or any of its offices. That's why they've worked very hard to support, sustain and encourage in the general population – about the President, senators, Congress, lawmakers in general, attorneys, people in government service – the belief that these people cannot be trusted and that the worst can be expected of them. All of that plays into the hands of the sinister secret government. That's why you have to guard against cynicism.

So the two major thrusts of the secret government are the crime gangs in cities and the encouragement of drug sales by recruiting runners and . . .

Understand that the sinister secret government does not recruit gang members; it does not recruit anybody. The sinister secret government is a very small group of people. It simply manipulates and dispatches things. The sinister secret government is what I would call a negative dispatcher. They move things around so different people are exposed to opportunities. They might talk to a few individuals who come to them, and they have many individuals who work for them unwittingly, but they don't go out and do something on their own. They're strictly behind the scenes. That's how they maintain their secret status. We need to make that clear so you can understand that people who do any level of recruiting might believe that they're a secret agent working for the intelligence forces of the world (not just the CIA) or are being looked upon benignly by some organized crime figure who will make them wealthy and powerful.

If you can move things around like a dispatcher, where this batch of cocaine goes unnoticed and is not seized by the legitimate government, trainloads of it, then you can provide lots of material. From their point of view it's good business to expand.

So the inner circle connects to the outer ring, then their agents and just keeps expanding . . .

I realize that what you're saying is that their influence goes to the outer ring. However, the outer ring people usually come to them. But yes, their influence goes out that way.

So the influence eventually reaches the street gangs and drug runners.

Yes. But it's always indirect so that there is never any way to trace it to them. They do this by moving things about.

But you might be able to trace it to some of the organized crime members, who might not realize that it goes beyond the person they report to.

That's right. You might even be able to trace it to an outer ring member, but because all of the outer-ring members are very respected in society, people would have a hard time believing that these individuals could in any way be working for the most evil institution on the planet. They have good offices and are respected. Sometimes when they're unwitting outer- ring members, they have no idea that they're serving some greater evil purpose. They think they're doing something that's worth doing and don't necessarily recognize that other people are feeding off it.

SSG Wants More Things Illegal

For example, there was the resistance in this last election to the idea of doctors providing marijuana to seriously ill patients for the relief of pain or various disease symptoms. A lot of the resistance you heard about was people saying, "This will lead to the legitimization of marijuana, and then children are going to go from marijuana to heroin and that's that," and 99% really believe it. But there are a few who are (wittingly or unwittingly) campaigning to keep marijuana and all other things illegal at all costs, because when it's illegal they can sell it for more. If every supermarket could sell its version of marijuana, a pack would eventually cost only about fifty cents more than a pack of regular cigarettes. This would make a lot of money, but not the kind of money they're making now. So it pays them to keep it illegal.

They do that by funding and falsifying research and putting out disinformation . . .

They do it by supporting organizations that fight legalization no matter what their political or religious affiliation is. They will see to it that those organizations never run out of money. If it ever looks like they're going to be exposed, they will drop their support of that group and start supporting another organization doing the same thing. They won't start organizations, but they'll see that they are supported.

You could say: "Well, these organizations are not made up of evil beings." Certainly not, but organizations that seem to hang on past their time are usually getting their money from those who stand to gain by keeping these drugs illegal.

Do they also give money to the political parties to influence them?

Yes. If your election laws weren't so stringent they would show up with a busload of money and just shovel it off the bus. Although there are pretty good controls on that right now, they're still able to sneak some money into politics. If you really want to do it, it can be done. Just don't leave footprints. If it's not logged in, it can be done anytime. You just pass somebody a suitcase.

But they support both sides to keep the illusion of the two-party system, even though these politicians do not really govern the country.

No, the two parties are more the bureaucratic level that keeps things going. If they didn't have this influence, the country would be quite a bit different – different *better*. The sinister secret government has no problems with your government making laws and so on as long as it does not support legalization of anything they want to keep illegal. Generally, the sinister secret government would like any restrictive acts by your government.

For example, at some time in the future there will be more people working secretly to support those individuals who want to commit suicide easily and gently. Suicide, while it has severe religious connotations in your society, is not always a terrible thing, especially if people are suffering physically with some terminal illness. In many civilizations, including higher ones, when someone is suffering they either replace their body (which to you would be like suicide), perpetuating their personality, or cure them in some way.

I'm not trying to say that suicide is okay, but that the sinister secret government will build private suicide clinics where they charge a lot of money because it's illegal. (I'm not in any way referring to the famous doctor who supports people to pass over who are suffering. He is doing this work from his heart because he doesn't want people to suffer. If there's no cure and they're just suffering, he sees no reason for that to be perpetuated.)

So you're saying that it's going to become an underground business where people will pay for this help?

The government is taking the position now that you don't have the right to tell your doctor, "Don't maintain my life." Until recently you could say, "Don't use heroic efforts to maintain my life."

Yes, in 1989 my mother had instructions not to mechanically prolong her life.

You can tell doctors that, but now the government is taking the position that it's *not* okay, and that medical science can take whatever efforts it must to preserve your life no matter what. Even though well-meaning people are involved in this, the sinister secret government thinks this is really wonderful. I don't want to scare you, but many hospitals are being purchased by legitimate fronts for organized crime. Organized crime, to become successful in the long run, must become involved in legitimate businesses and run them in a legal fashion, if not a moral one. I'm not saying that all hospitals are run by organized crime, but a significant number are. If you as a patient wanted to leave a certain amount of money to your family and you didn't want to go on suffering, you might say to your doctor, "Don't use any heroic efforts to keep me alive; I want to pass over naturally as I might do at home. And I want to leave something behind for my heirs." But if the government takes the position where that's not legal for doctors to do, then doctors and hospital administrations will, from a legal position, *have* to keep you alive no matter how much it costs, draining you of all funds and resources so that there's nothing left for your heirs—and unintentionally (from the doctors' perspective) keeping you suffering well past the time you would wish.

I'm not trying to say that physicians are evil—just the opposite. Most physicians are geared toward helping the public, not administering and running their organizations. They would like to have the administration taken care of so they can work with patients. Insurance companies have high rates due to high payouts for malpractice suits, so it's cheaper for doctors to work for large organizations. These organizations are easy targets for those who buy up these clinics, hospitals and large medical-plan organizations and who keep everything running legally but change the moral bent. You need to keep an eye on your federal government and what it does, because they often respond to those loud, squeaky wheels. They are being lobbied to maintain a position on moral and to some extent legal grounds because there have been some abuses where sometimes people have said they wanted to pass over when they didn't really want to. Your government might take a position that is truly unnatural: to keep a person alive past the time of the end of their natural cycle.

So doctors, keep an eye on things. Do your business; take care of the people that you want to take care of. But don't be blind to those who would say they're doing your work for you but are in fact trying to undermine you. Many doctors are being undermined by some of the more nefariously owned so-called medical organizations that are beginning to harm the people they're supposed to be helping. Many physicians know this already. I'm putting it out to the general public because I want you to become more politically involved. It's good to be lightworkers, but you also have to be grounded, down-to-earth, politically active. You don't have to run for President or senator or Congress, but you do need to attend school board meetings. If you can, move around, talk to people, bring the light through you when you're at meetings – it can only help.

It's important to understand how insidious it is – that the sinister secret government is not happy manipulating things behind the scenes; they won't be happy until they are manipulating and controlling *everything* within their venue. Then they'll want to go to other planets and do the same thing. There's no stopping this kind of lust, and there's never any satisfaction beyond the temporal. You might feel satisfied for a couple of days, but there's always more to do. This has to be experienced so that as you evolve to become Creator, you will recognize that one step in this direction can become seductive, becoming many steps.

At this time, then, you don't want to talk about North Africa, Korea, Vietnam and all that.

I think I'm going to skip over that because the present is more important. There's no question that many of these wars, certainly the Vietnam War, had to do with economics and so on, but I think others have said this pretty well.

Was there a connection between the HAARP project, which attempts to control and manipulate thoughts, and this latest satellite that started out for Mars and didn't get beyond the atmosphere?

This project called HAARP and other focused antenna arrays are able to broadcast a beam of electrical and electronic interference. This works on human beings, but it can also be broadcast into space and topple a satellite or a rocket. Why would the sinister secret government, utilizing through its own techniques the HAARP project, destroy the Russian satellite, several of them, heading toward Mars? Why would they interfere with the Martian project?

One of the foremost features of the Plan is to introduce extraterrestrials to you as a part of your normal space projects. This would involve primarily the Russians and the U.S. It was always intended that when you landed vehicles or pods on Mars, sometimes moving around but usually just sitting there, they would introduce extraterrestrial life to you. This satellite parked on the surface of Mars would sit there for a while and gather data. Then a ship would land nearby in full view of the cameras, and beings would get out and conduct business. They would not be human, but they would be pleasant-looking. This was always intended to take place, not just secretly for the scientists, but to be broadcast to the general public to introduce them to the fact that there are friendly ETs out there. This was part of the Plan.

The sinister secret government, of course, is desperate to destroy and interfere in any Mars project, whether launched by the U.S. or Russia, because they are aware of that aspect of the Plan and want everyone on Earth to be *afraid* of extraterrestrials. They desperately want that because they know that ultimately extraterrestrials will come and meet you. You'll like them, they'll like you; it'll be wonderful. They want to stop that, so they will use any means available even if they have to take serious risks —which they did when they used the HAARP array and another array of antennas to interfere with the Russian Martian project. They had to expose a couple of their people, for whom they then conveniently arranged car accidents. To do this they basically had to sacrifice some people in their organization, people they would rather not have sacrificed.

Was it the same in 1993 when our satellite almost got to Mars?

That's right. In 1993 there were some things going on in the planet where it was a little too soon to reveal that. Let's just say that when the sinister secret government interfered, nobody [ETs] made any attempt to save your probe. They could very easily have blocked the energy used to cripple your probe, but no one did because when your probe got closer to Mars it would have photographed things that would have been too soon to show on Earth. It's really now — around 1995, 1996 — that the Plan intended for these things to be seen. So your sinister secret government is corrupting the Plan a bit, but to put not too fine a point on it, "we'll be back."

Whose Plan is this?

It is the Plan to elevate all humankind to a higher consciousness in the best way for you.

But who wrote it, who instigated it?

The Creator, of course.

Oh, I see.

Granted, with a bit of a round-table discussion with friends of Creator.

All right. Our own God-selves are coming in on a wave of energy, then? It has nothing to do with the vehicle or the Hale-Bopp comet?

Your God-selves are coming from the future, that's right.

And they're doing this as much as possible.

That's right. That's why sometimes you'll reach out and go to them, and sometimes they can come back and come to you. But yes, there's definitely an attempt to connect more substantively.

47

Hale-Bopp Comet Brings Lightbeing-Filled Vehicle To Assist Humans

Zoosh through Robert Shapiro
November 19, 1996

Can you tell us about the vehicle four times the size of the Earth that is traveling with the Hale-Bopp comet? This is a picture taken November 14, 1996, that is on the Internet.

This vehicle traveling with the comet is studying it, but there's more. It's a somewhat long story; I'll condense it a bit.

As you know, for a long time planets beyond your own have been trying to bring your planet into the Network of Planets – planets with beings sufficiently similar to you that there would be no great cause for alarm if you saw them. The vehicle traveling with the comet, which is making itself obviously known, is a part of a "Hey, look, we're here!" outfit. And there's more.

This vehicle came to the Earth in 1896 and was involved in surveying Russia. It was also very interested in Russia as a potential place for colonization. Although the beings in that ship would never consider usurping control or doing any kind of forced colonization on the interior of your planet or the surface, a lot of the surface has been mapped by extra-terrestrials with the idea that if you someday want their help and have them live amongst you to share their wisdom, perspective and knowledge, they would find certain places

more comfortable than others — perhaps reminding them of their homeland in some ways. A southern mountainous area of the Soviet Union was surveyed then, a warmer area, not so cold. (I use the term Soviet Union because I think that they will become reconnected before too long, not under Communist control, but perhaps in a loose organization of states that might become closer in time.)

This vehicle is returning now. It might not come all the way to your planet, partly because of hostile forces — those individuals who try to keep enlightened beings away from the surface for fear of losing control. Even without any hostility, there is the slow breakdown in your planet's atmosphere. Some energies of discomfort, which you call negativity, are escaping and creating problems beyond your immediate planet. These areas of escaped discomfort are being shielded by a small device planted in the center of your planet that creates an artificial energy similar to magnetism, in the sense that it attracts and holds any negative energy escaping beyond your atmosphere. This is done to protect the citizens of other worlds and, to some extent, even your own astronauts — who, I might add, are actually more susceptible to earthly discomforts when they're in space than on the Earth! This is done to protect everybody beyond your atmosphere. Thus there is some control in place. Nevertheless, the ship will probably be cautious and not approach too closely.

You'll want to know, of course, where the vehicle is from. It's from a very distant star system in another galaxy. The travels of this vehicle take it all around your universe and occasionally, though not commonly, in the past to other universes. This was done largely to

organize their original intention, which was to monitor the development of civilizations of various cultural heritages so that when they would get to a certain point in their cultural, social and spiritual evolution they would be invited to join with other planets that have similar cultures. It is an unwritten law that no planet such as Earth, with its human culture and population, would be in any way initially involved in a network of planets that would connect you with races too dissimilar from your own. One step at a time, yes? Come to know the people that are like you and some that are sufficiently like you that you can ease into the reality of other-world culture and sophistication.

The origin of the ship has less to do with a planet than a feeling and a thought. The ship was created because there was no planetary body that could be utilized for such voyages that could tolerate and be tolerated by different solar systems. A ship was the logical choice. It was necessary to make it quite large because it has a permanent population—a civilization that lives on the ship all the time with all the equipment necessary for them and the crew.

It was always considered to have several functions, that of cultural or social observation, but also of potential rescue operations. At any given time the ship is no more than one-third to one-half full of the denizens of that culture and their guests. If it were necessary for some spiritual or other very specific purpose to rescue the population of any medium-sized planet (such as this one), the ship would have sufficient space for the population and for the material needed to support and sustain it, including the different cultural requirements.

Now, the ship is *not* coming toward Earth to rescue you, but on its route the original thought was that this might be the case. The mapping done was in case rescue wasn't necessary and for the time when people on that ship and from other places would someday come to mingle with you according to your desires. The focus, then, has been changed toward the desirable idea of contact rather than rescue.

Rescue has occurred, however, in previous times when civilizations have risen and fallen on this Earth. Rescue has taken place onboard that vehicle no less than twice by the entire citizenry that desired to leave the planet. Once a warlike culture on this planet was evacuated. You might ask, "Why were these people rescued?" Well, there were a couple of factors: First, they were actually welcome somewhere. In those days there were civilizations in other galaxies that were still training defense forces, and this warlike civilization was evacuated to places like that. At another time a civilization associated with the sea was rescued and taken to Sirius, where they blended their genetic material (which had evolved in a subtly different way here) to be with their root races. Both were perceived to be worthy rescues.

Now, you might ask, "There have been many other civilizations that have risen and fallen—why wasn't everybody rescued every time?" Well, evolved spiritual beings know (as well as most individuals who are in some way spiritual or religious) that there is life after life. The idea was that yes, the civilization and the people would die, but souls would go on; there would be no break in their existence. The rescues took place only when there was a need, desire or a purpose for that civilization elsewhere.

This ship heading your direction was originally coming in case rescue was necessary and desired. But now it is believed that this is no longer necessary. The ship, as I say, comes not from a *place* so much as a *need*. If I had to say where it was originally formed, it was close to the point of emergence of the matter that makes up your universe. So it travels very great distances with ease.

Is this a separate vehicle? Is this the planet that's four times the size of the Earth, or is this a separate vehicle?

This is a vehicle, not a planet.

Is it four times the size of the Earth?

Well, perhaps a little more than that, maybe 4.2.

It's the one that was sitting out by Saturn for a long time?

No, it is not the same vehicle that was sitting out by Saturn.

That one's still there?

That vehicle's a different shape, too, by the way. The one sitting out by Saturn is thousands of miles long, but it is more an elliptical shape. This vehicle in your photograph is spherical and has what I'll call a rim, used for its manner and means of motivation, meaning how it gets from here to there. Sometimes the rim is out, sometimes it's in, sometimes it's various lengths and distances. It is not a planet. Granted, it looks like one, but it is not.

Does it come every hundred years, or is it just toward the end of time now?

No. It doesn't come every hundred years (as one measures time here) but when civilizations are nearing either their break point or their transformation point. Other civilizations around the universe are like that too, but since discomfort does not exist much in other places, when it goes to other places usually it's for the purpose of education. Maybe a planet has a group of citizens numbering many millions or more and they need something. It might be possible to simply send individuals into their midst to help them if they desire it. Sometimes, if a lot of individual attention is needed, it's necessary to take them aboard the ship and put everybody through a process by which they can quickly relive a certain amount of their previous experience in infinite detail, but without loss of the intimacy of the experience. In this way the transformation (to give an example of what the ship has done) of that society was faster because things people had forgotten were replaced into their conscious memories so that they could remember as a group what they needed to remember and be motivated toward the leap they needed to make on their own. They were not given the leap, but mainly the reminders why they *needed* to make the leap.

Okay, if we looked at them what would we see? What shape, what dimension, what form?

The beings themselves on the ship?

Yes.

They have the ability to appear, not as *all* forms of life, but in anything from, say, a pinpoint of light to any physical being from the dimension 2.8 and up in this universe. So they are a little limited. They don't travel to anyplace less than 2.8 dimension because they are a little more difficult to synthesize, but basically they can appear as just about anything in your universe.

Have they been appearing on our planet? Have we been interacting with them without knowing?

I don't think you have had a mass experience with them. They have come from time to time, usually choosing to be someone sufficiently obscure that, although they might be well-known in their time, they would not have fame or recognition beyond that time. They would be seen perhaps as well-known teachers—not celebrities or someone who would espouse a clearly religious goal—but someone who would support and sustain purposes of morals and values.

Are there any names in our history we would recognize as these people?

We'll get into more of this with the book on the mythology of the Explorer Race. Once as Eros, also once as Atlas—that's their mythological versions. In terms of beings you might still know in your society, I don't think you know these beings, but you will probably rediscover them as beings of value. For example, I think there was once a being typified through Homeric writings—the Cyclops—as some horrible monster; but in fact, at the time Homer wrote of these things it was already a myth—and myths, as you know, tend to become clouded, in terms of the facts. The actual beings were much more enlightened. I think there's no one else you would recognize, but you might rediscover their knowledge.

Do they plan to interact with us now that they're here?

They might. If they do, it will again be in roles as teachers. They will make a great effort to look like you, sound like you, talk like you, act like you. In other words, they will be under cover. I do not think there is any way to detect the difference between them and another human being.

What would they look like if we visited them on the ship and they were in their natural state?

Oh, they would probably be irregular shapes of moving light whose colors would correlate with their mood.

Is there a dimension that would have any relevance?

Oh, perhaps around 32.

Thirty-two? Are these the god parts of ourselves, or totally separate, unrelated beings?

They are their own beings. They are their own civilization.

This is their work?

This is what they do, yes. This is their choice.

Is the reason there have been no photographs of the Hale-Bopp comet since (I think) May 1995 because no one wanted to point out that there was something along with it?

I think that to some extent, giving astronomers their due, the vehicle wasn't always there, and so one would question the scientific relevance. Understand that if one looked at it and said, "What is that? Why is it traveling with the comet?" not thinking of it as a ship —one moment it is there, but in the next picture, perhaps on the same reel of film, it's not—it would be very disquieting to the scientific community. This is more the reason the pictures are not being released. It also cannot be overlooked that because of these anomalous light patterns (as they're being referred to) it is now considered a matter of national security.

It is possible that some other countries will at times in the future release pictures as they see fit. However, it might not get into the mainstream press, because the mainstream press in this country and Europe and other places is to some extent controlled.

But the Internet is still open; these came from the Internet.

The Internet is open for the moment, and is considered a weathervane of people's feelings, even though putting something onto the Internet and accessing it usually requires a reasonable intelligence and at the very least computer literacy.

And that's a small proportion of the world's population.

Yes, exactly.

All right, how long will they be here?

That is not fixed. They will be here, as they say, as long as they like. The ship has the capacity to make itself unseen. It also has the capacity to move to higher dimensions very quickly to get out of the way of something.

Which is why you could see it in photos, then you couldn't?

Yes. Even when you can't see it, it's still there. When you can travel dimensionally, the easiest escape is to simply move dimensionally, then you are no longer tangible.

Is it going to go around the planet? Is it going to cut into the solar system?

I think if it comes into your solar system it probably won't come much closer than Saturn. This is probably because of the weapons systems associated with Earth. They're not at all concerned about your weapons, but they do not wish to create a stir on Earth, and the firing of weapons invariably does that. I'm sorry to say that there are some people who are basically afraid of anyone or anything that might approach from afar. Aside from that, nowadays keeping secrets is more difficult than it used to be. They do not desire to create problems.

Their very presence is going to make the energy frequency rise, isn't it? You've got 32nd-dimensional energy and . . .

Well, you have to remember that if they are focused in your dimension (visible), even though they might be based in 32nd dimension, they would not be emanating or radiating it, or it would breach the veils, which would be disastrous.

But they are connected to what we call the Federation and you call the Network?

They're connected to *all* networks in this universe and some beyond. They have no limit in this universe; they go wherever they feel needed.

Is this universe synonymous with what we call this creation?

Yes.

So they can go beyond this creation?

They can.

But they're not from ***this creation?***

No, I'm not saying that. They are from this creation, but they can go beyond it. They have not often done so, but they can.

Well, they must be doing something more than just sending one or two teachers down here if their interest is to raise our consciousness and move us up, right?

Understand that they are doing something that most other extraterrestrials don't do. Looked at directly in the eye, as it were, they are interfering.

How? Evidently they're allowed.

That's right, they are allowed a very minor degree of interference as long as they do not appear to be gods or anything like that. They've got to look like whoever is running around on the surface, emanate no greater energy than that and communicate in the same style of the culture they're in.

Are they going to bring people from Earth to their ship for anything?

Certainly nothing like what you'd call abduction, but they might inquire and open a certain amount of contact with certain representatives to the United Nations. They tend to perceive the United Nations as your world government even though they are aware that it is not yet. They see the U.N. as the nucleus of your world government, so if they were to approach anybody as a governmental representative, they'd go right to the U.N.

Is there a name we can use to identify them rather than "that ship with Hale-Bopp"? Is there some way they'd like to be known?

Well, let's see if they can give us . . . a moment. I will spell it roughly in English, Ahsaad-Hunie [ah-saad´ hu-nay´]. I will also, for your amusement, reproduce a little of their writing when they write physically. [He writes.] I'll give you a rough translation: "Greetings to our brothers and sisters of similar life."

What about the ship outside Saturn that is also four times the size of Earth? What is it doing? What is its purpose?

This is a vehicle that has been hanging around the general area for perhaps three or four hundred years.

Before the Hubble telescope, you couldn't see it.

That's right. Right now it's doing a lot of work. Saturn has some similarities to Jupiter—do you remember Jupiter being struck by that space debris [July 1994]? They are creating a link right now to transfer material mass from Saturn to Jupiter to repair it. Jupiter was so badly damaged by that strike that if left to its own resources, it might develop a sufficient orbital decay to grossly interfere with several other planets in your solar system.

So they're digging stuff out of Saturn and transporting it to Jupiter?

They're basically operating like a dentist, extracting matter—*only* the matter that's incompatible with Jupiter (if it's compatible, they will leave it)—and repairing stress fractures by transferring material from Saturn and using a fusing technique with a latticework that works not unlike a scab, although it's not as full as a scab from a cut on your hand. It is not unlike a glue, but it attracts similar particles, allowing the natural elements of the planet to grow together in time. It's like surgical sutures.

Who are these beings? Would we have heard of them? Where are they from and what do they do here?

They're from Orion future, so they have an interest in your culture. Their primary function for the past few hundred years has been to sustain the stability of your solar system while studying it. They're interested in your solar system because it is growing. When planets come together it is usually for a cause, not just casually. Your solar system is growing and will ultimately become at least thirteen planets. They're very interested in that process, so this is to some extent a scientific mission, though at the same time helpful.

Have any of these beings ever channeled through anybody? Are these ETs who are some of the technocrats who are helping us?

No, I don't think so. These beings would be disinclined to contact you directly. Their stock in trade (what they're good at) is tones, including those in your audible range and tones beneath and above it, as well as a set of tones more to the side of it. They are more inclined to communicate through tonal inspiration (I'm not going to take credit away from artists and musicians on your planet), so when a musician hears a tone that he or she cannot reproduce but knows it's perfect for a particular composition, it is sometimes from these people. They tend not to communicate or even inspire through audible signals—tones you can hear—because they do not wish to interfere with the inspirational process, but from time to time they communicate in tones that can be imagined. Thus the people they contact would usually be musicians.

Are they light? Do they have a form? What is their lifestyle? How do they entertain themselves?

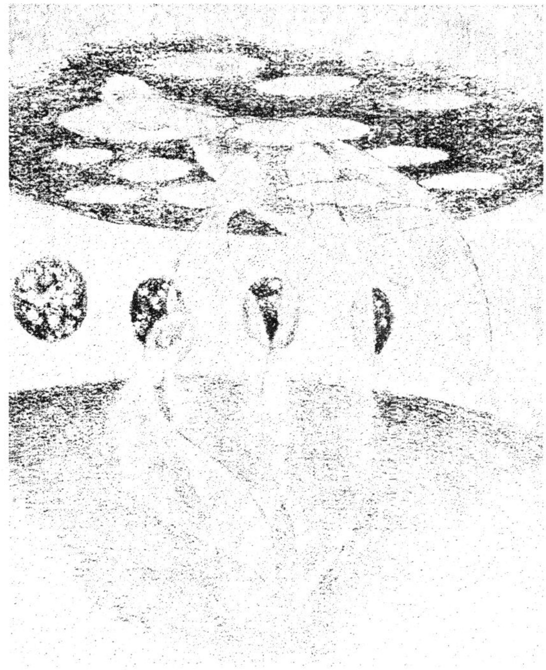

They're gaseous in nature if you were to see them. Unlike the beings on the other ship, they cannot take other form. They do have the capacity to utilize automation and speak through an automated synthetic being, creating something that would look, for instance, like a human being but would have no intellectual capacity of its own. It would basically be a tool of the beings aboard the ship. As I say, their culture is culture—music, art, dance, a celebration form, perhaps light and its variations. Emotionally speaking, they are usually happy and in what you would call a celebrating mood. They need to maintain this energy. Since they have contacts with Earth people through the means described, they need to maintain that mood so they don't get caught up in anybody's inflammatory passion. Thus they maintain that level of cheerfulness and happiness.

And yet they do scientific work instead of . . .

Well, science even now is beginning to understand a little of the potential of sound in manufacture, creation—and yes, re-creation, meaning the transformation of one thing into another.

So they're doing this with sound, then?

Yes, they are most adept at that.

Okay. What is is the purpose of the comet Hale-Bopp?

Well, it is a form of life, you know. All comets are forms of life. Ofttimes they recognize that they are utilized by and for those who wish to give signs to others and, obviously, those who need to receive the signs. So they are purposefully anomalous so that they will be seen. They are meant to be seen.

But they have some purpose. They're going to be coming in and going around the solar system and then where?

They are messengers. They do not create the message, but deliver it. That is what *any* comet is doing: delivering a message from one point to another.

It isn't a vehicle, but is there an energy in the comet, anything other than the living comet itself that is going to affect us?

It is possible that there will be some radiation – nothing to worry about – that could affect your imaginations and dreams, most likely in a benevolent way, possibly creating fantastic experiences in the dreams. Generally, what you remember of your dream life tends to relate in some way to your everyday life. This material might cause some of you to have dreams from your far-flung future existences that would cause you after waking to feel as if you've been in star fields or with the clouds of light or something. It won't relate directly to your life, but it will be a very benevolent, uplifting experience.

All astronomical photos were taken from the Internet site of artbell.com

48

The Ship: The New Collective Teacher

Aruthrra through Arthur Fanning
November 18, 1996

It is not Jehovah. It is power. The being, it, beingness, a group of be-ings, a collection, a tribe, a region of the ascended portions of every being on your planet and portions of beings from elsewhere that had reached their highest level of the wisdom of God, and those are your words. So understand that they [your words] are a limitation. Indeed? You would term it a greater thing, a spiritual hierarchy. They come when things need to be done.

These are ones. They come with authority. They are not given authority by anyone. They have it. They are this authority. And their resonance is like "I command." Yet it is not. As they move through systems, the energy is so powerful that you beings—humanity or any system—are automatically aligned unto their thought. Know you what I mean?

Now, you beings have read the words that they are a thought matrix in that verbiage of your remote viewers. Now, we've been working with you a long time. Indeed? And from back when we were speaking, the energy called I (and more indeed) is the will of God (your words). Now you can understand it a little more. In the presence of this energy you will not have the ability to think the game of not. You will be thinking the way these beings hold the thought. All right? The power here is outrageous. You have no understanding of it. You can conceptualize it a little bit, but you will be aligned unto their thought and you will think your free will is going down the tubes. But you will be aligned unto a more lovingness. Indeed?

It's going to happen, anyway. Have a grand time. It's the argumentative and the competitive that's going to have difficulty. Now, recall you meditations we've done on the other side of the black hole. Indeed? And the beings there we spoke of unto you. Because they are lovingly holding the thought of this system, this universe, that is why this universe exists. A lot of energy has been put toward this place. A lot of petitioning has come from this place and your star systems also. And the Earth is the last place to raise its frequency.

What they haven't told you is if you don't [raise it], you're going to kill your universe, because the beings on the other side [of the black hole] will figure it's not worth it and they will stop participating with their thoughts amongst themselves. They'll think the game (because to them it's a game) is not worth playing anymore. There's no joy there.

This ship is coming to align you unto joy. This is part of where this thought thing with some of your beings' information channeled this uncreation part. But you can't uncreate anything. It's always in the thought of it, and the soul holds memory. Know you what I mean?

So these beings that are coming are going to align unto a purity of thought what your religious beings, your churches will say is what God intended. But it's a little more than that. You're growing up and being responsible, and these energies are going to align those thoughts. Now, the name of the being in charge here of this ship, as close as we can come now . . . we'll have to let the vibration sit so the consciousness of the physical body can handle it, and then we'll change it later. But it will likened unto Aruthrra. A-R-U-T-H-R-R-A. That is the name of the being who would be said to be in charge of the collective consciousness of this ship, this energy field, these beings—Aruthrra. You will be speaking with this one shortly, within a month. And he will be doing some of the presentations in your intensives.

This energy has a sense of humor, but it's on the fringe. It's not within the core of its being. In the core of its being is pure love, and your system, your societies, can't handle that yet. So it will be around for a while. It's going to make interesting conversation.

Tell the one who wanted this information that you have it. It's a short explanation. I want it understood [that] in here is the power and the authority—as you would term it, the will of God. But there's much more there than the will of God. There are legions of them, what you would term millions or more, and as they move they gather more with them. So you can never tell their numbers, have no idea. And the power of it is love, you see.

So are these beings from the other side of the black hole?

They are, yes. The ship sent emissaries, so to speak, that are coming. Their allegiance is unto those beings on the other side, as you would say—the ones that hold the thought here. Their allegiance is unto them, for they are part of they. They are, in a manner, the thought from these beings as it be what's going on. Know you?

These are the beings that were involved in parting your Red Sea and destroying your cities and destroying Maldek and some other planets and some systems. But they didn't [really] destroy, only from your perspective. They simply came with so much love that everything had to vibrate to that love or be destroyed. That's what's happening now. There's going to be a great shift in your consciousness, but some beings aren't going to like it.

49

SSG's Worldwide Agenda

Aruthrra and Jehovah through Arthur Fanning
November 27, 1996

I would like some information about what's going on right now with the sinister secret government, with the beings that they are dealing with, what it's going to mean to humanity and what humanity can do about it. I want the information, not to scare anybody, but to empower them.

That can be done.

First I'd like to know who you are, where you've been, what you're doing.

Know you Shiva?

Well, I know what I've read about him and what I've been told.

Yes. One aspect is the mover and the destroyer. Indeed? The creation forces. The idea of Shiva existed as a thought – the idea. This was before Shiva. All there is is thought. There's much more thought than what you beings can utilize here. There are those beings who modify the stream of thought – [a] great river. [with] narrow channels to pass through certain canyons. I am in that band.

How wonderful! Anything like the Thought Adjusters in the **Urantia** ***book?***

They are copycat over the belief system of the understanding. They are part of the grouping that is working with your secret government.

Have you been here and channeled through anyone before?

No.

Well, welcome.

We are aligned unto the concept of the will of God – that is your concept. And we are aligned also unto the petitioning of beings as was told in your story from the Council of Nine. So in one way you beings move me. In another I adjust . . .

You adjust us.

Yes.

So is the flow of thought from Shiva, then? Is that what you're saying?

It is a concept that is beyond Shiva. And the word "beyond" is your hierarchical understanding. It is beyond the concept that is.

Well, when I figure out who Shiva is, then I'll ask you more.

Well, Shiva is everything you can see on your planet.

As well in all creations.

Yes. It will be there in layers.

All right. So what would you like to tell us about the situation right now that will expand our understanding of it and allow us to do something about it. This is the big hurdle before the fourth dimension, right? The last big one.

Yes. What will help you to assimilate some of these understandings is to recognize that you are divine. A symbol on your chest like a pyramid – in your dress, your shirts, your blouses, your clothing – will allow you a concept to think from here [soul/chest]. Now, it allows you to think from within your soul that you're in the safety of the soul – that energy field. You're in that safety. It was designed that way as a safe haven. The energies coming now that we are directing and aligned with and assisting are coming to . . . well, you beings say "awaken." Know you awaken?

In order to awaken, you have to remove some of the dust and some of the obsolete material that is covering ones. And most of the obsolete material is here [brain]. Well, we're bringing forth more light, and it's going to create great activity in the brain – a lot of pressure, particularly in the upper temple area here. There will be a tendency for beings to panic, for their consciousness will focus here [brain]. If you focus in the soul and understand that the body's a tool . . . it is necessary to have that understanding now, *not* metaphysically. That has taken you to where you are now. It is to really realize that you exist in here [soul] – your greater force in there, inside the body in safety. And that force can align to the thoughts that are around here – what you beings say is your lightbody. You will want to begin to vibrate that lightbody, to quicken it and feel the quickening inside the soul area, [so] that the flesh begins to change its texture – literally – so the membrane [becomes] permeable now for both energies to move freely through.

The higher frequency (as you say, the fourth dimension) is a vibratory understanding of God (your word). It is your ability to vibrate within the understanding of all that is and all thought that will assist you, that will assist the physical body in these changes – these (you would say) drastic changes. They are *not* drastic changes. The reason you have been so spiritually ignorant for so long is that you have not allowed yourself the incremental changes that were supposed to take place. You stacked them all up at one end.

And now we have to experience them all at once.

You have to complete. That is what is going on now. Now, there are those that you know of, what you term your secret government, that are aware of this process and they are aware of this reincarnational understanding and they are aware of control – power. They want it. They want to become God physically incarnate. They're going to come very close to it.

The concept of God, however, is love. It is not the game of *not.* So these beings – this grouping – will never make it, never complete in that way. That's why you were told that these beings that are playing these money games (and they're pretty outrageous now), that pretty soon they will know (and some of them are already feeling it because the energy is being pushed there). They'll be giving their money away because it's going to be understood that it's hurting them. Humanity is going to, in your next ten years, begin to go through the phase – the beginning – of understanding what the body is for and what the planet is for. It is for the attainment of your spiritual wisdom; not the attainment of reciting, not the attainment of building a church, not the attainment of having the only truth. It is the attainment of building power within the soul forces of the wisdom of spirit.

It is like you go through your colleges and you go through again and again and you never graduate, and you're the ultimate student. Everyone looks up to you. You never move into the real world, but you're pretty popular there. The real world is spirit and love.

There's going to be a movement where beings are going to spend their time understanding love and the frequency within the body. That is the purpose of life. It's not the accumulation of power. Spiritual understanding is the true power. The letting-go process is going to be the difficult process. Do you understand what I'm saying?

Yes.

So what is going on now with this grabbing and the manipulations, particularly over in your area of China, is [that this is] the last foothold left where there's a possibility of controlling the consciousness of the majority of mankind. Lot of population in China. If you can control the population and control the consciousness significantly enough (group together to control consciousness) you can affect the entire planet. That is what they are trying to do.

Zoosh said previously that the SSG [sinister secret government] created an earthquake to threaten them into submission.

In the manipulation of telling beings how to think. They must think this way.

Or they will be . . .

Punished.

Punished and forfeit their rights on the planet?

Yes.

So we don't know about that. It doesn't come out in our papers.

Yes. Going on within the now, you are having . . . and in part of this country (I might as well tell you) a movement to create the same energy fields, thought vortices that the entity called Hitler established in Germany. That is being worked in your country right now. The groundwork is being laid for the informers within the citizenry and the corporate safety nets are being set up. They'll get away with it for a little bit. That's why this energy is sort of accelerating in your December. There is this thing that we are doing that if enough energy comes in, this networking of these limiting structures [scenarios] will not complete satisfactorily.

In this country and China, or just in this country?

Primarily in this country for that Hitler energy, yes. But it will spread. Pretty outrageous.

I have questions at the end, but I don't want to influence what you say with what I'm hearing from another channel.

Yes. Right. One of the reasons you want to focus on the energy and the light that's coming is that you can then have the ability to handle these things coming. Then you will have the ability to successfully network with other beings of like mind in the feeling. And it can be altered. The importance of it is rather outrageously profound. What it means is that you must do it here on your planet — know that you are in the power and you can manipulate the thought so that certain beings can't go around establishing a thought for you to believe in. That is why it's so important for each one now to become empowered within self. Know you what I mean?

Yes.

Once you do, they can't manipulate you. They won't have enough ability to.

They'll try to project thoughts, then?

Yes. They're already doing that.

Well, they have been, but evidently they're going to increase it tremendously.

Yes. They're going to try to. They did their little experiment and one of the agents, your agents, our agents, sort of fixed it.

Are we back to the HAARP project now? Are they still using that technology to broadcast these thoughts?

Well, that is a part of it, yes.

So they've replaced that satellite* with something else to provide it with the power, or what?

*[*The electricity-generating satellite whose tether broke when being tested by U.S. astronauts on the shuttle Columbia on February 25, 1996.]*

Well, the things you sent that were supposed to be going to Mars?

The ones the Russians sent?

And one of yours.

Who are they going to try to focus on here in this country? Hitler had a particular group he focused on.

That was later.

Yeah, I guess first they just killed everybody.

Yes. Anyone of any intellectual bent was isolated. That will be the first step. It will be the metaphysical community, yes.

So they're going after the metaphysical community first?

First. You're the most dangerous to them. Know how the Buddhists—you know, the Buddhists, and the Tibetan Buddhists particularly—had a lot of energy focused on them and they had to move, flee? Go into exile?

Yes. From Tibet to India.

Why? Because they were working with what you term spiritual understandings. And there were certain groupings. Not just China; your England was involved here. They had a lot of influence over there, and England doesn't want too much spiritual understanding.

Why?

Because you wouldn't need a king or queen. People would begin to see for themselves, think for themselves, be themselves. Why do you need a king? So that is what is going to start. With your

United States — and you have a certain level of freedom here, more so than most. So it's going to be a lot [more] difficult for them to get on your case, so to speak. They might, oh, ridicule you a little bit. But here in your United States you've sort of gone over the hill. They can't do too much now. You have a greater network of beings now.

These beings who are leading this are in turn led by somebody, right? The secret government beings on the planet? They are in turn controlled by somebody?

They are being influenced, yes, by an extraterrestrial, yes.

Zoosh has been talking about this negative alternate future where these beings are coming in to influence . . .

There is one being, extraterrestrial in nature, that is situated in Europe who is orchestrating this thing. He knows he's being watched.

There are beings from this alternate negative future that are controlling the secret government?

Yes. They are desiring to influence it in their direction — the energy fields, yes. What you have to print is that each of you came to this planet at this time knowing what was going to happen. You have that concept metaphysically. Correct? You have the plan. You chose to be involved in these energies only because it was a great test of your accumulated spiritual wisdoms, and you wanted to get further wisdom. All right? So you are participating in these scenarios. A lot of you beings that have been working diligently for a number of years aren't so much threatened by that scenario. You are sort of above it, I'll say. And you are assisting the ones that are stuck in it, or [you are] going toward it to show them another way out. As you move one or two, you move yourself higher. You've scored a point. All right? So some of you across your America and across the planet are working from that perspective to build your spiritual forces, your spiritual bodies, your spiritual understanding (I'm using your words now; it is much more profound than that). You are working here in this greatest density to perfect all of your spiritual powers because this is the hardest density to do it in, right now.

And it's basically the end of the possibility of doing it?

It is the end of the possibility, yes, within the physical form — as you would say, the human form, yes. Eventually the human's condition is going to understand that that is all there is — the development of spiritual wisdom, not the perversion of it. And yet the perversion of it became the development of it. It was part of the journey. Know you? And that's all right.

In fact, Zoosh says that the Creator helped set up this . . .

Yes.

. . . this negative future as the final test.

Yes. To put you there, to let you make a choice again, you see. Yes. It is right in front of you, your labels good-bye. Choose your wisdom.

Okay, what can people do in their daily lives now? What's the most important thing they can do? They need to know that they're safe within their soul, but what are some other things they can do?

Be gentle to one another — be compassionate. If a being is angry at you and having an energy difficulty, if you lend assistance and it helps, fine. If you lend assistance and they become more angry, simply move away. Don't struggle and create a confrontation. There's going to be in your month December — that is next week — the great energy individually of surrendering to some power that you will say is outside of yourself. It is not your government, it is not the antichrist, it's not the christed energy. It is the last part of your battle against *yourself.* This month December you'll get a good taste of it. Surrender into the center. And even though you're in the middle of the storm, you're still in the middle of the storm — it's very quiet there.

The eye of the hurricane.

Yes. A lot of things are going to go on.

Amplify that a little. We're going to surrender . . .

To self.

. . . to ourselves, whether it's to our positive, loving side or to our baser side, you're saying.

You surrender into your loving self. The soul inside . . . you beings say it's your higher self. I prefer "your light." You just center there with it and feel safe and secure with it. And what you'll end up doing is drawing in more light and more light and more light. There's going to be a great tendency to argue this month from December, outrageous tendency. But that's all right. You're getting assistance from many beings, many energies. Even some of the extraterrestrials are going to start to show up simply to alter some of these thought patterns, to get you think[ing] in another way.

Did you bring that planet that's near the Hale-Bopp comet, or did you have anything to do with it?

I'm associated with that, yes. It is on one of my strings.

Well, I'm glad you pulled it this way.

We're moving it this way, yes. It's going to be very interesting.

In fact, the beings and the entities associated with that energy are the ones primarily responsible for the consciousness shift on your planet. They will be the ones that will be the intermediaries; they'll be the emissaries. They'll be the ones you'll be making contact with from that station.

Wonderful!

Yes, it is.

But that's a few years away yet.

The energy is going to start this month.

The energy's going to start, but the actual interaction physically with the beings . .

It will depend. Some beings are already being contacted.

They are?

Yes. . . . We're shifting. . . . [Pause while energy shifts.]

[Chuckling.] Some of the information you'll be getting a little bit later will have to do with this control, yes, energies of different extraterrestrials regarding this planet.

Excuse me. Who's here now?

This is Jehovah. Now, there is a favorite place for interference, so to speak. We're putting an end to that. You've heard of the battles in the skies that take place?

Yes.

They will. It is important what you're being told about this here [touches chest].

Centering in the heart.

Yes.

When you came here you told us that you said, "This is my planet. I want it back."

Yes.

Tell me who you are taking it back from.

Oh, from what you would term the Pleiadians as you understand it, from some beings on Orion (not all of them) and from some Sirian beings. Not too many Arcturians. Basically, this place has become a garbage dump throughout the universe.

All these beings you just named have got some controlling interest going on here?

They've been raping the planet for the minerals, etc. They've been . . . you beings can't understand it. They steal color. How can you steal color? You're the only planet that has this much color. They borrow the frequencies, so to speak.

Is this like siphoning it out like you siphon gas or water? I mean, can they just take

it?

Well, they rob your consciousness of it, is what they do.

How do they do that?

I don't want to get into it. They sort of . . . they let you forget.

And these are supposedly benevolent beings?

They are in one manner. But they don't know, either, know you? In the great energy, jealousy and greed seem to permeate in this sector – not just on your Earth here.

In this part of the galaxy?

Yes. And this was purposeful – experience.

Right. And we set it up that way, but now it's going to stop.

Now it's changing.

Right. Are some of these like the merchant ships who see this as just a place to trade?

Well, they're sort of moving away now. They know this conflict is coming. It's like refugee time out there. Those who stay, they're going to get it. They know it. So there's this, sort of leaving. Indeed? And your secret government think it's being aligned because some beings *are* staying; they want this confrontation. Well, they picked on the wrong one. They think they know who they're aligned unto and who's aligned unto them. But little do they know.

"They" being the secret government, or these . . .

Even the extraterrestrials that are aligned unto the secret government.

Who do they think they're aligned with?

They think they are aligned to very powerful beings, what you'd term, from other systems that have greater power. So they're going to be attacked from the inside out as well as from the outside in. Caught in the middle, you see. And that's the way the game is going to be played.

So it's going to play out where everyone really needs to focus on their heart and be loving and compassionate. But the end is basically assured.

The end has already been completed or I wouldn't be here.

All right. Zoosh told us a little bit about that alternate negative future, and I really got a little concerned.

That's all right. In one manner that's needed. Know you what I mean? I'll put it this way. There are beings that are going to need that platform to go to.

That negative future?

They will need it because there's going to come so much love to the planet that the love itself could destroy their consciousness. You see? So they must learn to develop it within a construct where they feel safe. Some beings feel safe in [the] negative; they *need* to be controlled.

Oh, but this one was 73% negative — horrible, ghastly.

Some beings require that identity. Make it not your choice. Know you what I mean? That is what is going to happen as we come forth with more light. Some beings will slide into that. And as long as you understand that there are levels of that negativity, there are dimensions within that negativity . . .

It doesn't have to be the extreme one we were talking about.

No, not unless you desire it or prove you're stronger than it is. It wouldn't be wise at this time. But we took care of that one.

It will be everyone who will be tied in. It will be . . . as you would term the movement, the antichrist move. That's why the [positive] energies of those ships are coming here, to adjust the energy of the soul. If the soul can adjust itself to love, then it will prevent. And it's also available that if a shifting [is] needed, beings in their loving nature will be left here and the others will be taken.

That is a possibility at this time?

Yes, it is. Negative energy over here placed there within different levels. That is what they want to do.

I know, but how would you take them? A war would have to happen in order for them to be killed, right?

We would shift the consciousness of it.

And let their bodies go.

Well, they can stay in the body and be in negative energy. You know, I have the ability to alter this planet in a moment?

But then we wouldn't learn anything.

You wouldn't. I can shift it in half—I can allow a dimensional activity to occur in a square mile. Pick one. Whoever's there has to relate to that activity.

But that's just someone else trying to control us.

Of course. But if it gets out of hand, I'm going to do it. It's not as bad as blowing up a planet. Then we create gateways for beings to come in and assist and back out and assist and teach. We've thought of that, too. Then what you call the Lemurians can come to the surface. They've been down there too long.

[There will be] a lot of things, particularly starting this December. Pay attention to your skies, entity. What you don't know is that you are so close to what would be termed a Sodom and Gomorra that you can't believe it. You can't see it. But from our perspective, you're that close. And the last time, we shifted it. It makes great table food now – salt!

It's gotten worse lately. Right? It has not gotten better, and it's because of this influence of the secret government. Right?

Within the grouping of those beings. A lot of you who have been working in your understanding of spiritual wisdoms have made it better. It would have been a lot worse a lot sooner.

But aren't they going to the past and trying to change it? You say you alter the time lines. But they are influencing the past, aren't they?

They're getting into it, yes. What you don't know, however, [is that] we are the group that was shifting your time lines, eh? It was pretty clever. They couldn't figure out what was going on. Now we have other groupings. We've been training you beings, believe it or not, when you play sleep, know you? When you can't sleep you have been on a journey for a little bit altering your time lines – not yours, but theirs. You're practicing to get it. You're doing it. You're in the process of it. That's particularly why some of you can't sleep. Sometimes you bring forth your judgments of what you're doing to this time.

Why do we judge ourselves if we think we're making a positive . . .

I don't know. It's something you're doing, something you beings do. You have fun with this thing. We have difficulty figuring it out. It's part of the process. Know you the Ten Commandments? They weren't commandments. They were pieces of wisdom for beings in this density. If they could not remember, they could read the wisdom and apply it in the soul so the frequency of God within the soul would not be trapped here. Because of this judgment you beings do, we put forth that information, having seen the future. We gave you the clues and someone took them and used them as rules. They were not rules; they're wisdoms here. And where does wisdom come from? It comes from the feeling. Know you the feeling? The feeling when you read those words is what is important, not the word. And if you maintain the feeling you could not be controlled.

And these were the things that we were most apt to judge ourselves on.

It's what you *did*. So I came and wrote them [the Ten Commandments] before, because I am in all places. I left you notes, many notes. And I am in your other futures, too. I'm coming back and leaving you notes, piece of a pie.

So we better start reading them.

You're doing it.

How are you connected to Aruthrra? He talked about the will of God also.

Yes, he's aligned unto that manner. Pretty outrageous. We will say he's the best tactician that exists. He is primarily involved with this comet. That's one of his strings.

All right. Do Id and YHWH have anything to say about this, or do they basically work with you? Do they have anything that they want to say?

YHWH is comfortable. And Id doesn't want to change the tone of the energy at this time.

Okay. What can we do about China?

Well, you can't interfere there. There's a wise man in China who's on his journey. He's sort of a seer there providing wisdoms for them in their journey. And he has to do battle with another seer.

What will be coming out pretty soon anyway is that a lot of your governments—all of your governments—use seers, know you? Astrology and this.

All right. What about Africa? This is an absolute atrocity. They're trying to kill all the Africans and take the minerals. What can be done about this?

Yes. Part of it is the karma of Africa.

What is the karma of Africa?

It is a denial of God in their understanding. They were nomadic people. And they were in freedom, the movement, and they sold out, you see?

For?

The monies. The beings . . . it's power, indeed. And it causes disruption of the peoples.

Beings in power of the countries that are fighting sold out?

The beings were set up prior to the arrival of the German people and the English people I be speaking of here (not this year; obviously, this all happened after the Second World War). You've heard the story. Your Earth was divided by the rich men prior to any of the wars.

So before the secret government became the sinister secret government, they divided up the planet and each took a big chunk of it?

They allocated what they were going to have at what you would term the end of tribulation. Yes.

At the end of tribulation. And what date did they give that?

They give that at 2010.

So they knew about that a hundred years ago.

Yes. It's pretty outrageous, yes. It is being played out. There's nothing you can do right now. You can send the light there and [to] the other scenes. But that continent is going to shake and split in half, anyway.

Vertically or horizontally?

Vertically.

The pyramid will be . . .

Opened.

Will be opened at the time of the earthquake?

Indeed.

Days, months, years? How long?

Depends on how the energy builds with all this murdering and fighting going on there. It will either speed up or slow down. The more the murders, the quicker the quake, sadly to say. Pretty outrageous.

But the people who are dying don't have the karma. The people who are suffering don't have the karma if the leaders sold out. Is this from some other time? Is it something they came here to experience now? They had to have chosen it.

Karma in a greater understanding doesn't exist. At the level that these beings are playing in, it does exist. All right? Some of them have to learn lessons. It evens itself. This is not the first time they've been involved in the game called murder — either side of it.

So this is an old battle being fought.

Yes.

Where did it start? On this planet, or before?

Well, it started on this planet, you could call it, but it has been incited . . .

Yes, definitely that's the point I was making.

. . . from other places on and on and on.

Because they want the minerals. They want to get rid of the people.

Yes.

So they seem like victims, although you say they have lessons to learn.

Yes. With these energies coming in to assist them, it's an alignment of the heart. I will talk to government leaders, I and my friends. And I suggest they listen when I talk. They'll know who's talking, because if they don't, I will harden their heart. And they know what I mean. That's one way to get attention on your planet.

How do they know that you're there? Is it thoughts in their mind or a dream or a

vision?

The dream will be so vivid, they'll be talking about it amongst themselves. And I'm not the only one.

What about our heart energy? What is the capacity right now? What is the percentage that we can really tune into that's available to us at the moment?

All of it. What do you mean?

Most of our heart energy is supposed to be locked up in the center of the Earth until . . . so we could play in polarity and negativity.

Oh, I understand what you're saying. As long as you agree to those rules. If you step outside of the box of those rules, you have it *all* open. The planet is not ready for that grand experience yet totally. All right?

I understood that the Council of Nine was stuffing it in as fast as we can hold it.

That is true.

Let's just say that the capacity must be increasing if we're going to integrate the energy. We can hold more if we work on it.

Yes. The soul can hold more. And the body will transform itself. Yes. You won't forget the experience. Yes. Anything else?

No, I think Zoosh gave us a really detailed analysis of how the sinister secret government got that way — you know, with the beings going back and forth in time and the Nazis and organized crime and everything. I think that's clear to people. I think you're giving people the feeling that there's something they can do. There are people helping them. There's something positive that's going to happen. They can get this information and they won't be afraid.

You wouldn't have Zoosh in this time if you weren't gaining wisdom from it. Know you? I'm not saying that it's not challenging times. I am saying that some of you later are going to learn that the only thing that is important is your spiritual wisdom: the accumulated wisdom of your soul and your accumulated spiritual power. Life is forever, and it's that spiritual wisdom accumulated in the darkest of times and the happiest of times that will take you into forever. Everything else will limit you and cause you fear. You will play in the fear individually. Be caught not up in fear; be into love. All right?

And this is a grand time to make a choice right now.

This is the time of choosing, yes. Be not swayed by your political leaders, either. They're not of the greatest wisdom.

Is the country going to fall apart into the separate states and sections? You said that what happened to Russia is going to happen here.

Yes.

Soon?

You're well on your way. Prepare yourself for more riots in your cities.

Instigated, or people who are . . .

Instigated, of course.

Are they going after the metaphysical people?

A little bit. They're going to be too busy with the cities.

So they're going to incite riots. Then what?

This will be the time of the segregation and the separation of peoples – the next two years. Don't just simply wire off the cities. Border them off.

You mean like separating rich people from poor people?

Yes.

So traveling will be curtailed?

Lot of limitations. You're going to start seeing a society created for the elite. And you beings will want it.

We will want it? Why?

A lot of beings do because they're not into understanding the power of their soul. They're into the churches telling them this good/bad thing, beings making decisions for them. They feel very safe in that manner. But the energies that are coming this month, December, are coming in to alter it. The energies coming in your March or April are coming in to alter a lot of these preconceptions – your preconceptions, your tendencies.

So the future's open.

Of course.

As much as we can open up, we can bypass a lot of this stuff, right?

Yes. With Africa, you can send them love. They need it there. Pretty outrageous what's going on.

Well, we're going to put it in big print what you said: Every time you look on TV and see war or violence, send them love. That's something that we can do.

You beings *will* stop your wars.

BOOK MARKET

A reader's guide to the extraordinary books we publish, print and market for your enLightenment.

ORDER NOW!
1-800-450-0985
or Fax 1-800-393-7017
Or use order form at end

VISA / MasterCard

✦ BOOKS BY ROBERT SHAPIRO AND ARTHUR FANNING

NEW!
THE EXPLORER RACE
Robert Shapiro/Zoosh

In this expansive overview, Zoosh explains, "You are the Explorer Race. Learn about your journey before coming to this Earth, your evolution here and what lies ahead." Topics range from ETs and UFOs to relationships.

$25.00 Softcover 574p ISBN 0-929385-38-1

NEW!
ETs AND THE EXPLORER RACE
Robert Shapiro/Joopah

The next book in the famous Explorer Race series. Covers the Grays, abductions, the genetic experiment, UFO encounters, contactees, the future of our relationship with various ETs and much more.

$14.95 softcover 238p ISBN 0-929385-79-9

SHINING THE LIGHT
BOOK IV

The latest book in the series tells of the incredible vehicle traveling with the Hale-Bopp Comet. Four times the size of the Earth it is filled with lightbeings. Also covers the Montauk project, the HAARP project and the uncreation of Hitler.

$14.95 Softcover 560p ISBN 0-929385-93-4

SHINING THE LIGHT

Revelations about the Secret Government and their connections with ETs. Information about renegade ETs mining the Moon, ancient Pleiadian warships, underground alien bases and many more startling facts.

$12.95 Softcover 208p ISBN 0-929385-66-7

SHINING THE LIGHT
BOOK II

Continuing the story of the Secret Government and alien involvement. Also information about the Photon Belt, cosmic holograms photographed in the sky, a new vortex forming near Sedona, and nefarious mining on sacred Hopi land.

$14.95 Softcover 422p ISBN 0-929385-70-5

SHINING THE LIGHT
BOOK III

The focus shifts from the dastardly deeds of the Secret Govern-ment to humanity's role in creation. The Earth receives unpre-cedented aid from Creator and cosmic councils, who recently lifted us beyond the third dimension to avert a great catastrophe.

$14.95 Softcover 512p ISBN 0-929385-71-3

THE SEDONA VORTEX GUIDEBOOK

by 12 channels

200-plus pages of channeled, never-before-published information on the vortex energies of Sedona and the techniques to enable you to use the vortexes as multidimensional portals to time, space and other realities.

$14.95 Softcover 236p ISBN 0-929385-25-X

NEW! GALAXY SEVEN

A novel by
Joseph David Collins

Various unrelated people establish contact with space visitors. As they start to go public, a secret, insidious government agency is out to silence them. A sort of cross between "Close Encounters of the Third Kind" and "The X Files."

$15.95 Softcover ISBN 0-9654285-4-0

COLOR MEDICINE

The Secrets of Color Vibrational Healing

Charles Klotsche

A practitioner's manual for restoring blocked energy to the body systems with specific color wavelengths by the founder of "The 49th Vibrational Technique."

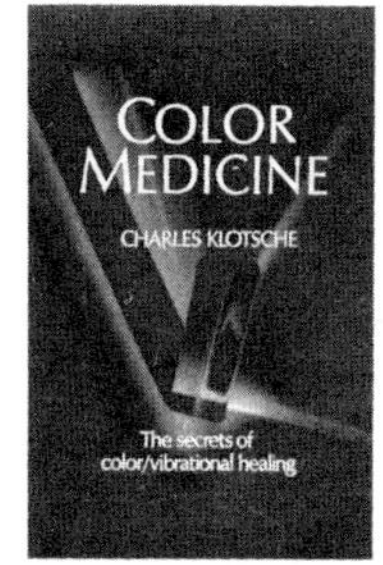

$11.95 Softcover 114p ISBN 0-929385-27-6

✦ BOOKS BY DOROTHY ROEDER

THE NEXT DIMENSION IS LOVE

Ranoash

As speaker for a civilization whose species is more advanced, the entity describes the help they offer humanity by clearing the DNA. An exciting vision of our possibilities and future.

$11.95 Softcover 148p ISBN 0-929385-50-0

REACH FOR US

Your Cosmic Teachers and Friends

Messages from Teachers, Ascended Masters and the Space Command explain the role they play in bringing the Divine Plan to the Earth now!

$14.95 Softcover 204p ISBN 0-929385-69-1

CRYSTAL CO-CREATORS

A fascinating exploration of 100 forms of crystals, describing specific uses and their purpose, from the spiritual to the cellular, as agents of change. It clarifies the role of crystals in our awakening.

$14.95 Softcover 288p ISBN 0-929385-40-3

BOOK MARKET

A reader's guide to the extraordinary books we publish, print and market for your enLightenment.

ORDER NOW!
1-800-450-0985
or Fax 1-800-393-7017
Or use order form at end

VISA MasterCard

THE ASCENSION BOOK SERIES by JOSHUA DAVID STONE, Ph.D.

THE COMPLETE ASCENSION MANUAL

How to Achieve Ascension in This Lifetime

A synthesis of the past and guidance for ascension. An extraordinary compendium of practical techniques and spiritual history. Compiled from research and channeled information.

$14.95 Softcover 297p ISBN 0-929385-55-1

SOUL PSYCHOLOGY

Keys to Ascension

Modern psychology deals exclusively with personality, ignoring the dimensions of spirit and soul. This book provides ground-breaking theories and techniques for healing and self-realization.

$14.95 Softcover 276p ISBN 0-929385-56-X

BEYOND ASCENSION

How to Complete the Seven Levels of Initiation

Brings forth new channeled material that demystifies the 7 levels of initiation and how to attain them. It contains new information on how to open and anchor our 36 chakras.

$14.95 Softcover 279p ISBN 0-929385-73-X

HIDDEN MYSTERIES

An Overview of History's Secrets from Mystery Schools to ET Contacts

Explores the unknown and suppressed aspects of Earth's past; reveals new information on the ET movement and secret teachings of the ancient Master schools.

$14.95 Softcover 333p ISBN 0-929385-57-8

THE ASCENDED MASTERS LIGHT THE WAY

Keys to Spiritual Mastery from Those Who Achieved It

Lives and teachings of 40 of the world's greatest saints and spiritual beacons provide a blueprint for total self-realization. Guidance from those who mastered the secrets in their lifetimes.

$14.95 Softcover 258p ISBN 0-929385-58-6

ASCENSION-ACTIVATION TAPES

How to anchor and open your 36 chakras and build your light quotient at a speed never dreamed possible. Scores of new ascension techniques and meditations directly from the galactic and universal core.

ASCENSION-ACTIVATION MEDITATION TAPE:

- S101
- S102
- S103
- S104
- S105

$12.00 each

Set of all 5 tapes **$49.95**

BOOK MARKET

A reader's guide to the extraordinary books we publish, print and market for your enLightenment.

ORDER NOW!
1-800-450-0985
or Fax 1-800-393-7017
Or use order form at end

VISA · MasterCard

✦ BOOKS BY LYNN BUESS

CHILDREN OF LIGHT, CHILDREN OF DENIAL

In his fourth book Lynn calls upon his decades of practice as counselor and psycho-therapist to explore the relationship between karma and the new insights from ACOA/ Co-dependency writings.

$8.95 Softcover 150p ISBN 0-929385-15-2

NUMEROLOGY FOR THE NEW AGE

An established standard, explicating for contemporary readers the ancient art and science of symbol, cycle, and vibration. Provides insights into the patterns of our personal lives. Includes life and personality numbers.

$11.00 Softcover 262p ISBN 0-929385-31-4

NUMEROLOGY: NUANCES IN RELATIONSHIPS

Provides valuable assistance in the quest to better understand compatibilities and conflicts with a significant other. A handy guide for calculating your/his/her personality numbers.

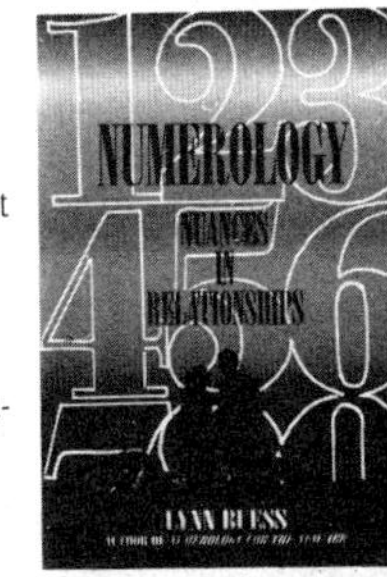

$12.65 Softcover 239p ISBN 0-929385-23-3

THE STORY OF THE PEOPLE

Eileen Rota

An exciting history of our coming to Earth, our traditions, our choices and the coming changes, it can be viewed as a metaphysical adventure, science fiction or the epic of all of us brave enough to know the truth. Beautifully written and illustrated.

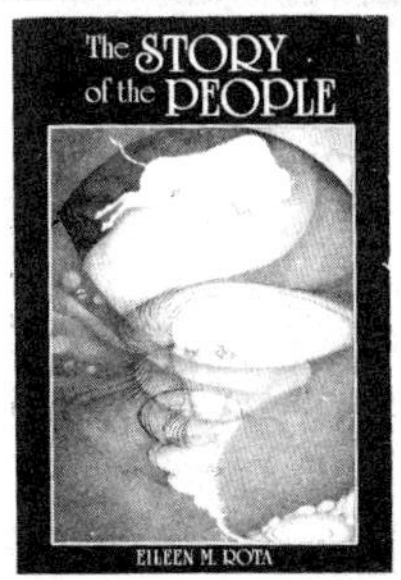

$11.95 Softcover 209p ISBN 0-929385-51-9

THE NEW AGE PRIMER

Spiritual Tools for Awakening

A guidebook to the changing reality, it is an overview of the concepts and techniques of mastery by authorities in their fields. Explores reincarnation, belief systems and transformative tools from astrology to crystals.

$11.95 Softcover 206p ISBN 0-929385-48-9

LIVING RAINBOWS

Gabriel H. Bain

A fascinating "how-to" manual to make experiencing human, astral, animal and plant auras an everyday event. Series of techniques, exercises and illustrations guide the reader to see and hear aural energy. Spiral-bound workbook.

$14.95 Softcover 134p ISBN 0-929385--42-X

ACUPRESSURE FOR THE SOUL
Nancy Fallon, Ph.D.

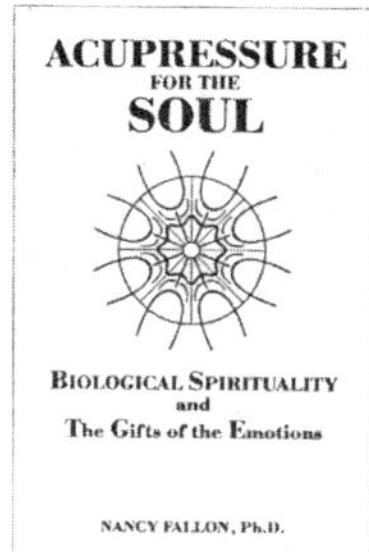

A revolutionary vision of emotions as sources of power, rocket fuel for fulfilling our purpose. A formula for awakening transformation with 12 beautiful illustrations.

$11.95 Softcover 150p ISBN 0-929385-49-7

◆ BOOKS BY RUTH RYDEN

THE GOLDEN PATH

"Book of Lessons" by the master teachers explaining the process of channeling. Akashic Records, karma, opening the third eye, the ego and the meaning of Bible stories. It is a master class for opening your personal pathway.

$11.95 Softcover 200p ISBN 0-929385-43-8

LIVING THE GOLDEN PATH
Practical Soul-utions to Today's Problems

Guidance that can be used in the real world to solve dilemmas, to strengthen inner resolves and see the Light at the end of the road. Covers the difficult issues of addictions, rape, abortion, suicide and personal loss.

$11.95 Softcover 186p ISBN 0-929385-65-9

◆ BOOKS BY WES BATEMAN

KNOWLEDGE FROM THE STARS

A telepath with contact to ETs, Bateman has provided a wide spectrum of scientific information. A fascinating compilation of articles surveying the Federation, ETs, evolution and the trading houses, all part of the true history of the galaxy.

$11.95 Softcover 171p ISBN 0-929385-39 X

DRAGONS AND CHARIOTS

An explanation of spacecraft, propulsion systems, gravity, the Dragon, manipulated Light and interstellar and intergalactic motherships by a renowned telepath who details specific technological information received from ETs.

$9.95 Softcover 65p ISBN 0-929385-45-4

FOREVER YOUNG
Gladys Iris Clark

You can create a longer younger life! Viewing a lifetime of a full century, a remarkable woman shares her secrets for longevity and rejuvenation. A manual for all ages. Explores tools for optimizing vitality, nutrition, skin care via Tibetan exercises, crystals, sex.

$9.95 Softcover 109p ISBN 0-929385-53-5

BOOK MARKET

A reader's guide to the extraordinary books we publish, print and market for your enLightenment.

ORDER NOW!
1-800-450-0985
or Fax 1-800-393-7017
Or use order form at end

✦ BOOK AND MEDITATION TAPES by VYWAMUS/BARBARA BURNS

CHANNELLING:
Evolutionary Exercises for Channels

A lucid, step-by-step guide for experienced or aspiring channels. Opens the self to Source with simple yet effective exercises. Barbara has worked with Vywamus since 1987.

$9.95 Softcover 118p ISBN 0-929385-35-7

THE QUANTUM MECHANICAL YOU

Workshop presented by the *Sedona Journal of Emergence!* in Sedona April 2-3, 1994

Barbara Burns through Vywamus explores the "mutational" process that humanity agreed to undertake at the time of the Harmonic Convergence. This fundamental biochemical and electromagnetic restructuring is necessary for those who have agreed to remain in body throughout the full shift. The "mutation" process is a complete reformatting of the human DNA.

B101-4 (6-tape set) $40

✦ BOOK AND MEDITATION TAPES by BRIAN GRATTAN

MAHATMA
I & II
Brian Grattan

Combined version of the original two books. Guidance to reach an evolutionary level of integration for conscious ascension. Fascinating diagrams, meditations, conversations.

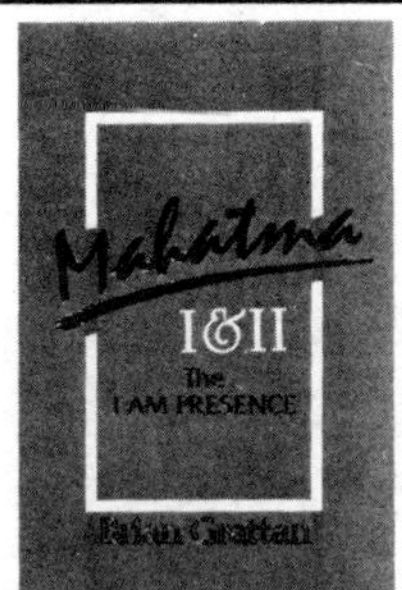

$19.95 Softcover 328p ISBN 0-929385-77-2

DNA FOR THE MULTIDIMENSIONAL MATRIX

Seattle Seminar, October 27-30, 1994

These 12 powerful hours of meditations lead to total spiritual transformation by recoding your 2-strand DNA to function in positive mutation, which finite scientists refer to as "junk" DNA. Ancient intergalactic civilizations altered humanity's DNA; the ultimate achievement now for Earth's inhabitants is to spiritualize the 12-strand DNA to achieve complete universal and monadic consciousness; these audio tapes are a profound step in that direction.

M102-12 $79.95 (12-tape set)

✦ BOOKS BY SCOTT FREE

LOOK
WITHIN
Scott Free

Transformational channeled poetry for the New Age removes past blockages — opens up memories of all that you are. If you are committed to changing your life, let your soul guide you to look within.

$9.95 Softcover 108p ISBN 0-9635673-0-6

FUTURE BOOKS IN THE EXPLORER RACE SERIES. WATCH FOR BOOKS ON:

✦ MYTHOLOGY ✦
✦ ORIGINS & the NEXT 50 YEARS ✦
✦ CREATOR & HIS FRIENDS ✦
✦ PARTICLE PERSONALITIES ✦
✦ THE IMMORTAL ENGINEERS ✦
✦ BEYOND THE EXPLORER RACE ✦

MEDITATION TAPES AND BOOKS by YHWH/ARTHUR FANNING

ON BECOMING

YHWH through Arthur Fanning

Knowing the power of the light that you are. Expansion of the pituitary gland and strengthening the physical structure. Becoming more of you.

F101 $10

HEALING MEDITATIONS/ KNOWING SELF

Knowing self is knowing God. Knowing the pyramid of the soul is knowing the body. Meditation on the working of the soul and the use of the gold light within the body.

F102 $10

MANIFESTATION & ALIGNMENT with the POLES

Alignment of the meridians with the planet's grid system. Connect the root chakra with the center of the planet.

F103 $10

THE ART OF SHUTTING UP

Gaining the power and the wisdom of the quiet being that resides within the sight of thy Father.

F104 $10

CONTINUITY OF CONSCIOUSNESS

Trains you in the powerful state of waking meditation.

F105 $25 (3-tape set)

MERGING THE GOLDEN LIGHT REPLICAS OF YOU

The awakening of the Christ consciousness.

F107 $10

NEW! SOUL EVOLUTION FATHER

Lord God Jehovah through Arthur Fanning

Jehovah is back with others, to lead humanity out of its fascination with density into an expanding awareness that each human is a god with unlimited power and potential.

Finally in stock!

$12.95 Softcover 200p ISBN 0-929385-33-0

SIMON

A compilation of some of the experiences Arthur has had with the dolphins, which triggered his opening and awakening as a channel.

$9.95 Softcover 56p ISBN 0-929385-32-2

THE SOUL REMEMBERS

A Parable on Spiritual Transformation

Carlos Warter, M.D.

What is the purpose of human life? What is the reality of this world I find myself in?
A cosmic perspective on essence, individuality and relationships.
Through the voices of archetypes of consciousness, this journey through dimensions will assist the reader to become personally responsible for cocreating heaven on Earth.

$14.95 210p ISBN 0-929385-36-5

MEDICAL ASTROLOGY

Eileen Nauman, DHM

The most comprehensive book ever on this rapidly growing science. Homeopath Eileen Nauman presents the Med-Scan Technique of relating astrology to health and nutrition. With case histories and guide to nutrition.

$29.95 339p ISBN 0-9634662-4-0

BOOKSTORE DISCOUNTS HONORED

☐ CHECK ☐ MONEY ORDER

CREDIT CARD: ☐ MC ☐ VISA

____

Exp. date: ______________

Signature: ______________

(U.S. FUNDS ONLY) PAYABLE TO:

LIGHT TECHNOLOGY PUBLISHING

P.O. BOX 1526 • SEDONA • AZ 86339
(520) 282-6523 Fax: (520) 282-4130
1-800-450-0985
Fax 1-800-393-7017

NAME/COMPANY ______________

ADDRESS ______________

CITY/STATE/ZIP ______________

PHONE ______________ CONTACT ______________

SUBTOTAL: $ ______________

SALES TAX: $ ______________
(7.5% – AZ residents only)

SHIPPING/HANDLING: $ ______________
($3 Min.; 10% of orders over $30)

CANADA S/H: $ ______________
(20% of order)

TOTAL AMOUNT ENCLOSED: $ ______________

All prices in US$. Higher in Canada and Europe.

CANADA: Cherev Canada, Inc. 1(800) 263-2408 Fax (519) 986-3103 • ENGLAND/EUROPE: Windrush Press Ltd. 0608 652012/652025 Fax 0608 652125
AUSTRALIA: Gemcraft Books (03)888-0111 Fax (03)888-0044 • NEW ZEALAND: Peaceful Living Pub. (07)571-8105 Fax (07)571-8513

BOOKSTORE DISCOUNTS HONORED

☐ CHECK ☐ MONEY ORDER

CREDIT CARD: ☐ MC ☐ VISA

____

Exp. date: ______________

Signature: ______________

(U.S. FUNDS ONLY) PAYABLE TO:

LIGHT TECHNOLOGY PUBLISHING

P.O. BOX 1526 • SEDONA • AZ 86339
(520) 282-6523 Fax: (520) 282-4130
1-800-450-0985
Fax 1-800-393-7017

NAME/COMPANY ______________

ADDRESS ______________

CITY/STATE/ZIP ______________

PHONE ______________ CONTACT ______________

SUBTOTAL: $ ______________

SALES TAX: $ ______________
(7.5% – AZ residents only)

SHIPPING/HANDLING: $ ______________
($3 Min.; 10% of orders over $30)

CANADA S/H: $ ______________
(20% of order)

TOTAL AMOUNT ENCLOSED: $ ______________

All prices in US$. Higher in Canada and Europe.

CANADA: Cherev Canada, Inc. 1(800) 263-2408 Fax (519) 986-3103 • ENGLAND/EUROPE: Windrush Press Ltd. 0608 652012/652025 Fax 0608 652125
AUSTRALIA: Gemcraft Books (03)888-0111 Fax (03)888-0044 • NEW ZEALAND: Peaceful Living Pub. (07)571-8105 Fax (07)571-8513